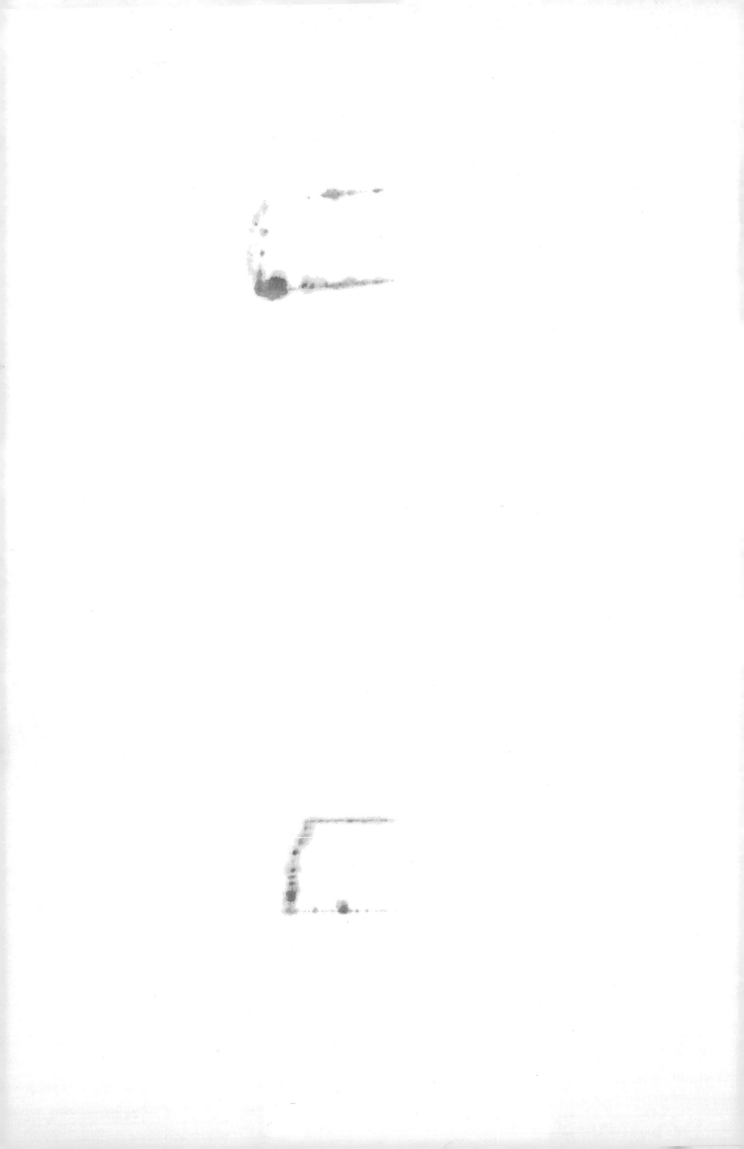

THE VICTORIA HISTORY
OF THE
COUNTIES OF ENGLAND

A HISTORY OF
SUSSEX

INDEX TO
VOLUMES I–IV, VII, AND IX

THE VICTORIA HISTORY
OF THE
COUNTIES OF ENGLAND

EDITED BY C. R. ELRINGTON

THE UNIVERSITY OF LONDON
INSTITUTE OF
HISTORICAL RESEARCH

Oxford University Press, Walton Street, Oxford OX2 6DP
London Glasgow New York Toronto
Delhi Bombay Calcutta Madras Karachi
Kuala Lumpur Singapore Hong Kong Tokyo
Nairobi Dar es Salaam Cape Town
Melbourne Auckland

and associated companies in
Beirut Berlin Ibadan Mexico City Nicosia

Oxford is a trade mark of Oxford University Press

Published in the United States by
Oxford University Press, New York

© University of London 1984

ISBN 0 19 722766 X

Produced by Alan Sutton Publishing Limited, Gloucester
Printed in Great Britain

INSCRIBED TO THE

MEMORY OF HER LATE MAJESTY

QUEEN VICTORIA

WHO GRACIOUSLY GAVE THE TITLE TO

AND ACCEPTED THE DEDICATION

OF THIS HISTORY

A HISTORY OF THE COUNTY OF

SUSSEX

INDEX TO
VOLUMES I–IV, VII, AND IX

EDITED BY SUSAN M. KEELING AND C. P. LEWIS

PUBLISHED FOR

THE INSTITUTE OF HISTORICAL RESEARCH

BY

OXFORD UNIVERSITY PRESS

1984

Distributed by Oxford University Press until 1 January 1987
thereafter by Dawsons of Pall Mall

EDITORIAL NOTE

SIX volumes of the Sussex *Victoria County History* were published between 1905 and 1953. They have remained until now without an index, apart from that to the Domesday Survey included in Volume I, in accordance with the early scheme of the *History* which provided that all the volumes of each county set would, when complete, be indexed collectively. The inevitably long interval between the publication of the first volume in a county set and the completion of the set has made that plan inadequate, and since 1953 each new volume of the *Victoria County History* has contained an index or been quickly followed by the publication of one. Under the new scheme *Sussex,* Volume VI (part 1), published in 1980, included an index, as will its successors, and the time seemed ripe to make good the long-standing absence of an index to the earlier volumes.

A most generous grant from the British Library Board, for which the University of London Institute of Historical Research is sincerely grateful, enabled the index to be compiled. It was a condition of the grant that the work should be done in a relatively short time, which made it necessary to recruit a team of six indexers. Volumes I and II were indexed by Mr. and Mrs. K. C. Leslie; Volume III was indexed by Mrs. M. Maloney, Volume IV by Dr. A. R. Rumble, Volume VII by Mr. L. J. Johnson, and Volume IX by Mr. D. W. Hutchings. The work of collating the separate indexes and of eliminating as far as possible the minor differences of method and style has been done by the editors, Dr. Keeling and Mr. Lewis.

The Introduction and Translation of the Domesday Survey are separately indexed in Volume I, pages 541–54.

An italic page number denotes an illustration on or facing that page.

*An asterisk indicates that the reference on the page concerned is subject to the corrigenda printed below, after the index.

Among the abbreviations used the following, sometimes with the addition of -s to indicate plurality, may require elucidation (some additional abbreviations being set out in the Victoria History's *Handbook for Editors and Authors*): A.-S., Anglo-Saxon; abp., archbishop; adv., advowson; agric., agriculture; Alex., Alexander; almshos., almshouses; And., Andrew; Ant., Anthony; archit. architecture; b., born; Bart., Bartholomew; Ben., Benedict, Benet; Benj., Benjamin; Bd., Board; boro., borough; bp., bishop; bro., brother; bt., baronet; *c.*, *circa*; Cant., Canterbury; cast., castle; cath., cathedral; Cath., Catherine, Catholic; cent., century; ch., church; chant., chantry; chap., chapel; char., charity; Chas., Charles; Chich., Chichester; Chris., Christopher; chyd., churchyard; coll., college; Com., Commission; ct., court; ctss., countess; d., died; Dan., Daniel; dau., daughter; dchss., duchess; dioc., diocese; dom., domestic; Edm., Edmund; Edw., Edward; Eliz., Elizabeth; fam., family; fl., flourished; Fm., Farm; Fred., Frederick; Geo., George; Geof., Geoffrey; Gilb., Gilbert; govt., government; grds., grandson; Hen., Henry; Herb., Herbert; Ho., House; hosp., hospital; Humph., Humphrey; hund., hundred; inc., inclosure; ind., industry; Jas., James; Jn., John; Jos., Joseph; jr., junior; Kath., Katharine; Ld., Lord; Laur., Laurence; Lawr., Lawrence; m., married; man., manor; Marg., Margaret; Mat., Matthew; Maur., Maurice; mchnss., marchioness; Mic., Michael; Min., Ministry; mkt., market; *n*, note; Nat., Nathaniel; Nic., Nicholas; nonconf., nonconformity; par., parish; parl., parliamentary; Phil., Philip; pk., park; pop., population; prehist., prehistoric; *q.v.*, *quod vide*; rd., road; Reg., Reginald; rem., remains; rep., representation; Ric., Richard; riv., river; rly, railway; Rob., Robert; Rog., Roger; Rom., Roman; s., son; Sam., Samuel; sch., school; Sim., Simon; sis., sister; sr., senior; Steph., Stephen; tax., taxation; *temp.*, *tempore*; Thos., Thomas; vct., viscount; vctss., viscountess; w., wife; Wal., Walter; Wm., William.

INDEX TO
VOLUMES I–IV, VII, AND IX

Aaron, a Jew, i. 506
Abadam, *see* Badeham
Abberbury:
  Sir Jn. de, iv. 52
  Ric. de, iv. 51–2
  Sir Ric., iv. 52
  Thos. de, iv. 52
Abberton, *see* Yapton
Abbey, Noel, iii. 139, 145
Abbey & Sons, ii. 263
Abbot's wood, *see* Arlington
Abbott, W.J. Lewis, i. 312
Abel Smith, *see* Smith, Anna; Smith, Jn.
Abell:
  Ric., prior of Pynham, ii. 81
  —— (fl. 1540), ii. 19
Abercrombie, Thos., iv. 57
Aberdeenshire, i. 291
Abergavenny, earl of, Ld., *and* marquess of, *see* Larnach-Nevill; Nevill
Abernon (Dabernoun):
  Jn. d' (fl. 1264), i. 500
  Jn. (fl. 1321), i. 508
Abingdon (Abyndon):
  Margery de, m. Jn. Torrel, iv. 42
  Steph. de, iv. 42
Abingdon (Berks.), i. 344 *n*
Abu Klea (Sudan), battle, i. 536
Abulci, iii. 6, 9
Abyndon, *see* Abingdon
Acdenne, *see* Adeane
Achescombe, Wm. de, vii. 34 *n*
Achingham, *see* Echingham
Ackling Dyke (Dors.), iii. 34
Acland:
  Sir Thos. Dyke, iv. 143–4
  and see Fuller-Palmer-Acland
Acra, Wm. del, iv. 230
Adam, abbot of Robertsbridge, ii. 73
Adam, priest of Ticehurst, ix. 257
Adam, sheriff of Lewes, vii. 1
Adam, ap, *see* Badeham
Adams (Adam, Addams):
  Abraham, vii. 144, 180
  Abraham Gray, vii. 180
  Alice, w. of Thos., iv. 179
  H.P., iv. 49 *n*
  Rob., iii. 75; ix. 230
  Theophilus, iii. 75; iv. 138, 170; ix. 230
  Thos., mayor of Chich., iii. 97
  Thos. (fl. 1564, ? another), ii. 24; iv. 179
  Thos. (d. 1785), vii. 180
  Wm. (fl. 1549), iv. 27
  Wm. (fl. 1626), ix. 113
  Mr., ii. 455
  ——, ii. 470
Adamson:
  J.E., ii. 476
  R.W., ii. 472 *n*
  W.R., ix. 235
Addams, *see* Adams
Addington, Dr., vii. 247
Addington (Surr.), iii. 43, 45; vii. 203
Ade:
  Hen., vii. 54
  Jn., vii. 54
  Ric., rector of Iden, ix. 156 *n*
  fam., vii. 54 *n*
Adeane (Acdenne, atte Dene):
  Agnes, w. of Ric., vii. 121
  Edm., vii. 122
  Hen., vii. 121
  Jn., vii. 121–2
  Kath., m. Jn. Rowe, vii. 122

(or Warren), Ric. (d. 1550), vii. 121
  Ric., vii. 121
  Rob., vii. 122
  Thos., ix. 145
  Wm. (fl. 1398), ix. 145
  Wm. (d. 1597), vii. 122
Adelaide, queen of Wm. IV, vii. 19, 37, 250
Adelize (Adelais, Adelisa, Adeliz, Adeliza, Aeliz), queen of Hen. I, m. 2 Wm. d'Aubigny, earl of Arundel (d. 1176), i. 490; ii. 80, 303; iii. 81, 84; iv. 1, 60, 120, 130
Adelize (Adelise, Alice), m. 1 Jn., count of Eu, 2 Alfred de St. Martin, ii. 71; ix. 14
Adelulf, sheriff of Lewes, vii. 1
Aderne, Giles de, vii. 203
Aderton:
  Rog., vii. 183
  Thos., vii. 183
  Thomasine, *see* Ockenden
Ades, Hen., iv. 64
Ades, *see* Chailey
Adingar, prior of Boxgrove, ii. 59
Adingers (unidentified), iv. 183 *n*
Adley, Thos., vii. 162
Adlington, Hen., ii. 22
Adman, Hen., and his w. Cecily, ix. 221
Admiral, Ld. High, ii. 141, 144, 146–7, 150, 152–4; *and see* Fitzwilliam, Sir Wm.; Howard, Chas.; Seymour, Thos.
Admiralty, Court of, *see* courts
Adrian V, pope, ii. 12
Adsdean:
  Clement de, iii. 98
  Thos. de, iii. 98
Adsdean, *see* Westbourne
Adur (or Shoreham), riv., i. 18, 473–4; ii. 139, 279; iii. 2, 47, 62; iv. 1; vii. 1
  estuary, i. 25; iii. 4, 10, 42–3, 52, 62; iv. 275, 277, 282
  natural history, i. 42, 54–5, 209, 303
  salt, ii. 232
  sport, ii. 451, 453, 465
  timber, ii. 306
  valley, i. 20; vii. 186
Adur Preservation Society, ii. 465
Adversane, *see* Billingshurst
Adye, Nic., ix. 178
Adyson, Jn., mayor of Chich., iii. 92
Aedric, *see* Edric
Aegelm, moneyer, iii. 83
Aelard, *see* Alard
Aeldret, *see* Aldret
Aelfech, *see* Alfech
Aelfer, *see* Alfer
Aelfric, *see* Alfric
Aelfstan, *see* Alfstan
Aelfwig, *see* Alfwig
Aelfwine, *see* Alfwine
Aeliz, *see* Adelize
Aelle (Aella, Elle), king of South Saxons, i. 334, 481–2, 494; ii. 1, 126, 291; iii. 4, 6, 10, 19, 82
Aelric, *see* Alfric
Aerated Bread Co., ix. 31
Aethelbert, *see* Ethelbert, king of South Saxons
Aethelburt, *see* Ethelbert, king of Wessex
Aethelm, *see* Ethelm
Aethelmar, *see* Ethelmar
Aethelred, *see* Ethelred
Aethelstan, *see* Athelstan

Aethelwalh, *see* Ethelwold
Affete, Rob., vii. 34
Agassiz, Jean L.R., i. 27, 32–5, 38
Agate:
  Hen., vii. 183
  Jn., vii. 183
  Mary, m. Ric. Blower, vii. 183
  Thos., vii. 183
  fam., vii. 188 *n*
Agatha, prioress of Lyminster, ii. 121
Agincourt (Pas de Calais, France), battle, i. 513; ii. 141; iv. 35; ix. 127, 133
Agmerhurst, *see* Ashburnham
Agnes, prioress of Rusper, ii. 64
Agricola, iii. 2, 15
agricultural education, ii. 213, 288–9; vii. 109
agriculture, ii. 170, 211–14, **273–90**; iii. 82; *and see* agricultural education; allotments and smallholdings; arable farming; assarting; beekeeping; Board of Agriculture; convertible husbandry; crops; customs and services; dairy farming; dairy produce; drainage; farm buildings; farm implements; farmers' clubs; fields, open; fruit growing; inclosure; livestock; manures; mkt. gardening; pastoral husbandry; rents, agricultural; Romano-British Suss.; shows, agricultural; tenancies, agricultural; wages; wool production
Agriculture, Central Chamber of, ii. 289
Aguiller, —— le, iii. 97
Aguillon:
  Alice, m. 1 Wm. Russell, 2 Rob. Haket, iv. 89, 111
  Cecily, m. Peter de Gatesden, iv. 89, 111
  Eleanor, w. of Ric., iv. 128
  Godehuda, m. Ralph de St. Owen, iv. 89, 111
  Godfrey, ii. 81
  Isabel, m. Hugh Bardolf, vii. 110, 203
  Joan, *see* FitzAilwin
  Jn., ii. 81
  Jn. (? another), iv. 111, 128
  Julian (Juliane), iv. 128, 195
  Manser (Manasses) (*temp.* Hen. I), iv. 128
  Manser (fl. 1195), iv. 128
  Margery, *see* Thorney
  Mary, m. Wm. de Covert, iv. 89, 111
  Mary, *see* Valle Pironis
  Reynold, iv. 89, 111, 145
  Ric. (fl. 1195), iv. 128
  Ric. (d. by 1308), iv. 128
  Rob. (fl. 1180), iv. 128
  Sir Rob. (d. 1286), i. 503–4; ii. 185, 295; iv. 161, 199 *n*; vii. 203–4
  Sir Rob. (? another), ii. 82
  Sarah (Sarra), m. Wm. Whateman, iv. 128
  Thos., iv. 128
  Wm. (fl. 1195), iv. 128
  Wm. (d. 1244), iv. 108, 128, 145, 195; vii. 203
  Wm. (fl. 1263–5), i. 498; iv. 197
  Wm. (fl. 1278, ? another), iv. 129
  fam., ii. 48; iv. 128–9
  arms, iv. *128*; vii. *203*
Aigle, *see* Laigle
Ailwin, reeve of Lewes, vii. 24 *n*
Ainsworth, Harrison, vii. 234
Airey, Geo., ii. 425

airfields, iv. 165, 237
Aiscough, Wm., bp. of Salisbury, vii. 4
Aishurst, *see* Ashurst
Aix (Bouches-du-Rhone, France), iii.
101
Akerman, Jn. Yonge, i. 336
Akingeham, *see* Echingham
Alan, abbot of Robertsbridge, ii. 73
Alan son of Conan, iv. 166
his s., *see* William son of Alan
Alan the cheesemonger, and his w.
Alice, ix. 23
Alan (fl. *temp.* Hen. I), iv. 47
Alan (? another, d. before 1140), iv. 84
his w., *see* Aveline
Alan (d. before 1201) and his widow
Hillary, ix. 180
Alard (Aelard), iv. 30
Alard:
Gervase (fl. 1295–1303), mayor of
Winchelsea, ii. 134; ix. 69, 71
Gervase (fl. 1331, d. by 1339), bailiff
of Winchelsea, ix. 68, 181
Hen., ix. 18
Jas., ix. 274
Jn. (fl. 1293), ii. 132 *n*
Jn. (d. *c.* 1377), ix. 61, 177
Jn. (b. 1348), ix. 92
Marg., w. of Gervase, ix. 181
Nic. (fl. 1298), ii. 132 *n*
Nic. (fl. *c.* 1300, ? another), ix. 177
Nic. (fl. 1347), ix. 92
Reynold (Reg.), ii. 132 *n*; ix. 74, 92
Rob. (fl. after 1312), ix. 75
Rob., bailiff of Winchelsea, ix. 61, 68,
177
Rob. (fl. 1430), ix. 181
Steph., ix. 75, 149, 177
Sybil, ix. 177 *n*
Thos. (? two of this name), ii. 132; ix.
71
——— (? Tallarte de Lajes), ii. 143
fam., ix. 70–1, 74
Albano, cardinal bp., *see* Duèse
Albemarle, earl of, *see* Keppel
Alberry, Jn., ii. 33
Albert, Prince Consort, vii. 250
Albert II, duke of Austria, ii. 68
Albert, prior of Lewes, ii. 70
Albert (fl. 1086), vii. 283
Albini, *see* Aubigny
Albo Monasterio, *see* Blancmuster
Albourne, ii. 43–4, 108
Bishopshurst, prebendary, *see* Hen-
shaw, Jos.
botany, i. 60
ch., ii. 351, 366
dom. archit., ii. 386
pop., ii. 219
Rom. rem., iii. 49, 58
textile ind., ii. 257
Wick Pond, i. 286
Albury (Surr.), ii. 271
Alcher (fl. 1086), iv. 161
Alchorne:
Agnes, vii. 106
Alice, vii. 106
Anne, *see* Chambre
Joan, vii. 106
Jn. (fl. 1523), vii. 106
Jn., his s., vii. 106
Jn. (fl. 1630), vii. 59
Marg., w. of Thos., vii. 106
Nic. (fl. 1559), vii. 106
Nic. (fl. 1624), vii. 106
Thos. (d. 1559), vii. 106
Thos. (fl. 1782), vii. 59
Wm., and his w. Eliz., vii. 59
arms, vii. *106*
Alciston, ii. 44, 382
adv., ii. 52
Alciston Place, ii. 384
Battle abbey estates, ii. 52; ix. 253
ch., ii. 340, 366, 371
earthworks, i. 480
hund., i. 538; ii. 225; iv. 133
insects, i. 148
man., ii. 175–6; vii. 14, 228; ix. 251

pop., ii. 225
roads, iii. 42
Tilton, *q.v.*
vicarage, ii. 9
Alcock (Allcock, Awcocke):
Anne, m. Geo. Bramston, iv. 35, 38,
163
Anne, w. of Laur., *see* Fuller
Chas., iv. 216 *n*
Eliz., m. 1 Ric. Paine, 2 Ric. Rideout,
vii. 230, 232
Hannah, m. Thos. Pellatt, vii. 37, 230
Jane, m. Jn. Radcliffe, iv. 35–6, 42–3,
163
Laur. (Lawr.), iv. 35, 42, 83, 163, 237
Laur., s. of Lawr., iv. 35, 38, 42,
163 *n*
Seth, vii. 37, 75
Thos., iv. 216
Wm. (d. 1662), vii. 37, 232
Wm. (fl. 1663), vii. 230
Wm. (fl. 1807), iv. 216
fam., iv. 42, 76, 216
Alcorn, Thos., ii. 253
Aldbricht, *see* Ealdberht
Alde, Jn., ix. 192
Alderson, ———, vii. 106
Alderton, Thos., vii. 179 *n*
Alderwych, Nic., ix. 3
Aldham, Francis de, vii. 256
Aldingbourne, i. 483; ii. 43; iii. 116; iv.
133, **134–8**, 166, 223
adv., iv. 138
bp.'s palace, iv. 134
char., iv. 138
ch., iv. 134, 136–8, *137–8*
accessories, ii. 350–3, 356, 360, 366,
368, 373–4
archit., ii. 333, 335, 340, 344, 347–
8, 350, 364–6, 368, 371, 373–4
dom. archit., iv. 134
Fontwell, iv. 134
Gates, prebend, ii. 408; iv. 136; prebendary, *see* Tireman, Ric.
glebe, ii. 5
Headhone, iv. 134–6
inc., iv. 134
insects, i. 200
Lidsey, *q.v.*
man., iv. 134–6, 142, 152
ho., ii. 186; iv. 134
mill, iv. 135
Norton, iii. 49; iv. 134
man., iv. 136
Nyton, iv. 134, 136
pk., ii. 297, 303, 315 *n*; iv. 135–6,
152–3, 202
pop., ii. 220
prebend, iv. 138
priest, iv. 135
rly., iv. 134
rds., iv. 134
Rom. rem., iii. 4, 46, 49
royal visits, i. 483, 491
sanatorium, iv. 134
streams, iv. 134; *and see* Aldingbourne Rife
tithes, iv. 138
Westergate (Westgates), i. 120; ii.
388; iv. 134–6
Rom. rem., iii. 4, 15, 46, 67
Woodgate, iv. 134
Aldingbourne Rife, iv. 134, 223, 226–7
Aldon:
Maud, *see* Burghersh
Thos. de (d. 1361), ix. 196
Thos. de (fl. 1365), ix. 196
Aldred (fl. 12th cent.), iv. 107
Aldret (Aeldret) (fl. 1066), ix. 213
Aldridge, fam., ii. 310
Aldrington (Eldretune), ii. 7, 43–4; iii.
62; vii. 265, 274, **275–6**, 277, 280,
282
adv., vii. 276, 283
angling, ii. 465
ch., vii. 276, *276*, 283
coastal erosion, ii. 224 *n*; vii. 275
coastguards, i. 507 *n*

insects, i. 207
man., vii. 2, 275–6, 283
pop., ii. 224
prehist. rem., i. 328
rly., vii. 275
rector, *see* Bolle, Wm.
Rom. rem., iii. 49
ship service, ii. 134
wrecking, ii. 148
Aldsworth, *see* Westbourne
Aldulf (Aldwulf, Ealdwulf, Eldwulf),
king of South Saxons, i. 482; ii. 3,
117; vii. 168, 196, 226 *n*, 239
Aldwick (in Pagham, later in Bognor),
iv. 226–7
adv., iv. 101
coastal erosion, iv. 230
coins, i. 326, 328
hund. (formerly Pagham hund.), i.
538; ii. 220; iii. 104; iv. 2, 88,
101, 133, **222**
insects, i. 113–14*, 116–17, 212, 214,
219, 225, 228, 230, 233, 236
man., iv. 130, 229–30
Aldwulf, *see* Aldulf
Alestan (fl. 1066), ix. 82
Alewin (Alewyn), *see* Aylwin
Alexander II, king of Scotland, vii. 99,
283
Alexander III, pope, ii. 47, 53, 121
Alexander IV, pope, ii. 72
Alexander, prior of Hastings, ii. 77
Alexander, prior of Lewes, ii. 65, 70
Alexander:
Boyd, i. 293
Wm., and his w. Peggy, vii. 235
———, iii. 64
Aleyn, *see* Allen
Alfech (Aelfech) (fl. 1066), vii. 206
Alfer (Aelfer) (fl. 1066), ix. 262, 266
Alfold (Surr. and Suss.), ii. 217
ch., ii. 328 *n*, 373
pop., ii. 217
Alfoldean, *see* Slinfold
Alford:
Edw. (d. 1631), vii. 85*
Sir Edw., vii. 85
Col. Edw., ii. 39 *n*
Frances, w. of Jn., vii. 85
Jn. (d. 1648), vii. 85*
Jn. (? another), ix. 146
Jn. (d. 1744), vii. 85
arms, vii. *85*
Alfray, *see* Allfrey
Alfred, king of Wessex, i. 349, 483; ii.
122, 126, 302, 323, 402; iv. 91, 135;
vii. 104, 275; ix. 144
Alfred, bp. of Selsey, iv. 215
Alfred (fl. 1086), vii. 189
Alfred (Alured) (fl. 1086, another), ii.
381
Alfred (Alured) (fl. *c.* 1160), iv. 154
Alfred (Alvred), Wm. s. of, *see* William
Alfrey, *see* Allfrey
Alfric (Aelric) cild, ii. 172
Alfric (Aelfric), moneyer, iii. 83
Alfric (Alvric) (fl. 1066), iv. 108
Alfric of Dungeness, *see* Dengemareis
Alfriston (Alfryssen), i. 56; ii. 44, 277
A.-S. rem., i. 336, 348
birds, i. 287
ch., ii. 9, 30, 78
accessories, ii. 250, 352–3, 356,
359–60
archit., ii. 334, 340, 346, 348, 350,
377–8
ch. ho., ii. 384, 389–90
coins, i. 326, 328
dom. archit., ii. 386, 390
earthworks, i. 480
fishes, i. 267
fossils, i. 33
Frog Firle, ii. 3, 122, 386; vii. 234
Hindover, i. 323 *n**
ind., ii. 250, 257
mkt. cross, ii. 394
militia, i. 534
pop., ii. 225

prehist. rem., i. 321–2, *322*, 328
sport, ii. 450, 460–1, 468
vicar, ii. 79
vicarage, ii. 9
Winton Street, ix. 251
Alfstan (Aelfstan), abp. of Cant., ix. 253
Alfwig (Aelfwig), abbot of Winchester, i. 487
Alfwine (Aelfwine), moneyer, iii. 83
algae, *see* freshwater algae; marine algae
Algar (fl. 1066), ix. 172
Algeria, i. 278 *n*
Algiers, ii. 154–5, 157
Alice, ctss. of Eu, m. Ralph de Exoudun (or Lusignan), i. 507; ii. 113, 324*; ix. 2, 10, 14–15, 79, 91, 119, 197, 199, 224
Alice, prioress of Easebourne, ii. 85; iv. 85
Alice, prioress of Rusper, ii. 64
Alice, daughter of Henry, ii. 397
Alice, daughter of Jocelin, iv. 60
Alice, daughter of Robert son of Edgar, m. Wm. de la Falaise, iv. 192–3*
Alice, *see* Adelize
alien houses, ii. 46, 119–24
Alin, *see* Allen
Alkmaar (Netherlands), i. 535
All Souls College, Oxford, ii. 421; ix. 265
Allcock, *see* Alcock
Allcroft, A. Hadrian, iii. 20, 46, 48
Allec, Wm. fitz, *see* FitzAllack
Allen (Aleyn, Alin, Alleyn, Alleyne):
    Abel, ix. 91
    Edith K., ix. 33
    Grant, ii. 431
    J. Romilly, i. 318
    Jn. (fl. 13th cent.), vii. 75
    Jn. (fl. early 17th cent.), ii. 155, 234; ix. 55
    Jn. (fl. 1719), vii. 217
    Ralph, prior of Sele, ii. 61–3
    Ric., cellarer of Battle, prior of Sele, ii. 61–2
    Thos. (fl. 1278), ii. 184
    Thos. (d. 1781), iii. 147
    Wm., ii. 207–8
    Mr., ii. 458
    and see Heron-Allen
Allfrey (Alfray, Alfrey, Allfray, Allfrye, Aulfrey):
    Edw., ix. 221
    Edw. Thos., vii. 177
    Eliz., w. of Thos., ix. 111
    Geo., vii. 177
    Hen., ix. 221
    Hen. W., ix. 221
    Joan, vii. 100 *n*
    Jn., vii. 229, 232
    Nat., ix. 241
    Ric. (fl. 1611), ix. 202
    Ric. (fl. 1609–37, ? another), ix. 241, 244
    Ric. (fl. 1665), ix. 120
    Ric. (? another), ix. 122
    Thos. (d. 1589/90), ix. 111, 116, 202, 242 *n*
    Thos. (d. by ? 1611), ix. 202, 241, 242 *n*
    Thos. (fl. 1678), ix. 241
    Wm., vii. 76
    fam., ix. 242
Allington (in St. John's Without, Lewes):
    Allington, East, vii. 34
    Allington, West, vii. 34
    man., vii. 2–4, 7, 33–4, 79, 89, 231
allotments and smallholdings, ii. 207–9, 212–13, 279, 285, 287
Alman, fam., ix. 208
Almar (fl. 1066), iv. 4
Almenesches (Orne, France), abbey, ii. 46, 121, 331
Almodington:
    Agnes de, m. Ric. Rumbregger, iv. 202
    Alice, w. of Jn. de, iv. 202

Clemence, w. of Jn. de, iv. 202
    Ernis de, iv. 202
    Hugh de, iv. 202
    Joan de, m. Thos. Shypwright, iv. 202
    Jn. de (fl. 1296), iv. 202
    Jn. de (sr.) (fl. 1337), iv. 202
    Jn. de (jr.) (fl. 1337), iv. 202
    Jn. de (d. by 1367), iv. 202
    Rob. de, iv. 202
    Wal. de (fl. *c.* 1260), iv. 202
    Wal. de (fl. 1300–32), iv. 295 *n*; iv. 202
Almodington, *see* Earnley
Almodington Green, *see* Sidlesham
Alms:
    Geo., iii. 144
    Jas. (d. 1791), iii. 144
    Jas. (d. 19th cent.), iii. 145
almshouses, *see* Arundel; Ashburnham; Birdham; Boxgrove; Boxgrove: priory; Chich.; Fairlight; Lewes; Oving; Rye
Alnod (fl. 1066), iv. 199; vii, 67, 228; ix. 137
alodial tenure, iv. 58, 108–9, 115, 199; vii. 68, 101
Alrehelle, *see* Auronhelle
Alric, bp. of Selsey, iv. 127; ix. 1, 253
Alschot (? in Folkestone, Kent), ix. 149
alsike, *see* crops
Alston, Avice, m. Thos. Forster, ix. 197
Alta Ripa, de, *see* Dawtrey
altar recesses, *see* architecture: ecclesiastical
altar slabs, *see* architecture: ecclesiastical
Altham:
    Eliz., *see* Sutton
    Sir Jas., iv. 224
Alured, *see* Alfred
Aluredesfeld, Humph. de, iv. 195
Alvered, Wm., ii. 78
Alvred, Wm. s. of, *see* William
Alvric, *see* Alfric
Alward the clerk, iv. 135
Alward (fl. 1066), iii. 84; iv. 142, 144
Alwin (fl. 1066), iv. 104
Alwin (fl. 1066, another), iv. 108
Alwin (fl. 1066–86), vii. 142
Alwold (fl. 1086), ix. 267
Alwyn, *see* Aylwin
Amberley, Rob. de, canon of Chich., iii. 166; iv. 171
Amberley, i. 539; ii. 24, 42–3, 298, 314 *n*
    birds, i. 277, 286–7, 293
    botany, i. 47, 60
    cast., i. 274; ii. 305, 333, 392, 394–5
    ch., ii. 5
        accessories, ii. 350–1, 353–4, 356, 361, 366
        archit., ii. 333, 339, 342, 349–50, 365–6, 371, 373–5
        dom. archit., ii. 337, 386, 391
    fossils, i. 33–4
    insects, i. 134, 136, 142, 144–6, 148–9, 151, 153, 157, 162–3, 186–7, 189–90, 193, 196, 207, 209–10, 233
    lime works, ii. 231
    man., ii. 404
    marshes, i. 274
    pop., ii. 218
    prehist. rem., i. 328
    Rackham, *q.v.*
    sport, ii. 466
    Stone gate, i. 328
    vicarage, ii. 9
    Wild Brooks, i. 54, 287
Ambersham, North and South (formerly in Steep, Hants), i. 536; ii. 217 *n*, 442; iv. 2, 40, 54
    North, i. 196, 200, 204, 206, 209
    pop., ii. 221
    South, iv. 60, 80
Ambroys, Jn., ix. 61
Amelia, Princess, dau. of Geo. III, ii. 204

America:
    North, i. 33, 281, 286, 293, 529; ii. 165–7, 239
    United States of:
        president, *see* Wilson, Woodrow
        and see Carolina, North; Maryland; Virginia; wars: American Independence
Amesbury (Wilts.), ii. 316
Amherst:
    Arthur, vii. 75
    Frances, vii. 35
    Geof., vicar of Southease, vii. 75
    Marg., m. —— Colbrand, vii. 35
    Ric., vii. 35, 239, 255
    his w., vii. 35
Amherst, ctss. of, *see* Sackville, Mary
Amicellis (Auncell), Rob., prior of Lewes, ii. 69–70
Amigo, P.E., bp. of Southwark, iii. 167
Amigoni, Jacopo, iv. 50
Amminius, Lucullus s. of, *see* Lucullus
Amport (Hants), iv. 154
Amundeville, Ric. de, i. 497
Amyand, Claudius, iv. 212
anchorage, right of, ix. 84
anchorites, ii. 46–7, 94; iv. 131, 233; vii. 40, 276
    cells, *see* architecture: ecclesiastical
Anderida, *see* Pevensey
Anderida forest, *see* Andredsweald
Anderson, J.G.C., iii. 14
Andred (Andredeslea) forest, *see* Andredsweald
Andredsceaster, *see* Pevensey
Andredsweald (Anderida, Andred, Andredeslea) forest, i. 49–50, 305, 334, 481, 536; ii. 126, 291–3, 313, 324
Andrewe (Andreu):
    Jn., ii. 257
    Lawr., ii. 24
Andrews (Andrewes):
    Edw., ii. 163
    Eliz., *see* Westbrook
    H.R., vii. 155
    Lancelot, bp. of Chich., ii. 32; iv. 134
    Mrs., ix. 221
Androin, abbot of Cluny, ii. 68*
Angell, Wm., ix. 53
Anger:
    Eliz., ix. 177
    Wal., ix. 177
Angieus, Ralph de, vii. 234
Anglesey, i. 344 *n*; ix. 37*
    high sheriff, *see* Sparrow, Bodychen; Sparrow, Hen.
angling, *see* sport
Anglo-Saxon remains, i. **332–49**, *332*
    anatomy, i. 335–6, 346
    burials, i. 334–48, 470; vii. 14
    coins, i. 344, 348–9
    glass, i. 342, *344*, 345
    ornaments, i. 343–5, *344*
    pottery, i. 338, 342–3
    religion, i. 333–7, 345, 347
    weapons, i. 341–2, 345
    and see parish names
Anglo-Saxon wars, *see* wars
Angmering, East and West, i. 483; ii. 42–3; iv. 42
    Barpham (Bargham), ii. 42–3
        chap., ii. 16, 105
        man., iv. 41
        prebend, ii. 16, 105; iii. 146
    char., ii. 437
    ch., ii. 124, 332, 339, 354, 368, 379
    dom. archit., ii. 386
    Harrow Hill, i. 467*, *467*
    man., ii. 109
        Ecclesden (Ecclesdon), ii. 190, 230; iii. 46, 58
    militia, i. 535
    natural history, i. 60, 199, 264, 283
    New Place, ii. 386
    pk., ii. 297
    pop., ii. 217
    roads to, iii. 46

Angmering (*cont.*):
Rom. rem., iii. 4, 20, 46, 49
sch., ii. 437
Angoulême, Isabella of, *see* Isabella
Anjou, count of, *see* Geoffrey
Ankas, Wm., iv. 39
Anker, *see* Aucher
Ankerwyke (Bucks.), priory, iv. 167
Anketil (Anketill, Ansketil, Ansketill),
prior of Boxgrove (? two of the
name), ii. 59; iv. 107, 157
Anketil (Anschitel) (fl. 1086), iv. 199
Anketil (Anschitil) (fl. 1086, another),
ix. 267, 278
Anknapp, Thos., ii. 308
Annadown (Enaghdun) (Irel.), bp., *see*
O'Tigernach
Anne, queen, ii. 444; iii. 89; vii. 239
Anne (Boleyn), queen of Hen. VIII, ix.
255
Anne (of Bohemia), queen of Ric. II, ix.
3
Anne (of Cleves), queen of Hen. VIII,
iv. 185; vii. 48, 57, 69, 83, 95, 105,
109, 123, 163, 169, 171, 217–19,
224, 227–8, 237, 257, 262
Anne (of Denmark), queen of Jas. I, iv.
208
Anne, dchss. of York, *see* Mowbray
Anne, Adam de, master of hosp. of St.
Jas. and St. Mary, Chich., ii. 100
Annebault, Claude d', ii. 145; vii. 63
Annesley:
Brian, vii. 217
Grace, m. Sir Jn. Wildgose, vii. 217–
18; ix. 220
Annington, *see* Botolphs
Anscher, *see* Aucher
Anschitel (Anschitil), *see* Anketil
Anselm, abp. of Cant., ii. 6, 53, 112,
303; iii. 106; iv. 229, 234; ix. 9
Ansevill, Reynold de, ix. 206
Ansfrid (fl. 1086), iv. 135
Ansketil (Ansketill), *see* Anketil, prior of
Boxgrove
Anslevill (Ansleville):
Rob. de, iv. 30 *n*
Wm. de, iv. 143 *n*
Anstey:
Aphorah, m. Thos. Battishill, vii. 179
Isaac, and his w. Sarah, vii. 179
and see Anstye
Anstie Grange, *see* Holmwood
Ansty, *see* Cuckfield
Anstye (or Holcombe):
Eliz., vii. 157
Joan, w. of Thos., m. 2 Wm. Cooke,
vii. 157
Thos. (d. 1597), vii. 157
Thos. (fl. 1640), vii. 157
Thos. (fl. 1688), vii. 157
Wal., vii. 157
and see Anstey
Anstye, *see* Cuckfield: Ansty
Ansye, Gerard, ii. 255
Anteny, Jn., prior of Dominican friary,
Chich., ii. 94
Anthemius, Rom. emperor, i. 337
Anthill, Edw., vii. 286
Antiquaries, *see* Society of Antiquaries
Antonio, Don, claimant to throne of
Portugal, ii. 153; vii. 63
Antwerp (Belgium), i. 536; ii. 27, 254
ap Adam, *see* Badeham
Apelderham, *see* Appledram
Apleye, *see* Apsley
Apperley, Chas. Jas. (Nimrod), ii. 444–
6
Appleby, Wm., iii. 80
Appledore (Kent), ii. 365; ix. 34, 40
Appledram (Apelderham, Apul-
derham):
Ric. de, dean of South Malling, ii. 119
Thos. de, iv. 117
Appledram (Apuldram), ii. 43; iii. 86,
102; iv. 133, **138–40**, 198
adv., iv. 140
angling, ii. 467

Appledram Place, *see* Appledram: Rymans
ch., ii. 112; iv. 138–40, *140*, 169
accessories, ii. 353, 356, 358, 362
archit., ii. 346, 348, 350–1, 366, 371
Dell Quay, i. 65; ii. 467; iii. 50, 71,
90, 100–2; iv. 138
dom. archit., ii. 384; iv. 138–9, *138*
guild, iv. 140
man., ii. 53, 176, 181–3; iv. 139–40
ho., iv. 138–9
mill, iv. 138 *n*
natural history, i. 181–2, 293
pop., ii. 220
prebend, ii. 110–12
prehist. rem., i. 310, 312–13, 328
roads, iv. 138
Rom. rem., iii. 49
Rymans (Appledram Place), ii. 384;
iv. 138–9, *138*
stream, iv. 138
trades and ind., ii. 232–3, 261, 270;
iv. 139
Applesham, *see* Coombes
Appleshaw (Hants), iv. 154
Appleton, Wm., iii. 93
apprentices, ii. 195–6
Apps, Thos., ii. 235
apses, *see* architecture: ecclesiastical
Apsley (Apleye):
Anne, *see* Mill
Ant., ix. 84, 254
Cordelia, m. Jas. Dalrymple, ix. 84
Cordelia, w. of Hen., ix. 84
Hen., s. of Ant., ix. 84, 254
Hen., s. of Randolph, ix. 84
Hen., s. of Hen., ix. 84 *n*
Jn. (fl. 1560), iv. 123
Jn. (fl. 1564, ? another), ii. 24
Jn. (fl. 1719–53), vii. 11
Jn. (? another), ix. 84
Judith, *see* Randolph
Nic., iv. 41, 123
Randall, rector of Pulborough, ii. 35
Randolph, ix. 84
Wm., iv. 123
Col., i. 525
Apulderham family, *see* Appledram
Apuldram, *see* Appledram
Aquila, *see* Laigle
Aquitaine (France), ii. 135
arable farming (vol. ii only), ii. 211,
274–6, 280–1, 285
Archdall:
Anna Maria, *see* Montagu
Ric., iv. 122
archdeacon, Ric. the, *see* Richard
Archdeacon, Wm., iv. 120
archdeaconries, *see* Chich.: dioc.:
archdeaconries
Archer:
Jn., iv. 29
Mary, ctss. of Plymouth, *see* Sackville
Other, earl of Plymouth, vii. 35
Arches, Court of, *see* courts
architects, *see* Adams, H.P.; Amigoni;
Barry, Sir Chas.; Blomfield, Sir
Arthur W.; Blomfield, Sir Reg.;
Bodley; Brooks, Jas.; Burges, W.;
Bushnell; Butler, Jos.; Butterfield,
Wm.; Carpenter, R.H.; Carpenter,
Ric. C.; Carpenter, Wm. (fl. 1830);
Chambers, Sir Wm.; Cheeseman,
G.; Christian; Clark, T. Chatfield;
Clarke, Somers (d. 1926); Clarke,
——; Elmes, Jas.; Emerson; Fel-
lowes-Prynne; Ferrey; Frewen,
Chas. Hay; Gibbins; Habershon,
W.G. & E.; Habershon and Brock;
Hill, Jn.; Johnston, Jn.; Johnston,
Phil.; Kay, Jos.; Kendall, H.; Lit-
tle; Macartney, Mervyn; Maw;
Nash, Jn.; Nash, T.; Norton, Jn.
(fl. 1881); Pearson, F.L.; Pearson,
Jn. L.; Pugin; Reveby; Rickman,
Thos.; Ridge, Lacy W.; Saunders,
——; Scott, Edm.; Scott, Sir
Gilb.; Scott, J. Oldrid; Slater, W.;

Slater & Carpenter; Smirke;
Streatfield, G.E.; Talman; Teulon,
S.S.; Teulon, W.H.; Troup;
Webb, Sir Aston; Woodman, Mr;
Wren, Sir Chris.; Wyatt, Jas.;
Wyon
architecture (vol. ii only), ii. **327–96**
building materials, *q.v.*
civil and dom., ii. **380–94**
brick, flint, and stone buildings, ii.
380–4, *385*, 386–8, *388*, 391–4
bridges, ii. 394
ch. hos., ii. 383–4, *385*, 392
crypts, ii. 384
decoration and fittings, ii. 389–90,
392–3
dovecots, ii. 382
farm buildings, ii. 393
man. hos., ii. 380–2
mansion hos., ii. 386–7
mills, ii. 393–4
timber-framed buildings, ii. 382,
384, *384*, *385*, 386–91, 393
village and mkt. crosses, ii. 394
weatherboarding, ii. 391
ecclesiastical (including accessories),
ii. **327–79**
altar recesses, ii. 351, 372
altar slabs, ii. 337, 351
anchorite cells, ii. 346–7
apses, ii. 331, 342, 364–7, 376
aumbries, ii. 351, 370, 372–3
bas reliefs, ii. 334, 336, 356, 362,
363, 365–6, 379
bells, ii. 249–51, 362
brasses, monumental, ii. 360–1
buttresses and pilasters, ii. 329–30,
335, 348–9, 363–4, 366–8, 370–
6
candelabra, ii. 362
chantry chapels, ii. 329, 332, 361,
378–9
chests, ii. 359–60, 371, 373
clerestories, ii. 342, 344, 366, 368,
370–4, 376
coffin slabs, ii. 261, 360, 362, 365,
368
corbel tables, ii. 329, 349, 366, 368,
373–4
cross, churchyard, ii. 348
crosses, consecration, ii. 350–1,
353–5, 366
crypts, ii. 329–30, 347, 373
decoration in stone (carvings,
mouldings, and sculpture), ii.
334, 336–8, 334 *n*, *345*, *347*,
347–50, *350*, 360–2, *363*, *364*,
364–8, *366*, *369*, *370*, 370–9,
373, *374*, *375*, *377*
dials, scratch (or mass), ii. 346, 350,
362
doors and doorways, ii. 349–50,
357, 362, *363*, 364–8, 370–2,
375–9
easter sepulchres, ii. 352, 378
floors, ii. 330, 338, 344, 353
fonts and font covers, ii. 337, 355–
7, 365–8, 370–3, 376, 378–9,
395
galleries, ii. 359, 379
glass, ancient, ii. 353, 375, 378
graffiti, ii. 350
grave slabs, cast-iron, ii. 360
image holders, ii. 352, 378
iron work, ii. 338, 346, 350, *357*,
357–8, 376
lectern, ii. 359
lych gates, ii. 348
misericords, ii. 358–9, 375
parapet walls, ii. 349
parvise chambers, ii. 346
piscinas, ii. 330, 338, 351–2, *363*,
364, 366–7, 370–8
plate, ii. 362
porches, ii. 332, 346, 349, 370–3,
376–9
pulpits, ii. 359, 377, 379
reliquary, ii. 367

reredoses, ii. 352–3
sacristies, ii. 332, 346, 371, 375, 378
screens, ii. 333, 346, 352, 357–8, *358*, 375–9
seating, ii. 333, 357–9, 375, 378
sedilia, ii. 330, 352, 370–8
spires, ii. 337, 340, 342, 374, 378–9
squints, ii. 346, 350–1, 368, 370
stoups, water, ii. 352, 376, 378–9
tabernacles, ii. 351, 367, 370, 378
tombs, ii. 309, 334, 337, 352, 361–2, 374, 376–9
towers, ii. 328, 334, 337, 339–40, 342, 362, 364–8, 370–4, 376–9
vaulting, ii. 329–30, 333, 344, 346–8, *347*, 367–8, 371–2, 378
wall paintings, ii. 353–5, 364, 366–7, 370–1, 377
wind vane, ii. 376
military, ii. **394–6**
Rom., *see* Romano-British Sussex: roads and camps
Arctic, i. 288
Arden (Ardenne), *see* Arderne
Arden, Ld., *see* Perceval, Chas. Geo.
Arden (Yorks. N.R.), priory, iv. 171*
Arderne (Arden, Ardenne, Ardern):
Nichole de, *see* Bardolf
Ralph de (fl. *c.* 1190–1212), ii. 81; iv. 67, 69, 77, 104, 106, 114
Ralph de (fl. 1239), ii. 81
Sir Rob. de, vii. 203
Thos. de, iv. 104, 114
Ardingly (Ardinglie), ii. 43–4, 311; vii. 125, **127–32**, 200, 225 *n*
adv., vii. 132
botany, i. 60–1
ch., vii. *128–9*, 129–32
accessories, ii. 353, 358, 361, 376
archit., ii. 336–7, 349–50, 376–7
Coll., *see* Ardingly: St. Saviour's sch.
dom. archit., vii. 127–9, *128*
man., vii. 2, 129
pop., ii. 223
rector, ii. 35
rivers, i. 464
roads, iii. 42; vii. 127
St. Saviour's sch., i. 536; ii. **432–4**, 476; vii. 127
Wakehurst, i. 174
man., vii. 129, 196
pk., ii. 310–11
Wakehurst Place, ii. 336, 386–7; iii. 42
Argenteyn (Argentein, Argentem, Argentham, Argentyn):
Alice de, m. Jn. de Chaggele, iv. 144
Christiane de, *see* Lovell
Jn. de, iv. 161, 199 *n*
Thos. de, iv. 144
Wm. de, iv. 144, 161, 199 *n*
fam., iv. 144–5
Argentina, *see* Buenos Aires
Argentyn, *see* Argenteyn
Arismandy, Jn., iv. 76
Arlington, ii. 44, 77; vii. 42
Abbot's wood, i. 56
insects, i. 115–17, 119–22, 127–9, 135, 137–41, 143, 147–69, 171–210, 212–13, 215–25
angling, ii. 464
Bramblegrove wood, ii. 322
Burghlow (Burlow) cast., i. 475–6; ii. 394
chant., ii. 13
Chilver Bridge, iii. 47
ch., ii. 30, 333; iii. 49
accessories, ii. 352, 354, 356, 359–61, 376
archit., ii. 328, 336–7, 344, 346, 348–51, 362, 368, 371, 376
Claverham, i. 477; ix. 56
earthworks, i. 475–7, 480
Hempstead, i. 68, 167
insects, i. 174, 179, 199–201, 203–4
man., ix. 193
Michelham, *q.v.*
Milton, ii. 122

half hund., i. 538
Hide, i. 193, 195
Street, i. 348
pop., ii. 226
roads to, iii. 47
Rom. rem., iii. 2, 49
Sessingham, ix. 193
Bridge, i. 477
vicar, ii. 35; *and see* Turner, Steph.
Wilbees, i. 477
Windover Hill, i. 328*; iii. 48
Arnald, *see* Ernald
Arnold:
Edith, *see* Wavell
F.H., iii. 16
Jn., iii. 146
Marion Harriet, iv. 118
Thos., iv. 129
Wm., ix. 111
Arques:
Emma de, m. Manasses, count of Guines, ix. 149
Wm. de, ix. 149
Artillery Ground, *see* London
Artington (Surr.), *see* Loseley House
Arton, riv., *see* Asten
Arun, riv., i. 18, 52, 108, 274, 473, 539; ii. 279, 291; iii. 35–6, 38–9, 41, 63, 71
as a boundary, ii. 303, 445
crossings, iii. 46, 60, 70
fossils, i. 25
mouth, i. 515; ii. 477; iii. 3–4, 10
natural history, i. 42, 53–4, 60, 109, 177, 190, 192, 198, 202, 209, 286, 303–4
prehist. rem., i. 310
settlement, iii. 2
sport, ii. 271, 453, 466
transport, ii. 241
Arundel (Arundell):
Eleanor, m. 1 Sir Thos. Browne, 2 Thos. Vaughan, iv. 92, 112, 168
Eleanor, w. of Sir Jn., iv. 160
Eliz. de, Lady la Zouche, w. of Sir Jn. de, iv. 202
Joan de *see* St. John
Jn. (fl. 1288), iv. 85
Jn. (fl. 1306), iv. 85
Sir Jn. (fl. 1376–97), iv. 52, 202–3
Jn., Ld. Maltravers, iv. 52, 60, 66, 90, 114, 202–3*
Jn., earl of Arundel, iv. 202–3
Jn., bp. of Chich., ii. 61–2, 117, 267, 378; iii. 111, 137, 145, 159; iv. 51, 210; ix. 157
Lady Kath., iv. 56
Sir Thos., iv. 168
arms, iii. *111*
Arundel:
ctss. of, *see* Adelize; Bohun, Eliz. de; Despenser, Isabel; Eleanor, dau. of Hen., earl of Lancaster; Fitz-Alan, Beatrice; FitzAlan, Eleanor; Marshall, Maud; Mortimer, Isabel; Stuart, Eliz.; Warenne, Isabel de
earls of, ii, 171; iii. 23, 40, 51, 59, 90, 97, 108, 111, 114, 122, 144, 176, 199, 235; vii. 145, 195, 206
bailiffs, ii. 301
earldom, iv. 66, 97, 127, 177, 202–3
and see Arundel, Jn.; Aubigny; Bel-leme; FitzAlan; Howard; Mont-gomery, Hugh de; Montgomery, Rog. de
Arundel, ii. 187, 217, 228; iii. 87; iv. 2; vii. 15
adv., ii. 108, 119
ale-hos., ii. 196
almshos., iv. 32
A.-S. rem., i. 346
birds, i. 284
botany, i. 46, 48, 54, 60
bridge, ii. 80
cast., i. 490, 493, 501, 503, 509, 515, 519; ii. 108, 120, 174, 271; iv. 1, 95

archit., ii. 334, 336, *394*, 394–5
Civil War, i. 522, 524–5, 528
coffin slabs, i. 360, 362
earthworks, i. *473*, **473–4**
gaol, i. 512
oratory, ii. 338
signal post, i. 533
wall, iv. 62
castlery, *see* Arundel: rape
causeway, ii. 80; iv. 130
ch., i. 155 *n*, 524; ii. 25, 33, 108–9, 119
accessories, ii. 352–4, 356–61, 377
archit., ii. 332, 336, 340, 344, 346, 350–1, 377–8
FitzAlan chap., ii. 344, 346, 348, 351, 358–9, 377
and see Arundel: colleges
Civil War, i. 522, 524–6, 528; ii. 39; iv. 16
clerks of St. Nic., *see* Arundel: col-leges
clubs, political, i. 532
colls.,
Holy Trinity, ii. 20, 46, 83, 93, 97, **108–9**, 120, 398; iv. 23, 45, 47, 129, 153, 172; hosp., *see* Arun-del: hosps.
St. Nicholas, ii. 4, 46, 119, 398; iv. 20, 23, 47
coroner, ii. 188
crustaceans, i. 264
deanery, ii. 42–3
dom. archit., ii. 231, 392
earthworks, i. 467–8, 473–4
forest, ii. 293–7, 300–6; iv. 45, 235
bounds, ii. 303
cts., ii. 304
fossils, i. 32
friary, ii. 45, 47, **93–4**
archit., ii. 331
priors, ii. 94
Friday's Church, i. 346
geology, i. 13
governor, i. 526–7
honor, i. 491; iv. 122
descent, ii. 304–5; iv. 1, 31, 44, 50, 77, 111, 115, 128, 130, 234
fees, iv. 4, 13, 30–1, 40–1, 45, 50, 58, 91, 95, 97–8, 111–12, 115, 118, 123, 127–8, 143, 145, 158, 166–8, 171, 234
franchises, iv. 1, 45
hunds., extrinsec, iv. 40, 133
revenues, iv. 21, 88
valuation, ii. 302
and see Arundel: rape
hosps.:
Holy Trinity (Maison Dieu), ii. 45, **97–8**, 331; iv. 31, 99, 124, 199; vii. 58; masters, ii. 98
St. Jas., ii. 46, **97**, 331
hund., ii. 217, 228
insects, i. 114, 119–20, 133, 136, 142, 153–6, 159–63, 173, 181–5, 190, 192–3, 195, 199–200, 202–6, 208–10, 212–13, 224–5, 235
Jews, i. 506
local govt.:
boro., i. 504; ii. 228
mayors, i. 521, 532; ii. 39
Maison Dieu, *see* Arundel: hosps.: Holy Trinity
mammals, i. 300, 305
man., iv. 95
mkt., ii. 194
militia, i. 507, 519, 528, 534–5
mills, ii. 97
naval recruitment, *see* Arundel: ship service
Nineveh, ii. 388
nonconf., ii. 33
pk., ii. 297, 303–6; iii. 49
deer, i. 306
Hiorne's Tower, ii. 395
insects, i. 117, 158, 162, 170–1, 177, 187, 190–2, 194–9, 201–10, 235

Arundel (*cont.*):
parl. rep., i. 532
M.P., *see* Weekes, Carew
piracy, ii. 149
poor relief, ii. 206
pop., ii. 217
port, ii. 28, 161, 194, 248, 270; iii. 102
prebend, ii. 119
priory, ii. 14, 46, 48, 108, **119–20**, 398; iv. 20, 23
ct., iv. 23
priors, ii. 57–8, 119–20; iv. 47; *and see* Denis
sch., ii. 120, 398
rape, i. 490; ii. 175; iii. 83, 96; iv. 1–2, 30, 47 *n*, 58, 65, 114, 222, 226–7, 234; vii. 4
ale-hos., ii. 195
apprentices, ii. 195–6
boundary, iv. 134
coastguards, i. 506 *n*
famine, ii. 194–5
franchises, iv. 1
hunds., iv. 1–2
sheriff, *see* Robert son of Tetbald
sub-bailiffs, ii. 171
vagrancy, ii. 196
and see Arundel: honor
Rewell (Rewel, Ruell, Ruelle):
Hill, iii. 64
wood, i. 121, 174, 193–207, 209, 213, 233; ii. 303–5
riots, i. 512; ii. 206 *n*
roads to, iii. 46
Rom. Cath., ii. 28, 217 *n*
Rom. rem., iii. 2, 46, 49
royal visits, i. 491–2, 505, 515, 527; ii. 61, 93
sch., ii. 120, 397–8
ship money, ii. 156
ship service, ii. 141, 153, 161
shipping, ii. 141, 148, 151
shire ct., iii. 96
sport, ii. 453, 466
Swanbourne, ii. 97
trades and ind., ii. 145–6, 164, 166, 233, 235, 253, 262, 270–1; *and see* Arundel: port
vicar, ii. 35
vicarage, ii. 37
water bailiff, ii. 270
and see shows, agricultural
Arundel and Portsmouth canal, ii. 241, 466
Aseville, Thos. de, iv. 23, 25
Ashburn (Ashbourn, Ashbourne), riv., i. 18, 56, 479; ii. 464; ix. 126
Ashburnham (Ashburneham, Oseburnham):
Adam, ix. 183
Alice, w. of Steph., ix. 127
Alice, w. of Wm., ix. 229
Sir Anchitil, i. 302; ii. 447, 470 *n*; ix. 181
Ann, w. of Chas., iii. 146
Ann Frances, iii. 146
Anne, m. Wm. Michelborne, vii. 239
Bart. (fl. 1253), ix. 127
Bart. (d. 1322), i. 508; ix. 127
Bertram, earl of Ashburnham, i. 306; ix. 112, 127
Bridget, m. Francis Dear, iii. 145
Lady Cath., ix. 107, 127, 130, 206, 233, 237
Chas. (d. 1762), ix. 181
Chas. (d. 1800), iii. 146
Chas. (d. 1810), iii. 146
Sir Denny, vii. 239; ix. 12, 181
Eliz., baroness of Cramond, w. of Sir Jn., m. 2 Sir Thos. Richardson, ix. 129
Eliz., w. of Sir Jn., *see* Kenn
Eliz., w. of Thos., *see* Dudley
Frances (Francis), *see* Holland
Geo., Vct. St. Asaph, later earl of Ashburnham, i. 535; ix. 130
Harriott, iii. 146
Isabel, *see* Grofhurst

Jane, m. Geo. Nevill, Ld. Bergavenny, vii. 185
Jane, w. of Wm., *see* Butler
Joan, w. of Rog., ix. 266
Jn. (fl. 1296), ix. 127
Jn. (d. 1335), ix. 127–8
Jn. (fl. 1371), ii. 325; ix. 127
Jn. (fl. 1415), ix. 127, 266
Jn. (fl. 1459), ix. 266
Jn. (d. 1563), ix. 127–8, 241
Jn. (d. 1591), ix. 106, 126–7, 244
Sir Jn. (fl. 1600), ix. 127, 129, 229, 241
Sir Jn. (d. 1671), iv. 212, 216; ix. 12, 126–30, 234
Jn., Ld. Ashburnham (d. 1710), ix. 127, 233, 249
Jn., earl of Ashburnham (d. 1737), ix. 127
Jn., earl of Ashburnham (d. 1812), ii. 325; ix. 107, 138–9, 196, 199, 206, 234–5, 238, 244
Revd. Sir Jn., chancellor of Chich., rector of Guestling, vii. 109*; ix. 181, 183
Jn. (fl. 1909), ix. 234
L., ii. 470 *n*
Lawr. (d. 1565), ii. 24; ix. 20, 181
Lawr., his grds., vii. 239; ix. 177, 180–1
Maria Eliz., ctss. of Ashburnham, ix. 139, 238
Sir Reg., ix. 179
Reynold de, ix. 127
Ric. de (fl. 1242), ix. 127
Ric. de (fl. 1275), ix. 127
Ric. de (fl. 1459), ix. 181, 266
Rog. (fl. 1371), ix. 127 *n*
Rog. (fl. 1417), ix. 266
Steph. de, ix. 127
Thos., ix. 127, 181, 266
Wm. (fl. early 16th cent.), vii. 185; ix. 229, 241
Wm. (d. 1679), ix. 129–30
Wm., Ld. Ashburnham (d. 1710), ix. 127, 236–7, 241
Wm. (another), iii. 146
Sir Wm. (d. 1755), ix. 177, 181
Sir Wm., dean, later bp., of Chich., ii. 51; ix. 71, 177, 181
Sir Wm. (d. 1823), ix. 181
Sir Wm. (d. 1843), ix. 181
——, w. of Lawr., *see* Levett
fam., ix. 128, 183, 237–8, 241–2, 244, 249, 261
arms, ix. *107, 127, 181*
and see Ashburnham-Clement
Ashburnham:
ctss. of, *see* Ashburnham, Maria Eliz.
earls of, ix. 113, 125; *and see* Ashburnham
Lds., *see* Ashburnham
Ashburnham, ii. 43, 464; ix. 125, **126–30**, 233, 247
adv., ix. 130
Agmerhurst, ix. 127–8
almshos., ix. 130
Ashburnham Place, ix. 126, *126*
birds, i. 291
Buckwell, ix. 126, 233
char., ix. 130, 234
ch., ii. 76; ix. *127–8*, 128–30
accessories, ii. 250, 356, 358; ix. *127*, 130
archit., ii. 336, 339, 346, 379
chyd., ix. 237
geology, ii. 243
insects, i. 116, 138–41, 145, 147, 152, 162, 164, 168, 173, 188, 201, 211, 225, 227–9, 232–4, 236
iron ind., ii. 229, 246, 249, 296; ix. 126, 232 *n*
mammals, i. 303
man., ii. 180–1; ix. 127–8
militia, i. 535
Panningridge, ii. 246, 249
pk., i. 306; ii. 297, 325
pop., ii. 222

roads, ix. 126
vicarage, ix. 238
woodland, ii. 324–5
Ashburnham-Clement (formerly Ashburnham), Sir Anchitil P., ix. 181
Ashby (Asheby, Assheby):
J.W., ii. 473–4
Jn., ix. 118
Kath., w. of Ric. de, ix. 240
Ric. de, ix. 240
Thos., ix. 240 *n*
Ashby & Co., ii. 263
Ashcombe, Ld., *see* Cubitt
Ashcombe (in Lewes):
Ashcombe Hill, i. 498
Ashcombe Pk., ii. 446
man., vii. 34
mill, vii. 58
vill, vii. 51
Ashdown (Ashdowne), Jn., prior of Lewes, ii. 70; vii. 49
Ashdown (Ashdowne, Assesdon, Asshedon, Asshedonne, Asshedowne, Eschedune, Essendon, Essesdoun, Evesfold, Pevensey), forest, i. 49, 110, 305; ii. 186 *n*, 230, 245, 291, 293–4, 296–9, 313–24; iii. 34, 44–6
assarts, ii. 189
birds, ii. 316
Blackbrooke (Black brook wood, Blackebrooke), i. 172; ii. 319
Bodinggeham, ii. 315
botany, i. 59–61
Bromknoll, ii. 314
coins, i. 326, 328
Colbebech, ii. 315
commons, ii. 319
cts., ii. 317–18, 320–2
customs and services, ii. 294, 314–16, 320–1
Duddles (? Duddleswell), ii. 317
Evesfold, ii. 315
fish ponds, ii. 321
forest rights, ii. 122
gates, ii. 319
gills, ii. 319
golf, ii. 477
Hamoda, la, *q.v.*
Heselwode, ii. 314
Honnywell, ii. 319
hunting, i. 512; ii. 316, 318, 322, 448
inc., i. 322
insects, i. 112, 121, 165–6, 168 *n*, 169, 172, 174–5, 177–9, 181–2, 184–6, 189, 192–4, 196, 202, 204, 215, 220, 228–9
Lancaster Great Pk., ii. 316–18, 321–2
Landwelheade, ii. 319
lodges, ii. 317, 319, 321
Loggebrok, la, ii. 315
Mayeslond, ii. 316
militia, i. 533
Redee, la, ii. 314
roads to, iii. 34, 44–6
Rom. rem., iii. 34, 44–6
Rottingeham, ii. 315
Stoneland pk., ii. 297, 318
tithes, ii. 315
Uleley (Uleleye, Oulele), ii. 314–15
Walheath, ii. 314
walks, ii. 319
wards, ii. 315, 317–9
Wigge, la, ii. 314
Ashdowne, *see* Ashdown
Ashe (Assh, Asshe):
Jas., ix. 180
Jn. de, ix. 180
Rog. de, i. 509
Thos., ix. 224
and see Nash
Asheby, *see* Ashby
Ashfield:
Dorcas, m. Maur. Kendall, iv. 224
Dorcas, w. of Sir Ric., *see* Hore
Eliz., *see* Sutton
Frances, m. Jn. Isham, iv. 224
Sir Jn. (d. 1635), iv. 224

Sir Jn. (d. 1714), iv. 224
Sir Ric., iv. 223–4
his w., see Rogers
fam., iv. 223
Ashford (Kent), ii. 193; ix. 40, 146, 244–5
Ashington, i. 513–14, 519; ii. 43
ch., ii. 352
earthworks, i. 477
insects, i. 164
pop., ii. 220
tanning, ii. 260
and see Frenchlands
Ashling, see Funtington
Ashtead (Surr.), iii. 33
Ashton:
Miss., iv. 39
Mrs., iv. 39
Ashurst (Assherst), Wm., ix. 177
Ashurst (Aishurst), ii. 43
ch., ii. 340, 344, 356, 368, 372
man., ii. 307
pk., ii. 297
pop., ii. 220
Ashurst House, see Coldwaltham
Ashwell, Rawson, canon of Chich., iii. 115–16
Asia Minor, i. 306
Aske:
Joan, see Shelvestrode
Jn. (d. 1397), iv. 56
Jn. (fl. 1542), iv. 56
Sir Rob., iv. 56
fam., iv. 56
arms, iv. 56
Askell, Tobias, ii. 257
Aslaby, Jn., master of Holy Trinity hosp., Arundel, ii. 98
assarting, ii. 187, 189, 273–4, 292 n, 306
Assefalde, Isabel le, iv. 61
Asser, i. 483
Assesdon, see Ashdown
Assh (Asshe), see Ashe
Assheby, see Ashby
Asshedon (Asshedonne, Asshedowne), see Ashdown
Assherst, see Ashurst
assize of bread and of ale, ii. 188; iii. 93, 95–6, 104; iv. 76, 131; vii. 2; ix. 51, 118, 196, 201, 221
assize of cloth, ii. 256
assizes, see courts
Asten (Arton), riv., ii. 464; ix. 9
Astley, D.G., ix. 221
Aston:
Jn., ii. 164
Sir Rog., vii. 227
Atchison, Jn. D., ix. 124
Athelstan (Aethelstan, Ethelstan), king of Wessex, ii. 3, 126; iii. 83; iv. 13, 202; vii. 14, 32
Athelstan (Aethelstan), aetheling, iv. 91
Athelstan, sub-king of South Saxons, i. 483
Athelstan (Aethelstan), moneyer, iii. 83
Atherfield (I.W.), i. 7
Atherington, see Climping
Atherton, Thos., vii. 183
Atherton, see Climping: Atherington
athletics, see sport
Athlone, earls of, vii. 132
Athlone (Irel.), rector, see Jones, Wm.
Atkins (Atkys):
Geo., iv. 112
Isabel, see Shales
Jas., and his w. Mary, iv. 163
Wm., vii. 266
Atkinson, Jn., ii. 408
Atkys, see Atkins
Atlantic Ocean, i. 268–9, 288
Atlingworth, see Portslade Atlingworth
Atrebates, i. 326*
Attacton, Thos., vii. 20
atte Dene, see Adeane
Attegildenehall, see Gildenhall
Attewelle, see Atwelle
Attewode, see Awood

Attree:
Edm., vii. 180
Jn. (fl. 1438), vii. 121
Jn. (d. 1665), vii. 180
Thos. (fl. 1502), vii. 121
Thos. (fl. 1537), vii. 121
Thos. (fl. 1852), vii. 258, 262
Wm. (fl. 1502), vii. 121
Wm. (fl. 1806), vii. 258*
fam., vii. 109
Atwelle (Attewelle), Thos., prior of Lewes, ii. 69–70
Atwood, see Awood
Aubigny (Albini, Daubeney):
Adeliza d', see Adelize, queen of Hen. I
Hen. d', iii. 82
Hugh d', earl of Arundel, ii. 304; iii. 82; iv. 2, 13, 96, 111, 115, 122–4, 127, 143, 145, 166–7, 171
coheirs of, iv. 2
Hugh d' (? another), iv. 89
Isabel de, see Warenne
Maud d', m. Rob. de Tattersall, iv. 13
Maud, w. of Hugh d', see Marshal
Nichole, m. Rog. de Somery, iv. 58, 115, 124, 166
Phil. d', i. 494; iii. 79
Wm. d', earl of Arundel, Chich., or Suss. (d. 1176), i. 490; ii. 57–8, 80, 303; iii. 80 n, 84, 102, 104, 119; iv. 1, 13, 23, 34, 59, 100, 120, 128, 130, 168; ix. 2
Wm. d', earl of Arundel (d. 1193), ii. 303–4; iii. 84; iv. 89, 99, 145
Wm. d', earl of Arundel (d. 1221), i. 491, 493–4; ii. 58, 119; iv. 30, 89, 96, 120
Wm. d', earl of Arundel (d. 1224), ii. 121, 304; iv. 167
arms, iii. 84
Aubigny, dukes of, see Lennox
Aucher (Anscher, Auscher), prebendary of Hastings, ii. 113, 410
Aucher (Anker), prior of Lewes, abbot of Reading, ii. 65, 69
Aucher, Wm. fitz, see William
Auchier (Aucher):
Alice, see Wells
Hen., ix. 144
Joan, see Wells
Jn., ix. 144
Nic., i. 507
Audeham:
Francis de, i. 508
Isabel, see Hay
Thos. de, i. 498; ii. 241–2, 317
Audele (Audeley), see Audley
Audenard, Giles de, dean of Hastings, ii. 117
Audhun (fl. 7th cent.), i. 482
Audley (Audele, Audeley):
(or Beauchamp), Alice, w. of Jas. de, ix. 176
Eleanor, m. Sir Rog. Lewknor, iv. 35
Sir Hen., iv. 64, 80, 109, 111
Hugh de, and his w. Marg., ii. 323
(or Beauchamp), Jas. de (d. by 1285), ix. 176
Jas. de (fl. c. 1300), ix. 176
Jas. de (fl. 1310, his s.), ix. 176, 178
Marg., w. of Jas., ix.. 176
Augmentations, Court of, see courts
Augustus, Rom. emperor, iii. 14
Augustus Frederick, duke of Sussex, ii. 209 n*
Aulfrey, see Allfrey
Aulus Plautius Silvanus, iii. 1
Aumary, warden of Cokeham hosp., Sompting, ii. 106
aumbries, see architecture: ecclesiastical
Auncell, see Amicellis
Aungier, Francis, ix. 156
Auronhelle (Alrehelle), hund., i. 537
Auscher, see Aucher
Austen (Austyn):
Jane (novelist), iv. 226
Jn. (fl. 1622), ix. 213

Jn. (fl. 1670), ix. 213
Margery, see Chauncy
Rob., ix. 213
Sarah, m. Ric. Righton, ix. 213
Susan, iii. 164 n
Thos. (d. by 1472), vii. 190, 280
Thos. (fl. 1541–2), vii. 183
Wm., ix. 213
and see Austin
Austin (fl. 1086), iv. 145
Austin, F., ix. 151; and see Austen
Australia, ii. 471–3, 481; and see Melbourne
Austria, duke of, see Albert II
Austyn, see Austen
Autresi, Rob., iv. 177
Aveline, dau. of Brian FitzRalph, m. Jn. de Say, iv. 45
Aveline, ? granddaughter of Rob. s. of Tetbald, m. 1 Alan, 2 Reynold de Windsor, iv. 44, 84
Avenel (Avenell):
Agnes, w. of Nic., iv. 135
Britell, ii. 361
Maud, w. of Nic., iv. 135
Nic. (fl. 1296), iv. 135
Nic. (fl. 1332), iv. 135
Wm., iv. 135 n
Averenches, see Avranches
Avery:
Nat., vii. 177
Thos., vii. 177
aves court (avesfeild), see courts
Avesford, see Avisford
aveshould, see courts: aves
Avignon, Jn. of, prior of Lewes, ii. 66–7, 70
Avisford (Avesford, formerly Binsted or Benestede), hund., i. 538; ii. 138 n, 217; iv. 1, 222, 234
Avisford, see Walberton
Avranches (Averenches), Wm. de, ix. 37
Avranches (Manche, France), dean, see Laigle, Nic. of
Awcocke, see Alcock
Awdry, W., bp. of South Tokyo, ii. 433
Awood (Attewode, Atwood):
Elias, ix. 128
Harman, vii. 280
Jn. (d. 1528), vii. 180
Sir Jn. (d. 1559), vii. 180
Jn. (fl. 1602), vii. 180
Nic., vii. 180
(or Thurstan), Thos., vii. 180
and see Bosco; Wood; Woods
Awsiter, Jn., ii. 203*; vii. 248
Aylardenne:
Isabel, see Grofhurst
Sim. de, ix. 127
Aylen, ——, i. 526
Aylesbury, Jn. de, dean of South Malling, ii. 119
Aylesbury Dairy Co., ii. 435
Aylesford, Hen. de, abbot of Battle, ii. 55
Ayleston, Jn., warden of St. Mary's hosp., Chich., ii. 102
Aylewyn (Aylewyne), see Aylwin
Ayling (Aylinge), see Aylyng
Ayloffe, Thos., ix. 181
Aylward, Revd. Augustus F.A., ix. 276
Aylwey, Hen., iv. 64
Aylwin (Alewin, Alewyn, Alwyn, Aylewyne, Aylwyn):
Eliz., iv. 13
Eliz., m. Sir Wm. Mannock, iv. 31
Hannah, m. Jn. Edes, iii. 73–4
Joan, w. of Wm., iv. 31
Jn. (fl. 1535–57), iv. 31, 99
Jn. (d. 1588), iv. 31
Jn. (d. 1604), iv. 99
Jn. (fl. 1604–22), iv. 90, 99
Jn. (fl. 1613), vii. 75
Jn. (fl. 1634–49), iv. 163
Kath., w. of Wm., iv. 31
Magdalen, w. of Ric., iv. 31
Mary, m. Chas. Talbot, iv. 31
Ric. (fl. 1545), iv. 99

Aylwin (cont.):
  Ric. (fl. c. 1677–89), iv. 31, 62
  Rob. (d. 1607), iv. 31, 44 n
  Rob. (d. by 1689), iv. 31
  Rob. (d. 1736), iv. 31
  Rob. (d. 1740), iv. 31
  Thos. (d. 1594), iv. 62, 99
  Thos. (fl. 1617), iv. 163
  Wm. (fl. 1571), iv. 31
  Wm. (d. 1585, another), iv. 31
  Wm. (d. by 1678), iv. 30–1
  Wm. (fl. 1688), iv. 31
  Wm. (d. 1737), iv. 31
  fam., ii. 388; iv. 99
  arms, iv. 31
Aylyng (Ayling, Aylinge):
  Joan, m. Edm. Gray, iv. 85
  Wm., prior of Pynham, ii. 80–1
  Wm. (d. 1583), iv. 62, 85
  Wm., cricketer, ii. 475
Aynscombe, Thos., ix. 254
Ayot (Eyott):
  Eliz. de, m. Valentine Bromdene, iii. 105
  Hen., iv. 168
  Isabel, w. of Nic., iii. 105
  Jn. de, iii. 105
  Nic. de, iii. 105
  Wm. de (d. 1325), iii. 105; iv. 168
  Wm. de (fl. 1332), iii. 105
Ayscue, Sir Geo., ii. 157–8
Azo, abp., ii. 92
Azo, Geof. s. of, see Geoffrey
Azor (fl. 1066), iv. 44, 234; vii. 80, 141–2, 179, 202, 225–6, 228, 280
Azores, i. 253; ii. 154

Babington, J., ii. 461
Babinrerode (Babirote), see Gostrow
Bachelor (Bacheler):
  Agnes, m. Thos. Fawkenor, iv. 179
  Edw., ix. 241
  Geo., ix. 181
  Goddard, ix. 214
  Jn., rector of All Saints in the Pallant, Chich., iii. 104
  Jn. (fl. 1546), ix. 181
  Jn. (d. 1558, ? another), iv. 179
  Marion, see Fowle
  Rob., ix. 181
  Thos., prior of Pynham, ii. 81
  Thos., (fl. 1605), ix. 214
  Wal., ii. 311
  and see Batchellor
Back, Fanny, ix. 33
Backshell:
  Jn., canon of Chich., iii. 126
  Mary, w. of Jn., see Mill
  Mary, w. of Jn., see Miller
Bacon (Bacoun):
  Edm., ix. 139
  Francis, rector of Birdham, ii. 408
  G.A., ii. 260
  Margery, w. of Edm., see Poynings
  Wm., vii. 122
Badby, Jn., ii. 15
Badeham (Abadam, ap Adam):
  Eliz. de, see Gurney
  Sir Jn. de, iv. 144
  Thos. de, iv. 144
badger baiting, see sport
Badlesmere:
  Bart. de, i. 508; iv. 167
  Eliz. de, m. 1 —— Mortimer, 2 Wm. de Bohun, earl of Northampton, iv. 167
  Eliz., w. of Giles de, m. 2 Hugh le Despenser, iv. 167
  Giles de, iv. 167
  fam., ii. 317
Badly, Edw., vii. 85
Badworth, see Lyminster: Batworth
Bageley (Baguley):
  Jn., ii. 408
  Mic., M.P. for Midhurst, iii. 94; iv. 76, 79
  Thos., ii. 15*; iii. 94; iv. 79 n
  Wm., iii. 94

Bagshawe, Mrs., ix. 29
Baguley, see Bageley
Bahamas, gov. of, see Shirley, Wm.
Baildon, W. Paley, i. 310, 331
Bailie, see Bayley
Bailiffscourt, see Climping
Bailinghill, see Warnham
Baillie, Wm., Ld. Forester, ii. 441
Bailly, see Bayley
Baird:
  D., ii. 459
  ——, i. 264
Baker (Bakere):
  Ann, see Colman
  Chas., iv. 192
  Constance, see Kingsmill
  Gilb. le, Wm. s. of, see William
  Hen. (fl. 1404), ii. 86
  Sir Hen. (d. 1623), ix. 20
  Hen., rector of Linch, iv. 67
  Hen. (d. 1730), and his w. Penelope, iii. 144
  Jas., iv. 70
  Jane, see Trafford
  Jn., prior of Pynham, ii. 81
  Sir Jn., chancellor of exchequer etc., ix. 20, 120, 130, 233–4, 257
  Jn. (d. 1596), ix. 20
  Jn. (fl. 1614), ix. 83 n, 254
  Sir Jn. (fl. 1623), ix. 20
  Jn. (fl. 1632), iv. 172
  Sir Jn. (fl. 1661), ix. 20
  Jn. (fl. 1663), iv. 190 n
  Jn. (fl. 1671), ix. 83 n
  Jn. (d. c. 1725), ix. 92
  Jos., iii. 145
  Mic. (fl. 1730), ix. 92
  Mic. (fl. 1750, ? another), ii. 439
  Mic. (fl. 1771, another), ii. 439
  Penelope, m. Thos. Hayley, iii. 144
  Peter, ix. 92
  R., ii. 473
  Ric. (fl. 1558), iv. 101, 103, 238; vii. 60, 78
  Sir Ric. (fl. 1579), iv. 238
  Sir Ric. (d. 1594, ? another), ix. 20, 120, 232–3
  Ric. (fl. 1605–35), ix. 202
  Ric. (fl. 1622, ? another), ix. 120
  Rob., vii. 96, 238
  Ruth, see Farnden
  Thos., vicar of Cocking, iv. 238
  (or Sherman), Thos. (fl. 1450), vii. 34
  Sir Thos. (d. 1625), ix. 120, 233–4
  Thos. (fl. 1647), and his w. Alice, ix. 120, 233
  Thos. (fl. 1660), ii. 408
  Thos. (fl. 1701), ii. 408
  Thos. (fl. 1781), ii. 439
  Thos., warden of St. Mary's hosp., Chich., canon of Chich., ii. 102; iii. 147
  (or Lewes), Wm., see Lewes
  Mr., ii. 101
  Mrs., vii. 204
  ——, ii. 35
  fam., vii. 159; ix. 20
  arms, ix. 20, 233
Baker and Bennett, Messrs., iii. 76
Bakere, see Baker
Balcombe, ii. 43–4; vii. 92, 125, 127–8, 132–6
  adv., vii. 135
  botany, i. 60
  Brantridge:
    Forest, vii. 132
    Pk., vii. 132
  ch., vii. 135, 136
  dom. archit., vii. 132–3
  Down, i. 55
  forest, vii. 132
  Highley, vii. 134, 195, 199 n
  inc., ii. 313
  insects, i. 137, 139, 142, 151, 154, 158, 162, 194, 200, 206, 208–10, 225
  mammals, i. 301, 304
  man., vii. 2, 92, 133–5

  pop., ii. 223
  rly., ii. 223; vii. 132
  rectors, ii. 416–17, 420; and see Chatfield, Thos.; Routh, Dan.; Spicer, Wm.
  Tilgate forest, q.v.
  trades and ind., ii. 247; vii. 132
  Worth forest, q.v.
Baldeslei (Baldeslowe), see Baldslow
Baldewyn, see Baldwin
Baldred, king of Kent, ii. 118
Baldshill (unidentified), vii. 4
Baldslow (Baldeslei, Baldeslowe), hund., i. 537; ii. 222; ix. 3, 19, 76
Baldslow (in Ore), see Ore
Baldwin, abp. of Cant., ii. 53, 63
Baldwin (Baldewyn):
  Edwin, vii. 280
  Nic., sub-prior of Bayham, abbot of Durford, ii. 90–1
  Stanley, iii. 130
  Wm. (? two of this name), iv. 99, 195
Baley, see Bayley
Balfour, A.J., vii. 173
Balger (fl. 1058), ii. 2
Baliol, see Balliol
Ball (Balle):
  C.H., ii. 474
  Hen., archdeacon of Chich., iii. 125
  Isabella, see Franks
  Marg., w. of Thos., see Mill
  Thos., warden of St. Mary's hosp., Chich., dean of Chich., ii. 51, 102; iii. 144–5
  W.H., ii. 474
  Wal., ii. 296
Ballard:
  Adolphus, iii. 83, 90
  Eliz., vii. 50
  ——, iii. 77
Balle, see Ball
Ballett:
  Chas., iv. 161, 163
  (formerly Halfpenny), Jn., iv. 161
  Jn. (d. 1755), iv. 161
  Susanna, m. Cholmely Brereton, iv. 161
Balliol (Baliol):
  Gilb. de, ix. 118
  Jn., i. 499
  Ralph de, vii. 234
  Ric. de, vii. 234
  Widelard de, ix. 118
Balliol College, Oxford, ii. 432
Ballowe:
  Martha, m. —— Grane, iii. 126
  Thos., iii. 126
Bally, H., ii. 470 n
Balmer, see Falmer
Balneath (in Barcombe and Chailey), vii. 80, 95–6
Balsdean, see Rottingdean
Baltic sea, ii. 162, 165, 167
Baltine, Maj., ix. 240
Bamford, Jn., ii. 29
Bamsteed (? Banstead, Surr.), ii. 408
Banassac (Lozère, France), iii. 69
Banaster, see Bannister
Banbury (Oxon.), ii. 406
Banham (? Bineham in Chailey), vii. 4
Banister, see Bannister
Banks:
  Dorothea, see Hugessen
  Geo., vii. 199
  Geo. Wilson, vii. 199
  Jn., ii. 411
  Sir Jos., ix. 145, 273
Bannister (Banaster, Banister, Bannaster):
  Edw. (d. 1606), iv. 92
  Sir Edw. (fl. 1640), iv. 118
  Hugh, vii. 259
  Sir Humph., vii. 258–9
  Mary, iv. 111 n
  Peter, and his w. Constance, iv. 163
  Thos., ii. 276
Banstead (Surr.), see Bamsteed

Banvilla, Wm. de, prior of Wilmington, ii. 123
Baptists, ii. 38–9, 41; iii. 88, 164, 168; iv. 227; vii. 42, 62, 87, 103, 119, 136, 144, 147–8, 172, 179, 181, 263; ix. 61–2, 112, 123, 200, 206, 257
Bar (Barre):
  Eleanor, see Eleanor, dau. of Edw. I
  Hen., count of Bar, iv. 233; vii. 3
  Joan de, m. Jn. de Warenne, earl of Surrey, vii. 3, 12 n
  Theobald de, rector of Pagham, ii. 12; iv. 233
Barantyne, see Barrington
Barbados, attorney gen., see Hooper, Rob.
Barbican ho., see Lewes
Barclays Bank, vii. 32
Barcombe (Bercham, Bercompe, Berecompe, Middleborgh), i. 498; ii. 43–4; vii. 79–83, 87, 89, 226
  adv., vii. 83
  agric., vii. 80
  Balneath, q.v.
  Barcombe Mills, ii. 465; vii. 82
    angling, ii. 465
    insects, i. 116
    roads to, iii. 44, 69
    Rom. rem., iii. 69
  ch., vii. 79, 82–3, 112
    accessories, ii. 356
  cts., vii. 81
  dom. archit., vii. 80
  hund., i. 537; ii. 223; vii. 1, 3 n, 33, 36, 44, 54 n, 79
  insects, i. 121, 137–63, 186, 212–14, 217–18
  man., ii. 173 n; vii. 80–2, 84, 190, 226
  pop., ii. 223
  rly., vii. 80
  Spithurst, vii. 80, 83
  trades and ind., ii. 253, 259–60
Barcroft:
  Mary (d. 1741), iii. 126
  Mary, w. of Wm., see Blaker
  Ric., iii. 126
  Wm., canon of Chich., iii. 126
Bardi, the, iii. 101
Bardney (Lincs.), abbey, ix. 103 n
Bardolf:
  Agnes, w. of Wm., m. 2 Sir Thos. Mortimer, vii. 110
  Anne, m. 1 Sir Wm. Clifford, 2 Sir Reynold Cobham, vii. 110
  Beatrice, m. Hubert de Burgh, vii. 283
  Beatrice, w. of Doun, see Warenne
  Doun, vii. 80, 110
  Hugh, Ld. Bardolf, vii. 80, 110, 203
  Isabel, see Aguillon
  Joan, m. Sir Wm. Phillips, vii. 110
  Jn., Ld. Bardolf, vii. 110
  Margery, vii. 203
  Nichole, m. 1 Sir Rob. de Arderne, 2 Sir Thos. Wale, vii. 203–4
  Thos., Ld. Bardolf (d. by 1328), vii. 67 n, 110, 203 n
  Thos., Ld. Bardolf (fl. 1405), vii. 110
  Wm. (d. 1275), i. 498–9; vii. 66, 80, 110, 226, 283
  Wm. (fl. 1275), vii. 110, 113
  Wm. (fl. 1385), vii. 110, 203
  Sir Wm. (d. 1423), vii. 110
  fam., vii. 80, 168, 228
    arms, vii. 67
Bardolf, Ld., see Bardolf; Beaumont, Wm.
Bardown, see Ticehurst
Barenten (Barenton, Barentyn, Barentyne), see Barrington
Baret, see Barrett
Bargham, see Angmering: Barpham
Baring, F., ii. 128
Barkeley, see Berkeley
Barker:
  Ant., ii. 407
  Hugh, ii. 407
  Susan, see Bateman

Sir Thos., iv. 35
Wm., ii. 34
Barkhale, see Bury
Barkham, see Birkham
Barking (in Wandsworth, London, formerly Surr.), iv. 92
Barlavington, ii. 43
  botany, i. 49
  ch., ii. 351, 357, 368
  earthworks, i. 480
  man., iv. 108
  pop., ii. 218
Barley:
  Alice, ix. 24
  Jn., ix. 24
  Thos., ix. 24
barley, see crops
Barline, see Peasmarsh
Barlow:
  Randoll, warden of St. Mary's hosp., Chich., ii. 102
  Wm., bp. of Bath and Wells, bp. of Chich., ii. 23–4; iii. 124; iv. 208; vii. 262
Barlow, see Pratt Barlow
Barman, Ric., iv. 73
Barmling:
  Mabel de, see Waliland
  Steph. de, ix. 267
Barnam:
  Anne, iv. 167
  Rob., iv. 167
Barnard (Bernardi):
  Dan., and his w. Anna, iii. 115
  Eliz., iv. 130
  Frances, m. Ezekiel Dickenson, vii. 74 n
  Jn., and his w. Mary, iii. 144
  Lambert, ii. 16*, 354*, 392*; iii. 112, 114, 116, 132–4, 148, 151; iv. 146
  Osmond, iv. 208
  Thos. (fl. 1735–49), vii. 74
  Sir Thos. (fl. 1756–67, ? another), vii. 74
  Wm., iv. 130
  and see Bernard
Barnes:
  Agnes, ii. 99
  Wm., ix. 183
Barnfield, East (Kent), hund., ii. 223 n
Barnham:
  Alice (fl. 1602), vii. 180
  Alice, w. of Francis, see Bradbridge
  Francis, iii. 145
  Martin (? two of this name), vii. 50, 180
  Steph., vii. 180
Barnham, i. 483; ii. 42–3, 56; iv. 226
  ch., ii. 7, 9, 56
    accessories, ii. 351, 356, 358, 360, 368, 379
    archit., ii. 329, 335, 339–40, 346, 365–6, 368, 371–3, 379
  ct., ii. 388
  insects, i. 197, 208
  man., iv. 143
  pop., ii. 217
  prehist. rem., i. 328
  sport, ii. 452*, 453
Barnhorne, see Bexhill
Barnsley:
  Geo. (fl. 1708), ix. 232
  Revd. Geo. (d. 1723, ? another), ii. 437–8
Baron, Jn., prior of Hardham, ii. 75
baronial cts., see courts
Barons' war, see wars
Barpham, see Angmering
barracks, see Blatchington, East; Chich.; Climping; Lewes; Ringmer
Barratt, see Barrett
Barre, see Bar
Barrentyn, see Barrington
Barrett (Baret, Barratt, Barret):
  Agnes, prioress of Rusper, ii. 64
  Anne, m. Thos. Spence, iv. 193 n
  Bridget, ii. 34
  Jn., ix. 119

Nic., ii. 159
Serenus, rector of New Fishbourne, ii. 428*
Thos., ix. 119
Barrington (Barantyne, Barenten, Barenton, Barentyn, Barentyne, Barrentyn, Baryngton):
  Alex. de, iv. 192
  Aubrey de, iv. 193
  Daines, i. 291
  Drewe, ii. 24; ix. 153, 242
  Geo. de, and his w. Emma, iv. 135; vii. 99
  Joan, see Lewknor
  (or Hedehone), Nic. de, iv. 135
  Ric. de, iv. 192–3
  Thos. de, iv. 193
  Sir Wm., iv. 35; ix. 263
Barrow Hill, see Henfield
Barrowe, see Bergen op Zoom
barrows, see earthworks
Barry:
  Sir Chas., vii. 177, 259, 267
  Ric., earl of Barrymore, ii. 449; vii. 249
  Willoughby, ii. 414
Barrymore, earl of, see Barry, Ric.
Bartelot (Bartelott), see Barttelot
Barter, Jn., ii. 166
Bartholomew, Wm., mayor of Chich., iii. 87
Barthropp, P.G., ii. 447
Bartie, see Bertie
Bartlett:
  Barbara, see Smith
  Wal., iv. 90
  (later Smith), Wal., iv. 90
  Wm., J.P., ii. 24
  Wm. (another), iii. 164
  and see Barttelot; Stone and Bartlett
Barton:
  Geo., ii. 470
  Hen. de, iv. 62
  Humph. C., ix. 216–17
  Rob. G., ix. 216
  Thos., vii. 204
Barton, see Pagham: Nyetimber
Barton (Hants), i. 29
Barttelot (Bartelot, Bartelott):
  Cath., m. Wm. Luntley, iv. 161
  Edw. (d. by 1474), iv. 161
  Edw. (d. by 1501), iv. 202, 212
  Edw. (fl. 1558), iv. 202, 212
  Eliz., m. Jn. Burdeville, iv. 5
  Jas. (d. 1474), iv. 161
  Jas. (fl. 1494), iv. 5
  Joan, w. of Edw., iv. 202 n, 212
  Jn., iv. 212
  Thos., iv. 5
  Thos. (? another), iv. 212
    his w., see Okehurst
  fam., i. 513; iv. 212
  and see Bartlett
Barwell:
  Cath., w. of Ric., m. 2 Edw. Miller Mundy, iv. 172, 189 n, 190, 195; ix. 224
  Ric., iv. 112, 121–2, 124, 127, 129–30, 172, 185, 189–90, 195, 223; ix. 224
Barwick (Barwicke, Barwyke):
  Alfred, and his w. Agnes, vii. 158
  Amy, m. Jn. Gratwick, iv. 93
  Curtis, iv. 93
  Jn., iv. 93
  Ric., vicar of Compton, iv. 93
  Ric., (fl. 1641), iv. 93
  Rog., iv. 93
  Rog. (another), iv. 93, 112 n
  Wm., ii. 308
Baryngton, see Barrington
bas reliefs, see architecture: ecclesiastical
Base:
  Hen., ii. 407
  Jn., ii. 407
  Owen, ii. 407
Baseville (Basevile):
  Alan de, and his w. Isabel, iv. 41

Baseville (cont.):
Alice de, m. 1 Wm. Torrell, 2 Jn. de Teuelby, iv. 42
Alice de, see Dunstanville
Sir Gilb. (d. by 1258), iv. 6 n
Gilb. de (fl. 1241, ? another), iv. 41–2, 85
Hawys de, iv. 42
Joan de, m. Wm. Paine, iv. 42
Ladereyna (Laderena) de, m. 1 Jn. de Wykes, 2 Wm. de Valoynes, iv. 42, 171
Marg. de, m. Jn. de Wykford, iv. 42
Bashurst, see Itchingfield
Basilia, w. of Hugh son of Gold, vii. 33
Basing (Hants), i. 525; iv. 143, 199
Basok:
Adam de, ix. 278
Rob., ix. 278–9
Basok, fee of, ix. 202, 278
Bass (Basse):
Issac, vii. 263
Ric., ii. 406–7
Mr., ii. 460–1
Bassano:
Agnes, see Warren
Wm., vii. 106
Basse, see Bass
Basset (Bassett):
Alan, iv. 41
Alice (fl. 1340), iv. 144
Alice, w. of Wm., iv. 41
Cecily, see Dunstanville
Hawise, see Vilers
Joan, m. Rog. Dore, iv. 144
Joan, w. of Ralph, Ld. Basset see Montfort
Joan, w. of Sir Wm., iv. 42
Jn., vii. 158
Laur., iv. 41
Lucy, ii. 84
Marg., see Somery
Nic., i. 512
Ralph (fl. 1293), iv. 167
Ralph, Ld. Basset, ix. 3
Thos., iv. 15
Sir Wm. (d. by 1283), ii. 84
Wm. (d. 1305), iv. 41
Sir Wm. (d. c. 1333), iv. 41–2
Wm. (fl. after 1333), iv. 42
Bassett Smith:
W., vii. 37
——, i. 265
Bassingburn, Alex. de, ix. 15
Basyng:
Marg., w. of Wm. de, m. 2 Edm. de Passeley, ix. 154
Wm. de, ix. 154, 176, 254
Bat, Ralph, ix. 128
Bataille, see Batayle
Batan, Wm., ii. 95
Batayle (Bataille):
Rob., ii. 136
Wm., abbot of Robertsbridge, ii. 74
Batchellor (Batchelor):
Sam., iv. 38
——, iii. 57
and see Bachelor
Bate, see Bates
Bately:
Cath., m. Chas. Heath, iii. 126
Wm., iii. 126
Bateman:
Eliz., m. Hen. Watkinson, iv. 35
Eliz., w. of Thos., see Foster
Philadelphia, m. Wm. Rochester, iv. 35
Susan, m. 1. Hen. Taylor, 2 Sir Thos. Barker, iv. 35
Thos., (fl. 1588), vii. 54
Thos., (fl. 1643), iv. 35
Wm., iv. 234
Batemans, see Burwash
Bates (Bate, Batys):
Agnes, m. Thos. Selwyn, ix. 229
Jn., ix. 229, 232
Jn. Lockington, ix. 156
Sim., ix. 229

Spence, i. 259, 261
Bath (Som.) ii. 431, 467 n; iii. 2, 18; iv. 38; ix. 50
Bath and Wells, bp., see Barlow, Wm.
Bathoni, Hen. de, iv. 34 n
Batisford, see Batsford
Batley:
Cath. Anna Cockburn, ix. 179
Wm., ix. 178
Batner:
Anne, see Wane
Jn., vii. 144
Ric., vii, 144
batrachians, i. 271–2
Batsford (Batisford, Battesford):
Alice, ix. 118
Eliz., ix. 118
Joan, m. 1 Jn. de Coding, 2 Wm. Brenchley, ix. 118–19, 123, 266
Margery, see Peplesham
Wm. (? two of this name), i. 510; ii. 104; ix. 92 n, 118–19, 123, 266
arms, ix. 216
Battel, see Battle
Batten, Oliver, ix. 207
Battesford, see Batsford
Battishill:
Aphorah, see Anstey
Thos., vii. 179
Batthyany-Strattmann, Prince Edm., ii. 457
Battle (Battel, de Bello), i. 57, 501; ii. 43, 206 n, 228, 464; iv. 78; ix. 76, 97–112
abbey, i. 486, 496, 500, 502; ii. 4, 6, 16, 45, 54, 52–6, 57, 87, 176–7, 294; iv. 133, 139–40, 183; vii. 14, 210, 228; ix. 92, 94, 97, 103, 118, 135, 189, 207, 209
abbots, i. 510–11, 514, 538; ii. 14, 55, 72, 115, 139–40; ix. 148–50; and see Blancard, Rob.; Coventry, Ralph de; Dover, Jn. de; Gausbert; Hammond, Jn.; Henry; Lucy, Wal. de; Ludlow, Thos. de; Odo, prior of Christ Church, Cant.; Offington; Ralph, prior of Rochester; Reynold; Retlyng; Richard; Warner
accessories, ii. 353
archit., ii. 230, 329, 366, 371, 373, 378, 382, 395; ix. 102–5
arms, i. 139; ix. 102
cellarer, see Allen, Ric.
dissolution, i. 515; ix. 115
dorter, ix. 102
endowments, ii. 328–9
estates, i. 538; ii. 171–8, 252, 295, 297–8, 384; ix. 75, 82, 106, 112–13, 128, 145, 147, 180–1, 242, 253, 255, 262, 267, 278
gateho., ix. 96
lowey (leuga, liberty), ii. 42, 52, 172, 177; ix. 79, 82, 84, 95, 101, 106–7, 119, 226
royal visits, ii. 53–5
ship service, ii. 134
adv., ix. 111
apprentices, ii. 196
batrachians, i. 272
Beauport Pk., i. 57; iii. 29, 31–2, 49; ix. 81, 101
insects, i. 123, 125*
iron ind., ii. 241
mammals, i. 302–3
Beech (Westbece), ix. 95, 106
botany, i. 68
char., ix. 111–12
ch., ix. 108, 110
accessories, ii. 351, 353–4, 356–8, 360–1; ix. 111
archit., ii. 328–9, 336, 339–40, 342, 344, 346–7, 349–50, 366, 368, 370–1, 378; ix. 109–11, 136 n
coins, i. 326, 328
Dallington forest, q.v.
dean, ii. 42; ix. 106; and see Clere,

Rob.; Crake, Edw. Neville; Richard; Torkesey; Wythines
Deanery, ii. 387
dom. archit., ii. 391; ix. 97–101
fairs, ix. 102
fossils, i. 35–7
gaol, i. 503
geology, i. 2, 4–5
guilds, ix. 102
High Wood, i. 57
hosp., ii. 45, 98
hund., i. 537–8; ii. 222, 228; ix. 95–6, 115, 164, 226
inns, ii. 196
insects, i. 116–17, 120, 122–3, 125–7, 129, 132, 137–8, 140–7, 150–9, 161–3, 166–8, 171–6, 178–90, 192, 194–5, 199, 208, 215–22, 224, 226–37
liberty, see Battle: abbey: lowey
local govt., i. 539; ix. 101
mammals, i. 301–3
man., ii. 177; ix. 20, 106–7, 113, 118, 128, 147, 180, 221
mkt., ii. 183; ix. 102
militia, i. 534
mills, ix. 101, 109
Netherfield, q.v.
nonconf., ix. 112
Oaklands Pk., see Westfield
pks., ii. 294; ix. 106–8
Peppering (Peperynge):
insects, i. 120, 125–8, 148
powder mill, ii. 238
Petley wood, ii. 298; ix. 106
poor relief, ii. 191, 209
pop., ii. 222; ix. 101
prehist. rem., i. 328
rly., ii. 222 n; ix. 97, 131, 247
rebellion, i. 514
roads, ix. 97, 101
Rom. Cath., ii. 25, 28; ix. 106
Rom. rem., iii. 49
royal visits, i. 491–2, 496, 501, 505
Sandlake (Sanglake, Senlac, Sentlache), i. 486 n; ix. 95, 101, 106
sch., ii. 397, 440
master, ii. 25, 397
Senlac (Sentlache), battle, see Hastings: battle; and see Battle: Sandlake
smuggling, ii. 200
sport, ii. 447, 468, 470, 477
Telham, i. 487; ii. 172; ix. 95
fossils, i. 38
prehist. rem., i. 328
Telham Hill, ii. 52
trades and ind., ii. 230, 238, 241, 249, 252, 260; ix. 101–2, 109
Uckham, ix. 95, 106
U.D., ii. 228
Batworth, see Lyminster
Batys, see Bates
Baude, Peter, ii. 246
Baudefar, Hugh, ii. 77; vii. 257
Baume (Doubs, France), ii. 70 n
Bavaria, ii. 72
Bavent:
Adam de, iv. 45
Joan de, m. Sir Jn. de Dantesey, iv. 45
Jn. de, iv. 45
Rog. de (d. by 1279), iv. 45
Rog. de (fl. 1316), iv. 45
Rog. de (d. 1355), iv. 45
Sarah de, see Sarah
arms, iv. 45
Baxter:
Geo., ii. 239
Jn., ii. 239
Wynne E., mayor of Lewes, vii. 29*, 38
——, ii. 470, 475
Bay (Poll Bay), riv., ix. 217
Baybush, see Beeding: Bewbush
Bayeux, Thos. of, abp. of York, ii. 6
Bayeux (Calvados, France):
abbey, ii. 331
bp., see Odo

Tapestry, i. 476, *488*; iv. 182; ix. 14
Bayfield, Mat. Albert, ii. 434
Bayham abbey (in Frant), ii. 8, 13, 16–17, 45, 77–8, **86–9**, 323, 329–30
  abbots, ii. 14, 86–9; ix. 127; *and see* Chetham, Jn.; Jordan, abbot of Otham
  accessories, ii. 351, 353
  archit., ii. 330, 342, 347, 371
  estates, ix. 139–40, 214, 230, 255
  polo, ii. 461
  royal visit, ii. 87
  wool trade, ii. 188, 256
Bayle, Jn., ii. 237
Bayley (Bailie, Bailly, Baley, Bayly):
  Abraham, ix. 197
  Arthur, iv. 112
  Eliz., iv. 112
  Jn., prior of Arundel friary, ii. 94
  Jn. (fl. 1807), iii. 168
  Mat., ii. 204 *n*
  P., ii. 166
  Ric., ix. 241
  Wm., ii. 428–9
  Wm. Goodenough, ii. 429
  and see Baillie
Baylis, Jn., and his w. Sarah, iv. 202
Bayly, *see* Bayley
Bayne, Nic., ii. 422*
Baynham:
  Diana, *see* Covert
  Rob., vii. 280
Bayntun, Hen., vii. 180
Bayonne (Pyrénées-Atlantiques, France), ii. 132–3; iii. 101
Beach, Ric., ii. 271; *and see* Beche
Beachy Head (Eastbourne), i. 56, 72; ii. 127–8, 146, 157–62; iii. 55; vii. 244; ix. 13
  angling, ii. 467
  battery, ii. 163
  battle, ix. 10
  earthworks, i. 455
  fishing, ii. 271
  fossils, i. 11
  geology, i. 1, 10, 18–19, 274
  lighthouses, ii. 163
  natural history, i. 45–6, 48–9, 62–3, 83, 98, 125, 169, 172, 185, 254, 282, 286, 297
  prehist. rem., i. 313, 316, 320, 329
Beacon Hill, *see* Harting: Harting Beacon
Beadufrid (fl. 714), iv. 211
beagling, *see* sport: hunting
Beakesbourne, *see* Bekesbourne
Beale:
  Jerome, and his w. Anne, vii. 227
  Jerome (another), vii. 227
  Ric., iv. 192
  Steph., iii. 146
  Mrs., ix. 232
Bean, Messrs., ii. 280
Bean Lodge (unidentified), ii. 388
beans, *see* crops
Beard:
  Ann, vii. 178, 196
  Caroline, m. Jn. Evans, vii. 177
  Cecily, vii. 236
  Chas., vii. 228
  Dan., vii. 177
  Eliz., m. Hen. Streatfield, vii. 228, 236
  Jn. (fl. *c*. 1556), ii. 309
  Jn. (fl. 1745), vii. 235
  Kitty, vii. 177, 235
  Mary, vii. 178, 236
  Nic. (fl. 1594), ii. 29
  Nic. (fl. 1699), vii. 177, 234–5
  Ric., vii. 228, 234, 236
  Stenning (fl. 1772), vii. 235
  Steyning (fl. 1903), ii. 451
  Thos. (fl. 1656–79), vii. 105, 236
  Thos. (fl. 1699), vii. 105
  Miss, vii. 234
  Mr., vii. 228
Beard & Co., ii. 263
Beasley, W.C.T., ii. 472 *n*

Beaston:
  Ruth, *see* Covert
  Sam., iv. 162
Beaton, Nehemiah, rector of Wiston, ii. 36
Beatrice, prioress of Easebourne, ii. 85
Beatrice, dau. of Hen. III, m. Jn. de Brittany, duke of Brittany, ix. 2
Beaubush (Beaubusson), *see* Beeding: Bewbush
Beauchamp:
  Alice, w. of Guy de, earl of Warwick, *see* Thony
  Alice, w. of Jas. de, *see* Audley
  Alice, w. of Rob. de, *see* St. Leger
  Eliz., m. Edw. Nevill, Ld. Bergavenny, vii. 3–4, 19, 53, 70–1, 81, 95, 101, 202–3, 209, 216–17*, 234
  Eudes de, iv. 115, 117
  Guy de, earl of Warwick, iv. 171
  Jas. de, *see* Audley
  Joan, *see* FitzAlan
  Jn. de, iv. 112
  Ralph de, iv. 115, 117
  Ric., earl of Warwick, ii. 324
  Rob. de (fl. 1242), iv. 115
  Rob. de (d. by 1270, ? another), ix. 176
  Rog. de, iv. 115
  Thos., earl of Warwick (d. 1369), vii. 3
  Thos., earl of Warwick (d. 1402), iv. 171
  Wm. (d. by 1288), iv. 117
  Sir Wm. (fl. 1386), capt. of Calais, ix. 67
  Wm (another), vii. 3
  fam., iv. 115
Beauclerk:
  Chas., duke of St. Albans, ii. 442–3
  Ld. Hen., ii. 441–3
  Ld. Wm., M.P. for Chich., ii. 441; iii. 72, 89
Beaufitz (Beaufiz):
  Steph., ix. 145
  Wm. (fl. 1235), ix. 50
  Wm. (fl. 1462), iv. 162
Beaufort:
  Edm., duke of Somerset, ii. 143
  Jn., ix. 144
  Jn., duke of Somerset, ix. 153
  Marg., mchss. of Somerset, *see* Holland
Beaulieu, *see* St. Leonards (in Hastings)
Beaumeis, *see* Belmeis
Beaumes:
  Bonenee de, *see* Wolbedinge
  Wm. de, iv. 84
Beaumont (Beaumund):
  Alfred, i. 124
  Cath., ix. 32
  Eleanor, *see* Eleanor, dau. of Hen., earl of Lancaster
  Eliz., w. of Jn., Vct. Beaumont, *see* Phillips
  Eliz., w. of Wm., Vct. Beaumont, *see* Scrope
  Geo., warden of St. Mary's hosp., Chich., ii. 102
  Jn., Vct. Beaumont, vii. 110
  Sir Wm., vii. 203
  Wm., Vct. Beaumont, Ld. Bardolf, vii. 67, 82, 110
Beaumont, Messrs., ix. 169
Beaumont (unidentified), i. 121
Beaumoys (in Swallowfield, Berks.), ix. 139
Beaumund, *see* Beaumont
Beauport, *see* Battle
Beause, *see* Bexhill
Beazley:
  Eliz., iii. 169; iv. 188
  Mrs. (? another), ix. 31
Bec (Beck, Bek):
  Ant., bp. of Durham, iv. 74, 76–7; vii. 207–8
  Hugh de, ii. 129 *n*; ix. 36

  Theobald of, *see* Theobald
  Toustain of, i. 487
Bec (Eure, France), abbey, ii. 46, 331; ix. 244
  arms, ix. *244*
Becchenridere, Ingelram, *see* Northeye
Becco, Wm. de, ix. 180
Beche (Beech):
  Agnes, m. Wm. Stent, vii. 34
  Ann, m. Wm. Breche, vii. 34
  Denis de, ix. 106
  Elias de, ix. 106
  Gilb. de, ix. 106
  Giles de la, ii. 311
  Hen. de, ix. 106
  Hugh de, ii. 53
  Isabel de la, m. 1 Jn. de Langford, 2 Wm. FitzElys, ix. 139, 153
  Joan, vii. 34
  Joan, w. of Nic. de la, ix. 139
  Jn. de la (fl. *c.* 1320), ix. 139
  Jn. de (fl. before 1347), ix. 187
  Jn. de (fl. 1347), ix. 187
  Jn. (d. by 1474), vii. 34
  Margery de la, *see* Poynings
  Mic. de, ix. 106
  Nic., ix. 139, 153, 177, 235
  Reinhert de, ix. 106
  Reynold de, ix. 106
  Ric. de, ix. 106
  Ric. atte, vii. 34
  Rog. de, ix. 106
  and see Beach
Bechere, Wal., and his w. Lora, iv. 98
Beck, *see* Bec
Beckenham (Kent), iii. 70
Becket, St. Thos., abp. of Cant., i. 499; ii. 6–7, 11, 17, 19, 114, 353–5; iv. 79, 163, 182–3; ix. 14
Becketwesell, *see* Salehurst: Bexwesell
Beckford, Ric., and his w. Frances, ix. 198
Beckley, i. 483; ii. 43, 104; ix. **143–8**, 156
  adv., ix. 148
  agric., ix. 143–4
  bridges, ix. 144
  char., ix. 148
  ch., ii. 113; ix. *144*, 147–8
    accessories, ii. 352, 376
    archit., ii. 342, 344, 376
  dom. archit., ii. 389; ix. 143–4
  earthworks, i. 477
  heronry, ix. 153 *n*
  Knelle (Knell), ix. 55, 142, 144–5
  Ludley, ix. 145 *n*, 147
    Hill, ix. 143
  man., ix. 144–7
  Massines, ix. 157
  mills, ix. 143, 147
  nonconf., ix. 144, 148
  pop., ii. 222
  rector, *see* Sharp, Thos.
  roads, ix. 143
  trades and ind., ii. 255; ix. 143
  Watcombe, ix. 142
  and see Wyke, cross of
Becku (or Dolyn), Ant., ii. 254
Beconsawe:
  Benj., iv. 24
  Peter, iv. 24
Beddingham (Belingham), i. 11, 483; ii. 44, 46
  A.-S. rem., i. 337–8, 349
  ch.:
    accessories, ii. 250, 354, 356, 376
    archit., ii. 342, 344, 349, 366, 368, 370–1, 376, 378
  earthworks, i. 480
  Grestain abbey estates, ii. 122
  insects, i. 159
  man., ii. 106; ix. 193, 195*
  pop., ii. 227
  prehist. rem., i. 321, 328
  Rom. rem., iii. 49, 60
  signal post, i. 533
  vicar, ii. 37

Beddingham (*cont*):
  and see Bedinghommes
Beddington, Rob., prior of Winchelsea
  Franciscan friary, ii. 96
Beddoe (Bedoe):
  Rob., ii. 191
  Dr., i. 346
Bede, Ven., i. 49, 305 *n*, 334; ii. 264,
  291–2
Bede, Thos., *see* Twisden
Bedford (Bedeford):
  Edith, *see* Scrase
  Geo., vii. 85 *n*
  Jn., master of Playden hosp., ii. 105
  Thos. (fl. 1848), ix. 163
  Revd. Thos. (fl. 1863–80, ? another),
    vii. 57
Bedford:
  dukes of, *see* Lancaster, Jn. of; Rus-
    sell, Francis
  earl of, *see* Russell, Francis
Bedfordshire, i. 511; *and see* Eaton
  Socon
Bedhampton (Hants), ii. 449; iii. 47; iv.
  113
Bedingfield:
  Sir Edw., ix. 146 *n*
  Humph., ix. 146
  Marg., *see* Scott
  Mary, *see* Browne
  Sir Ric., vii. 142
  Capt., ix. 242 *n*
Bedinghommes (Beddingham or Beed-
  ing), ii. 3
Bedoe, *see* Beddoe
Bedyng, *see* Beeding
Beech, fam., *see* Beche
Beech, *see* Battle
Beecham, W.P., ii. 470 *n*, 471
Beecher:
  Ant., ii. 414
  Edw., ii. 414
Beeching:
  And., ix. 174
  Clemence, *see* Burdett
  Jn. (fl. 1578), ii. 407
  Jn. (fl. 1626), ix. 174
Beeding (Bedyng):
  Nic. de, prior of Shoreham friary, ii.
    97
  Rob. de, prior of Sele, iii. 62
Beeding, Lower and Upper, i. 483; ii.
  43–5, 219, 280, 306; ii. 49; vii. 147
  Bewbush (Baybush, Beaubush,
    Beaubusson, Bewbushe, Boghe),
    iii. 296–7, 306–10
  bridge, ii. 60–1
  Buchan Hill, ii. 462
  chap., ii. 60–1
  ch., ii. 60–1
    accessories, ii. 61, 250*
    archit., ii. 329, 334, 337, 379
  Colgate, i. 53*, 58, 68*; 228–37; ii. 44
  earthworks, i. 478
  ferry, ii. 60
  Gosden, ii. 253
  Holmbush, i. 302; ii. 310
  Leonardslee, i. 289, 307; ii. 310
  man., ii. 306, 309; vii. 92, 275
  Monk's Gate, i. 53
  natural history, i. 112, 289–90, 302,
    307
  New Lodge, ii. 310
  Newells, ii. 310
  Plummer's Plain, i. 53, 55
  roads to, iii. 47
  Rom. rem., iii. 49
  Sele priory, *q.v.*
  Shelley (Shullegh) pk., ii. 43–4, 296–
    7, 306–10
  shooting, ii. 462
  signal post, i. 533
  Stone Lodge, i. 53
  trades and ind., ii. 231–2, 253
  vicarage, ii. 8
  woodland, ii. 306
  and see Bedinghommes
Beedle, Mary, ii. 201

beekeeping, ii. 287
Beeleigh (Bileigh) (Essex), abbey, ii. 90
Beer (Beere):
  Geo., ii. 285
  Jn., prior of Winchelsea Franciscan
    friary, ii. 96
Beer (Devon), ii. 335
Beere, *see* Beer
Beeston, Anna, ix. 162
Befs, Sir Jn., i. 499
Beggars Bush, *see* Hartfield
Bek, *see* Bec
Bekesbourne (Beakesbourne) (Kent), ii.
  129 *n*, 130; ix. 4, 36
Belasye, Barbara, m. Jn. Webb, ix. 121
Belchamber, Thos., ii. 229
Belcher, Thos. Hayes, rector of Bram-
  ley, ii. 431
Belet, Ralph, and his w. Sybil, iv. 168
Belgae, iii. 1
Belgic pottery, *see* Romano-British
  Suss.: pottery
Belgium, i. 16, 29–30, 36–7
  and see Antwerp; Bruges; Brussels;
    Flanders; Huy; Ostend; Swyn,
    the; Waterloo; Wynendaal
Belingham, *see* Beddingham
Belknap:
  Alice, m. Hen. Finch, ix. 92, 107
  Alice, m. Sir Wm. Shelley, ix. 144
  Edw., ix. 144
  Hamon de, ix. 144
  Hen., ix. 144
  Jn., ix. 144
  Julian, w. of Rob., *see* Goldingham
  Juliana, w. of Sir Rob. (? another), ix.
    144
  Marg., w. of Hen., ix. 144
  Rob. (fl. 1373), ix. 84
  Sir Rob. (fl. 1388, ? another), ix. 144
  Wm., ix. 144
  arms, ix. *145*
Bell:
  Geo., bp. of Chich., iii. 130
  Ingress, ii. 436
  T., i. 245–55, 257–8, 300
Bell Banks, *see* Hailsham
Bell Hanger (unidentified), i. 175, 194
Bell House, *see* Horsham
Bell Vale (unidentified), i. 173
Bell woods, *see* Fernhurst
Bellagio (unidentified), i. 116
Bellamy, Jn., iv. 23
Belle Tout, *see* Eastdean: Beltout
Belleme (or Montgomery), Rob. de, earl
  of Arundel and Shrewsbury, i. 490;
  ii. 303; iii. 84; iv. 1, 13
Bellemonte, Geof. de. vii. 203
bellfounders, *see* Allen, Jn. (fl. 13th
  cent.); Bullisdon; Carter, Jos.; Cat-
  lin; Chapman & Mears; Cole, Jn.;
  Edric; Eldridge, Brian; Eldridge,
  Ric.; Eldridge, Wm.; Founder;
  Giles, Edm; Giles, Thos.; Halton;
  Higden; Hill, Ric. (fl. *c.* 1420–40);
  Hull, Wm.; Hunneman; Iacobus;
  Jannaway; Jordan, Hen.; Kipling,
  Joshua; Knight, Sam.; Landen;
  Lawrence, Thos.; Lester; Lester &
  Pack; Mears & Co.; Mears & Stain-
  bank; Mote, Rob.; Nicholas; Oliv-
  er, C.; Pack and Chapman; Palmer,
  Jn. (fl. 1649); Phelps; Rudhall,
  Thos.; Tapsell, Rob.; Tapsell,
  Rog.; Tonne; Tosear; Wakefield,
  Ant.; Wakefield, Thos.; Warner,
  Jn., & Sons; Waylett; White, Jn.
  (fl. *c.* 1520); Wilner; Wimbis, Ric.
bellfounding, ii. 249–51
Bellhurst, *see* Etchingham
Bellingham:
  Cecily, m. 1 Thos. West, 2 Hen. Rolt,
    vii. 6, 157, 230, 232
  Cecily, w. of Edw., *see* Clarke
  Edw. (d. 1589), ii. 24; iv. 20; vii. 207,
    275
  Edw. (d. 1605), vii. 6, 230, 276, 279,
    281

  Sir Edw. (d. 1637), iv. 26; vii. 6, 157,
    180, 230, 276
  Sir Edw. (d. 1640), vii. 207
  Edw. (fl. 1660), vii. 207
  Eliz., iv. 20
  Geo., vii. 286
  Hen. (fl. 1550), vii. 230
  Capt. Hen. (fl. 1588, ? another), ii.
    149
  Hen. (fl. 1638), vii. 160
  Jn. (fl. 1580), vii. 286
  Jn. (fl. 1610, ? another), iv. 26
  Jn. (fl. 1660), vii. 207
  Mary, w. of Ric. (d. by 1535), *see*
    Everard
  Mary, w. of Ric. (d. 1592), *see*
    Whalley
  Parnel, *see* Cheney
  Ric. (d. by 1535), vii. 275–6
  Ric. (d. 1550), vii. 6, 207, 230, 232,
    277, 279
  Ric. (d. 1592), vii. 6, 207, 230, 279
  Ric. (fl. 1597), vii. 279, 281
  Thos. (fl. 1550), vii. 230
  Thos. (d. *c.* 1648), vii. 207
  Wal., vii. 207
  Wm., vii. 286
  fam., ii. 387; iv. 20 *n*; vii. 179
  arms, vii. *207*
Bello, Rob. de, abbot of Battle, ii. 55
Bello, de, *see* Battle
Belloc, Hilaire, iii. 32
bells, *see* architecture: ecclesiastical
Belme, Wm., ii. 257
Belmeis (Beaumeis):
  Ric. de, bp. of London (1108–27), iii.
    84; iv. 73, 229
  fam., iv. 73
Belstead (unidentified), ii. 408
Belton (Lincs.), ii. 56
Beltout (Belle Tout), *see* Eastdean
Belvoir (Leics.), ii. 444
Belyncham (or Velingham), Jn., sacrist
  of Bosham coll., ii. 112
Bembridge (I.W.), ii. 477; iv. 138
Benbricke, Jos., ii. 34
Benbridge:
  Jn., ix. 137 *n*
  Mary, *see* Creed
  ——, iv. 13
Benderton, *see* Binderton
Bendeville:
  Alured de, and his w. Sybil, ix. 201
  Sara, m. Steph. de Danmartin, ix.
    201
Benedict, abbot of Bayham, ii. 88
Benedict, a Jew, i. 506, iii. 80
Benedict the seneschal, ii. 172, 174
Benedict (fl. 1224), vii. 24 *n*
Benefeld, *see* Benfield
Benenden (Kent), ix. 270
  cricket, ii. 470
  Hempstead, ix. 151
Benestede, Jn. de, master of Bidlington
  hosp., ii. 98
Benestede, hund., *see* Avisford
Benet, *see* Bennett
Benetfeld, *see* Benfield
Benett-Stanford, J.M., *see* Stanford
Benfield (Benefeld, Benetfeld, Benfeld,
  Beningfeld, Beningfield):
  Agnes de, *see* Meyners
  Hen. de, vii. 189
  Jas. de, vii. 189
  Joan, m. Jn. Chauncy, vii. 190
  Jn. de (d. 1274), vii. 189
  Jn. de (d. 1325), vii. 15 *n*, 189, 280
  Jn. de (fl. 1378), vii. 189
  Jn. de (fl. 1412), vii. 189, 280
  Jn. de (fl. 1448), iv. 157
  Ric. de, vii. 189, 280
  Sim. de, vii. 189
  Thos., ix. 146
  Wal. de, vii. 189
  Wm. de (fl. 1226), vii. 189
  Wm. de (d. by 1247, another), vii. 68,
    189, 280
Benfield, *see* Hangleton

Benger, Dorothea, ix. 235
Beningefeld (Beningfield), see Benfield
Bennett (Benet, Bennet):
  Camilla, w. of Chas., earl of Tanker-
    ville, iv. 113
  Chas., Ld. Ossulstone, earl of Tank-
    erville (d. 1722), iv. 16
  Chas., Ld. Ossulstone, earl of Tank-
    erville (d. 1753), iv. 16
  Chas., Ld. Ossulstone, earl of Tank-
    erville (d. 1767), ii. 442–3
  Fred. Geo., ii. 409
  Geo., ii. 471
  Jos., rector of Brightling, ii. 39
  Sir Levin, iv. 213
  Mary, m. Ric. Lewknor, iv. 199
  Mary, w. of Chas., earl of Tankerville,
    see Grey
  Nic., prior of Castle Acre and Lewes,
    ii. 69–70
  Rebecka, m. Geo. Taylor, iv. 211 n
  Thos. (fl. 1599–1609), iv. 144
  Thos. (d. 1611, ? another), iv. 82
  Thos. (fl. 1611), iv. 213
  Thos. (fl. c. 1617), alderman of Lon-
    don, iv. 199
  Thos. (fl. 1622), ix. 192
  Wm., iv. 82
  fam., iv. 213
    arms, iv. 11 n, 100, 211 n
Bennett, see Baker and Bennett
Benson, Edw., and his w. Mary, vii. 190
bent-wood making, ii. 300
Benthall, W.H., ii. 472
Bentinck:
  C., ii. 443
  Ld. Geo., ii. 458–9
  and see Cavendish-Bentinck
Bentley, see Framfield
Beorhthelm (Brihthelm, Brithelm), bp.
  of Selsey, iv. 142, 166
Beorhthelm (Bristelm) the priest, vii. 40
Beorhtmaer (Bricmaer) (fl. 1066), vii.
  228
Beorhtnoth (Brihtnoth), moneyer, iii. 8
Beorhtric (Brihtric) (fl. 1009), i. 484
Beorhtric (Brictric) (fl. 1066), vii. 253
Beorn, earl, i. 484; iv. 182; ix. 9
Beornheah (Beornege, Beornheage), bp.
  of Selsey, iii. 83; iv. 202
Bepton, ii. 43; iv. 40, 41–3, 65, 67
  adv., iv. 41–3
  Bepton Common, iv. 41
  Bepton Down, i. 121, 184, 186, 232–4
  birds, i. 292
  Brookham, Gt. and Lt., iv. 41, 67
  ch., iv. 42–3, 42–3
    accessories, ii. 352, 355, 361, 376
  dom. archit., iv. 41
  earthworks, i. 480
  foxhunting, ii. 442
  Linch, q.v.
  man., iv. 41–4
  pop., ii. 221
  roads, iv. 41
  textile ind., ii. 257
  tithes, iv. 43
Bercamp, Maud de, vii. 81
Bercham (Bercompe), see Barcombe
Berde, Jn., ii. 308
Berebrewer, Dirik, ii. 261
Berecompe, see Barcombe
Berelynde, Maud de, see Dene
Berelynde, see Peasmarsh
Berengar, abbot of Welbeck, ii. 89
Beresford:
  Ld. Wm., ii. 460
  Wm. Carr, Vct. Beresford, ix. 217,
    257
Berewyk, see Berwick
Bergavenny, Lds., see Hastings, Jn. de
  la; Nevill
Bergen op Zoom (Barrowe) (Nether-
  lands), i. 535–6; ix. 151
Berges (unidentified), iv. 65 n, 66 n
Berghsted (Berksted, Bersted, Burgh-
  stede):
  Steph. de, bp. of Chich., ii. 500; ii.

    49, 57, 87; iii. 110, 144; iv. 53,
    210, 215
  Thos. de, dean of Chich., ii. 51; iii.
    139
Bergue (Nord, France), ii. 2
Berhthun (Berthun) (fl. 7th cent.), i.
  482
Berhtwald (Berthwold, Bertuald) (fl.
  795), ii. 3; ix. 8
Berie, see Bury
Berkeley (Barkeley):
  Anne, see Bolney
  Augustus, Vct. Dursley, earl of Ber-
    keley, ii. 443
  Chas., Ld. Fitzhardinge, iv. 184*
  Eliz., Lady Berkeley, m. 2 Thos.
    Chamberlayn, iv. 163
  Fred. Augustus, earl of Berkeley, iv.
    184
  Geo., earl of Berkeley, iv. 187
  Grantley, i. 287
  Hen., vii. 129, 138
  Maur., Ld. Berkeley, iv. 184; vii. 5,
    254
  Sir Maur. Fitzhardinge, Ld. Fitzhard-
    inge, iv. 184*
  Wm., Earl Marshal, earl of Notting-
    ham, marquess of Berkeley, iv.
    184; vii. 5, 35, 254
  Wm. Hen., Ld. Portman, i. 306
  fam., iv. 122, 163, 184, 197
    arms, iv. 184; vii. 5
Berkhale, see Bury: Barkhale
Berkshire, iii. 1, 4; iv. 83, 172; and see
  Abingdon; Beaumoys; Bradfield;
  Bray; Brightwalton; Chipping
  Lambourne; Hinksey; Newbury;
  Reading; Shefford, East;
  Uffington; Wallingford; Windsor;
  Wokingham
Berksted, see Berghsted
Bermondsey (London, formerly Surr.),
  ii. 260; iv. 36
  priory, ii. 115
    prior, see Cusancia, Jn. de
Bernak (Bernake):
  Alice, see Driby
  Joan, w. of Jn., iv. 123
  Jn. (d. 1346), iv. 123
  Jn. (fl. 1348), iv. 98, 123
  Sir Wm. de, iv. 14, 41, 98, 115, 123,
    168
Bernard:
  Geo., ii. 308
  Jn., iv. 176
  and see Barnard
Bernardi, see Barnard
Bernehus:
  Agnes, see Salnervill
  Wm., ii. 106; iv. 98
  fam., ii. 92
Berners:
  Hatton, vii. 71
  Sir Jas., ii. 123
  Jn. de, vii. 257
  Wm., iv. 99
Berry (Berrye):
  Jn., ix. 149
  Capt. Jn., ii. 164–5
  Miss, vii. 249–50
  and see Bury
Bersted, fam., see Berghsted
Bersted, North and South, ii. 43; iv.
  222, 223–5, 226
  adv., iv. 225, 233
  chapelry, iv. 227
  Chich. Prebendal sch. estates, ii. 408
  ch., iv. 223–5, 225, 226, 238 n
    accessories, ii. 250, 354, 359, 371
    archit., ii. 333, 335, 340, 342, 345,
    368, 371*, 372
  dom. archit., iv. 223
  guild, iv. 225
  insects, i. 114, 118, 120, 131, 216,
    224–5, 228, 234–6
  man., iv. 222–4, 229–30
    ho., iv. 223
  pop., ii. 220

  roads, iv. 223
  Rom. rem., iii. 50
  sch., iv. 134
  Shripney, ii. 284; iv. 135, 223
    dom. archit., iv. 223
    man., iv. 223–4, 229
    pk., iv. 224
  streams, iv. 223
  vicar, ii. 16; iv. 226
  vicarage, ii. 16
Berthar, Thos., ix. 230
Berthun, see Berhthun
Berthwold, see Berhtwald
Bertie (Bartie):
  A., ii. 166
  Eliz., see Montagu
  Sir Montagu, Ld. Willoughby d'Eres-
    by, vii. 117
  Peregrine, Ld. Willoughby d'Eresby,
    ii. 235
  Rob., Ld. Willoughby d'Eresby, earl
    of Lindsey, ii. 155; vii. 117
Bertuald, see Berhtwald
Berwick (Berewyk):
  Curtis, iv. 129
  Joan de, see Vilers
  Jn. de, dean of S. Malling, ii. 119
  Jn. de (fl. 1385), iv. 31
  Maud, w. of Jn. de, m. 2 Phil. de
    Egerton, iv. 31
  Ric., iv. 129
Berwick, i. 56; ii. 44
  Berwick Common, iii. 47
  ch.:
    accessories, ii. 250, 352, 355–6, 361,
    376
    archit., ii. 340, 342, 371, 376, 379
  dovecot, ii. 382
  insects, i. 172, 187, 194, 200–1, 206,
    208
  man., ii. 186
  parsonage, ii. 186
  pop., ii. 226
  roads to, iii. 47
  Rom. rem., iii. 47
  tithes, ii. 122
Berwick (Northumb.), ii. 134
Berwick, North (East Lothian), ii. 480
Beselyngford, see Buslingthorpe
Bessborough, earl of, see Ponsonby,
  Vere
Bessole, see Bexley
Best:
  Hen., iv. 123, 200
  Mary, see Covert
  Nic., vii. 190
  Ric., ix. 88
  Thos., iii. 142
Bestenoure:
  Gervase de, i. 502
  Rob. de, i. 502
  Wm. de, i. 502
Beston, Jn., canon of Durford, iv. 27
Besyll:
  Margery, see Hannys
  Sir Peter, ix. 206
Betchworth (Surr.), iv. 168; vii. 2
Bethell:
  Chris., dean of Chich., ii. 51
  Chris. (fl. 1774–95, ? another), iv. 96
  Mary, see Michelborne
Bethune:
  Ann, see Eversfield
  C.C., ii. 474
  Chas. Goodwin, vii. 136; ix. 85
  (later Eversfield), Edw., ix. 85
  Geo., rector of Worth, vii. 134
  Geo. Cuddington, vii. 134, 136, 199
  Geo. Maximilian, vii. 134, 136
  (later Eversfield), Isabella Cath.
    Mary, ix. 85
  (later Eversfield), Sophia Beatrice, ix.
    85–6
  fam., vii. 192 n, 199
Bettesworth:
  Ann, m. Thos. Riggs, iv. 63 n
  Anne, m. Benj. Birch, iv. 152
  Arthur, iv. 5

Bettesworth (*cont.*):
Arthur (? another), iv. 65
Chas., iv. 23, 64
Charlotte, m. Jn. Sargent, iv. 59
Charlotte, w. of Ric., *see* Orme
Chris. (fl. *temp.* Eliz. I), iv. 63
Chris. (fl. *c.* 1700), iv. 152
Edith, m. Thos. Bilson, iv. 24–5
Eliz., iv. 24
Eliz., w. of Peter, *see* Mervyn
Eliz., w. of Sir Peter, m. 2 Jn. Harris,
iv. 23, 64
Peter (fl. 1556–72), iv. 5, 24, 28
Peter (d. 1613), iv. 5
Peter (fl. 1613), iv. 24
Peter (d. after 1613, another), iv. 24
Peter (d. 1634, another), iv. 5
Sir Peter (d. 1636), iv. 23, 64, 70
Peter (fl. 1654), iv. 35; vii. 101
Peter (fl. 1710), iv. 66
Ric. (d. 1613), iv. 24–5, 27
Ric. (fl. 1758), iv. 59
Susan, *see* Bilson
Thos. (d. 1594), iv. 23, 36, 64, 70
Thos. (? d. by 1715), iv. 24–5
Thos. (fl. 1743), iv. 5
(later Bettesworth Bilson), Thos., iv.
24–5
Thos. (fl. 1754), iv. 25
W.A., ii. 476
fam., iv. 20 *n*
arms, iv. *24*
Beuford, Rob., rector of Northiam, ix.
275
Bevan:
D.B., ix. 171
David, ix. 171
J.O., i. 336
Bevendean, *see* Falmer
Beveridge, Jas., ii. 477
Beverishe, Wm., iv. 150
Beverley (Yorks. E.R.), i. 535; ii. 398,
402, 404
Beverston (Glos.), iv. 144
Bevile, *see* Bevill
Bevilham, *see* Mayfield: Bibleham
Bevill (Bevile, Bevyl):
Eliz., ix. 146
Isabel, vii. 203
Kath., m. Sir Jn. Hewett, ix. 146 *n*
Rob. (fl. 1387), vii. 203
Sir Rob. (fl. *c.* 1621), ix. 146 *n*
W., ii. 455
Bewbush (Bewbushe), *see* Beeding
Bexhill (Beause, Bexle, Bexlei), i. 56–7,
247; ii. 34, 43; ix. 77, 79, 86,
116–24, 226, 237
adv., ix. 123
Barnhorne, ix. 115–16, 118
dovecot, ix. 118
man., ii. 176–8; ix. 118
mill, ix. 118
Bexhill Common, i. 44
birds, i. 281, 293, 298
bp. of Chich.'s residence, ii. 333; ix.
116
Bollington, ix. 9, 115, 119
boro., ix. 116
botany, i. 44, 59, 61, 68
boundaries, ix. 116
Buckholt, i. 505; ii. 297; ix. 116, 118,
120, 240 *n*
chant., ix. 123
char., ix. 123–4
ch., ii. 3, 112; ix. *121*, 121–3
accessories, ii. 350, 360, 362
archit., ii. 334, 364, 367, 376
coastguards, i. 502
Cooden (Coding, Cooding), i. 507 *n*;
ix. 116, 239
Down, ii. 451
earthworks, i. 477
man., ix. 117–19
crustaceans, i. 261, 265
dom. archit., ix. 116
fossils, i. 36
Galley Hill, ii. 163
Gotham, ix. 116, 120

hosp., ix. 124
hund., i. 537; ii. 222; ix. **115**, 239, 248
insects, i. 113, 115–17, 119–21, 123,
129, 131–2, 134–5, 137–8, 141–2,
146, 148–50, 152, 156–7, 159–63,
173, 175–6, 178–9, 186–7, 197,
204, 212–13, 221, 223–36
Liberty of the Sluice, *see* Hastings
Little Common, ix. 116
local govt., ix. 116
cts., i. 504
mammals, i. 302
man., ii. 146, 169; ix. 117–21, 123,
201
ho., ii. 451; ix. *120*
marine zoology, i. 85
mayors, ix. 124
militia, i. 534
nonconf., ix. 123–4
Northeye, ii. 130; ix. 36, 116
ch., ix. 123
man., ix. 120
pk., ii. 297; ix. 117–18
Pebsham (Peplesham), ix. 115, 119,
221, 233
insects, i. 142–3, 161
man., 119–20, 123
pop., ii. 222
prehist. rem., i. 327
rly., ii. 240
roads, ix. 116
Robertsbridge abbey estates, ii. 72; ix.
119
Rom. Cath., ix. 123
smuggling, ii. 160 *n*
sport, ii. 451–2, 470–1, 477, 481
trades and ind., ix. 116, 120
U.D., ix. 116
vicar, ii. 36; *and see* Delves, Thos.;
Pye, Thos.
vicarage, ix. 228
Bexwesell, *see* Salehurst
Bexley, Ric., abbot of Bayham, ii. 88–9
Bexley (Bessole) wood (near Halnaker),
ii. 303
Beyvill:
Agnes de, *see* Wappenbury
Alice de, *see* Ryslee
Fresent de, vii. 229
Ric. de (fl. 1261), vii. 229
Ric. de (d. by 1295, ? another), vii.
229
Ric. de (fl. 1316), vii. 229
Ric. de (fl. 1332), and his w. Eliz., vii.
229
Ric. (fl. 1400), and his w. Agatha, vii.
229
Rob. de (fl. 1332), and his w. Eliz.,
vii. 229
Rob. de (fl. 1375), vii. 229
Rob. de (fl. 1375, another), vii. 229
Thos. de, vii. 229
arms, vii. *229*
Bible Bottom, *see* Malling Without,
South
Bibleham, *see* Mayfield
Bickley:
Brune (or Brewen) (d. before 1707),
iv. 189
Brune (fl. 1719), iv. 195, 197
Cicely, *see* Ryman
Hen. (d. 1570), iv. 189, 195
Hen. (d. 1707), iv. 189
Honor, iv. 189
Ric., iv. 189
Thos. (d. 1588), iv. 189
Thos., bp. of Chich., iii. 116, 135
Thos. (fl. 1614), iv. 195
Thos. (d. 1640, ? another), iv. 189–90
Thos. (d. 1667), iv. 195
Thos. (fl. 1677–81, ? another), iv. 161
Mr., i. 529
——, ii. 469
fam., iv. 190 *n*; 197
arms, iii. 116; iv. *189*
Biddulph:
Sir Ant. Jn., i. 289, 306
Chas., ii. 442

Ric., ii. 442
Bidlington, *see* Bramber
Bidoux, Prégent de (Prior John), ii. 143;
vii. 245
Biffen, Jas., iii. 90
Bifrons (in Patrixbourne, Kent), i. 344
Bigg:
Chas., rector of Fenny Compton, ii.
431
Edw. Francis, ii. 480
Biggs:
Jn. (fl. 1639), iv. 155
Sir Jn. (fl. 1662), iv. 155, 156 *n*
Rob., ii. 166
——, w. of Jn., m. 2 Jn. Tredcroft,
iv. 155
Bigham, Chas., Vct. Mersey, iii. 35
Bignor, ii. 43; iv. 47 *n*, 114
Bignor Down, iii. 34–5
Bignor Hill, i. 60
Bignortail wood, iii. 35
botany, i. 60
Buddington, *see* Easebourne
chant., ii. 20
ch.:
accessories, ii. 355, 358, 376
archit., ii. 339, 364, 373
dom. archit., ii. 384
earthworks, i. 479–80
Glatting Down, iii. 56
Gumber Corner, iii. 32, 34; *and see*
Slindon: Gumber, the
man., iv. 23, 51, 58, 114, 216
pk., ii. 296–7, 305
pop., ii. 217
prehist. rem., i. 328
roads to, iii. 34–5; *and see* Stane
Street
Rom. rem., ii. 229, 251; iii. 4, 20–3,
21–3, 25, 34–5, 47, 56
tithes, ii. 263
trades and ind., ii. 230, 251
Westburton Hill, i. 328
Bignortail wood, *see* Bignor
Bigod (Bigot):
Alice, w. of Rog., earl of Norfolk, iv.
183
Hugh, earl of Norfolk, iv. 183; vii. 2
Hugh le (d. 1266), i. 499, 501; iv. 122,
163, 183, 195, 197
Jn., iv. 183
Maud, *see* Marshal
Rog., earl of Norfolk (d. 1270), iv.
122, 183, 195–6
Rog. le, earl of Norfolk, Earl Marshal
(d. 1306), iii. 85; iv. 122*, 183,
188, 191, 193
fam., iv. 163, 193
Bileigh, *see* Beeleigh
Billingshurst, i. 53; ii. 43; iii. 39
Adversane, iii. 39, 49
adv., ii. 108, 119
beagling, ii. 452–3
birds, i. 287
ch., ii. 340, 348, 368, 371
fence making, ii. 234
fossils, i. 38
guild, ii. 398
pop., ii. 218
prehist. rem., i. 328
roads to, iii. 39; *and see* Stane Street
Rom. rem., iii. 39, 49–50
sch., ii. 397–9
vicar, *see* Foster, Wm.; Wilson, Wm.
Billingsley:
Jn., iv. 168
Jn. Fred., iv. 168
Sam., iv. 168
Sarah, *see* Hughes
Bilsham, *see* Yapton
Bilsington (Kent), ii. 57
priory, ii. 57; ix. 148
Bilson:
Edith, *see* Bettesworth
Hen., *see* Legge
Leonard (fl. 1647), iv. 24
Leonard (d. 1715), iv. 24, 26
Susan, m. Thos. Bettesworth, iv. 25

Thos., bp. of Winchester, iv. 26
Thos. (fl. 1647), iv. 24–5
Thos. Bettesworth, see Bettesworth
Binderton (Benderton), ii. 36; iv. 88, **89–91**, 97, 99, 139, 163, 204
    adv., iv. 90, 100, 120
    ch., iv. 90
    dom. archit., iv. 89–90, *90*
    foxhunting, ii. 443
    Goosehill, i. 466
    Lambdown Hill, iii. 50
    man., iv. 89–90, 139, 185
    pop., ii. 221
    prehist. rem., iv. 89
    rly., iv. 89
    Rom. rem., iii. 50
    sch., iv. 91
    tithes, ii. 36; iv. 91
Bineham, see Banham
Bingley, Geo., iv. 223
Binstead (I.W.), ii. 335
Binsted, i. 505; ii. 42–3
    ch.:
        accessories, ii. 351, 353–4, 356–7, 367
        archit., ii. 327, 330, 339, 348, 367
    hund., see Avisford
    insects, i. 118*, 194, 196, 199–200, 204–5, 227, 236
    pop., ii. 217
    roads to, iii. 46
Birch (Burch, Byrch):
    Anne, see Bettesworth
    Benj., iv. 152
    Jane, m. Thos. Bowyer, iv. 161
    Jn. (fl. before 1580), iv. 161
    Jn. (fl. c. 1595), iv. 90 n
Bird:
    Drury, vicar of Bolney, vii. 140
    Sir Wm., iv. 152
    Mr., ii. 460
Bird Brow, see Iford
Birdham, ii. 43; iii. 71; iv. 198, **199–201**, 204
    adv., iv. 201
    almshos., iv. 201
    angling, ii. 466–7
    boundary, iv. 198
    Broomer, iv. 165, 199
    ch., ii. 56; iv. 199–201, *200*
        archit., ii. 376
    dom. archit., iv. 199
    guild, iv. 201
    inc., iv. 199
    Itchenor, East, ii. 16, 43; iv. 198–9
        adv., iv. 201
        chap., iv. 201
        ch., iv. 201
        man., iv. 200
    Manhood End, iv. 171, 198 n, 199
    man., iv. 161, 199–201
    mill, iv. 138, 199
    par., ii. 16*
    pop., ii. 221
    rector, see Bacon, Francis
    roads, iv. 199
    salt pans, iv. 156 n
    tithes, iv. 165, 200
    birds, i. **273–98**; ii. 292, 306
    game, ii. 292, 295, 312, 316, 322
Birkett, see Courtney & Birkett
Birkham (? Barkham in Fletching), ii. 316
Birling, see Eastdean
Birmingham, ii. 285
Bise, Jn. de la, vii. 217
Bishop (Bishopp, Bisshopp, Busshoppe, Bysshop, Bysshoppe):
    Sir Cecil, Ld. Zouche, iv. 157
    Sir Edw. (fl. 1637), iv. 216
    Sir Edw. (fl. 1643, another), i. 522, 524
    Harriett Anne, m. Rob. Curzon, iv. 157
    Jane, ix. 201
    Jn., iv. 216
    Kath. Annabella, m. Sir Geo. Brooke Pechall, iv. 157

Ric., ix. 201
Thos. (d. 1560), iv. 157, 167, 216
Sir Thos. (d. 1626), iv. 157*, 216
Wm. (fl. 1640), ix. 201
Wm. (d. 1730), ix. 177
Mr., ii. 29
Mrs., ii. 25
fam., iv. 157, 167
    arms, iv. *157*
Bishopeston, see Bishopstone
Bishop's Stortford (Herts.), ii. 411
Bishopsgate, see London
Bishopshurst, prebendary, see Henshaw, Jos.
Bishopstone (Bishopeston, Bissopeston, Busshopeston):
    Alice de, prioress of Rusper, ii. 64
    Jn. de, chancellor of Chich., ii. 84, 103, 401; ix. 228
Bishopstone, ii. 44; vii. 9, 14, 62–4; ix. 197
    birds, i. 291
    ch., ii. 401
        accessories, ii. 346, 350, 352, 354, 356, 360, 362, 368
        archit., ii. 332, 339, 342, 346, *347*, 349, 362, 366–8, 371
    earthworks, i. 480
    hund., i. 537–8; ii. 225
    hunting, ii. 443, 450
    insects, i. 138–9, 144, 147, 150, 153, 157, 159–63, 218, 224
    man., ii. 170 n, 186, 190; iv. 152; ix. 201
        ho., vii. 12
    militia, i. 534
    Norton, ii. 284
    pop., ii. 225
    printing, ii. 239
    tide mills, vii. 63–4
    vicarage, ii. 9
Bishopstone (Bucks.), i. 344
Bissel, Damette de, vii. 211
Bisshopp, see Bishop
Bissopeston, see Bishopstone
Biterley, see Buterley
Bitterne (Clausentum) (Hants), iii. 9–10, 47
Blaber, see Geere and Blaber
Blachington, Rob. de, rector of Hailsham, ii. 87
Black, see Clayton and Black
Black, riv., i. 55
Black brook wood, see Ashdown forest: Blackbrooke
Black Death, see epidemics
Black Down, see Lurgashall
Black Herry, friar of Lewes, ii. 96
Black Rock, see Brighton
Blackboys, see Framfield
Blackbrooke, see Ashdown forest
Blackdown, see Lodsworth
Blackebrooke, see Ashdown forest: Blackbrooke
Blackford, see Herstmonceux
Blackham, see Withyham
Blackheath hund. (Surr.), ii. 217 n
Blackman, W., ii. 476
Blackmore, Steph., i. 313
Blackstone, Hen., ii. 28, 407
Blackthorn Hill (near Rotherfield), i. 57
Blackwell, Francis, iv. 24
Blagden:
    Bragg, iii. 160
    Frances, see Nixon
    Geo., iii. 160
    Hannah, iii. 160
    Jas., iii. 160
    Jane, m. Jn. Dawes, iii. 162
    Jane, w. of Geo., see Bragg
    Jn., iii. 147
    Mary, m. Jn. Gruggen, iii. 160; iv. 212
    Mary, w. of Bragg, iii. 160
    Phil., iii. 160
    R.A., ii. 477
Blagrave, Jn., ix. 197
Blainville (Blanville), Wm. de, prior of

Wilmington, ii. 123
Blakborne:
    Edm., vii. 263
    Rog., vii. 263
Blake:
    Geo., iv. 217
    Geo. Hans, iv. 217
    Jn. (fl. 1387), iv. 42
    Jn. (fl. 1487), vii. 263
    Rob., ii. 157–8
    Wm., iv. 152
Blakemore, Wm., iv. 200
Blaker:
    Edw., vii. 144
    Ernest Hen., iv. 213
    Geo., ii. 450
    Mary, m. Wm. Barcroft, ii. 126
    Wm., ii. 144
Blancard, Rob., abbot of Battle, ii. 52, 55
Blancmuster (Albo Monasterio):
    Gaudin de, iv. 152
    Lucy de, see Clifton
Blanesburgh, Ld., see Younger
Blangii, Geof. de, ii. 113
Blanville, see Blainville
Blast, Wm., vii. 146
Blatchington (Blaxinton):
    bridge, ii. 108
    insects, i. 189, 195–7, 207
    rector, ii. 40
Blatchington, East, ii. 44, 228
    barracks, ii. 226 n, 450
    ch.:
        accessories, ii. 350–2, 371
        archit., ii. 337, 339, 367, 371
    defences, ii. 152, 161
    earthworks, i. 480
    foxhunting, ii. 450
    militia, i. 534–5
    pop., ii. 226
    prehist. rem., i. 321
    Rom. rem., iii. 50
Blatchington, West, ii. 43–4; vii. 215, 225, 241, **242–4**, 245, 253, 262, 265
    adv., vii. 244
    ch., ii. 367; vii. *241*, 243, *243*
    hare hunting, ii. 450
    man., vii. 2, 242–3
    mill, vii. 242
    pop., ii. 225
    rector, see Michell, Mr.
    rectory, vii. 262
    Rom. rem., iii. 28, 50; vii. 242
Blaxinton, see Blatchington
Blaxton:
    Edw., iii. 145
    Hen., and his w. Joan, iii. 145
Blencowe:
    Charlotte Eliz., see Poole
    Jn., vii. 98
    Rob. Campion, vii. 98
Blinstone, Hen., ii. 166
Bliss, Geo., ii. 409; iii. 166
Bloet (Blouet):
    Rob., bp. of Lincoln, ii. 112; ix. 9
    Roland, i. 493; ii. 296, 307
    Wilkin, i. 493
    and see Bluett
Blois, Hen. of, bp. of Winchester, ii. 6
Blomer:
    Frances, see Montagu
    Jn. (fl. 1628), ix. 121
    Jn. (fl. 1661), ix. 121
    Mary, m. Sir Jn. Webb, ix. 121
Blomfield (Bloomfield):
    Sir Arthur W., iii. 81; iv. 227; vii. 261, 272; ix. 25–6
    Edwin N., rector of Guestling, i. 43, 61, 64, 71, 111, 114, 124, 130, 136, 210, 247, 260; ix. 183
    Sir Reg., iv. 121
Blondel, see Blundell
Bloodworth, Sir Thos., iv. 144 n
Bloomfield, see Blomfield
Blosseville, Jordan de, vii. 225, 228
Blouet, see Bloet

Blount (Blund, Blunde):
Alice, m. Sir David Owen, ix. 273
Alice, see Oxenbridge
Anne, m. Sir Thos. Oxenbridge, ix. 181 n
Anne, w. of Edw., see Cobham
Edw., Ld. Mountjoy, ix. 120
Eliz., m. And., Ld. Windsor, ix. 181 n, 273
Jn. le (fl. 1304), iv. 98
Jn. (fl. 1348), and his w. Thomasine, iv. 98
Marg., see Echingham
Mary le, iv. 98
Peter, iv. 97
Ric., ii. 29
Thos. le, iv. 97
Wm. le (fl. 1264), i. 498, 500
Wm. (fl. c. 1482), ix. 212 n, 273
arms, vii. 272
Blower:
Francis, ix. 160
Mary, see Agate
Ric., vii. 183
Bluett, T., ii. 24; and see Bloet
Blund (Blunde), see Blount
Blundell (Blondel, Blundel):
Agatha, m. —— Ramsyn, iv. 231
Alice, iv. 231
Edith de, w. of Rob., iv. 171
Hen., iv. 135
Iden, iv. 231
Jn., iv. 231
Julian, w. of Rob., m. 2 Rob. Oakeley, iv. 231
Ric., iv. 135
Rob. (d. by 1377), iv. 171
Rob. (another), iii. 92
Rob. (fl. 1394, another), iii. 92
Rob. (d. by 1474), iv. 231
Blunt:
Lady Anne Isabella, see King-Noel
Chas., vii. 38
Sir Chas. R., ix. 203
Charlotte, vii. 195
Frances Scawen, vii. 195
Judith Anne Dorothea, Baroness Wentworth, vii. 195
Sam., vii. 111, 145, 195
Sarah, see Gale
Lady Sophia, ix. 203
Thos., ii. 414–15; vii. 12–13, 17, 37, 42
Sir Wal., ix. 203
Wilfred Scawen, ii. 313; vii. 195
Winifred, see Scawen
Blythe, J., ii. 164
Board, see Boord
Board of Agriculture, ii. 280, 289; vii. 168
Boarzell, see Ticehurst
Bochard, Iterus, ii. 325; ix. 228
Bochehordea, see Buckworth
Bocher, see Butcher
Bocking:
Alice de, w. of Jn., vii. 206
Jn. de, vii. 206, 208
Ralph, ii. 93
Ralph de (another), iv. 176
Bockland, Wal., vii. 101
Bocse, see Box and Stockbridge
Boddington, Miss M.A., vii. 109
Bodeketon, Rob. de, see Glottyngs
Bodiam fam., see Bodiham
Bodiam, ii. 43, 142; ix. 34, 82, 85, 235, 258, 259–65, 274
adv., ix. 264
angling, ii. 463
batrachians, i. 272
cast., i. 512, 515; ii. 242; vii. 257; ix. 153, 258, 260, 259–63, 265, 267
archit., ii. 394–5
chap., ii. 338, 352; ix. 261
earthworks, i. 477
char., ix. 265
ch., ii. 113; ix. 264
accessories, ii. 360; ix. 264
archit., ii. 371; ix. 264

earthworks, i. 477
fair, ii. 223 n; ix. 263
insects, i. 116, 118, 125, 180
man., ix. 127, 242, 262–4, 266
mkt., ix. 263
pk., ix. 263 n
pop., ii. 223
prebend, ii. 113; ix. 264, 268
rly., ix. 259
roads, ix. 259
wharf, ii. 463
Bodicca Aelia Cauva, iii. 15
Bodiham (Bodiam):
Emma de, ix. 262 n*
Hen. de (fl. temp. Ric. I), ix. 87, 92, 262
Hen. de (d. c. 1287), ix. 262
Isabel de, m. Wm. de Siwell, ix. 262
Margery, ix. 92
Osbern de, ix. 262
Rog. de, ix. 262
Wm. de (fl. after 1166), ix. 262
Wm. de (fl. c. 1210), ix. 92, 127, 262
Wm. de (fl. 1261), ix. 262
fam., ii. 72; ix. 92
arms, ix. 262
Bodinggeham, see Ashdown forest
Bodle Street Green (in Herstmonceux and Warbleton), i. 140, 153; ii. 43; ix. 204, 206, 209
Bodleian, see Oxford: University
Bodley, G.F., vii. 261
Boduni, see Dobunni
Boghe, see Beeding: Bewbush
Boghounte, Peter, iv. 23 n
Bognor Regis (formerly Bognor), i. 111, 119; ii. 43; iv. 222–5, 226–7, 227
adv., iv. 233
Aldwick, q.v.
beagling, ii. 452
birds, i. 281
Bognor Lodge, ii. 204; iv. 226
botany, i. 63
chap., ii. 16; iv. 226
ch., iv. 226–7
coins, i. 326, 328
crustaceans, i. 245–6, 248–9, 251–3, 255–60
defences, ii. 152
dom. archit., iv. 226, 227
fishes, i. 270
fossils, i. 28–30
geology, i. 13–14
hosp., iv. 226
insects, i. 111–15, 117–21, 126, 130–5, 143, 145, 148–50, 152, 157, 160, 165, 167, 169 n, 171–7, 179–93, 195–7, 200–9, 211–37
local govt., iv. 226
man., iv. 223, 229
mkt., iv. 226
mill, iii. 50; iv. 226, 229
navigation lights, ii. 163
nonconf., iv. 227
Owers, see Cymenesore
pop., ii. 220
port, iv. 226
prehist. rem., i. 328
priory, iv. 227
rly., iv. 226
resort, ii. 204; iv. 226
Rom. Cath., iv. 227
Rom. rem., ii. 50
sch., iv. 226
signal station, ii. 163
tithes, iv. 226
trades and ind., ii. 269–70; iv. 226
U.D., iv. 223, 226
vicarage, ii. 16
Bohemia, Anne of, see Anne
Bohemia, see St. Leonards
Bohun (Boun):
Cecily, w. of Sir Jn. de, iv. 36, 52, 77*
Eleanor de, m. Thos., duke of Gloucester, ix. 87
Eliz. de, m. Hen. Hussey, iv. 14
Eliz. de, m. Ric. FitzAlan, earl of Arundel, vii. 3

Eliz., w. of Wm. de, see Badlesmere
Engeler de (fl. 1086), iv. 111, 113, 185 n
Engeler (Enjuger) de (d. 1180), iv. 76–7
Engeler (Enjuger) de (d. 1218), iv. 23, 77, 104, 114
Frank de (d. 1192), iv. 77, 104
Frank de (d. by 1270), iv. 25, 51
Sir Frank de (d. 1273), iv. 77
Humph. de (fl. 1264), i. 497
Humph. de, earl of Hereford (d. 1322), i. 508; vii. 283 n; ix. 87, 221
Humph. de, earl of Hereford (d. 1361), ix. 87
Humph. de, earl of Hereford (d. 1373), ix. 87
Sir Humph. (d. 1468), iv. 76–7*; vii. 207
Jas. de, iv. 52, 77; vii. 207
Joan de, m. —— de Lisle, iv. 92, 115
Joan, w. of Sir Jn. de, see Chapelle
Jocelin de, bp. of Salisbury, iv. 117 n
Sir Jn. de (d. 1284), i. 498–9; ii. 84; iv. 25, 40, 53, 76–7, 114, 152; vii. 206–8
Jn. de (d. 1295), iv. 77; vii. 207
Jn. de (fl. c. 1300), ii. 185, 295
Sir Jn. de (d. 1367), ii. 84; iv. 14, 36, 52, 77; vii. 207–8
Sir Jn. de (d. 1433), iv. 52, 76–7; vii. 207
Jn. de (d. 1440), iv. 56
Jn. (d. 1492), iv. 77; vii. 207
Lucy de, m. Ric. de Meri, iv. 77
Mary de, m. Sir David Owen, iv. 77; vii. 207
(or Meri), Muriel de, m. Savaric fitz Cane, iv. 53, 77, 113–14, 117
Nichole de, see Chapelle
Rohese, w. of Frank de, iv. 77
(or Ford), Savaric de (fl. c. 1154), ii. 81; iv. 114
Savaric de (d. 1246), iv. 73, 76–7
Savaric de (fl. c. 1290), iv. 152
Sibyl de, see Ferrers
Ursula de, m. Sir Rob. Southwell, iv. 77; vii. 207
Wm. de, earl of Northampton, iv. 167; vii. 3; ix. 87
fam., ii. 84, 386, 394; iv. 23–4, 49, 52, 56, 74, 78, 104, 114, 152 n
arms, iv. 77, 116–17; vii. 186; ix. 81
Bokerly Dyke (Dors.), iii. 34
Bolebrook, see Hartfield
Boleworth:
Edm., ix. 191
Grace, ix. 191
Boleyn (Bolyn):
Anne, queen of Henry VIII, see Anne
Anne, see Hoo
Geof., ix. 254
Sir Jas., ix. 255
Thos. (d. 1463), ix. 255
Thos., earl of Wiltshire, ii. 245, 317; ix. 255
Sir Wm., ix. 255
Bolingbroke, Eliz., m. Sir Jn. Cornwayle, ix. 169
Bolkestrode, see Bulstrode
Bolle:
Wm. (fl. 1280), ii. 307
Wm., rector of Aldrington, ii. 47; iii. 111
Bollington, see Bexhill
Bolmer, see Falmer: Balmer
Bolney (Bolne):
Anne, w. of Jn., m. 2 Thos. Culpeper, 3 Hen. Berkeley, vii. 129, 138, 225
Bart. de (fl. c. 1284), vii. 138, 271
Bart. de (fl. 1476), i. 514; vii. 138; ix. 177, 241
Edw., vii. 138; ix. 177
Jn. de (fl. 1296–1310), vii. 138
Jn. de (fl. c. 1350), vii. 138
Jn. de (fl. 1426), vii. 138

Jn. de (d. by 1461), vii. 138; ix. 177
Jn. de (fl. 1500), vii. 138; ix. 241
Jn. de (d. 1558), ii. 379; vii. 138–9; ix. 241*
Jn. de (fl. 1586), vii. 138; ix. 177, 241
Ric. de, vii. 138; ix. 177, 241
Rob. de, vii. 138
Wm. de, vii. 138
arms, vii. *138*, 140
Bolney, ii. 43–4; vii. 1, 125, **136–40**, 271
adv., vii. 140
ch., vii. *137, 139*, 188, 265
accessories, ii. 20 *n*; vii. 140
archit., ii. 230, 339, 349, 351, 364–5, 379; vii. 139–40
dom. archit., vii. 136–8
fossils, i. 37
man., vii. 1–2, 138–9, 225
mill, vii. 137
natural history, i. 60, 164, 289
pop., ii. 223
quarrying, ii. 230
Bolnore, Wm. de, vii. 157 *n*
Bolton, Francis, ix. 69
Bolton, duke of, *see* Paulet, Chas.
Bolton-Clark:
Chas. J.J., ix. 153, 158, 266, 273
Jn. Percival, ix. 153, 266
Bolyn, *see* Boleyn
Bon Johan (Bonion):
Agnes, iv. 61; *and see* Percy
Rob., iv. 61
Bonaparte:
Jerome, vii. 234
Napoleon, ii. 125, 128, 160 *n*, 162, 299
Bonar Law, And., vii. 173
Bond:
Denis, and his w. Eliz., iv. 135–6
Fred., i. 300
Rob., ii. 166
Bone:
Hen., ix. 61
Jn. (fl. 1281), ix. 61
Jn. (d. by 1320, ? another), ix. 187
Boneham, Ric., prior of Boxgrove, ii. 59
Bonfoy, Hugh, ii. 166
Bongar (Bougan):
Jn., ii. 255
Peter, ii. 255
fam., ii. 254
Bonham:
Alice, *see* Young
Thos., iv. 56
Boniface VIII, pope, iv. 34
Boniface IX, pope, ii. 57, 118; vii. 219
Boniface, abp. of Cant., ii. 48, 63, 113, 295; iii. 110; ix. 2
Boniface, C.H., ii. 453
Bonion, *see* Bon Johan
Bonner, Edm., bp. of London, iv. 73
Bonsignori, iv. 177
Bonville (Bonvyle):
Cecily, m. 1 Thos. Grey, marquess of Dorset, 2 Hen. Stafford, earl of Wiltshire, iv. 159
Eliz., m. Sir Thos. West, Ld. de la Warr, iv. 51, 143–4, 177
Eliz., w. of Jn., *see* Martel
Joan, *see* Poynings
Sir Jn. (d. 1396), iv. 159
Jn. (d. 1495), iv. 143
Kath., w. of Jn., iv. 143
Wm., Ld. Bonville, iv. 159
arms, iv. *159*
Bonwick, Ric., ii. 38
Booker, Agnes, iii. 145
Boord (Board, Boorde, Bord, Borde):
And., ii. 262
Edw., vii. 159
Geo., vii. 34, 89, 159, 183, 235
Herb., ix. 242
Hugh, vii. 183
Joan, vii. 95
Jn., vii. 89, 159
Mary, *see* Burrell
Ninian, ix. 242
Ric., ii. 18

Steph. (d. 1567), iv. 82, 123; ix. 242
Sir Steph. (d. 1630), vii. 34, 89, 159, 183, 235
Thos., iv. 82, 123; ix. 242
Sir Thos. Wm., vii. 127, .129
Thomasine, *see* Ockenden
Wm. (fl. 1659–95), vii. 95, 159
Wm. (his s.), vii. 89, 158–9
arms, vii. *89*
Booth:
E.T., ii. 470 *n*
Humph., warden of St. Mary's hosp., Chich., ii. 102
W., ii. 465
——, i. 275, 278, 280
Booth museum, *see* Brighton: museums
Booty, Jas., ix. 30
Boouns, Rob. le, iv. 23 *n*
Bopeep (in St. Leonards), *see* St. Leonards
Bord (Borde), *see* Boord
Bordeaux, Steph. of, iv. 98
his w., Claremunde, *see* Hampton
Bordeaux (Gironde, France), ii. 132; ix. 70
Boreham:
Harvey de, i. 497
Jn., ii. 15
Boreham, *see* Wartling
Borell, *see* Burrell
Borle, Jn., rector of West Tarring, ii. 106
Bormer, *see* Falmer: Balmer
Borne:
Jn. de, ii. 93
Steph. le, ix. 266
Borne, *see* Eastbourne
borough English, ii. 170; vii. 29–30, 34, 55, 64, 66, 70–1, 74, 77, 96, 101, 104, 115, 117, 134–5, 142, 157, 180, 183, 225, 284; ix. 106, 117, 128
Boroughbridge (Yorks. N.R.), battle, ix. 212
Borrer (Bourere):
Alice, w. of Jn., iv. 229–30, 233
Carey Hampton, vii. 178
Hen. Hall, iv. 213
Jn. (fl. 1377), iv. 229-30, 233
Jn. (fl. 1833–70), vii. 284
Jn. (fl. 1843–66, ? another), iv. 213
Nat., vii. 178
Wm. (d. 1797), vii. 177
Wm (d. 1832), sheriff of Suss., vii. 177, 284
Wm. (fl. 1821, ? another), iv. 213
Wm. (d. 1862), i. 42–3, 54, 64, 273, 276–7, 279, 281–2, 286, 289, 293, 300
Wm. (d. 1872), vii. 177
Wm. (d. 1898), vii. 177
Wm. (d. 1920), vii. 177
Canon, vii. 178
arms, vii. *177*
Borrer collection, i. 273 *n*, 276, 279, 284–5, 287, 289, 291, 293, 302
Boscawen:
Sir Edw., ii. 166
Evelyn, Ld. Falmouth, ii. 459
Jn., ii. 443
Bosco:
Geof. de, ii. 263
Sim. de, ii. 108
Wm. de, dean of South Malling, ii. 118
and see Awood; Wood; Woods
Boseham, *see* Bosham
Boselinthorpe, *see* Buslingthorpe
Boseney (Bosene):
Adam de, ix. 155
Ralph de, ix. 155
Thos. de, ix. 155
Bosgrave, *see* Box and Stockbridge
Bosham (Boseham):
Dicul of, ii. 1, 3, 109; iv. 187
Herb. of, ii. 7; iv. 182
Peter de, iii. 93
Bosham (Boseham), i. 484–5, 492, 501; ii. 43, 127 *n*, 291; iii. 83, 169; iv.

181, **182–8**, 192, 204
adv., iv. 187–8
Bosham channel, *see* Chich.: harbour
Broadbridge (Bradbridge), iii. 50, 93 *n*; iv. 181–2, 184–5, 191
mills, iv. 182, 184–5
chant., iv. 188
chapelry, iv. 181, 183, 185, 188, 192, 195
char., 149, 188
ch., ii. 110; iii. 56; iv. 90, 182, *184–5*, 188, 193; vii. 110
accessories, ii. 351–2, 354, 356, 359, 361, 366, 371, 373, 376; iv. 187
archit., ii. 334–5, 337, 339–40, 344, 346–8, 362, 366, 371, 373, 376, 380; iv. 119, 185–7
coll., ii. 1, 3–4, 12, 20, 42, 46, **109–12**; iv. 185, 189
dean, ii. 42
prebendaries, ii. 110–12; *and see* Courtenay, Ric.
prebends, ii. 110; iv. 139 *n*, 140, 188, 190, 192
sacrist, ii. 111–12; iv. 192; *and see* Taverner, Nic.
vicar choral, *see* Digby, Rob.
cts., iv. 184
Creed, iv. 181, 184
dom. archit., ii. 392; iv. 182–3, *184*
Fishbourne, Old, iv. 154, 181, 184–5
hund., i. 538; ii. 145, 220, 295; iv. 133, 181
inc., iv. 182
local govt., iv. 183–4
man., iii. 83, 100; iv. 3, 122, 139, 162–3, 181, 183–5, 191, 193, 196, 204; vii. 207
ho., iv. 182, 184
mkt., iv. 183
mills, ii. 394; iv. 155, 182–3
mon., iv. 187
natural history, i. 165, 168, 185, 189, 291–2
Old Fishbourne, *see* Bosham: Fishbourne, Old
Old Pk., i. 113, 452; ii. 50; iv. 182
pk., iv. 182–3
pop., ii. 220
prehist. rem., i. 328
rly. station, iv. 182
reeves, *see* Roger; Simon; Thomas
roads, iv. 182
Rom. Cath., iv. 188
Rom. rem., iii. 20, 50; iv. 182
royal visit, i. 505
sch., ii. 398
Southwood, iv. 181, 184
Stonewall Farm, i. 477; iii. 50; iv. 182
stream, iv. 182
tenures, iv. 184
timber, ii. 294
trades and ind., ii. 131, 145, 235, 271
vicar, ii. 110–11
Walton, iv. 181–2, 184
Bostock (Bostocke):
Alfred, iii. 146
E.J., ii. 480
Ellis, vii. 169
Grissell, w. of Thos., vii. 157
Jas. Bethune, vii. 169
Rob. (fl. 1731), vii. 169
Rob. (fl. 1790), vii. 169
Thos., ix. 157
Boston (Lincs.), ii. 325
Bosvile:
Eliz., *see* Morgan
Hen., ix. 242, 263
Leonard, ix. 242, 263
Sir Ralph, vii. 101; ix. 242, 263
Bosworth (Leics.), battle, vii. 5, 254
botany, i. **41–69**, *41*
Boteler, *see* Butler
Botevilleyn, Wm., vii. 204
Bothamley, *see* Bottomley
Botiler (Botiller), *see* Butler
Botolphs:
Annington, ii. 60

Botolphs (*cont.*):
Botolphs Down, iii. 51
ch., ii. 250, 350, 357, 359, 362, 371, 375
insects, i. 190, 204
pop., ii. 219
Rom. rem., iii. 51
Bottingelle (Bottingill), *see* Buttinghill
Bottomley (Bothamley):
H., ii. 461
Hen., vii. 115
Kath., *see* Lane
Bottynghill, *see* Buttinghill
Bouch, H.E., ii. 476
Boucicaut, Jn. le Meingre II de (sire de Bursegard), i. 513
Boudon:
Eliz. de, m. Jn. de Gildesburgh, iv. 153
Jn. de, i. 508; iv. 153
Sir Jn. de, iv. 153
Mary de, iv. 153
Bougan, *see* Bongar
Boughen, Edw., vii. 75
Boughton, Ld. Montagu of, *see* Montagu, Edw.
Boughton-Leigh, Theodosius C.H., ix. 217
Bould, Rob., vii. 279
Boulogne, count of, *see* Eustace; William, count of Mortain
Boulogne (Pas-de-Calais, France), ii. 160, 162, 233, 237; iii. 8
Boun, *see* Bohun
Bourdillon, Mrs., ix. 33
Bourere, *see* Borrer
Bourgneuf (Bourneuf), bay (Loire Atlantique, France), ii. 139, 233
Bourn (Bourne):
Jas., ix. 230
Jn., i. 94
Bourne, *see* Eastbourne
Bourne, stream, ix. 8
Bourneuf, *see* Bourgneuf
Bouverie, Mr., ii. 456
Bouvier, ——, i. 252
Bovey Tracy (Devon), i. 23
Bow, *see* Stratford le Bow
Bow Hill, *see* Stoughton
Bowden, T., vii. 132
Bowell, Wm., iv. 52
Bower, Fred., iv. 31, 97, 122
Bowerbank, J.S., i. 71
Bowers, Thos., bp. of Chich., iii. 126
Bowes:
Cicely, m. Ric. Covert, vii. 186
Mr., ii. 458–9
arms, vii. 186
Bowet, *see* Bowett
Bowetby, Jn., master of Playden hosp., ii. 105
Bowett (Bowet):
Amy, vii. 36
Ela, w. of Ric., vii. 175
Eliz., m. Sir Thos. Dacre, vii. 36, 175, 177
Joan, w. of Sir Wm., vii, 175
Ric., vii. 175
Sir Wm., vii. 36, 117, 175
Bowler:
Geo., iv. 129
Jane, *see* Wavell
Bowley, Jn., ii. 246
Bowley, *see* Mundham, North
bowls, *see* sport
Bowman, Seymour, ix. 222
Bowyer:
Anne, ix. 249
Anne, m. —— Hendley, vii. 156
Anne, m. Sir Jn. Morley, iv. 161
Anne, w. of Hen., *see* Salter
Anne, w. of ——, *see* Stoughton
Denise, ii. 246
Eliz., ix. 249
Eliz., w. of Francis, iv. 155, 172
Eliz., w. of Hen., *see* Vaux
Francis, alderman of London, iv. 155, 172

Hen. (d. 1589), vii. 150, 156–7, 162, 196
Sir Hen. (d. 1606), vii. 156, 196
Hen. (fl. 1609), iv. 155, 172
Sir Jas., iv. 161
Jane, *see* Birch
Joan, w. of Thos., m. 2 Alex. Nowell, iv. 158, 161
Jn. (? two of this name), vii. 196; ix. 249
Mary, w. of Sir Wm., iv. 155
Rob., (fl. 1540), iii. 99
Rob., (fl. 1652), vii. 179
Thos. (d. 1558), iv. 82, 123, 158, 161–2, 165
Thos. (fl. 1588), ii. 28
Thos. (d. 1595, ? another), iv. 161, 167
Thos. (fl. 1626–38), iv. 193
Sir Thos., M.P. for Bramber, i. 522; iv. 161, 163 *n*, 231
Sir Thos. (d. 1659), iv. 161–2
Wm. (fl. 1540), iv. 163
Sir Wm. (d. 1615), iv. 155, 172
Wm. (d. 1632), vii. 196
Wm. (fl. 1633), iv. 155, 172
fam., iv. 160, 161 *n*, 163
arms, iv. *161*; vii. 150
Box:
Hen., iv. 64
Martha, iv. 64
Mary, iv. 64
Mary, m. Sir Everard Fawkenor, iv. 64
Ralph, iv. 64
Ruth, m. Sir Chas. Peyton, iv. 64
Thos., ii. 468–70
Box hund., iii. 98; iv. 1–2, 216 *n*, 222
Box (Bocse, Bosgrave) and Stockbridge (Estocbridge) hund., i. 538; ii. 220; iv. 1, **133**
Boxforde, Gilb., master of hosp. of St Jas. and St. Mary, Chich., ii. 100
Boxgrove, Jn. de, mayor of Chich., iii. 91
Boxgrove, iv. 133, **140–50**
adv., iv. 149, 201
almshos., ii. 439; iv. 104, 149, 239
chant., iv. 116, 146–7, *146*, 220
char., ii. 439; iv. 149–50, 188
ch., ii. 7, 37, 56; iv. *140*, 141–2, 146–9
accessories, ii. 59, 351–4, 360–1, 376, 379; iv. 149
archit., ii. 58, 327, 329–30, 332–4, 337, 340, 346–9, 367–8, 371, 375–6, 379; iv. 146–8
coll., ii. 4, 56
Crocker Hill, ii. 303; iv. 141, 145
deanery, ii. 42–3
dom. archit., iv. 141–2
Goodwood, ii. 24, 277, 284, 439; iii. 13–14; iv. 144
botany, i. 46, 48–9, 65
coins, i. 329
Goodwood Ho., iv. 118 *n*, 142*, 144
horse racing, ii. 455, 457–61
hunting, ii. 443–5, 452–3
insects, i. 112, 114, 155, 166, 169, 216, 222–3, 226–8, 232, 235
pk., i. 21; ii. 297, 301, 303; iv. 140, 142, 144, 175–6; vii. 267
guild, iv. 149
Halnaker, *q.v.*
Hampnett, East, iv. 133, 145, 200
man., iv. 144–5
mill, iv. 144
insects, i. 236
man., iv. 36, 142–6, 149
mill, iv. 142
Oldbury, iv. 141, 145
pk., iv. 143
pop., ii. 220
priory, ii. 4, 7, 45, **56–60**, 82, 121, 232, 303; iv. *141*, 143, 179
almsho., ii. 59
archit., ii. 382; iv. 141
char., ii. 191

estates, iv. 8–9, 36, 51, 56, 64, 80, 107, 109, 122, 136, 142, 144–5, 156–7, 162, 167, 170 *n*, 171, 199, 204, 213, 231
patronage, ii. 7; iv. 10, 158, 165, 179, 201
priors, ii. 14*, 16, 56–60, 62; iv. 6 *n*, 53, 177, 180; *and see* Anketil; Chese, Ric.; Dumo; Myles, Thos.; Nicholas; Rickman, Jn.; Robert
sch., ii. 59
roads, iv. 140–1
sch., ii. 439
Seabeach, iii. 32–3; iv. 140, 142, 145
Strettington, iv. 133, 142
chap., iv. 145
man., iv. 145, 180
Strettington Ho., iv. 142
tithes, ii. 56; iv. 145
tithes, iv. 142, 149
vicar, ii. 58
Boxhull (Buxhull):
Alan de (d. 1325), i. 507; ii. 325; ix. 229
Sir Alan (d. 1381), ix. 229
Sir Alan (fl. 1405), ix. 169
Elias de, ix. 220
Wal., de, ix. 220
Wm., de, ix. 220
Boxley (Kent), ii. 115 *n*
abbot, ii. 72
Boyce:
Eliz., m. 1 Jn. Morton, 2 Jn. Sparrow, vii. 254
Eliz., w. of Wm., *see* Shirley
Wm., vii. 254
and see Boys
Boyd-Dawkins, W., i. 470; ii. 241; iii. 37
Boyle, Ric., earl of Burlington, ii. 441
Boys (Boyse):
Alice, m. Jn. Dawtrey, iv. 174
Cordelia, *see* Wildgose
Eliz., *see* Harcourt
Hannah, m. Sam. Ridge, vii. 36
Jn. de (fl. 1318), iv. 190 *n*
Jn. (d. by 1547), iv. 210
Jn. (fl. 1656), vii. 218
Jn. (fl. 1783), vii. 36
Randolph, iv. 174 *n*
Sam., vii. 218
Thos., vii. 218
Sir Wm. (fl. 1654), vii. 218; ix. 221
Wm. (fl. 1694), ix. 152
Wm. (fl. 1783), vii. 36
Wm. H., ix. 222
fam., iv. 218 *n*
and see Boyce
Braban, *see* Brabon
Brabant, ix. 151
Braberry Hatch, *see* Maresfield: Braby's Hatch
Brabon (Braban):
Eliz., w. of Martin, ix. 220
Jn. (fl. 1589), ii. 262
Jn., vicar of Udimore, ix. 174
Jn. (fl. c. 1700), ix. 220
Martin, ix. 220
Sarah, *see* Burdett
fam., ix. 220
Braby:
Ernest E., ii. 276
Jas., ii. 276
Braby's Hatch, *see* Maresfield
Brack Mount, *see* Lewes
Bracklesham (Brakelsham), Wm. de, dean of Chich., ii. 51, 77; iii. 119, 139; iv. 117–18, 155
Bracklesham (in East Wittering), ii. 43; iv. 198, 215, 217
adv., iv. 217
Bracklesham Bay, ii. 467
chap., iv. 215
farm, i. 15
fossils, i. 15–16, 27–30, 32
man., iv. 200, 216
prebendaries, iv. 215–17
prehist. rem., i. 328

Bradbridge (Bradbrigge, Bradebridge, Bradebrugge):
  Aernald of, iv. 184
  Alice de, iv. 184
  Alice, m. Francis Barnham, iii. 145
  Alice, w. of Thos. de, see Hunston
  Alice, w. of Wm. de, iii. 145
  Isabel de, iv. 184
  Jn. de, iv. 153
  Nic., ii. 405
  Thos. de (d. by 1438), iv. 157 n
  Thos. (fl. 1548), ii. 308
  Wm. de (fl. 1316), iv. 184
  (or Broadbridge), Wm., mayor of Chich., iii. 92, 145
  and see Broadbridge
Bradbridge, see Bosham: Broadbridge
Bradbrigg, see Bradbridge
Bradbury, Jn., see Norton
Braddock, Francis, iv. 231
Brade (or Helling):
  Ralph, ii. 86
  Randolph, ii. 86
  Rikeward, ii. 86
  Wybert, ii. 86
  fam., ii. 86
Bradebridge, see Bradbridge
Bradebrigg (unidentified), ii. 316
Bradebrugge, see Bradbridge
Bradfield (Berks.), ii. 432
Bradford (Braydforde):
  Jn., rector of St. Michael's, Lewes, vii. 39
  Susannah, vii. 98
  Thos., vii. 35–6
Bradford, earl of, see Bridgeman
Bradford (Dors.), iv. 34
Bradford on Avon (Wilts.), ii. 366
Brading (I.W.), ii. 351
Bradley, Jn., ix. 61
Bradley (Wilts.), see Maiden Bradley
Bradshaw (Bradshawe):
  Agnes, iv. 195
  Dorothy, m. Rog. Drew, iv. 185, 191 n, 195 n
  Ebenezer, vii. 245
  Ellis, iv. 185, 191
  G.W., i. 292
  Rob., ii. 439; ix. 183
  Wm., iv. 185
Bradsole (in Poulton, Kent), abbey, vii. 276, 286
Bradwell (Essex), iii. 5
Brady, ——, i. 264
Braganza, Cath. of, see Catherine
Bragg:
  Jane, m. Geo. Blagden, iii. 162
  Jane, see Braman
  Mary, m. —— Eede, iii. 162
  Mr., ii. 459
Braid, Jas., ii. 478–80
Brain:
  Anna, m. Geo. French, ix. 235
  Diana, ix. 235
Braiose, see Braose
Brakelsham, see Bracklesham
Braman:
  Jane, m. —— Bragg, iii. 162
  Jn., iv. 172–3
  Ric., mayor of Chich., iii. 162
Bramber, i. 501; ii. 43
  Bidlington:
    hosp., ii. **98–9**
    man., ii. 98
  borough, i. 504
  botany, i. 46
  Bramber Rife, see Bremere Rife
  bridge, ii. 230, 394
  cast., i. 493, 508, 512; ii. 174; iii. 51; iv. 1
    archit., ii. 394–5
    constables, i. 493; ii. 188
    earthworks, i. 474, 474–5
    insects, i. 179, 181
    signal post, i. 533
  ch., ii. 60
    archit., ii. 332, 340, 349, 366
  Civil War, i. 524, 528

coins, i. 326, 328
coll., ii. 60
  dean, see Herbert
dom. archit., ii. 386
ferry, ii. 60
honor, i. 492, 508
insects, i. 167 n, 179, 181, 185, 191, 194, 197–207, 210, 214
man., ii. 306
militia, i. 507
parl. rep., i. 521, 531–2
M.P.s, see Bowyer, Sir Thos.; Temple, Jas.
pop., ii. 219
rape, ii. 171, 175, 219 n, 307; iv. 51; vii. 1, 175, 201, 204, 275
  ale-hos., ii. 196
  coastguards, i. 506 n, 507 n
  franchise, i. 532
  poor relief, ii. 196
  roads, ii. 240
roads to, iii. 47
Rom. rem., iii. 2, 51
royal visits, i. 491, 505; ii. 296, 307
salt making, ii. 89, 232
Bramblegrove wood, see Arlington
brambles, i. **67–9**
Brambletye, see Grinstead, East
Bramley (Hants), rector, see Belcher
Bramshott (Brembelschete):
  Ant., ii. 405
  Eliz., m. Sir Jn. Dudley, iv. 28, 92
  Eliz., w. of Jn., see Lisle
  Jn. de (fl. 1370), iv. 92, 115
  Jn. de (d. by 1428), iv. 28
  Jn. de (d. 1479), iv. 28, 92, 116
  Kath., see Pelham
  Marg. de, m. Sir Jn. Pakenham, iv. 28, 92, 116
  Wm. de (fl. 1338), iv. 28
  Wm. de (d. by 1449), iv. 28, 116
  fam., iv. 28
  arms, iv. 28
Bramshott (Hants), ii. 217 n, 220; iv. 22
  rector, see Titherington
Bramston:
  Anne, see Alcock
  Geo., iv. 35, 38, 163
  Jas., vicar of Harting, iv. 13
Brand, moneyer, iii. 83
Brand:
  Chas., ii. 446
  Hen. Bouverie Wm., Vct. Hampden, ii. 277, 446
  Thos. S., ii. 277, 284
Brann, Geo., ii. 470, 476
Branthwaite:
  Jn., ii. 432
  Ric., vii. 239
Brantridge, see Balcombe
Braose (Braiose, Brewes, Brewose, Brous):
  Aline de, m. Jn. de Mowbray, i. 508; ii. 307
  Beatrice de, see Mortimer
  Giles de, bp. of Hereford, i. 493
  Sir Jn. de (d. 1232), ii. 60, 63, 98, 361
  Jn. de, master of Bidlington hosp., ii. 98
  Jn. de (fl. 1315), vii. 207
  Marg., w. of Sir Thos., m. 2 Sir Wm. Burcester, ix. 196
  Mary de, ii. 306
  Peter de, ii. 98
  Phil. de, ii. 60
  Reg. de, i. 494
  Thos., Ld. Braose (d. 1361), i. 509; iii. 72; iv. 184
  Thos., Ld. Braose (d. 1395), ii. 361, 378; ix. 196
  Wm. de (d. 1093 × 1096), ii. 60, 306; iv. 1, 121; vii. 1, 70, 275, 279
  Wm. de (d. 1192), ii. 89, 306
  Wm. de (d. 1211), ii. 63, 296
  Wm. de, Ld. Braose, ii. 60, 132, 171, 188
  Wm. de (d. 1326), i. 506; ii. 97–8, 307
  fam., ii. 63, 261, 332, 371

arms, vii. 272
Brasenose College, Oxford, iv. 82; vii. 144, 181; ix. 199
brasses, monumental, see architecture: ecclesiastical
Brassey:
  Idina, w. of Thos., Earl Brassey, ix. 242, 244–5
  T.A., ii. 447
  Thos. (d. 1870), ix. 240, 242, 245
  Thos., Earl Brassey (d. 1918), ii. 447, 472; ix. 12, 240, 242
  Thos., Earl Brassey (d. 1919), ix. 118, 242
  arms, ix. 242
Brassey Institute, see Hastings
Brasyer, Wm., vii. 34
Braund, Leonard Chas., ii. 474
Braunson (Brianson):
  Giles de, ii. 180; ix. 138
  Isabel de, see St. Leger
Bray:
  Cath., see Hussey
  Edm., iv. 15
  Sir Edw. (d. by 1509), iv. 15
  Sir Edw. (fl. 1529–53), ii. 144 n; vii. 121, 270
  Eliz., see Lovell
  Hen., vii. 76
  Margery, m. Wm., Ld. Sandys, iv. 15
  Mildred, vii. 136
  Reynold, iv. 11, 15
  Sarah, m. Thos. Chatfield, vii. 76, 136
  ——, ii. 29
  fam., iv. 25
Bray (Berks.), vicar of, ii. 35
Brayboef, Wal. de, ii. 316
Braydforde, see Bradford
Braysher, Ric. and Sarah, ii. 252
Breakspear, Sir Harold, vii. 46
Bréauté, Falkes de, ix. 15
Breche:
  Ann, see Beche
  Wm., vii. 34
Brecon (Brecknock), ii. 52, 54, 431, 434
Breda (Netherlands), ii. 158
Brede:
  Adam de, ix. 92
  Rob., ii. 132 n
Brede, ii. 43; ix. 34, 164, **165–7**, 258
  adv., ix. 3, 169, 171
  boundaries, ix. 165
  Brede, Little, ix. 165
  Brede Place, ii. 384, 386; ix. 165–7, 166, 169
  bridge, ix. 168 n
  Broad Oak, ix. 165, 167
  char., ix. 171
  Chitcombe, iii. 29, 32; ix. 258
  ch., ix. 169–71, 170
    accessories, ii. 353, 378; ix. 171
    archit., ii. 332, 339, 344, 371, 378–9; ix. 169–71
  cts., ix. 168–9
  dom. archit., ix. 165–8
  Fécamp abbey estates, ii. 124, 295; ix. 168
  half hund., ix. 164
  hop growing, ix. 165
  hosp., ix. 168
  man., ix. 9, 26, 40, 56–7, 61, 168–9, 181
  mills, ix. 168
  natural history, i. 125–6, 286, 302–3
  nonconf., ix. 168, 171
  pop., ii. 222
  rector, ii. 19; and see Laurence
  riots, ii. 206 n
  roads, ix. 165
  Rom. rem., iii. 3, 7, 29, 31–2
  sch., ix. 168
  Smegle, ix. 164
  trades and ind., ii. 236, 238, 241, 242, 252; ix. 168
  woodland, ii. 295; ix. 168
Brede, riv., i. 57; ii. 463–4; ix. 63, 168, 276

Bredford, *see* Brightford
bredgeld, ix. 80
Breeds & Co., ii. 263
Breeds, *see* Hamilton and Breeds
Breggel:
    Adam, ix. 202
    Wal., ix. 202
Brembelschete, *see* Bramshott
Brembre, Ralph de, master of Bidlington
    hosp., ii. 98
Bremelhangere, Alan de, iv. 191
Bremere (Bramber) Rife (Bremersdytch,
    Brimesdik, Unredisditch), iv. 198,
    210, 227
Brenchley (Brenchesle, Brenchly):
    Joan, *see* Batsford
    Thos., ix. 80
    Wm., ix. 119, 123, 266
Brenchley and Horsmonden hund.
    (Kent), ii. 226 n
Brent:
    Nat., vicar-general of abp. of Cant., ii.
        33; iii. 87
    Thos., master of Playden hosp.,
        dean of South Malling, ii. 105,
        119
Brentford, Vct., *see* Joynson-Hicks
Brentingham, Thos. de, bp. of Exeter,
    ii. 110–11
Brenzett (Kent), ix. 150
Brereton:
    Cholmely, iv. 161
    Mary, iv. 168
    Susanna, *see* Ballett
    Thos. (d. 1699), iv. 168
    Thos. (fl. after 1701), iv. 68
    Thos. Wm., iv. 168
    Wm., iv. 161, 223, 233
    fam., iv. 107
Brest (Finistère, France), ii. 138
Bretagne, *see* Brittany
Bretford, *see* Brightford
Breton (Bretun, Bruton):
    Joan, *see* Dive
    Nic. le (fl. 1275), ii. 184
    Nic. (fl. 1652), ix. 92
    Ric. le, iv. 102
    Wm. le, iv. 102
    Sir Wm. (another), iv. 59
Brett:
    Eliz., w. of Rob., iv. 129
    Jn., ii. 262
    Jn. (? another), iv. 129
    Rob., iv. 129
    Thos., ii. 34
    Wal., vii. 36
Brettell, Ric., iv. 208; ix. 173
Bretun, *see* Breton
Brewen:
    Jn., ix. 156
    Nic., iv. 77
Brewes, *see* Braose
brewing, ii. 260–3; iii. 75; vii. 32; ix. 56,
    162
Brewose, *see* Braose
Brian, Eudes s. of, *see* Eudes
Brian son of Ralph, *see* FitzRalph
Brian:
    Anne, *see* Brooke
    Thos. (fl. 1514), vii. 24 n
    Thos. (d. by 1655), ix. 177
    and see Bryan
Brianson, *see* Braunson
Bricet, Sir Wal., ii. 75
Bricklehurst, *see* Ticehurst
brickmaking, ii. 198, 253–4; iv. 71, 226;
    vii. 103, 109, 179; ix. 87, 131, 184,
    240, 247
Brickwall, *see* Northiam
Bricmaer, *see* Beorhtmaer
Brictric, *see* Beorhtric
Bridford, Jn. de, ii. 89
Brideoake (Brideoke), Ralph, bp. of
    Chich., iii. 112 n, 133
Bridge:
    A.J., ii. 479
    Arthur, rector of Worth, vii. 199
    Mrs. E.N.W. Waller-, vii. 199

Bridgeman, Orlando, earl of Bradford,
    ii. 459
Bridger:
    Harry, vii. 142, 257
    Jn. (fl. 1717), vii. 142
    Jn. (fl. 1762, ? another), vii. 85
    Sir Jn. (fl. 1777, another), vii. 85,
        87
    Mary, m. Geo. Shiffner, vii. 85
    Mary, w. of Jn., *see* Rivers
    Ric., vii. 84, 232
    W., ii. 451
    Wakeford, iii. 162
    Wm., iv. 36
    fam., vii. 85, 87
    arms, vii. *85*
Bridges:
    Edw., iii. 77
    H.C., ii. 166
    Jn., ii. 299
    Timothy, ii. 165
bridges, *see* architecture: civil and dom.;
    and see parish names
Bridgnorth (Salop.), i. 490
Brienne:
    Jn. de, count of Eu (d. 1294), i. 507
    Jn. de, count of Eu (d. 1302), ix. 267
Briet, Pierre, ii. 254
Briggs:
    David, ii. 442
    Eliz., vii. 111
    Eliz., m. Jn. Shore, iii. 147
    Eliz., w. of Thos., *see* Stapley
    Joan, w. of Steph., iii. 145
    Jn. (fl. 1655), ii. 408
    Jn. (d. 1723), iii. 144
    Marg., *see* Thomas
    Mary, iii. 144
    Steph., iii. 145
    Thos., chancellor of Chich., iii. 147;
        iv. 36, 204
    Thos. (? another), vii. 217
Brigham (Brygham):
    Ric., iv. 116
    Thos., vii. 183
Brightford (Bredford, Bretford) hund.,
    i. 538; ii. 218
Brighthelmstone, *see* Brighton
Brighthis, Laur., ix. 181
Brightling, ii. 31–2; ix. 224, 226, **227–
    32**, 233
    adv., ix. 228, 232
    Brightling Pk., i. 306; ii. 325; ix. 227
    Cackle Street, ix. 227
    char., ix. 232
    ch., ii. 30, 113; ix. 230–2, *230, 231*
        accessories, ii. 353; ix. 231–2
        archit., ii. 336, 344, 346, 376; ix.
        230–1
    Dallington forest, *see* Dallington:
        forest
    dom. archit., ix. 227–8
    fair, ix. 228
    forest, *see* Dallington: forest
    fossils, i. 38
    insects, i. 150–2, 157, 159
    iron ind., ii. 230, 241 n, 242, 245, 247,
        253–4; ix. 227–8
    man., ix. 228–30
    mill, ix. 228
    Oxleys Green, ix. 227
    pop., ii. 223
    prebend, ii. 113; ix. 228
    rectors, *see* Bennett, Jos.; Burrell,
        Wm.; Hayley, Wm.; Pye, Thos.;
        Rush
    roads, ix. 227
    sch., ii. 438
    Socknersh, ii. 242, 247; ix. 138, 227,
        227–9
    woodland, ix. 227–8
Brighton (Brighthelmstone), i. 54, 72,
    305; ii. 158, 162, 197; iii. 102; vii.
    19, 216, 241–5, *244, 245, 246, 247*,
    244–63, 269; ix. 90
    adv., vii. 262–3*
    ale-hos., ii. 196
    A.-S. rem., i. 340

    Aquarium, i. 82, 268, 270, 304, 307
    batteries, i. 535; ii. 152, 161–2
    birds, i. 275–81, 283, 285–6, 291, 293
    Black Rock, i. 23, 313
    blockho., ii. 152, 161; vii. 246
    botany, i. 43, 45–7, 55, 59, 62–4, 67–8
    chap. (St. Bart.'s), vii. 252, 263
    char., ii. 439
    Charles II, escape, i. 528; vii. 246–7
    ch., ii. 37, 265, 333; iii. 123; vii.
        259–62*, *260*
        accessories, ii. 356, 358, 378
        archit., ii. 348, 376, 378
    ch. wardens, ii. 265
    coaching, ii. 204–5; vii. 9, 248
    coastguards, i. 507 n
    coins, i. 326, 328
    cts., ii. 152; vii. 251–3
    crustaceans, i. 247, 253, 260, 264
    curate, ii. 29
    deanery, ii. 43
    defences, i. 518; ii. 265; vii. 245–6
    dom. archit., ii. 392; vii. 251
    downs, i. 23, 133, 135, 199, 201,
        203–4, 206, 210
    earthworks, i. 458; *and see* Brighton:
        Hollingbury
    Elm Grove, i. *322*, 323
    fair, vii. 253
    fishes, i. 267, 269
    fossils, i. 13, 22, 28, 32, 35
    French raids, i. *518*; ii. 143–5; vii. 245
    geology, i. 1, 12–13, 19, 21, 26, 274
    Hollingbury, i. 169–70, 172, 319, 328,
        455, 458, 460, 470–1, 533; iii. 58
    hosp., ii. 254
    inns, i. 528; ii. 456; vii. 247–8
    insects, i. 111, 115–16, 131–46, 148–
        63, 164 n, 165–7, 169–99, 201–3,
        207, 210, 213–18, 220, 223–5
    Kemp Town, i. 137, 145–6; ii. 241;
        iii. 24, 51; vii. 250
    local govt., ii. 24, 146; vii. 251–3
        constable, ii. 197, 235
        mayor, burgesses, and aldermen,
        vii. 78
        Society of Twelve, vii. 241, 252
    mammals, i. 300, 303–5, 307
    man., vii. 2–4, 6–7, 251–9, 263
    marine zoology, i. 82–5, 93–101, 105–
        7
    mkt., vii. 253
    Michelham priory estates, ii. 77
    militia, i. 518, 533–6
    mills, vii. 245
    molluscs, i. 109
    museums:
        Booth museum, i. 287–8, 291–2;
        vii. 250 n
        Brighton museum: A.-S. rem., i.
        340; fossils, i. 30–5, 37, 39; pre-
        hist. rem., i. 309, 313, 316, 318,
        318, 321, *322*, 329–31; Rom.
        rem., iii. 16, 17 n, 24, 37, 41, 49,
        51–2, 55–62, 64, 66, 68
    nonconf., ii. 22; vii. 251, 263
    Park Bottom, iii. 62
    parl. rep., i. 532; vii. 252–3
    Pavilion, ii. 203; vii. 249–51
    piers, ii. 163; vii. *247*, 250
    piracy, ii. 147; vii. 246
    poor law, ii. 206
    pop., ii. 225, 275
    prehist. rem., i. 310, 313, 316–17,
        319–20, 328
    rly., ii. 205, 240–1; vii. 250
    rates, vii. 252
    resort, ii. 203–4; vii. 244, 247–51
    riots, ii. 206 n
    roads, ii. 240; iii. 47; vii. 62, 76,
        102–3
        from London, vii. 136, 144, 172,
        181–2, 186, 192, 204, 212, 244,
        248
    Rom. rem., iii. 3, 23–4, 51–2; vii. 244
    sch., ii. 397, 431, 439; vii. 247
        Coll., ii. 430–1, 473, 475–6
        and see Telscombe

ship money, ii. 156
ship service, ii. 134, 153
shipping, ii. 151, 156, 159
signal station, ii. 163
smuggling, vii. 246
spiders, i. 239–43
sport, ii. 448–52, 455–7, 460–1, 467–
71, 473, 475, 478–9, 481
trades and ind., ii. 233, 235–7, 262–3
fisheries, ii. 146, 151, 157, 160, 235,
264–71; vii. 244–6, 253
union, i. 539
vicar, ii. 265; vii. 252, 262; and see
Hannah, Jn. Julius; Michell, Mr.
vicarage, ii. 8
White Hawk Hill, iii. 51
earthworks, i. 458, 462, 464
prehist. rem., i. 458, 470
Brighton and Lewes races, ii. 454–5
Brighton and Sussex Natural History
Society, i. 59
Brighton Gazette, ii. 161 n, 162 n, 239
Brightwalton (Berks.), ii. 52
Brihthelm, bp. of Selsey, see Beorh-
thelm
Brihtnoth, moneyer, see Beorhtnoth
Brihtric, see Beorhtric
Brimesdik, see Bremere Rife
Brine, Hen., ii. 166
Brinley:
Kath., iv. 129
Laur., iv. 129
Ric., iv. 129
Rob., iv. 129
Brisco:
Eliza, ix. 29, 83
Frances, w. of Musgrave, m. 2 Chas.
Frewen, ix. 83
Maria, ix. 29, 83
Mary Fletcher, see Dyne
Musgrave, ix. 92
Musgrave (another), ix. 83, 187
Sir Musgrave Horton, ix. 83
Sarah, ix. 29, 33, 83
Wastel (d. by 1836), ix. 83, 92, 187
Wastel (d. 1878), ix. 83, 180, 187
arms, ix. *83*
Bristelm the priest, see Beorhthelm
Bristlinga forest, see Dallington: forest
Bristol:
earl of, see Digby, Geo.
marquess of, see Hervey, Fred. Wm.
Bristol, i. 490, 527; ii. 132, 135, 140,
142–3, 277; iii. 101 n, 102
Clifton coll., ii. 433
Bristow (Bristowe):
Edw., ix. 274
Geo., i. 277–9, 284, 303
Thos., ix. 169
Wal., prior of Wilmington, ii. 123
Brithelm, see Beorhthelm
Brithelmston, Jn. de, vii. 262
British Museum:
A.-S. rem., i. 337, 344–5
crustaceans, i. 246–7, 257, 259–60,
265
fossils, i. 28–31, 33–9
insects, i. 114
Newcastle papers, i. 530
prehist. rem., i. 309, 316, 319–22,
328–31
Rom. rem., iii. 12, 18, 25 n, 51, 57,
60–1, 63, 67
British Ornithologists Club, i. 277–8,
280, 293, 298
Brittan, see Britten
Brittany (Bretagne):
Alan of, count of Brittany, earl of
Richmond, i. 487
Arthur of, duke of Brittany, ix. 2
Beatrice, see Beatrice, dau. of Hen.
III
Jn. de, duke of Brittany, earl of Rich-
mond (d. 1286), ix. 2
Jn. de, duke of Brittany, earl of Rich-
mond (d. 1305), ix. 2, 142, 175–
6, 196, 235, 266
Jn. de, duke of Brittany, earl of Rich-

mond (d. 1334), ix. 2–3, 21, 83,
88, 112, 127, 187, 196, 254, 279
Jn. de, duke of Brittany, earl of Rich-
mond (d. 1341), ii. 138, 325; ix.
2, 15
fam., ix. 2
Brittany:
dchss. of, see Holland, Joan
dukes of, i. 509; ix. 79, 196–7*; and
see Brittany; Dreux; Montfort,
Jn.
Brittany (France), i. 20, 318, 518; ii.
138, 141, 143, 148, 161; ix. 15
Britten (Brittan):
Edw., iv. 123
Jn., ix. 195
Brittiffe, Chas., ii. 165
Britton, see Carlyon–Britton
Broad, E.F., ii. 481
Broad, the, see Hellingly
Broad Oak, see Brede
Broad Rife, iv. 201, 210
Broadbridge (Brodbridge):
Hen., vii. 190
Jas. (Jem), ii. 468, 470
Jn., vii. 190
Wm., mayor of Chich., see Brad-
bridge
Wm., ii. 468
and see Bradbridge
Broadbridge, see Bosham
broadcloths, see textile industries: wool
Broadford Green, see Chiltington, West
Broadhurst, see Horsted Keynes
Broadstairs (Kent), i. 315
Broadstone, see Forest Row
Broadwater, ii. 43; iv. 147 n
chant., ii. 20
Charmandean, i. 193–5, 198
ch.:
accessories, ii. 351, 354, 358–9, 361
archit., ii. 332, 334, 340, 347, 367,
376
golf, ii. 478
man., vii. 275
natural history, i. 65, 169, 183, 193,
205, 207, 209
poor law, ii. 210 n
pop., ii. 218
prehist. rem., i. 309, 312, 328
rectory, ii. 12
Rom. rem., iii. 3, 52
Broadwater Down (Kent, formerly
Suss.), i. 287, 536; ii. 44
Broc, see Brok
Brocas:
Alice, see Peverel
Jn., i. 510; iv. 168; vii. 233; ix. 202*
Marg., see Hevere
Sir Oliver, iv. 168; ix. 202
Sybil, w. of Jn., m. 2 Jn. de Uvedale,
iv. 168
Brock, see Habershon and Brock
Brockett, Ninian, ii. 39
Brockley abbey, see Deptford
Brockman:
Anne, see Glydd
Jas., ix. 230
Wm., ix. 230
Brodbridge, see Broadbridge
Brodestone, see Forest Row: Broadstone
Brodhull, see Dymchurch
Brodhull, ct., see Cinque Ports: cts.
Brodnax (later May, later May Knight),
Thos., iv. 97*, 104
Broglie, Charles François, comte de, ii.
125
Broile, la, park, see Ringmer: Broyle
Brok (Broc):
Alice (or Felice) de, m. Wm. Hareng,
iv. 168 n
Ingram (Ingelram) de, iv. 152, 202
Niel de (fl. 1189), iv.. 167
Niel (Nigel) de (fl. c. 1260), ii. 108
Niel de (fl. 1286, ? another), vii. 204
Niel de (fl. 1310, ? another), iv. 152,
202
Ranulf de, iii. 81

Rob., ii. 187
Broke:
Agatha, see Radmylde
Jn., vii. 71, 73 n, 229
Rob., vii. 177
and see Brook; Brooke
Broke, Ld. Willoughby de, see Verney
Brokere, Jn., vii. 203
Brokers, Thos., ii. 260
Brokysby (or Roksbye), Ric., dean of
Hastings coll., ii. 117
Bromdene:
Eliz., see Ayot
Valentine, iii. 105
Brome, fam., arms, iv. 100
Bromfield (Broomfield):
Edw., ld. mayor of London, ix. 127,
174, 237
Sir Edw., vii. 142
Eliz., ix. 83
Eliz., w. of Jn., see Weekes
French, ix. 173
Jn. (d. 1623), ix. 173, 266
Jn. (fl. 1724), ix. 173
Jn. (d. 1735, ? another), ix. 83
Jn. (d. 1792), ix. 83
Rob., vii. 141
Thos. (d. 1612), ix. 173
Thos. (fl. 1623–42), ix. 173–4, 266
Thos. (d. 1690), ix.. 169, 173–4
fam., ix. 61
arms, ix. *173*
Bromham:
Geof. de, ix. 201
Rob. de, ix. 201
Rog. de, ix. 229
Wm. de (? two of this name), ix. 201,
242
Bromham (Wilts.), ii. 52*
Bromham, see Heathfield: Broomham
Bromholm (Norf.), ii. 115 n
Bromknoll, see Ashdown forest
Bromley (Bromlee):
Clobery, vii. 224
Hen. Wm., vii. 224
Jn., prior of Shoreham friary, ii. 97
Kath., see Cloberry
Lucy, see Throckmorton
Ric., vii. 239
Wm., vii. 224
Wm. Throckmorton, vii. 224–5
Bromore, Rob. de, iv. 199
Brook:
A.J., ii. 451, 471–2
Jn. (fl. 1384), ix. 144
Jn. (fl. 1400), vii. 232
Jn. (fl. c. 1800), ii. 451
and see Broke; Brooke; Brooks
Brooke:
Anne, m. 2 Thos. Brian, ix. 177
Sir Basil Stanlake, vii. 156
Cynthia, see Sergison
Frances, see Mills
Hen., Ld. Cobham, warden of Cinque
Ports, ix. 53
Jn. (fl. 1646), ix. 177
Jn. Warden, vii. 156
Thos., ix. 246
W.H., iv. 179
Wm., Ld. Cobham, warden of Cinque
Ports, ii. 262
and see Broke; Brook; Brooks; Ser-
gison-Brooke
Brooker, E., ii. 448
Brookham, see Bepton
Brookhampton (Glos.), i. 513
Brookland (Kent), ii. 104
Brooks:
Amy, iv. 80
Charlotte, w. of Wm., iii. 162
Jas., ix. 26
Jn., and his w. Mary, iii. 162
Wm., iii. 162
and see Brook; Brooke
Broomer, see Birdham
Broomer's Hill, see Pulborough
Broomfield, see Bromfield
Broomhall, see Warnham

Broomham (in Catsfield), *see* Catsfield
Broomham (in Guestfield), *see* Guestfield
Broomham (Bromham) (in Heathfield),
see Heathfield
Broomham (in Penhurst), *see* Penhurst
Broomhill (Promhelle):
Adam de, ix. 149 *n*
Ailwin de, ix. 149 *n*
fam., ix. 149
Broomhill (formerly partly Kent), ii. 43;
ix. 142, **148–50**, 151, 175, 177
adv., ix. 149–50
boundary, i. 536; ix. 148–9
Camber Sands, ix. 148
chap., ix. 150
ch., ix. 149–50
coastguard, ix. 148
marsh, ix. 149–50
pop., ii. 222
sea defences, ix. 149
Brotherhood Hall, *see* Steyning
brotherhoods, *see* guilds, religious
Brotherton:
Alice de, w. of Thos., iv. 188
Thos. de, earl of Norfolk, Earl Mar-
shal, iv. 122, 183–4, 188, 193
his dau., *see* Margaret, dchss. of
Norfolk
his son, *see* Edward
fam., iv. 122
Brougham, Hen., Ld. Brougham, ii. 429
Brouncker, Wm., Vct. Brouncker, iv.
172
Brounyng, *see* Browning
Brous, *see* Braose
Brown:
D. Burns, *see* Burns
Edw., iv. 136
Frances, ix. 250
Francis, iv. 16 *n*
G., ii. 469
G.H., ii. 474
Geof., iv. 136
Jn. (fl. 1290), iv. 136
Jn., prior of Dominican friary,
Chich., ii. 94
Jn. (fl. *c.* 1551), vii. 263
Jn. (d. 1592), iv. 16 *n*
Jn. (fl. 1693), ix. 168
Rob. (d. by 1299), iv. 136
Rob. (fl. *c.* 1555), ii. 312
T.C., ii. 473
Thos., rector of St. Peter's, vicar of
St. Paul's, Chich., ii. 404*, 409*
Mrs., vii. 146
and see Browne; Stewart-Brown
Brown, Messrs., i. 321
Brown, *see* Edwardes, Brown and Oliver
Browne:
Alice, w. of Sir Ant., vii. 209; ix. 110
Sir Ambrose, iv. 168
Sir Ant. (d. 1548), i. 515–16; ii. 361;
iii. 149; iv. 25 *n*, 49, 61, 73, 77,
80, 93, 130; vii. 34, 204, 208–9;
ix. 17, 20, 26, 47, 75, 81, 85, 96,
102–7, 109–11, 113–14, 118, 128,
141, 148, 156–7, 160, 162, 169,
171, 180, 230, 246, 249, 255, 264,
268, 276, 278
Sir Ant., Vct. Montagu (d. 1592), i.
519; ii. 55, 117, 150, 234, 255,
362, 441; iv. 25 *n*, 42, 45, 50, 52,
56, 61, 66, 74, 77–8, 80, 83, 93*;
vii. 34, 141, 208–10, 212; ix. 81,
106–7, 109, 121, 128, 156–7, 160,
169, 181
Ant. (d. by 1592), iv. 80; ix. 169
Ant., Vct. Montagu (d. 1629), ii. 196–
7; iv. 52, 77, 80; vii. 208; ix. 106,
121, 147, 169, 268
Ant., Vct. Montagu (d. 1767), iv. 79;
ix. 20, 106, 141
Ant., Vct. Montagu (d. 1783), iv. 76
Eleanor, w. of ——, m. 2 ——
Gaynesford, iv. 112
Eleanor, w. of Thos., *see* Arundel
Eliz., w. of Sir Ant., ix. 157

Eliz., w. of Sir Geo., iv. 92, 112, 168
Eliz., w. of Sir Thos., ii. 117
Eliz. Mary, m. Wm. Steph. Poyntz,
iv. 77; vii. 142, 204, 208, 210
F.M.B., ii. 476
Francis, Vct. Montagu (d. 1682), iv.
76, 80; vii. 142, 208; ix. 80, 85,
106, 128, 160, 232, 246, 268
Francis, Vct. Montagu (d. 1708), i.
530; iv. 76; ix. 106
Frideswide, w. of Sir Mat., iv. 112
Sir Geo., iv. 92, 112, 168
Geo. Sam., Vct. Montagu, iv. 77; vii.
210 *n*
Sir Hen (fl. 1609), ix. 169
Hen., Vct. Montagu, iv. 67; ix. 106*
Jane, *see* Radcliffe
Jn. (fl. 1594), ix. 106
Jn. (d. 1608), vii. 169
Jn. (fl. 1626), ii. 248
Jn. (fl. 1695), vii. 169
Lucy, *see* Nevill
Magdalen, w. of Ant., Vct. Montagu,
ix. 106
Marg., m. Wm. Fenwick, iv. 168
Marg., w. of Ant., Vct. Montagu, *see*
Dacre
Mark Ant., Vct. Montagu, vii. 204,
208–9
Mary, m. —— Bedingfield, vii. 142
Mary, w. of Ant., m. 2 Sir Edm.
Uvedale, 3 Sir Thos. Gerard, iv.
80; vii. 208
Mary, w. of Weston, iv. 191
Sir Mat., iv. 92, 112
Oliver, iv. 39
Ric. (fl. 1577), iv. 112
Ric. (fl. 1702), ii. 165
Thos. (fl. 1444), ii. 90
Sir Thos. (fl. 1461), iv. 92, 112, 168
Thos. (fl. 1560), vii. 169
Thos. (fl. 1602), iv.. 92
Thos. (fl. 1726), vii. 144
Weston, iv. 191
Revd., ii. 420
fam., iv. 43 *n*, 50, 69–70, 76, 112; vii.
142, 212; ix. 20, 26, 80, 114, 160,
162, 268, 276, 278
arms, iii. 149; iv. 50, 77; vii. 142;
ix. *106*
and see Brown
Browning (Brounyng, Brownyng):
Ant., vii. 82, 101
Beatrice, vii. 82
Gilb., ii. 314
Jn., ii. 310
Thos., ii. 263
Broyle, the, *see* Fishbourne, New
Broyle park, *see* Ringmer
Bruce (Brus):
Rob. (d. 1295), i. 499
Rob. (d. 1329), i. 507; ii. 135
Thos., earl of Elgin, vii. 248
Mr., ii. 460
——, iii. 18
Brudenell:
Geo., earl of Cardigan, ii. 442
Hon. ——, ii. 443
Bruges, Wm., ii. 317
Bruges (Belgium), ii. 162
Bruhl, Hans Maurice, count de, ix. 215
his w. Eliz., *see* Chowne
Brunching (fl. 1190), ii. 113
Brunman, moneyer, iii. 83
Brunning (Brunyng):
Ant. (fl. 1617), iv. 163
Ant. (fl. *c.* 1643), iv. 35
Beatrice, *see* Wallcott
Ric., and his w. Helen (Ellen), iv.
163
Brunswick, Caroline of, *see* Caroline
Brunyng, *see* Brunning
Brus, *see* Bruce
Brussels (Belgium), ii. 335
Bruton (Som.), priory (later abbey), ii.
46, 121; iv. 145 *n*, 160, 162, 165,
175, 179
Bruton, *see* Breton

Bruyn:
Joan, *see* Rykhill
Ric., ix. 118
Bryan:
Jn., vii. 159, 171
Thos., vii. 159
Wm., vii. 159, 171
Wm. (another), vii. 159
and see Brian
Bryant, Wm., vii. 111
Bryce, G.H., ii. 472 *n*
Brygge, Thos., master of Playden hosp.,
ii. 105
Brygham, *see* Brigham
Buchan Hill, *see* Beeding
Buchanan:
Jas., Ld. Woolavington, iv. 58–60
Mr., ii. 461
and see Macdonald-Buchanan
Buchenet, Jn., vii. 36 *n*
Bucher, *see* Butcher
Buck, Geo., ii. 407
Buckberd, Ralph, vii. 284
Buckholt, *see* Bexhill
Buckhurst:
Baroness, *see* Sackville, Eliz.
Ld., *see* Sackville, Thos.
Buckhurst, *see* Withyham
Buckingham, dukes of, *see* Stafford,
Hen.; Villiers, Geo.
Buckinghamshire, earl of, *see* Hobart
Buckinghamshire, i. 68; ii. 276, 472; iv.
97 *n*
and see Ankerwyke; Bishopstone;
Eton; Hambledon; Taplow;
Tring
Buckland:
Beatrice, *see* Wallcott
Frank, i. 245, 256
Helen, vii. 82
Maurice, iv. 35
Wal. (fl. 1635), vii. 82
Wal. (fl. *c.* 1643, another), iv. 35, 39
Buckland, *see* Falmer
Buckle:
Chris., iv. 24
Lewes (fl. 1692), iv. 24
Lewes (d. 1785), iv. 24
Wm., iv. 24
arms, iv. 24
Buckner:
Jn., bp. of Chich., ii. 42; iii. 126, 148
Mary (d. 1772), w. of Ric., iii. 161
Mary (d. 1852), w. of Ric., iii. 126
Ric., mayor of Chich., iii. 95, 161
Ric. (d. 1837), iii. 126
arms, iii. *148*
Bucknill, S.P., ii. 472 *n*
Bucksteed, *see* Buxted
Bucksteep, *see* Warbleton
Buckwell, *see* Ashburnham
Buckworth (Bochehordea) (Hunts.), ii.
113
Bucler, Wal., ix. 150
Bucston, *see* Buxton
Budd (Budde):
E.H., ii. 468
Hen., iv. 231
Thos., iv. 157
Wm., ix. 249
Buddington, *see* Easebourne
Budleigh Salterton (Devon), i. 256
Budlett's Common, *see* Uckfield
Buenos Aires (Argentina), ii. 167
Bugsell (Buxhull):
Alan de (d. 1325), ix. 220
Sir Alan de (d. 1381), ix. 213*, 220
Sir Alan de (fl. 1443), ix. 220
Jn. de (fl. 1293), ix. 220
Jn. (fl. 1553), ix. 220
Sir Thos., ix. 220
——, w. of Sir Alan, m. 2 Jn. Monta-
gu, earl of Salisbury, ix. 220, 229
arms, ix. *220*
Bugsell, *see* Salehurst
building materials, ii. 327, 329, 333–8,
342, 351, 353, 355–6, 361, 366–7,
371, 379–81, 392–3, 395; *and see*

Caen stone; Horsham stone; Petworth marble; Portland stone; Purbeck marble; Sussex stone
Bulkestrode, *see* Bulstrode
Bull:
 Jn. (d. 1710), iii. 147
 Jn. (fl. 1770), vii. 255
 Mary, *see* Whitwood
 Rob. (? two of this name), iv. 177 *n*, 212
 ———, iii. 77, 90
Bull Ho., *see* Lewes
bull baiting, *see* sport
Bullisdon, Thos., vii. 171
Bullock:
 (later Bullock Fetherstonhaugh), Frances, iv. 16, 21
 ———, m. Sir Hen. Fetherstonhaugh, iv. 16
Bullock Down, *see* Eastbourne
Bulluc, Alwin, iv. 24–5
Bulstrode (Bolkestrode, Bulkestrode):
 Hen. de (fl.. 1312), iv. 128, 195
 Hen. (fl. 1657), iv. 98
 Mary, *see* Hall
 Maud de, w. of Hen., iv. 128, 195
 Nic. de, iv. 157
Bulverhythe (in Hastings), i. 57, 247, 495; ii. 177; ix. 9, 13, **20–1**, 138
 bailiffs, ii. 131
 Bulverhythe Salts, ix. 8
 chap., ii. 112; ix. 20–1
  archit., ii. 367
 coastguards, i. 507 *n*
 defences, ii. 152
 fair, ix. 21
 ferry, ix. 21
 harbour, ii. 125, 144–5
 inns, ix. 20
 mkt., ix. 21
 natural history, i. 139–40, 161, 175, 228, 265
 pop., ii. 228
 prebend, ii. 113, 116; ix. 21
 prehist. rem., i. *318*, 327–8
 ship service, ii. 130; ix. 36
 shipping, ii. 131
Bulwer-Lytton, Edw. (later Ld. Lytton), vii. 234
Bumenore, Jn. de, ii. 270
Bumsted, Steph., ix. 179
Bunbury:
 Sir Chas., ii. 455–6
 Thos., and his w. Bridget, ix. 160
Bunchgrove, *see* Maresfield: Buntisgrove
Buncton, *see* Wiston
Buntingehill, *see* Buttinghill
Buntisgrove, *see* Maresfield
Bunyard, Mr., ii. 33
Burarches, *see* Burleigh Arches
Burbeach (Burbece, Burbeche, Burgebeche) hund., i. 537–8; ii. 219
Burbridge, Mr., ii. 469–70
Burcester:
 Eliz., w. of Jn., ix. 158
 Jn. (fl. *c*. 1390), ix. 196
 Jn. (fl. *c*. 1470, ? two of this name), ix. 158
 Marg., w. of Sir Wm., *see* Braose
 Marg., w. of Sir Wm., *see* Burghersh
 Willelme, m. Wal. Urry, ix. 196
 Sir Wm., ix. 196
Burch *see* Birch
Burchell, ———, ii. 470
Burdett:
 Anne (or Agnes, or Alice), m. Wm. Jordan, ix. 174
 Clemence, m. And. Beeching, ix. 174
 Jn., ix. 174
 Rob., ix. 56
 Sarah, m. Jn. Brabon, ix. 174
 Wm. (d. 1592), ix. 174
 Wm. (d. 1624), ix. 174
Burdeville:
 Eliz., *see* Barttelot
 Jn., iv. 5

Ric., iv. 5
 Thos., iv. 5
Burdun, Wm., master of hosp. of St. Jas. and St. Mary, Chich., ii. 100
Bures, Jn. de, ix. 153
Burfield, W., ii. 471 *n*
Burfield & Sons, ii. 238
Burgebeche, *see* Burbeach
Burgelstaltone (? in Willingdon), ix. 251
Burges:
 Sir Chas. Montolieu, *see* Lamb
 W., vii. 261
 arms, ix. *91*
Burgess (Burgis):
 Jn. (fl. 1563), ii. 259
 Jn. (fl. 1788), ii. 202 *n*
 Rob., ix. 225
 Thos. (fl. 1450), ii. 230
 Thos. (fl. 1691), ii. 159
 Thos., bp. of St. David's, iv. 121
 Wal., ii. 13
 Wm., ix. 155
Burgess Hill (formerly in Clayton and Keymer), ii. 44; vii. 179
 golf, ii. 478
 insects, i. 167, 175, 187, 191, 193, 196–9, 201–2, 204–5, 207–10
 roads to, iii. 42–3
 Rom. rem., iii. 42–3
 St. John's Common, i. 198, 201, 208; iii. 42
  A.-S. rem., i. 337
  sheep fair, iii. 281
 trades and ind., ii. 254; vii. 179
 U.D., vii. 103, 119, 141, 179
Burgh:
 Anne, *see* Cobham
 Beatrice de, *see* Bardolf
 Benedict, dean of Hastings coll., ii. 117
 Divorguilla, m. Sir Rob. FitzWalter, vii. 283
 Edw., Ld. Burgh, ix. 120
 Hawise de, m. Sir Rob. de Greyly, vii. 99, 283
 Hubert de, earl of Kent, warden of Cinque Ports, i. 495; vii. 99, 275–6, 283, 286
 Jn. de (d. 1274), i. 497; vii. 229, 275, 283, 286
 Jn. de (d. 1280), vii. 283
 Sir Jn. (fl. 1589), i. 519
 Marg. de, m. Ric. de Clare, earl of Gloucester, vii. 283
 Marg. de, w. of Hubert, vii. 99, 275–6, 286
 Margery de, vii. 283
 Ulick Jn. de, marquess of Clanricarde, iv. 10, 31, 122, 208
Burgh Castle (Suff.), iii. 5
Burgherse forest, *see* Dallington: forest
Burghersh (Burghershe):
 Bart. de (? two of this name), i. 508–9; ii. 323; ix. 196
 Cecily, w. of Steph. de, ix. 196
 Hen. de, iv. 91, 143
 Herb. de, ix. 196
 Isabel de, *see* St. John
 Jn. de (d. ? 1256), ix. 196
 Jn. de, prior of Lewes, ii. 68, 70
 Marg., w. of Bart. de, m. 2 Sir Wm. Burcester, ix. 196
 Maud, m. 1 Wal. de Paveley, 2 Thos. de Aldon, ix. 196
 Reynold, ix. 196
 Rob. de, ii. 114; ix. 196
 Steph. de (fl. 1272), ii. 325
 Steph. de (d. 1310), ix. 196, 202
 fam., ix. 195
 arms, ix. *196*
Burghersh, Ld., *see* Fane, Francis
Burghershe, *see* Burghersh
Burghlow castle, *see* Arlington
Burghstede, *see* Berghsted
Burgis, *see* Burgess
Burgon, Jn. Wm., dean of Chich., ii. 51; iii. 115, 132, 155

Burgoyne, Jn., M.P. for Midhurst, iv. 76
Burgundy (France), ii. 328
burials:
 Romano-British, *see* Romano-British Sussex: burials
 Saxon, *see* Anglo-Saxon remains: burials
Buriton (Hants), *see* Sunworth; Weston
Burkitt, Wm. T., ix. 89-90
Burlamack, Phil., ii. 248
Burle (? Kent), ix. 148
Burleigh Arches, *see* Worth
Burleigh Arches (Burarches) hund., i. 537; ii. 225
Burley, Thos., sacrist of Bosham coll., ii. 112
Burlington, earls of, *see* Boyle; Cavendish
Burlow castle, *see* Arlington: Burghlow
Burne:
 Christine de, *see* Socknersh
 Jn. de, ix. 229
 Thos. de, ii. 80
 Wm., iv. 25
Burne, *see* Eastbourne; Westbourne and Singleton hund.
Burne-Jones, Sir Edw., vii. 234, 237
Burnell, Wm., vii. 75
Burnett:
 Jn., ii. 200
 Ric., i. 531
Burney, Fanny, vii. 248–9
Burnham (Essex), ii. 271
Burns Brown, D., vii. 259
Burpham, ii. 42–3
 adv., iv. 173
 ch., ii. 124
  accessories, ii. 351, 354, 356, 359
  archit., ii. 328, 333, 339–40, 347–8, 365, 367–8, *369*, 370, 373, 376, 378
 dom. archit., ii. 386
 earthworks, i. 468; vii. 7 *n*
 man., ii. 230; iv. 111, 128
 natural history, i. 131, 133, 198–201, 208, 225–7, 231, 264, 300
 Peppering (Pipering), i. 28, 302*
  insects, i. 120–1, 126–7, 138, 142–9, 151–4, 157–64
  man., ii. 109
 pop., ii. 217
 prehist. rem., i. 327
 Rom. rem., iii. 2, 52, 67
 Wepham, i. 495; iii. 2, 67
Burr, J., ii. 166
Burrell (Borell):
 Alberic, vii. 158
 Anne, m. Wm. Hayley, ix. 228
 Sir Chas., ii. 415
 Eliz., ix. 159
 Eliz., w. of Peter, vii. 158
 Eliz., w. of Ninian, *see* Penhurst
 Eliz., w. of Wm., *see* Noakes
 Gerard, archdeacon of Chich., vicar of Cuckfield, vii. 162
 Honor, *see* Wotton
 Jane, m. Peter Short, vii. 158
 Jane, w. of Ninian, vii. 157
 Jn. (fl. 1651), vii. 158
 Jn. (fl. *c*. 1760), ix. 228
 Mary, m. Wm. Board the younger, vii. 89, 158
 Matilda, ix. 32
 Sir Mayrick (Merrick), i. 306; ii. 278
 Ninian, vicar of Cuckfield, ii. 416
 Ninian (fl. 1562), ix. 237
 Ninian (fl. 1576, another), ix. 237
 Ninian (d. 1614), vii. 157–8, 162
 Ninian (d. 1629), vii. 162
 Ninian (d. 1674), vii. 158, 235
 Ninian (fl. 1683), vii. 158
 Peter, vii. 158–9
 Peter, Ld. Gwydir, vii. 158
 Peter Rob., Ld. Gwydir, vii. 158
 Thos. (fl. 1562), ix. 237
 Thos. (fl. *c*. 1682), ii. 414

Burrell (*cont.*):
Timothy (fl. 1682), ii. 414
Timothy (d. 1717, ? another), ii. 264; vii. 89, 95, 159, 173
Wal. (d. 1671), vii. 142, 158, 235
Wal. (d. 1683), vii. 158, 235
Wm., rector of Brightling, ix. 228
Wm., rector of Burwash, vicar of Icklesham, ix. 199, 228
Wm. (fl. 1737), ix. 228
Sir Wm. (d. 1796), iii. 12, 111; iv. 100, 158, 186 *n*; vii. 49, 230; ix. 207, 227–9
fam., vii. 148, 162
arms, ix. *228*
Burrey, *see* Bury
Burrows, Winfrid, bp. of Chich., iii. 126
Burry, *see* Pullen-Burry
Bursegard, *see* Boucicaut
Burstow (Burstowe):
Jn. de, ix. 150
Steph. de, ix. 149
Burstow (Surr.), ii. 328 *n*, 446, 448; vii. 199
Burstowe, *see* Burstow
Burt:
Eliz., m. Nic. Hardham, vii. 159–60
Jn., vii. 159
Burtenshaw:
Jn., vii. 176
Jn. (another), vii. 176
Ric., vii. 177
Burton:
Alice, *see* Warbleton
Decimus, ii. 204
Edw., ii. 34
Eliz. de, *see* Hartridge
Jas., ix. 5
Jn., ii. 202–4, 239, 253, 310
Marmaduke, ix. 162
Phil., iv. 10
Rob. de, master of Playden hosp., ii. 104–5
Wal. de, ix. 206
Wm. de, vii. 147
Burton, ii. 43; ix. 92
Burton Down, iii. 34
ch., ii. 327, 334, 338, 354–5, 358–9, 361, 365
earthworks, i. 480
man., ix. 193
mill, ii. 382
natural history, i. 282, 285, 289, 297, 303, 306
pk., i. 28, 306; ii. 297, 301
pop., ii. 218
roads to, iii. 34
Rom. rem., iii. 34
textile ind., ii. 257
Burton Lazars (Leics.), prior, iv. 17
Burton, West, *see* Bury
Burwash, Geo., and his w. Susan, ix. 56
Burwash. i. 57, 514; ii. 43, 196; ix. 127, 158, 193, **194–200**, *198*, 251
adv., ix. 209
assarting, ii. 189
Batemans, ii. 387; ix. *195*
char., ix. 199–200
ch., ii. 38, 40; ix. 195, 198–9, *198*
accessories, ii. 242, 356, 360; ix. 199
archit., ii. 336, 339–40, 342, 366, 376; ix. 198–9
Dallington forest, *see* Dallington: forest
dom. archit., ii. 391; ix. 194–5, *194*
fair, ix. 196
forest, *see* Dallington: forest
fossils, i. 37
halemote, ix. 1
Holmshurst, ii. 334; ix. 195
imparking, ii. 295
man., ii. 173 *n*, 325; ix. 2–3, 79, 91, 195–8, 202
mkt., ix. 195–6
mill, ix. 197–8
natural history, i. 167, 276–7, 284
nonconf., ix. 200

pk., ix. 97
pop., ii. 222–3
rectors, ix. 199; *and see* Burrell, Wm.
rectory, ix. 199
Rom. Cath., ix. 200
sch., ii. 438; ix. 200
smuggling, ii. 200
trades and ind., ii. 263; ix. 195
vicars, ix. 199; *and see* Goldham, Thos., Otley, Thos.
Bury (Burrey):
Thos., iii. 96
Wm., prior of Shulbred, ii. 82–3
and see Berry
Bury, Vct., *see* Keppel
Bury (Berie), i. 526; ii. 42–3; ix. 9
Barkhale (Berkhale), ii. 303
botany, i. 47
Burton, West, ii. 109; iv. 188
cider making, ii. 264
char., iv. 188
ch., ii. 42
accessories, ii. 250, 352–4, 356–7, 379
archit., ii. 337, 339–40, 342, 346, 348, 374, 376, 379
ch. ho., ii. 384
earthworks, i. 480
Grevatts wood, iii. 35
hund., i. 538; ii. 217; iv. 1
insects, i. 160, 168, 182, 184, 191, 193, 196–7, 199–200, 202
man., ii. 4, 109, 124
pop., ii. 217
roads to, iii. 35
and see Paplesbury; Swanbridge
Buryman, Jn., prior of Pynham, ii. 81
Busbridge:
Joan, *see* May
Jn. (d. by 1616), ix. 214, 230, 233
Jn. (fl. 1659), vii. 218; ix 214, 230
Mary, m. Jas. Temple, ix. 214
Busby, *see* Wilds and Busby
Bushby:
J., ii. 167
Wm., master of Holy Trinity hosp., Arundel, ii. 98
Bushnell, Jn., iv. 106; ix. 130
Buslingthorpe (Beselyngford, Boselinthorpe):
Isabel, *see* Percy
Jn., iv. 61*
Ric., iv. 61*
Bussey, Hugh de, ii. 295
Busshopeston, *see* Bishopstone
Busshoppe, *see* Bishop
Bust:
Ric., vii. 121
Wm., vii. 121
Buston, Paul, ix. 209
Bustow, Rob., ix. 252
Butcher (Bocher, Bucher):
Jn., ix. 86
Thos. (fl. 1549), vii. 42
Thos. (fl. 1763), vii. 177
Butcher's Cross, *see* Maresfield
Buterley (Biterley):
Marg., *see* Hussey
Ric., iv. 5, 14
Butler (Boteler, Botiler, Botiller, Butiler, Butiller):
Alice, w. of Rob. le, *see* Picheford
Alice, w. of Sir Thos., *see* Dalingridge
Ann, iv. 121, 203
Chas., earl of Ossory, ii. 454
E.A., i. 71, 136, 247
E.T., iv. 39
Edm. le, vii. 189
Hen., master of hosp. of St. Jas. and St. Mary, Chich., ii. 100
J., ii. 481
Jas., Ld. Boteler, ix. 130
Jas. (fl. 1734), i. 531
Jane, m. 1 Jas. Ley, earl of Marlborough, 2 Wm. Ashburnham, ix. 129–30
Joan, vii. 189
Joan le, w. of Theobald, vii. 258

Jn. le (fl. 1352), iv. 130
Jn. (fl. 1727), iv. 112
Jn. (fl. *c.* 1762), iv. 54
Jos., iii. 82, 113
Marg., m. Lawr. Washington, vii. 155
Phil., ii. 166
Rob. le (fl. 1308), iv. 167 *n*, 168, 171
Rob. (fl. 1610), ix. 68
Rog., vii. 160
Theobald le, vii. 258
Sir Thos., vii. 54 *n*; ix. 263
Wal., iv. 172
Wm. (fl. 1585), vii. 155, 160
Wm. (fl. 1814), iv. 195
Wm. (d. *c.* 1925), iii. 16–17, 167
Butler's Green, *see* Cuckfield
Butt, H.R., ii. 473
Butterfield:
Ruskin, i. 273, 275–80, 282, 284, 293
Wm., iv. 65
Butterie, Thos., iv. 199
Butterwick, Geo., vii. 95
Buttinghill, *see* Clayton
Buttinghill (Bottingelle, Bottingill, Bottynghill, Buntingehill) hund., i. 538; ii. 311; vii. 1, 3 *n*, 92, 116, **125–6**, 140
buttresses and pilasters, *see* architecture: ecclesiastical
Buxhull, fam., *see* Bugsell
Buxhull, *see* Boxhull
Buxted (Bucksteed), ii. 44, 280, 292
Ashdown forest, *q.v.*
assarting, ii. 189
char., ii. 438
ch., ii. 13, 118
accessories, ii. 352, 356, 359, 361, 375
archit., ii. 333, 336, 340, 344, 346, 348, 373, 375
dom. archit., ii. 381, 387
earthworks, i. 477–8
Etchingwood, ix. 193*
Five Ash Down, i. 57
Gilderigge, ii. 13
Hendall (Hindall), ii. 381
hermitage, ii. 47
Hindall, *see* Buxted: Hendall
hosp., ii. **99**
natural history, i. 50, 155, 168, 217
Newnham (Newenden) pk., ii. 297, 317 *n*, 318, 320
pk., i. 306; ii.297, 322–3
poor relief, vii. 266
pop., ii. 226
Pound Gate, ii. 319
prehist. rem., i. 328
rector, ii. 13, 118; *and see* Clarke, Wm.; Gage, Jas.
royal visit, i. 505
sch., ii. 438
Shepherd's Hill, i. 477
trades and ind., ii. 242, 246, 259, 296
Buxton (Bucston):
Mildred, w. of Sydney, Earl Buxton, vii. 207
Sydney Chas., Earl Buxton, vii. 207
Wm., ix. 69
Byatt, Horace, ii. 429
Byfleet (Surr.), i. 171 *n*
Bykenaker hund., i. 538
Bykewell manor (unidentified), iv. 128
Byndloss, Mr., ii. 457
Byne:
Anne, *see* Wane
Hen., vii. 81 *n*
Magnus, vii. 144
Steph. (fl. 1671), vii. 144
Steph. (fl. 1724), vii. 144
Steph. (fl. 1792), vii. 208
Byng, Geo., Ld. Torrington, ii. 159, 164–5
Byrch, *see* Birch
Byron:
Geo. Gordon, Ld. Byron, ix. 8
Maj.-Gen., iv. 155
Bysshe (Byshe, Bysse):
Chris., ii. 420

Jn., vii. 196
Lora de la, m. Steph. le Chamberlayn, iv. 61
Thos., rector of West Tarring, vicar of Eastbourne, ii. 420
fam., ix. 209
Bysshop (Bysshopp, Bysshoppe), *see* Bishop
Byworth, *see* Petworth
Byzantium, i. 343

cabbages, *see* crops
Caburn, Mount, *see* Glynde: Mount Caburn
Cackham, *see* Wittering, West: Cakeham
Cackle Street, *see* Brightling
Cacqueray, fam., ii. 254
Cadborough, *see* Rye: Gateborough
Cade, Jack, *see* rebellions
Cade Street, *see* Heathfield
Cadiz (Spain), ii. 153–5, 165
Caedwalla (Cadwalla, Ceadwalla, Cedwalla), king of Wessex, i. 347, 482; ii. 1, 303; iii. 134; iv. 135–6, 161–2, 198–9, 207, 211, 215, 218, 223–4, 229, 233, 237; vii. 101
Caen stone, ii. 52, 327, 333–6, 361, 367, 371, 379–81, 395; vii. 21, 40, 45–7, 259
Caerwent (Mon.), i. 344 *n*
Caesar, Julius, Rom. emperor, i. 324; ii. 241, 291; iii. 30
Caesar, *see* Cesar
Caffyn:
 Mat., ii. 38
 ——, ii. 469
Cahaignes, Hugh de, ii. 122
Cailli (Cailly, Kailly):
 Adam de, iv. 123
 Emma de, *see* Tattersall
 Osbert de, vii. 217
 Rob. de, iv. 111
 Thos. de, iv. 98, 123, 128
Caisneto, Ralph de, vii. 253
Cakebred, Rob., vii. 30 *n*
Cakeham, *see* Wittering, West
Calais (Callice) (Pas de Calais, France), i. 515; ii. 68, 124, 129, 133, 138–9, 141, 143–4, 153, 160, 233–4, 267; iii. 97, 101–2; iv. 15; ix. 67
Calceto priory, *see* Lyminster: Pynham priory
Caldecott museum, *see* Eastbourne: museums
Caldecourt, Wm. Hen., ii. 468
Cadicott (Chaldecott):
 Cordelia, w. of Matthias, vii. 218
 Grace, vii. 218
 Matthias, vii. 64, 218
 Ric., vii. 64
 Thos., iii. 81
Calland, Jn., ix. 152, 156, 163
Calleva Atrebatum, *see* Silchester
Callice, *see* Calais
Calvert, Col., ii. 447
Calvinists, ii. 32, 41; vii. 80; ix. 247, 257
Camber, *see* Icklesham
Camber Sands, *see* Broomhill
Cambrai (Nord, France), ii. 258
cambric, *see* textile inds.: linen
Cambridge:
 Philosophical Society, museum, i. 286
 St. Radegund's priory, ii. 87
 University, ii. 399, 404–5, 408, 420, 427, 432–3, 435, 471–3, 476
  anatomical museum, i. 346
  colleges, *see* Clare; Corpus Christi; Jesus; King's; Magdalene; Pembroke; Queens'; St. Catharine's; St. John's; Sydney Sussex; Trinity
Cambridgeshire, i. 186, 290; *and see* Ely; Gog Magog Hills; Madingley; Stretham; Thorney; Wicken Fen
Camden, Wm., i. 42; ii. 170–1, 324; iii. 62
Camden, Lady, *see* Pratt, Clementina

Camehide (unidentified), ix. 87
Camelsdale, *see* Fernhurst
Camilla, Tedisius de, rector of West Tarring, ii. 12
Camoys (Camois):
 Eleanor de, m. Sir Rog. Lewknor, iv. 24, 35; vii. 81, 226
 Eliz. de, w. of Ralph, *see* Rogate
 Eliz., w. of Thos., *see* Mortimer
 Hugh, Ld. Camoys, iv. 35, 37; vii. 81, 226
 Sir Jn. de (d. 1298), iv. 8, 34, 36, 58; vii. 81
 Jn. (fl. *c.* 1350), iv. 35
 Marg. de, m. Ralph Radmylde, iv. 35; vii. 81, 226
 Marg., w. of Sir Jn. de, *see* Gatesden
 Marg., w. of Thos., iv. 35
 Ralph de (fl. 1264–92), i. 497, 505
 Ralph de (d. 1336), ii. 106; iv. 8–9, 24–5, 28 *n*, 34–5, 85; vii. 81
 Ralph de (d. by 1372), iv. 35
 Ric., iv. 35, 37
 Rog., iv. 35
 Sir Thos. de (d. 1372), iv. 31, 35; vii. 81
 Sir Thos de, Ld. Camoys, i. 512–13; ii. 360, 394; iv. 24, 35, 37, 61 *n*; vii. 81
 fam., ii. 394; iv. 24–5
 arms, iv. *35*, 38, 100; vii. 10, *81*
Camp Hill, *see* Maresfield
Campbell:
 Alex. B., ii. 451–2
 Maxwell, ii. 480
 R.J., iii. 130
Camperdown (Netherlands), battle, ii. 153
Campion:
 Barbara, w. of Hen., *see* Courthope
 Barbara, w. of Wm., *see* Springett
 F.H., ii. 479
 Hen. (fl. 1614), vii. 144
 Hen. (d. 1761), vii. 173, 176
 Hen. (fl. 1766), ix. 202
 Hen. Courthope, vii. 176, 262 *n*
 Wm., vii. 111, 176
 Wm. Hen., ii. 479; vii. 176, 178
 Wm. Jn. (d. 1855), vii. 9, 119, 142, 176
 Wm. Jn. (d. 1869), vii. 176
 Sir Wm. Rob., vii. 115, 119, 142, 172, 176
 arms, vii. *176*
camps, *see* Romano–British Suss.: roads and camps
Canada, *see* Cape Breton: Louisberg; Newfoundland; Quebec
canals, *see* Arundel and Portsmouth; Chichester; Rother Navigation; Royal Military; Wey and Arun
Cancellario, Emericus de, ii. 304
candelabra, *see* architecture: ecclesiastical
Candelsby, Jn., warden of Windham hosp., ii. 108
Candy:
 Jn. Hen., iv. 190
 Jn. Wm., iv. 190 *n*
Cane (fl. before 1066), ix. 212
Cane, Savaric fitz, *see* Savaric
Cannon, M., ii. 457
Canterbury (Kent), i. 484; ii. 172, 404, 469; iv. 223
 abps., ii. 6, 30, 87, 106; iii. 89 *n*, 95; iv. 134, 233; vii. 258; ix. 35, 278; *and see* Alfstan; Anselm; Baldwin; Becket; Boniface; Chicheley; Courtenay, Wm.; Cranmer; Dover, Ric. of; Dunstan; Escures; Ethelgar; Grindal; Howley; Islip, Sim.; Juxon, Wm.; Kilwardby; Lanfranc; Langton, Steph.; Laud; Parker, Mat.; Peckham, Jn.; Poole, Reynold; Rich, Edm.; Sancroft; Stafford, Jn.; Stigand; Stratford, Jn.; Sutton, Chas. Manners;

Theobald; Theodore; Walter, Hubert; Warham, Wm.; Winchelsea, Rob.; Wulfred
 arms, iii. *103*; iv. 225, *229*
 ct., ii. 90
 estates, i. 538; ii. 1, 3, 118, 231, 292, 295, 297, 300, 303–5, 311, 316, 322–3, 333, 371, 380, 383; iii. 81; iv. 45, 69, 80, 88, 101–2, 133, 135, 161–2, 183, 222–3, 229–31, 234–5; vii. 14, 239; ix. 10, 148
 jurisdiction, i. 502–3; iii. 164; iv. 206; vii. 30
 patronage, ii. 36, 333, 403; iii. 165; iv. 103–4, 225, 227, 233, 237, 239; vii. 227, 239–40; ix. 123
 peculiars, ii. 1, 3, 9, 42, 44 *n*, 48, 333; iii. 103–4; iv. 2, 101–2, 222, 234–5
 province, ii. 87
 vicar general, *see* Brent, Nat.
cath., ii. 11, 50, 229, 400; iv. 148 *n*
Christ Church cath. priory, ii. 54; vii. 41
 estates, iv. 101, 165, 226, 233–4; vii. 101; ix. 149
 monks, ii. 53, 73, 87
 prior, ii. 67, 118; *and see* Henry; Odo
 prior and chapter, ii. 11, 16; iv. 237
 dean, *see* Turner, Thos.
 dean and chapter, iv. 165, 233; vii. 41, 101; ix. 130, 189, 249, 257
 arms, vii. *101*
dioc., ii. 54, 103
 chancellor, *see* Wych, Ric. de
 roads, ii. 240
St. Augustine's abbey, ii. 78
St. Gregory's priory, ii. 63
 sch., ii. 437
Canterbury College, Oxford, ii. 54; iv. 233
Cantwara, i. 347
Canute, *see* Cnut
Capcot, Capt., i. 524
Cape Breton (Canada), ii. 165
Cape Finisterre (Spain), i. 296
Cape of Good Hope (South Africa), ii. 167
Capel (Capell):
 Edw., ix. 7
 Frances, m. Jn. Shirley, vii. 37
 Wm., earl of Essex, ii. 454
Capella, *see* Chapelle
Capron:
 Ant. (fl. 1700), iv. 56
 Ant. (fl. *c.* 1800), iv. 56
Carausius, Rom. emperor, iii. 4, 7
Cardiff, *see* Ely
Cardigan, earl of, *see* Brudenell
Cardinal College, Oxford, ii. 16, 80, 88; iv. 80, 130
Cardonell:
 Adam, iv. 180
 Mary, m. Wm., Ld. Talbot, iv. 180
Cardwell, W.A., ii. 448
Careso, H., ii. 167
Carew (Carewe):
 Eleanor, *see* Hoo
 Eliz., w. of Nic., vii. 67, 80, 110
 Francis, vii. 67, 80, 110–11, 159, 213
 Sir Geo., rector of Harting, iv. 20
 Sir Jas., ix. 138, 229*
 Maline, w. of Ric., ix. 138
 Sir Nic., vii. 67, 80, 110, 209, 213; ix. 138
 Sir Ric., ix. 138, 229
Carisbrooke (I.W.), iii. 5
Carless, Wm., ii. 472 *n*, 473
Carleton:
 Edw., ix. 237
 Geo., bp. of Chich., ii. 32; iv. 134
 Guy, bp. of Chich., i. 529; iii. 88, 134; vii. 17–18, 232
 Steph. de, master of hosp. of St. Jas. and St. Mary, Chich., ii. 100
 ——, i. 524

Carlisle (Cumb.), i. 535
Carlyle, Thos., vii. 234
Carlyon-Britton, P.W.P., iii. 15–16, *16*, 51, 69
Carmelites, ii. 45, 97
Carolina, North (U.S.A.), ii. 166
Caroline (of Brunswick), queen of Geo. IV, vii. 19*, 249
Caroloco (or Cherlew), Jn. de, prior of Lewes, ii. 68–71, 77
Carpender (Carpynder):
    Agnes, w. of Thos., iii. 105
    Phil., iv. 163
    Thos., iii. 105; iv. 163, 199
Carpenter:
    Hen., and his w. Mary, iv. 221
    Jn., dean of Hastings coll., ii. 117
    R.H., iii. 123
    Ric. C., ii. 433; iii. 137, 160; vii. 259, 262
    Wm. (fl. 1605), vii. 96
    Wm. (fl. 1830), iii. 113
Carpenter, *see* Slater & Carpenter
Carpynder, *see* Carpender
Carr (Carre):
    Anne (? w. of Geo.), ix. 181
    Anne, w. of Jn., ix. 86
    Geo., ix. 181
    Jn., vicar of Hollington, ix. 86
    Rob., ii. 166
    Rob. Jas., bp. of Chich., ii. 404, 409
    Thos., iii. 99
Carré, Jean (Jn.), ii. 254–5
Carreghofa (Carrechova) (Mont., formerly Denb.), castellan, *see* Strange, Ralph le
Carrill, *see* Caryll
Carrington, Ld., *see* Smith, Rob.
Carryll, *see* Caryll
Carsfelde, Peter, sacrist of Bosham, ii. 111–12
Carson:
    Eliz., *see* Manning
    Rob., ix. 207
Cartar, *see* Carter
Cartaret, Peter, ii. 166
cartbote, ii. 310
Carter (Cartar):
    Dorothy, m. Jn. Jeffrey, ii. 424
    Edw., and his w. Eliz., iii. 163
    Jn. (fl. 1524), iii. 86
    Sir Jn. (fl. after 1776), iv. 212
    Jos., iv. 93; vii. 171; ix. 279
    Martha, m. Hen. Smart, iii. 147
    Mary, iii. 163
    Thos., iv. 237
Carter's Corner, *see* Hellingly
Carthusians, Old, ii. 473
Cartwright:
    Adam, vii. 246, 252
    Edm., rector of Earnley, vicar of Lyminster, ii. 327; iii. 20, 25, 47, 63–4; iv. 203
Carver, Derrick, ii. 22, 262; vii. 251
Carver, *see* Corney and Carver
Carver & Co., ii. 164
Caryll (Carrill, Carryll):
    Anne, m. Sir Wm. Ford, iv. 16
    Cath., *see* Petre
    Sir Edw. (d. 1610), ii. 244, 247, 309; iv. 16, 20, 25; vii. 55
    Sir Edw. (fl. 1634), ii. 244
    Edw. (d. 1766), ix. 88–9
    Jn. (fl. 1509), vii. 158, 258
    Jn. (d. 1566), ii 20, 246; iv. 159, 167, 212; vii. 258
    Jn. (fl. 1584), vii. 55
    Jn. (fl. 1590, ? another), ii. 310; iii. 80
    Sir Jn. (d. 1652), i. 523; ii. 309; iii. 88; iv. 13, 16, 167, 212
    Jn. (d. 1681), iv. 16, 20, 144; ix. 71
    Jn., Ld. Caryll of Durford, i. 530; ii. 40 *n*; iv. 16–17, 20; ix. 88
    Jn. (fl. 1736), iv. 17, 21 *n*
    Jn. (fl. 1736–71), iv. 17, 20, 159; ix. 88
    Mary, w. of Sir Jn. (d. 1652), iv. 16

Mary, w. of Sir Jn. (fl. 1736–71), ix. 88
    Sir Ric. (d. 1616), iv. 16, 20
    Ric. (fl. *c.* 1690), iv. 17
    Thos. (d. 1566), vii. 55
    Sir Thos. (d. 1617), iv. 16
    fam., ii. 27, 29, 247, 310, 362; iv. 11, 20, 25, 159, 167
    arms, iv. *16*
Case:
    T.E., ii. 459
    T.K., ii. 453
Casingham, Wm. de, i. 494
cask making, ii. 236–7
Cassingham, *see* Ticehurst
Cassye, Rob., iv. 62 *n*
Castile, Eleanor of, *see* Eleanor
Castile (Spain), iii. 130
Castle Acre (Norf.), i. 337; ii. 65
    priory, ii. 65, 68
        priors, *see* Bennett, Nic.; Oke, Jn.
Castle Cary (Som.), iv. 144
Castle Goring, *see* Goring
castle guard service, ii. 173–4; ix. 15, 79, 84, 87–8, 92, 133, 180, 206, 212–15, 248, 263, 266
Castle Hill (in Hartfield), *see* Hartfield
Castle Hill (in Hastings), *see* Hastings
Castle Hill (in Newhaven), *see* Newhaven
Castle Hill (in Rotherfield), *see* Rotherfield
castles, ii. 394–6; *and see* Amberley; Arundel; Bodiam; Bramber; Chich.; Deal; Deal: Sandown; Dover; Fulking; Guildford; Hastings; Herstmonceux; Icklesham: Camber; Lamberhurst: Scotney; Leeds; Lewes; Midhurst; Nuthurst: Sedgewick; Perching; Pevensey; Reigate; Rye; Shipley: Knepp; Winchester
Castor ware, *see* Romano-British Sussex: pottery
Castre, Rob. de, and his w. Joan, vii. 203
Caterham (Surr.), iii. 42
Catherine (of Braganza), queen of Chas. I, vii. 270
Catherine, abbess of Guines, ix. 150
Catia Censorina, iii. 15
Catley, Thos., ix. 25
Catlin, P., vii. 140
Cato, ii. 418
Cator, Maj., ii. 446
Catsfield, ii. 43; ix. 20, 77, 88, 146, 226, 239, **240–4**
    adv., ix. 240, 243–4
    brickmaking, ix. 240
    Broomham, ii. 295; ix. 242, 244
    chap., ix. 243
    char., ix. 234, 244
    ch., ix. *242*, 243, *243*
        accessories, ii. 251; ix. 243
        archit., ii. 336, 371, 376; ix. 243
    dom. archit., ix. 240
    foxhunting, ii. 447
    man., ix. 240–2, 244
    ho., ix. 242
    mill, ix. 241 *n*
    natural history, i. 132, 140, 158, 167, 171, 232–5, 279, 286, 301–2
    Normanhurst, i. 132, 301; ix. 240, 242
    pop., ii. 223
    rector, ii. 34
Catt (later Willett), Wm., iv. 237
cattle, *see* livestock
Caurden, Ric., dean of Chich., ii. 51
Causays, Rob. le, vii. 106
Cauz:
    Agnes, w. of Rob. de, iv. 58
    Denise de, m. —— Trotemenu, iv. 58
    Emma de, m. 1 Jn. de Segrave, 2 Jn. de Grey, iii. 105; iv. 168
    Godfrey de, iv. 58
    Hugh de, iv. 58
    Nichola de, *see* Leigh
    Rob. de, iv. 58

Rog. de, iii. 105
    fam., iv. 58
Cave:
    Sarah, *see* Tufton
    Wm., ix. 169
Cavendish:
    Eliz., *see* Compton
    Geo., earl of Burlington, ii. 456; ix. 173
    Ld. Jn., ii. 443
    Louise, dchss. of Devonshire, ii. 277
    Phil., ii. 165
    Spencer Compton, duke of Devonshire, ii. 461, 478
    Wm., marquess of Hartington, duke of Devonshire (d. 1707), ii. 441, 443
    Wm., duke of Devonshire (d. 1891), ii. 434
    Wm., earl of Burlington, ix. 173
Cavendish-Bentinck, Sir Wm., duke of Portland, ii. 460
Cawley:
    Eliz., w. of Wm., iv. 172
    Jn., mayor of Chich., iii. 161; iv. 212
    Wm., M.P. for Midhurst and Chich., i. 522, 525–6; iii. 75, 80–1, 87–8, 99; vii. 50, 136, 146, 155–6, 172, 173 *n*, 177, 199, 212, 238
    Wm. (another), iv. 172–3
    arms, iii. *81*
Cawthorn, *see* Scott and Cawthorn
Cayley, F., vii. 168
Cayme, *see* Kyme
Caynsham, Rob., ii. 412
Ceadwalla, *see* Caedwalla
Ceawlin (Ceaulin), king of Wessex, i. 482 *n*
Ceccano, Hannibal, cardinal bp. of Tusculum, rector of E. Grinstead, prebendary of Fittleworth, ii. 12
Cecil:
    Brownlow, earl of Exeter, ii. 458
    Rob., i. 520
    Wm., ii. 145
Cedwalla, *see* Caedwalla
Celestine V, pope, iv. 233
Celpham (Kent), ix. 149
Celts, iii. 1, 15, 62
cement industry, ii. 231–2; ix. 235
cemeteries, *see* A.-S. remains: burials
Ceolwulf, king of Wessex, i. 347, 482, 494
Cerdicsore, i. 334
Cerne Abbas (Dors), i. 323–4
Cesar (Caesar):
    F., ii. 471
    Thos., iv. 144
Chads, Hen., and his w. Susannah, iii. 161
Chadwick (or Evans), Owen, iv. 157
Chaggele:
    Alice de, *see* Argenteyn
    Jn. de, iv. 144
Chailey, ii. 43–4; vii. 2, 34, 53 *n*, 87, 92, **94–8**, 225
    Ades, ii. 277
    adv., vii. 97–8
    Balneath, *q.v.*
    Bineham, *see* Banham
    botany, i. 60
    ch., vii. 94, 96–7, *96*, 97
        archit., ii. 340, 348, 373, 375; vii. 96–7
    dom. archit., vii. 94–5
    earthworks, i. 477, 480
    inc., vii. 95
    insects, i. 166, 169, 172, 194–6, 198, 200–2, 204, 208–10, 218–19
    Institution, vii. 94, 98
    man., vii. 95–6
    nonconf., vii. 94
    pop., ii. 225
    potteries, ii. 252–3, *252*; vii. 94
    prehist. rem., i. 329
    rly., vii. 94
    R.D., vii. 31

union, i. 539
Wapsbourne (Wapsburn, Werples-burn), ii. 311
   chap., vii. 53 *n*
   man., vii. 4, 54, 95–6
Warningore, *see* Chiltington, East
Chaldamby, *see* Cholmondeley
Chaldecott, *see* Caldicott
Chaldese, Sir Ric., and his w. Joan, ii. 92
Chalfhunte:
   Idonia de, *see* Passeley
   Thos. de, ix. 145
Challen:
   Hen., warden of St. Mary's hosp., Chich., ii. 102
   Jn., vii. 230, 276
   Ric. (sr.), and his w. Anne, iv. 83
   Ric. (jr.), iv. 83
   Steph., iv. 169
   W.H., iv. 32, 43 *n*
   Wm., iv. 213
Chaloner (Challenor):
   Eliz., w. of Jn., vii. 78
   Francis (fl. 1583), ii. 318
   Francis (d. 1624, ? another), vii. 100
   Francis (d. by 1680), vii. 41, 78
   Jn. (d. 1520), vii. 100
   Jn. (fl. 1532), vii. 158
   Jn. (d. by 1694), vii. 78
   Mary, w. of Francis, vii. 78
   Nic. (d. 1566), vii. 100
   Nic. (d. 1613), vii. 100
   Nic. (d. 1646), vii. 100, 117
   Nic. (fl. 1714), vii. 100
   Ninian, vii. 158
   Ric. (d. 1610), vii. 100
   Ric. (fl. 1627), ii. 420
   Ric. (fl. 1727), vii. 100
   Thos. (fl. 1456), vii. 235
   Thos. (fl. 1729), vii. 100
   Wm., vii. 158, 235
   fam., ii. 389; vii. 99–100
   arms, vii. *100*
Chalvington, ii. 34, 44, 475; ix. 226, 251
   ch., ii. 339–40, 353, 375
   pop., ii. 227
Chalwood, *see* Danehill: Chelwood
Cham, Petronilla (or Pernel) de, ii. 103, 411; ix. 31
Chamberlayn (Chambyrleyn, Chaum-berleyn, Chaumberlyn):
   Eliz., *see* Berkeley
   Joan, w. of Wm. le, iv. 52, 61
   Jn. le, iv. 61
   Lora le, *see* Bysshe
   Rob., prior of Boxgrove, ii. 59
   Steph. le, iv. 61
   Thos. le (fl. 1340), iv. 61
   Thos. (fl. 1623), iv. 163
   Wm. le (d. by 1346), iv. 52, 61
   Wm. le (d. by 1391), iv. 61
Chambers:
   Jn., master of Holy Trinity hosp., Arundel, ii. 98
   R. Halley, ii. 431
   Rob., ix. 197
   Tom, ii. 443
   Sir Wm., iv. 142, 176
Chambre:
   Anne de la, m. —— Alchorne, vii. 59
   Eliz. de la, m. —— Scrase, vii. 59
   Jane de la, m. 1 Thos. Michell, 2 Steph. Ridge, vii. 59
   Jn. de la (fl. 1600), vii. 36, 59, 70, 123
   Jn. de la (fl. 1643), vii. 70, 73 *n*
   Laur. de la, vii. 70
   Mary de la, ? m. —— Thorpe, vii. 59
   Ric. de la, vii. 70
   Thos. de la, master of Playden hosp., ii. 105
   fam., vii. 69
   arms, vii. *70*
Chambyrleyn, *see* Chamberlayn
Champion:
   Geo., ii. 444
   Jn. (fl. 1475), warden of St. Mary's hosp., Chich., ii. 102

Jn. (fl. 1535), warden of St. Mary's hosp., Chich., ii. 102; iii. 139 *n*
Laur., abbot of Battle, ii. 55
Chance:
   Sir Wm., vii. 151
   Lady, vii. 152
chancellor of England, vii. 41, 50, 83, 208, 212; *and see* Nevill, Ralph de
Chancery Lane, *see* London
Chanceus (Chaunceus, Chaunceux):
   Aylmer de, ix. 139
   Cecily de, m. Wm. Filliol, ix. 139
   Giles de (fl. by 1269), iv. 199
   Giles de (fl. 1318), iv. 199
   Joan de, *see* St. John
   Jn. de, iv. 199
   Thos. de, iv. 199
Chanctonbury, *see* Washington
Chandler (Chaundler):
   Geo., dean of Chich., ii. 51; iii. 113, 137
   Hen., ii. 256
   Ralph, iii. 80
Channel Islands, i. 20, 266; ii. 132; *and see* Guernsey; Jersey
Chantler (Chantelor):
   Hen., vii. 89
   Rafe, ii. 24
chantries, ii. 13–14, 20; *and see* Bexhill; Bosham; Boxgrove; Chich.: cath.; Chich.; Cuckfield; Fairlight; Gor-ing; Halnaker; Hastings; Hove; Icklesham; Lewes; Midhurst; Mundham, North; Pagham; Poyn-ings; Rye; Sidlesham; Ticehurst; Trotton; Warbleton; Winchelsea
chantry chapels, *see* architecture: ecclesiastical
Chantry Hill, *see* Storrington
Chapel, N., iv. 54
Chapelayn, Rob. le, chaplain of Todham, iv. 53
Chapelle (Capella):
   Bart. de la, iv. 77; vii. 206
   Joan de la, m. Sir Jn. de Bohun, iv. 77; vii. 206
   Nichole, w. of Bart., m. 2 Sir Frank de Bohun, iv. 77
chaplain, Ric. the, *see* Richard
Chaplin, Mr., ii. 459
Chapman:
   Abraham, and his w. Cicely, iv. 179
   Cath., *see* Hammond
   F.H., ix. 173
   Hen., ix. 29
   Sir Jn., iv. 177, 179, 211
   Jn. (another), iv. 179
   Jos., vii. 34
   Thos., vii. 196
   Wm., ix. 238
   Mr., ii. 450
   and see Pack and Chapman
Chapman & Mears, iv. 20; *and see* Mears & Co.
Chapper, Rob., ii. 257
charcoal burning, ii. 237, 240–2, 247, 296, 310, 397; iv. 154; ix. 55
Charles I, i. 520; ii. 32, 48, 156–7, 163, 318, 320; iii. 73, 87–8; iv. 208, 223, 231; vii. 217, 224, 270
   relics, ix. 126–7, 129
Charles II, i. 305, 528; ii. 158, 310, 437, 458; iii. 88, 112; iv. 115; ix. 134
Charles V, emperor, ii. 150
Charles II, king of France, i. 527
Charles III Honore, prince of Monaco, i. 250, 252
Charles:
   Alice, w. of Ric., m. 2 Sir Nic. Haute, ix. 187
   Joan, m. Wm. Repoun, ix. 187
   Ric. (d. 1378), ix. 187
   Ric. (d. by 1392), ix. 187
   Rog., ix. 187
Charleton, Wal. de, iv. 118
Charlotte, Princess, dau. of Geo. IV, iv. 226; vii. 250
Charlston, *see* Westdean

Charlton (in Singleton), iv. 118
   adv., iv. 101
   cricket, ii. 467
   dom. archit., iv. 118
   forest, i. 50, 305; ii. 304–5; iv. 43, 118, 174
      birds, i. 283, 285
      insects, i. 111, 114, 165–6, 168–9, 171, 178–9, 181–9, 196, 212–13
   Fox Hall, ii. 441–2; iv. 118
   hunting, ii. 304, 441–3; iv. 118
   man., ii. 176, 303; iv. 97, 118, 229
   tanning, ii. 259
Charlwood, *see* Danehill: Chelwood
Charmandean, *see* Broadwater
Charney (or Chernell), Jn., prior of Pynham, ii. 81
Charnock:
   Rog., vii. 135
   Wm., vii. 135
Charterhouse, *see* London: schs.
Chartres:
   Alan de, iv. 111–12
   Christiane de, w. of Rog., iv. 112
   Joan de, *see* Maufe
   Rob. de, iv. 111
   Rog. de, iv. 111–12
   fam., iv. 111
Chartres, Phillippe, duc de, ii. 456; vii. 249
Chase, Thos., master of Playden hosp., chancellor of Oxford University, ii. 105
chase, right of, *see* hunting
Chasemore, P., ii. 480
Chatfield (Chatfyld):
   Bernard, ii. 424 *n*
   Caroline, vii. 136
   Harriet, vii. 136
   Hen., vii. 76, 136
   Jn., lecturer at Horsham, ii. 36
   Jn. (d. 1778), vii. 76, 136
   Mary, vii. 136
   Ric., iv. 31
   Rob., ii. 159
   Sarah, *see* Bray
   Thos., rector of Balcombe, vii. 76, 136
   Thos., his s., vii. 75–6
Chatham (Kent), ii. 140, 157, 298, 322
Chatham Rly., *see* South Eastern and Chatham Rly.
Chaucier, Jn., iii. 101 *n*
Chaumberleyn (Chaumberlyn), *see* Chamberlayn
Chaunceus (Chaunceux), *see* Chanceus
Chauncy:
   Joan, *see* Benfield
   Jn., vii. 190
   Margery, m. 1 —— Thwaytes, 2 Thos. Austen, 3 Jn. Williams, iv. 157; vii. 190*, 280
Chaundler, *see* Chandler
Chawner, Ethel, i. 119
Chaworth (Chaworthe):
   Sir Geo., i. 521
   Jn., prior of Boxgrove, ii. 59
   Thos., ii. 58
Cheale (Cheele):
   Jn., vii. 204
   Wm., vii. 115
Cheapside, *see* London
Checeham, *see* Peasmarsh: Kitchenham
Cheele, *see* Cheale
Cheeseman (Cheesman):
   Chas., iv. 189; vii. 122
   G., vii. 37, 260–1
   Mrs. Wal., ii. 453
cheesemonger, *see* Alan
Cheesman, *see* Cheeseman
Cheke, Sir Jn., ix. 245
Chekenora, *see* Kechenore
Chelchester, Jn., abbot of Durford, ii. 91
Cheleshunt (or Elding), Wm. de, and his w. Avice, ix. 180
Chelmsford (Essex), ii. 430

Chelsea (London, formerly Mdx.), ii. 407; ix. 133
Chelsfield, Sim. de, iv. 152
Chelsham, Margery, ii. 256
Chelsworth, see Horsham: Chesworth
Cheltenham (Glos.), ix. 50
Chelwood, see Danehill
Cheney (Cheny, Chesney, Cheyne, Cheyney):
  Alex. de (d. 1296), vii. 114
  Alex. (fl. 1437), ix. 91
  Alice de, m. Geof. de Say, vii. 114, 207, 225
  Alice, w. of Thos. de, see Sturmy
  Amice, w. of Sir Wm., iv. 204
  Bart. de, vii. 203
  Elias, iv. 204 n
  Eliz., m. Thos. Culpeper, ix. 181, 183, 190
  Eliz., w. of Jn., see Palmer
  Frances, ix. 154
  Hen. de, iv. 98
  Hugh de (fl. 1086), vii. 84
  Hugh de (fl. 12th. cent., another), iv. 59
  Hugh de (fl. c. 1244), iv. 98
  Isabel de, m. Peter FitzAilwin, vii. 203
  Itaria de, see Salnervill
  Joan, see Filliol
  Jn. de (fl. 1147), vii. 114, 253, 255, 258
  Jn. de (fl. 1229), iv. 23
  Jn. (fl. 1346), iv. 204
  Sir Jn. (fl. 1487), ix. 154
  Jn. (d. 1494, another), ix. 91
  Jn. (d. 1603), ix. 181, 183
  Lucy de, m. Guy de Dive, ix. 59
  Mabel, w. of Hugh de, iv. 98
  Marg. de, m. Hugh de Cressy, vii. 236
  Margery, see Cralle
  Maud de, m. Wm. Sanzaver, iv. 23
  Maud, w. of Hugh de, iv. 51
  Maud, w. of Ralph de, see Watevile
  Nic. de, iv. 128
  Sir Oliver, ix. 91, 207
  Parnel, m. Ric. Bellingham, vii. 207, 279
  Pelham, ix. 91, 207
  Ralph de (fl. 1086), iv. 50–1, 58–9; vii. 33, 83–4, 114, 135, 171, 179, 181, 203, 206–7, 253, 255, 262, 275–6, 279
  Ralph de (d. by 1147), ii. 65; vii. 33, 84, 114, 171, 253, 262, 275
  Ralph de (fl. 1170), iv. 51, 59
  Ric. (fl. 1207), iv. 23
  Ric. (fl. c. 1430), ix. 91, 207
  Ric. (fl. 1559), ix. 91
  Rob. de, vii. 114
  Rog. de, iv. 59–60
  Sim., ix. 91, 154, 207
  Thos. de (fl. 1220–45), iv. 199, 204
  Sir Thos. (fl. 1377), i. 510; vii. 233
  Thos. (fl. 1478), iv. 136
  Thos. (fl. 1522), vii. 207
  Sir Thos., warden of Cinque Ports (? another), ix. 154
  Thos. (d. 1565), ix. 181
  Wm. de (fl. c. 1150), vii. 236
  Wm. de (fl. 1158–70, ? another), iv. 23, 59–60
  Wm. de (fl. 1296), vii. 114
  Wm. de (d. 1334, another), vii. 114
  Sir Wm. (fl. 1324–46), iv. 204
  Wm. (fl. 1398), iv. 136
  Wm. (fl. 1419), vii. 229
  Sir Wm. (d. by 1434), vii. 147
  Wm. (d. 1487), ix. 91, 154
  Wm. (d. 1508), ix. 91
  Wm. (fl. 1508), ix. 91
  fam., ix. 206
Cherleton, see Cherlton
Cherlew, see Caroloco
Cherlton (Cherleton):
  Wal. de, iv. 145
  Wm. de, iv. 98
Chernell, see Charney

Cherry, Hen., ix. 198
Chertsey (Surr.), ii. 250, 252
Cheryman, Thos., ii. 260
Chese, Ric., prior of Boxgrove, ii. 59; iv. 147
Cheshire, i. 168 n; and see Chester; Macclesfield; Vale Royal
Chesney, see Cheney
Chester, vii. 5–7
Chesterfield, earl of, see Stanhope, Geo.
chests, church, see architecture: ecclesiastical
Chesworth, see Horsham
Chetel the huntsman, iv. 73
Chetel (fl. 1147), vii. 256 n
Chetham, Jn., abbot of Bayham, ii. 88–90
Chetwynd, Sir Geo., ii. 457
Chevalier, Jn., ii. 254
Chevening (Kent), ix. 133
Chewitt, see Chowte
Cheynall, see Cheynell
Cheyne, see Cheney
Cheynell (Cheynall):
  Francis, rector of Petworth, ii. 35, 39; vii. 269
  Hen., iii. 147
  Mary, w. of Hen., see Miller
Cheyney, see Cheney
Chich (Essex), iv. 73
Chicheley, Hen., abp. of Cant., ii. 49, 118; iv. 234; vii. 219
Chichester:
  F.G., ii. 472 n
  Jas. of, iv. 157 n
  Jane Whitchurch, vii. 163
  Mat. de, dean of Chich., ii. 50
Chichester:
  earls of, vii. 101, 238; ix. 27; and see Aubigny, Wm. d'; Pelham
Chichester (Noviomagus Regnum, Regnum), i. 501, 508, 529; ii. 111, 160, 169, 187, 461–2; iii. frontispiece, 71–169, 71, 73, 89; iv. 154, 167–8; vii. 14
  ale-hos., ii. 196
  almshos., iii. 167–8
    Cawley almshos. (St. Bart.'s hosp.), iii. 81, 82, 87, 88
  A.-S. rem., i. 346
  archit., ii. 382 n, 392; iii. 13, 72–8, 87, 89–90
  bailiwick, iv. 2
  barracks, ii. 227 n; iii. 81
  battle, i. 483
  birds, i. 282, 293
  Bp. Otter Coll., iii. 81
  bps., i. 504; ii. 42, 50, 61, 72, 104, 110, 112-14, 117, 122–3, 189, 366, 424–5, 432; iii. 71–3, 80 n, 84–5, 96–7, 102–3, 112, 124, 146, 164–7; iv. 21, 47, 66, 106, 113; vii. 266, 276; ix. 111; and see Andrews, Lancelot; Arundel, Jn.; Ashburnham, Sir Wm.; Barlow, Wm.; Bell, Geo.; Berghsted, Steph. de; Bickley, Thos.; Bowers; Brideoake; Buckner, Jn.; Burrows; Carleton, Geo.; Carleton, Guy; Carr, Rob. Jas; Christopherson, Jn.; Climping; Curteis, Ric.; Day, Geo.; Duppa; Durnford, Ric.; FitzJames; FitzRobert; Gilbert, Ashurst Turner; Godfrey; Greenford; Grove, Rob.; Hare, Francis; Harsnett; Hilary; King, Hen.; Laigle, Nic. de; Lake, Jn.; Langton, Jn. de; Lenne; Luffa; Maltby, Edw.; Manningham; Mitford, Ric.; Moleyns, Adam; Montagu, Ric.; Nevill, Ralph; Otter; Patrington; Peacocke; Poor; Praty; Read, Rob.; Read, Wm.; Rickingale; Ridgeway; Rushook; Sampson, Ric.; St. Leofard, Gilb. de; Scory; Seffrid I; Seffrid II; Sherburne, Rob.;

  Shuttleworth; Stigand; Story, Edw.; Stratford, Rob.; Sydenham; Waddington, Edw.; Ware, Hen.; Wareham; Watson, Ant.; Wilberforce, Ernest; William; Williams, Jn.; Wych, St. Ric. de
  estates, i. 491, 538; ii. 173; iv. 134–6, 152, 154, 202, 208, 211–12, 216–17, 219; vii. 1 n, 9, 138, 264, 266, 269, 271; ix. 115, 117, 122–3, 193, 197, 201
  hunting rights, iv. 217
  palace, iii. 13–14, 50, 74, 81, 107, 146, 165; archit., ii. 370, 371–2, 392, 395; iii. 79, 147–53, 151–2, 156 n; chap., ii. 338, 350, 354, 358, 371; iii. 108, 146, 148–50, 149–50, 152, 165
  patronage, ii. 333, 349; iii. 165; iv. 10, 29, 32, 39, 58, 63, 70, 96, 108, 110, 120, 125, 138, 152, 154, 170, 188, 190, 192, 201, 203, 210, 215, 217, 221, 227; vii. 40–1, 69, 73, 113, 140, 147, 163, 181, 200, 238, 262–3, 268, 276; ix. 26–8, 81, 94, 123, 141, 156, 162, 189, 195, 212, 217, 234, 257
  right of wreck, iv. 206
  steward, see Senliz
  Black Friars, see Chich.: friaries
  botany, i. 42, 65–6
  boundaries, iii. 71, 82; iv. 150, 165, 171
  Broyle, the, see Fishbourne, New
  canal, see Chich.: Chich. canal
  Canon Gate, ii. 395; iii. 98, 158
  captain, i. 520
  cast., i. 493–4; ii. 95, 101, 394–5; iii. 72, 78–80; iv. 1
  earthworks, i. 474
  cath., i. 523; ii. 4, 10, 17, 35, 47–51, 52–3, 72, 82; iii. 13, 74, 84, 86, 88–90, 96, 103, 104 n, 104–5, 105–46, 112, end paper; ix. 36 n
    accessories, ii. 229, 333–4, 350–4, 357–62, 371, 375–8; iii. 126
    anchorite, ii. 47; vii. 276
    archit., ii. 6–7, 16, 327, 329, 332–5, 337–8, 340, 342, 346–50, 365–6, 366, 368, 371, 373, 375–8; iii. 106–46, 116–19, 122–3, 128–9, 134–5; iv. 124, 146 n, 147 n; vii. 210
    beadman, see Chich.: cath.: precular
    bell tower, ii. 333, 335, 340, 378; iii. 72, 73–4, 104, 110–11, 113, 159–60
    bursar, see Chich.: cath.: communar
    canons, ii. 46; iii. 86, 102–3, 146; iv. 125, 198; and see Amberley; Ashwell; Backshell, Jn.; Baker, Thos.; Barcroft, Wm.; Courtenay, Ric.; Cross, Thos.; Darrell, Ivo; Edes, Hen.; Eston, Wal.; Frankland, Jn.; Geoffrey; Hickes; Hurdis, Thos.; Kainesham; Mitford, Jn. de; More, Edw.; Mortlock; Northburgh; Paxton, Jn.; Richard; Sanderson, Rob. Edw.; Snatt, Wm.; Wood, Geo.; Woodward, Thos.
    chancellor, ii. 47–8, 50, 399–401, 404; iv. 138; vii. 109; and see Ashburnham, Jn.; Bishopstone, Jn. de; Briggs, Thos.; Nevill, Wm.; Pagham, Ric. de
    chanter, iv. 51
    chantries, ii. 57; iii. 86, 92, 111–14, 119, 124, 129, 131, 137, 139–40, 142, 153; iv. 51, 98, 118, 170, 210; vii. 217
    Chantry, the, iii. 111, 156–7, 156
    chapter, ii. 48–50, 101, 399–404; iv. 98, 134, 138
    chapter ho., iii. 110–11, 113, 135
    choristers, ii. 49–50

churchyard, iii. 89, 92; *and see* Chich.: cath.: Paradise
cloisters, ii. 50; iii. 110–11, 122, 141, 146–7, 153–5
close, ii. 227, 349, 377; iii. 73, 87, 92, 96, 100, 102, 106, 111, 146–8, 152–9, *156, 158*
communar (bursar), iv. 98
dean, ii. 26, 47–51, 57, 399, 402–3; iii. 72, 75 *n*, 86, 92–3, 146; iv. 79, 106, 138, 152; jurisdiction, ii. 13–14, 48; iii. 96, 103, 164–6; *and see* Ashburnham, Sir Wm.; Ball, Thos.; Berghsted, Thos. de; Bracklesham; Burgon; Chandler, Geo.; Cloos; Curteis, Ric.; Dee; Duncan–Jones; Fleshmonger; Freton; Garland, Hen. de; Gloucester, Wal. de; Greenfield, Wm. de; Greenford; Gulston, Jos.; Hannah, Jn.; Hargraves, Jas.; Harward; Haselee; Hayley, Thos.; Hayley, Wm.; Henshaw, Jos.; Hook, Wal.; Laigle, Nic. de; Lenne; Lichfield; Lullington; Matthew; Maydenhithe; Miller, Combe; Milton, Wm.; Perigord; Pigou; Pye, Wm.; Randall, Ric.; Reeves, Bruno; Rush; Sampson, Thos.; Scrope, Ric. le; Seffrid II; Sherlock; Slade, Sam.; Thomas, Lambrook; Thorne; Traheron; Turnbull; William; Young, Jn.
dean and chapter, ii. 49, 80, 82, 105, 400, 406–7, 409; iii. 72, 86, 88, 92, 95, 103–4, 143 *n*, 167; iv. 27; vii. 266; estates, ii. 123, 296, 404; iii. 73; iv. 7, 90–1, 96, 99–100, 120, 125, 131, 135 *n*, 162–4, 170, 185, 199–200; vii. 235; patronage, ii. 101; iii. 146, 165–6, 333; iv. 7, 39, 90–1, 100, 117–18, 140, 154, 173, 188, 192, 201, 217; seal, ii. *16*, 51; iii. 93
deanery, iii. 12–13, 72, 88, 90, 146, 155–6
library, iii. 88, 98 *n*, 108–9, 111–14, 125, 128–30, 137 *n*
minster, iii. 71, 83, 105–6, 124 *n*, 146, 165–6
organists, ii. 49
Paradise (graveyard), ii. 50; iii. 111, 126, 146–7
prebendal sch., *see* Chich.: schs.
prebendaries, ii. 26, 36, 48, 50; iii. 146
prebends, ii. 12, 43, 105, 108, 123; iv. 30; *and see* Aldingbourne: Gates; Aldingbourne; Eartham; Ferring; Firle; Gates; Heathfield; Hove; Marden, East; Oving: Colworth; Seaford: Sutton; Selsey; Sidlesham: Highleigh; Sidlesham; Singleton; Waltham, Up; Wittering, East: Somerley; Wittering, East: Thorney, East
precentor, ii. 40, 47–8, 399–400, 404; iv. 98, 166, 170; *and see* Edes, Hen.; Ernis; Henshaw, Jos.; St. Lucy in Silice
precular (beadman), ii. 407
Reformation in, ii. 23, 50
residentiaries, ii. 48–9; iii. 106–7, 111, 146, 153–6
revenues, ii. 36
Royal Chantry, iii. 153–4
sacrists (sacristans), ii. 48, 50
St. Faith's chap., *see* Chich.: chaps.
service, form of, ii. 49
shrine of St. Richard, ii. 11, 19, 49–50, 305, 377; iii. 85–6, 103, 110, 112–13, 123
spire, ii. 164
subdean, ii. 48, 402, 404
succentor, ii. 400
treasurer, ii. 47–8, 399–400; *and*

see Seffrid the treasurer
treasury, iii. 111, 147, 155
verger, ii. 50
vicars, ii. 49–50, 100
Vicars' Hall, ii. 383; iii. 76, 92, 153, 157–8, *157*, iv. 218
visitations, ii. 14, 50
Wiccamical prebendaries, ho. of, iii. 146, 154–5
chant., iii. 82; iv. 216 *n*
chaps., iii. 72, 75, 77, 81–2, 90, 92
St. Cyriac, ii. 11, 46, 121; iii. 75; iv. 162
St. Faith, iii. 146–7, 153; iv. 170
St. Jn. the Evangelist, iii. 163–5
char., iii. 90, 93, 166–9
charters, iii. 82–6, 90–2, *90*, 94, 96, 98–100, 102, 104, 112
Chich. canal, i. 48, 113; ii. 466; iii. 71, 76, 102; iv. 134, 150, 156, 158, 160, 165
chs., iii. 75
adv., iii. 104–5, 164–6
All Saints in Portfield, iii. 161, 165
All Saints in the Pallant, ii. 371; iii. 90, 103–4; rector, *see* Bachelor, Jn.
Holy Trinity, iii. 102; iv. 30
St. And. (in the Market), East St., ii. 333; iii. 12, 161, *161*, 163 *n*, 165, 169; rector, *see* Holland, Wm. Woollams
St. And. in the Pallant, ii. 94; iii. 77, 86, 90, 165
St. Bart., iii. 74 *n*, 161–2
St. Martin, iii. 86, 90, 162–3, 165, 168; iv. 209; rector, *see* Holland, Wm. Woollams
St. Mary in the Market, ii. 100; iii. 75, 86, 166
St. Olave, ii. 333–4; iii. 73, 90, 162–3, *162*, 165–6; accessories, ii. 350, 352–4, 359–60, 376; iii. 162; archit., ii. 365; iii. 162; rector, *see* Collings, Rog.; Gyldesburgh, Thos.
St. Pancras, i. 522; ii. 33; iii. 74 *n*, 83 *n*, 87, 105, 163, 166, 168; rector, *see* Speed, Wm.
St. Paul, iii. 81, 163, 166; vicar, *see* Brown, Thos.
St. Peter in the Market, ii. 100, iii. 165–6
St. Peter sub Castro, iii. 166
St. Peter the Great (subdeanery), ii. 4, 47–8; iii. 15, 75, 93, 111, 113, 128 *n*, 137, 160, 165–6, 168
St. Peter the Less, iii. 78, 90, 93, 163, *163*, 166; iv. 118; rector, *see* Brown, Thos.
and see Chich.: friaries
Civil War in, i. 522–3, 525, 527–8; ii. 35, 50, 229; iii. 79 *n*, 82, 87–8, 102, 112, 148, 155, 165–6; vii. 217
clubs:
athletic, ii. 480
Corp. of St. Pancras, i. 530; iii. 89
cricket, ii. 475
golf, ii. 480
coaching, ii. 204; iii. 71
coins, i. 329
coll., *see* Chich.: Bp. Otter
cts., ii. 401; iii. 86, 90, 94–6, 98
abps.', iii. 103–4
county, i. 504; ii. 188; iii. 86, 95–6; vii. 15
customary, iii. 103
dean's, iii. 103
hund., iii. 94, 103
Palace, iii. 103
pie-powder, iii. 96, 98, 159
view of frankpledge, iii. 94–6, 103–4
crosses, iii. 71 *n*, 76, 82, 89, 103–4
mkt. cross, ii. 394; iii. 13, 73, *74*, 87, 89–90, 92
St. Jas.'s cross, iii. 82
customs, iii. 90, 96, 98, 100–2, 104

deanery, ii. 43
defences, i. 509–10; iii. 72, 84–8, 102; *and see* Chich.: walls
dioc. (see), ii. 305, 328; iii. 71, 83–4, 102, 124; iv. 2, 142 *n*, 207; ix. 150
archdeanconries, ii. 42–3, 99; iv. 1; vii. 123
archdeacons, ii. 23, 110; iii. 167; iv. 10, 66, 106; *and see* Ball, Hen.; Burrell, Gerard; Hoskins, B.G.; Seffrid II; Silvester; Whitby arms, iii. *106*; iv. *135, 208*; vii. 269; ix. *117, 201*
board of patronage, iv. 70; vii. 124
deaneries, ii. 42–4
estates, ii. 297, 303, 314 *n*, 315, 381; iv. 217
Purity Assoc., vii. 42
seal, iii. 105
dispensary, *see* Chich.: hosps.
earthworks, i. 470–2
East Gate, ii. 201; iii. 71–2, 75, 77, 82, 87, 95
entrenchments, iii. 18–19, *19*, 81
fairs, iii. 71 *n*, 90, 97–8
Sloe Fair, iii. 98, 153, 159
fee farm, iii. 72, 84–6, 91, 94, 96, 101
fields, iii. 82–3
fires, iii. 84, 103, 106–8, 113, 116, 118, 129, 135, 142, 146, 148
fishes, i. 269
forest, iii. 81
friaries:
Dominican (Black Friars), ii. 45, **94**, 263; iii. 75, 77, 86, 164; archit., ii. 331; prior, ii. 122
Franciscan (Grey Friars), i. 474; ii. 45, 90, **95**, 101; iii. 71, 75, 77, 80, *81*, 86, 93, 165–6; accessories, ii. 352, 358, 361; archit., ii. 327, 331, 348–9, 373, 395; iii. 80
gaol, ii. 201; iii. 72, 104
geology, i. 13, 19, 45
Graylingwell, iii. 81
Grey Friars, *see* Chich.: friaries
Guildhall (Shire Hall), iii. 78, 80, 81, 92–3, 95–6, 100, 157
guilds:
merchant, ii. 188; iii. 82, 84, 87, 90–4, 96–7, 99–100
St. George's, ii. 20; iii. 92–3, 142
harbour, i. 45, 466, 485; ii. 125, 128, 145, 152, 159, 303; iv. 188, 199, 204, 217
angling, ii. 467
Bosham channel, i. 45; iv. 182
boundary, i. 536
Chich. channel, i. 15; iv. 204
coastguards, i. 506 *n*
Emsworth channel, iv. 195
Great Deep, iv. 195
Horemouth, i. 506 *n*; iii. 90, 96, 100–1; iv. 198
insects, i. 191
prehist. rem., i. 313
Thorney channel, iv. 127, 195
Underyng, iii. 100
waterways, ii. 241
haws, iii. 83–4, 166; iv. 4, 13, 41, 44, 63, 65, 80, 83, 111, 118, 121, 127, 145, 150, 156, 158, 162, 176, 183, 208, 216, 218
heretic burnt at, ii. 22
hermitage, ii. 46
hosps.:
Chich. infirmary, iii. 167
dispensary, iii. 81, 168
Loddesdown, *see* Westhampnett
Royal West Suss., iii. 81, 167–8
St. Bart., *see* Chich.: almshos.
St. Jas. and St. Mary, ii. **99–100**; iii. 82, 86, 90, 98, 166–7; iv. 143; masters, ii. 99–100; *and see* Doyly, Francis; Lawes; Lewes, Peter; Odeby; Walker, Wm; proctor, *see* Egle, Wm.
St. Jn.'s, iii. 80 *n*, 104 *n*

Chichester
  hosps. (cont.):
    St. Mary's, ii. 45, 48, **100–2**; iii. 71, 75 *n*, 80, *78–81*, 86, 88, 90, 91 *n*, 119, 165–7; iv. 153, 165, 176–7; accessories, ii. 352–3, 357–8, *358*, 375; archit., ii. 331, 342, 375; iii. 78–9; chaplain, ii. 13, 101; wardens, ii. 101–2; *and see* Ball, Thos.; Champion, Jn.; Darrell, Ivo; Edes, Hen.; Fleshmonger; Frankland, Jn.; Gooch, Sir Thos.; Harward; Hayley, Thos.; Hayley, Wm.; Hurdis, Thos.; Miller, Combe; Pye, Wm.; Reeves, Bruno; Sherlock; Shiffner, Geo.; Toghill; Turnbull; Webber; Whitby
    Stockbridge, ii. **103**
    West Suss. County Mental, iii. 81
    West Suss. Infirmary, iii. 81
  inns, iii. 74–5, 77, 88–9, 93 *n*
  insects, i. 113, 118, 154, 167, 171–4, 176–89, 197, 204, 208, 226, 234
  Jews, i. 506; iii. 80–1
  Kingsham, iii. 71, 83, 105; iv. 133, 150, 168
    man., iii. 104–5, 166
    North, iii. 73
  local govt.:
    aldermen, ii. 26; iii. 87, 95–6; *and see* Cox, Peter; Holland, Wm.
    bailiffs, iii. 71–2, 86, 91, 93–6, 99, 101; *and see* Steele, Wm.
    burgesses, iv. 143
    clerks, iii. 89, 93, 96
    common council, iii. 95–6, 99
    corp., ii. 101, 458; iii. 71, 85, 90, 93, 97, 99–100; iv. 222
    cts., *see* Chich.: cts.
    elections, iii. 93
    jurisdiction, iv. 206
    mayor and corp., iii. 81, 88–9, 102, 104
    mayors, i. 508, 529; ii. 33, 101, 149, 401; iii. 72, 82, 85–9, 91–103, 142, 167–8; *and see* Adams, Thos.; Bartholomew; Bradbridge, Wm.; Braman, Ric.; Buckner, Ric.; Cawley, Jn.; Cressweller, Jn.; Daniel, Ric.; Eartham, Wm.; Exton, Ric.; Exton, Rob.; Garland, Sharp; Harris, Geo.; Hilly; Holland, Wm.; Jacob; Lane, Jn.; Lane, Wm.; Merricks, Ric.; Neel, Wm.; Newland, Jn.; Patching, Thos.; Rouen; Sherer, Jn. (fl. 1438); Sherer, Jn. (d. *c.* 1730); Stubbe, Jn.; Wyn, Jn.; Young, Ric.
    other officers, iii. 87, 95–7, 99
    recorders, iii. 91 *n*, 95–6, 99; *and see* Lewknor, Chris.; Lewknor, Ric. (fl. to 1592)
    reeves, iii. 90–2, 94, 96, 98, 100, 103–4
    seal, iii. 93–4, *94*, 96
    sheriffs, iii. 86–7, 90, 96, 98, 103
    and see Chich.: charters
  Lytton, the, iii. 75, 82
  mammals, i. 305
  man., iii. 81, 83–4, 96, 104–5
  mkt. cross, *see* Chich.: crosses
  Mkt. ho., iii. 73, 77, 89
  Mkt. Place, iii. 73, 84, 87, 166
  mkts., ii. 190; iii. 17, 77–8, 82, 89, 95–8
  mayors, *see* Chich.: local govt.
  messuages, iv. 230
  militia, i. 507, 519, 527, 533–4
  minister, *see* Corbett, Jn.
  mint, i. 348–9; ii. 126; iii. 83–5
  molluscs, i. 108
  museum, i. 295, 309; iii. 15–17
  naval recruitment, ii. 161
  New Fishbourne, *see* Fishbourne
  nonconf., i. 528; ii. 33, 41; iii. 74, 82, 88, 164–5, 168

  North Gate, iii. 71–2, 82, 87, 94, 98
  nunnery of St. Peter, ii. 4, 45, 47
  Pallant, the, ii. 42, 48, 392; iii. 71, 76, 89, 95, 103–4, 165; iv. 180, 222
    coins, i. 326, 329
  parishes, ii. 37; iii. 73, 88, 164
    All Saints, ii. 37, 227; iii. 71, 76, 165, 169
    St. And. (in the Market), East St., ii. 37, 43, 277; iii. 165
    St. Bart., ii. 37, 43, 227
    St. Jas. (extra parochial), ii. 227
    St. Jn., ii. 43
    St. Martin, ii. 37, 43, 227; iii. 165–6
    St. Mary in the Market, ii. 43 *n*; iii. 166
    St. Olave, ii. 37, 43, 227; iii. 165–6
    St. Pancras, ii. 43, 227; iii. 165
    St. Paul, ii. 43; iii. 166
    St. Peter in the Market, iii. 166
    St. Peter Subdeanery, iii. 71, 166
    St. Peter the Great, ii. 37, 42, 227; iii. 71, 165, 168
    St. Peter the Less, ii. 37, 43, 227; iii. 81, 165–6
  parl. rep., ii. 36; iii. 92, 98–100
    elections, i. 504, 531; iii. 99–100
    M.P.s, ii. 207; iii. 98–100; *and see* Beauclerk, Wm.; Cawley, Wm.; Huskisson; Lewknor, Chris.; Lewknor, Ric.; Miller, Sir Jn.; Miller, Sir Thos.; Page, Jn.; Steele, Thos.; White, Geo.; Wyn, Jn.
  pest ho., iii. 82
  pirates, ii. 148–9
  poor relief, ii. 206–7; iii. 71, 81, 86, 95
  pop., ii. 227
  port, ii. 125, 247–8; iii. 3, 14, 29, 71, 76, 82–3, 87–9, 90, 94, 96, 99–102; ix. 70
    officials, iii. 101
    Staple, iii. 94, 101
  Portfield, *see* Chich.: suburbs
  postern gate, iii. 72, 88
  prehist. rem., i. 321, 329
  Priory Pk., iii. 77, 79–80, 166
  public health, iii. 86
  rly., i. 23; ii. 240; iii. 18, 71
  rape, ii. 196; iii. 83, 87–8, 96, 100; iv. **1–2**, *1*
    boundary, iv. 2, 226–7
    coastguards, i. 506 *n*
    ho. of correction, ii. 195–6
  rebellions, i. 514
  Reformation in, ii. 26
  riots at, ii. 13–14; iii. 86
  roads to, ii. 229; iii. 71, 102; iv. 223, 227
  Rom. Cath., ii. 28; iii. 88, 164, 167
  Rom. rem., i. 471, 481; ii. 333, 362; iii. 1–4, 9–19, *11*, *16–17*, *19*, 50, 69, 72, 73 *n*, 103
  royal visits, i. 505, 515–16, 520; ii. 94, 271, 294; iv. 184 *n*
  Rumboldswick, *q.v.*
  schs., ii. 437–8; iii. 75–6, 90
    Prebendal (Bp. Story's) sch., ii. 16, 48, 397, 399–409; iii. 74, *74*, 90, 92
    Whitby's Free (Bluecoat) sch., ii. 437–8, iii. 74, 90; iv. 13, 219
  seal, *see* Chich.: local govt.
  see, *see* Chich.: diocese
  sheep auctions, ii. 282
  ship·money, ii. 156
  ship service, ii. 135, 137–8, 153
  shipping, ii. 137–9, 142, 148, 151, 153, 155
  Shire Hall, *see* Chich.: Guildhall
  South Gate, iii. 15, 71–2, 76–7, 82–3, 87, 90, 102
  Spitalfield, iii. 82
  sport, ii. 460, 475, 480; iii. 89
  Staple, *see* Chich.: port
  streets, iii. 10, 77, 82, 89–90, 94–5, 98, 104
    Baffins Lane, iii. 75, 77, 90, 164

  Broyle Rd., iii. 81, 163
  Chapel St., iii. 74, 164
  College Lane, iii. 81–2
  East Pallant, iii. 76, 104
  East St., ii. 94; iii. 12–13, 73, 75, 77, 89, 93 *n*, 95, 97, 161, 165; iv. 127
  Eastgate Square, iii. 82, 88
  Fore St., iii. 76, 83
  Hog Lane, iii. 78, 90
  Hornet, the, iii. 46, 82, 88
  Little London, iii. 79, 89, 104 *n*
  North Pallant, iii. 12, 76, 164 *n*, 167
  North St., iii. 12, 73, 77–8, 83, 89–90, 93–5, 97, 103
  Priory Rd., iii. 166–7
  Shamble Lane, iii. 90
  South Pallant, iii. 12, 76, 104
  South St., iii. 76, 88, 95, 157–8, 164, 166
  Spitalfield Lane, iii. 82
  St. Martin's Square, iii. 78, *78*, 165
  St. Martin's St., iii. 78, 165
  Tower St., iii. 74–5; iv. 162, 173
  West Pallant, iii. 76, 77, 160
  West St., iii. 13, 69, 72, 73–4, 83, 84 *n*, 89, 92, 95, 113, 146, 152, 160, 166
  suburbs, iii. 87, 99; iv. 177
    New Town, ii. 227; iii. 77
    Portfield, ii. 43; iii. 46, 82, 93; iv. 165, 170
    St. Bartholomew, iii. 71, 88, 165, 169
    St. Pancras, ii. 37, 229; iii. 71, 82, 83 *n*, 84, 88, 90, 97, 104, 105 *n*, 165–8; iv. 143, 222
  taxation, ii. 189; iii. 85–6, 88, 90 *n*, 96, 100, 104
  Technical Inst., iii. 77
  Town Hall, iii. 87, 90
  trades and ind., ii. 131, 145; iii. 89–90, 93, 95–8, 101–2, 104
    bellfounding, ii. 249–50
    brewing, ii. 261–2; iii. 75
    cider making, ii. 263–4
    cloth trade, ii. 256–7; iii. 97, 102
    corn trade, iii. 89, 102
    fishing, ii. 146
    malting, ii. 199
    mercers, iii. 93, 95, 97
    needle making, ii. 199, 229
    printing, ii. 239
    shipbuilding, ii. 164, 166; iii. 90, 102
    tanning, ii. 259–60; iii. 75
    wool trade, ii. 188, 204, 284; iii. 91, 97, 101–2
  tramway, *see* Hundred of Manhood and Selsey
  union, i. 539
  Vicars Hall, *see* Chich.: cath.
  Vintry, the, iii. 71
  walls, i. 492, 509–10, 520; ii. 395; iii. 9–12, 18, 71–2, 77, 82–3, 85–90, 103, 146, 156–7
  West Gate, iii. 12, 71–2, 72, 75, 88, 102, 169
    A.-S. rem., i. 349
  woodland, iii. 81
  workho., iii. 81
  Y.M.C.A., iii. 167
Chichester and West Sussex Natural Hist. Soc., i. 42, 64, 66
Chiddingfold (Surr.), ii. 254, 328 *n*, 353, 445, 448
Chiddingly, ii. 44, 206, 280, 297, 416; iv. 179
  bellfounding, ii. 250
  ch., ii. 11, 250, 339–40, 354, 361
  dom. archit., ii. 384, 386–7, 390–1
  fair, ii. 281
  Friths, ii. 387
  insects, i. 221, 223
  pop., ii. 227
  puritanism, ii. 32 *n*
  Rom. rem., iii. 29, 31
  vicar, ii. 40

Chidham, ii. 43; iv. 124, 181, **188–90**
  adv., iv. 190
  char., iv. 190
  ch., ii. 348, 355, 371–2; iv. 188–90, *190*
  Cobnor, iv. 188
  ct., iv. 184
  dom. archit., iv. 188
  guild, iv. 190
  Hambrook, iv. 188
  inc., iv. 188
  man., ii. 184; iv. 8–9, 183, 185, 188–9, 192, 195
  mere, iv. 188 *n*
  molluscs, i. 109
  pop., ii. 220
  prebend, ii. 110
  quarrying, ii. 232
  ripereeve, iv. 189
  roads, iv. 188
  tithings, iv. 188–9
  wheat, iv. 188
Chifney, Mr., ii. 458
Chikehull, Hen. de, iii. 80
Chilbolton (Hants) rector, *see* Oliver, Ric.
Child:
  Agatha, iv. 36
  Bob, ii. 447
  Coles, i. 335
  Jn. le, iv. 98
  Sam., iv. 35
  Thos., iv. 98
  Wm. le, iv. 98 *n*
Child-Villiers, Geo., *see* Villiers
Chilgrove, *see* Dean, West
Chilleye:
  Amice de, ix. 241 *n*
  Isabel de, *see* Somery
  Thos. de, ix. 240
Chillingworth, Wm., ii. 39; iii. 47
Chiltington (East or West?), i. 61
Chiltington, East (formerly in Westmeston), vii. 42, 92, **98–102**, 116, 225
  agric., vii. 98
  char., vii. 102
  ch., vii. *97*, 101–2, *102*, 112
  dom. archit., vii. 98–9
  man., vii. 67, 99–101
  pop., ii. 225
  Warningore (Wanningore, Warrengore), i. 157, 187, 212, 215–16, 218–19, 223–6; ii. 310; vii. 33, 54, 92, 95–7, 101
  Wootton, vii. 101
    Farm, vii. 98
    man., ii. 179, 186 *n*; vii. 101
Chiltington, West, i. 53–4; ii. 43
  Broadford Green, i. 53
  ch., ii. 340, 344, 346, 348–9, 351, 354, 359, 367–8
  Coneyhurst, i. 53
  iron ind., ii. 244
  pop., ii. 218
  sch., ii. 437
Chilver Bridge, *see* Arlington
Chilworth (Surr.), iv. 115
Chipping Lambourne (Berks.), iv. 172
Chiselbergh:
  Jn., ii. 181
  Reg., ii. 181
Chitcombe, *see* Brede
Chitecroft, Jn., and his w. Marg., ix. 56
Chithurst, Morin de, iv. 4
Chithurst, iv. **3–6**, 25, 28, 32, 63, 82
  adv., iv. 4–6, 65
  ch., iv. 5–6, *6*, *10*, *157**
    accessories, ii. 351, 360, 362
    archit., ii. 339, 351, 366; iv. 5–6
  common, iv. 4
  dom. archit., ii. 388; iv. 4
  Durford abbey estates, ii. 302
  Hammer Pond, *q.v.*
  inc., iv. 4
  Kingsham, iv. 4, 63–4
  man., iv. 4–5
  marsh, iv. 4
  mill, iv. 4

pop., ii. 220
rector, iv. 4, 6
streams, iv. 4
tithes, iv. 6
waste, iv. 4
woods, iv. 4
Chittenden, And., vii. 158
Chitty (Chittey):
  Hen., i. 522
  Justice, ii. 436
Chitty and Vernon, ii. 164
Cholmeley, Mary, iii. 145, 161
Cholmondely (Chaldamby), Lady Charlotte, vii. 250
Cholynton, *see* Eastbourne
Choute, *see* Chowte
Chowne:
  Anne, *see* Wane
  Bray, vii. 179
  Eliz., m. Hans Maur., count de Bruhl, ix. 215
  (formerly Tilston), J.H., *see* Tilston
  Phoebe, *see* Westbrook
  Thos. (sr.), ix. 214
  Thos. (jr.), ix. 214–15
  Wm., vii. 144 *n*
Chowte (Chewitt, Choute, Chute):
  Cecily, *see* Freake
  Eliz., vii. 158
  Sir Geo., vii. 158; ix. 152, 154
  Phil., ii. 144; ix. 185
  Mr., ii. 200
Christ Church, Oxford, ii. 407, 409, 431, 434; ix. 139, 214*, 230
Christchurch (Hants), i. 287
Christian, Ewan, iii. 159; vii. 87
Christian Society, *see* Shoreham: clubs
Christie:
  A.L., ix. 145
  Jessie, vii. 178
  Jn., vii. 74; ix. 213, 220
  W. Langham, ii. 446; vii. 74; ix. 145
Christmas, Capt., i. 519
Christopherson:
  Cecil, ix. 29
  Jn., bp. of Chich., ii. 22; vii. 220, 227
Christ's Hospital, *see* Horsham
Chuck Hatch, *see* Hartfield
Chulmestride, Marg. de, ix. 139
Church, Prof., i. 343
Church Borough (in Brede half hund.), ix. 164
church houses, *see* Alfriston; architecture: civil and dom.; Bury; Coombes; Denton; Eastbourne; Hailsham; Hartfield; Kingston near Lewes
Church Norton, *see* Selsey: Norton, Church
Church of England Temperance Soc., iii. 167
Church Pastoral Aid Soc., vii. 50
Church Patronage Soc., vii. 65, 263; ix. 28, 86
Churcher, Geo., vii. 232
Churchill:
  Jn., duke of Marlborough, iii. 89; iv. 121
  Winston S., vii. 173
  Gen., ii. 443
Churton, H.B. Whitaker, ix. 189
Chute, *see* Chowte
Chyntriaco, Hugh de, prior of Lewes, ii. 69–71; iv. 106
Chyntynge, Phil., master of St. James's hosp., Seaford, ii. 105
Chytynglegh (Chytyngele):
  Beatrice de, vii. 169
  Jn. de, vii. 169
  Marg., w. of Jn. de, vii. 169
  Ric. de, vii. 169
  Wm. de, vii. 169
Cicero, ii. 406
cider making, ii. **263–4**
Cinque Ports, i. 501; ii. 127–56, 158, 161; ix. 13, **34–9**, *34*, 90
  charters, ix. 37–8
  Civil War, i. 522

cts., ix. 36, 38–9
  Admiralty, ii. 146, 152; ix. 38–9
  Brodhull, ix. 37, 39, 50
  Shepway (Shipweye), i. 503; ix. 35–8, 51
custumals, ix. 35, 37, 52, 55
fisheries, ii. 127, 132–3, 140, 142 *n*, 145, 156; ix. 36–7
fleet, i. 496
liberties, i. 538; ix. 35, 37
limits, ii. 146
local govt.:
  barons, i. 493; ix. 36–8, 53
  jurats, ix. 36, 53
  mayors, ix. 35–6
  other officers, ix. 37
  and see Cinque Ports: wardens
militia, i. 535–6
peculiar jurisdiction, i. 503
piracy, ii. 131–2, 136–7, 141–2, 147–9, 155
privateering, ii. 154
ship service, ii. 130, 134–6, 140–5, 150, 152–6; ix. 34–6, 39
taxation, ii. 189; ix. 115
wardens, ii. 67, 131, 135–7, 140–1, 144, 146–7, 148 *n*, 149–50, 154–5, 267; ix. 37–8, 53, 68, 80; *and see* Burgh, Hubert de; Brooke, Hen.; Brooke, Wm.; Cheney, Sir Thos.; Cobham, Reynold; Mortimer, Rog.; Pencestre
and see Bekesbourne; Dover; Grange; Hastings; Hydney; Hythe; Pevensey; Romney; Rye; Sandwich; Seaford; Tenterden; Winchelsea
Cirencester, Ric. of, iii. 47
Cirencester (Glos.), i. 508
Cissa, king of South Saxons, i. 334, 481–2; ii. 291; iii. 4, 6, 10, 71 *n*, 82
Cissbury, *see* Findon
Cîteaux (Côte d'Or, France), ii. 71
Citizen, Jn., rector of Westham, vii. 276; ix. 207
Citolin, ——, vii. 18
Civil Service Cricket Club, ii. 472
Civil War, *see* wars
Clairvaux, Payn de, iv. 13
Clairvaux (Jura, France), ii. 71
Clancarty, Ld., *see* MacCarthy
Clanricarde, marquess of, *see* Burgh, Ulick Jn. de
Clapham, ii. 42–3
  ch., ii. 37, 124, 354, 361
    archit., ii. 340, 344 *n*, 348, 350, 366, 368, 371–2, 378
  Clapham Down, i. 191–2, 194–5, 204, 206–7, 209
  Clapham Woods, i. 187, 189, 192, 195, 200–1, 203, 210, 302
  dovecot, ii. 382
  insects, i. 191–2, 194–6, 198, 200, 203–4, 206–9
  Michelgrove:
    horse racing, ii. 460–1
    mammals, i. 302
    pk., ii. 297
  pop., ii. 218
  puritanism, ii. 33
  rectors, *see* Nye, Hen.; Spencer, David; Wilmer
  Rom. rem., iii. 53
Clare:
  Amice de, m. Baldwin de Redvers, earl of Devon, iv. 230
  Bogo de, ii. 12
  Geof. de, dean of Hastings coll., ii. 116–17
  Gilb. de, earl of Pembroke, i. 490
  Gilb. de, earl of Gloucester (d. 1230), iv. 230
  Gilb. de, earl of Gloucester (d. 1295), i. 496–7, 500; ii. 89, 323; vii. 2; ix. 229, 235
    his seneschal, ii. 171
  Hen. de, iv. 184
  Isabel de, m. Hen. atte Hook, iv. 184

Clare (*cont.*):
Isabel, w. of Gilb. de, *see* Marshal
Marg. de, *see* Burgh
Ric. de, earl of Clare, ii. 323
Ric. de, earl of Gloucester, i. 495; vii. 283; ix. 77, 79
Wm. de, i. 495; ii. 89; ix. 79
fam., ii. 323; vii. 194
and see Clere
Clare, earls of, *see* Clare, Ric. de; Pelham-Holles
Clare College, Cambridge, ix. 183
Claremont (in Esher, Surr.), ii. 443
Clarence, duke of, *see* Lancaster, Thos. of
Clarendon, earls of, *see* Hyde
Clarendon, constitutions of, ii. 6
Clares (Claris, Cleres, Clers) chase, ii. 295, 298, 311–12; vii. 3
Clark:
A., ii. 473
Bart., ix. 267
E.K., ix. 86
G.T., i. 474–5
Jn., ix. 267
T. Chatfield, iv. 126
Maj., i. 528
and see Bolton-Clark; Clarke; Clerk
Clark, Messrs. Thos. and Wm., ii. 235*
Clarke:
Anne, ii. 34
Ant., prebendary of Firle, ii. 406
Bart., dean of the Arches, vii. 230
C.L.S., rector of St. Barnabas, Bexhill, ix. 123
C. Somers-, vii. 180
Cecily, m. Edw. Bellingham, vii. 230
Dennis, vii. 129
Edm. S., vii. 190
Evelyn S., ix. 123–4
Jn. (fl. 1601), ix. 3
Jn. (another), iv. 173
Mrs. M. C. Somers-, vii. 180
Mary, *see* Hendley
Ric. (fl. 1674), vii. 4
Ric. (fl. 1757), vii. 129
Rob., and his w. Anne, vii. 256
Somers (d. 1892), vii. 180
Somers (d. 1926), iii. 123; vii. 180, 259, 261–2
Stephenson, vii. 172
Stephenson R., vii. 190
Wm. (fl. 1687), vii. 156–7
Wm., rector of Buxted, vii. 49, 244*, 247–8
Wm., warden of St. Mary's hosp., Chich., ii. 102; iii. 126
Wm. (fl. 1853), ii. 469
——, vii. 261
and see Clark; Clerk
Classis Britannica, iii. 5, 8, *8*
Claudius, Rom. emperor, iii. 9
Clausentum, *see* Bitterne
Claverham, *see* Arlington
Claveridge (Claverige, Claveringge) forest, ii. 301, 315, 318
Clavir, Wal. le, iii. 104 *n*
Claye (Cleye):
Ellis de la, iii. 166
Ralph de la, iii. 166
Wm. atte, iv. 145
Clayton:
Anne, *see* Parker
Jas. (fl. 1743), iii. 160
Jas. (fl. 1928), iv. 210
Clayton, i. 31–5; ii. 43–4; vii. 105, 140–4, *144*, 179
adv., vii. 108, 144, 171
agric., vii. 141
Burgess Hill, *q.v.*
Buttinghill, vii. 125
ch., ii. 30, 48; vii. *141*, 142–4, *144*
accessories, ii. 250, 328, 354; vii. 144
archit., ii. 337–8, 348, 351, 362, *364*, 372; vii. 142–3
wall paintings, vii. 143
dom. archit., ii. 387; vii. 141

downs, i. 60
fair, vii. 142
foxhunting, ii. 446
man., vii. 2–4, 6, 141–2*, 212
mills, vii. 140
natural history, i. 60, 170, 178, 181, 199
pop., ii. 223
prehist. rem., i. 316, 320, 329
rly., ii. 223 *n*
rector, *see* Halliwell
rectory, vii. 181
roads to, iii. 42–3, 47
Rom. rem., iii. 3–4, 42–3, 53
royal visit, i. 505
Wickham, vii. 125, 141–2
Clayton and Black, vii. 268
Cleare, Fanny Jemima, vii. 163
Clemenceau, Georges, ix. 167
Clemens, son of Pudentius, iii. 14
Clement VI, pope, ii. 73, 95
Clement VII, pope, ii. 80
Clement:
Ann, iii. 146
Jn., and his w. Ann, iii. 146
Mary, iii. 146
Clements:
J., iv. 203
Miss, iv. 203
Clement's Inn, *see* London
Chelmsfold, *see* Slinfold
Clenlow, Wm., ix. 216
Clere:
Avice de, *see* Gurney
Hawise, w. of Rog. de, vii. 189
Ralph de (sr.), vii. 258
Ralph de (jr.), vii. 258
Rob., dean of Battle, ix. 111
Rog. de (fl. 1147), vii. 258
Rog. de (fl. 1180), vii. 258
Rog. de (fl. 1242), vii. 189
and see Clare
Cleres chase, *see* Clares
clerestories, *see* architecture: ecclesiastical
clerk, *see* Alward the clerk; Peter the clerk; Robert the clerk; Stephen the clerk; William the clerk
Clerk (Clerke):
Jn., ii. 252
Ric. le, vii. 24
Wm., vicar of Falmer, vii. 230
and see Clark; Clarke; Le Clerk
Clerkson, Jn., iv. 202
Clermont, earl of, *see* Fortescue, Wm. Hen.
Clers chase, *see* Clares
Cleveland:
dchss. of, *see* Vane; Villiers, Barbara
duke of, *see* Vane
Cleves, Anne of, *see* Anne
Cleye, *see* Claye
Cliff End, *see* Pett
Cliffe (in South Malling, suburb of Lewes), ii. 44, 196; vii. 7–8, 16, 21 *n*, 28
benefice, ii. 9, 12
ch., ii. 33, 118, 250–1
Cliffe Hill, ii. 479
man., ii. 292, 296
prehist. rem., i. 329
rector, ii. 35
sch., ii. 414; vii. 18
trades and ind., ii. 231, 263
Clifford (Clyfford):
Anne, *see* Bardolf
Eleanor, *see* Mowbray
Sir Lewis, vii. 283
Ric. de, ii. 263
Ric., dean of Hastings coll., ii. 117
Rog. de, iv. 167
Sir Wm. (fl. c. 1408), vii. 110
Wm. (fl. 1791), vii. 168
Clifton:
Adam de, iv. 123
Agnes de, iv. 152 *n*
Sir Clifford, ix. 161
Constantine de, ix. 123

Eliz. de, m. Sir Jn. Knyvett, iv. 123
Sir Jn. de, iv. 123
Lucy de, m. Gaudin de Blancmuster, iv. 152
Reynold de (sr.), iv. 152
Reynold de (jr.), iv. 152
Clifton college, *see* Bristol
Climping, Jn. de, bp. of Chich., ii. 108; iii. 124, 129, 139
Climping (Clymping), ii. 37, 42–3
Atherington (Atherton), i. 515
Bailiffscourt, i. 478; ii. 381
ballivate, ii. 46, **120**; bailiffs, ii. 120; iv. 170 *n*
chap., ii. 120, 338, *339*, 366, 373, 375, *375*, 381
dovecot, ii. 382
earthworks, i. 478
barracks, ii. 217 *n*
ch., ii. 121, 333, 338 *n*; iv. 236
accessories, ii. 350–1, 353–4, 356, 358–9, 373
archit., i. 332–4, 340, *341*, 342, *345*, 348–9, 368, 371–4, *373*
Climping Sands, i. 54
Cudlow (Codelawe, Codlow, Cudlo), i. 506 *n*; ii. 42–3, 138, 185, 303; iv. 31
coursing, ii. 453
dom. archit., ii. 386, 388, 391
fishing, ii. 265
Ilsham, ii. 93, 265
ch., ii. 8, 82
man., iv. 145
man., ii. 121
natural history, i. 177–8, 185, 189–93, 195–6, 201–4, 207–9, 291
pop., ii. 217
tithes, ii. 265
Climpsfold, *see* Slinfold: Clemsfold
Clinton:
Cath., *see* Pelham
Edw. Fiennes de, Ld. Clinton and Say, iv. 145; vii. 74
Hen. Fiennes, earl of Lincoln, duke of Newcastle, ii. 443; ix. 139, 196
Jn. de (fl. 1307), iii. 85
Jn., Ld. Clinton (d. 1464), vii. 84, 87
Jn., Ld. Clinton (fl. 1484), vii. 84
Jn., Ld. Clinton (another), vii. 84
Marg., *see* St. Leger
Wm., Ld. Clinton, vii. 84, 114
Clipsham, Jn., i. 514
Clitherow:
Jas. (sr.), vii. 111, 145, 195
Jas. (jr.), vii. 145
Philippa, *see* Gale
Thos. Claude, vii. 147
Col., vii. 145
fam., vii. 147
Cliveshend, *see* Pett: Cliff End
Cloberry:
Sir Jn., vii. 224
Kath., m. Wm. Bromley, vii. 224
clockmaking, ix. 46, 60
Cloos, Jn., dean of Chich., ii. 51; iii. 110, 142, 145
Clothale:
Adam de, iv. 195, 197
Christine de, *see* Grenested
Cloustiere (Gloustiere, Glovernestre), Georgia la, prioress of Lyminster, ii. 121
clover, *see* crops
Clowes, Wm., iii. 90
Clubmen's rising, *see* wars: Civil War
Clue, —— de la, ii. 166
Clun, Alan of, Wm. s. of, *see* William son of Alan of Clun
Clun, fam., arms, iv. 131
Clune, Thos., prior of Shulbred, ii. 82
Cluny (Saône-et-Loire, France), abbey, ii. 64–9, 70 *n*; vii. 46–7, 55, 224
abbot, ii. 411–12; *and see* Androin; Hugh, prior of Lewes
Clutton, Jn., vii. 136
Clyfford, *see* Clifford
Clymping, *see* Climping

Clyveshend, *see* Pett: Cliff End
Cnapp (Cnep, Cnepp), *see* Shipley: Knepp
Cnut (Canute), king of England, i. 348, 484; iv. 182, 186 *n*; vii. 33; ix. 8, 34, 49, 62, 168, 253
coaching, ii. 204–5
Coachman, Revd. ——, ii. 420
Coast, Wm., and his w. Marg., vii. 100
coast, defence of, iii. 5, 87–8; vii. 63, 245–6, 249; *and see* maritime hist.
coastal erosion, ii. 72, 76–8, 95–7, 106–7, 116, 169, 199, 224 *n*, 233; iv. 195, 198, 230; vii. 275; ix. 239 *n*
coastguards, i. 502, 506, 507 *n*; ix. 27, 148
Coates, Wm., iii. 145; *and see* Cotes
Coates, ii. 43, 388
  ch., ii. 339, 346, 350, 356–7, 366
  pop., ii. 217
  prehist. rem., i. 310, *310*, *312*, 329
Cobbett, Wm., ii. 206
Cobden:
  Edw., iv. 99
  Ric., iv. 60, 65
  Wm., iv. 106
  Miss, m. T. Fisher Unwin, iv. 60
Cobden Memorial Association, iv. 60
Cobehay, Hen., ii. 261
Cobham:
  Anne, m. 1 Edw. Blount, Ld. Mountjoy, 2 Edw., Ld. Burgh, ix. 120
  Anne, w. of Sir Reynold, *see* Bardolf
  Jas., ix. 150
  Sir Jn. de, vii 196
  Marg., m. Ralph Nevill, earl of Westmorland, ix. 120
  Ralph de, vii. 134, 196
  Reynold de, Ld. Cobham, warden of Cinque Ports, ix. 120, 244
    his w., ix. 120
  Reynold de (d. 1403), ix. 120
  Sir Reynold (fl. *c.* 1423), vii. 110
  Reynold de (d. 1446, ? another), ix. 120
  Thos., ix. 120
  arms, ix. *120*
Cobham, Ld., *see* Brooke; Cobham, Reynold
Cobhambury, *see* Edenbridge
Cobnor, *see* Chidham
Coburg, prince of, *see* Leopold
Coby, Wm., vii. 235
cock fighting, *see* sport
cock scailing, *see* sport
Cocke, Wm., ii. 257
Cockeram, Phil., ix. 149
Cockes, Thos., vii. 227
Cockfield:
  Adam de (sr.), vii. 279
  Adam de (jr.), vii. 279
  Lucy de, w. of Adam, vii. 279
  Rob. de (sr.), vii. 279
  Rob. de (jr.), vii. 279
  arms, vii. *279*
Cocking, i. 505; ii. 43, 303; iv. 40, **43–7**
  adv., ii. 108, 119; iv. 47, 70
  ch., ii. 81; iv. 45–7, *43*, *46*
    accessories, ii. 250, 351–2, 354–5, 360–1, 366; iv. 46–7
    archit., ii. 339, 342, 366, 373, 375; iv. 45–6
  Cocking Causeway, iv. 44, 65
  Cocking Down, i. 111, 121, 170
  dom. archit., ii. 393; iv 44
  earthworks, i. 480
  fair, iv. 45
  Foundry Pond, iv. 44
  foxhunting, ii. 442
  insects, i. 111–12, 117, 119, 121, 164, 166–70, 177–90, 212, 216, 218, 224–6, 231, 234, 236–7
  ironworks, iv. 44 *n*
  man., iv. 44–5, 69
  mkt., iv. 45
  mills, ii. 394; iv. *43*, 44–5
  Pitsham, iv. 44
  pop., ii. 221

rly., iv. 44
roads, iv. 43–4
Rom. rem., iii. 47, 53
streams, iv. 44
tithes, iv. 47
vicars, *see* Baker, Thos.; Skynner, Melmoth
woods, iv. 43, 45
Cockmarling, *see* Udimore
Cocquerell, *see* Coquerell
Code, Jn., rector of Ovingdean, vii. 230
Codelawe, *see* Climping: Cudlow
Coding (Codyng, Goding):
  Hugh de, ix. 119
  Joan de, *see* Batsford
  Jn. de (d. by 1332), ix. 119
  Jn. de (fl. *c.* 1340), ix. 266
  Jn. de (fl. 1346), ix. 119
  Jn. de (d. by 1382), ix. 266
  Jn. (d. *c.* 1397), ix. 119
  Maud de, *see* Wacelyn
  Ric. de (fl. 1305–32), ix. 266
  Ric. de (fl. 1332, another), ix. 119
  Sarah, w. of Jn., ix. 119
  Thos. de, ix. 266
  Wm. de, ix. 119
  fam., ix. 119
Coding, *see* Bexhill: Cooden
Codington, Jn. de, dean of Hastings coll., ii. 117
Codlow, *see* Climping: Cudlow
Codmore Hill, *see* Pulborough
Codrington, Thos., iii. 32, 34, 42
Codulf (fl. 1066), iv. 80
Codwell, Jn., vii. 263
Codyng, *see* Coding
Coenwulf, king of Mercia, i. 349
coffin slabs, *see* architecture: ecclesiastical
Cogan:
  Hen., vicar of East Dean, iv. 96
  Horace Barbutt, vicar of East Dean, iv. 96
  Thos. White, vicar of East Dean, iv. 96
Cogger:
  Eliz., ix. 168 *n*
  Wm., ix. 168 *n*
Cogges (Oxon.), prior, ix. 50 *n*, 63
Coggeshall (Essex), iii. 49
  abbey, ii. 73
Coghlan, Mary E., ix. 178
Coghurst, *see* Guestling
Cogidubnus, king of the Regni, iii. 1–2, 9–10, 14
Cohen, Mrs. J.M., vii. 171
coins:
  A.-S., *see* Anglo-Saxon remains: coins
  Celtic, i. **324**, **326**, 328–31
  Rom., *see* Romano–British Suss.: coins
Coitere, Rob., prior of Pynham, ii. 80–1
Cokayne:
  Chas., Vct. Cullen, vii. 111
  Chas., vii. 111
  Mary, m. Chas. Howard, earl of Nottingham, vii. 111
  Sir Wm., vii. 111
Coke:
  Alan, ii. 308
  Hen., vii. 80
  Sir Jn., ii. 238
  and see Cook; Cooke
Coke-Richards, Miss, vii. 115, 117
Cokeham, *see* Sompting
Cokelers, *see* Independents, Soc. of
Cola (fl. 1066), vii. 34, 189
Colbebech, *see* Ashdown forest
Colbrand (Colbrande, Colbrond):
  Agnes, *see* Pelham
  Jas., iii. 77
  Jn. (fl. 1435), ix. 133
  Jn. (fl. 1600), iii. 77
  Marg., *see* Amherst
  ——, i. 514
  fam., ii. 386; ix. 140
Colby, Sam., and his w. Mary, iv. 189
Colchester (Essex), i. 349, 534; ii. 247;

iii. 51, 60
Cold Harbour, *see* Maresfield: Coldharbour
Coldam, *see* Coldham
Coldell, Jn., prior of Shulbred, ii. 82
Coldham (Coldam):
  Alice, w. of Wm., iv. 93
  Jn., iv. 24 *n*
  Ric., iv. 51
  Wm., iv. 51, 83, 93
  ——, iv. 25 *n*
  fam., iv. 51
  arms, iv. *83*
Coldharbour (in Maresfield), *see* Maresfield
Coldharbour (in Pulborough), *see* Pulborough
Coldharbour Green, *see* Titsey
Coldone, Luke de, abbot of Bayham, ii. 89
Coldwaltham, ii. 43
  Ashurst Ho., iii. 35
  ch., ii. 359, 373, 375
  insects, i. 205
  pop., ii. 217
  roads to, iii. 35
  Rom. rem., iii. 35, 53, 64
  Watersfield, iii. 4, 35, 53, 64
Cole:
  Chas., iv. 99
  Eliz., w. of Thos., iii. 146
  Jn., iv. 239
  Sim., ii. 398
  Thos., iii. 146
  Wm., iii. 90
Colebrook (Colebrooke):
  Anne, w. of Jn., iv. 5
  Jas., iv. 150
  Jas. (? another), and his w. Barbara, iv. 163
  Jn. (fl. 1709), iv. 10
  Jn. (d. 1772), iv. 5
  Jn. (fl. 1775), iv. 5
Colegrove, *see* Rotherfield
Coleman, *see* Colman
Coleman's Hatch, *see* Hartfield
Colepeper (Colepepper), *see* Culpeper
Coles, *see* Cowper-Coles
Colespore, *see* Goldspur
Colet, Jn., dean of St. Paul's, ii. 404, 421–2
Colevile:
  Alice de, iv. 213
  Geof. de, iv. 213
  Guy de, iv. 213
  Jn. de, iv. 213
  Julian, w. of Sir Rob. de, iv. 213
  Lucy, w. of Sir Rob. de, iv. 213
  Sir Rob. de, iv. 213
  Rog. de, iv. 213
  Wal. de (fl. *c.* 1225), ii. 95
  Wal. de, prior of Sele, ii. 62–3
  Wm. de, and his w. Alice, iv. 213
Colgate, Thos., vii. 64
Colgate, *see* Beeding
Coline, Jn. (Ihone), ii. 360
Collard, Mrs., vii. 124
Collett:
  And., and his w. Jane, iv. 231
  Peter, ii. 426
  and see Colet
Collier (Collyer, Colyer):
  A., ii. 453
  Cecilia, m. Jas. Murray, ix. 86
  Dorothie, ii. 421
  Geo., ii. 421
  Henrietta, m. Hen. Jackson, ix. 86
  Jane, m. Wm. Green, ix. 86
  Jn., mayor of Hastings, ii. 391; ix. 24, 86
  Kath., w. of Ric., later Lady Dormer, ii. 421–2
  Mary, m. Edw. Milward, ix. 86
  Mary, w. of Jn., *see* Cranston
  Ric., ii. 421–2
  Sarah, m. Hen. Sayer, ix. 86
  and see Colyear

Collings:
Rog., rector of St. Olave, Chich., iii. 162
Wilmot, w. of Rog., iii. 162
and see Collins
Collingwood, R.G., iii. 14, 59, 68
Collins (Collyns, Colyn):
Alex. (d. 1550), ix. 229
Alex. (d. by 1565), ix. 229
Anne, m. 1 Hugh Sempill, 2 Revd. —— Durnford, iii. 90, 161
Anne, w. of Edw., ix. 177
Edw. (fl. 1697), ix. 227
Edw. (fl. 1803), ix. 177
Eliz., ii. 34
Eliz., w. of Alderman ——, iii. 161
Fred., ii. 235
Geo., ii. 408
H., i. 42
Hen. (fl. 1583), and his w. Alice, vii. 67
Hen. (fl. 1724), ix. 229
Hen. (d. 1753, another), ix. 229
Increased, ix. 229
Jn. (d. *c.* 1350), ii. 242
Jn. (d. 1537), ix. 229
Julia, w. of Alex., ix. 229
Mary (d. 1648), ix. 231
Mary, w. of Thos., ix. 229
R., ii. 423
Thos. (d. 1612), ix. 229
Thos. (fl. 1660), iii. 93
Thos. (d. 1667, ? another), ix. 229, 242
Thos. (d. 1709), ix. 229
Thos. (fl. 1814), iii. 81
Wm. (fl. 1632), iv. 172
Wm. (fl. *c.* 1691), ii. 159
Wm. (d. 1759), iii. 90, 97, *135*, 145, 161
Wm. (fl. 1783), ix. 266
Alderman ——, iii. 161
arms, ix. *229*
and see Collings
Collock, Wm., iv. 90, 100
Collyer, *see* Collier
Collyer's school, *see* Horsham: sch.
Collyns, *see* Collins
Colman (Coleman):
Ann, m. Jas. Baker, iv. 70
Beatrice, w. of Jn., iv. 62
Jn. (d. by 1240), iv. 62
Jn. (fl. 1807), ix. 197
Wm., iv. 123
Colmorde, Jn., master of Arundel coll., ii, 109
Colnet, Nic., master of Playden hosp., ii. 105
Columb, Phil. Howard, ii. 139
Colpece (Colpys):
Isabel, iv. 39
Jn. (d. 1580), iv. 123
Jn. (fl. 1607), iv. 123
Colshill, Thos., ii. 151; vii. 63
Colstaple, *see* Horsham
Colte:
Edw., ix. 86
Jn., ix. 86
Thos., ix. 86
——, *see* Kyme
fam., ix. 86
Columbiers, Miles de, prior of Lewes, ii. 70
Columbus, Chris., ii. 143
Colwell (Colwyll):
Jn., prior of Arundel friary, ii. 94
Thos., vii. 204
Colworth, *see* Oving
Colwyll, *see* Colwell
Colyear, Chas., earl of Portmore, ii. 454
Colyer, *see* Collier
Colyn, *see* Collins
Combe:
Edw., vii. 242
Hen., prior of Hardham, ii. 75
Jn., ix. 119
Jn. de (another), vii. 242
Jn. (another), vii. 242

Ric. de, vii. 87
Thos. (d. by 1501), vii. 242
Thos., and his w. Eliz. (? two of this name), iv. 202; vii. 242
and see Cumbe
Combe (in Peasmarsh), *see* Peasmarsh
Combe (unidentified), ii. 93
Combe forest, *see* Dallington forest
Combe Haven, riv., ix. 20–1, 77
Comber (Coumber):
Jn. (fl. 1561), vii. 85
Jn. (fl. 1615), vii. 75
Jn. (d. 1623, another), iv. 155
Jn. (d. 1684), iv. 144 *n*, 155, 156 *n*, 213, 230
Kath., m. —— Madgewick, iv. 155, 230
Mat., ii. 318
Rob., ii. 73
Thos. (d. *c.* 1613), vii. 75
Thos. (d. 1634), iv. 155
Wm., and his w. Martha, vii. 85
fam., vii. 33 *n*
Combert, Lambert, ii. 34
Combes (Combs, Coombes):
A.H., ii. 433
Jn., iv. 192
Louisa, ix. 200
Combwell, *see* Goudhurst
Commios (Commius), i. 326; iii. 9; iv. 205
Comper:
Alfred, iii. 160
Chas., iii. 160
Eleanor, iii. 160
Emma, iii. 160
Harry, iii. 160
Hen., iii. 160, 169
Jas., iii. 160
Maria, w. of Harry, iii. 160
Wm., iii. 160
Comport, Ambrose, ix. 106
Compostella (Spain), ii. 142
Compton:
Cath., m. Ric. Infield, vii. 165 *n*, 166, 197
Chas., earl of Northampton, ix. 173
E.D., ii. 476
Eliz., m. Geo. Augustus Hen. Cavendish, earl of Burlington, ix. 61, 173
Eliz., w. of Wm., iv. 5
Eliz., w. of Wm., Ld. Compton, *see* Spencer
Geo., earl of Northampton, ix. 173
Sir Hen., ii. 319; iv. 212; ix. 89
Ric., and his w. Joan, vii. 197
Sir Spencer, earl of Wilmington, ii. 468; ix. 61, 173
Thos., iv. 101
Wm. (fl. *c.* 1520), iv. 42
Wm., Ld. Compton, vii. 217
Gen., ii. 441
fam., iv. 144; ix. 61
Compton, i. 483, 502; ii. 43, 302–3; iv. 88, **91–4**, 107, 110, 149
adv., iv. 93, 113
char., iv. 93–4
ch., ii. 9, 15–16, 84, 368, 376; iv. *90*, 91–3
Compton Down, iii. 29; iv. 91
dom. archit., iv. 91
glebe, ii. 5
Little Green, iv. 91–2
man., iv. 91–3, 109, 111–12
Pk., iv. 91
pop., ii. 221
Rom. rem., iii. 29
vicarage, ii. 9
vicars, iv. 93; *and see* Langdale
Compton (Surr.), ii. 89
Compton by Winchester (Hants), *see* Sparkford
Compton Place, *see* Eastbourne
Compton Wasseling (Hants), ix. 266 *n*
Comyn:
Jn., i. 499
Mary, *see* Wilson

Steph., ix. 229
Conan, Alan s. of, *see* Alan
Conan, Wm., iv. 166
Coney, Wm., ii. 164–5
Coneyhurst, *see* Chiltington, West
Conghurst:
Bridget, w. of Jn., ix. 213
Joan, w. of Jn., ix. 213
Jn. (fl. 1448), ix. 213
Jn. (fl. 1517), ix. 213
Mary, ix. 213
Thos., ix. 213
Congregationalists and Independents, ii. 35, 39; iii. 164; iv. 77, 190, 193 *n*, 227; vii. 42, 62, 109, 119, 127, 132, 144, 147–8, 163, 179; ix. 29–30, 62, 112, 123–4, 131, 137, 141, 200, 201, 265
Congreve, Wm., ii. 159
Connell, Susan, ix. 179
Connold, E., i. 122
Conny, Jn., ii. 153
constable, Joslen the, *see* Jocelin
Constable:
A.J., ii. 477
Chas., ii. 165
Capt. Jn., ii. 165
Jn. (fl. 1698), ix. 215
Jn. (d. by 1786), ix. 197–8
Jos., vii. 106
L.L., ii. 452
Wm. (fl. 1730), ix. 197–8
Wm. (d. before 1776, another), ix. 198
Wm. (fl. 1786–96), ix. 197, 215, 254
Wm. (d. 1811, ? another), ii. 438
——, ii. 457
Constable & Sons, ii. 263
Constantine, Rom. emperor, iii. 9, 68
Constantius II, Rom. emperor, i. 344; iii. 4
convertible husbandry, ii. 273
Conway, Francis, Ld. Conway, ii. 442
Conyngsby, Ric., ix. 245
Cooden (Cooding), *see* Bexhill
cook, Rob. the, *see* Robert
Cook:
Jas., vii. 177, 235
Jn., ii. 160
Lucy, m. Sir Sam. Gerrard, ix. 207
Mary, vii. 177, 235
Rob. le (d. 1350), iv. 105
Rog., iv. 153
Thos., iv. 111
Thos. Wm., bp. of Lewes, ii. 433; iii. 126
Tommy, ii. 443
and see Coke; Cooke
Cooke:
Eliz. Ward, m. Hen. Nailand, vii. 158, 180
Isaac, ii. 165
Jas., vii. 157, 180
Jane Frazer, *see* Piggott
Joan, *see* Anstye
Jn. (fl. 1468), ii. 230
Jn. (fl. 1561), vii. 85
Jn. (fl. 1564, another), ii. 24
Jn. (fl. 1564, ? another), ii. 256
Ric. (fl. *temp.* Hen. VIII), iv. 117 *n*
his w., *see* Hall
Ric. (fl. 1689), ix. 152
Simon Frazer, *see* Frazer Cooke
Thos., vii. 180
W., i. 64, 66
Wm., vii. 157
arms, iv. 117; vii. 186
and see Coke; Cook
Cooksbridge, *see* Hamsey
Cookson, Jas., vicar of Harting, iv. 13
Coolhurst, *see* Horsham
Coombe Place, *see* Hamsey
Coombe Plantation (unidentified), i. 147–8, 159
Coombes, *see* Combes
Coombes, i. 511; ii. 43, 232, 384
Applesham, i. 302
ch., ii. 337, 339, 349–51, *350*, 353,

366, 373–4, 379
ch. ho., ii. 384
insects, i. 207–8
pop., ii. 219
Cooper (Coopere):
  Allan, ii. 284
  Anna Maria, iv. 132
  Benj., ix. 181
  C.E., vicar of Portslade, ii. 433
  Isabella, see Franks
  Jn., ii. 165
  Martha, ii. 147
  Mary, see Peckham
  N.C., ii. 476
  Ralph, iv. 129
  Ric., iv. 80
  Rob. Chester, vii. 31
  T.H., i. 42
  Thos. (fl. 1791), ix. 181
  Thos. (fl. 1878), ii. 474
  Wm. (fl. 1526), iii. 77
  Wm. (fl. 1678), iii. 88
  Wm. (fl. 1775), ix. 181
  Wm. Durrant, ii. 312; ix. 168
  Sir Wm. Hen., ix. 187
  Mr., ii. 25
  ——, ii. 185
  and see Cowper
Coote (Cootte):
  I., ii. 453
  Mary, w. of Thos., ii. 145
  R., ii. 453
  Thos. (sr.), iii. 145
  Thos. (jr.), iii. 145
Cootham, see Storrington
Cootte, see Coote
Cope:
  Arabella Diana, m. 1 Jn. Fred. Sack-
    ville, duke of Dorset, 2 Chas.
    Whitworth, earl Whitworth, vii.
    35, 257
  Sir Chas., vii. 257
  Jn., iv. 76
Copenhagen (Denmark), ii. 167
Cophall, see Maresfield
Copis, Geo., iv. 216
Copley:
  Anne, see Hoo
  Ric., ix. 196
  Sir Rog., ix. 196
  Thos., ii. 27
  Lady, ii. 28
  Mr., ii. 20
  fam., ii. 27
Copper, Geo., and his w. Mary, ix. 181
Copperas Gap (? in Shoreham), i. 173
Copthorne, see Worth
Coquerell (Cockquerell):
  Geo. (fl. 1615), iv. 61
  Geo. (fl. 1669), iv. 62
  Geo., his s., iv. 62
  Marg., see Yalding
  Martha, m. Chas. Randall Covert, iv.
    62
Corbeaux, ——, ii. 258
corbel tables, see architecture: ecclesias-
  tical
Corbelin (fl. 1086), iv. 108
Corbett (Corbet):
  Ann, see Norton
  Edm., vii. 96
  Hadwissa, ii. 82
  Jn., minister of Chich., ii. 37
  Thos., ii. 420
Corbridge (Northumb.), iii. 18
Cordall (Cordell), Jn., iv. 64, 80, 109,
  111
Cordwaner, Phil., ii. 108
Corfe Castle (Dors.), i. 183, 191
Corfu (Greece), i. 536
Corle, Jn., vii. 40
corn, see crops
Cornell, Mary, iv. 93
Cornewall, Sir Geo., iv. 212; and see
  Cornwayle
Corney and Carver, ii. 164
Cornhill, see London
Cornish, Sir Sam., i. 531

Cornwall, earls of, see Edmund; Richard
Cornwall, i. 44, 68, 516, 520; ii. 134,
  138, 141, 148; iii. 68; iv. 41
  and see Dodman; Fowey; Glasney;
    Marazion; Scilly Isles
Cornwallis, Jas., Earl Cornwallis, ix. 20
Cornwayle:
  Eliz., see Bolingbroke
  Sir Jn., ix. 169
  and see Cornewall
Corpus Christi College, Cambridge, ii.
  431
Corpus Christi College, Oxford, ii. 408,
  432
correction, hos. of, see prisons
Corry, Sarah, ix. 32
Corsica, ii. 162
Corteney, see Courtenay
Cortesley, see Hollington
Cosby, Phillips, ii. 166
Costantin, Anne-Hilarion de, count de
  Tourville, ii. 159
Coste, Jacques Meud de, vii. 146
Costune, Jn., prior of Boxgrove, ii. 59
Cotelege, Rob. de, ix. 27
Cotes:
  Elias de, iv. 219
  Geof. de, iv. 219
  Jn., vii. 34
  Louisa Harriet, see Jenkinson
  Rob. de, iv. 219
  Sim., ii. 46; iv. 131
  Steph. de, iv. 219
  Wm. de, iv. 219
  fam., iv. 219
  and see Coates
Cotesmore, Thos., ii. 25
Cotille, Nic., master of hosp. of St. Jas.
  and St. Mary, Chich., ii. 100
Cotnall, Wm., ii. 85
Cotterill (Cotterell):
  G.H., ii. 476
  Hen., bp. of Grahamstown (South
    Africa), ii. 430–1
  Jn., rector of Hollington and Winford,
    ix. 86
Cottingham, Thos., abbot of Bayham,
  ii. 89
Cotton:
  Chas., vii. 230, 232
  Francis, and his w. Mary, vii. 256
  Sir Jn. Hynde, ix. 91
  Marg., see Cragg
  Ric., ii. 165
  Rob., iv. 224
  Sir Thos. (fl. 1549), ii. 145
  Thos. (fl. 1643), i. 523
  ——, vii. 230
cotton, see textile inds.
Cotyng, Jn., i. 514
Couchman:
  J.E., iii. 43 n, 57–8
  Thos., ix. 235
Coudenne (Kudenn):
  Isabel de, m. Jn. de Peplesham, ix.
    138
  Jn. de, and his w. Joan, ix. 138
  Steph. de, ix. 138
Coulsdon (Surr.), iii. 42
  Farthingdown, i. 341
Coulstock (Cowstock), Rob., ii. 312
Coumber, see Comber
Counte, Sim. le, ii. 92
Countess of Huntingdon's Connexion,
  vii. 42, 119, 164, 192, 263
County Agric. Coll., see Plumpton
county court, see courts
Courage:
  Archibald Vesey, vii. 139
  H.E., vii. 139
  Hen., vii. 139
Courcy, fam., arms, vii. 10
Courderay, Jn., warden of St. Mary's
  hosp., Chich., ii. 102
coursing, see sport
Court (Courte):
  Hen., iv. 79
  Jn. (fl. 1553), iv. 118

Jn. (fl. 1640), and his w. Kath., iv.
  118
Wm., iv. 118
Court Bushes, see Hurstpierpoint
Courtail:
  Jn., warden of St. Mary's hosp.,
    Chich., ii. 102
  —— (? another), ix. 199
Courte, see Court
Courtenay (Corteney, Courtney):
  Cath., see Smith
  Hugh de, earl of Devon, ii. 67
  Isabel de, m. Jn. de St. John, iv. 143,
    199
  Jn. de, ii. 67
  Ric., dean of South Malling coll., etc.,
    ii. 118–119
  Wm., abp. of Cant., iv. 226, 233
  Sir Wm., vii. 111
  arms, ix. 216
Courthope:
  Barbara, m. Hen. Campion, vii. 173,
    176, 217
  Eliz., see Saunders
  Geo. (d. 1577), ix. 255
  Sir Geo. (d. 1642), ix. 255
  Sir Geo. (d. 1685), ix. 255–6
  Geo. (fl. 1788), ix. 254–5
  Geo. (fl. 1825), ix. 142, 255
  Geo. (d. 1835), ix. 255
  Geo. Campion, ix. 254–5, 257
  Geo. Jn., ix. 255
  Sir Geo. Loyd, ix. 253–5
  Jn. (fl. 1513–39), ix. 255
  Jn. (fl. 1541, another), ix. 255
  Jn. (d. 1615), ix. 253, 255
  Mary, ix. 256
  Peter (d. 1657), vii. 176
  Peter (d. 1724), vii. 36 n, 176, 217
  Philadelphia, see Stapley
  fam., vii. 9; ix. 255
  arms, ix. 255
Courtney, see Courtenay
Courtney & Birkett Ltd., ii. 235
courts:
  Admiralty, ii. 141, 148 n
  Arches, ii. 17
  dean, see Clarke, Bart.
  assize, vii. 16
  Augmentations, iii. 93; iv. 106; vii. 75
  aves (avesfeild, aveshould), ii. 320–1
  baronial, i. 503; ii. 320
  Brodhull, see Cinque Ports: cts.
  county, i. 504; ii. 172 n; iii. 96; vii.
    15–16
  forest eyres, ii. 292–3
  hund., i. 504, 538; ii. 171–2, 184, 187;
    vii. 51, 58, 61, 125, 201, 221–2
  leet, i. 514
  lodemanage, ix. 39
  manorial, see parish names
  pannage, ii. 293, 322
  pie-powder, iii. 98
  quarter sessions, i. 521; vii. 16
  Shepway, see Cinque Ports: cts.
  shire, iii. 96
  swain-motes, ii. 292–3, 317, 320
  wood, ii. 317
  wood-motes, ii. 292, 311, 320–1
  wood playt, ii. 304
  and see Chich.; Cinque Ports; Lewes:
    barony; Lewes; Shoreham: coun-
    ty ct.
Coutances (Manche, France), bp., see
  Geoffrey
Cove:
  Eve de, see Tattersall
  Jn. de, iv. 115 n
Covehurst, see Fairlight
Coveney:
  Mary, ix. 197
  Thos., ix. 197
Coventry (Covintre):
  C.J., ii. 471 n
  Eliz., m. Sir Wm. Keyt, ix. 207
  Eliz., w. of Francis, see Manning
  Francis, ix. 207
  Ralph de, abbot of Battle, ii. 53, 55

Covert (Coverte):
Alex., vii. 186
Ann (fl. 1579), vii. 186
Ann (fl. 1643), vii. 280
Ann, w. of Ric., see Hendley
Anne, m. Sir Jas. Morton, vii. 145, 156, 183
Anne, w. of Sir Wal., vii. 156, 190, 204
Benj., iv. 161–2
Blanche, see Vaughan
Chas. Randall, vicar of Hunston, iv. 62, 129, 158
Cicely, see Bowes
Diana, m. 1 Rob. Baynham, 2 Jn. Palgrave, vii. 226, 280
Diana, w. of Sir Thos., see Goring
Dulcibella, vii. 186
Eliz., vii. 186
Eliz., w. of Ric., see Faggar
Eliz., w. of Ric., see Nevill
Ellen, vii. 186
Francis, vii. 186
Geo., vii. 159
Humph., i. 518
Isabel, see Pelham
Jane, m. 1 Sir Francis Fleming, 2 Sir Jn. Fetyplace, vii. 185
Jane, w. of Wal., see Shirley
Joan (fl. 1512), ii. 85
Joan (fl. c. 1579), vii. 186
Jn. (fl. 1487), iv. 171
Jn. (d. 1503, ? another), vii. 159, 185, 190, 226; ix. 229
Jn. (d. c. 1558), vii. 190
Jn. (fl. c. 1579), vii. 186
Sir Jn. (d. 1680), ii. 312; vii. 156, 183, 190, 280
Kath., m. Sir Jn. Gaynesford, vii. 230
Marg., ii. 99, 106
Margery, vii. 186
Martha, see Coquerell
Mary, vii. 186
Mary, m. 1 Hen. Goring, 2 Nic. Best, vii. 190
Mary, w. of Wm. de, see Aguillon
Mynors, vii. 186
Nic., iv. 161–2, 165 n
Ric. (fl. before 1517), ix. 229
Ric. (d. 1547), vii. 159, 185, 190
Ric. (d. 1579), ii. 24; vii. 34, 186, 190, 204
Sir Rog., ii. 307, 316
Ruth, m. 1 Wm. Wharry, 2 Sam. Beaston, iv. 162
Thos. (fl. c. 1579), vii. 186
Sir Thos. (d. 1643), ii. 312; vii. 156, 183, 190, 204, 226, 280
Sir Wal. (d. 1632), ii. 28, 31, 152, 312; vii. 145, 156–7, 182, 186, 190, 195–6, 204, 226
Sir Wal. (fl. 1632), vii. 156, 190, 204
Wal. (d. 1672), vii. 190
Wm. de (fl. 1236), iv. 89, 111
Wm. (d. 1494), vii. 100, 159, 183, 190, 230, 280; ix. 229
Wm. (fl. c. 1579), vii. 186
Wm. (fl. 1613, ? another), vii. 184
fam., i. 513; ii. 84, 361–2, 379, 387; vii. 145, 159, 191
arms, vii. 10, 182, 183, 185–6
Covintre, see Coventry
Cow, J., ii. 480
Cowbeach (Cowbeech), see Herstmonceux
Cowden (Kent), ii. 77; iii. 44–5
Cowden (in Wartling), see Wartling
Cowdray, Vcts., see Pearson
Cowdray, see Easebourne
Cowfold (Cuffold), i. 302; ii. 43–4, 230, 253
birds, i. 273 n, 277, 284
ch., ii. 70 n, 309, 339, 356, 358, 361
insects, i. 136, 143, 146–8, 152, 156–9, 163–4, 178
mammals, i. 300–1
Parkminster, ii. 231
pop., ii. 220

vicar, see Winter, Geo.
Cowlden:
Ric., ii. 257
Wm., ii. 257
Cowley:
Thos., vicar of Ticehurst, ii. 19
Wal., and his w. Mabel, ix. 207
Wm., ix. 86
Cowper:
Edw., ix. 83
Jane, see Weekes
Jn. (fl. 1532), ix. 176–7
Jn. (d. 1618), iv. 20
Jn. (d. 1620), iv. 20
Jn. (fl. 1691), ix. 224
Marg., see Lewknor
Ric., ix. 119
Rob., ix. 157
Thos., vii. 52
Wm., Earl Cowper, ii. 443
Wm., iv. 152
Mr., ii. 454
and see Cooper
Cowper-Coles, A.R., ii. 472 n
Cowstock, see Coulstock
Cox (Coxe):
Francis, warden of St. Mary's hosp., Chich., ii. 102
Peter, alderman of Chich., ii. 407
Ric., ii. 21, 417
Mr., ii. 26
Coxon, Wm., ii. 153
Cozens:
Rose, iv. 191
Wm. (? two of this name), iv. 191
Crabbet Park, see Worth
Crabhouse nunnery (Norf.), ii. 85 n
crafts, see industries, crafts, and trades
Cragg:
Anne, m. —— Knight, ix. 91
Eliz., m. —— Elliott, ix. 91
Jas., ix. 91
Marg., m. Sir Jn. Hynde Cotton, ix. 91
R., ii. 423
Crake:
Edw. Neville, dean of Battle, ix. 100, 112
V.B., ii. 470 n
Cralle:
Isabel, m. Vincent Finch, ix. 91–2
Jas., de, ix. 207
Marg. de, see Peplesham
Margery, m. Ric. Cheney, ix. 91, 207
Ric., ix. 91–2, 207
Rob. de (fl. before 1278), ix. 207
Rob. de (fl. 1327–50), ix. 207
Rob. (fl. before 1412), ix. 91, 207
Cramesham:
Muriel de, iv. 230
Rog. de, iv. 230
Cramond, baroness of, see Ashburnham, Eliz.
Cranbrook (Kent), i. 293; ii. 434, 448; ix. 254
Crane:
And., vii. 58
Jn., abbot of Battle, ii. 55
Jn. (fl. 1546), vii. 58
Nic. de la, iii. 103
Peter, vii. 58
Ric., vii. 58
Crane Down, see Southover
Cranfield, Lionel, earl of Middlesex, vii. 64, 254
Cranhalls, ——, ix. 12
Cranmer, Thos., abp. of Cant., ii. 145, 305; vii. 101, 223, 230–1, 234, 238; vii. 286
Cranston:
Cordelia, see Delves
Jas., ix. 86
Mary, m. Jn. Collier, ix. 86
Craucumbe (Crawcombe):
Clarice de, see Sartilli
Godfrey de, iv. 144; ix. 15
Craven:
C.J., ii. 446

Eliz., ix. 154
Eliz., w. of Wm., Ld. Craven, see Skipwith
Fulwar, Ld. Craven, vii. 224–5
Thos., vii. 225
Wm., Earl Craven (d. 1697), iv. 223; vii. 224; ix. 138, 154
Wm., Ld. Craven (d. 1711), vii. 224
Wm., Ld. Craven (d. 1769), ii. 454; vii. 224
Wm., Ld. Craven (d. 1791), iv. 223; vii. 224–5; ix. 138
fam., iv. 223
arms, iv. 223
Crawcombe, see Craucumbe
Crawford (Crawfurd):
Anne (Anna), see Paine
Chas. Payne, vii. 169
Gibbs, vii. 169, 197
O.G.S., iii. 47
Sir Patrick, i. 532
Rob., vii. 169
W.S., ii. 457, 459
Mr., i. 532
Crawford, earl of, see Lindsay, Ludovic
Crawfurd, see Crawford
Crawle, Jn., prior of Shoreham friary, ii. 97
Crawley:
Harriet, m. O.H.A. Nicholls, iii. 146
Wm., ix. 138
Crawley, ii. 44, 206, 301, 311–12; vii. 125, 144–7, 146
adv., vii. 146–7
agric., vii. 144
char., vii. 147
ch., ii. 40, 339, 348, 352, 356; vii. 145, 146
dom. archit., vii. 144–5
fair, vii. 145
man., vii. 145–6
mkt., vii. 145
mon., vii. 144
natural history, i. 68, 213
poor relief, ii. 208
pop., ii. 223
prehist. rem., i. 329
rly., vii. 144
rector, ii. 40
roads, ii. 240
sport, ii. 445–9, 481
trades and ind., ii. 236, 242, 256, 259
Crawley and Horsham foxhounds, i. 302
Crawley Down, see Worth
Crawshaw, Mr., ii. 457
Crécy (Aisne, France), ii. 138
Creed:
Jas., iv. 191
Mary, m. Jn. Benbridge, ix. 137 n
Sam., ii. 420
Creed, see Bosham
Cremesham, see Pagham: Crimsham
Crepyn, Edm., and his w. Mary, iv. 135
Cresselinus, iii. 80
Cresset (formerly Pelham), Hen., see Pelham
Cressi, see Cressy
Cressingham, Jn. de, ix. 198
Cresswell:
Edw., vii. 230
Eliz., m. Sir Hen. Goring, vii. 230
Cressweller:
Augustine, iv. 39
Jn., mayor of Chich., iii. 86, 92, 104; iv. 39
Wm. (sr.), iv. 16
Wm. (jr.), iv. 16
Cressy (Cressi):
Alice de, w. of Jn., ix. 91
Hugh de, vii. 236
Jn. de (fl. 1262), ix. 91
Jn. de (fl. 1339), ix. 91
Jn. de (fl. 1351, another), ix. 91
Marg. de, see Cheney
Oliver de, ix. 91
Rog. de, vii. 236
Rog. de (another), vii. 236
Thos. de, ix. 91

Wm. de, vii. 236
Crete, Hen., iv. 79
Creule, Rob. de, ii. 175
Crevequer:
  Alice de, w. of Hamon, ix. 153
  Dan. de, ix. 153
  Hamon (Hamo) de (fl. 1235), ix. 37, 153
  Hamon de (fl. 1284), ix. 153
  Rob. de (d. by 1166), ix. 153
  Rob. de (fl. c. 1200), ix. 146, 153
  Rob. de (fl. before 1269), ix. 146
  Rob. de (fl. 1284), ix. 153
  Rob. de (fl. 1320), ix. 247
  arms, ix. *154*
Crewe (Crew):
  Nat., Ld. Crewe, dean of Chich., ii. 51
  Thos., vii. 78
  Sir Vauncey, i. 298
Crichett:
  Ric., iv. 168
  Sarah, *see* Hughes
cricket, *see* sport
Criel:
  Sir Peter de, ii. 53
  Rob. de, ii. 93
Crimean War, *see* wars
Crimsham, *see* Pagham
Criol (Crioil, Cruel):
  Bertram de, ix. 37
  Edm. de, ix. 127 *n*
  Jn. de, ix. 127 *n*
  Rob. de, ix. 117, 127
  Sim. de, ix. 127 *n*
  fam., ix. 127
Cripps:
  Jas., vii. 188 *n*
  Jn., vii. 100
  Jn. Marten, vii. 100–1
  Mary, *see* Wood
  Rush Marten, vii. 100
  arms, vii. *100*
Crisp (Crispe):
  Eliz., m. Jn. Harrington, ix. 88
  Wm., ix. 88
  fam., ix. 89
Crispyn, Peter, prior of Wilmington, ii. 123
Croche, Ric., ix. 61
Crochon, Wal., iv. 62
Crocker, Chas., iii. 90
Crocker Hill, *see* Boxgrove
Crockett, Ralph, ii. 28
Crockham Hill, *see* Edenbridge
Crockhurst, *see* Horsham
Croft (Crofte):
  Denis de, iv. 177
  Hen., ii. 166
  Hugh de, iv. 8, 36
  Phil. de, iv. 8, 36
  Rob. de, iv. 8
  arms, iii. 151
  and see Crofts
Croft (near Hastings), i. 134
Crofte, *see* Croft
Crofts:
  Hen. Peter, vii. 41
  Jn. (fl. 1728), vii. 37
  Jn. (fl. 1774), vii. 41
  Peter Guerin, vii. 41
  fam., vii. 37
  and see Croft
Croke, Wm., iv. 229
Cromer:
  Frances, *see* Sommer
  Francis, ix. 154
  Jas., ix. 154
Crompe, *see* Crumpe
Crompton, Thos., iv. 238
Cromwell:
  Agnes, iii. 145
  Gregory, vii. 16
  Oliver, Ld. Protector, i. 526–8; ii. 38–9, 101, 321, 424; iii. 88; iv. 72 *n*
  Ralph, ii. 104
  Ric., Ld. Protector, i. 528; iv. 50,

173; vii. 17
  Thos., Ld. Cromwell, earl of Essex, ii. 17–19, 54, 58–9, 69, 75, 79, 83, 91, 96, 103, 118, 144; iii. 86 *n*; iv. 64, 84, 230; vii. 16, 41, 48, 50, 55–6, 58, 65, 69, 83, 89, 91, 95, 105, 109, 123, 135, 144, 163, 171, 214, 217–19, 224, 226–8, 235, 237, 257–8, 262, 276; ix. 151
Crookenden, ——, ii. 164
Crookshank, Edgar March, i. 306
crops (vol. ii. only):
  alsike, ii. 281
  barley, ii. 212, 280
  beans, ii. 274
  cabbages, ii. 281–2, 286
  clover, ii. 274, 281, 285–6
  corn, ii. 211–12, 273–5, 280, 286
  gratton, ii. 281–2
  hops, ii. 209, 213, 237, 261, 275, 278, 286, 298
  mangolds, ii. 281. 286
  mustard, ii. 281
  oats, ii. 274, 280–2, 285
  peas, ii. 274
  rape, ii. 280, 282, 286
  roots, ii. 274, 286
  rye, ii. 280
  swedes, ii. 281, 286
  tares, ii. 280–2
  timber, ii. 233, 294–301, 303, 306–7, 309–10, 312–25
  trefoil, ii. 280–1
  wheat, ii. 274–5, 280–1, 283, 285
crops, rotation of, ii. 211
Cros, *see* Du Cros
Crosbie (Crosseby):
  Chas., iv. 150
  Frances, *see* Thomas
  Jn. Gustavus, iii. 77; iv. 150
  Wm., master of St. James's hosp., Seaford, ii. 105
Cross:
  Edgar Herman, vii. 41
  Mrs. Odo, ix. 229
  and see Crosse
cross, churchyard, *see* architecture: ecclesiastical
Cross-in-Hand, *see* Waldron
Crossbush, *see* Lyminster
Crosse:
  Thos. Francis, warden of St. Mary's hosp., Chich., canon of Chich., ii. 102; iii. 121
  and see Cross
Crosseby, *see* Crosbie
crosses, consecration, *see* architecture: ecclesiastical
crosses, village and market, *see* architecture: civil and dom.
Crouch, Jn., vii. 58–9
Crouch Ham, *see* Earnley
Croucher (Crowcher):
  Alice, m. Thos. Greenfield, iv. 109
  Hen., iv. 109
  Jn., warden of St. Mary's hosp., Chich., ii. 102
  Jn. (d. 1562), iv. 109
  Jn. (fl. after 1744), iv. 191
  Marg., iv. 99
  Ric., iv. 109
  Wm. le (fl. 1332), iv. 136
  Wm. (fl. 1543), iv. 109
  fam., iv. 109
Crow:
  Fred., iii. 134
  Josiah, ii. 165
Crowborough (Crowborrow) (formerly in Rotherfield), i. 49; ii. 389
  Beacon, i. 43
  common, ii. 319
  Crowborough Gate, i. 55; ii. 319
  golf, ii. 477–8
  man., ii. 478
  natural history, i. 185, 187, 211–12, 215, 290
  prehist. rem., i. 329
  sch., ii. 438

Stone Cross, i. 55
Walsh (Walshes), ii. 389
Crowcher, *see* Croucher
Crowden, Chas., ii. 434, 476
Crowe, Sackville, ii. 248
Crowfoot, Eliz., iv. 53
Crowham, Rob., prior of Lewes, prebendary of Lincoln, ii. 69–70; vii. 105, 224, 235, 238
Crowham, *see* Westfield
Crowhurst, ii. 43, 301, 324; ix. 76, **77–81**, 196
  adv., ix. 81
  agric., ix. 79–80
  batrachians, i. 272
  birds, i. 283
  char., ix. 81
  ch., ii. 76; ix. 77, 79–81
    accessories, ix. 81
    architt., ii. 328 *n*, 336, 339, 378; ix. 80–1
  Crowhurst Pk., i. 53; ix. 77–8, 80
  dom. architt., ix. 77–9
  insects, i. 116, 122–3, 129, 152, 155, 174, 187, 230, 233, 235
  mammals, i. 303–4
  man., ii. 325; ix. 3, 19, 79–80, 120, 180, 241, 257
    ho., ii. 186 *n*, 325, 382; ix. 77, 76–7
  otter hunting, ii. 453; vii. 192
  pop., ii. 222
  prebend, ii. 113; ix. 81
  rly., ii. 222 *n*, 240
  trades and ind., ii. 229; ix. 77–9
  water mill, ix. 80
  woodland, ix. 80
Crowmarsh (Oxon.), ii. 52, 179
Croydon (Surr.), i. 345, 518; ii. 240; iii. 42
  Norwood, Upper, ii. 41
Cruel, *see* Criol
Crulie, Ric., *see* Ernele
Crullfield, *see* Stoneleigh
Crumpe (Crompe):
  Jn., ii. 73
  Nic., ix. 177
crusades, ii. 11, 241, 359, 367; iii. 84; ix. 2, 9, 35 *n*, 262
Cruso, Aquila, rector of Sutton, ii. 36
crustaceans, i. **245–65**
Crutchere, Jn., dean of Chich., ii. 51
Cruttenden, Eliz., ix. 200
Cryfield, *see* Stoneleigh
crypts, *see* architecture: civil and dom.; architecture: ecclesiastical
Crysford, Wm., ix. 268
Cubitt:
  Geo., Ld. Ashcombe, ii. 464; ix. 264–5
  Hen., Ld. Ashcombe, ix. 264
  Thos., ix. 265
Cuchenovere, *see* Kechenore
Cuckfield, i. 55, 533; ii. 43–4, 310, 312; vii. 5, 92, 125, 132, **147–63**
  adv., vii. 163
  agric., vii. 147
  Ansty (Anstye), i. 35; iii. 3, 53; vii. 147, 152
  Butler's Green, i. 55; iii. 42
  char., vii. 163
  ch., ii. 34; vii. *150*, 160–3, *161*
    accessories, ii. 352, 354, 356, 373; vii. 163
    architt., ii. 337, 339–40, 348–9, 370, 373, 378; vii. 160–2
  chant., ii. 419
  cts., vii. 156, 159
  Cuckfield Pk., i. 306; ii. 297, 311–12; vii. 2–3, 149–51, *150*, 157, 213
  dom. architt., ii. 386–7, 396; vii. 148–58
  fair, vii. 148, 156–7
  fossils, i. 35–9
  Hayward's Heath, *q.v.*
  inc., ii. 191
  man., vii. 2–4, 6–7, 156–60
  mkts., vii. 148, 156–7
  natural history, i. 42, 171, 174–5

Cuckfield (*cont.*):
pop., ii. 223
rly., ii. 223 *n*
rectors, ii. 416–17
roads, ii. 240; iii. 42
Rom. rem., iii. 3, 53
R.D., vii. 179
schs., ii. 397, 399, 416–21
Slough Green, i. 55
sport, ii. 446–7, 465, 480–1
Staplefield, ii. 44, 447; vii. 148, 155, 163
tanning, ii. 259–60
union, i. 539
U.D., vii. 119, 148
vicarage, ii. 8
vicars, ii. 34, 40, 416, 420–1; *and see* Burrell, Ninian; Curteis, Edm.; Fearon; Henshaw, Tobias; Vickers
Whiteman's Green, i. 55
Cuckmere, riv., i. 18, 55, 58, 475–6; iii. 2, 65
natural history, i. 43, 56–7, 62, 172, 183, 186–7, 198–9, 216, 262, 267
sport, ii. 446, 453, 464
Cuckmere Haven, *see* Seaford
Cuckney, Wm., ii. 252 *n*
Cuddington, Peter de, iv. 45
Cuddon:
Anne, m. Dan. Shilfox, iv. 212
Eliz. Henrietta, m. Jn. Sutton, iv. 212
Sir Thos., chamberlain of London, iv. 212
cudgeling, *see* sport
Cudlow (Cudlo), *see* Climping
Cuffold, *see* Cowfold
Cullen:
Chas., iii. 145
——, iii. 100 *n*
Cullen, Vct., *see* Cokayne, Chas.
Culliford, Ric., ii. 165
Cullompton (Devon), ii. 52
Culpeper (Colepeper, Colepepper, Culpepper):
Agnes, *see* Gaynesford
Anne, *see* Bolney
Benj., vii. 129
Cath., m. Ric. Infield, ii. 387
Cheney (fl. 1624), ix. 222
Sir Cheney (fl. 1635, ? another), ix. 181
Sir Edw., ii. 387; vii. 127, 129, 131–2, 142, 195–6, 218, 225–6
Eliz., w. of Jn., ix. 220 *n*
Eliz., w. of Sir Edw., *see* Farnfold
Eliz., w. of Nic., *see* Wakehurst
Eliz., w. of Thos., *see* Cheney
Jane, *see* Pellatt
Joan, *see* Holden
Sir Jn. (fl. 1348–72), ix. 222
Sir Jn. (fl. 1460), vii. 129, 225 *n*
Jn. (d. 1565), vii. 129, 132, 142, 225; ix. 220 *n*
Sir Jn. (fl. 1624), ix. 222
Marg., *see* Wakehurst
Martin, dean of Chich., ii. 51
Nic., vii. 129, 131; ix. 273
Ric. (d. by 1516), vii. 100, 129, 131; ix. 235, 273
Ric. (d. 1539), vii. 129; ix. 235
Ric. (fl. 1588), vii. 141
Thos. (d. 1321), i. 508; ii. 316, 323
Sir Thos. (d. by 1348), ix. 222
Sir Thos. (fl. 1407), ix. 222
Thos. (d. 1541), ix. 255
Thos. (fl. 1543), ix. 255
Thos. (d. 1571, ? another), vii. 142, 196, 225
Thos. (fl. 1598), ix. 56*
Thos. (d. by 1635, another), ix. 181, 222, 224
Sir Wal., ix. 222
Wm. (fl. 1535), ix. 75
Wm. (fl. 1564, ? another), ii. 24
Sir Wm. (d. 1678), M.P. for East Grinstead, vii. 129, 138, 142, 218, 226

Sir Wm. (fl. 1694), vii. 129, 138
Capt., i. 528
fam., i. 513; ii. 387; vii. 127; ix. 222–3, 255
arms, vii. 127, *129*, 131; ix. *222*
Culverden, Wm., ii. 250
Cumba forest, *see* Dallington forest
Cumbe:
Christiane de, *see* Falaise
Mat. de la, vii. 190
Mat. de la (another), vii. 190
Ric. de (fl. 1200), and his w. Sybil, ii. 123
Ric. de la (fl. before 1260), vii. 190
Ric. de la (fl. after 1260), vii. 190
Sim. de, iv. 102
and see Combe
Cumberland, duke of, *see* Henry Frederick
Cumberland, i. 168 *n*, 187; iii. 88; *and see* Carlisle
Cumbwood, *see* Dallington forest
Cuming, Jn., ii. 478
Cumpayn:
Cecily, *see* Folet
Ric., ix. 267
Cumpton, Wm. de, and his w. Mary, iv. 199
Cunna, moneyer, iii. 83
Cunningham, W., ii. 183
Curson, *see* Curzon
Curteis (Curteys, Curtis):
Augustine, ii. 407
Caroline, *see* Mascall
Cath. Sarah, m. Jn. Luxford, ix. 151
Edm., vicar of Cuckfield, ii. 27
Edw., ix. 155
Edw. Jeremiah, ix. 56, 145, 161, 273
Herb., ix. 134
Herb. Barett, ix. 71, 134, 158
Herb. Mascall, ii. 447, 470 *n*, 471–2; ix. 145, 158, 273
Jeremiah (fl. 1697), ix. 151
Jeremiah (d. 1806), ix. 145, 151, 154–5, 158, 181
Jn., ix. 62
L., ii. 167
Martha, m. Rob. Mascall, ix. 158
R.M., ii. 472 *n*
Ric., dean of Chich., bp. of Chich., ii. 26, 29, 51, 255
Rob., master of Holy Trinity hosp., Arundel, ii. 98
Whitfield, ix. 199
fam., ix. 137, 145, 149, 160
Curthose, Rob., *see* Robert, duke of Normandy
Curtis, *see* Curteis
Curwen:
E. Cecil, iii. 50, 52, 66, 68
E.V.M., *see* Ogle
Eliot, iii. 33–4, 50, 52
Curzon (Curson):
Geo., Ld. Curzon, ix. 259, 264–5
Harriett Anne, *see* Bishop
Rob. (fl. 1548), iv. 36, 64
Rob. (fl. 1835), iv. 157
Rob., Ld. Zouche, i. 306
Mr., ii. 454
Cusancia:
Jas. de, prior of Prittlewell, ii. 67
Jn. de, prior of Bermondsey, ii. 67
Wm. de, prebendary of Thurrock, ii. 115
Cust:
Pury, vii. 207
Ursula, *see* Woodcock
Custard, W.G., ii. 471 *n*
customs and services, ii. 171–83, 292, 294, 314–16, 320–1; iii. 85, 100, 105; *and see* borough English; bredgeld; castle guard; gavel; gavelkind; heccage; heriot; mede panes; tallage; works, villeins'
Cut, riv., i. 116
Cutbeard, Thos., i. 512
Cuthman, St., ii. 2; iv. 190
Cutt, Constance, ii. 99

Cutts, Jn., Ld. Cutts of Gowran, iv. 17
Cuyp, Jn., ix. 126
Cwmaman (in Aberdare, Glam.), ii. 244
Cyletona (unidentified), ii. 113
Cymen, son of Aelle, i. 334, 481; ii. 291; iii. 82
Cymenesore (Cymensora, Cymenes ora, the Owers), i. 256, 334, 481; ii. 126, 163, 291; iv. 205

Dabernoun, *see* Abernon
Dabe?usen, Heinrich van, iv. 66
Dacre:
Anne, m. Thos. Howard, duke of Norfolk, vii. 6
Eliz., *see* Bowett
Joan, m. Ric. de Fiennes, vii. 36, 114, 175, 177, 213; ix. 133
Marg., m. Ant. Browne, Vct. Montagu, iv. 52
Philippa, m. Rob. Fiennes, vii. 172, 213
Thos., Ld. Dacre, vii. 175; ix. 133
Sir Thos., i. 513; vii. 36, 175, 177
arms, ix. 171
Dacre, Lds., *see* Dacre, Thos.; Fiennes; Lennard
dairy farming, ii. 208, 212–13, 274–7, 280, 285, 289–90
Dalbiac:
Eleanor, *see* Shelley
Geo. Jn., vii. 77
Mary, vii. 77
Dalby:
Hannah, ix. 124
Wm., i. 513
Dale, Valentine, iii. 99
Dale Park (in Madehurst and Slindon), i. 48, 113, 119, 218, 220, 234, 236, 302, 305
Dalingridge (Dalingerigge, Dalingregge, Dalingrugge, Dalyngridge, Dalyngrigge, Dalyngruge, Dalyngrygge, Dalynrugge):
Alice, w. of Sir Jn., m. 2 Sir Thos. Butler, vii. 54, 257; ix. 82, 153, 263
Alice, w. of Rog., *see* Ratenden
Alice, w. of Rog., *see* Seymour
Sir Edw., i. 512; ii. 123; vii. 106 *n*, 257; ix. 79, 82, 153, 259, 261, 263
Eliz., *see* Wardedieu
Joan, vii. 54 *n*
Jn. (fl. 1309), ii. 315
Sir Jn. (d. 1417), i. 513; ii. 323; vii. 54, 101, 257; ix. 82, 153, 263
Philippa (Philippe), m. Sir Thos. Lewknor, vii. 54, 258; ix. 153, 263
Sir Ric., ii. 305; vii. 54, 257; ix. 82, 263
Rob., i. 510
Rog. de (fl. 1273), ii. 315
Rog. (d. c. 1380), vii. 106 *n*, 257
Thos., vii. 257
Wal., vii. 54, 257; ix. 153, 263*
Wm. (fl. 1309), ii. 315
Wm. (d. by 1443), vii. 257
fam., ii. 360–1; vii. 97; ix. 270
arms, vii. *54*; ix. *82*, 216, *263*
Dalkeith, earl of, *see* Scott, Francis
Dallaway, Jas., iii. 10, 12, 15–16, 18, 66; iv. 203
Dalling, Rob., ii. 61
Dallingridge, *see* Dalingridge
Dallingridge, *see* Forest Row
Dallington (Dalynton), i. 57; ii. 43, 324; ix. 125, 138, 193, 210, 226, **232–4**
adv., ix. 234
botany, i. 61
Buckwell, *see* Ashburnham
char., ix. 234, 244
chase, ii. 189
ch., ii. 76; ix. 233–4, *236*
accessories, ii. 356; ix. 234
archit., ii. 336, 339–40, 378; ix. 233–4
deanery, ii. 42–3

dean, ii. 42
dom. archit., ii. 386; ix. 232–3
fair, ix. 233
forest (or Brightling, Bristlinga, Burgherse, Burwash, Combe, Cumba, Cumbwood, Werth forest), i.
   50; ii. 291, 293–7, 324–5; ix. 230,
   233; and see Dallington: chase
   bounds, ii. 324
   quarrying, ii. 230
insects, i. 112, 121, 125–7, 129, 134,
   138–9, 141, 150, 154, 157–9, 194,
   216, 218, 220, 224, 227–30, 232,
   236–7
man., ix. 226, 229, 233
pop., ii. 223
Rom. rem., iii. 29, 31
trades and ind., ii. 247; ix. 126
vicar, ii. 35; ix. 234; and see Green,
   Thos.
Dally, Ric., iv. 172
Dalrymple:
   Cordelia, see Apsley
   Jas., ix. 84
   Jn. Apsley, ix. 84, 254
Dalton:
   Sir Jn., ix. 139
   Margery, see Poynings
Dalyngridge (Dalyngrigge, Dalyngruge,
   Dalyngrygge, Dalynrugge), see
   Dalingridge
Dalynton, see Dallington
Damme (unidentified, ? Netherlands),
   ii. 134
Danebury, see Wallop, Nether
Danecombe, Wm., ii. 242
Daneghithe, see Hurstpierpoint: Danny
   Pk.
Danehill, ii. 44
   Chelwood (Chalwood, Charlwood), ii.
   319
   Danehurst, ii. 463
Danehill Horsted hund., i. 537–8; ii. 225
Danehurst, see Danehill
Danes, i. 483; iii. 83, 166; ix. 1
Dangstein House, see Terwick
Daniel, prior of Sele, ii. 62
Daniel (Danyel, Danyell):
   Eliz., vii. 96
   Jn., prior of Lewes, ii. 69–70
   Ric., mayor of Chich., iii. 91
   Rob., vii. 96
   Rog., ii. 113; ix. 26
   Wm. Barker, ii. 449
Daniel-Tyssen, Amherst, ii. 249
Danmartin:
   Sara de, see Bendeville
   Steph. de, ix. 201
Dann (Danne):
   Thos., iv. 39
   W., ii. 253
Danny, see Hurstpierpoint
Dantesey:
   Joan de, see Bavent
   Sir Jn. de, iv. 45
Dantzig, see Gdansk
Danvers:
   Muriel, see Dunstanville
   Rob., iv. 41
Danyel (Danyell), see Daniel
Danzig, see Gdansk
Darby (Darbie, Darbye):
   Anne, see Smith
   Jn., ii. 41
   Mic., ii. 251
   Susan, see Wetherell
   Thos., vii. 266
   fam., ii. 41
Darbysher, Father, i. 518
Darcy:
   Hen., iv. 42
   Thos., Ld. Darcy, iv. 42; ix. 133
Dare, Rob., ix. 248
Darel, see Darrell
Darent, riv., 453
Darnall (? in Fletching), ii. 463
Darrell (Darel, Dorrell):
   Bridget, w. of Thos., iv. 163

Edw., iv. 163, 231
Ivo, canon of Chich., warden of St.
   Mary's hosp., Chich., ii. 101–2;
   iii. 139 n
Joan, see Knottesford
Marg., m. Edw. Darrell, iv. 163
Marmaduke, iv. 163
Thos. (fl. 1564), ii. 24
Thos. (fl. 1603), iv. 163, 231
Wm., iv. 163
Mrs., ii. 29
fam., ii. 27, 29
   arms, vii. 10
Dartford (Kent), ii. 238
Dartmouth, earls of, iv. 128; and see
   Legge, Wm.
Dartmouth (Devon), ii. 135, 137, 155,
   247; ix. 68
Darvel forest (Darum wood), ii. 296,
   298, 325
Darwell, see Mountfield: Derfold
Darwell, riv., ix. 217
Daubeney, see Aubigny
Daundevill:
   Jn., iv. 136
   Rog., iv. 136
Dautreye, see Dawtrey
Daves, see Davis
David, prior of Sele, ii. 62
David the parson, vii. 276
Davidson:
   Blanche, vii. 189
   Charlotte, see Wood
   Randall Geo., vii. 180
   Wm., vii. 189
Davie:
   Geo., vii. 157
   Mary, m. Ric. Ward, vii. 157
Davies:
   Eliz., m. Thos. Phillips Lamb, vii.
   258, 284
   Eliz., w. of Wm., see Watson
   Mary, vii. 258
   Phil., ii. 165
   Wm., vii. 258, 284
   Mr., ix. 264
   his w., see Sivier
   and see Davis
Davington (Kent), priory, ix. 144
Davis (Daves):
   Barnard, i. 335–6
   David, ii. 409
   F.B., iii. 70
   Jane, m. —— Weekes, vii. 57
   Jn., ix. 156
   Sir Jn. Brewer, ix. 235
   Launcelot, ix. 235
   his w., see Michelborne
   Ric., vii. 41, 57
   Wm. (fl. 1569), ii. 25
   Wm. (fl. 1741), vii. 41, 57
   fam., ix. 53, 156, 235
   and see Davies
Dawe (Daw):
   Rob., iii. 165; vii. 40; ix. 257
   Wm., ix. 207
Dawes (Daws):
   Anne, iii. 162
   Jas., ix. 224
   Jane, see Blagden
   Jn., iii. 162
   Mary E., ix. 268
   Wal., ix. 54
Dawestone hund., ix. 164
Dawkins, see Boyd-Dawkins
Dawnay, Hen., Vct. Downe, ii. 443
Daws, see Dawes
Dawson:
   Chas., i. 323 n, 326–7, 478; ix. 15,
   17–18
   Thos., ix. 202
   Thomasin, ix. 202
   Wm., ii. 431
Dawtrey (Alta Ripa, Dautreye,
   Dawtry):
   Alice, iv. 128
   Alice, w. of Jn., see Boys
   Alice, see Lovell

Alice, see Mill
And. (fl. 1296), iv. 174 n
And. (fl. 1440), iv. 174
Anne, m. Thos. Stanley, iv. 128
Cecily, see Roche
Dorothy, see Stoneley
Eve, m. 1 Rog. de Shelvestrode, 2
   Wm. Paynel, 3 Edw. de St. John,
   iv. 34–5, 56, 85, 108, 110, 145*,
   176, 213
Sir Francis (fl. 1548), iv. 157, 216
Francis (fl. 1624–33), iv. 98, 128
Isabel, see Shirley
Jn. (fl. 1292), iv. 58, 128
Jn. (d. 1398), iv. 174
Jn. (fl. 1403), iv. 174
Jn. (fl. 1498), iv. 98 n, 216
Sir Jn. (d. 1518), iv. 157
Sir Jn. (d. 1542), iv. 128
Sir Jn. (d. 1549), iv. 98*, 128
Nic., iv. 128
Ric., iv. 128
Sarah, m. Edw. Luther, iv. 174–5
Wm. (fl. 1246–99), i. 506; iv. 108,
   110, 144–5, 212
Wm. (fl. 1534–73), ii. 24; iv. 115, 128,
   174
Wm. (fl. 1573, another), iv. 174
Wm. (d. 1758), iv. 174
fam., iv. 56, 58 n, 98, 174
   arms, iv. 128, 174; vii. 10
Day (Deye):
   A.R.W., ii. 470 n
   Frances, see Middleton
   Geo., bp. of Chich., ii. 21–2, 404,
   406; iii. 112, 124
   Jn., master of Playden hosp., ii. 105
   Jn. (fl. 1835), ii. 458
   Jn. (fl. 1873), ix. 207
   Rob., vii. 34, 124
   arms, iii. 112
de la Warr:
   Earls, see Sackville-West; West
   Lds., see Warr; West
De Laet, Mr., ix. 235
Deacon, Ronald, iii. 105
Deal (Kent), ii. 143, 160
   cast., ii. 395; ix. 185
   Sandown cast., ii. 395; ix. 185
Dealtry, Miss, vii. 158
Dean (Deane, Deen):
   Jas., ii. 469
   Ric., sacrist of Bosham, ii. 112
   Thos., iv. 149
   and see Dene
Dean, East (E. Suss.), see Eastdean
Dean, East (W. Suss.), i. 11, 287*; ii.
   36, 43; iv. 58, 88, 94–6, 118
   adv., 90, 95–6, 100–1, 120
   chase, iv. 94
   ch., ii. 48; iv. 94–6, 96
      accessories, ii. 356; iv. 96
      archit., ii. 332, 340, 350, 371–2; iv.
      95–6
   dom. archit., iv. 94
   Hugabeorg, q.v.
   hunting, ii. 442
   man., ii. 305; iv. 94–7, 118, 174; ix.
   193
   pk., ii. 297, 303; iv. 94–5
   pop., ii. 221
   rectory, ii. 408
   roads, iv. 94
   royal visit, i. 505
   Selhurst pk., ii. 297, 303; iv. 94
   tithes, ii. 408; iv. 96
   woodland, iv. 94
   Winkins wood, ii. 303; iv. 94
Dean, Forest of (Glos.), i. 165; ii. 241;
   iii. 29
Dean, West (E. Suss.), see Westdean
Dean, West (W. Suss.), i. 108; ii. 43,
   206; iv. 24 n, 31, 88–9, 97–101, 118
   adv., iv. 90–1, 100–1, 120
   Chilgrove, i. 282; ii. 467; iii. 53; iv.
   97, 99
      adv., iv. 90, 100–1, 120
      man., iv. 97–8

Dean, West (W. Suss.)
  Chilgrove (cont.):
    prehist. rem., i. 329
    ch., ii. 48; iv. 90, 97, 99–100
      accessories, ii. 356; iv. 100
      archit., ii. 349, 365; iv. 99–100
    Civil War, i. 524; ii. 36
    dom. archit., iv. 97
    earthworks, i. 480
    insects, i. 180, 186, 189
    man., ii. 176; iv. 90, 94–5, 97–9, 118, 122, 199
    pk., i. 180; ii. 303, 462; iv. 97
    pop., ii. 221
    rly., iv. 97
    rectory, ii. 408; iv. 99
    roads, iv. 97
    Rom. rem., iii. 53, 66
    royal visit, i. 505
    sport, ii. 442–3, 467
    tithes, ii. 408; iv. 100
    vicarage, ii. 8; iv. 100
    woods, iv. 43, 97
Dean hund., ii. 224; vii. 1, **215**, 241
Deane, see Dean
deaneries, see Chich.: dioc.
Deanton (? Denton or Dentun), ii. 3
Dear:
  Bridget, see Ashburnham
  Francis, iii. 145
  Jn., iii. 162
  Martha (d. 1807), iii. 162–3, 165, 168
  Martha (another), iii. 162
  Sarah, iii. 162
Dearden, Capt., vii. 158
Dearling:
  Hannah, w. of Jas., iii. 164
  Jas. (d. 1781), iii. 164, 168
  Jas., s. of Jas., iii. 164
  Jas., s. of Jn., iii. 164
  Jn., iii. 164
  Jn., s. of Jas., iii. 164
  Mary, iii. 164
  Mary, w. of Jn., iii. 164
  Sarah, iii. 164
  Sarah, w. of Jas., see Furlonger
  Wm., iii. 105
Decheham, fam., ix. 92 n
decoration and fittings, see architecture: civil and dom.
decoration in stone, see architecture: ecclesiastical
Dee, Francis, dean of Chich., bp. of Peterborough, ii. 51; iv. 233
Deeds:
  Eliz., see Drake
  Julius, ix. 230
Deen, see Dean
deer, i. **305–7**; and see livestock
Defoe, Dan., ii. 160, 298; iii. 89; vii. 18; ix. 5
Delahay, Godfrey, ii. 255
Delap, Jn., rector of Iford and Kingston, vii. 53, 249
Delapré (Northants.), abbey, vii. 279
Dell, R.B., ii. 480
Dell Quay, see Appledram
Delmé, Mr., ii. 460
Delves:
  Cordelia, m. Jas. Cranston, ix. 86
  Nic., ix. 24, 181
  Thos. (d. by 1669), ix. 24
  Thos., vicar of Bexhill (1661–77), ix. 86*, 122
Delvey, Eliz., ii. 362
Demesford, see Dumpford
Den, see Dene
den, see strand and den
Denbighshire:
  Carreghova, castellan, see Strange, Ralph le
Dendy, Geo., iii. 161
Dene (Den):
  Alice, iv. 5
  Aubrey of, ix. 14–15
  Ela de, m. 1 Jordan de Sackville, 2 Wm. de Marci, ii. 86
  (or Berelynde), Maud de, ix. 146

Ralph de, ii. 86
Rob. de (fl. c. 1100), i. 539
Rob. de (fl. after 1180), ii. 86, 189, 298
Rob. de (fl. 1281), ix. 10
Sibella, w. of Rob., ii. 298
Thos., master of Holy Trinity hosp., Arundel, ii. 98
Wm. de, prior of Hastings, ii. 76–7
  and see Adeane; Dean
Deneswyrth, see Densworth
Dengayne, see Engayne
Dengemareis, Alfric (Aluric) de, ii. 172, 174
Dengemarsh, see Dungeness
Denham:
  Atherton, vii. 183
  Benj., and his w. Marg., vii. 183
  David (fl. 1678), ix. 88
  David (fl. 1702–26), ix. 192
  Dorothy, w. of Atherton, vii. 183
  Thos., ii. 414
  Mr., ix. 101
Denis, abbot of Robertsbridge, ii. 71, 73
Denis, prior of Arundel, ii. 120, 398
Denman:
  Sir Thos., Ld. Denman, vii. 132
  Wm., vii. 227
Denmark, Anne of, see Anne
Denmark, i. 318; ii. 47, 126–9, 365
  king, see Swegen
  prince of, see George
  and see Copenhagen
Denne, La, see La Denne
Denne Park, see Horsham
Dennett:
  Jn. (d. 1727), vii. 138, 140
  Jn. (d. 1759), vii. 138
  Susannah, m. Jn. Lintott, vii. 138
  Thos., vii. 138
Dennis (Dennys, Denys):
  Geo., iv. 52
  L., ii. 477
  Marg., m. 1 Wm. Rose, 2 Wal. Dobell, iv. 52
  Maur., and his w. Eliz., ix. 150
  Rog., iv. 73
Denny, Anne, m. Geo. Goring, i. 527
Dennys, see Dennis
Denstone (Staffs.), ii. 432–3
Densworth (Deneswyrth), Wal. de, iv. 191
Densworth, see Funtington
Denton, Wm., iv. 83–4
Denton, ii. 3, 44, 225; iv. 66; vii. 42, 62
  ch., ii. 339–40, 352–3, 356, 358, 361, 376, 378
  ch. ho., ii. 383
Denton Island, see Newhaven
Dentun, see Deanton
Denys, see Dennis
deodands, vii. 254
Deopham (Norf.), vii. 4
Dependents, iii. 164
depopulation, vii. 66; ix. 27
Deptford (London, formerly Kent):
  Brockley abbey, ii. 86
  New Cross, iii. 45
Derby:
  ctss. of, see Morley, Mary
  earls of, see Ferrers, Wm.; Stanley
Derbyshire, i. 318, 344 n; iii. 63; iv. 167
  and see Matlock
Derfold, see Mountfield
Dering:
  Dan., ii. 165
  Eleanor, see Dyke
  Hen., iv. 110
  Nic., iv. 110
  Thos., iv. 110
  Unton, ii. 165
  Wm., iv. 108, 110
Dertmouth, Ric., abbot of Battle, ii. 55
Despagne, Nic., ix. 127
Despenser (Despencer):
  Eliz. le, see Badlesmere
  Hugh le, earl of Winchester (d. 1326), i. 508; ii. 67, 323; ix. 127, 195

Hugh le (fl. 1338), iv. 167
Isabel, m. Ric. FitzAlan, earl of Arundel, vii. 3
Thos. le, Ld. Despenser, ii. 323
fam., i. 508; ix. 195
Despenser, baroness, see Nevill, Mary
Deulebenie, Jew of Chich., i. 506; iii. 80
Devenish (Devenishe):
  Anne, see Tawke
  Cecily, w. of Wm., iv. 176–7
  Eliz., see Hoo
  Jn. (fl. 1439), ii. 79; ix. 119
  Sir Jn. (fl. 1465), ix. 119, 233, 248
  Marg., see Hurst
  Ric., ix. 120, 138, 233, 248*
  Thos., iv. 51, 177, 230; ix. 120, 123, 207, 233, 248
  Wm., M.P. for Lewes, vii. 31
  Wm. (fl. 1564, ? another), ii. 24
  Wm. (fl. to 1584, ? another), iv. 106, 176–7; ix. 138 n, 207, 233, 248
  fam., ix. 229
Deveral, Wm. de, master of hosp. of St. Jas. and St. Mary, Chich., ii. 100
Devereux:
  Sir Jn., ix. 79
  Rob., earl of Essex (d. 1601), i. 518, 520
  Rob., earl of Essex (d. 1646), ix. 234
Devil's Dyke, see Poynings
Devon:
  ctss. of, see Clare, Amice
  earl of, see Courtenay, Hugh de; Redvers
  Devonshire, dukes of, ix. 61; and see Cavendish
Devonshire, i. 41, 44, 68, 180, 191; ii. 141, 158, 286, 472; iv. 52; ix. 52
  North Devon Regiment, i. 534
  Torre abbey, canon of, see Speer
  and see Beer; Bovey Tracy; Budleigh Salterton; Cullompton; Dartmouth; Exeter; Plymouth; Tavistock; Torbay; Torquay
Devonshire Park, see Eastbourne
dew-ponds, i. 311, 460–1
Dewé, Mr., ii. 450
Dewsbury (Yorks. W.R.), ii. 67
Dewyas:
  Alice, see Tregoz
  Jn., iv. 167
Deye, see Day
dials, scratch (or mass), see architecture: ecclesiastical
Diamond Shoal, see Hastings
Dickens, Chas., ii. 431
Dickenson:
  Bernard, vii. 74
  Ezekiel, vii. 74
  Frances, see Barnard
  Mrs., vii. 74
Dicker, see Hellingly
Dickins, Chas., see Scrase Dickins
Dicul of Bosham, see Bosham
Didling, iv. 3, **6–7**, 30, 39
  adv., iv. 7, 32, 90, 100, 120
  ch., iv. 6–7, 7
    accessories, ii. 355, 359; iv. 7
    archit., ii. 339; iv. 7
  Civil War, ii. 36
  dom. archit., iv. 6
  man., iv. 6–7, 9, 34, 36, 56
  pop., ii. 220
  roads, iv. 6
  tithes, iv. 7
  woods, iv. 6
Dieppe (Seine-Maritime, France), i. 516; ii. 27, 158, 192, 234, 263, 268
Digby (Dygby):
  Geo., earl of Bristol, ii. 322
  Rob., vicar choral of Bosham, ii. 111
  Wriothesley, ix. 88
Diggens (Diggons):
  Edw., iv. 202
  Francis, iv. 202
  Thos., ix. 202
Digges (Diggs, Dyges):
  Sir Dudley, ix. 145

Judith, *see* Rose
Sir Maur., iv. 52
Thos., ix. 155
Diggons, *see* Diggens
Diggs, *see* Digges
Dilft, Cornelius van der, ix. 151
Dilke:
  Chas., iii. 147
  Emma, iii. 147
  Mary, iii. 147
  Sarah, w. of Chas., iii. 147
  Wm., iii. 147
  Wm. Wentworth, iii. 147
Dill (La Tille, Latille, Thille) hund., i. 537; ii. 182 *n*, 226; ix. 1
Din, Thos., *see* Wood
Dingley:
  Anne, *see* Harleston
  Chas., iv. 230
  Jn. (fl. 1588), iv. 230
  Jn. (fl. 1615), iv. 230
  Jn. (fl. 1675), iv. 230
  Jn., his s., iv. 230
  Ric., iv. 230
  arms, iv. *230*
Diocletian, Rom. emperor, ii. 241; iii. 4
Diosza (fl. *c.* 740), iv. 218 *n*
Ditchfield, Edw., iv. 223; vii. 224
Ditchling, i. 55, 483; ii. 43–4, 310; vii. 3, 51, 92, **102–9**, *103*, 217
  adv., vii. 108–9*, 171
  char., vii. 109
  ch., ii. 48, 68; vii. 106–8, *107, 108,* 123
    accessories, ii. 352–4, 356, 359, 361; vii. 108
    archit., ii. 231, 340, 344, 348, 373, 375–6; vii. 106–8
  convent, vii. 102
  cts., vii. 105
  Ditchling Beacon, i. 55; vii. 102–3
    earthworks, i. 455, **460–1**, *461*, 466, 469–70
  Ditchling Pk., ii. 295–7, 310, 312; vii. 104–5, 203, 213
  dom. archit., ii. 384, *384*, 386, 391; vii. 103–4
  Dominican community, vii. 103
  earthworks, i. 479
  fair, vii. 104
  Fragbarrow (Frekeburgh), vii. 105
  hunting, ii. 296
  inc., vii. 104–5
  insects, i. 171–2, 181, 185, 187–9, 192, 195–7, 199–201
  man., vii. 2–4, 89, 104–6, 129, 133–4, 168, 175, 179, 280
    Piddingworth, vii. 2, 106
  mkt., vii. 104
  nonconf., vii. 103
  poor relief, vii. 109
  pop., ii. 225
  riots, ii. 206 *n*
  Rom. rem., iii. 54
  royal visits, i. 508; ii. 296
  St. Dominic's Press, vii. 103
  stud farm, vii. 3, 105
  trades and ind., ii. 254, 259, 262; vii. 103
Ditton's Wood (unidentified), i. 68
Dive (Dyve):
  Guy de, iv. 59
  Hen., iv. 59
  Hugh de, vii. 96
  Joan, w. of Jn., m. 2 Sir Wm. Breton, iv. 59
  Jn. (fl. 1310), and his w. Margery, iv. 59
  Jn. (fl. 1327, another), iv. 59
  Lucy de, *see* Cheney
  Marcia, w. of Hen., iv. 59
  Maud de, vii. 96
  Wm. de, iv. 59
Dixon:
  Augustina Ivens Mary, *see* Wilder
  Chas., iv. 122, 126–7
  F., iii. 68
  Fred., i. 27

Geo. (sr.), iii. 147
Geo. (jr.), iii. 147
Mary, iii. 147
Dixter, *see* Northiam
Dixterue (Dykesterue):
  Florence de, ix. 273 *n*
  Steph. de, ix. 273 *n*
Dobbs, Ric., ld. mayor of London, ii. 435
Dobell:
  Barnham, iv. 212; vii. 114
  Eliz., m. Thos. Peckham, iv. 200 *n*
  Grisel, *see* Farrington
  Marg., *see* Dennis
  Mary, vii. 114
  Mary, m. Thos. Lane, vii. 89, 114–15
  Mary, *see* Stapley
  Wal. (d. 1558), vii. 224
  Wal. (fl. 1574), vii. 224
  Wal. (d. 1625), vii. 89, 100, 113–14, 117, 224
  Wal. (d. 1640), vii. 114, 224, 227
  Wal. (fl. *c.* 1650), iv. 52
  Wal. (d. 1661, ? another), i. 529; vii. 114
  Wal. (d. 1694), sheriff of Suss., vii. 114, 117
  Wm., iv. 212; vii. 111, 114
  arms, vii. *114*
Dober, Rog., vii. 36
Dobson:
  Eliz., vii. 106
  Jn., vii. 106
Dobunni (Boduni), iii. 1
Docwra, Sir Thos., prior of the Knights Hospitaller, iv. 76
Dodd:
  Bart., iv. 155–6
  Francis, iv. 155–6
  Moses, ii. 409
Doddridge, Jn., rector of Whatlington, ix. 114
Dodman, the (Cornw.), ii. 165
Dodson:
  Sir Jn., vii. 80
  Jn. Chas., Ld. Monk Bretton, vii. 81, 85
  Jn. Wm., Ld. Monk Bretton, vii. 85
  fam., vii. 32
  arms, vii. *81*
dog fighting, *see* sport
Doget (Dogett):
  Jn., master of Arundel coll., ii. 109
  Maud, *see* Socknersh
  Rog., ix. 229 *n*
Dogger bank, ii. 165
Doisnel, Juliana, m. Wm. FitzAudelin, ix. 206
Dollfus, M., i. 260
Dollyng, Thos., abbot of Durford, ii. 91
Dolman, Mr., ii. 25
Dolyn, Ant., *see* Becku
Domesday survey, i. **351–451**
domestic architecture, *see* architecture: civil and dom.
Domitian, Rom. emperor, i. 344
Donaldson, Anna Maria, *see* Montagu
Doncaster (Yorks. W.R.), Wheatley Hall, ix. 132
Donewico, Clement de, ii. 93
Donne:
  Jn. de la, *see* Ottehale
  Maud de la, m. —— Ottehale, vii. 121
  Ric. de la, vii. 121
  and see Dunn
Donnington, i. 188; ii. 43, 466; iv. 133, **150–2**, 165, 198
  adv., iv. 152
  ch., iv. 150–1, *151*
    archit., ii. 340, 373; iv. 150–1
  dom. archit., iv. 150
  guild, ii. 21; iv. 152
  inc., iv. 150
  Kingsham, *see* Chichester: Kingsham
  man., iv. 150, 152
  pop., ii. 220
  Rom. rem., iii. 54
  tithes, iv. 152

vicarage, ii. 8
Donovan, A., ii. 446
Donzy, Hervé de, count of Nevers, i. 495
doors and doorways, *see* architecture: ecclesiastical
Dore:
  Joan, w. of Rog., *see* Basset
  Rog., iv. 144
d'Orival, *see* Orival
Dorking (Surr.), ii. 240, 306; iii. 38; vii. 1, 6
  Leith Hill, i. 49, 290; iii. 32–3, 39
Dorkynge, Jn., ii. 261
Dormar, Lady, *see* Collier, Kath.
Dormer, Chas., Ld. Dormer, and his w. Eliz., iv. 109
Dormer, Lady, *see* Collier, Kath.
Dorrell, *see* Darrell; Dorrill
Dorrien:
  Henrietta, *see* Le Clerk
  Jn., iv. 104
Dorrill, Ric., ii. 166
Dorset:
  dukes of, *see* Sackville; Sackville-Germain
  earls of, ii. 322; vii. 69; *and see* Sackville
  marquess of, *see* Grey: Hen., Thos.
Dorset, i. 5, 19, 44, 47, 111, 164 *n*, 180, 535; ii. 127, 136, 141, 253; ix. 52; *and see* Ackling Dyke; Bokerly Dyke; Bradford; Cerne Abbas; Corfe Castle; Lyme Regis; Purbeck; Shaftesbury; Sherborne; Sturminster Marshall; Swanage; Tarrant; Tyneham; Weymouth
Douglas:
  And., ii. 164–5
  Jas., vicar of Preston, i. 337; iii. 50; vii. 269
  Stair, ii. 166
  Wm., duke of Queensberry, ii. 456
Dove:
  Jane, vii. 71
  Thos., ii. 166
dovecotes, *see* architecture: civil and dom.
Dover (Dubra):
  Jn. de, abbot of Battle, ii. 53, 55, 65, 73
  Ric. of, abp. of Cant., ii. 53, 63
Dover (Dubrae, Dubris) (Kent), i. 495, 501; ii. 11, 67, 129–30, 134, 157, 233; iii. 5, 10; ix. 9, 34–5, 55
  bp., ii. 94–7; *and see* Yngworth
  cast., i. 300, 500–1; ii. 142, 155, 307, 325; ix. 35
  constables, ix. 37, 50
  charters, ii. 127; ix. 38
  Chronicle, i. 499
  cts., ii. 146; ix. 38–9
  defences, ii. 144, 158
  fishing, ii. 235
  geology, i. 8
  local govt., ix. 10–11
  mint, i. 349
  port, ii. 154–5; ix. 38
  privileges, ix. 37
  Rom. rem., iii. 8
  royal visit, i. 492
  Shakespeare's Cliff, i. 49
  shipping, ii. 155
  straits, i. 18; ii. 125, 130, 148
Dow, Ellen, ix. 32
Downe, Vct., *see* Dawnay
Downes: •
  Jn., M.P. for Arundel, i. 529; iv. 166, 199
  Ric., iv. 166
Downing, Edw., iv. 152
Downley, *see* Singleton
Downs, North, i. 18; iii. 34, 45
Downs, South, i. 19, 55–6, 155, 235, 274, 333, 524; iii. 2–4
  A.-S. rem., i. 335
  birds, i. 275–6, 278, 290–1
  botany, i. 46, 60, 65

Downs, South (*cont.*):
  geology, i. 9, 12, 14, 19, 23–5
  hunting, i. 302, 305
  prehist. rem., i. 311, 313
  roads, iii. 32, 42, 47, 68–9
Downs, the (English Channel), ii. 158, 160, 162, 165
Downshire, mchnss. of, *see* Hill, Caroline Frances
Downton, Jn., ix. 279
Downton, *see* Duncton
Doyly:
  Francis, master of St. Jas.'s hosp., Chich., iii. 162, 167 *n*
  Mary, m. Rog. Tupper, iii. 162
drainage, agric., ii. 274; iv. 195
Drake:
  Eliz., m. Julius Deeds, ix. 230
  Sir Francis, ii. 153
  Jas., ii. 166
  Martha, m. —— Griffiths, ix. 230
  Martha, w. of Ralph, *see* Glydd
  Ralph (d. 1694), ix. 230
  Ralph (d. 1731), ix. 230
Drakys, Jn., vii. 183
draper, Sim. the, *see* Simon
Draper:
  Jn., ii. 165
  ——, iii. 164
Drayton, Mic., ii. 192; iii. 62
Drayton, *see* Oving
Dresser, H.E., i. 278 *n*
Dreux, Peter de, duke of Brittany, i. 495
Drew (Drewe):
  Beatrice F., ix. 257
  Bradshawe, iv. 185, 191 *n*, 195
  Dorothy, m. Harpocrates de Otten, iv. 191 *n*
  Dorothy, w. of Rog., *see* Bradshaw
  Francis (sr.), iv. 185
  Francis (jr.), iv. 185
  Jn. (fl. 1404), ii. 86
  Jn. (fl. 1788), iv. 213
  Martha, m. 1 Sir Greg. Norton, 2 Rob. Gordon, Vct. Kenmure, iv. 185, 195
  Rog., iv. 185, 191 *n*
Drewell (Druell):
  Marg., *see* Wood
  Thos., iv. 51
  Wm., iv. 51
Drewitt:
  Ellen Charlotte, iv. 170
  R.D., i. 302
Driby (Dryby):
  Alice de, m. Wm. de Bernak, iv. 14, 41, 98, 115, 123, 168
  Joan de, *see* Tattersall
  Sim. de, iv. 123
Drigsell, *see* Salehurst
Drinkwater:
  Jas., iii. 164
  Mary, w. of Jas., iii. 164
  Ric., iii. 164
  Ruth, w. of Ric., iii. 164
  Thos., iii. 164
  Woodruffe, iv. 210
Dripping Pan, *see* Southover
Droseto:
  Geof. de, vii. 224
  Rob. de, vii. 224
  Wm. de, vii. 224
Drosey, *see* Rosey
Drove, *see* Singleton
Druell, *see* Drewell
Drummond, Hugh, iii. 126
Dry Hill, *see* Lingfield
Dryby, *see* Driby
Du Cros, Sir Art., iv. 226; ix. 30
Du Mont, A. Neven, ii. 447
Dubletmaker, Thos., iii. 97
Dublin (Irel.), i. 344 *n*; ii. 134, 236, 254, 423
  Trinity Coll., *q.v.*
Dubois, N., vii. 9
Dubra (Dubrae, Dubris), *see* Dover
Duddington, *see* Hailsham
Duddles, *see* Ashdown forest

Duddleswell, *see* Maresfield
Dudeney:
  Mrs. Hen., vii. 20
  Jn., ii. 284; vii. 221
Dudley:
  And., ix. 196
  Ann, m. Rob. Hall, ix. 191
  E., ii. 452
  Edm., i. 515; ii. 412; iv. 92; vii. 84, 87, 242; ix. 3, 196
  Eliz., m. Thos. Ashburnham, ix. 190–1
  Eliz., w. of sir Jn., *see* Bramshott
  Jas. de, ix. 177
  Jane, *see* Guldeford
  Sir Jn. (fl. 1479), iv. 28, 92
  Sir Jn., Vct. Lisle, earl of Warwick, duke of Northumberland, ii. 145; iv. 92, 231 *n*; vii. 85, 87; ix. 151, 177, 196
  ——, w. of Sir Edm., *see* Windsor fam., ix. 183
Dudley, earl of, *see* Ward, Jn. Wm.
Dudney & Co., ii. 263
d'Udy, Mrs., iv. 4
Duer, Roland, iii. 146
Duèse, Jocelin, cardinal bp. of Albano, rector of Pagham, ii. 12*; iv. 233
Duffield, Geo., and his w. Anne, ix. 233, 237
Duffus (Morayshire), vii. 268
Duguay-Trouin, ——, ii. 166
Duke:
  Edw., ix. 177
  Sir Jas., ii. 277
  Mat., ix. 177
  Ric., ix. 177
  Thos., ix. 177
  (or Francis), Wm., iv. 5
  Wm. (fl. 1607), ix. 177
  Wm. (fl. 1860), iii. 74, 76
Dumare:
  Gilb. de, ix. 113
  Warin de, ix. 113
Dumbrell (Dumrell):
  Jn. (fl. 1577), vii. 238
  Jn. (fl. *c.* 1637), and his w., ii. 34
  Ric., vii. 224
  Misses, vii. 109
Dumfries (Scot.), i. 535
Dummer (Dummere, Dunmere):
  Ric. (fl. 1316), iv. 213
  Ric. le (fl. 1336), iv. 177
  Thos. de (sr.), iv. 213
  Thos. de (jr.), iv. 213
Dumo, Ralph de, prior of Boxgrove, ii. 57, 59
Dumouriez, General, ii. 125
Dumpford, *see* Trotton
Dumpford (Demesford, Hamesford) hund., i. 504, 538; ii. 220–1; iv. 1, **3**
  constable, iv. 28
  ct., iv. 30
Dumrell, *see* Dumbrell
Duncan-Jones, A.S., dean of Chich., iii. 111, 130
Duncombe:
  Geo. (fl. 1650), iv. 24
  Geo. (fl. 1692), iv 24
  Jane, *see* Stynt
  Jn., iv. 24
  Martha, iv. 24
Duncton (Downton), i. 49, 109*; ii. 43, 207, 218, 468; iii. 47
  ch., ii. 362
  Duncton Common, i. 52
  Duncton Hill, i. 47
  paper ind., ii. 238
  pk., ii. 297
  rectors, ii. 439
  Rom. rem., iii. 4, 24, 47
Dundas, Lawr., earl of Zetland, ii. 444
Dungate:
  Ric., and his w. Mary, vii. 190
  Thos. Huett, vii. 190
Dungeness (Dengemarsh, Dungemarsh) (Kent), i. 2, 72; ii. 52, 128, 136, 157–8, 161–2, 172; ix. 34 *n*, 35, 55

levels, ii. 159
light, ii. 155, 269
Dunk (Dunke):
  Anne, m. Geo. Montagu, earl of Halifax, ix. 264, 274
  Anne, m. 1 Jn. Luxford, 2 Thos. Ray, ix. 248
  Beatrice, ix. 248
  Bryan, ix. 248
  Bryant (? another), ix. 235
  David, ix. 197
  Denny, ix. 248
  Edw., ix. 248
  Frances, ix. 248
  (formerly Montagu), Geo., earl of Halifax, iv. 93, 113, 122, 127, 131; ix. 264, 274
    his dau., *see* Montagu, Anna Maria
  Jn., ix. 26, 235
  Mary, ix. 248
  N., ii. 471
  Ric., ix. 235
    his w., *see* Michelborne
  Sir Thos., ix. 264, 274
Dunkirk (Nord, France), ii. 148–9, 156–8, 160, 268
Dunmere, *see* Dummer
Dunn:
  Francis Guerant, ix. 209
  H.L., ii. 472 *n*
  Harriet Louisa, ix. 209
  Thos., ii. 477
  and see Donne
Dunning, J., iii. 42
Dunsfold (Surr.), ii. 328 *n*
Dunstan, St., abp. of Cant., ii. 2–3
Dunstanville:
  Alan de (sr.), iv. 41
  Alan de (jr.), iv. 41–2
  Alice de, m. —— de Baseville, iv. 41
  Cecily de, m. Wm. Basset, iv. 41
  Emma de, m. —— de Englefeld, iv. 41
  Muriel, w. of Alan, m. 2 Rob. Danvers, iv. 41
  Pernel, m. Rob. de Montfort, iv. 41
  Rainald de, iv. 41
  Wal. (sr.), iv. 41
  Wal. (jr.), iv. 41
  fam., iv. 41 *n*
Dunster, Dorothy, iii. 145
Dunwich (Suff.), ii. 131
Duplex, C.R., ii. 430
Duppa, Brian, bp. of Chich., bp. of Winchester, ii. 34; iii. 133
Dupuis:
  Martha, *see* Skelton
  Thos. Sanden, iv. 202
Durand, Wm. s. of, *see* William
Durante, Ric., iv. 10
Duredent:
  Gerard, vii. 229
  Margery, *see* Wappenbury
Durford (Dureford) abbey (in Rogate), ii. 45, **89–92**, *92*, 294, 329–30*; iv. 14, 109
  abbots, ii. 90–2; iv. 10, 17, 24; *and see* Baldwin, Nic.; John; Kypping; Mene; Mersey, Steph.; Simpson, Jn.; Ultyng
  accessories, ii. 252, 330, 353
  archit., ii. 230, 330
  canon, *see* Beston Jn.
  char., ii. 191
  estates, ii. 103, 232, 302, 330; iv. 17, 21, 24–6, 36, 51, 56, 61, 64, 99, 109
  patronage, ii. 89; iv. 20 *n*, 27
  royal visit, ii. 90
  tithes, ii. 302
  wool trade, ii. 188, 256
Durham:
  Sarah, ix. 148
  Simeon of, ii. 127
Durham, i. 168 *n*, 187, 328
  bp., ii. 295; *and see* Bec, Ant.; Flambard
  cath. priory, iv. 148 *n*; ix. 103 *n*

sch., ii. 432–3
Durham, County, iv. 211; *and see*
    Shields, South
Durnford:
    Anne, *see* Collins
    Emma, iii. 146
    Ric., bp. of Chich., ii. 404, 409; iii.
        142, 145; iv. 179
    Dr. ——, iii. 90, 161
Durobrivae, *see* Rochester
Durrant:
    Jn. Mercer Bosville, vii. 48
    Nic., vii. 24 *n*
    Ric., ix. 202
    Sam. (d. 1782), vii. 48
    Sam. (d. 1783), vii. 48
    Sam. (d. 1822), vii. 48
    Wm., vii. 37
    fam., ix. 202
    arms, vii. *48*
Durrington, ii. 218
    ch., ii. 338, 373
    insects, i. 198, 200, 202, 206
    Offington, i. 197
    roads, iii. 47
    Rom. rem., iii. 54
    Salvington, ii. 107
        insects, i. 188–90, 196, 199, 201–2,
            205, 207, 209
Dursley, Vct., *see* Berkeley, Augustus
Dutch wars, *see* wars
Duvall, Steph., ii. 255
Duverent, Ralph de, vii. 236
Dyblocke, Gilb., ii. 257
Dychenynge, Jn. de, vii. 105
dyeing, *see* textile inds.
Dyere, Sim., mayor of Chich., iii. 92
Dygby, *see* Digby
Dyges, *see* Digges
Dyke:
    Anne, w. of Ric., m. 2 Hen. Horne
        Haviland, ix. 197
    Constance, m. Jn. Goring, iv. 108,
        110
    Eleanor, m. Wm. Dering, iv. 108, 110
    Eliz., *see* St. John
    Hen., iv. 108, 110
    Kath., w. of Sir Thos., ix. 237
    Ric. Still, ix. 197
    Sir Thos. (sr.), ix. 169, 237
    Sir Thos. (jr.), ix. 236–7, 248–9
    Sir Wm. (d. *c.* 1671), ix. 165
    Wm. (fl. 1676), iv. 62
    fam., ix. 169, 197
    arms, vii. 10
Dykere, Wal. le, ii. 316
Dykesterue, *see* Dixterue
Dyll (? in Warbleton), ix. 125
Dymchurch (Kent), Brodhull, ix. 39
Dymmok (Dymok):
    Jn., ii. 312; vii. 106 *n*
    Ric., vii. 106 *n*
Dyne:
    Edw., ix. 92
    Jn., ix. 92
    Mary, *see* Fletcher
    Mary Fletcher, m. Musgrave Brisco,
        ix. 92
    Timothea, m. Jn. Dyne, ix. 92
    Thos., ix. 92
    Thos. (another), ix. 92
    Wm. ix. 152
Dyve, *see* Dive

Eadberht, *see* Edberht
Eadgar, *see* Edgar
Eadie, Albert, iv. 189, 191
Eadnoth, *see* Ednoth
Eadric, *see* Edric
Eadulf, *see* Edulf
Eadwig (Eadwi, Eadwy), *see* Edwy
Eagle, honor of, *see* Laigle, honor of
Eagles, Edw., ii. 257
Ealdberht (Aldbricht) (d. 725), i. 482
Ealdwulf, *see* Aldulf
Ealfred, and his w. Ealsware, iv. 110
Ealweald, king of South Saxons, i.
    482

Eames, Louisa, m. Thos. Rog. Ridge,
    iv. 25
Eanfrid, king of the Hwiccas, ii. 1
    his dau., *see* Ebba
Earl Marshal, i. 494–5; ii. 294; *and see*
    Berkeley, Wm.; Bigod, Rog. le;
    Howard, Jn.; Marshal, Ric.; Mar-
    shal, Wal.; Mowbray, Thos.
early man, i. **309–31**
Earnley:
    Wm., iii. 154 *n*
    Mr., iv. 238
    fam., ii. 361
Earnley, ii. 43; iii. 82; iv. 198, **201–3**,
    212, 215; vii. 271 *n**
    adv., iv. 203, 217
    Almodington, ii. 43; iii. 4, 54; iv. 198,
        201–3
    boundary, iv. 198, 202
    char., iv. 203
    ch., ii. 37, 339, 376; iv. 202–3, *203*
    man., iv. 202–3
    mill, iv. 201–2
    pop., ii. 221
    rector, *see* Cartwright, Edm.
Eartham, Wm. (or Wal.) de, mayor of
    Chich., iii. 91, 98
Eartham, ii. 43; iii. 90; iv. 133, 145,
    152–4; vii. 271 *n*
    adv., iv. 154
    ch., ii. 362; iv. 152–4, *154, 156*
        archit., ii. 327, 335, 339, 366, 373
    Copyhold plantation, iii. 34
    Crouch Ham, iv. 152
    Eartham Ho., iv. 152
    foxhunting, ii. 443
    ind., iv. 152
    insects, i. 112, 114, 121, 169, 172,
        191, 212, 227, 231, 236
    Long Down, iii. 34
    man., iv. 114, 152–3
    mill, iv. 152
    Nore Hill, iii. 54
    pop., ii. 220
    prebend, ii. 48; iv. 154
    prebendary, *see* Shiffner, Geo.
    roads, iii. 34; iv. 152
    Rom. rem., iii. 34, 54
    tithes, iv. 152–4
    vicarage, ii. 9
    woods, iv. 152, 174
earthworks, i. 311, **452–80**
    barrows (tumuli), i. 311, 317–18, 320,
        336–7, 346, 479–80
    and see parish names
Easebourne (Eseborne, Eseburne), ii.
    43, 81, 217 *n*; iv. 40, **47–53**, 56, 62
    adv., iv. 53, 73, 78, 120
    Buddington, ii. 217 *n*; iv. 40, 47,
        49–51, 56, 58
    char., iv. 53, 77
    ch., ii. 84–5; iv. *48*, 50, 52–3, 57
        accessories, ii. 250*, 356, 361–2,
            368
        archit., ii. 331, 335–6, 339, 366, 368
    Cowdray, i. 524–5, 528; ii. 55; iv. 74,
        76, 83, 85
        ho., ii. 196–7, 336, 386, 394–5; iv.
            49–50, *48*–9; chap., ii. 338, 379;
            iv. 50 *n*
        man., iv. 34, 42, 45, 49–50, 56–7,
            66–7, 69, 73, 78, 80
        mill, ii. 394
        Pk., i. 306; ii. 301; iv. 49, 76; vii.
            210
        royal visits, i. 515–16; ii. 301, 441;
            iv. 50
        timber, ii. 295
    dom. archit., ii. 386; iv. 49–50
    earthworks, i. 480
    Hollist, iv. 47, 51
    hund., i. 538; ii. 171–2, 221; iv. 1, **40**
    man., iv. 50–3, 77, 114
    pop., ii. 221
    priory, ii. 45, **84–5**; iv. 47–9, *48*, 52–3,
        56–7, 93, 113
        archit., ii. 331, 347
        prioresses, ii. 84–5; iv. 79, 85; *and*

see Alice; Edith; Pygon
    roads, iv. 47
    Rom. Cath., iv. 77
    tithes, ii. 263
    Todham, iv. 40, 47, 65, 77
        chap., iv. 51, 53
        man., iv. 51–2, 165
        mill, iv. 51
        tithes, ii. 56; iv. 51, 53
Easewrith (Easewrithe), *see* Easwrith
East Anglia:
    A.-S. rem., i. 339
    bp., *see* Grimketel
East Borough (in Udimore half hund.),
    ix. 164
East Hill, *see* Hastings
East India Company, i. 536; ii. 238
East Lothian, *see* Berwick, North
East Sussex County Council, *see* Sussex
East Sussex Cricket Club, ii. 470–2
East Sussex Farmers' Club, ii. 289
East Sussex hunt, ii. 446–8, 452, 460
East Sussex Subscription Pack, ii. 446
Eastbourne (Borne, Bourne, Burne,
    Estborne), i. 294, 509, 514; ii. 44,
    159, 206, 209, 275; ix. 1
    allotments, ii. 208
    batrachians, i. 272
    battery, ii. 163
    Beachy Head, *q.v.*
    birds, i. 281, 289–96
    botany, i. 41, 43, 45–6, 61–8
    Bourne Place, *see* Eastbourne: Comp-
        ton Place
    Bullock Down, iii. 55
    chant., ii. 20
    Cholynton, ii. 181
    ch., ii. 251, 265; ix. 182
        accessories, ii. 351–4, 356, 358, *358*,
            361, 376, 378
        archit., ii. 332, 337, 339, 344, 346,
            350, 368, 376–8, *377*
    ch. ho., ii. 383–4
    coaching, ii. 204
    coastguards, i. 507 *n*
    coll., *see* Eastbourne: schs.
    Compton (formerly Bourne) Place, ii.
        277, 391, 441
    Devonshire Pk., ii. 474
    dom. archit., ii. 338, 391
    earthworks, i. 477, 480
    fossils, i. 8
    geology, i. 2, 7, 9–10, 12, 17, 72, 274;
        ii. 337, 356, 395
    Gildridge, ii. 446, 474
    guilds, ii. 20–1
    Holywell, ii. 231
    hund., i. 537; ii. 226
    insects, i. 112, 115, 124–5, 133–5,
        137, 140–1, 144–6, 149, 151, 153,
        155–7, 159–66, 167 *n*, 168–80,
        182–3, 185–91, 193–6, 199, 201–
        3, 205, 208–10, 218–19, 221, 223,
        225, 227, 229, 231, 234
    Langport, iii. 55; ix. 34
    man., ii. 173, 186, 189–90
        ho., ii. 391
    militia, i. 534–5
    molluscs, i. 109
    museum, i. 309, 329–31; iii. 8, 24,
        54–5
        Caldecott museum, i. 323
    Natural Hist. Soc., i. 66
    Ocklynge, ii. 93
    parl. rep., i. 532
    pier light, ii. 163
    poor law union, i. 539; ii. 205
    pop., ii. 226
    prehist. rem., i. 313, 316–17, 320–1,
        329, *330*
    rly., i. 348; ii. 205, 240–1
    resort, ii. 204
    roads to, iii. 47–8, 55; vii. 8
    Rom. rem., iii. 4, 20, 24, *25*, 54–5
    St. Anthony's Hill, i. 8; ii. 162
    schs., ii. 397
        coll., ii. 434–5, 476
    Sea Houses, ii. 162, 204

Eastbourne (*cont.*):
  ship service, ii. 138
  smuggling, ii. 200
  sport:
    angling, ii. 467
    athletics, ii. 474, 480–1
    cricket, ii. 468, 470, 474–6
    foxhunting, ii. 446–8
    golf, ii. 478
    hare hunting, ii. 452
    horse racing, ii. 460
  telegraph, ii. 163
  trades and ind.:
    brewing, ii. 262–3
    fishing, ii. 145, 235, 265, 269–70
    pottery, ii. *252*
    quarrying, ii. 230–1
    salt, ii. 232
    ship building, ii. 235
  Upperton, iii. 55
  vicar, ii. 265; *and see* Bysshe, Thos.;
    Hoo, Wm.
  vicarage, ii. 9
  Wish Tower, i. 8
Eastdean (E. Suss.), i. 313; ii. 44, 138,
    227
  Beltout (Belle Tout):
    earthworks, i. 455, *456*, 469–70
    prehist. rem., i. 328
  Birling:
    Farm, iii. 54
    Gap, ii. 152
    man., ii. 146, 163
    man. ho., ii. 382
  ch., ii. 48, 122–3
    accessories, ii. 352, 356, 359–60
    archit., ii. 329 *n*, 332, 337, 340,
      342, 348, 365, 370
  earthworks, i. 480
  prehist. rem., i. 310, 316, 329
  Rom. rem., iii. 54
easter sepulchres, *see* architecture: eccle-
    siastical
Eastergate, i. 526; ii. 42–3, 217; iv. 134
  ch., ii. 334–5, 338, 340, 353–4, 362,
    364, 377–8
  dom. archit., ii. 388, 393
Easthothly, *see* Hoathly, East
Eastland's Farm, *see* Slaugham
Easton:
  Geo., ii. 426
  Wm., ix. 111
Easton, *see* Sidlesham
Eastry (Kent), lathe of, ix. 38
Easwrith (Easewrith, Easewrithe, Ese-
    writhe):
  East, hund., i. 538; ii. 219
  hund., iv. 1
  West, hund., i. 538; ii. 218
Eatendon, *see* Mountfield
Eaton:
  C., ii. 473
  Col., ix. 253 *n*
Eaton Socon (Beds.), iv. 115
Eatonden, *see* Mountfield: Eatendon
Ebba, dau. of King Eanfrid, m. Ethel-
    wold, ii. 1
Ebden, C.J., ii. 472 *n*
Ebernoe, *see* Kirdford
Eburne, Jas., iv. 91
Ecclesbourne, *see* Fairlight
Ecclesden (Ecclesdon), *see* Angmering:
    man.
ecclesiastical   architecture,   *see*
    architecture
ecclesiastical history, ii. **1–44**
Eccleston, Ric., ii. 39
Echingham (Achingham, Akingeham,
    Etchingham):
  Alice, w. of Sim., ix. 222
  Eliz., ix. 216
  Eliz. de, m. 1 Rog. Fiennes, 2 Sir
    Goddard Oxenbridge, ix. 169,
    212, 220
  Eliz., m. Jn. de Lunsford, ix. 214
  Eliz., m. Sir Ric. de Wakehurst, ii.
    361; vii. 129, 131; ix. 273
  Eliz., m. 1 Sir Thos. Hoo, 2 Sir Thos.

  Lewknor, ix. 118, 138, 196 *n*
  Eve (Eva) de, *see* Stopham
  Sir Jas., ix. 212
  Joan de, ii. 72
  Joan, w. of Rob., *see* Gate
  Joan, w. of Sir Wm. de, ix. 216
  Jn. de, dean of South Malling coll., ii.
    119
  Jn. (fl. 1485), ix. 212
  Marg., m. 1 Wm. Blount, 2 Sir Jn.
    Elrington, ix. 173, 212, 220, 273
  Margery, w. of Rob., *see* Socknersh
  Margery, w. of Wm., ix. 112
  Parnel, w. of Rob., ix. 213
  Pauline, w. of Sim. de, ix. 112
  Ric. (d. by 1340), ix. 212
  Ric. (fl. 1412), ix. 212
  Rob (fl. *c.* 1293), ix. 229
  Rob. de (d. 1328, another), i. 507; ix.
    107, 112, 212–13, 235
  Rob. (fl. *c.* 1340), ix. 273
  Rob. (fl. 1412), ix. 273–4
  Sim. de (d. by 1166), ix. 212
  Sim. de, sheriff of Suss., i. 492; ii. 52;
    ix. 112–13, 212, 223–4
  Sim. de (fl. 1253), ix. 112, 212
  Sir Sim. de (fl. 1333), ii. 72
  Sim., rector of Herstmonceux, ix.
    112, 212
  Sim. de (fl. 1348), ix. 222
  Sim. de (one of the above), ix. 1
  Sir Thos. (d. 1444), ii. 79, 324; ix.
    212, 214, 216, 220
  Sir Thos. (d. 1482), ix. 164, 169, 173,
    212, 216, 220, 229, 273
  Sir Thos. (fl. 1483), i. 515
  Wal. de, ii. 324
  Wm. de (fl. 1166), ix. 212
  Wm. de (d. 1252 or 1253), ix. 112–
    113, 212
  Wm. de (d. 1293 or 1294), i. 504; ix.
    113, 164, 212, 229, 235
  Wm. de (d. 1326), i. 505; ii. 67, 72;
    iv. 66; vii. 70 *n*; ix. 112, 139,
    212–13, 214 *n*, 220, 224, 229, 235
  Wm. de (d. 1389), ii. 360; ix. 120,
    172, 212, 215–16
  Wm. de (d. 1412), ii. 360; ix. 138,
    190, 212, 216
  ——, m. Wm. de St. Leger, ix. 176
  fam., ii. 72; ix. 82, 164, 170–2, 212,
    235–6, 254, 256, 270
  arms, vii. 272; ix. *212*, 216, 223
Eckington, *see* Ripe
Edberht (Eadberht), abbot and bp. of
    Selsey, ii. 2; iv. 94
Edburton, ii. 44, 219, 224; vii. 201–2,
    204
  ch., ii. 118, 250, 333, 346, 350, 356,
    370, 373
  earthworks, i. 462–3, 476, *476*, 479–80
  Edburton Hill, *see* Fulking
  Perching, *q.v.*
  pop., ii. 219
  prehist. rem., i. 329
  roads to, iii. 47
  Rom. rem., iii. 47, 56
  and see Fulking
Eddeva, *see* Edith
Edelingedene, iv. 94
Eden, Rob., *see* Hedon
Eden, riv., ii. 453; iii. 43
Edenbridge (Kent), ii. 453; iii. 43–5, *44*,
    69–70
  Cobhambury, iii. 44, 46
  Crockham Hill, iii. 44–5, 70
Edendon (Edington), Wm., bp. of Win-
    chester, ii. 63
Edes (Eedes):
  Hannah, *see* Aylwin
  Hen., canon and precentor of Chich.,
    warden of St. Mary's hosp.,
    Chich., ii. 101–2; iii. 73, 79; iv.
    116 *n*, 185, 187
  Hen. (d. 1722), iii. 74
  Jn., iii. 73–4
  Mary, m. Jn. Frankland, iii. 74; iv.
    185

  fam., iv. 188
    arms, iii. 74, *74*
  and see Eede
Edgar (Eadgar), king, iv. 13, 83, 150;
    vii. 32, 73, 75–6, 206; ix. 62
Edgar (fl. 1066), iv. 192
  his s., *see* Robert
Edge, Peter, master of St. James's hosp.,
    Chich., iii. 167 *n*
Ediall, Hen., master of Arundel coll., ii.
    169
Edinburgh, ii. 236, 431
Edington, *see* Edendon
Edith, queen of Edw. the Confessor, ii.
    3; vii. 53, 224 *n*
Edith, prioress of Easebourne, ii. 85; iv.
    196
Edith Swan-neck (Swanneshals), i. 489
Edith (Eddeva) (fl. 1066), iv. 83; vii. 33,
    36, 228
Edith (fl. 1066, another), ix. 242
Edivestone, *see* Shiplake
Edmer (fl. 1086), ix. 132
Edmond:
  Jn., iv. 223
  Thos., dean of South Malling coll., ii.
    119
Edmondes, *see* Edmunds
Edmonton (Mdx.), ii. 473
Edmund, St., abp. of Cant., *see* Rich
Edmund, king, iv. 215
Edmund, earl of Cornwall, i. 504; ii. 94,
    190; iii. 77, 85, 93, 94 *n*, 97–8, 103;
    iv. 42 *n*
Edmund, earl of Kent, iii. 85; iv. 59,
    122; ix. 153
Edmunds (Edmondes):
  Frances, ix. 181
  Hannah, ix. 181
  Jn., vii. 276
  Wal., vii. 276
Ednod (fl. 1086), ix. 152, 160, 279
Ednoth (Eadnoth), moneyer, iii. 83
Edolphe, Thos., ix. 53
Edred, king, vii. 73, 75–6
Edric (Eadric), king of Kent, i. 482
Edric (Eadric), moneyer, vii. 32
Edric (fl. 1009), i. 484
Edric (Eadric) (fl. before 1066), ii. 350
Edric (fl. 1066), ix. 158
Edric (Aedric), bellfounder, ii. 249; ix.
    101
education, *see* Chich.: Bp. Otter coll.;
    schools
education, agric., *see* agricultural educa-
    tion
Education, Board of, ii. 430
Edulf (Eadulf) (d. 897), i. 483
Edward the Elder, king, ii. 126
Edward the Confessor, king, i. 348–9,
    484–5; ii. 3, 46, 109, 112, 122, 124,
    126–7, 302, 306, 310, 324; iii. 83–4;
    iv. 183, 185, 233; vii. 104, 275; ix.
    8–9, 34, 49
Edward I, i. 502–7; ii. 11, 49, 54, 61, 78,
    93–4, 96, 107, 129, 131–3, 261, 271,
    294, 296, 307, 316, 324, 333; iii. 85,
    91, 98, 100, 110; iv. 14, 66, 127,
    183, 193, 233, 235; vii. 3; ix. 37–8,
    63, 69–71, 87, 153, 171, 217
  as prince, i. 496, 498–501; ii. 131–2;
    iv. 14; vii. 21; ix. 2, 15, 50, 79
  his s., *see* Brotherton, Thos. de
Edward II, i. 507–8; ii. 54, 67, 73, 87,
    90, 135–6, 296, 307, 325; iii. 85, 91,
    100; vii. 15 *n*, 223, 253; ix. 2, 38,
    81, 139, 153, 217
  as prince of Wales, i. 508; ii. 133; vii.
    3, 105
Edward III, i. 508–10; ii. 67–8, 72, 111,
    115, 124, 129, 136–9, 316–17, 325,
    353; iii. 85–6, 95–6; iv. 167; vii. 3,
    196; ix. 15, 61, 172
  arms, ix. 216
  as prince, ii. 135
  his dau., ii. 68
Edward IV, i. 515; ii. 113, 141; iii. 86,
    96, 114, 142, 153; iv. 122, 162, 168;

ix. 3, 169
as earl of March, ix. 40
Edward VI, ii. 21–2, 197, 435; iv. 50, 56, 73, 145; vii. 33, 239; ix. 245
Edward VII, ii. 284; iii. 81
as prince of Wales, ii. 435
Edward, the Black Prince, ii. 139; iii. 85 n; ix. 172, 216
Edward, prince, son of Geo. III, ii. 204
Edward, son of Ric., king of the Romans, i. 499
Edward, son of Thos. de Brotherton, iv. 183–4
his w., see Mortimer, Beatrice
Edwardes, Brown and Oliver, ii. 164
Edwards (Edwardes):
Abraham (fl. 1601), ix. 229
Abraham (d. 1615, ? another), vii. 258, 284
Abraham (d. 1643), vii. 256, 284
Abraham (d. 1643, another), vii. 256, 284
Abraham (fl. 1670), vii. 256, 275–6, 284
Bryan, iii. 100
David, ii. 166
Feregod, ii. 32 n
Francis, ii. 28
G.S., ii. 455, 457
Hen., vii. 159
J.D., ii. 457
Jas., ii. 236 n
Jn., ii. 236 n
Timothy, ii. 166
——, ii. 164
and see Powell Edwards
Edwin, (fl. 1066), iv. 50
Edwine, moneyer, iii. 83
Edwy (Eadwig, Eadwy), king, iii. 83; iv. 142
Edwy (Eadwi), moneyer, iii. 83
Edwyne, Rob., iv. 95
Eede:
Mary, w. of Ric., iii. 162
Mary, see Bragg
Ric., iii. 162
and see Edes
Effingham, Ld. Howard of, see Howard, Wm.
Egan, Helen, iii. 167
Egbert, king of Wessex, i. 483; ii. 118, 292
Egdean, ii. 43, 218, 379
Egendon, Wm. de, preceptor of Shipley, ii. 92–3
Egerton:
Chas., Augustus, ii. 447; ix. 235
Edw., ix. 235
Edw. Chris., ix. 235
Francis, earl of Ellesmere, ii. 460
Helen, iv. 192
Hugh Sydney, ix. 235, 249
Jn., ix. 199
Jn. Coker, rector of Burwash, ix. 199
his w., ix. 199
Maud de, see Berwick
Phil. de, iv. 31
(formerly Grosvenor), Thos., earl of Wilton, ii. 459
Eggar, Jn., iv. 70
Egglestone (Yorks. N.R.), abbey, ii. 87
Egle (Egles, Egly):
Dorothy, w. of Wm., ii. 99
Gabriel, and his w. Martha, ix. 266
Wm., proctor of hosp. of St. Jas. and St. Mary, Chich., ii. 99
Egley, see Oving
Eglinton, earl of, see Montgomery, Archibald
Egly, see Egle
Egmont, earls of, see Perceval
Egremont, earls of, see Wyndham: Chas., Geo. O'Brien
Egypt, i. 16; and see wars
Eldeid (fl. 1086), vii. 36
Elderton, Ric., ii. 190
Elding (or Cheleshunt), Wm. de, see Cheleshunt

Eldretune, see Aldrington
hund., see Fishersgate
Eldridge:
Brian (Bryan), ii. 250; iv. 27, 60, 73, 113, 170, 236; vii. 73, 91, 113, 119, 132, 286
Ric., ii. 250; iv. 73
Wm., iii. 160; iv. 53, 63, 103, 149; vii. 140, 286
Eldritune, see Fishersgate
Eldwulf, see Aldulf
Eleanor (of Castile), queen of Edw. I, ii. 94; iii. 77, 110; iv. 8, 89, 167
Eleanor (of Provence), queen of Hen. III, ii. 92, 132; ix. 36, 50
Eleanor, dau. of Edw. I, m. Hen., count of Bar, vii. 3 n
Eleanor, dau. of Hen., earl of Lancaster, m. 1 Jn. de Beaumont, 2 Ric. Fitz-Alan, earl of Arundel, ii. 68, 108; iii. 144 n; iv. 45; vii. 3
Eleanor, dau. of King Jn., m. 1 Wm. Marshal, earl of Pembroke, 2 Sim. de Montfort, earl of Leicester, i. 501
Eleanor, dau. of Jocelin, iv. 60
elections, see parl. rep.
Eley, W.H., ix. 217
Elfalm, ix. 240
Elficke, see Elphick
Elfred, Geo., ix. 171
Elgar (Elger):
Geo., ii. 407
Jn., iv. 27
Elgin, earl of, see Bruce, Thos.
Elibank, Ld., see Murray, Alex.
Elizabeth I. i. 305, 516; ii. 22–3, 27, 48, 55, 101, 143, 147–50, 152–4, 254, 301, 318, 441; iii. 75, 86, 96, 165; iv. 50, 123, 143, 152, 199, 206, 208, 212, 219, 224; vii. 91, 105, 227, 239, 257–8, 270; ix. 28, 31, 44, 54, 64, 67, 201, 230, 268
as princess, ix. 105, 245
Elizabeth, princess, dau. of Geo. III, ii. 204
Elizabeth, prioress of Easebourne, ii. 85
Elizabeth, prioress of Rusper, ii. 64
Elizabeth (Woodville), m. 1 Sir Jn. Grey, 2 queen of Edw. IV, iii. 142; iv. 122, 159; vii. 71
Elkham:
Agnes, w. of Jn. de, iv. 5
Alice de, see Vesseler
Jn. de (fl. 1330), iv. 5
Jn. de (d. by 1398), iv. 5
Elle, see Aelle
Ellesmere, earl of, see Egerton, Francis
Elliott (Elliot):
Chris., ii. 165
E.A., i. 124
E.W., ix. 179
Eliz., see Cragg
Geo. Augustus, Ld. Heathfield, ix. 200
Lucy E., ix. 200
Ellis:
Bernard, ii. 473
Chas. Howard, ii. 469–70
Dorothy, ii. 438
Fred. Geo., Ld. Howard de Walden, ii. 457
Jn., and his w. Cath., vii. 54, 190
Steph. ii. 427
Thos. (fl. 1687), vii. 184
Thos. (fl. c. 1690, ? another), ii. 159
W.B., i. 300
——, ii. 79
Ellman:
Jn., ii. 282–5
Wm., vii. 135
Ellsworth, Ric., ix. 28
Elm Grove, see Brighton
Elmer, see Middleton
Elmes:
Ant., vii. 217
Jas., iii. 163

Elmeton, Jn., master of Playden hosp., ii. 105
Elmham, bp. of, see Ethelmaer
Elnested (Elnestede), see Elsted
Elphege, Steph. de, ii. 187
Elphick (Elficke):
Edw., ix. 80
Jn. (fl. 1588), ix. 202
Jn. (fl. 1614), ix. 80
Rob., ix. 80
Steph., ix. 80
Thos. (fl. 1600), ix. 197
Thos. (d. 1614, ? another), ix. 80
Thos. (d. 1628), ix. 80
W., iii. 61
Elphinstone, Sir Howard, ix. 88
Elrington:
Edw. (d. 1515), vii. 270, 272; ix. 172 n, 173, 220
Edw. (fl. 1536), ix. 173, 220
Sir Jn., clerk of hanaper, treasurer of household, etc., ix. 212 n, 220, 273
Mary, see Shirley
Marg., w. of Sir Jn., see Echingham
Ric., vii. 258, 270; ix. 220
arms, vii. 272
Elsefeld, Jn. de, ix. 153
Elson:
Ann, m. Sir Jn. Miller, iii. 125
Jn., iv. 163
Wm., iv. 208
fam., iv. 166
Elstead (Surr.), ii. 328 n
Elsted (Elnested, Elnestede):
Sir Bart. de, iv. 8, 107
Clemence de, w. of Sir Bart., iv. 8
Hugh de, iv. 230
Rob. de (fl. c. 1200), iv. 8, 107
Rob. de (fl. 1340), and his w. Agatha, iv. 230
Rob. de (fl. 1360, ? another), iv. 230
Sim. de, rector of Elsted, iv. 107
Wm. de, iv. 107
Elsted, ii. 16, 43, 185; iv. 3, 8–10
adv., iv. 8, 10, 32
Beacon Hill, see Harting: Harting Beacon
ch., ii. 250; iv. 8–10, 9, 30
accessories, ii. 354, 360
archit., ii. 334–5, 339, 346, 365–6, 373, 379
dom. archit., iv. 8
glebe, ii. 5
inc., iv. 8
man., iv. 173 n; iv. 8–9, 185
mill, iv. 8
pk., iv. 8
pop., ii. 221
prehist. rem., iv. 8
rly. station, iv. 8
rector, see Elsted, Sim. de
tithes, iv. 8
Elstree (Herts.), ii. 434
Elsworth, ——, ix. 20
Elverton, Ric., ii. 24
Ely, Talfourd, iii. 29
Ely (Cambs.):
abbey, iv. 13
bp., see Eustace; Kirkby, Jn. of
canon, see Lowe, Edw. Clarke
Ely (in Cardiff, Glam.), iii. 70
Emerick, bailiff of Atherington, ii. 120
Emerson, Sir Wm., vii. 261
Emfred, son of Wm. Treiponters, iv. 102
his s., see William
Emia (Italy), iii. 41
emigration, ii. 223; ix. 30–1
Emma, queen of Ethelred, ix. 8
Emmes, Fleetwood, ii. 165
Empson:
Agnes, see Lovell
Jn., iv. 15
Ems, riv., i. 48, 52, 62; iv. 113, 121
Emson, Ric., vii. 242
Emsworth (Hants), i. 25, 45, 119, 168 n, 169, 171–83, 188–91; ii. 161; iii. 29,

Emsworth (*cont.*):
47, 100; iv. 195
channel, *see* Chich.: harbour
Emsworth Common, iv. 113
fishing, ii. 270–1
Watergate, i. 166, 174
Enaghdun, bp., *see* O'Tigernach
Ends Place, *see* Warnham
Engayne:
Sir Jn., iv. 115
Kath. d', ix. 144
Engehame:
Jn. (sr.), ix. 241
Jn. (jr.), ix. 241
Philippe, *see* Mavesyn
Engeler (Engelram), iv. 185
his s., *see* Turstin
Enghere, Adam, mayor of Chich., iii. 91
Englefeld (Englefield):
Emma de, *see* Dunstanville
Sir Phil. de, iv. 42
Wm. de (fl. 1341), iv. 41
Wm. (fl. 1653), and his w. Mary, ix. 191
Englescheville, Theobald de, ii. 92
English:
Edw., ix. 227
Hen. (fl. 1625), ix. 217–18, 222, 235
Hen. (fl. 1662), ix. 235
Persis, w. of Hen., ix. 218, 235
Wm., ix. 217, 222
English Channel, i. 4, 18–19, 22, 282, 286, 289, 295–8, 307
English Linen Co., ii. 258; ix. 67
Enham (unidentified), ix. 169
Enock, Mr., i. 238
Enthoven:
Ernest J., vii. 121
Roderick Eustace, vii. 121
Eolla, bp. of Selsey, ii. 2
epidemics, ii. 54
Black Death, i. 511; ii. 9, 14, 54, 68, 78, 81, 84, 179 *n*, 182–3, 186; iii. 86; iv. 91, 124, 177, 233; ix. 65
plague, ii. 39, 54, 90, 199, 417
smallpox, ii. 199; ix. 269 *n*
Eppillos, i. 326
Epsom (Surr.), ii. 455, 468
Erasmus, ii. 419
Erburie, ——, ii. 31
Eresby, Lds. Willoughby d', *see* Bertie
Erham, *see* Ertham
Eridge (in Frant and Rotherfield), ii. 44, 242, 301, 323–4
botany, i. 60–1, 65
Eridge Pk., i. 57, 306; ii. 297, 299, 324, 448; iii. 31
insects, i. 212–15, 218–21, 232, 234–5
sport, ii. 446–8, 461
Erith, Thos., and his w. Denise, vii. 82
Erley (Erleigh):
Agnes, m. Clement Poggesley, vii. 256
Alice, vii. 256
Ann, m. Wm. Hawle, vii. 256
Giles de, vii. 255–6
Isabel, vii. 256
Jane, m. Wm. Newton, vii. 256
Jn. de (fl. 1196), vii. 255–6
Jn. de (fl. 1332), vii. 256
Jn. de (d. c. 1393), vii. 256
Jn. (fl. 1457), vii. 256
Jn. (fl. 1500), vii. 256
Jn. (d. 1538), vii. 256
Marg., vii. 256
Maud de, vii. 255
Rob. de, vii. 256
fam., vii. 255
arms, vii. *255*
Erlham, Thos. de, ii. 296
Ernald (Arnald), ? prior of Lewes, ii. 69
Ernald (Arnald) (fl. 1086), iv. 58, 145, 174
Ernele (Erneley, Ernle, Ernley):
Amice de, w. of Luke, iv. 202 *n*
Bridget, *see* Spring
? Eliz., w. of Wm., iv. 220–1
Francis, iv. 92, 157, 216, 218 *n*
Joan de, iv. 202

Jn. de (fl. 1284), iv. 202
Jn. de (fl. 1318), iv. 202
Jn. de (fl. 1427), iv. 202
Jn. (d. by 1467), iv. 202
Jn. (fl. 1480), iv. 202
Sir Jn. (d. 1519), iv. 92, 157, 216
Luke de (fl. c. 1200), iv. 202
Luke de (fl. c. 1260), iv. 202
Marg., w. of Jn., m. 2 Jn. Lunsford, iv. 202
Ric. (fl. 1337), iv. 202
(or Crulie), Ric., ii. 24
Ric. (d. by 1609), iv. 157, 202, 216, 219
Ric. (fl. 1630), iv. 157, 202, 216
Susan, w. of Ric., iv. 216
Wm. (fl. 1431), iv. 202
Wm. (d. 1546), ii. 50; iv. 92, 157, 216, 220–1*
fam., iv. 202
arms, iv. *202*; vii. 10
Ernesbeme:
Geof. de, iv. 136
Jn. de, iv. 136
Peter de, iv. 136
Rob. de, iv. 136
Thos. de, iv. 136
Wm. de, iv. 136
Ernest, prince of Mecklenburg-Strelitz, vii. 19
Ernis, precentor of Chich., iv. 98
Ernle (Ernley), *see* Ernele
Ernulf, Wm. s. of, *see* William
Erringham, *see* Shoreham
Errington, Geo., iv. 95
Ersfield, Sir Thos., ii. 309
Erskine, Sir Jas., i. 535
Ertham (Erham, Irham):
Adam, master of Arundel coll., ii. 109
Gervase de, iv. 152
Joan de, w. of Jn., iv. 153
Jn. de, iv. 153
Ric. de, iv. 152 *n*
Wal. de, iv. 153
Wm. de (fl. 1171), iv. 152 *n*
Wm. de (fl. 1300), iv. 153
Esam, Mr., i. 124
Eschedune, *see* Ashdown
Escures, Ralph d', abp. of Cant., iv. 91, 239; vii. 218, 237–8, 281
Eseborne (Eseburne), *see* Easebourne
Esewrithe, *see* Easwrith
Esher (Surr.), *see* Claremont
Esmerewic, *see* Hangleton
Espagnols sur Mer, battle of l', ii. 139
Essarz, Ric. de, vii. 58
Essay (Manche, France), abbey, ii. 303
Essendon (Essesdoun), *see* Ashdown
Esseswelle, *see* Shoyswell hund.
Essex:
Eliz., *see* Rogers
Thos. (fl. 1488), iv. 172
Thos. (fl. 1543), iv. 172
Wm. (fl. 1513), iv. 172
Sir Wm. (fl. 1543, ? another), iv. 172
Essex, earls of, *see* Capel; Cromwell, Thos.; Devereux
Essex, i. 30, 41, 169, 333, 483, 508, 511, 516; ii. 52, 170 *n*, 451, 471; iii. 1; iv. 58, 79 *n*; vii. 1; ix. 139 *n*
Hornchurch, vicar, *see* Levett, Hen.
and see Beeleigh; Bradwell; Burnham; Chelmsford; Chich; Coggeshall; Colchester; Fawkesbourn; Fordham; Harlow; Harwich; Hoo; Kelvedon Hatch; Lexden; Pleshey; Prittlewell; Rickling Green; Saffron Walden; St. Osyth; Sisteleberg; Stanesgate; Thorpe; Thurrock, West; Tilbury; Tolleshunt D'Arcy; Waltham; Walton-on-the-Naze
Estapona Roads (Spain), ii. 166
Estborne, *see* Eastbourne
Estdene, Hen. de, iv. 177
Esteham (unidentified), ii. 113, 410
Esterman, *see* Sturmy

Estgrenestede, *see* Grinstead, East
Estling, *see* Guestling
Estocbridge, *see* Box and Stockbridge
Eston:
Jn., ii. 412
Wal., canon of Chich., iii. 111 *n*
estover, iv. 11
Estrange:
Hamon l', iv. 166
Jn. l', iv. 166–7
Estrat, *see* Streat
Estur, Maud, m. Baldwin de Lisle, iv. 91, 115
Esturmi, *see* Sturmy
Etaples (Pas-de-Calais, France), iii. 8
Etchingham family, *see* Echingham
Etchingham, ii. 43; ix. 1, 173 *n*, 210, **211–17**, 251
adv., vii. 140; ix. 216–17
agric., ix. 212
Bellhurst, ix. 213, 220
char., ix. 217, 224
ch., ii. 333; ix. 211, 215–16, *215, 216*
accessories, ii. 352–3, 356, 358, 360, 376
archit., ii. 336, 340, 346, 349, 376
earthworks, i. 477; ix. 211
Glottenham (Glottingham), ii. 384; ix. 210, 213
Haremere, ii. 386; ix. 211, 213, *217*, 220
Hurst Green, *see* Salehurst: Hurst Green
insects, i. 157, 226
iron ind., ix. 211
Kitchingham, ix. 211, 214, *216*
Lundsford, ix. 197, 214–15
man., ix. 172, 212–13, 220, 235, 254
pk., ii. 295; ix. 212
pop., ii. 223
rly., ii. 222 *n*
station, ix. 211
roads, ix. 211
Shoyswell, ii. 386, 389; ix. 215, 251
tithes, ii. 112
woods, ix. 212–13
Etchingwood, *see* Buxted
Ethelbert, king of Kent, i. 334
Ethelbert (Aethelbert), king of South Saxons, i. 482; iii. 82; iv. 218 *n*
Ethelbert (Aethelburt), king of Wessex, i. 483
Ethelgar, abbot of Winchester, bp. of Selsey, abp. of Cant., ii. 2
Ethelm (Aethelm), nephew of Alfred, king of Wessex, i. 483; iv. 91, 135
Ethelm (Aethelm), moneyer, iii. 83
Ethelmaer, bp. of Elmham, ii. 3
Ethelmar (Aethelmar), ix. 49
Ethelred (Aethelred) II, i. 349, 484; iii. 83; iv. 30 *n*, 94, 166; ix. 8, 49, 62
Ethelric II, bp. of Selsey, ii. 3
Ethelstan, *see* Athelstan
Ethelwold (Aethelwalh, Aethelwald), king of South Saxons, i. 333, 482; ii. 1; iv. 207
his w., *see* Ebba
Ethelwold, bp. of Winchester, iv. 13
Ethelwold, nephew of Alfred, king of Wessex, i. 483
Ethelwulf (Ethelwolf), king of Wessex, i. 483; ii. 118, 122
Ethiopia, *see* Magdala
Eton (Bucks.), coll., ii. 121, 405, 408, 414, 417, 421; iv. 162; ix. 244
Eu (Ow):
Hen. de, dean of Hastings coll., ii. 114, 117
Jn. of, ix. 2
Ralph (Raoul) of, ix. 2
Eu:
counts of, ix. 2, 9, 19, 115, 118, 183, 197, 232, 244; *and see* Brienne; Exoudun, Ralph de; Henry; John; Robert; William
ctss. of, *see* Alice
Eudes son of Brian, iv. 45
Eugenius III, pope, ii. 47

Eustace, bp. of Ely, ii. 65
Eustace, count of Boulogne (fl. 1066), i. 487–8, 489 n; ix. 9
Eustace, count of Boulogne (d. 1153), i. 490
Eustace the monk, i. 495; ix. 10
Eustace (fl. 1086), vii. 225
Evans:
  A.A., iii. 16, 18
  Caroline, see Beard
  Jn. (fl. 1828), vii. 177
  Sir Jn. (fl. 1905), i. 310, 314, 320, 326; iii. 15
  Lewis, ii. 480
  (or Chadwick), Owen, see Chadwick
  R.S., ii. 455
  W.H., iii. 144
Evelyn:
  Annabella, see Medley
  Sir F., ii. 456
  Jn. (d. 1706), ii. 299, 414; vii. 18, 45
  Jn. (fl. 1796), vii. 33
  Julia Medley, m. Sir Geo. Shuckburgh, vii. 33; ix. 180, 191
  Ric., vii. 64, 254
Everard:
  Dorothy, m. Hen. Goring, vii. 10, 230, 232
  Francis, master of St. James's hosp., Chich., iii. 167 n
  Joan (fl. 1546), w. of Wm., vii. 6, 157, 228, 230
  Joan (d. 1550, ? another), iv. 92
  Jn., vii. 230, 232
  Mary, m. 1 Ric. Bellingham, 2 Geo. Goring, iv. 5; vii. 6, 10, 230, 232, 275, 279
  R. Guy, ii. 451
  Wm., vii. 10, 228 n, 230, 275
  arms, vii. 10
Everenden, see Evernden
Evererde, Francis, master of hosp. of St. Jas. and St. Mary, Chich., ii. 100
Evernden (Everenden):
  Jn., ix. 264
  Wal., ix. 106
  Capt., i. 524
Eversfield:
  Ann, m. Chas. Goodwin Bethune, ix. 85
  Anne, w. of Thos., vii. 134
  Chas. (fl. 1703–29), ix. 20, 89
  Sir Chas. (d. 1784), ix. 20
  Chas. (d. 1818), ix. 20
  Chas. Cyril St. Leonards, ix. 85
  Chas. Gilb., ix. 28, 32, 84
  Edw., vii. 134
  (formerly Bethune), Edw., see Bethune
  Herb., vii. 134
  Isabella Cath. Mary, see Bethune
  Jas., ix. 20, 84, 242
  Jn. (d. 1595), vii. 105, 134
  Jn. (fl. 1660), i. 529; ix. 20
  Mary, ix. 242
  Mary, m. Jas. Markwick, ix. 20
  Mary, w. of Thos., see Levett
  Nic., sheriff of Suss., ix. 19–20, 92
  Olive, ix. 20
  Sophia Beatrice, see Bethune
  Thos. (d. 1612), ix. 20, 241
  Sir Thos. (d. 1616), vii. 105, 134
  Thos. (fl. 1621), vii. 89, 105
  Sir Thos. (fl. 1629, another), ix. 12, 20
  Wm., vii. 105
  (formerly Markwick), Wm., ix. 20
  Mrs., i. 306
  fam., ii. 312; ix. 19, 21, 81, 84, 86, 242
  arms, vii. 134; ix. 241
Evershed:
  Sarah, iii. 168
  Thos., ix. 203
Evesfold, see Ashdown forest
Evesham, Rob. de, iii. 92
Evesham (Worcs.), i. 501; ii. 15, 131
  battle, ix. 10

Evreux (Eure, France), i. 488
Ewen:
  Eliz., m. Jn. Staker, iv. 231
  Ric. (fl. 1709), and his w. Mary, iv. 83
  Ric. (fl. 1754), iv. 231
Ewhurst, ii. 43, 71; ix. 85, 169, 226, 258, 262, **265–8**
  adv., ix. 268
  agric., ix. 267
  char., ii. 224, 268
  ch., ii. 113, 356, 370, 376; ix. 267–8, 267, 268
  dean, ii. 42
  dom. archit., ix. 265, 265–6
  hund., see Wyndham and Ewhurst hund.
  insects, i. 112, 115, 117, 129, 133, 137–8, 140, 155, 159, 163, 183, 195, 199, 202, 213, 217, 220–1, 223–6, 237
  mans., ix. 266–7, 273
  nonconf., ix. 265
  pop., ii. 223
  prebend, ii. 71, 113; ix. 264, 268
  rly., ix. 265
  roads, ix. 265
  Staple Cross, ix. 258, 265
Ewhurst (in Shermanbury), see Shermanbury
Ewhurst Place, see Ifield
Ewitt:
  Mary, vii. 190
  Thos., and his w. Sarah, vii. 190
Exanta, Sondaye, ii. 255
Exceit (in Westdean), ii. 15, 44
  man., ii. 87
  prebendary, iii. 146
  tithes, ii. 122
Exeter:
  duke of, see Holland, Jn. de
  earl of, see Cecil, Brownlow
Exeter (Devon), i. 349, 483; ii. 52, 54, 409
  bp., ii. 12, 42, 110; iv. 8–9, 90, 129, 197
    arms, iv. 8, 185
    estates, i. 492; ii. 184; iv. 8–9, 181, 188, 192–3, 195–6
    and see Brentingham; Grandison, Jn.; Lacy, Edm.; Osbern; Quivil; Stapleton, Wal.; Veysey; Warelwast
Exeter College, Oxford, ii. 437; vii. 140, 191
Exouden (Issounden):
  Alice de, see Alice
  Maud de, ix. 87 n
  (or Lusignan), Ralph (Raoul) de, count of Eu, i. 491, 493; ii. 116, 174, 324; ix. 2, 14, 79, 87 n, 91, 133, 220
Exton:
  Jn., mayor of Chich., iii. 92
  Ric., mayor of Chich., iii. 92, 104
  Rob., mayor of Chich., iii. 87–8
Eye, see Opton
Eynsham (Oxon.), abbey, iv. 59; ix. 49
Eyott, see Ayot
Eyre (Eyr):
  Dorothea (Dorothy), 'ctss. of Newburgh', m. Chas. Leslie, iv. 153, 235
  Francis, iv. 153, 235
  Giles, dean of Chich., ii. 51
  Jn., dean of Hastings coll., ii. 117
  Kath., see Kemp
  Phil., iv. 234
  Thos. (fl. before 1660), iv. 234
  Thos. (fl. 1779), and his w. Ann, ix. 150
Eyston:
  Mary, see Thatcher
  Wm. (sr.), ix. 191
  Wm. (jr.), ix. 191
Eythorne (Kent), iv. 153

Fabricius, Otto, i. 258
Fagg, see Fagge

Faggar:
  Eliz., m. Ric. Covert, vii. 185
  Jn., and his w. Eliz., vii. 185
  arms, vii. 186
Fagge (Fagg):
  Christian, ix. 202
  Jn. (d. 1645), ix. 202
  Jn. (fl. 1651), ix. 202
  Jn. (d. 1701), i. 528; iv. 50
  Jn. Meeres, iv. 76
  Marg., ix. 202
  Mary, m. Jn. Spence, vii. 35
  Sir Rob., ii. 454
  Wm., ix. 202
  arms, ix. 202
Fair Mile (unidentified), i. 111
Fairfax:
  Denny, vii. 259
  Sir Thos., i. 526; iii. 88
Fairhazel Brocks, see Uckfield
Fairlight, ii. 43, 153; ix. 34, 175, **176–9**
  adv., ix. 157, 178
  almshos., ix. 178
  chant., ix. 178
  char., ix. 178–9, 183
  ch., i. 533; ii. 160; ix. 177–8, 178
  Covehurst, ix. 149, 177
  cricket, ix. 178
  dom. archit., ix. 176
  Ecclesbourne, i. 65, 125, 127–8, 134–5, 143–4, 146–8, 163, 171, 188, 196, 259, 265, 303
  Fairlight Beacon, ix. 175
  Fairlight Down, i. 49, 57; ii. 163
  Fairlight Glen, i. 109; ix. 176
  man., ix. 149, 176–7, 180, 187
  natural history, i. 61, 65, 67–8, 112, 114, 116–18, 120–3, 125–9, 131, 133–5, 138–40, 142–8, 150–63, 172, 176, 184, 186, 189, 194, 196–201, 203–4, 207–9, 212, 216–17, 222–5, 227–37, 261–2, 272, 279, 284, 300, 303
  pop., ii. 222
  signal station, i. 533; ii. 163
  Stonelink, ix. 71, 149, 177
  vicarage, ix. 156
  vicars, see Elliott, E.W.; Frewen, Steph.; Stephen
  ward, ix. 1
Fairlight (in East Grinstead), see Grinstead, East
Fairmanner (Fayremanner):
  Alice, w. of Wm., iv. 123
  Edm. (sr.), iv. 111
  Edm. (jr.), iv. 111
  Jn., iv. 123
  Marg., iv. 123
  Marg., w. of Wm., see Jenman
  Nic., iv. 123
  Thos., iv. 123
  Wm. (d. 1550), iv. 123
  Wm. (d. 1558), iv. 123
  Wm. (fl. 1574), iv. 123
  Wm. (fl. 1668), iv. 109
Fairmile Bottom, see Slindon
fairs, see Battle; Bodiam; Brightling; Brighton; Bulverhythe; Burgess Hill: St. John's Common; Burwash; Chich.; Chiddingly; Clayton; Cocking; Crawley; Cuckfield; Dallington; Ditchling; Findon; Guestling; Harting; Hastings; Heathfield; Hoathly, West; Hurstpierpoint; Lavant, East; Lewes; Lindfield; Midhurst; Pagham; Playden; Portslade; Preston; Robertsbridge; Rogate; Rudgwick; Rye; St. Leonard's forest; Selsey; Ticehurst; Westbourne; Westmeston; Winchelsea; Yarmouth, Great
Fairwarp, see Maresfield
Falaise (Falaisa, Faleyse):
  Agnes de, m. Hugh de Gundeville, ii. 103; iv. 17, 145
  Alice de la, iv. 102
  Alice de la, w. of Peter, iv. 102

Falaise (*cont.*):
  Alice de la, w. of Wm., *see* Alice, dau. of Rob. s. of Edgar
  Christiane de la, m. Sim. de Cumbe, iv. 102, 193
  Elias de la (d. by 1242), iv. 193
  Elias de la (fl. *c.* 1270), iv. 193, 195
  Elias de la, his s., iv. 193
  Emma de, iv. 145
  Emma de, m. Gilb. de Sartilli, iv. 179
  Hugh de, iv. 108, 115, 145
  Margery de la, *see* Grenested
  Peter de la, iv. 102, 193
  Ralph de la, iv. 193
  Wm. de la (fl. 1210), iv. 102, 193
  Wm. de la (d. 1255), iv. 193
  Wm. de la (fl. after 1255), iv. 193
falconer, Seffrid the, *see* Seffrid
falconer, king's, *see* Ralph the king's falconer; Richard the king's falconer; Silvester the king's falconer
Falconer (Faulconer):
  Agnes, *see* Infield
  Geof., iii. 80
  Hen., vii. 165, 168, 171
  Rob., and his w. Maud, ii. 86
  and see Faulkner; Fawkenor
Falemere, *see* Falmer
Falemere hund., i. 537
Faleyse, *see* Falaise
Falkland Islands, ii. 166
Fallesly (Fallisle), Sir Jn., i. 510, 512; vii. 233
Falmer (Falemere), i. 31, 55; ii. 43–4, 284; vii. 81, **223–7**, 253
  adv., vii. 227
  agric., vii. 223
  Balmer (Bolmer, Bormer), ii. 64; iii. 56; vii. 223, 225
  chap., vii. 227
  prehist. rem., i. 321, 328
  Bevendean, i. 165 *n**, 172*, 191–2; vii. 216, 223
  Bormer, *see* Falmer: Balmer
  Buckland, iii. 56; vii. 223
  ch., ii. 30, 40; vii. 226–7, *232*
  cts., vii. 224–5
  dom. archit., vii. 223
  earthworks, i. 480; vii. 223
  hund., vii. 1, 221; *and see* Younsmere
  Lewes priory estates, ii. 64
  man., ii. 104, 186; iv. 223 *n*; vii. 221–6, 234, 242
  mill, vii. 224
  natural history, i. 174–5, 179, 185, 190–1, 197, 200, 206–10
  Newmarket Plantation, i. 478
  pop., ii. 225
  prehist. rem., i. 329
  rly., vii. 224
  Rom. rem., iii. 56; vii. 223
  smuggling, vii. 224
  vicarage, vii. 239–40
  vicar, *see* Clerk, Wm.
Falmouth, Ld., *see* Boscawen, Evelyn
Falvesley:
  Eliz. de, *see* Say
  Sir Jn. de, vii. 114
Family of Love, ii. 29
famine, ii. 193–5
Fancourt, R.D., ii. 166
Fane:
  Sir F., iii. 87
  Francis, Ld. Burghersh, ix. 195
  Sir Hen., ix. 12
  Mary, *see* Nevill
Fane-Benett:
  Ellen, *see* Stanford
  Vere, *see* Stanford
Farewell, Sir Geo., ix. 207, 248
Farhill:
  Geo. (d. 1790), iii. 126
  Geo. (d. 1795), iii. 126
  Geo. Parker, iv. 195
  Jn. (fl. 1740), iv. 195, 213
  Jn. (d. 1830), iii. 116
  Sarah, *see* Peckham

Faringdon, Thos., ii. 24
Farington, *see* Farrington
Farley (Farlegh):
  Adam de, ix. 190
  Joan, w. of Adam de, m. 2 Rog. de Mosewelle, ix. 190, 192
  Rog. de, ii. 315
  Wm. of, ix. 14
Farley Heath, *see* Guildford
Farley priory, *see* Monkton Farleigh
farm buildings, ii. 280–1, 287–8, 393
farm implements, ii. 288, 300
farmers' clubs, ii. 212–13, 289
Farmor:
  Mary, *see* Morgan
  Peter, ix. 191
Farncombe (Farnecombe):
  C., ii. 470 *n*
  E., ii. 470 *n*
  Hen., vii. 218
  Jos. (fl. 1730), vii. 122
  Jos. (d. 1775), vii. 122
  Jos. (d. 1812), vii. 122
  Maline (or Maud), *see* Godfrey
  Sim., ix. 75
Farnden:
  Joan, m. Sam. Gott, ix. 88, 92
  Peter (fl. 1614–28), ix. 88, 93, 147, 169
  Peter (d. 1681), ix. 88, 91, 147, 167 *n*, 168 *n*
  Ruth, m. Jn. Baker, ix. 92
  Tobias, ix. 147
  ——, ix. 276
Farndon, Sarah de, *see* Passeley
Farne islands (Northumb.), i. 295
Farnebergh, Jn. de, and his w. Eliz., vii. 147
Farnecombe, *see* Farncombe
Farnefold, *see* Farnfold
Farnese, Alex., duke of Parma, i. 518
Farnfold (Farnefold):
  Agnes, w. of Ric., iv. 213
  Eliz., m. Sir Edw. Culpeper, vii. 131
  Jn., iv. 231
  Ric., iv. 213
  Rose, iv. 213
  ——, ii. 84
  arms, vii. 141
Farnham, Jn., vii. 134
Farnham (Surr.), i. 494, 522, 524; iii. 87, 89, 102
Farnhurst, Wm., mayor of Chich., iii. 92
Farnhurst, *see* Fernhurst
Farnlegh, Jn. de, ii. 315
Farquhar:
  Horace Brand Townsend, Ld. Farquhar, ii. 457
  Wm., ii. 442
Farrington (Farington):
  Anne, m. Wm. Vinall, iv. 212
  Eliz., iii. 168
  Grisel, m. Barnham Dobell, iv. 212
  Jn. (fl. 1660), iii. 99; iv. 62
  Sir Jn. (d. 1685), iii. 78
  Jn. (fl. 1707), iii. 99
  Jn. (d. by 1736), iv. 213
  Jn. (fl. 1744), iv. 177 *n*
  Sir Ric., iii. 76, 99; iv. 62, 191, 212–13
  his w., iii. 73, 76, 89
  Thos., iv. 206
  ——, iii. 88
  arms, iii. 73
Farthingdown, *see* Coulsdon
Faukeham, *see* Fawkham
Faukener, *see* Fawkenor
Faukes, Jn., master of Playden hosp., ii. 105
Faulconer, *see* Falconer
Faulkner:
  Thos., ix. 24
  and see Falconer, Fawkenor
Fausta, ii. 344
Faversham, Wm. of, ii. 114
Faversham (Kent), ii. 237; ix. 38

Fawkenor (Faukener, Fawkener):
  Agnes, *see* Bachelor
  Anne, m. Arthur Middleton, vii. 34
  Sir Everard, iv. 64
  Georgiana Anne, w. of Wm., iv. 64
  Harriet, m. Ld. Rob. Spencer, iv. 64 *n*
  Mary, *see* Box
  Thos. (fl. *c.* 1558), iv. 179
  Thos. (d. 1613), vii. 34
  Wal., vii. 34, 236
  Wm., iv. 64
  and see Falconer, Faulkner
Fawkesbourn (Essex), iv. 15
Fawkham (Faukeham):
  Wm. de, canon of Steyning, ii. 122
  Wm. de (another), ii. 314
Faxberwe, *see* Flexborough
Faxe, Jn., sacrist of Bosham coll., ii. 112
Faxeburgh, *see* Flexborough
Fay, Jn., ii. 185
Faygate, *see* Rusper
Fayremanner, *see* Fairmanner
Fearon, Francis Jos., vicar of Cuckfield, ii. 421
Featherstonhaugh, *see* Fetherstonhaugh
Fécamp (Seine-Maritime, France), i. 528
  abbey, ii. 60, 122, 331; ix. 8, 10, 23, 26, 40, 49, 61, 75, 160, 171
  abbots, ii. 104, 122, 234, 265; ix. 10, 14, 49–51, 55, 62, 67, 70, 107, 142, 168–9, 171; *and see* Henry; Ralf
  estates, i. 485; ii. 3–4, 42, 46, 104, 122, 124, 127, 232; ix. 8–9, 23, 34, 39, 62, 164, 168–9, 175
Feckham, *see* Felpham
Feilder:
  Agnes, iv. 61
  Jn., iv. 61
  and see Fielder
Felbridge, *see* Grinstead, East
Felde:
  Bart. at, ix. 213
  Geof. at, ii. 179
  his s., *see* William
  Jn. at, ii. 179
  Kath. at, m. Jn. Nicoll, ix. 213
  Mabel at, m. —— Neyr, ix. 213
  Mabel, w. of Jn. at, ii. 179
  and see Field
Feldwicke, fam., ii. 387
Felesmere (unidentified), vii. 224
Felix, Mr., ii. 469
Fellowes-Prynne, G.H., iv. 227
Felpham:
  Hamo de, iii. 103
  Ric. de, iii. 103
Felpham (Feckham), i. 483; ii. 42–3; iii. 90, 100, 102; iv. 226
  boundary, iv. 2
  bridge, iv. 226
  ch.:
    accessories, ii. 250, 356, 359, 370
    archit., ii. 334, 339, 342, 344, 348, 365, 370, 372, 374–5
  coastguards, i. 506 *n*
  defences, ii. 152
  dom. archit., ii. 392
  fishing, ii. 265; iv. 229
  Flansham, i. 187, 190
  guild, ii. 21
  man., iii. 84
  natural history, i. 114, 117, 120, 135, 196, 198–9, 201, 215–17, 222, 224–6, 229, 232–7, 252
  nonconf., ii. 33
  pop., ii. 217
  shipping, ii. 151, 155
  tithes, ii. 265
  vicar, *see* Hill, Wm.
  vicarage, ii. 9
Felton:
  Eleanor, m. Sir Thos. Hoo, ix. 138
  Thos., ix. 138
Feltwell (Norf.), ii. 68
fence and wattle making, ii. 234, 300

Fenne (Fenn):
Jas. del, iv. 229
Thos. de la, preceptor of Shipley, ii. 93
Wm. de la, ii. 92
Mr., ii. 271
Fenner:
Dudley, iv. 172
Edw., ii. 149 n, 153
Geo. (fl. 1561), iv. 202
Geo. (fl. 1577, ? another), ii. 148–9, 153 n
Jn. (d. 1566), iv. 155–6, 172
Sir Jn. (fl. 1623), iv. 116
Thos. (fl. 1568), iv. 20*
Thos. (fl. 1587, ? another), ii. 149 n, 153 n
Wm., ii. 149 n, 153
Fennex, Wm., ii. 467
Fennour, Jn., ii. 24
Fenny Compton, rector of, see Bigg, Chas.
Fenton, Jn., ii. 39
Fenwick:
Marg., see Browne
Wm., iv. 168
Fenys, see Fiennes; Fynes
Ferguson, Mr., ii. 458
Feringes (Fering), see Ferring
Ferle, see Firle, West
Ferles, Jn. de, and his w. Maud, vii. 189, 234
Fermor, Sir Hen., ii. 438
Ferne:
Elwyn de, ix. 235
Jn. de, ix. 235
Wal. de, ix. 235
Wm. de, ix. 235
Ferneth, see Frant
Fernhurst (Farnhurst), ii. 43, 218 n; iv. 40, 54–8, 67
adv., iv. 57–8
Bell woods, 175, 195
Camelsdale, chap., iv. 58
ch., ii. 354–5; iv. 53, 56–8, 57, 60
dom. archit., iv. 54–6, 69
Henley, iv. 53
Henley Hill, i. 174, 190, 194, 202; ii. 336; iv. 54
insects, i. 172–9, 181–9, 191–210
man., iv. 51, 56
Moses Hill Farm, iv. 54, 56
pop., ii. 221
roads, iv. 54
tithes, iv. 56–7
trades and ind., ii. 249; iv. 54
Verdley (Verdly), ii. 394; iv. 49 n, 54–6
pk., ii. 297; iv. 56
Ferour, Jn., vicar of West Dean, iv. 100
Ferrers (Ferrariis, Ferrer):
Edw., iv. 21
Joan de, prioress of Lyminster, ii. 121
Mary Anne, see Wriothesley
Sibyl de, m. Sir Frank de Bohun, iv. 77
Wm. de, earl of Derby, iv. 77
Ferrey, B., vii. 163, 261
Ferring (Fering, Feringes, Ferryng, Feryng):
Agnes de, m. —— atte Stone, vii. 100
Agnes, w. of Ric. de, iv. 24; vii. 99–100
Alfred de, vii. 99, 283
Amfrey (Amfrid, Aumfrid), i. 492; ii. 7, 74; iv. 135–6; vii. 34
Amice, w. of Sim. de, iv. 24; vii. 99
Isabel de, m. Jn. atte Nash, vii. 100
Isabel, w of Amfrey de, vii. 34
(or Palyng), Jn. de, see Palyng
Ric. de, iv. 24; vii. 99
Sim. de, iv. 24, 135; vii. 99
arms, vii. 100
Ferring, ii. 43, 293; iv. 135
A.-S. rem., i. 341
ch.: i. 3, 37, 351–2, 356, 370
archit., ii. 332, 337, 339, 349, 365, 370

High Down:
A.-S. rem., i. 340, 341–2, 343, 344, 345–7
earthworks, i. 464, 466, 466, 470
High Down Hill, iii. 47, 58
insects, i. 191, 193, 195, 197–9, 201, 203–4, 206, 208–9
Miller's Tomb, i. 340, 467 n
prehist. rem., i. 329
signal post, i. 533
Kingston, see Kingston (by Ferring)
man. ho., ii. 381
pop., ii. 217
prebend, ii. 48
roads to, iii. 47
Rom. rem., iii. 56
vicar, ii. 40
Ferro, Wilhelm Karl, iv. 208
Ferryng (Feryng), see Ferring
Fetcham (Surr.), ii. 373
Fetherstonhaugh (Featherstonhaugh, Fetherstonehaugh, Fetherston):
Frances, see Bullock
Sir Hen., ii. 456, 460; iv. 13, 16, 92 n
Sir Herb., see Meade
Keith Turnour, see Turner
Sir Mat., ii. 298, 454; iv. 16–17, 20, 95
Lady, iii. 123
Miss, i. 306
——, w. of Sir Hen., see Bullock
arms, iv. 11, 16
Fetyplace:
Jane, see Covert
Sir Jn., vii. 185
Marg., see Rogers
Thos., iv. 172
Fevere:
Hen. le, iii. 94
Juliana le, iii. 94
Nic. le, iii. 94
Wal. le, iii. 94
Wm. le, iii. 94
Feversham, Nic., prior of Shulbred, ii. 82
Feythfull, Wm., mayor of Chich., iii. 92
Fidder, Edw., iv. 70
Fidges Gate, see Withyham: Fishers Gate
Field:
Thos., iv. 57–8
W., ii. 478
and see Felde
Fielder, ——, ii. 470; and see Feilder
fields, open, ii. 191; vii. 66, 76, 183; and see parish names
Fiennes (Fenys):
Anne, m. Sir Goddard Oxenbridge, ix. 169
Anne, w. of Gregory, Ld. Dacre, see Sackville
Eliz., w. of Rog., see Echingham
Gerard de, ix. 133 n
Sir Giles de, ix. 139, 177
Gregory, Ld. Dacre, vii. 89, 175, 213; ix. 116, 133, 248
Sir Jas., Ld. Saye and Sele, ix. 120, 248
Joan, w. of Jn. de, see Say
Joan, w. of Ric. de, see Dacre
Jn. de (fl. 1346), ix. 139
Jn. de (d. 1375), ix. 133, 139
Sir Jn. (d. before 1483), ix. 133, 266
Marg., Lady Dacre, m. Sampson Lennard, ix. 133–4, 266, 274
Mary, see Nevill
Maud, see Monceaux
Philippa, see Dacre
Sir Ric., Ld. Dacre, sheriff of Suss. and Surr., i. 514–15; vii. 36, 114, 126, 175, 213; ix. 118, 125, 133, 266
Rob., vii. 177, 213
Sir Rog. (d. 1449), i. 513; ii. 78–9; vii. 114; ix. 125, 131, 133–4, 244, 266
Rog. (fl. c. 1482), ix. 212 n
Sybil, see Filliol

Thos. (d. before 1533), ix. 135
Thos., Ld. Dacre (d. 1533), ii. 352; vii. 175, 177; ix. 118, 133, 135, 137, 140
Thos., Ld. Dacre (d. 1541), ii. 144 n, 197; vii. 175; ix. 133
Thos. (d. 1553), ix. 133
Wm. de (fl. 1217), i. 495
Wm. de (d. 1359), ix. 133, 139
Sir Wm. (d. 1403), ii. 361; ix. 133, 136
fam., ix. 120, 135, 171, 267
arms, vii. 175; ix. 133
and see Fynes
Fifhide (Fifhyde), Wm. de, i. 510; ii. 316; vii. 275 n, 276
Fifield, Jn., ii. 310
Filching, see Jevington
Fillery, Ric., ii. 470, 472, 475
Filliol:
Cecily, see Chanceus
Joan, w. of Wm., m. 2 Sir Wm. Cheney, vii. 147
Jn., vii. 147
Jn. (another), vii. 147
Mary, m. Jn. de Percy, vii. 147
Sybil, m. Giles de Fiennes, ix. 139
Wm. de (fl. c. 1250), ix. 139
Wm. (fl. 1318), ii. 123
Wm. (d. by 1420), vii. 147
Wm. (fl. 1420), vii. 147
fam., ix. 135
Filsham, see Hollington
Finch (Fynch):
Agnes, w. of Wm., m. 2 Babilon Grauntford, ix. 107 n
Alice, see Belknap
Ant., ix. 107
Cath., see Moyle
Clement (d. 1597), ix. 113
Clement (d. 1650), ix. 113
Denise, ix. 107
Eliz., ctss. of Maidstone and Winchilsea, see Heneage
Geo., earl of Winchilsea, ii. 467 n
Heneage (d. 1631), ix. 53
Heneage, earl of Maidstone and Winchilsea, ix. 107, 235
Hen., mayor of Winchelsea, ix. 71 n
Hen. (d. 1384, ? another), ix. 107, 146, 187
Hen. (d. 1494), ix. 92, 107
Hen. (d. 1554), ix. 113
Isabel, see Cralle
Jn. (fl. 1341), ix. 71 n
(or Herbert), Jn., ix. 107, 146
Jn. (d. 1549), ix. 113
Jn. (d. 1637), ix. 113
Jn. (fl. 1656), ix. 113
Lawr., ix. 107
Mary, w. of Clement, ix. 113
Mary, w. of Lawr., ix. 107
Sir Moyle, iv. 212; ix. 71, 107
Parnel, ix. 107
Theophilus, ix. 107
Thos. (fl. 1549), ix. 113
Sir Thos. (d. 1563), ix. 107
Thos., earl of Maidstone and Winchilsea, ix. 107
Vincent (fl. before 1343), ix. 107
Vincent (fl. 1349, another), ix. 107
Vincent (fl. 1411), ix. 107, 146, 187
Vincent (fl. 1466), ix. 113
Vincent (fl. 1476, ? another), ix. 177
Wm. de (fl. c. 1443), ix. 106–7, 158
Sir Wm. (d. 1553), ix. 92, 107
Wm. (fl. 1623), i. 521
Wm. (another), ix. 149
fam., ix. 71, 92, 235, 240
arms, ix. 107
Finch Dean (Hants), hund., ii. 220 n
Fincham (Norf.), vii. 4
Findon, i. 53, 505, 524; ii. 43
ch.:
accessories, ii. 250, 352, 354
archit., ii. 337, 344, 366, 370, 372, 376

Findon (*cont.*):
 Cissbury, i. 12
  earthworks, i. **464–5**, *465*, 466, 470
  flint mines, i. 314–16, *315*
  natural history, i. 114, 173, 189–93, 196–7, 200–7, 226, 228–9, 235, 262
  prehist. rem., i. 313, 329
  Ring, iii. 53
  signal post, i. 533
 fair, ii. 281–2
 fish trade, ii. 266
 geology, ii. 306
 insects, i. 181, 188, 195, 209–10
 pk., ii. 297
 pop., ii. 218
 prehist. rem., i. 329
 Rom. rem., iii. 3, 56
 sport, ii. 442, 445, 448, 461
 tithes, ii. 60
 vicar, ii. 397; *and see* Story, Thos.
Finnie, Jn., iv. 195
Finsbury Court, *see* London
firebote, ii. 303, 310; vii. 105
Firle, West (Ferle, Firles), ii. 44, 289; vii. 4, 224; ix. 251
 A.-S. rem., i. 341
 ch., ii. 48, 122–3, 344, 352–3, 362, 376–8
 earthworks, i. 480
 Firle Beacon, i. 336; iii. 3, 48
 Firle Place, ii. 277, 289, 386
 foxhunting, ii. 446, 450
 insects, i. 165, 167 *n*, 168, 171, 219–21
 man., ii. 92–3
 pk., ii. 297
 pop., ii. 227
 prebend, ii. 406
 prebendary, *see* Clarke, Ant.; Webb, Percival
 prehist. rem., i. 329
 roads to, iii. 47–8
 Rom. rem., iii. 3, 47–8, 56
 union, i. 539
 vicar, ii. 40
First World War, *see* wars
Fishbourne (Fisshebourne, Fisseburne), Wm. (? more than one of the name), iii. 72; iv. 184, 188
Fishbourne, New (or East), ii. 43, 303; iv. 133, **154–6**
 adv., iv. 156
 botany, i. 67
 Broyle, the, i. 522; iii. 18–19, 81, 87, 94; iv. 154
 forest, ii. 296, 303
 Heath, ii. 28
 man., iii. 81
 shooting, ii. 463
 char., iv. 156
 ch., ii. 48, 373; iv. 155–6
 dom. archit., iv. 154–5
 harbour, iii. 18, 100, 102
 man., iv. 155, 156 *n*, 183
 mills, iv. 155
 pop., ii. 220
 prehist. rem., iv. 154
 rector, ii. 37; *and see* Barrett, Serenus
 roads, iv. 154
 Rom. rem., iii. 16, 18, 47, 57
Fishbourne, Old, *see* Bosham
Fisher:
 Edw., ix. 197
 Jn., ix. 197
 Mary, w. of Ric., iii. 81
 Philadelphia, w. of Edw., ix. 197
 R.C., i. 309
 Ric., iii. 81
 Thos., iv. 189, 195
 (or Fitzwilliam), Thos., *see* Fitzwilliam
 W., ii. 167
 Mrs., ix. 247
Fisher Unwin, T., iv. 60
 his w., *see* Cobden
Fishergate, *see* Fishersgate
fisheries, ii. **264–71**; *and see* Brighton: trades; Cinque Ports; Hastings:

trades; Rye: trades; Shoreham: trades; Winchelsea: trades; Yarmouth, Great
Fishers Gate, *see* Withyham
Fishersgate (Eldretune, Eldritune, Fisheresgate, Fishergate) hund., i. 537; ii. 219, 224, 228; vii. 1, 3 *n*, 251, 258, **274**
Fisherton (Wilts.), i. 23
fishes, i. **267–70**
fishing, *see* sport: angling
fishing (fishery), right of, ii. 60, 75; iv. 162, 183, 199, 229; vii. 3, 73, 80, 85; ix. 82, 84, 153, 213, 273
Fishmongers' Company, *see* London: guilds
Fissch, Wm., master of hosp. of St. Jas. and St. Mary, Chich., ii. 100
Fisseburne (Fisshebourne), *see* Fishbourne
Fistinden, *see* Vistynden
Fittleworth, ii. 314 *n*, 391; iv. 5, 128
 angling, ii. 467
 bridge, ii. 394
 ch.:
  accessories, ii. 250, 351, 356, 360, 373
  archit., ii. 339, 346, 349, 365, 373
 Lee, iv. 217
 pop., ii. 217
 prebendary, *see* Ceccano
 prehist. rem., i. 310, *310*, 329
 Sond (Sonde), vii. 4
Fitton:
 Edw., ix. 83
 Sir Edw., ix. 83
 Mary, *see* Harbotell
FitzAilwin:
 Hen., ld. mayor of London, vii. 203
 Isabel, *see* Cheney
 Joan, m. 2 Wm. Aguillon, vii. 203
 Peter, vii. 203
FitzAlan:
 Alice (Alesia), *see* Warenne
 Anne, w. of Hen., Ld. Maltravers, iv. 128
 Beatrice, w. of Thos., earl of Arundel, iv. 59, 111, 114, 124, 153; vii. 3, 5 *n*, 58, 64, 157, 175, 234, 253, 256, 279
 Edm., earl of Arundel, i. 508; ii. 93, 295, 302; iii. 59, 94, 109, 124, 144 *n*; iv. 59, 96, 98; vii. 3
 Eleanor, w. of Jn., earl of Arundel, iv. 122
 Eleanor, w. of Jn., Ld. Maltravers, iv. 177
 Eleanor, w. of Ric., earl of Arundel, *see* Eleanor, dau. of Hen., earl of Lancaster
 Eliz., m. 2 Thos. Mowbray, duke of Norfolk, 3 Sir Rob. Goushill, vii. 5, 117, 253–4
 Eliz., w. of Ric., earl of Arundel, *see* Bohun
 Hen. (fl. 1272), iv. 59
 Hen., Ld. Maltravers (d. 1556), iv. 89, 128
 Hen., Ld. Maltravers, earl of Arundel (d. 1580), i. 516, 519; ii. 25, 109, 144 *n*, 302, 397; iv. 23, 31, 36, 45, 59, 85, 89–90, 111, 115, 118, 122, 124, 127–9, 143, 153, 172, 203, 216; vii. 55, 251–2
 Isabel, w. of Jn., earl of Arundel, *see* Mortimer
 Isabel, w. of Ric., earl of Arundel, *see* Despenser
 Jane (or Joan), m. Jn., Ld. Lumley, ii. 302; iv. 31, 45, 59, 85, 97, 111, 118, 122, 127, 143, 153, 176, 203
 Joan, m. Wm. Beauchamp, vii. 3
 Jn. (d. 1262), ii. 97
 Jn., ld. of Arundel (d. 1267), i. 496, 499, 501; iv. 2, 31, 59, 96, 128, 145, 167–8, 235
 Jn., ld. of Arundel (d. 1272), iv. 10, 59, 97, 118

 Jn., Ld. Maltravers, earl of Arundel (d. 1421), iv. 98, 177
 Jn., earl of Arundel (d. 1435), ii. 305; iv. 122, 168
 Marg., m. Sir Rowland Lenthall, vii. 3
 Mary, m. Thos. Howard, duke of Norfolk, iv. 143; vii. 6
 Ric., earl of Arundel (d. 1302), ii. 305; iii. 98; iv. 10, 45, 94–5, 122, 127
 Ric., earl of Arundel (d. 1376), i. 509; ii. 80, 82, 97, 108–9, 119–20; iii. 72, 144; iv. 31, 44, 51–2, 58–9, 66, 85, 98, 111, 129, 144–5, 152–3, 168, 176, 238; vii. 36, 71, 208 *n*
 Ric., earl of Arundel (d. 1397), i. 510–12; ii. 72, 82–3, 108, 312, 398; iii. 96, 144; iv. 23, 36, 47; vii. 3, 16, 20–1, 58, 208
 Thos., earl of Arundel and Surrey (d. 1415), i. 513; ii. 69, 75, 98, 109, 124, 312; iv. 14, 31, 42, 90, 93, 123, 128–9, 153, 199; vii. 3, 5, 58, 110, 117
 Thos., Ld. Maltravers, earl of Arundel (d. 1524), ii. 441; iv. 115, 121
 Wm., earl of Arundel (d. 1487), i. 514–15; ii. 85; iv. 12, 45, 121, 218 *n*; vii. 283
 Wm., earl of Arundel (d. 1544), ii. 144 *n*, 296, 305, 441; iv. 131, 153; vii. 55
 fam., ii. 361, 441; iv. 59, 123; ix. 216
 arms, iv. *127*, 131; vii. *3*
FitzAlan-Howard, Hen., duke of Norfolk, i. 306
FitzAlan of Clun, Wm., *see* William son of Alan of Clun
FitzAllack (fitz Allec), Wm., ii. 112; ix. 123
FitzAudelin:
 Juliana, *see* Doisnel
 Wm., ix. 206
FitzBernard, fam., ix. 149
FitzElys:
 Isabel, *see* Beche
 Jn., ix. 153
 Wm., ix. 153
FitzErnis, Oliver, vii. 20
Fitzgerald:
 Jas., earl of Kildare, duke of Leinster, ii. 443
 ——, ii. 472
Fitzhall, *see* Iping
Fitzhardinge, Lds., *see* Berkeley, Chas.; Berkeley, Sir Maur.
Fitzherbert:
 Alice, m. Sir Thos. West, ix. 202
 Sir Edm., ix. 202
 Lucy, *see* Peverel
 Mat., iii. 79
 Peter, i. 494–5
 Mrs., vii. 249–50
FitzHugh:
 Emily, vii. 115
 Osbern, ix. 262
 W.R., vii. 89, 115, 117
 Wm. Ant., vii. 115
 arms, ix. 135
FitzJames, Ric., bp. of Chich., iii. 74 *n*
FitzJohn:
 Hen., and his w. Beatrice, iv. 195
 Jn., i. 497
FitzLambert:
 Wal. (fl. 1086), ix. 79, 253, 278
 Wal. (? another), ii. 112–13
FitzOsbern, Wm., i. 487
Fitzpatrick, Mrs., vii. 35
FitzRalph, Brian, iv. 44–5, 47, 69, 80
 his daus., *see* Aveline; Sarah
 his w., *see* Mauden
FitzReynold:
 Ela, *see* Martel
 Joan, *see* Martel
 Peter, i. 507–8; iv. 158
 Reynold, iv. 159

FitzRichard, Hen., iv. 114
FitzRobert (or Wells), Sim., archdeacon of Wells, bp. of Chich., i. 492; ii. 9, 57, 63*; iii. 84–5, 107, 108 n; iv. 27, 120
FitzRoger, see Martel, Hen.; Martel, Jn.
Fitzroy:
  Anne, m. Thos. Lennard, Ld. Dacre, ix. 134
  Chas., duke of Grafton, ii. 441
  H., ii. 467 n
  Hen., M.P. for Lewes, vii. 9
FitzWalter:
  Divorguilla, see Burgh
  Sir Rob., vii. 283
FitzWarren, Fulk, i. 500
FitzWibert, Wm., see William son of Wibert
Fitzwilliam:
  Edm., ii. 61
  Ela, see Warenne
  Mabel, w. of Sir Wm., earl of Southampton, iv. 84
  (or Fisher), Thos., iv. 61
  Wm., vii. 235
  Sir Wm., earl of Southampton, Ld. High Admiral, ii. 85, 144 n, 386; iii. 100, 149; iv. 17, 25, 27, 49–50, 56–7, 61, 69–70, 76–7, 84, 93, 99, 106, 162, 179
  fam., iv. 50
  arms, iii. 49
Five Ash Down, see Buxted
Five Mile Bottom (unidentified), i. 213
Flambard, Ranulph, bp. of Durham, ix. 9*
Flamme (fl. 1066), iii. 84
Flanders, i. 484, 518; ii. 88, 126, 133; ix. 172
  count of, ii. 129
  fishing, ii. 267
  glass, ii. 353
  persons from, ii. 22, 27, 261–2; ix. 56, 61
  shipping, ii. 136, 147
  trade with, ii. 188, 255; iii. 101–2; ix. 70
  wars, i. 493, 505, 516, 519
Flansham, see Felpham
Flatman, ——, ii. 459
Flaviobriga (Spain), iii. 30
flax, see textile inds.: linen
Flaxman, Jn., ii. 362; iii. 90, 145–6; iv. 152
Fleetwood, Mr., ii. 454
Fleming:
  Sir Francis, vii. 185
  Jas., iv. 226
  Jane, see Covert
  arms, vii. 185
Fleshmonger, Wm., dean of Chich., warden of St. Mary's hosp., Chich., ii. 51, 101–2, 405, 407
Fletcher:
  H.B., iv. 158
  Jn. (fl. 1544), ii. 145
  Jn. (fl. c. 1650), iii. 130
  Jn. Ballett, iv. 161, 223, 226, 230
  Jn. Chas. Ballett, iv. 158, 165
  Judith, w. of Jn., iii. 130
  Mary, m. Edw. Dyne, ix. 92
  Wm., ix. 183
  Wm. Holland Ballett, i. 124; iv. 161, 223, 230–1, 233
Fletching, i. 496–7; ii. 44, 313, 322
  angling, ii. 464–5
  Barkham, see Birkham
  ch., ii. 9, 78
    accessories, ii. 352–3, 358, 360–1, 375
    archit., ii. 339–40, 344, 366, 372–3, 375
  Danehill, q.v.
  Darnall, q.v.
  insects, i. 156, 174
  man., i. 496; ii. 173 n, 317
  Piltdown, i. 50, 188; ii. 465, 479
  pop., ii. 227

Searles, ii. 463–4
Sheffield:
  iron ind., ii. 247
  Pk., i. 165–6; ii. 277, 300, 464
  textile ind., ii. 257
  vicarage, ii. 9
Flexborough (Faxberwe, Faxeburgh, Flexberghe) hund., i. 537; ii. 182 n, 226, 228
Flimwell, see Ticehurst
flint mining, i. 314–16, 464
Flisco, Jn. de, rector of West Tarring, ii. 12
Flocer (Floc, Floscis):
  Geof. de, ii. 112; ix. 180, 183
  Hugh de, ii. 112; ix. 183
Flodwine, moneyer, iii. 83
Floid, see Floyd
Flood, Wm., ii. 237
floors, see architecture: ecclesiastical
flora, see botany
Florence (Italy), ii. 188
Floscis, see Flocer
flotage, ix. 84
Flower, Edm., ii. 416–17, 419–20
Flowers Green, see Herstmonceux
Floyd (Floid):
  Wm. (fl. 1685), iii. 96
  Wm. (d. 1716), iii. 145
Fludd, Sir Thos., iv. 152
Flynt, ——, i. 516
Flyrdar, Jn. le, iv. 80
Fogg (Fogge), Sir Jn., vii. 110; ix. 244
Fokinton:
  Egeline, w. of Hugh de, vii. 225
  Hugh de (sr.), vii. 225
  Hugh de (jr.), vii. 225
  Olimpia de, m. Jn. de la Warr, vii. 225
  Reynold de, vii. 225
Folet:
  Burgunnia, w. of Wal., m. 2 Jn. Winde, ix. 267
  Cecily, m. Ric. Cumpayn, ix. 267
  Elias, ix. 267
  Mabel, see Waliland
  Wal., ix. 267
Foley, Thos., vii. 284
Foljambe:
  Geo. Saville, vii. 34
  Selina, see Jenkinson
Folkestone (Kent), i. 8, 72, 239; ii. 162, 235; iii. 8, 102; ix. 38, 149
  and see Alschot
Folkington, ii. 44, 184; iv. 62, 204; vii. 225
  ch., ii. 339–40
  dean, ii. 42
  earthworks, i. 480
  Gnat (Nat) wood, i. 56, 167–8; ii. 122
  insects, i. 165–7
  man., ii. 276; vii. 4
  pop., ii. 226
  rector, ii. 40
  wood, i. 56
  Wootton, q.v.
Folks, Thos., ii. 96
Folsalre, see Foxearle
Fonnereau, ——, iii. 80
Fontanis, Torstin de, iv. 162
Fontevrault (Maine-et-Loire, France), abbey, iv. 91 n
Fontridge, tithing, ix. 210
fonts and font covers, see architecture: ecclesiastical
Fontwell, see Aldingbourne
Fooks, Wm., ii. 166
football, see sport
Footlands, see Sedlescombe
Forbes:
  Geo., Ld. Forbes, ii. 166
  Rob., ii. 167
Ford (Forde):
  Anne, see Caryll
  Cath. (Kath.), m. Ralph, Ld. Grey of Warke, iv. 16, 20
  Dorothy, m. Francis Fortescue, iv. 15
  Edm. (d. 1568), ii. 24; iv. 10–11, 13, 15–17*, 20, 24–6, 83, 129

Edm. (fl. 1607), iv. 24
Sir Edw., i. 522–5; ii. 298; iii. 87; iv. 13, 16, 20
Erasmus, iv. 10
Frances, see Knottesford
Sir Francis, ii. 450
Hen., ii. 321
Joan atte, ix. 169
Jn., iv. 16, 24
Magdalen, m. 1 Jn. Ford, 2 Hen. Knyvett, iv. 24
Mary, w. of Edm., iv. 24
Rob. atte, ix. 169
(or Bohun), Savaric de, see Bohun
Thos., iv. 15, 24
Sir Wm., i. 522; ii. 298, 309; iv. 13, 16, 20, 24, 118
fam., i. 526; iv. 18, 25
arms, iv. 16, 20
Ford, ii. 42–3; iii. 71; iv. 114; ix. 254
  ch., ii. 37, 108, 121, 331; iv. 77 n
    accessories, ii. 350–1, 354–5, 359, 362, 370
    archit., ii. 327, 332, 334, 338, 340, 346, 348, 350–1, 364, 366, 370, 376, 379
  dom. archit., ii. 392–4
  insects, i. 187, 197, 206
  man., ii. 121
  pop., ii. 217
  roads to, iii. 46
  Rom. rem., ii. 46
  ship service, ii. 138
  sport, ii. 453, 466
Fordcombe, see Penshurst
Forde, see Ford
Forden, Wm., master of hosp. of St. Jas. and St. Mary, Chich., ii. 100
Fordham, ——, ii. 459
Fordham (Essex), ii. 409
Fordwich (Kent), ix. 38
Foreland, North (Kent), ii. 127
Foreland, South (Kent), ii. 163
forest eyres, see courts
Forest of Dean, see Dean
Forest Row, ii. 44
  Broadstone (Brodestone), ii. 319
  Dallingridge, ii. 319
  Forest Row Green, ii. 319
  Hammerwood, ii. 44
  Highgate, ii. 319
  Hindleap, ii. 319
  Homestall, ii. 387
  insects, i. 112, 166
  Kidsbrooke gate, ii. 319
  Leggesheath gate, ii. 319
  Mudbrooke gate, ii. 319
  Plaw (Plagh, Plow) Chase, ii. 316
  Plaw Hatch, ii. 319, 322
Forester, Ld., see Baillie
forestry, ii. 170, 192, 278, **291–325**; vii. 168
forests, i. 305; and see Andredsweald; Arundel; Ashdown; Balcombe; Charlton; Clares chase; Claveridge; Dallington; Darvel; Dean, Forest of; Fishbourne, New: Broyle, the; Houghton; New Forest; Oving: Colworth; St. Leonard's forest; Shepherds Field; Singleton; Stansted; Tilgate; Waterdown; Windsor; Worth
Forman:
  Blanche, see Reynolds
  Sir Wm., ix. 139
Forrest, Jn., and his w. Marg., ix. 213
Forrey, Wal., warden of St. Mary's hosp., Chich., ii. 102
Forsham:
  Aveline de, see Gotele
  Steph. de, ix. 274
Forster:
  Anne, vii. 131, 165
  Avice, see Alston
  Jn., ix. 197
  (or Foster), Ric., ix. 197
  (or Foster), Sir Rob., and his w. Eliz., ix. 197

Forster (cont.):
Thos., ix. 197
and see Foster
Fortescue:
Anne, Lady Fortescue, vii. 89
Dorothy, see Ford
Edm., iv. 16
Francis, iv. 15–17
Henrietta Ann, w. of Mat., vii. 89
Jn., iv. 16
Mat., vii. 89, 91
Wm. Hen., earl of Clermont, ii. 456
fam., iv. 11, 20, 25
Forth, Mr., ii. 458
Forth, riv. (Scot.), i. 289
Forward:
Jn., vicar of Iford, vii. 57
Patience, w. of Jn., vii. 57
Fos, Jn., vii. 36
fossils, i. **27–39**
Foster:
Ant., iv. 7, 35–6, 38; vii. 54, 82, 101
Constance, see Lewknor
E., ii. 471
Eliz., m. Thos. Bateman, iv. 35
Fred., ix. 90
Giles, vii. 226
Godard, ix. 153
Jn., ix. 153
Mary, ix. 153
Mary, m. Chas. Wallcott, iv. 35
R.S., ii. 470
Rob., ix. 180
Thos. (fl. c. 1550), iv. 35; vii. 81
Thos. (d. 1605), ix. 153
Thos. (fl. 1638), ix. 153
Wm., vicar of Billingshurst, ii. 25
and see Forster
Fotherby, Chas., ii. 165
Foucarmont (Seine-Maritime, France), abbey, ix. 2
Founder, Wm., iv. 63, 239
Foundry Pond, see Cocking
Fountayne, Wm., vii. 171; ix. 183
Foville, Wm. de, prior of Lewes, ii. 66, 70
Fowey (Cornw.), ii. 136
Fowkes, Jn., see Fox
Fowle:
Alex., vii. 217
Anne, see Wildgose
Annesley, vii. 218; ix. 221
Ant., vii. 134
Eliz., vii. 218
Humph., vii. 134
Jn. (fl. 1526), ix. 214
Sir Jn. (d. 1637), vii. 218; ix. 221
Jn. (fl. 1699), and his w. Dorothy, ix. 221
Lucy, m. Wal. Roberts, ix. 221
Marion, m. Goddard Bachelor, ix. 214
Mildred, ix. 214
Ric., vii. 97
Rob., vii. 218; ix. 221
fam., ii. 247
Fowler:
Frances, w. of Wm., iii. 145
Jn., iv. 109
Mary, iii. 145
T.H., ii. 476
Wal., iv. 235
Wm. (fl. 1788), iv. 213
Wm. (fl. c. 1808, ? another), iii. 145
Fox:
Chas. Jas., M.P. for Midhurst, ii. 456; iv. 76
Geo., ii. 38
Hen., M.P. for Midhurst, iv. 76
(or Fowkes), Jn., dean of Hastings coll., ii. 117
Mr., vii. 248
Fox, Lane, see Lane Fox
Fox Hall, see Charlton
Foxborough Marsh (unidentified), i. 166
Foxearle (Folsalre, Foxelere, Foxelre, Foxer), hund., i. 537; ii. 222; ix. 3, **125**
foxhunting, see sport: hunting

Foxle (Foxele):
Alice de, iv. 171
Eliz. de, m. Thos. Uvedale, iv. 171
Sir Jn. de (fl. 1312), iv. 171, 173
Jn. de (fl. 1364), and his w. Agnes, vii. 58 n
Sir Jn. de (fl. 1377, another), iv. 171, 173
Jn. de (d. 1420), iv. 171
Ric. de, iv. 171
Thos. de (fl. 1338), iv. 171
Thos. de (fl. 1377, another), iv. 171, 173
Thos. de (fl. 1446), iv. 171
Foyce, Hen., ii. 308
Foyle, Jn., ix. 26
Foyster:
G.A., ix. 26
H.S., ix. 26
Jn. Goodge, ix. 26
Fragbarrow, see Ditchling
Fraine, Jn., iv. 35–6
Framelle hund., see Loxfield
Framfield, ii. 44, 189, 206 n, 292
Bentley, ii. 27, 297
Blackboys, i. 215, 217–18, 223
ch., ii. 118, 358
archit., ii. 336–7, 344, 348, 351, 375, 379
inc., ii. 190
insects, i. 217–19, 222
Plottesbridge pk., ii. 298
pop., ii. 226
trades and ind., ii. 257, 318
vicar, ii. 37
vicarage, ii. 8
Frampton:
E. Reg., ix. 22
Harriet, iii. 163
France:
Eliza, iii. 115
Wm., iii. 115
France, i. 343, 512; ii. 68, 87, 129, 164, 302, 400, 441–2; iv. 13
archit., ii. 332
Avranches, dean, see Laigle, Nic.
Coutances, bp., see Geoffrey
fishing, ii. 267–8; ix. 13, 55
flight to, i. 491, 494, 499–500
invasion, i. 517–18; ii. 125–6
kings, i. 496; ix. 2–3; and see Charles II; Francis I; Henry IV; Louis VIII; Louis XIII; Louis XIV; Louis Philippe; Philip II, Augustus
militia, i. 518
natural history, i. 13, 18, 28, 111, 141 n, 253, 255, 266, 278 n
persons from, i. 533; ii. 255, 258; ix. 56, 61, 226
prehist. rem., i. 312
privateers, ii. 147; ix. 5
queen, i. 500
raids, i. 518; ii. 259
Reformed ch., ii. 234
Revolution, see wars: French revolutionary
seneschal, see Bursegard, Sire de
shipping, ii. 158
trade with, ii. 232, 397; ix. 70
wars:
with Spain, i. 516
and see wars: with France
and see individual place names
Franceis, see Francis
franchises and customary rights, i. 502;
and see anchorage; assize of bread and ale; assize of cloth; bredgeld; cartbote; deodands; estover; firebote; fishing, right of; flotage; frankpledge, view of; free warren; gallows; haybote; hedgebote; herbage, right of; housebote; hunting rights; infangthief; lastage; measurage; mede panes; murage; outfangthief; palebote; pannage; passage; pasture; pillory; plowbote; pontage; quarrying, right of;

quayage; rivage; sac and soc; soilage; sponsage; stakebote; stallage; strand and den; treasure trove; tumbrell; waifs and strays; wainbote; withernam; wood allowance; wreck, right of
Francigena, Wal., ii. 174
Francis I, king of France, ii. 145
Francis (Franceis, Fraunceis, Fraunceys):
Dan., i. 304
Edm., ii. 420*
Sir Edw. (fl. 1609), iv. 144
Edw. (fl. 1617), vii. 230
Jn., ii. 325
Wm. le, and his w. Juliana, ix. 146 n
(or Duke), Wm., see Duke
Frankewelle, see Frankwell
Frankham park, see Mayfield
Frankland:
Hen., iii. 145
Jn., canon of Chich., warden of St. Mary's hosp., Chich., ii. 102; iii. 74, 147; iv. 185
Mary, see Edes
Sir Thos., iii. 80
Franklin (Franklen, Fraunkeleyne):
Dyrild, vii. 121
R., iv. 39
Lady, ii. 201
frankpledge, view of, iii. 94–6, 103–4; iv. 188; vii. 2–3, 26, 29–30, 93, 271; ix. 3, 82, 125, 153, 196, 201, 221
Franks:
Isabella, m. 1 —— Ball, 2 Sir Wm. Hen. Cooper, ix. 187
Jacob, ix. 187
Jacob Hen., ix. 187
Moses, ix. 187
Priscilla, w. of Jacob, ix. 187
Franks, iii. 3–5
Frankwell (Frankewelle, Fraunkwell):
Wm., ii. 259
Mr., ii. 318
fam., ix. 128
Frant (Ferneth), ii. 44, 229, 323–4; iv. 62
Bayham abbey, q.v.
boundary, i. 536
Eridge, q.v.
insects, i. 175, 179, 188–9, 212–15, 219–20, 224, 227, 230, 232–3, 235
pop., ii. 237
Rumbold's Hill, i. 477
textile ind., ii. 257
Fraser:
A.B.S., ii 277, 453
Jn. Hen., iii. 145
Maria Anne, see Hobart
Fraunceis (Fraunceys), see Francis
Fraunkeleyne, see Franklin
Fraunkwell, see Frankwell
Frawell, ——, ii. 31
Fraxineto (Fraxino), see Fresne
Fraye:
Anne, m. —— Lewknor, ix. 187
Jn. (d. 1592), ix. 187, 189
Jn. (fl. 1592), ix. 187
Wm., ix. 187
Frayes Gate, see Withyham: Friar's Gate
Frazer Cooke (later Piggott), Sim., iv. 5
his w., see Piggott, Jane
Freake (Freakes, Freke):
Cecily, m. Sir Geo. Chowte, ix. 154
Jas., see Parson
Jane, see Shirley
Jn., vii. 146
Ralph, ix. 154
Rob., vii. 238, 257
Thos., vii. 238
Freavill, see Freville
Frederick, Barnard, ii. 439
Fredesend, dau. of Hugh son of Rainer, vii. 110, 213, 226
Fredri (fl. 1086), vii. 99
free warren, i. 503; ii. 171, 294–5, 304–

5, 307, 311, 314, 316–17, 323–5; iii. 81; iv. 17, 23, 25, 28, 31, 34, 36, 42, 45, 61, 66, 85, 123, 135, 144, 155, 168, 202, 213, 217, 231, 235; vii. 2, 36, 73, 80, 105, 110–11, 133, 157, 183, 196, 203, 226, 271, 283; ix. 79–80, 82, 106–7, 117, 127–8, 134, 138–9, 144–5, 152–4, 176–7, 180, 187, 196, 201, 206, 213–14, 220–1, 228–9, 235, 254, 258, 264, 273

Freebody (Freebodye):
  Jn. (d. 1578), ix. 174
  Jn. (d. 1612), ix. 174
  Jn. (d. 1715), ix. 174
  fam., ix. 172

Freeland, Arthur Raymond Stilwell, iv. 239

Freeland, see Johnson, Price, and Freeland

Freeman:
  Alex., ii. 264
  Mrs. C., ix. 173
  Mrs. E.E., ix. 173
  Edw. Augustus, ii. 128
  Eliz., see Hammond
  Hen., vii. 34
  Luke, ii. 444
  and see Williams-Freeman

Freeman-Thomas, F., ii. 277

Freemantle, Jn., ii. 475

Freemantle (Hants), ii. 241

Freind, see Friend

Freke, see Freake

Frekeburgh, see Ditchling: Fragbarrow

Fremlin Bros., ii. 263

Fremlyn, Geo., ii. 263

French (Frenche):
  Anne, see Brain
  Eliz., m. Chas. S. Mortimer, ix. 181
  Geo., ix. 235
  Jeremiah, ix. 181
  Judith, ix. 215
  Winifred, ix. 181
  fam., ii. 247

'French John', see Huntrye

French revolutionary wars, see wars

Frenchlands Woods (? Ashington), i. 164, 169

Frend, see Friend

Frendesbury, Rob., abbot of Bayham, ii. 89

Frenyngham, Wm., i. 514

Frere:
  Rob., vii. 111
  Wm., ix. 235

Freschville (Fressenville):
  Ansel de, ix. 83, 161
  Auker de, ix. 83
  Ingelram de, ix. 221, 278
  Maud de, m. Reynold de Meyners, ix. 221, 278
  Ralph de, ix. 83
  Rog., ix. 83
  fam., ix. 83
  and see Freville

Freshfield, Mr., ix. 64 n

Freshwater (I.W.), i. 192

freshwater algae, i. 61–2

Fresne (Fraxineto, Fraxino):
  Conan de, iii. 104
  Rog. de, ii. 105, 122
  Wm. de (fl. temp. Hen. I), iii. 104; iv. 167
  Wm. de (d. 1223), iv. 167

Fressenville, see Freschville

Freton, Rog. de, dean of Chich., ii. 51; iv. 136 n

Freville (Freavill, Friville):
  Agatha, m. Hamon le Strange, vii. 231 n
  Jn. de, vii. 228, 231
  Ric. de, vii. 228, 231
  Rob. de, vii. 228
  Rog. de, and his w. Sybil, ix. 83 n
  and see Freschville

Frewen:
  Accepted, abp. of York, ix. 272 n
  Chas., ix. 83

Chas. B., ix. 187
Chas. Hay, ix. 25
Dorothy, see Scott
Sir Edw. (fl. 1712), ix. 165
Edw. (fl. c. 1730, ? another), ix. 167 n
Edw. (fl. 1768), ix. 224
Edw. (fl. 1882), ii. 447
Edw. (fl. 1905, ? another), i. 306
Frances, see Brisco
Jn. (fl. 1583), ix. 269
Jn. (fl. 1628, another), ix. 274
Jn. (another), ix. 274
Kath., see Scott
Oswald, ix. 169
Palacia, see Jenkin
Steph. (fl. 1666), ix. 146, 269, 272, 276
Steph., vicar of Fairlight, ix. 178
Thankful, ix. 264, 275–6
Thos. (fl. 1694), ix. 152, 156, 276
Thos. (fl. 1731-43), ix. 224, 276
Dr. Thos. (fl. 1749), vii. 18 n; ix. 269 n
Thos. (fl. 1784, ? another), ix. 147
Thos. (fl. 1849), ix. 171
fam., ix. 147, 169, 171, 224, 269, 274, 276

Friar's Gate, see Withyham

Friday Street, see Horsham

Friday's Church, see Arundel

Friend (Freind, Frend):
  Jn. (fl. 1577), vii. 96
  Jn. (fl. 1592), vii. 263
  Jn. (fl. 1725), vii. 256
  Mary, vii. 257
  Ric., vii. 96
  Thos. (d. 1762), vii. 19, 255, 257, 262
  Thos. (d. 1763), vii. 19, 255–6
  Wm., ii. 405
  fam., vii. 250

Friends, Society of, see Quakers

Frisby, Geo. Wm., iv. 21

Friston, i. 310; ii. 44, 86, 138; iv. 64
  ch., ii. 123, 354, 362
    archit., ii. 329 n, 337–8, 340, 348–9, 351, 364, 366, 376
  earthworks, i. 480
  Friston Place, ii. 384
  pop., ii. 227
  prehist. rem., i. 310, 329

Friths, see Chiddingly

Friville, see Freville

Frobisher, Martin, ii. 148 n

Frog Firle, see Alfriston

Froissart, Jean, i. 510, 512; ii. 139

Fromond:
  Bart., ix. 191
  Dorothy, see Thatcher
  Eliz., m. Sir Ant. Morgan, ix. 191
  Rob., ix. 191
  Susan, see Thatcher
  Wm. (d. 1504), prior of Pynham, ii. 81
  Wm. (fl. after 1612), ix. 191

Frostenden (Suff.), i. 285

Froyle (Hants), iv. 70, 155

fruit growing, iv. 197, 285–6, 299, 309; vii. 58, 87

Fry:
  C.B., ii. 470, 474
  Thos., and his w. Mary Hannah, ix. 198

Fuce, Jos., ii. 38

Fulcui (fl. 1066), iv. 85

Fulk (fl. 1066), iv. 114

Fulk (fl. 1086), iv. 80, 108

Fulking (formerly in Edburton), vii. 201, 202–4
  agric., vii. 202
  cast., vii. 202
  dom. archit., vii. 202
  Edburton Hill, iii. 3; vii. 202
  fields, vii. 202
  Fulking Hill, iii. 62
  inc., vii. 203
  man., vii. 202–4
  mills, vii. 204
  Perching, q.v.

pop., ii. 219 n
Rom. rem., iii. 3, 56, 62; vii. 202

Fullagar, Jn., iii. 164

Fuller:
  Anne, m. Laur. Alcock, iv. 35, 163 n
  Augustus Eliot, ix. 245, 264
  David, vii. 100
  Sir Dowse, iv. 83
  Dowse, iv. 83
  Edw., iv. 163 n
  Eliz., see Rose
  Eliz. L., ix. 75
  Hen., iv. 93
  Hugh, vii. 275
  Jane, see Grey
  Jn. (fl. 1610), ix. 202
  Jn. (fl. 1693), ix. 248
  Jn. (d. 1745), ix. 227
  Jn. (d. 1755), ix. 227*, 230
  Jn. (fl. 1775), ix. 245
  Jn. (fl. 1781, ? another), vii. 124
  Jn. (fl. 1788, ? two of this name), ix. 118, 245
  Jn. (fl. 1795, ? another), ix. 244
  Jn. (d. by 1815), ix. 231
  Jn. (fl. c. 1820), ix. 242
  Jn. (d. 1834, ? another), ix. 264
  Lydia, w. of Ric., iii. 147
  Marg., m. Sam. Pargitter, iv. 83
  Mary, ix. 147
  Ric. (fl. 1659), ix. 203
  Ric. (d. 1842), iii. 147
  Rose, ix. 227, 230
  Sam. Pargitter, iv. 83
  Thos. (d. 1611), ii. 236
  Thos. (fl. 1705), ix. 227
  Thos. (d. by 1790), ix. 230, 245
  Thos. (fl. after 1813), ix. 242
  fam., ii. 247–8; ix. 201, 228, 245
  arms, ix. 245

Fuller-Meyrick, Owen J., ix. 264

Fuller-Palmer-Acland (formerly Palmer-Acland), Sir Peregrine Palmer, ix. 242*, 245

fulling, see textile inds.

fulling mills, see mills

fungi, i. 66–7

Funtington, ii. 43, 442; iv. 181, 184, 190–2
  adv., iv. 192
  Ashling:
    East Ashling, iv. 181, 184, 190–2
    natural history, i. 65, 171
    West Ashling, iv. 181, 184, 190–2
  char., iv. 192
  ch., ii. 344, 373; iv. 190–2
  Densworth, iii. 4, 15, 17–18, 49, 53–4, 67; iv. 190
    man., iv. 185, 191, 195
  dom. archit., iv. 190–1
  inc., iv. 182
  man., ii. 53; iv. 183, 191
  mill, iv. 190
  nonconf., iv. 190
  Oakwood, i. 67; iv. 190
  pop., ii. 220
  prebend, ii. 110; iv. 188
  prehist. rem., i. 329; iv. 190
  Ratham:
    mill, iv. 190
    natural history, i. 277, 305
  roads, iv. 190
  Rom. rem., iii. 54
  Sennicots, iv. 190
    adv., iv. 192
    chap., iv. 192
    tithes, iv. 192

Furby, Ric., vii. 286

Furlonger:
  Eliz., iii. 164
  Jas., iii. 164
  Sarah, m. Jas. Dearling, iii. 164

Fursby, Jn., ii. 39

Fust (Fuyst):
  Marg., see Whelton
  Jn., iv. 195
  Ric., iv. 185, 195
  Wm., and his w. Joan, iv. 195

Fust (*cont.*):
 fam., iv. 195
fustian, *see* textile inds.: wool
Fuyst, *see* Fust
Fynch, *see* Finch
Fyner (or Mayer), Harry, *see* Mayer
Fynes (Fenys):
 Agnes, w. of Edw., *see* Holden
 Ant., vii. 177
 Edw., vii. 176
 Francis, vii. 177
 Giles, ix. 56
 Jn. (fl. 1555), ix. 56*
 Jn. (d. 1629), vii. 176
 Jn. (d. 1632), vii. 176–7
 Phil., ix. 92
 Sir Thos., ix. 56
 and see Fiennes
Fyneux, Sir Jn., vii. 242
Fyning, Rob. de, iv. 24
Fyning, *see* Rogate

gabulum, *see* gavel
Gadesden, *see* Gatesden
Gael, Ralph de, *see* Wader
gafol, *see* gavel
Gage (Gayge):
 Benedicta, w. of Thos., ix. 191
 Sir Edw., sheriff of Suss., ii. 22–4, 26, 317; vii. 105
 Edw. (fl. 1573), ix. 138
 Edw. (fl. 1580, ? another), ii. 27–8
 Edw. (fl. 1606, another), ix. 138
 Edw. (fl. 1717), ix. 191
 Hen., Vct. Gage, ii. 301
 Hen. Chas., Vct. Gage, ii. 277, 289
 Hen. Edw. Hall, iii. 115
 Hen. Hall, Vct. Gage, ii. 209 n, 446
 Jas., rector of Buxted, ii. 22
 Jas. (fl. 1569), ii. 24–6
 Jas. (d. 1573, ? another), ix. 138, 140
 Sir Jn., constable of Tower of London, i. 515; ii. 54, 144 n; vii. 37, 105; ix. 106, 140, 255
 Jn. (fl. 1580), ii. 27–8; vii. 105
 Jos., ix. 191
 Thos., Vct. Gage, ii. 444
 Thos. (fl. 1577), vii. 105
 Thos. (fl. 1717), ix. 191
 Wm. (d. 1333), ii. 297
 Sir Wm. (fl. 1730), ii. 454, 467
 Wm. Hall, Ld. Gage, i. 338
 Mr., ii. 457
 fam., ii. 27, 362
Gairdner, Jas., ii. 143
 and see Gardener; Gardiner
Gale:
 Eliz., m. Hen. Humphrey, vii. 111, 145, 195
 Geo. Alex., iv. 150
 Leon, vii. 111, 145, 147, 195, 199
 Philippa, m. Jas. Clitherow, vii. 111, 145, 195
 Sarah, m. Sam. Blunt, vii. 111, 145, 195
 ——, m. Arthur C. Harris, iv. 150
galleries, *see* architecture: ecclesiastical
Galley Hill, *see* Bexhill
Gallipoli, bp. of, *see* Young, Jn.
Galloway:
 Ambrose, ii. 38
 Jas., vii. 139, 158
gallows, iv. 71; vii. 2; ix. 11, 118, 196, 201, 221
Galys, Wm., abbot of Bayham, ii. 89
Game:
 E.J., ii. 476
 W.H., ii. 476
Gamull, Jn., dean of Hastings coll., ii. 117
Ganges, riv., i. 28
gaols, *see* prisons
Garbard (Harbarde, Jarbarde), Thos., ii. 406
Gardener (Gardner):
 Harry, ii. 474
 Thos., master of hosp. of St. Jas. and St. Mary, Chich., ii. 100

Wm., iii. 73
 and see Gairdner; Gardiner
Gardin:
 Alexandra, *see* Hay
 Cecily, *see* Thorney
 Maud, w. of Wm., iv. 163
 Wm. (d. by 1225), iv. 163
 Wm. (d. by 1230), iv. 163
 Wm. (fl. 1254), iv. 164
 and see Jardyn
Gardine Hill, *see* Hartfield
Gardiner, Steph., bp. of Winchester, iv. 13
 and see Gairdner; Gardener
Gardner, *see* Gardener
Gardner Street, *see* Herstmonceux
Gare, Luke de la, bailiff of Rye, ix. 51
Garfoot, Wm., vii. 76
Gargrave, Thos., iv. 27
Garland (Garlaunde):
 Hen. de, prebendary of Thorney, dean of Chich., ii. 51; iii. 114, 153; iv. 90, 170, 215
 Hen. de (fl. c. 1300, ? another), ix. 240
 Sam., iv. 64
 Sharp, mayor of Chich., iii. 163
 Wm. de, ix. 242
Garlethorpe, Jn. de, master of Playden hosp., ii. 105
Garnier, Wm., ii. 166
Garraway (Garway):
 Bart., and his w. Marg., ix. 181
 Hen., alderman and ld. mayor of London, vii. 228; ix. 245
 Marg., w. of Hen., ix. 245
 Powle, ix. 181
 Rice R., vii. 87
 Sir Wm. (fl. 1624), ix. 245 n
 Wm. (fl. c. 1670), ii. 392
Garrett, Ric., rector of Stedham, iv. 77
Garrick, David, iii. 90; ix. 7
Garth:
 Jos., iv. 144
 Sarah, *see* Turner
 Maj.-Gen., i. 535
Garthwaite, Jas., i. 534
Garton:
 Dorothy, w. of Hen., iii. 77
 Francis, iv. 59
 Giles (fl. 1588), and his w. Marg., vii. 158
 Giles (d. 1592, ? another), iv. 59
 Giles (fl. 1645), ix. 83
 Hen., iii. 77; iv. 59, 95
 Jane, m. Thos. Stoughton, iv. 212
 Judith, *see* Shirley
 Mary, ? m. Baynham Throckmorton, ix. 83
 Mary, m. Rob. Orme, iv. 59
 Sir Peter, iv. 59, 95*
 Rob., iii. 77; iv. 59, 95
 Sir Thos., iv. 59, 95
 Wm., iii. 77*; iv. 59, 95
 fam., iv. 96; vii. 36, 59
 arms, iv. 59
Garuerd, Griffin s. of, *see* Griffin
Garway, *see* Garraway
gas well, *see* Heathfield
Gascoigne (Gascoyn):
 Jn., ix. 255
 Sir Thos., ii. 444
Gascony (France), ii. 132; iii. 101 n; ix. 3
Gascoyn, *see* Gascoigne
Gate:
 Hamon atte, ix. 273
 Hen. atte, ix. 273
 Joan at, m. Rob. Echingham, ix. 273
 Jn. atte (d. c. 1284), ix. 273
 Jn. atte (or de la) (fl. to 1340), ix. 144, 273
 Ralph atte, iii. 75
 Rob. atte, ix. 273
 Sarah, w. of Hen. atte, ix. 273
 fam., ix. 273
 arms, ix. 274
 and see Gates

Gateborough, *see* Rye
Gatecourt, *see* Northiam
Gates:
 F.C., ii. 478
 Geof. de, iv. 135
 Jas., iii. 163
 Jn., iii. 163
 Mary, iii. 163
 Wm. de, iv. 157
 and see Gate
Gates, prebend, *see* Aldingbourne
Gatesden (Gadesden, Gatesdene):
 Cecily de, *see* Aguillon
 Hawise de, *see* Savage
 Jn. de (fl. 1231), ii. 99
 Jn. de (d. c. 1262, ? another), iv. 6 n, 8, 34, 36, 59, 107, 167; vii. 81, 226
 Jn., his s., iv. 8, 34
 Marg. de, m. 1 Sir Jn. de Camoys, 2 Wm. Paynel, ii. 84, 360; iv. 6 n, 8, 34, 36 n, 38, 213; vii. 81
 Margery, w. of Jn. de, iv. 34; vii. 81 n
 Peter de, iv. 89, 111
Gathole, ——, ii. 34
Gatland:
 Anne, vii. 154 n
 Dorothy, *see* Whitson
 Hen., vii. 154 n
 Wal., vii. 135
Gaucelin, rector of Pagham, *see* Duèse
Gaul, ii. 125; iii 1, 7, 9, 30, 55, 66, 69; *and see* Romano-British Suss.: pottery
Gaunt (Ghent), Jn. of, duke of Lancaster, earl of Richmond, i. 509–12; ii. 123–4, 139–40, 316–17; vii. 3; ix. 3, 77, 172, 196, 216
Gausbert, abbot of Battle, ii. 52, 55
Gausden, Chas. Hen., ii. 470
Gausden & Sisk, ii. 235
gavel (gabulum, gafol), iii. 83, 91, 104
gavelkind (gavelmerke), ii. 177; iv. 218; ix. 149
Gaveston:
 Marg., w. of Piers, iii. 85
 Piers, i. 508; iii. 85, 91
Gawen:
 Allan, iv. 136
 Ric., iv. 136
Gay, L.H., ii. 476
Gayge, *see* Gage
Gaynesford:
 Agnes, m. Sir Jn. Culpeper, vii. 225
 Eleanor, *see* Browne
 Jn. (d. 1450), vii. 225, 229–30
 Jn. (d. 1464), vii. 230
 Sir Jn. (fl. 1464), vii. 230
 Sir Jn. (d. c. 1494), vii. 230
 Kath., *see* Covert
 fam., ix. 270
 arms, vii. 230
Gdansk (Danzig, Dantzig) (Poland), ii. 233
Geere (Geare):
 Chas., vii. 226, 233, 235
 Diones, ix. 192
 Eliz., w. of Chas., vii. 233, 235
 Grace, ix. 192
 Ruth, m. —— Nixon, iii. 147
 Ruth, w. of Thos., iii. 147
 Thos. (sr.), iii. 147
 Thos. (jr.), iii. 147
Geere and Blaber, ii. 164
Geeringe, Ric., vii. 216
Geldart, Sarah Laura, ix. 33
Geldwin, son of Savaric, iv. 23, 25, 34, 77; vii. 208
Gem, Arthur, iii. 145
Gencelin, ix. 278
 his s., *see* Gilbert
Genebelli, ——, ix. 55
Genoa (Italy), ii. 132, 137 n
Gensing:
 Gilb., ix. 19
 Parnel (Pernel) de, m. Jn. Read, ix. 19
 Rob., ix. 19
 Wm. (fl. 1189), ix. 19

Wm. (fl. 1265), ix. 19
Gensing, see St. Leonards
Gentelman, Jn., vii. 61 n
Gentil, Nic. (? two of this name), i. 507;
iv. 177 n
Geoffrey, bp. of Coutances, i. 487
Geoffrey, canon of Chich., iii. 72 n
Geoffrey, count of Anjou, vii. 2
Geoffrey, dean of Chich., ii. 51
Geoffrey, monk of St. Carileff, ii. 53
Geoffrey, ? prebendary of Chich., iv.
174–5, 208
Geoffrey fitz Piers, vii. 258 n
his s., see John fitz Geoffrey (fl. 1243)
Geoffrey son of Azo, iv. 107, 110,
145
his w. Agnes, see Gundeville
Geoffrey, clerk (fl. 1086), ix. 123
Geoffrey (fl. 1086), iv. 41, 91, 118
Geoffrey (fl. 1086, ? another), ix. 82,
152
Geoffrey, Jn. fitz, see John
Geoffrey, Thos. s. of, see Thomas
geology, i. 1–26, 26, 43, 45–6, 49; and
see parish names
George, St., i. 499; iii. 92
George I, ii. 305; iii. 89
George II, ix. 12
as prince of Wales, ii. 305; iii. 89
George III, ii. 258; iv. 226
his dau., see Amelia
George IV, as prince of Wales, ii. 203,
444, 455–8, 460, 467; vii. 19, 247,
249–50, 260
George V, iii. 81, 130; iv. 226; ix. 29
George, prince of Denmark, ii. 239
Gerard (fl. 1086), see Girard
Gerard (Gerarde, Gerrard):
Jn., i. 41
Lucy, see Cook
Mary, see Browne
Sir Sam., ix. 207
Sam., ix. 207
Thos., master of St. Jas.'s hosp., Sea-
ford, ii. 105
Sir Thos., iv. 80
Gering:
Jn., vii. 225
Thos., vii. 225
Wm., vii. 225
German, see Jermyn
Germanicus, iii. 50, 50
Germany, i. 44, 58, 278 n; ii. 233, 246,
249, 342, 353, 442
and see Bavaria; Hanover;
Heiligenberg; Mainz; Rhein-
zabern; Trier; Wörth
Germayn, Rog., mayor of Chich., iii. 91
Germon, see Jermyn
Gernagan, and his w. Basile, iv. 24–5
his s., see Ralph
Gernagod, iv. 23–4
Gerpunville:
Alice de, ix. 149
Aubrey, w. of Wm. de, ix. 149
Wm. de, ix. 149
Gerrard, see Gerard
Gervase, prior of Arundel, ii. 120
Gervase, Wm. s. of, see William
Gerves, Jn., and his w. Eliz., vii. 177
Gestling (Gestlinge, Gestlinges), see
Guestling
Gethin-Jones, O., ii. 478
Ghent, see Gaunt
Ghidentroi hund., i. 538; iv. 88
Gibbings, Harrison & Co., ii. 260
Gibbins, J.G., vii. 261
Gibbon (Gibbons, Gybbon):
Edw. (fl. 1730), vii. 64, 67
Edw. (d. 1794), vii. 67
Hester, ii. 161; vii. 64, 67
Phillips, ix. 53, 151
Maj., i. 527
Gibbs:
H., ii. 480
Hen. Martin, ii. 432
W., ix. 143
Gibet, Wm., iii. 103

Gibson:
Edm., warden of St. Mary's hosp.,
Chich., ii. 102
Jn., iii. 134
Rob., and his w. Susan, iv. 202
T., ii. 253
Thos., iv. 180
Gida (Gytha), w. of Godwin, earl of
Wessex, iii. 84; iv. 13, 34, 89, 111,
161
Giffard:
H.A., ii. 423, 426 n
Osbert, vii. 236
Wal., ix. 238
Gifford (Gyfford, Gyfforde):
Edric Fred., Ld. Gifford, iv. 184, 189
Emmanuel, ix. 53
Geo., vii. 204, 209
Jn., prior of Pynham, ii. 80–1
Sophie, w. of Edric, ii. 452; iv. 189,
191
Wm., ix. 268
Gilbert the marshal, iv. 183
Gilbert, warden of St. Mary's hosp.,
Chich., ii. 101–2
Gilbert, warden of St. Mary's hosp.,
Chich. (? another), ii. 102
Gilbert, son of Gencelin, ix. 278
Gilbert the stranger, ii. 172
Gilbert (fl. 1086), iv. 202, 211
Gilbert:
Ashurst Turner, bp. of Chich., ii.
432; iii. 114–16; iv. 179
Chas., vii. 38
Davies, ii. 163
his w., ii. 208
Jn., master of hosp. of St. Jas. and St.
Mary, Chich., ii. 100
Mary, m. Jn. Weekes, ix. 83 n
Nic., ii. 423
Thos., ii. 423
Wm. Buchan, ix. 30, 32
Mr., ii. 460
Gilborne, Nic., iv. 152
Gildenhall (Attegildenehall):
Ric., iii. 92
Wm. de la, iii. 92
Gilderigge:
Eliz., see Levett
Wm., ix. 120
Gilderigge, see Buxted
Gildesburgh:
Eliz. de, see Boudon
Jn. de, iv. 153
Gildridge, see Eastbourne
Giles, abbot of Robertsbridge, ii. 73
Giles the smith, ix. 80
Giles (Gyles):
Edm., ii. 250; iv. 225; vii. 38–9, 123,
286; ix. 22
Francis, vii. 169
Joan, see May
Jn. (d. by 1655), ix. 160, 230, 235–7
Sir Jn. (fl. 1695), vii. 169
Jn., rector of Penhurst, ix. 238
Thos., ii. 250; iv. 170, 225
——, ii. 33
Gill's, clockmakers, ix. 46
Gillam:
Jn., vii. 183
Mr., ii. 465
Gillham, Geo., ix. 257
Gillman:
Alex. Wm., vii. 220
Jas., vii. 220
Gillon, Jn., ix. 134
Gills Lap, see Hartfield
Gilmore, Wm., ii. 238
Gipps, ——, iv. 173
Girard (fl. 1086), ix. 128, 137
Girdlers' Company, see London: guilds
Gise, Jn. de, vii. 283 n
Glamorgan:
Constance de, see Lisle
Rob. de, iv. 34
Wm. de, iv. 34
Glamorgan, militia, i. 534; and see
Cwmaman; Ely

Glande, Jn., ii. 246
Glanville, Wm., iv. 208
Glasewryth, Jn., ii. 254 n
Glasgow, ii. 285
Glasney (Cornw.), ii. 410
glass, ancient, see Anglo-Saxon remains:
glass; architecture: ecclesiastical
glass blowing, i. 305; ii. 254–5, 318; ix.
6, 168
Glassenbury, Jn., ii. 412
Glassonbury (Kent), ix. 205
Glastonbury (Som.), ii. 6
abbot, see Seffrid I
Glatting Down, see Bignor
Glazier, Thos., ix. 237
Glemham:
Constance, see Lewknor
Edw., iv. 35; vii. 54, 81, 101; ix. 242,
263
Glen, Great (Leics.), iv. 159*
Glesham:
Jn. de (fl. 1296), ix. 145
Jn. de (fl. 1381), ix. 145
fam., ix 145
Glocestria, see Gloucester
Gloria, Vincent, and his w. Jane, ii. 258
Glottenham (Glottingham), see
Etchingham
Glottingham:
Idonea de, see Idonea
Rob. de, ix. 80
fam., ix. 213 n
Glottyngs (or Bodeketon), Rob. de,
prior of Hardham and Shulbred, ii.
74–5, 82
Gloucester (Glocestria, Gloucestre):
Laur. de, prior of Boxgrove, ii. 59
Rob. of, i. 499
Wal. de, dean of Chich., ii. 51; iii.
140
Wm., warden of Windham hosp., ii.
108
Gloucester:
duke of, see Thomas
earls of, see Clare, Gilb. de; Clare,
Rob. de; Robert; William
Gloucester, bp., iv. 121
Gloucestershire, i. 169 n; ii. 241, 473,
476
and see Beverston; Bristol;
Brookhampton; Cheltenham;
Cirencester; Dean, Forest of;
Gloucester; Hartpury; Longney;
Salmonsbury; Slaughter, Lower;
Tewkesbury; Winchcombe; Wot-
ton under Edge
Gloucestre, see Gloucester
Gloustiere, see Cloustiere
Glovere, Hen., ii. 259
Glovernestre, see Cloustiere
Glydd (Glyd):
Anne, m. Wm. Brockman, ix. 230
Eliz., m. Hilkiah Reader, ix. 273
Jn. (d. by 1643), ix. 273
Jn. (d. 1689), ix. 230
Martha, ix. 231
Martha, m. Ralph Drake, ix. 230
Rachel, m. Thos. Mills, ix. 273
Ric. (fl. 1531), ix. 230
Ric. (d. 1618), ix. 231
Ric. (fl. after 1619), ix. 230
Rob., ix. 230
Susan, m. Jn. Wallis, ix. 273
Thos., ix. 230
Glyn, Fred., Ld. Wolverton, ii. 460
Glynde, i. 31–3, 503; ii. 44, 277, 282–5,
301
A.-S. rem., i. 338
chant., ii. 13
ch., ii. 118, 250, 279
earthworks, i. 480
Glynde Place, ii. 277, 387
Glynde Reach, iii. 47–8
Glyndebourne, i. 337; ii. 446, 465
insects, i. 133, 143*, 147–8, 150, 160,
171–2, 218, 222–3
Mount Caburn, i. 481, 533; iii. 2, 52
coins, i. 328

Glynde
  Mount Caburn (*cont.*):
    earthworks, i. **458–9**, *458*, 460, 464,
      466
    prehist. rem., i. 322–4, *323*, 328,
      459, 471
    pk., ii. 297
    pop., ii. 227
    roads to, iii. 47–8
    Rom. rem., iii. 2, 42, 47, 56–7
    trades and ind., ii. 231, 239
    vicarage, ii. 8
    and see More park
Glynn:
  Anne, *see* Manning
  Sir Jn., ix. 207
  Thos., ix. 207
Gnat Wood, *see* Folkington
Goater:
  Francis, iii. 126
  Mary, iii. 126
  Mary, w. of Francis, *see* Palmer
Goatley, *see* Northiam
Goble, Ric., ii. 257
Goda (Gueda), ctss., ii. 324; vii. 116; ix.
  107, 206, 220, 235, 278
Goda, moneyer, iii. 83
Goda (fl. *c.* 900), iv. 110
Godalming (Surr.), ii. 239–40; iv. 56;
  vii. 119
Godard, vii. 68
Goddard, Jn., vii. 199
Godfray, *see* Godfrey
Godfrey, bp. of Chich., ii. 5; iii. 126; ix.
  117
Godfrey, prior of Boxgrove, ii. 59
Godfrey, rector of Stoughton, iv. 117
Godfrey the priest, ii. 113
Godfrey (fl. 1086), iv. 176
Godfrey (Godfray):
  C.J.M., ii. 472 *n*, 473
  Francis, ii. 30
  Jn., and his w., ix. 75
  Maline (or Maud), m. Sim. Farn-
    combe, ix. 75
  Marg., ix. 74
  Thos., ix. 149
Godindon:
  Adam de, iv. 163 *n*
  Alexandra de, *see* Hay
Goding, *see* Coding
Godley, Thos., vii. 105
Godman:
  C.B., ii. 447
  Edw., vii. 121
  Eliz., ii. 34
  Eliz., m. —— Shirley, vii. 121
  Jn., vii. 121
  Mary, vii. 120
  Ric. (d. 1562), vii. 121
  Ric. (fl. 1778), iv. 159
  Ric. Temple, vii. 121
  Thos. (d. 1559), vii. 121
  Thos. (d. 1612), vii. 120–1
  Thos. (d. 1624), vii. 121
  fam., iv. 159; vii. 121
    arms, iv. *159*; vii. *121*
  and see Goodman
Godric, moneyer, iii. 83
Godric (fl. 1066), vii. 99, 101
Godstone (Surr.), iii. 42–3
Godswewd, *see* Goudeswode
Godwin (Godwine), earl of Wessex, i.
  484; ii. 4, 126–7, 302, 306–7, 324;
  iii. 83–4, 166; iv. 4, 13, 30, 34,
  50–1, 80, 83, 89, 91, 95, 104, 111,
  118, 121, 127, 161, 176, 182–3, 185,
  204; vii. 68, 80, 110, 175, 207, 224
  n, 234, 253; ix. 1, 8–9, 34, 168, 172,
  176, 190, 244, 272
  his fam., i. 484–5
  his w., *see* Gida
Godwin the priest, iv. 185; vii. 110, 207
Godwin (fl. 1066), iv. 104
Godwin (fl. 1066, another), iv. 145, 174
Godwin (? Golduin) (fl. 1066–86), ix.
  82, 84
Godwin, Wm. s. of, *see* William

Godwine, earl, *see* Godwin
Godwine, moneyer, iii. 83
Goffe (Goff):
  Ewen C.R., ii. 453
  Steph., and his w. Deborah, vii. 239
  Thos., ii. 259
  Wm., i. 529
  Dr., vii. 266
  Maj.-Gen., vii. 17
  and see Gough
Gog Magog Hills (Cambs.), i. 291
Gold, Jos., ix. 199
Gold (Golda, Golde), Hugh s. of, *see*
  Hugh
Goldfinch, H.H., ii. 477
Goldham, Thos., vicar of Burwash, ii.
  38
Golding (Goulding):
  Capt., i. 522
  Mr., ii. 414
Goldingham:
  Sir Alex. de, ix. 84
  Eleanor de, w. of Jn., ix. 84
  Jn. de, ix. 84, 92
  Julian de, m. Rob. Belknap, ix. 84
  Wm. de, i. 502
Goldsmid, Sir Isaac Lyon, vii. 267
Goldsmith:
  Francis, iv. 212
  Sam. (fl. 1633), iv. 212
  Sam. (fl. 1700), iv. 212
  Wal., iii. 104
  ——, ii. 31
Goldspur (Colespore) hund., i. 537; ii.
  222; ix. 3, 57, **142**
Golduin, *see* Godwin (fl. 1066–86)
Goldyff, Jn., ii. 405
golf, *see* sport
Gollan, Spencer, ii. 479
Gooch:
  Hannah, w. of Thos., *see* Miller
  Jn., iii. 147
  Sir Thos., warden of St. Mary's
    hosp., Chich., bp. of Norwich, ii.
    102; iii. 147
Good, Bart., ii. 468
Goodall, Jn., ii. 165
Goodenough, Thos., and his w. Marg.,
  ix. 22
Goodman, Hen., vii. 70; *and see*
  Godman
Goodwin (Goodwyn):
  Geo., iv. 36
  Jane, m. 1 —— Roundean, 2 Wm.
    Vigor, iv. 62
  Jn., abbot of Robertsbridge, ii. 74
  Jn. (fl. 1629), ix. 270
  Mercy, *see* Morton
  Ric. (fl. 1491), ix. 269
  Ric. (fl. 1730), iv. 195
  Ric. (d. 1756, ? another), iv. 62
  Ric. (fl. *c.* 1774), iv. 36
  Wm., ix. 269
  fam., vii. 192 *n*
Goodwood, *see* Boxgrove
Goodwyn, *see* Goodwin
Goodyer, Ric., and his w. Mary, ix. 88
Goosehill, *see* Binderton
Gordon:
  Anne, *see* Lutman
  Arthur Hamilton, vii. 178
  Arthur Pitman, vii. 208
  Chas., vii. 208
  Ethel, m. —— Hort, vii. 208, 214
  Martha, *see* Drew
  Rob., Vct. Kenmure, iv. 185
  Wm., ix. 91
Gordon-Lennox, *see* Lennox
Gore, Jn., iv. 144
Gorham, Ambrose, vii. 78
Goring (Goringe, Gorringe, Goryng):
  Anne, w. of Geo., vii. 114, 117
  Anne, w. of Geo., earl of Norwich, *see*
    Denny
  Chas., earl of Norwich, vii. 35, 71,
    176
  Chas. (d. by 1825), vii. 59
  Sir Chas. (fl. 1887), vii. 191

  Sir Chas. Foster, vii. 126
  Sir Chas. Mat., iv. 43; vii. 190
  Constance, *see* Dyke
  Diana, m. 1 Sir Thos. Covert, 2 Geo.
    Porter, ii. 312; vii. 71, 226
  Dorothy, *see* Everard
  Edw., vii. 227
  Eliz., *see* Cresswell
  Geo. (d. by 1595), ii. 24, 28; iii. 80;
    iv. 5, 64; vii. 6, 9–10, 80, 96, 179,
    227, 230
  Geo. (d. 1602), iv. 231; vii. 35, 39,
    89, 114, 117, 172–3, 175–6
  Geo. (d. 1657), vii. 175
  Geo., earl of Norwich, i. 527; iv. 231;
    vii. 31, 35, 70–1, 89, 100, 114,
    117, 175–6, 234
  Geo. (d. 1727), vii. 81
  Sir H.D., vii. 191
  Sir Harry, vii. 190
  Sir Hen. (d. 1594), ii. 24, 28, 257; vii.
    10, 96, 230, 232
  Hen. (fl. 1596), vii. 227
  Hen. (fl. 1660), i. 529; vii. 85
  Hen. (fl. 1671, ? another), ii. 39 *n*
  Hen. (d. by 1689, ? another), vii. 190
  Hugh, ii. 450
  Jn. (fl. 1467), iii. 142
  Jn. (d. 1495, ? another), iv. 64
  Jn. (fl. 1512), iv. 64, 108, 110
  Revd. Jn. (fl. 1858), vii. 59
  Revd. Jn. (fl. 1905), i. 306; ii. 300
  Mary, vii. 59
  Mary, w. of Geo., *see* Everard
  Mary, w. of Hen., *see* Covert
  Thos., vii. 81 *n*
  Sir Wm. (d. 1554), ii. 50, 75, 83; iv.
    5–6; vii. 96
  Sir Wm. (d. 1602), vii. 230
  Mr. (fl. *c.* 1528), ii. 20
  Mr. (fl. 1835), ii. 458
  fam., vii. 10, 41, 59, 96, 126
    arms, vii. *35*
Goring, ii. 43, 109, 263; iv. 123
  adv., ii. 109
  A.-S. rem., i. 341
  Castle Goring, i. 178, 205
  chant., iv. 39
  ch., ii. 37, 340, 359, 370; iv. 39
  Civil War, i. 527
  dom. archit., ii. 381, 386
  man., iv. 123
    ho., ii. 381
  natural history, i. 166, 173, 178, 187,
    189, 192–3, 196–7, 199–210, 218,
    220, 263
  pop., ii. 217
  prehist. rem., i. 329
  rectory, ii. 12
  vicarage, ii. 9
Gormunvill, David de, ix. 79, 83
Gornage, Geo., iii. 77
Gorringe, *see* Goring
Gort, *see* Gurth
Goryng, *see* Goring
Goschen, Sir Geo., Vct. Goschen, ix.
  211, 257
Gosden, Fred., ii. 447
Gosden, *see* Beeding
Gosetrowe, *see* Gostrow
Goslyng (Gosselyn):
  Rog., ii. 77
  Thos., ix. 120
Goss, Jessy, vii. 147
Gossaert, Jan, *see* Mabuse
Gosselyn, *see* Goslyng
Gostrow (Babinrerode, Babirote, Gose-
  trowe) hund., i. 537; ii. 222; ix.
  158, **164**, 175
Goswell, Jn., warden of St. Mary's
  hosp., Chich., ii. 102
Gotele (Gotlee):
  Anne, m. Jn. Piers, ix.. 91, 274
  Aveline de, m. Steph. de Forsham, ix.
    274
  Hen., ix. 91
  Jas. de, ix. 274
  Jn. de, ix. 91, 274

Juliana de, ix. 274
Peter de, ix. 274
Ric. de, ix. 274
Rob. de, ix. 274
Steph. de, ix. 274
Goteley, *see* Northiam: Goatley
Gotham, *see* Bexhill
Gotlee, *see* Gotele
Gott:
  Eliz., ix. 273
  (formerly Greening), Sir Hen. Thos.,
    ix. 273
  Joan, *see* Farnden
  Martha, vii. 115
  Mary, ix. 273
  Maximilian, ix. 92
  Peter (d. by 1724), ix. 92, 145, 273
  Peter (d. 1732), vii. 239; ix. 273
  Peter (fl. 1823), ix. 5
  Rob., vii. 115
  Sam. (fl. *c.* 1680), ix. 92, 145, 273
  Sam. (fl. 1713), vii. 239
  Sam. (d. 1724), ix. 92, 145
  Sam. (d. 1731), ix. 88, 147
  Sarah, ix. 273
  Thos. (d. by 1730), ix. 92
  Thos. (d. 1733), vii. 115
  Thos. (fl. 1773), ix. 88
  fam., ix. 92, 167 *n*, 273
    arms, ix. *273*
Goudeswode (Godswewd):
  Geof. de, iv. 204 *n*
  Godfrey de, iv. 204
  Lettice, w. of Geof. de, iv. 204 *n*
  Sarah de, *see* Sturmy
Goudhurst (Kent), i. 66; ix. 211, 254
  Combwell:
    man., ix. 255
    priory, ix. 27, 255
Gough:
  A.D., ix. 25
  Ric., iii. 12, 14–15
  Wm., ii. 166
  Capt., ix. 214
  and see Goffe
Gould:
  I. Chalkley, i. 476
  Jos., and his w., ix. 199
Goulding, *see* Golding
Gounter, *see* Gunter
Goushill:
  Eliz., *see* FitzAlan
  Joan, vii. 5
  Sir Rob., vii. 5
Gower, Peter, ix. 238
Gower, Earl, *see* Leveson-Gower, Jn.
Gowran, baron, *see* Cutts
Goze (fl. 1086), vii. 225
Gozelin, *see* Jocelin
Grace:
  Harvey, iii. 130
  Mat., vii. 101
  W.G., ii. 472
Graffham, ii. 43, 221; iv. 40, **58–60**, 80
  adv., iv. 59–60
  ch., ii. 250, 355, 370; iv. 58–60, *60*
  dom. archit., iv. 58
  earthworks, i. 480
  foxhunting, ii. 442
  Graffham Down, iv. 58, 94
  man., iv. 51, 58–9, 65, 145, 174
  mill, iv. 61
  natural history, i. 52, 109
  rectors, ii. 18; iv. 58, 60; *and see*
    Manning, Hen.
  tithes, iv. 60, 145
  trades and ind., ii. 232, 252; iv. 58
graffiti, *see* architecture: ecclesiastical
Grafham, Isabel de, iv. 58
Grafton, Fred. Wm., iv. 208
Grafton, duke of, *see* Fitzroy, Chas.
Grafton (Northants.), iv. 111 *n*; vii. 132
Graham:
  David, iv. 231
  G., iii. 70
  Jas., duke of Montrose, ii. 441
  Jas., iii. 44
  T., ii. 454

Grahamstown (South Africa), bp., *see*
  Cotterill, Hen.
Grampian mountains, i. 291
Grancurt, Wal. de, ii. 65
Grand Military Canal, *see* Royal Milit-
  ary Canal
Grandison:
  Jn., bp. of Exeter, ii. 73, 111
  Sybil de, *see* Tregoz
  Wm. de, ix. 71, 152
Grandison, Ld., *see* Villiers, Wm.
Grandyn, Sir Wm., vii. 204
Grane, Martha, *see* Ballowe
Grange (Greenech, Grench) (Kent), ii.
  130; ix. 4, 36
Grangiis, Valentine de, ix. 190
Grant, Tom, ii. 443
Grantham:
  Geo., vii. 82
  Thos., iv. 17 *n*
  Sir Wm., vii. 80, 82, 96
  Wm. Wilson, vii. 82, 96
  fam., vii. 83
    arms, vii. *82*
Grantham (Lincs.), ii. 88, 431
Gratian, prior of Arundel, ii. 119–20
gratton, *see* crops
Gratwick (Gratwicke, Gratwyke):
  Amy, *see* Barwick
  Anne, m. Hugh Keate, vii. 235
  Eliz., m. Rog. Gratwick, vii. 235
  Francis, vii. 235
  Jn. (fl. 1642), ii. 309
  Jn. (fl. *c.* 1700), iv. 93
  Mary (d. 1603), vii. 235 *n*
  Mary (fl. 1750), iv. 93
  Phil., vii. 235
  Ric., and his w. Anne, vii. 235
  Rog. (d. 1596, ? two of this name), ii.
    230, 244, 253; vii. 35, 235
  Rog. (d. by 1598, another), vii. 235
  Rog. (d. 1653), vii. 235
  Steph., ii. 22
  Thos., vii. 74, 77, 105, 235 *n*
  Sir Wm. (fl. 1609), vii. 235
  Wm. (d. 1664), vii. 235
  Wm. (fl. 1830), ii. 458
Graufesenque, La (Aveyron, France),
  iii. 17–18, 28, 57, 68–9
Grauntford:
  Agnes, *see* Finch
  Babilon, ix. 107 *n*
Grauntson:
  Beatrice de, *see* Malemayns
  Sir Otto de, iv. 229
  Pernel de, m. Thos. de St. Omer, iv.
    229–30
  —— de, m. Wm. de Hardeshulle, iv.
    229–30
Grave:
  Jn. de la, iv. 168
  Ralph de la, iv. 168
  Rog. de la, iii. 153; iv. 170
grave slabs, cast-iron, *see* architecture:
  ecclesiastical
Gravelines (Nord, France), ii. 153
Gravelye, *see* Lindfield
Gravenor, Goddard, and his w. Anne,
  vii. 227
graves, *see* burials
Gravesend, Thos., M.P. for Lewes, vii.
  31; ix. 119
Gravesend (Kent), i. 519
Gravett, Thos., ix. 242
Gravetye:
  Bart. de (? two of this name), vii. 168
  Mic. de, vii. 168
Gravetye, *see* Hoathly, West
Gray (Graye):
  Edm., iv. 61, 85
  Geo. H., mayor of Bexhill, ix. 124
  Hester, iv. 64
  J.E., i. 246
  Joan, *see* Aylyng
  Ric., rector of Withyham, ii. 25
  Rob., iv. 160
  Thos., iv. 93
  Wm., iv. 61

  and see Grey
Graylands, *see* Warnham
Graylingwell, *see* Chich.
Great Deep, *see* Chich.: harbour
Great Exhibition, ii. 235–6
Greatham, ii. 43; iv. 7, 35
  ch., ii. 339, 373
  common (? Gritham common), i. 194,
    202, 209
  man., iv. 41
  pop., ii. 218
  prehist. rem., i. 310, *310*, 329
  quarrying, ii. 230
  Rom. rem., iii. 57
Greaves, Sir Edw., ii. 310
Grebbell, fam., ix. 53
Gredle, *see* Greyly
Greece, i. 306
  and see Corfu; Ionian Islands
Green (Greene, Grene):
  Ant., iii. 147
  Chas., ix. 32
  Clementina, *see* Pratt
  Cornelius, iv. 29, 197
  Edw. (fl. 1606), iv. 111
  Edw. (fl. 1686), iv. 191
  Geo., iv. 192, 212
  Geo. Rob., ii. 434
  Jane, *see* Collier
  Marg., w. of Thos., iv. 111.
  Phil., ii. 461
  Ric., and his w. Anna, iii. 147
  Thos., vicar of Dallington, ii. 77
  Thos., iv. 111–12*, 212
  Thos. Hen., vii. 57
  Wm. de (fl. 1369), ii. 307
  Wm. (fl. 1802), and his w. Jane, ix. 86
  Capt., ii. 446
  ——, ii. 475
  ——, iv. 115
Green and Sons, ii. 238
Green Street, *see* Seaford
Greenech, *see* Grange
Greenfield (Grenefeld, Grenefield):
  Alice, *see* Croucher
  Eliz., m. Hen. Peckham, iv. 200
  F.F.J., ii. 476
  Jn., iv. 200
  Ric., iv. 200
  Thos., iv. 109
  Wm. de, dean of Chich., ii. 51; iii. 139
Greenford (Greneford, Grenford):
  Jn. of, dean and bp. of Chich., ii. 7,
    48, 50, 53; iii. 126; iv. 154, 179,
    205
  Jn., ix. 187
Greenhill, David, ii. 166
Greening (later Gott), Thos., *see* Gott,
  Sir Hen. Thos.
Greenway, Edw., and his w. Mary, ix.
  177
Greenwell:
  Lancelot, ii. 149
  Canon, i. 314
Greenwich (London, formerly Kent), ii.
  135, 305; iii. 45; vii. 207
  East Greenwich, man., iii. 104; iv. 42;
    vii. 57, 217
  West Greenwich, ch., ii. 86
Greenwood, ——, ii. 164
Greer, Capt., ii. 460
Greet, Hen., ii. 257
Gregory IX, pope, ii. 53, 66, 87
Gregory XI, pope, ii. 83, 404
Gregory:
  Jn., prior of Tortington, ii. 83
  Rob., dean of St. Paul's, iii. 124
Gregson:
  Jesse, ix. 232
  Jn., ix. 222
Grele (Grelle), *see* Greyly
Grench, *see* Grange
Grene, *see* Green
Grenefield (Grenefeld), *see* Greenfield
Greneford, *see* Greenford
Grenested (Grensted):
  Christine de, m. Adam de Clothale,
    iv. 195, 197

Grenested (*cont.*):
 Emma de, *see* Thorney
 Jn. de, prior of Arundel friary, ii. 94
 Margery de, m. Elias de la Falaise, iv. 193, 195, 197
 Ric. de, iv. 145, 195
Grenestede, *see* Grinstead, East; Grinstead, West
Grenford, *see* Greenford
Grenlef, Hen., mayor of Chich., iii. 92
Grensted, *see* Grenested
Gresle, *see* Greyly
Gressenhale, Reg. de, dean of South Malling coll., ii. 119
Grestain (Grestein) (Eure, France), abbey, ii. 8, 46, 48, 122, 329, 331
 abbot, *see* Robert
Grevatts Wood, *see* Bury
Greve, Nic., ix. 127
Greville, Chas., ii. 458–9; vii. 250
Grey:
 Ant., iv. 93
 Cath., *see* Ford
 Cecily, *see* Bonville
 Edw., vii. 238
 Eliz., *q.v.*
 Emma, *see* Cauz
 Ford, Ld. Grey of Warke, earl of Tankerville, ii. 441; iv. 16
 Hen., marquess of Dorset, iv. 159–60
 Lady Jane, iv. 234
 Jane, m. Dowse Fuller, iv. 83
 Jn. de (d. 1256), iii. 105; iv. 168
 Jn. de (fl. 1256), iv. 168
 Mary, m. Chas. Bennett, earl of Tankerville, iv. 16
 Peter (sr.), vii. 238
 Peter (jr.), vii. 238
 Ralph, Ld. Grey of Warke, iv. 16, 20
 Reg. (Reynold), iii. 105; iv. 168
 Thos., marquess of Dorset, iv. 159
 Thos. (fl. 1664), iv. 111
 Thos. (fl. 1684, ? another), iv. 83
 Wm. (sr.), iv. 111
 Wm. (jr.), iv. 111
 fam., ii. 475
 arms, iv. 131; ix. 135
 and see Gray
Grey Friars, *see* London
Greyly (Gredle, Grele, Grelle, Gresle):
 Amice, w. of Hen., iv. 230
 Hawise de, *see* Burgh
 Hen., iii. 92; iv. 230
 Joan de, m. Jn., Ld. de la Warr, vii. 99, 283
 Marg., w. of Wm., m. 2 Jn. Peachey, iii. 92; iv. 230
 Sir Rob. de, vii. 99, 283
 Thos. de, iv. 230; vii. 283
 Wm. (fl. 1226), iv. 230
 Wm. (d. by 1288, ? another), iii. 92; iv. 230
 fam., iii. 92
Griffin of Wales (Griffin de Sutton), s. of Garuerd, vii. 229*
 his w., *see* Strange, Maud le
Griffin:
 Jas., ix. 29
 Watson, ii. 477
Griffith:
 Geo., ii. 469–71
 Jn., ii. 431
Griffiths, Martha, *see* Drake
Grigge:
 Jn., prior of Sele, ii. 61–3
 Ric., ii. 62
Grimes Graves, *see* Weeting
Grimketel, bp. of East Anglia and Selsey, ii. 3
Grimm, Sam., iii. 12
Grimmett, Wm., ii. 439
Grimsby (Lincs.), ii. 235
Grindal, Edm., abp. of Cant., ii. 29
Grinstead, East (Estgrenestede, Grenestede), i. 505, 539; ii. 22, 43–4, 205, 313, 319; vii. 101
 ale-hos., ii. 196
 assizes, ii. 201; vii. 16 n

Brambletye, i. 477; ii. 20, 387
 ch., ii. 11, 40, 230, 379
 dom. archit., ii. 386, 389
 Fairlight, vii. 104
 Felbridge, iii. 43
 geology, ii. 336
 guild, ii. 21
 hund., i. 537; ii. 182 n, 226, 241, 316; vii. 1, 224
 mkt., ii. 183
 militia, i. 534–5
 natural history, i. 112–13, 166, 179, 189, 230, 234, 240–1, 277
 parl. rep., i. 504, 532
 M.P., *see* Culpeper, Sir Wm. (d. 1678)
 pop., ii. 226
 rector, *see* Ceccano
 rectory, ii. 12
 Ridge Hill, iii. 2, 29–31
 roads, ii. 240; iii. 43
 Rom. rem., iii. 2, 29–31
 Sackville coll., ii. 193, 358, 387
 Saint Hill, i. 306; ii. 323
 sch., ii. 398, 430
 Serreys Farm, ii. 430
 Standen, *q.v.*
 Stonequarry Hill, ii. 230
 tithes, ii. 9
 trades and ind., ii. 229, 236, 241, 257, 263; vii. 104
 Tyes Cross (Tyne's Cross), i. 55
 union, i. 539
 vicarage, ii. 9
 vicars, ii. 35, 37
 Walesbeach (Walesbeech), iii. 29, 31; iv. 101
Grinstead, West (Grenestede, Westgrenestede), ii. 43
 ch.:
 accessories, ii. 351, 353–4, 356–8, 370
 archit., ii. 328, 334, 337, 340, 344 n, 346, 348–9, 366, 370, 372–3, 377
 earthworks, i. 478
 foxhunting, ii. 448
 hund., i. 538; ii. 220
 mammals, i. 301
 Pk., i. 306; ii. 301, 310
 Partridge Green, i. 169
 pop., ii. 220
 rector, *see* Tredcroft, Jn.
Gritham common, *see* Greatham: common
Grobham, Sir Ric., iv. 62
Grofhurst:
 Hen. de, ix. 127
 Isabel, w. of Jn. de, m. 2 Jn. de Ashburnham, 3 Sim. de Aylardenne, ix. 127
 Jn. de, ix. 127
 Thos. de, and his w. Margery, vii. 147
Groombridge, Hen., ii. 200
Groombridge, *see* Withyham
Groome:
 Jn., iv. 237 n
 Thos., iv. 237
 Wm., iv. 237 n
Grosvenor:
 Hugh, duke of Westminster, ii. 460
 Ric., earl Grosvenor, ii. 456, 460
 (later Egerton), Thos., earl of Wilton, *see* Egerton
Grove:
 Geo., iv. 153
 Gilb. atte, ix. 84
 Nic. atte, ix. 84
 Ralph atte, vii. 190 n
 Rob., bp. of Chich., iii. 134
 Sarah, m. Sir Edw. Turner, iv. 144 n
 Thos., and his w. Christian, ix. 264
 Wm. atte (fl. 1296), vii. 190 n
 Wm. atte (fl. 1374), and his w. Maud, ix. 84
 Brig.-Gen., ii. 200
Grove, the, *see* Hollington
Grovehurst (Kent), ix. 113

Grover:
 Thos., ix. 121
 Wm., vii. 54
Groves, Jas., ix. 200
Gruggen:
 Charlotte, iii. 160
 Emma (d. 1825), iii. 160
 Emma (d. 1909), iii. 160; iv. 212
 Harriet, iii. 160
 Jn. (d. 1846), iii. 160
 Jn. (d. 1848), iii. 160
 Mary, w. of Jn., *see* Blagden
 Mary, w. of Wm., iii. 160
 Sarah, w. of Wm., iii. 160
 Wm. (d. 1828), iii. 160
 Wm. (d. 1846), iii. 160
Grundy, G.G., iii. 472 n
Gryndon, Hugh, master of hosp. of St. Jas. and St. Mary, Chich., ii. 100
Grysell, Wm. de, dean of Hastings coll., ii. 117
Gualo (fl. 1216), ix. 15
Guar, prior of Sele, ii. 62
Gubbit, Eliz., iv. 173
Gueda, ctss., *see* Goda
Guermonprez, H.L.F., i. 111, 119, 246, 250, 252–3, 255–63, 265
Guernsey, i. 164 n
Guestling (Estling, Gestling):
 Agatha, m. Hen. de Ore, ix. 87, 180
 Alice, w. of Geof., ix. 180
 Geof., ix. 180
 Isabel, m. Jn. de Guestling, ix. 180
 Jn. de (d. c. 1220), ix. 70, 149, 180, 182
 Jn. de (fl. c. 1243), ix. 180
 Phil. de, ix. 180
 Rob. de (fl. 1130), ix. 180
 Rob. de (fl. 1223), ix. 180
Guestling (Gestling, Gestlinge, Gestlinges), ii. 43, 173, 178, 206 n; ix. 175, **179–84**
 adv., ix. 183
 botany, i. 61, 65, 67
 Broomham, i. 302–3; ix. 177, 181–2
 char., ii. 439; ix. 179, 183–4
 ch., ii. 112; ix. *178, 182,* 182–3
 accessories, ii. 351–2, 359, 370; ix. 183
 archit., ii. 332, 339, 344, 366, 368, 370, *370,* 375; ix. 89, 182–3
 Coghurst, i. 109, 265; ix. 183
 dom. archit., ix. 179–80
 fair, ix. 180
 hare hunting, ii. 451
 hund., i. 537; ii. 222; ix. 3, **175**
 insects, i. 112–13, 115–23, 125–35, 137, 163, 167 n, 171–91, 193–209, 211–37
 mammals, i. 300–2
 man., ix. 177, 180–1
 Maxfield, ix. *179,* 180–1
 molluscs, i. 109
 pop., ii. 222
 prebend, ii. 113
 rly., ii. 222 n; ix. 179
 rectors, *see* Ashburnham, Revd. Sir Jn.; Blomfield, Edwin
 sch., ii. 439
 Snailham, ix. 180–1
Guildford (Surr.), i. 310, 328; ii. 256, 406; vii. 119; ix. 1
 cast., i. 503
 Farley Heath, iii. 42, 52
 gaol, i. 503, 510; vii. 20
guilds, religious (brotherhoods), *see* Appledram; Battle; Bersted; Billingshurst; Birdham; Boxgrove; Chich.; Chidham; Donnington; Eastbourne; Felpham; Grinstead, East; Horsham; Hunston; Itchenor, West; Pagham; Petworth; Rumboldswyke; Selsey; Sidlesham; Singleton; Slindon; Southwick; Steyning; Tarring, West; Wittering, West
guilds, trade, *see* Chich.; Lewes; London; Rye

Guinea, ii. 166
Guines, count of, *see* Manasses
Guines (Guisnes, Guynes), (Pas-de-Calais, France), iv. 15; ix. 149–50
Guinness, Sir Rupert, earl of Iveagh, iv. 181, 184, 189
Guinness, Messrs. A. & Co., ix. 267
Guise, Mr., i. 258
Guise, dchss. of, ii. 268
Guisnes, count of, *see* Manasses
Guisnes, *see* Guines
Guizot, François, ix. 5
Gulafre;
  Maud, *see* Lunsford
  Wm., ix. 214 *n*
Guldeford:
  Sir Edw. (fl. 1506), ii. 144; ix. 151, 177, 185
  Edw. (fl. 1625), ix. 151
  Edw. (d. 1678), ix. 71, 151
  Hen. de (fl. 1302), iv. 95, 97
  Hen. (fl. 1625), ix. 151
  Jane, m. Sir Jn. Dudley, ix. 151, 177
  Sir Jn., sheriff of Suss., ix. 151
  Mary, w. of Sir Jn., ix. 151
  Sir Ric., bailiff of Winchelsea, ix. 68, 75, 149, 151, 177, 185
  Ric., ix. 151, 177
  Sir Rob., ix. 151–2
  Sir Thos., ix. 151
  fam., ix. 54, 71, 151
  arms, ix. *151*, 152
Guldeford, East, ix. 40, 54, 142, 149, **150–2**
  adv., ix. 151–2
  ch., ii. 378; ix. 151–2
  dom. archit., ix. 150
  ferry, ix. 151
  pop., ii. 222
  rectory, ix. 163
  sea defences, ix. 151
Gulderig, Wm. de, ii. 316
Gully, Mr., ii. 458
Gulston:
  Frances, iii. 126
  Jos., dean of Chich., ii. 51; iii. 126
Gumber Corner, *see* Bignor
Gumber, the, *see* Slindon
Gundeville (Gundevile, Gundevill):
  Agnes de, m. Geof. son of Azo, iv. 107–8, 145
  Agnes, w. of Hugh de, *see* Falaise
  Hugh de, ii. 103; iv. 17, 115, 145
  Sibyl de, iv. 34
  Wm. de, iv. 104
  ——, m. Ric. Murdac, iv. 145
Gundewyn, Nic., iv. 229
Gundrada, m. Wm. de Warenne, earl of Surrey, ii. 4, 64, 294, 360; vii. 2, 19 *n*, 48–9, 213, 224, 281
Gunn (Gunne):
  Ric., vii. 218, 256
  Thos., vii. 218
gunpowder making, ii. 237–8; vii. 137; ix. 102, 109, 168
Gunpowder Plot, *see* rebellions
Gunston:
  Jn., ix. 197
  Thos., ix. 197
  Wm., ix. 197
Gunter, abbot of Thorney, ii. 53
Gunter (Gounter):
  Arthur (d. 1576), ii. 24–5; iv. 115, 128
  Arthur (fl. 1637), iv. 193
  Eliz., *see* Sherrington
  Sir Geo. (fl. 1576), iv. 115
  Sir Geo. (d. 1624), and his w. Ursula, iv. 116
  Col. Geo., i. 527, 529; iv. 115; vii. 247
  Geo. (fl. 1695), iv. 115
  Giles, and his w. Eliz., iv. 115
  Jn. (fl. 1434), iv. 231
  Jn. (fl. 1475), iv. 115
  Jn. (d. 1511), iv. 114–15
  Jn. (d. 1558), iv. 115–16
  Judith, *see* Nicholl
  Kath., m. Sir Hen. Maynard, iv. 115

Marg., *see* Troghton
Mary, *see* Stoughton
Rog. (fl. 1327), iv. 114
Rog. (d. 1437), iv. 114–15, 231
Wm., iv. 231
fam., iv. 114–15, 116 *n*, 138
  arms, iv. *115*, 116–17
Gunter Nicholl, Sir Chas., *see* Nicholl
Gunwardby, Rob. de, sacrist of Bosham coll., ii. 112
Gurney (Gurnard):
  Avice de, m. Rog. de Clere, vii. 258
  Eliz. de, m. Jn. de Badeham, iv. 144
  J.H., i. 278
  Jn. de, iv. 144
  Olive de, *see* Lovell
  Sir Ric., ld. mayor of London, vii. 76
Gurth (Gort, Gyrth), earl, i. 348–9, 487–8; iv. 158
Guthrie, Jn., vii. 268
Guy (Wido) (fl. 1086), iv. 104
Guy (fl. 1147), vii. 1
Guy:
  Jn., ii. 165
  Mary, w. of Thos., ii. 161
  Thos. (d. 1788), iii. 161
  Thos. (d. 1804), iii. 161
  Mr., ii. 415
Guynes, *see* Guines
Gwent, Ric., ii. 17
Gwydir, Lds., *see* Burrell: Peter, Peter Rob.
Gwymund, ii. 112
Gwynne, J.E.A., ii. 276
Gybbon, *see* Gibbon
Gybrisshe, Rob., iv. 78
Gyfford (Gyfforde), *see* Gifford
Gyldesburgh, Thos., rector of St. Olave's, Chich., ii. 401
Gyles, *see* Giles
Gyllyng, Wm., warden of Windham hosp., ii. 108
Gymming (Wyming) (fl. *c.* 1080), ii. 410
Gypsum Mines Ltd., ii. 232
Gyrth, *see* Gurth
Gytha, *see* Gida

Haben, *see* Rogate
Habershon, W.G. and E., vii. 267
Habershon and Brock, Messrs., ix. 89
Habin, Ric., iii. 88
Habington:
  Ant., ix. 145
  Thos., ix. 145
  Wm., ix. 145
Hachescumb, Jn. de, vii. 34 *n*
Hackett, *see* Haket
Hackney and New Coll., iv. 21
Hada, ii. 410
Haddock, Jn., ix. 146
Hadlow Down, ii. 44
Hadrian, Rom. emperor, ii. 241
Hague, Jenkin, ix. 61
Hague, the (Netherlands), ii. 160
Haia, *see* Hay
Hailesaltede hund., *see* Netherfield
Hailey park, *see* Westmeston
Hailsham, ii. 23, 32, 44, 112, 122, 206
  adv., ii. 87
  Bell Banks, ii. 249
  birds, i. 277
  botany, i. 68
  ch., ii. 13, 23
    accessories, ii. 249, 251, 356
    archit., ii. 230, 334, 339, 378
  ch. ho., ii. 392
  Duddington, ii. 174, 178
  Highlands, ii. 77
  hund., i. 538
  insects, i. 115–17, 164–8, 171, 175, 177, 185–7, 197, 219
  Jews, i. 506
  mkt., ii. 278
  militia, i. 534
  Otham, *q.v.*
  parl. rep., i. 531
  Polegate, *q.v.*
  poor relief, ii. 205

pop., ii. 226
rly., ii. 240
rector, *see* Blachington
rectory, ii. 8, 77–8
sport, ii. 448–52
tithes, ii. 8
trades and ind., ii. 230, 236, 238–9, 249, 253, 259, 262
union, i. 539
vagrancy, ii. 210
vicar, ii. 8
vicarage, ii. 8
Woodside, ii. 451
Hailstone, S., i. 248, 250–3, 255, 258–60
Haines (Haynes):
  Arthur, ix. 276
  C., ii. 474
  Sir Fred., ii. 429
  Ric., ii. 264
  Thos., ix. 82
Haire, *see* Hare
Hake:
  Sir And., iv. 14
  Ankarette, *see* Hussey
Haker, Wm., master of St. Jas.'s hosp., Seaford, ix. 105
Haket (Hackett):
  Alice, *see* Aguillon
  Jn. (fl. 1296), iv. 111
  Jn. (fl. 1327, ? another), iv. 111
  Jn. (fl. 1347, ? another), iv. 111, 145
  Jn. (d. by 1364, another), ix. 118, 240 *n*
  Lydia, vii. 226
  Margery, *see* Stokes
  Maud, w. of Jn., iv. 111
  Ric., ix. 118
  Rob., iv. 111
  Thos., iv. 111
Haldelegh, Jn. de, vii. 157 *n*
Halden, fam., arms, ix. 152
Hale:
  Barnard, ix. 145
  Grace, iv. 200
  Martha, ix. 145
  Peter, iv. 200 *n*
  Ric., iv. 200
  Rog., iv. 200–1
Hales:
  Edw., ix. 213
  Sir Edw., vii. 255; ix. 154
  Sir Jn., ix. 154
Half Smock (? in Worth), i. 55
Halfpenny (later Ballett), Jn., *see* Ballett
Halifax, earls of, *see* Dunk, Geo.; Montagu, Geo.
Halifax (Yorks. W.R.), ii. 65, 393
Hall (Halle, Haule, Haull):
  Amice, *see* Ore
  Ann, *see* Dudley
  Cecily, w. of Godard, ix. 88
  Eardley, i. 295, 300
  Edw., ii. 196 *n*
  Godard, ix. 19, 87–8, 191
  Hen. (fl. 1469), ix. 19, 87, 254
  Hen. (fl. 1535), vii. 275
  (or Ore), Jn. (d. 1422), ix. 19, 87, 89, 190, 192
  Jn. (d. after 1432), ix. 119
  Jn. (d. 1521), ii. 398
  Jn. (fl. 1524), iii. 104
  Jn. (fl. 1525, another), iv. 13
  Jn. (d. 1638), iv. 98
  Jn. (fl. 1638), iv. 98
  Marg., *see* Hurst
  Mary, iv. 98
  Mary, w. of Jn., m. 2 Hen. Bulstrode, iv. 98
  Ric., ix. 127
  Rob., ix. 19, 87, 191
  Spencer, ix. 211
  Thos., sacrist of Bosham coll., ii. 112
  Thos., ii. 398
  Wm. (d. 1449), ix. 87, 192
  Wm. (fl. 1540), ix. 19, 87–8
  Wm. (fl. 1657), iv. 98
  ——, m. Ric. Cooke, iv. 117 *n*
  arms, iv. 117; ix. *88*

Halland, *see* Hoathly, East
Halling (Kent), i. 34
Halliwell, Hen., rector of Clayton, iii. 53
Hallowell, Ben, ii. 166
Halnaker (in Boxgrove), iv. 133, 141, 145–6, 165
  chant., iv. 149, 165
  chap., ii. 57; iv. 143
  foxhunting, ii. 443
  Halnaker Hill, iii. 33; iv. 142
  Halnaker Ho., i. 515; ii. 382; ii. 57, 155–7; iv. *140*, 142
    chap., ii. 338, 349, 370, 372, 382
  honor of, i. 491; ii. 56; iv. 2, 51, 142–3, 145, 156, 176–7, 199, 212
  man., ii. 303; iii. 84; iv. 91–2, 101, 142–5, 147 *n*, 161–2, 177, 199, 201, 238
  mill, iv. 143
  pk., ii. 297, 301, 303–4; iv. 143–4
  roads to, iii. 33
  Rom. rem., iii. 33, 57
  tithes, ii. 303
  Warehead Farm, iii. 33
  wood, ii. 303
Halsham:
  Hugh, iv. 143
  Maud, *see* Poynings
  fam., i. 513
Halton, ——, iv. 100
Halton (in Hastings), *see* Hastings
Halton (in Selsey), *see* Selsey
Haltone, le, *see* Rye
Hamble (Hants), ii. 139
Hambledon (Bucks.), iv. 213
Hambledon (Hants), i. 527; ii. 445, 467; iv. 60, 190
  Windmill Down, ii. 475
Hambrook, *see* Chidham
Hamedon, Jn. de, preceptor of Shipley, ii. 93
Hamelin (fl. 1278), vii. 20
Hamerden, *see* Ticehurst: Hammerden
Hamesford hund., *see* Dumpford
Hamfelde hund., *see* Tipnoak
Hamilton:
  Ant., iv. 139
  Capt. Archibald, ii. 166
  Sir Archibald, ii. 452; iv. 64
  Sir Chas., ii. 166; iv. 64
  Sir Chas. Jn. Jas., iv. 64
  Sir Edw. Archibald, ii. 452; iv. 64
  Emma, w. of Sir Wm., iv. 13, 76
  Mary, *see* Smith
  Rob. Wm., iv. 139
  Sir Sydney, iv. 64
  Sir Wm., M.P. for Midhurst, iv. 76
  Capt. Wm., ii. 166
  Wm. (d. by 1767), iv. 90, 139
  Wm. (fl. 1796), iv. 139
  Wm. Gerard, iv. 139
  Wm. Jn., iv. 139
  Wm. Ric., iv. 139
  arms, iv. *64*
Hamilton and Breeds, ii. 164
Hamilton & Co., ii. 164
Haminc (fl. 1066–86), vii. 234
Haming, Ric. s. of, *see* Richard
Hamme:
  Gilb., vii. 229
  Hamon de, iv. 212
Hammer, *see* Linchmere
Hammer Pond (in Chithurst and Iping), iv. 4, 63
Hammer Stream, iv. 4, 63
Hammerden, *see* Ticehurst
Hammerwood, *see* Forest Row
Hammes (Hammessey), *see* Hamsey
Hammond (Hamond, Hamonde):
  Cath., m. Jos. Chapman, vii. 34
  Chas., ii. 475
  Eliz., m. —— Freeman, vii. 34
  Francis, vii. 34
  Jn., abbot of Battle, ii. 54–5; ix. 106, 111, 180
  Jn. (fl. 1676), ii. 238
  Jn. (fl. 1769), vii. 34

Jn. (fl. 1791, another), ii. 467, 469, 475
Mary, m. —— Woolven, vii. 34
Ric., iv. 157
Wm., ii. 238
——, burgess of Rye, ix. 53
Hamms, Steph., and his w. Thomasine, ix. 241
Hamoda, la (? Homewood or part of Ashdown forest), ii. 298
Hamon, Thos., mayor of Rye, ix. 60
Hamond (Hamonde), *see* Hammond
Hampden, Vcts., *see* Brand, Hen.; Trevor, Jn.
Hamper, Wm., vii. 178
Hampnett, East, *see* Boxgrove
Hampnett, West, *see* Westhampnett
Hampshire, i. 333, 482–4, 495 *n*; ii. 127, 158, 161, 217 *n*; iii. 1–2, 19; iv. 69
  boundary, i. 536; iv. 67
  Bramley, rector, *see* Belcher
  Bramshott, rector, *see* Titherington
  Chilbolton, rector, *see* Oliver, Ric.
  ch. archit., ii. 328
  Civil War, i. 526
  forests, ii. 291, 306
  fortifications, i. 520
  geology, i. 16, 19, 45–6, 274
  militia, i. 508, 516, 525, 534
  natural history, i. 44, 47–8, 50, 67, 110–11, 164, 183, 285, 288
  nonconf., ii. 25, 28
  ports, ii. 136, 141
  sheriff, *see* Mill, Sir Jn.
  sport, i. 305; ii. 445, 453, 468–70, 474–5
  Titchfield, abbot, *see* Simpson, Jn.
  and see individual place names
Hampstead, prebendary, *see* Wilford, Thos. de
Hampton (Hamton):
  Brune de, iv. 98
  Carey, vii. 199
  Charity, m. Ric. Weekes, vii. 113
  Claremunde, w. of Brune de, m. 2 Steph. of Bordeaux, iv. 98
  Jas. de, iv. 115
  Joan de, *see* Tracy
  Jn. de, ii. 412
  Leger de, master of hosp. of St. Jas. and St. Mary, Chich., ii. 100
  Wm., vii. 113
Hampton Court (Mdx.), i. 58; ii. 31; iv. 49–50
Hamptonette:
  Hen. de, iv. 177
  Hen. de (another), iv. 177
  Rog. de, iv. 177
  Wal. de, iv. 177
Hamsey (Hammes, Hammessey), i. 32, 498, 539; ii. 43–4, 209; vii. 33–4, 79, **83–7**
  adv., vii. 87
  angling, ii. 465
  ch., vii. 85–7, *86*
    archit., ii. 337, 339, 348, 366; vii. 90
  Cooksbridge, i. 212, 217; vii. 83
  Coombe Place, iii. 60
  cts., vii. 85
  dom. archit., vii. 83–4
  earthworks, i. 480
  Hewen Street, vii. 83
  man., ii. 311–12, 413; vii. 33–4, 84–5, 87, 206
  Midewinde fishery, ii. 311
  Mount Harry, i. 321, 479, 497
  Offham, ii. 93*; vii. 83
    A.-S. rem., i. 349
    ch., vii. 87
    Down, iii. 60
    Hill, i. 498
    natural history, i. 139, 154, 158, 284*
  pop., ii. 223
  rector, vii. 87; *and see* Wenham, Jn.
  Southborough, vii. 33, 79
  trades and ind., ii. 256, 259

Hamshar, Ric., vii. 139
Hamshaw, Jn., vii. 106
Hamton, *see* Hampton
Hanbery, Thos., iv. 10
Handcross, *see* Slaugham
Handroune, Mic., iv. 175
Haner, Susan, vii. 183
Hanger, Maj., vii. 249
Hangleton:
  Alice, w. of Ric. de, vii. 280
  Cardo de, vii. 280
  Ralph de, vii. 280
  Ric. de (fl. 1215), vii. 280
  Ric. de (d. by 1349), vii. 275 *n*, 280
  Sim. de, vii. 280
Hangleton, ii. 43–4; vii. 2, 4, 226, 265, 274–6*, **277–81**
  adv., vii. 281
  Benfield, ii. 387–8
  ch., ii. 40, 334–5, 344, 365; vii. 276, 281, *281*
  earthworks, i. 480; vii. 277
  Esmerewic, vii. 280
  man., vii. 275–6, 279–81
    ho., ii. 381, 386–7, 393; vii. 277–9
  pop., ii. 224
  prehist. rem., i. 320, 329
  rector, *see* Shales, Hen.
  roads to, iii. 43
  Rom. rem., iii. 57
  sport, ii. 450, 478
Hankerson, Thos., ii. 166
Hankey:
  Sir M.P.A., vii. 173
  Col. Wal. A., ii. 276, 472 *n*
Hankham, *see* Westham
Hanmer, Sir Jn., ix. 234
Hannah:
  Ian, iii. 153, 154 *n*, 156
  Jn. Julius, vicar of Brighton, dean of Chich., ii. 51; iii. 113 *n*, 123–4, 159; vii. 263
Hannam, Gilb., ii. 257, 427–8, 430; iv. 74
Hannay, Jos., ii. 411
Hannington:
  C. Smith, vii. 176
  Sam., vii. 178
Hannys, Margery, m. 1 Sir Peter Besyll, 2 Wm. Warbleton, ix. 206
Hanover (Germany), i. 534
Hanslap, Jn., vii. 36, 58
Hant, Hen., sacrist of Bosham coll., ii. 112
Hanwelle, Thos., dean of South Malling coll., ii. 119
Harbarde, *see* Garbard
Harben:
  Eliz., w. of Thos., vii. 57
  Thos., vii. 32 *n*, 57
Harbotell:
  Bertram, ix. 83
  Eleanor, m. Thos. Percy, ix. 83
  Geo., ix. 83
  Isabel, *see* Monboucher
  Mary, m. Edw. Fitton, ix. 83
  Ralph, ix. 83
  Rob., ix. 83
  Wychard, ix. 83
Harcourt (Harecourt):
  Caroline Mary, *see* Peachey
  Edith, *see* St. Clare
  Eliz., m. Wm. Hooper Boys, ix. 222
  Eliz., w. of Sir Phil., *see* Lee
  Francis Vernon, vii. 34
  Sir Jn., vii. 96, 226
  Kath. Julia, *see* Jenkinson
  Leveson Vernon, iii. 53; iv. 97, 122, 208
  Miles, vii. 257
  Phil. de, ii. 92
  Sir Ric., vii. 256
  Ric., ix. 222
  Sim., Earl Harcourt, ii. 441–3
  fam., iv. 10
Hardenburg, baron, ii. 443
Hardes, *see* Hardys

Hardeshulle:
  Marg. de, iv. 229
  Wm. de, sacrist of Bosham coll., ii. 112
  Wm. de, iv. 229
  ——, see Grauntson
Hardham:
  Eliz., see Burt
  Jas., vii. 160
  Jn., mayor of Chich., iii. 92
  Jn. (fl. 1594), and his w. Mary, vii. 159–60
  Jn. (d. 1772), iii. 90, 167
  Nic., vii. 159–60
Hardham, ii. 43, 47, 217, 301, 466
  ch., ii. 12, 74
    accessories, ii. 328, 354–5, 359
    archit., ii. 47, 334, 339, *339*, 346–8, 365, 372–3
  dom. archit., ii. 386, 391
  earthworks, i. 470, *471*; iii. 67
  insects, i. 201, 205
  man., ii. 75
  prehist. rem., i. 329
  priory, ii. 58, **74–5**, 82–3, 106; iii. 70
    archit., ii. 330, 372
    priors, 74–5; and see Glottyngs
  rly., iii. 37
  roads to, iii. 32, 35–6, 38, 41
  Rom. rem., iii. 2, 32, 35–8, *36*, *38*, 41, 64, 70
Harding, Wm., ii. 165
Hardingham (Norf.), iv. 35
Hardlestone, Jn. de, dean of Hastings coll., ii. 117
Hardman, Jn., vii. 226
Hardresse (Hardres):
  Geo., ix. 241
  Jas., vii. 242; ix. 241
  Thos., ix. 241
  fam., vii. 242
  arms, ix. *241*
Hardson, Hen., and his w. Barbara, ix. 120
Hardwick:
  Jas., vii. 163
  fam., vii. 279 *n*
Hardwick Hall (near Bury St. Edmunds, Suff.), ix. 122
Hardwicke, earl of, see Yorke
Hardy:
  Capt. Chas., ii. 165
  Chas., ix. 224
  Eliz., iv. 104
  Jn., ix. 224
Hardys (Hardes), Thos., vii. 180
Hare (Haire):
  Bethia, see Naylor
  C., ii. 166
  Francis, bp. of Chich., ix. 134, 138 *n*
  (later Naylor), Francis (d. 1775), ix. 134, 138 *n*
  (later Hare-Naylor), Francis (fl. 1807), ix. 134
  Henrietta, ix. 134
  Julius, rector of Herstmonceux, archdeacon of Lewes, ii. 41; ix. 131
  Mary Anne, vii. 42–3
  Rob., ix. 118, 134
hare hunting, see sport: hunting
Hare-Naylor, Francis, see Hare
Harecourt, see Harcourt
Haremere:
  Joce de, ix. 113
  Jn. de (fl. 1339), ix. 213
  Jn. (fl. 1469), ix. 213
  Kath., m. Jn. Sessely, ix. 213
  Laur., ix. 213
  Maud, w. of Wm. de, ix. 213
  Miles de, ix. 213
  Osbert de, ix. 213
  Thos. de, ix. 113
  Wm. de (fl. before 1200), ix. 213
  Wm. de (fl. 1200), ix. 213
  Wm. de (fl. 1296), ix. 213
  Wm. de (fl. 1332, ? another), ix. 213
  Wm. de (fl. 1428), ix. 213

——, w. of Wm. de, ix. 213
  fam., ix. 113, 213, 254
Haremere, see Etchingham
Hareng:
  Alice (or Felice), see Brok
  Emma, m. —— de Hotot, iv. 168
  Felice, m. —— de Wauncy, iv. 168
  Ralph, iv. 168
  Reynold (Reg.), iii. 104; iv. 168
  Reynold (another), iv. 168
  Wm. (d. c. 1230), iv. 168
  Wm. (? another), ii. 80
Harengod (Harengot, Haringod):
  Sir Jn., ix. 187
  Nic., ii. 52; ix. 187, 189
  Ralph, ix. 187, 189
  Steph., iv. 237
  Sybil, see Icklesham
  Thos., ix. 187
  Sir Wm., ix. 187
  arms, ix. *187*
Harethorn, Wm., prior of Shulbred, ii. 82
Harfield, Rob., iv. 195
Harfleur (Seine-Maritime, France), ii. 142 *n*
Hargraves:
  Jas., dean of Chich., ii. 51; iii. 126
  Mary, w. of Jas., see Williamson
Haringod, see Harengod
Harleston, Anne, m. 1 Ric. Dingley, 2 Edm. Mervyn, iv. 230
Harlow (Essex), iii. 52
Harlowe:
  Sarah, m. Thos. Hayley, iii. 144
  Thos., iii. 144
Harman:
  Ezekiel, vii. 74 *n*
  Jas. Ambrose, vii. 77
  Jn., ii. 248
  Revd. Jn., vii. 74
  Jonathan, vii. 13
  and see King-Harman
Harmer:
  Alice, see Wardedieu
  Hen., ix. 263
  Jn., ix. 263
  Mary, iv. 193
  Ric., iv. 193
  Rose, w. of Ric., iv. 193
  Thos., prior of Hastings, ii. 77
  Wm., ix. 263
Harmes, Mic., vii. 140
Harmondsworth (Mdx.), priory, ix. 27
Harney common, see Maresfield: Horney
Harold, king, i. 485–9; ii. 52, 55, 122, 128, 301; iv. 13, 155, 158; ix. 102
  coins of, i. 348–9
  as earl of Wessex, i. 484; ii. 3, 127, 302, 306–7, 324; iv. 182; vii. 70, 216; ix. 79, 112
Harold, king of Norway, ii. 128
Harold Hardrada, i. 485
Harper, J., ix. 244
Harpeting, see Piddinghoe
Harpetynge (Herbertinges, Herbeting):
  Ismania de, vii. 67
  Joan, w. of Sim. de, vii. 67
  Muriel, w. of Sim. de, vii. 67
  Peter de, vii. 67
  Sim. de (fl. 1170), vii. 67–8
  Sim. de (fl. 1224), vii. 67
  Sim. de (d. by 1344), vii. 67
  Wm. de, vii. 67
Harre, Alfred, ii. 425
Harries, see Harris
Harrington:
  Eliz., see Crisp
  Jn., ix. 88
Harrington, earl of, see Stanhope, Chas. Augustus
Harris (Harries, Harrys, Herris):
  Anne, see Salter
  Arthur C., iv. 150
    his w., see Gale, ——
  David, ii. 475
  Eliz., see Bettesworth

Geo., mayor of Chich., iii. 73 *n*, 134
H.E., ii. 477
H. Martyn, vii. 78 *n*
Jas. Hen. Bereford, iv. 195
Jn. (fl. 1548), ix. 157
Jn. (fl. 1615), iv. 150 *n*
Jn. (fl. 1638, ? another), iv. 23, 64
Jn. (fl. 1690), ix. 75
Jn. (d. 1730), iii. 147
Lucy, see Whalley
Rachel, w. of Geo., iii. 134
Renatus, iii. 128
T., ii. 471 *n*
Thos., vii. 74
Harrison:
  Cecil A.H., vii. 53
  Fred., iii. 51
  Geo., ii. 160
  J. Park, iii. 53
  Jn., ii. 447
  Jos., ii. 453
  Thos., ix. 206
  W., ii. 453
Harrison, see Gibbings, Harrison & Co.
Harrogate College Trust Ltd., ix. 178
Harrow Hill, see Angmering
Harry:
  Jn., i. 512
  Jn. (another), ii. 252
Harrys, see Harris
Harsnett, Sam., bp. of Chich., ii. 32, 50; vii. 262
Hart:
  David, ix. 246
  Thos., ix. 246
  ——, i. 287
Hart Hall, Oxford, ii. 407, 420; and see Hertford College, Oxford; Magdalen Hall, Oxford
Hartele, see Hartley
Hartert, Ernst, i. 277, 293
Hartfield, ii. 44, 77, 313, 317, 319
  adv., ii. 123
  Beggars Bush, ii. 319
  Bolebrook:
    archit., ii. 334, 387, 396
    pk., ii. 297
  Castle Hill, iii. 44–5
  Chuck Hatch, ii. 319, 322
  ch., ii. 316, 336, 348, 356, 377–8
  ch. ho., ii. 386
  Coleman's Hatch, ii. 319, 322
  Gardine Hill, ii. 316
  Gills Lap, ii. 322
  Holtye, iii. *40*, 44–5
  hund., i. 537; ii. 182 *n*, 188, 226
  iron ind., ii. 242, 245–6
  New Lodge, ii. 319
  Newbridge, ii. 245, 317, 319–20
  pop., ii. 226
  Quabrook, ii. 319
  rector, see Rands
  roads to, iii. 44–6
  Rom. rem., iii. 44–6
  sch., ii. 427, 437
  vicars, see Rands; Shaw, Geo.
Hartfield and Withyham Harriers, ii. 322
Harthacnut, i. 348; ix. 8
Harthill (Yorks. W.R.), vii. 286
Harting, J.E., i. 108, 287, 290, 301
Harting, i. 108; ii. 43, 89, 302; iv. 3, 8, **10–21**, 23, 56
  adv., iv. 14–16, 20–1, 27
  anchorite, iv. 21
  angling, ii. 466
  A.-S. rem., i. 349
  bridge, iv. 12–13
  char., ii. 437; iv. 21
  ch., iv. 10, *11*, 13–14, 18–20, *20*
    accessories, ii. 352–4, 362
    archit., ii. 335, 340, 346, 348–9, 372–3, 375, 379
  dom. archit., ii. 393; iv. 11–12
  fair, ii. 103; iv. 14–15
  fields, iv. 17
  Harting, East, iii. 57; iv. 3, 10, 12, 15, 20, 21 *n*
  man., iv. 13, 15–16, 92 *n*

Harting (cont.):
    Harting, South, iii. 90; iv. 3, 10–11, 15, 20, 21 n, 23
        Civil War, i. 523–5
        man., iv. 15–16
        prehist. rem., i. 329
    Harting, West, iii. 57; iv. 3, 10, 12–13, 17, 20–1, 159
        man., iv. 14–18, 20, 25
    Harting Beacon (Beacon Hill), iii. 3, 57; iv. 8
    hosp., ii. 89, **103**; iv. 14, 17
    inc., iv. 13
    Ladyholt, i. 108, 306; iv. 11, 15–17
        pk., ii. 303; iv. 10–11
    man., ii. 173 n; iv. 3–4, 13–18, 20–1, 24–5, 105
    mkt., iv. 14
    mills, iv. 11, 13, 17, 21 n, 24–5
    natural history, i. 48–9, 67, 121, 124–9, 132–3, 168, 174, 228, 288
    Nyewoods (Nigh woods), i. 301
    pks., ii. 297; iv. 10–11, 13–15, 17, 20; and see Harting: Ladyholt; Harting: Up Park
    poor ho., iv. 11
    pop., ii. 221
    prehist. rem., iv. 10 n
    rly., iv. 10
    rectors, see Carew, Sir Geo.; Poole, Reynold; Seager; Seton, Jn.
    Rom. rem., iii. 3, 47, 57, 70; iv. 13
    royal visit, i. 505
    sch., iv. 11
    Tarberry Hill, iv. 10, 17
    tithes, iv. 20–1
    trades and ind., ii. 252, 259, 262; iv. 25
    Up Park (Uppark), ii. 441
        archit., ii. 387; iv. 11
        deer, i. 306
        horse racing, ii. 460
        molluscs, i. 109
        pk., ii. 297; iv. 10–11, 15–16, 91
        timber, ii. 298
    Upperton (Upton), ii. 103; iv. 12, 17
    vicars, see Bramston, Jas.; Cookson; Roberts, A.J.
    woods, iv. 15, 17
Hartington, marquess of, see Cavendish, Wm.
Hartley (Hartele, Hertley):
    Jos., iv. 136
    Rob., abbot of Bayham, ii. 88–9
    Rob., iv. 136
    Thos., iv. 136
Hartman, F.W., vii. 71
Hartpury (Glos.), ii. 428
Hartridge:
    Eliz. de, m. 1 Jn. de Percy, 2 Wm. de Burton, vii. 147
    Jn. de, vii. 147
    Nicole de, see Hautentoft
Hartshorn:
    Eliz., m. Sam. Jeake, ix. 48
    Mr., ii. 425
    ——, iii. 65
Hartyngdon:
    Jn., iv. 173
    Marg., w. of Jn., iv. 173
Harvey:
    Mic., and his w. Agnes, iv. 102
    Capt., ii. 163
    Mr. ii. 238
    and see Hervey
Harvey and Staffele, ii. 164
Harvey, Messrs. J. & W.B., ii. 235
Harvey-Bloom, J., ii. 238
Harvey Smith, E. and N., vii. 41
Harward, Chas., dean of Chich., warden of St. Mary's hosp., Chich., ii. 51, 102
Harwich (Essex), ii. 136, 158, 159 n
Haselee, Jn., dean of Chich., ii. 51, 99
Haseling, Sir Arthur, i. 523
Hasker, Marianne Francis, ix. 29, 31–2
Haskyn (or Jonson), Jn., prior of Hardham, ii. 75

Haslemere (Surr.), i. 4, 183
Hasler:
    Jn., iv. 224 n
    Ric., iv. 134
Hassard, Rob., and his w. Anne, vii. 38
Hassell:
    Ann, vii. 101
    Mary, see Luxford
    Wm., vii. 101
Hassocks, see Keymer
Hassok, Jn., prior of Hastings, ii. 76–7
Hastings:
    Aline, w. of Wm. de, ix. 82
    Andrea (Audrey), w. of Mat. de, ix. 56, 118
    Edm. de, ix. 180
    Edw., Ld. Hastings, ix. 3*
    Francis, earl of Huntingdon, ix. 3
    Geo., Ld. Hastings, earl of Huntingdon, ix. 3
    Gilb. of, bp. of Lisbon, ix. 9
    Hen. de, i. 497–8
    Hen., earl of Huntingdon, ix. 3, 191
    Ida, see Ida
    Ingelram de, sheriff of Hastings, ix. 82, 84, 88, 244
    Joan, w. of Thos. de, ix. 82, 120
    Jn. de la, Ld. Bergavenny, ii. 174; iv. 85, 176
    Jn. de, earl of Pembroke, ii. 139
    Jn. de, ix. 146
    Juliana de, see Leyburne
    Laur. de, earl of Pembroke, iv. 85, 176
    Sir Mat. de, sheriff of Suss., bailiff of Rye, i. 498, 501; ii. 295; vii. 99 n, 104; ix. 50–1, 56, 82, 107, 118, 120, 235
    Rob. de (fl. 1086), ix. 168
    Rob. de (fl. 1166), and his w. Isabel, ix. 82
    Rob. de (fl. 1210, ? two of this name), ix. 1, 82, 107
    Rob. de (fl. 1306), ix. 82
    Sigar of, ix. 118
        his s., see Siward
    Thos. de, ix. 82, 88, 107, 118, 120, 186–7, 279
    Thos. de, his s., ix. 107
    Thos. (fl. 1870), ii. 447
    Warren, iv. 121; vii. 88
    Wm. de (fl. before 1207), ix. 1
    Wm. de (d. by 1325), ix. 82, 107, 118, 120, 235, 242
    Sir Wm. de (d. c. 1350), ix. 82, 107, 187
    Sir Wm., Ld. Hastings, ii. 117, 325*; vii. 110; ix. 3, 75, 79, 171 n
    fam., ix. 88, 107, 235, 240, 242
    arms, ix. 81
Hastings, Ld. see Hastings; Hoo, Sir Thos.
Hastings, i. 484–6, 495, 503; ii. 127, 177, 192; iv. 31; vii. 14; ix. **4–33**, 34–6, 39, 49, 168, 175
    bailiffs, ix. 10
    barons (or freemen), i. 493–4; ix. 10–12, 24
    barony, see Hastings: honor
    (or Senlac) battle, i. 349, 486, **486–9**; vii. 1; ix. 8–9, 14
    birds, i. 276
    borough, ix. 4, 8–12, 81
        arms, ix. 4
    botany, i. 43, 60–7
    boundaries, ix. 4–5
    Brassey Institute, i. 313, 327, 329; ix. 8
    Bulverhythe, q.v.
    cast., i. 472, 493, 496, 507, 509; ii. 115–16, 174, 295; ix. 1–2, 9–10, 14, **14–19**
        archit., ii. 336, 394–5; ix. 15–19
        chap., see Hastings: coll.
        constable, ii. 114, 116; ix. 15, 67
    earthworks, i. 476, 476–7
    Castle Cliff, ix. 8
    Castle Hill, i. 312; ix. 6

    Castle Place, ii. 411
    Central Recreation Ground, ii. 471–3
    chant., ix. 10, 28
    char., ii. 411; ix. 28–33
    charters, ix. 10–11, 37
    chs., ii. 160; ix. 21–8
        adv., ix. 26–8
        All Saints, ii. 43; ix. 8, 10, 21–3, 22, 31; accessories, ii. 249–50, 352, 354, 356*, 360, 378; adv., ix. 3, 26; archit., ii. 230, 334, 336, 339, 346–7, 350, 378; ix. 21–2; rector, ii. 410
        All Souls, ix. 25, 28
        Christ Church, Blacklands, ix. 25, 28
        Emmanuel, ix. 25, 28, 32
        Fisherman's, ix. 7, 25–6, 31
        Holy Trinity, ix. 25, 27
        St. Andrew, ii. 43, 113; ix. 25–6, 27 n, 32
        St. Clement, ii. 43, 154; ix. 3, 6, 10, 23, 23–5, 27–8, 31; accessories, ii. 249, 251, 352, 356, 378; adv., ix. 26; archit., ii. 334, 336, 339, 346–7, 350, 378; ix. 23–4; rector, ii. 410
        St. Ethelburga, ix. 25, 28
        St. Margaret, ii. 43, 76, 116; ix. 27
        St. Mary in the castle, ix. 1, 11, 17, 25, 27, 32; and see Hastings: coll.
        St. Mary Magdalen, ix. 26–9, 33
        St. Matthew, ix. 26, 28, 33
        St. Michael, ii. 43, 76, 116; ix. 27
        St. Paul, ix. 26, 28, 33
        St. Peter, ii. 43, 76, 116; ix. 27
    Civil War in, ii. 157
    Clive Vale reservoir, ix. 8
    clubs:
        Natural History, i. 66
        Old Hastings, ix. 6
        sports, ii. 473, 479, 481; ix. 8
    coastguards, i. 507 n
    coins, i. 326, 329
    coll. of St. Mary in the castle, ii. 11, 46, **112–17**, 265; ix. 9, 15–20, 16, 123, 215
        accessories, ii. 351, 370
        adv., ix. 2
        archit., ii. 338, 370, 395; ix. 14, 17–18, 89
        canons, ii. 72, 76, 410; ix. 145, 148, 155–7, 162, 183, 223, 228
        dean, ii. 42, 72, 117, 232; ix. 85; and see Hugh; Lewes, Wm. of; London, Edm. de; Lyndrigge; Ow; Prestwick, Wm.; Vincent; Wade, Jn.
        prebendary, see Aucher
        prebends, ii. 12, 71–2, 112–14, 116–17, 410; ix. 19–21, 81, 84–5, 123, 140–1, 148, 156, 174, 183, 223–4, 228, 232, 234, 246, 249, 264, 268
        sch., see Hastings: sch.
    Conqueror's stone, ix. 5
    convalescent homes, ix. 8, 28–9, 32
    cts., ix. 11, 36
    ct. ho. (or hall), ix. 5, 8 n, 11–12
    crustaceans, i. 245, 247–53, 255, 257, 259–66
    Custom ho., ix. 13
    deanery, ii. 42–3
    defences, i. 492; ii. 152, 156, 158, 160–2; ix. 5, 7, 10–11, 40
    Diamond Shoal, i. 247
    dom. archit., ii. 384, 386, 389, 391–2; ix. 6–8
    Dutch war, ii. 158
    East Hill, ii. 470–1; ix. 6, 9, 27
        earthworks, i. 468–9, 469
    fairs, ix. 13–14
    fishes, i. 267
    fossils, i. 28, 35–9
    freemen, see Hastings: barons
    French raids, i. 510, 530; ii. 138–40, 156, 159, 162; ix. 10, 15, 66
    geology, i. 274; ii. 242, 255, 336

Halton, ix. 11, 25, 27
harbour, *see* Hastings: port
Hollington, *q.v.*
honor (or barony) of, ix. **1–8**, 147,
164, 172, 175, 206, 220, 254; *and
see* Hastings: rape
ct. (le Lathe), ix. 1, 3
hosps., ix. 32–3
Royal East Suss., ix. 8, 28–9
St. Mary Magdalen, ii. 45, **103**; ix.
27, 31
hund. place, ix. 10–11
insects, i. 111–67, 136, 169, 171–205,
207–9, 211–16, 218–37
inns, ix. 5
liberties, ix. 9–10
Liberty of the Sluice, ii. 228, 247; ix.
4, 115–16, 123
local govt., ii. 24; ix. 10–11
corporation, ii. 410–11; ix. 10–11,
20
cts., *see* Hastings: cts.
jurats, ii. 156, 158, 410; ix. 10, 38,
90; *and see* Murray, Jas.
mayors, ii. 156, 410, 470 *n*; ix. 10,
12, 90; *and see* Collier, Jn.;
Hutchins, Geo.; Milward, Edw.
other officers, ix. 11
police, ix. 11
seals, ix. 11–12
mail coaches, ii. 204; ix. 4
mammals, i. 299, 301–2, 304, 307
man., ii. 3; ix. 9, 19–20, 84
marine zoology, i. 71–107
mkts., ix. 14
militia, i. 515, 517, 534–5, 536 *n*
mint, i. 348; ii. 126; vii. 14; ix. 8
molluscs, i. 108–9
museum, i. 124–5, 127–8, 301, 309,
313, 316
navigation lights, ii. 163; ix. 13
nonconf., ii. 32; ix. 7, 29–30
Ordinances of, ix. 10
Ore, *q.v.*
parishes, ix. 26–8
All Saints, ii. 228
Holy Trinity (the priory), ii. 228
St. Andrew, ii. 228
St. Clement, ii. 228
St. Mary in the castle, ii. 222, 228;
ix. 19, 28, 76
St. Mary Magdalen, ii. 228; ix.
27–8
St. Michael, ii. 228
pks., ix. 5, 8
parl. rep., ix. 4, 12
elections, i. 521; ix. 11
piers, ix. 10, 13
piracy, ii. 147, 160; ix. 27
poor relief, ii. 193, 205
pop., ii. 228, 275; ix. 5
port and harbour, ii. 3, 125, 129–30,
144, 169, 247, 464; iii. 102; ix.
12–13
prehist. rem., i. 311–12, 316, 329
priory, ii. 58, **75–7**, 78, *92*, 124, 331;
ix. 10, 27–8, 79, 81, 234, 257
estates, ix. 20, 130, 233
patronage, ix. 27, 81, 130, 234, 238
priors, ii. 14, 76–7
prisons, ix. 10–11
public services, ix. 8, 26
rly., ii. 205, 223 *n*, 240; ix. 4, 40
rape, ii. 174, 194, 222–3, 293; iii.
96 *n*; ix. 1–4, 38
apprentices, ii. 196
boundaries, ix. 1
coastguards, i. 507 *n*
descent of, ix. 1–4, 79, 84, 91, 118,
127, 133, 142, 153, 196, 210, 212,
226, 239–40, 258
militia, i. 535
musters, ix. 76
sheriff, *see* Hastings, Ingelram de;
St. Martin, Alfred de
vagrancy, ii. 196
wards, ix. 1, 4
woodland, ix. 1

rebellions, i. 514
reptiles, i. 272
roads to, ix. 4
Rom. Cath., ix. 6, 28, 33
Rom. rem., iii. 2, 58
St. Clement's caves, i. 327; ix. 6
St. Leonards, *q.v.*
sch., ii. 410; ix. 28–9, 33
coll. ch., ii. 113, 398, 409–10; ix.
17
grammar, ii. 113, 397–8, 409–11;
ix. 33
sea bathing, ii. 203–4
Sea Fencibles, ii. 162
ship money, ii. 156–7
ship (or sea) service, ii. 126–7, 129–
32, 134–5, 138, 141, 144, 150,
153–4; ix. 8–9, 36, 49
shipmasters, ix. 9
shipping, ii. 127–8, 130, 132–3, 137–
8, 142, 151–2, 155–6; ix. 10, 13
Silver Hill, i. 272; ii. 450
smuggling, ix. 13
Spanish Armada, ii. 153
spiders, i. 238–44
sport, ii. 460, 467, 470–4, 479, 481;
ix. 8, 29
Stone, ii. 113; ix. 19–20
streams, ix. 9, 11–12
streets, ix. 4–8, *6*
theatres, ix. 7
town hall, ix. 5–6, 8
trades and ind.:
basket making, ii. 236
bellfounding, ii. 249–50
brewing, ii. 262–3
brickmaking, ii. 254
fisheries, ii. 132, 145–6, 148, 151,
159, 163, 264–70; ix. 10, 12, 55
glass, ii. 255
lime burning, ii. 231; ix. 13
salt, ii. 233
shipbuilding, ii. 164, 167, 235; ix.
13
textiles, ii. 257–8; ix. 13
tile making, ii. 252; ix. 13
timber, ii. 233
union, i. 539
White Rocks, ii. 159, 162
wreck, right of, ii. 146
Hastings Cottage Improvement Soc., ix.
7
Hatch, Jos., ix. 159, 174
Hatchard, J.A., and his w., ix. 12
Hatfield (Herts.), iv. 114
Hathorne, Jn., vii. 9
Hatton, Sir Chris., iv. 99
Hatzell:
Sir Hen., vii. 270
Judith, *see* Shirley
Haubedene, fam., ix. 25 *n*
Haubois, *see* Hautbois
Haule (Haull), *see* Hall
Hautbois (Haubois):
Helewise de, vii. 177 *n*
Wm. de, vii. 67, 177
Haute:
Alice, *see* Charles
Sir Nic., ix. 187
Hautentoft:
Lucy de, vii. 147
Nicole de, m. Jn. de Hartridge, vii.
147
Olive de, m. —— de Northo, vii. 147
Thos. de, vii. 147
Wm. de, and his w. Isabel, vii. 147
Hauterive, fam., ii. 332
Havant (Hants), iii. 47; iv. 159 *n*
Haverfield, F., i. 343; iii. 9–10, 14–15,
30, 42, 47, 55, 59–60, 62, 68
Haviland:
Anne, *see* Dyke
E.A., ix. 209
Hen. Hone, ix. 197
Mrs., ix. 227
fam., ix. 209
Havre, Le (Seine-Maritime, France), i.
516; ii. 143, 145, 152

Hawe, Wm., dean of Hastings coll., ii.
117
Hawes, Jn., ii. 246
Hawke, Martin Bladen, Ld. Hawke, ii.
473
Hawkes, Chris., iii. 69
Hawkesborough, *see* Hawksborough
Hawkesbury, Cecil, Ld. Hawkesbury,
ix. 191 *n*
Hawkesley, Rob., and his w. Kath., ix.
255
Hawkeswurth, *see* Hawksborough
Hawkhurst (in Kent and Suss.), ii. 223;
ix. 210–11, 251
Hawkhurst Common, *see* Hoathly, East
hawking, *see* sport
Hawkins:
Francis, dean of Chich., ii. 51
Phil., and his w. Anne, ix. 178
Hawksborough (Hawkesborough, Haw-
keswourth) hund., i. 537; ii. 222;
ix. 3, **193**
Hawksbourne, *see* Horsham
Hawkshaw, Sir Jn., iv. 23, 65, 83
Hawksworth, Anne, ix. 209
Hawle:
Ann, *see* Erley
Wm., vii. 256
Hawley:
Hen., ii. 442–3
Jos., ii. 459
Hawney, Wm., ii. 426
Haworth, T.W., ix. 33
Hay (Haia, Haye):
Adam, ix. 180
Alex., iii. 12, 18, 83, 89–91
Alexandra de, m. 1 Adam de Godin-
don, 2 Wm. Gardin, iv. 163 *n*
Cecily de, m. Rog. St. John, ii. 53; iv.
143
Eliz., ix. 111
Emma, w. of Rog., iv. 156
Frances, ix. 213
German, iv. 157
Henrietta, ix. 213
Herb., ix. 141, 213
Isabel, w. of Ralph de la, m. 2 Thos.
de Audeham, ii. 241–2
Jn. de la, constable of Rye and Win-
chelsea, i. 498, 501, 504; ii. 77;
ix. 50
Jn., mayor of Chich., iii. 91
Jn. (d. 1605), ix. 141, 160, 213
Jn., M.P. for Rye and Suss., ix. 213
Ralph de la, ii. 241–2
Ralph, ix. 180
Rob. de (fl. 1105), ii. 56, 303; iv. 51,
142–3, 149, 156, 158, 179,
201
Rob., and his w. Levota, ix. 180
Rob., his s., ix. 180
Rog. (fl. *c.* 1187), iv. 156–7
Rog. (d. by 1230), iv. 156–7
Rog. (fl. 1230), iv. 156–7
Sarah, m. Jn. Langham, ix. 213
Thos. (d. by 1230), iv. 156
Thos. de (another), iv. 163 *n*
Thos. (fl. 1553), ix. 220
Thos. (d. 1786), ix. 213
Thos. (fl. 1907), ii. 429
Wm. (d. 1755), ii. 301; vii. 111
Wm. (d. *c.* 1823), ix. 213
——, ? m. Wm. de St. John, iv. 157 *n*
fam., ii. 303; ix. 220
arms, ix. *213*
haybote, ii. 294, 315; iv. 124; vii. 105
Hayden, Wm., i. 310, 313, 328
Haye, *see* Hay
Hayes, *see* Hays
Hayes Down, *see* Lavant
Hayley:
And. B., ix. 228
Anne, *see* Burrell
Burrell, ix. 242
his w., *see* Pilkington, ——
Jn. Burrell, ix. 141, 228
Penelope, *see* Baker
Sarah, *see* Harlowe

Hayley (*cont.*):
Thos., dean of Chich., warden of St. Mary's hosp., Chich., ii. 51, 102; iii. 144
Thos. (fl. 1745), i. 533; iv. 152
Thos. (d. 1800), iv. 152 *n*
W.B., ix. 242
Wm., dean of Chich., warden of St. Mary's hosp., Chich., ii. 51, 102
Wm., rector of Brightling, ix. 207, 227–8, 232
Wm. (d. 1820), ii. 239; iii. 90; iv. 152
Wm. Burrell, ix. 228
Miss, ix. 232
arms, ix. *228*
Hayley park, *see* Westmeston: Hailey pk.
Hayling (Hants), iv. 191
priory, ii. 109
Hayling Island (Hants), i. 45, 191, 194; ii. 269
Hayllyng, Ric. de, ii. 259
Haynes, *see* Haines
Hays (Hayes):
Eliz., ii. 64
——, ii. 35
Hayter, G.C.F., iii. 16, 39
Hayward:
Jn., ii. 164
Ric., iv. 190 *n*
Haywards (Hayward's) Heath, i. 55, 522; ii. 276; vii. 148
natural history, i. 59–60, 131–5, 137, 142, 153–6, 159, 165–7, 168 *n*, 169, 171–90
Rom rem., iii. 58
sport, ii. 448, 481
Hayward, Wm., ix. 160
Hayworthe, *see* Heyworth
Hazelrigg, Sir Arthur, ii. 454
Hazelwood, *see* Horsted Keynes
Head:
Alban, iii. 16
Edw., vii. 236
Jn., and his w. Jane, vii. 235
Headhone, *see* Aldingbourne
Heath (Heth):
Cath., *see* Bately
Chas., iii. 126
Frances, m. Hen. Pelham, ix. 197
Martha, m. Hen. Shelley, vii. 68
Nic., dean of South Malling coll., ii. 119
Ric., vii. 67
Rob., vii. 40, 64, 67, 254
Wm., mayor of Chich., iii. 92
Wm., vii. 67
Heath Common (in Sullington, Thakeham, Warminghurst, and Washington), i. 53
Heather:
Mary, iv. 163
Mary, m. Jn. Quantock, iii. 145; iv. 163
Ric., iv. 163
Thos., iv. 163
Heathfield:
Dan., and his w. Judith, vii. 183
Susannah, ix. 31
Heathfield, Ld., *see* Elliott, Geo. Augustus
Heathfield, ii. 43, 279–80, 295, 464; ix. 193, 195, **200–4**, 209
adv., ix. 203
apprentices, ii. 196
Broomham (Bromham), ix. 201
Cade Street, i. 57; ix. 201
char., ix. 203
ch., ix. 202–3, *203–4*
archit., ii. 336, 342, 347, 351, 373, 375
earthworks, i. 478
fair, ix. 201
fossils, i. 38
foxhunting, ii. 447–8
gas well, i. 6
insects, i. 186, 216, 226, 235
man., ix. 201–2

mkt., ix. 201
nonconf., ix. 201
Pk., i. 57; ix. 200
pop., ii. 222
prebend, ii. 48; ix. 203
Punnett's Town, i. 57; ix. 201
rebellions, i. 514, 516
Tottingworth (Toddingworth), ix. 193, 202, 278
trades and ind., ii. 249, 260; ix. 201
vicar, *see* Killingbeck
Heaver, Steph., vii. 58
Heawulf, moneyer, iii. 83
Hebbe:
Jn., mayor of Chich., iii. 91
Jn. (? another), iv. 5
Hecca, bp. of Selsey, ii. 3
heccage, i. 492
Hedehone, Nic., *see* Barrington
hedgebote, ii. 294, 302, 309–10; vii. 105
Hedger:
Edw., ix. 177
Jn., ix. 177
Hedol, Rado de la, iv. 43
Hedon (Eden), Rob., ii. 419
Heene, i. 53; ii. 43
chant., ii. 20
coins, i. 330
insects, i. 172, 203
pop., ii. 218
Heere, Lucas de, ix. 126
Heghested:
Helewise de, vii. 190 *n*
Maud de, vii. 190
Wm. de, vii. 190
Heighton, ii. 122; ix. 55, 142
Heighton, South, ii. 44; vii. 73; ix. 226
birds, i. 295*
foxhunting, ii. 450
pop., ii. 226
Rom. rem., iii. 61
Heiligenberg (Germany), iii. 41
Helde, Jn., mayor of Winchelsea, ix. 63
Hele, R.H.S., ix. 171
Helghi, iv. 216
Helling, *see* Brade
Hellingly, Ric. of, ii. 5
Hellingly, i. 56; ii. 44, 86, 197, 297, 313; vii. 33
adv., ii. 86
Broad, the, ii. 86, 392
Carter's Corner, i. 68; ii. 387
ch., ii. 5, 7, 13, 86–7
archit., ii. 332, 336, 367–8, 374–5
ch. yard, ii. 5
Dicker, i. 56; ii. 44, 297, 313–14
stud, ii. 461
trades and ind., ii. 247, 252, 254
wood, ii. 298
glebe, ii. 5
Horselunges, i. 477; ii. 384
Melgrave, ii. 86
natural history, i. 148, 154, 157–8, 165–6, 301
poor relief, ii. 209
pop., ii. 226
rly. station, ix. 131
tanning, ii. 260
vicarage, vii. 227, 240
Helyer, Jn., iv. 216
Heming:
Amelia, iii. 144
Emma, iii. 144
Geo., iii. 147
Sam., iii. 164
T., ix. 54
Hemingburgh, Wal. of, ii. 132 *n*
Hemmings, H., ii. 474
hemp, *see* textile inds.
Hempstead, *see* Arlington
Hempsted (in Benenden), *see* Benenden
Hempsted, prebendary, *see* Wilford, Thos. de
Hemsley, W.B., i. 42
Hendall, *see* Buxted
Henden, Jn., ix. 169
Henderfoot, Francis, ix. 156

Hendley:
Ann, m. Ric. Covert, vii. 186
Anne, *see* Bowyer
Mary, m. 1 Wm. More, 2 Wm. Clarke, vii. 156, 196
Sir Thos., vii. 6 *n*, 156–7
Sir Wal., vii. 156, 163, 196
arms, vii. 186
Heneage (Henneage):
Eliz., ctss. of Maidstone and Winchilsea, m. Sir Moyle Finch, ix. 71, 107
Sir Thos., iv. 212; ix. 71
Henfield, i. 54, 300; ii. 43–4; vii. 276
Barrow Hill, iii. 58
birds, i. 279, 295
botany, i. 42, 59–60, 62
ch., ii. 3, 354, 356, 358
archit., ii. 372, 378
insects, i. 165, 169, 172, 176, 190, 192, 198, 203, 206–8
mammals, i. 300–1, 304
man., vii. 14
militia, i. 535
Mockfords, ii. 393
pop., ii. 219
roads to, iii. 47
Rom. rem., iii. 2, 47, 58
sport, ii. 449, 465, 475
Streatham, i. 477; iii. 58
tanning, ii. 260
tithes, ii. 7–8
vicarage, ii. 7, 9
Henfield Anglers' Assoc., ii. 465
Henhurst and Robertsbridge hund., i. 506, 537; ii. 222 *n*, 223, 259; ix. 3, **210**, 227
Henistone (unidentified), ii. 56
Henley:
Rob., Ld. Keeper, ii. 423
Mr., ii. 454
Henley, *see* Fernhurst
Henneage, *see* Heneage
Hennezel:
Balthazar de, ii. 254
Thos., ii. 254
fam., ii. 254
Henrietta Maria, queen of Chas. I, iv. 13
Henry I, i. 490; ii. 6, 53, 56, 65, 109, 129, 303; iii. 71, 82, 84, 90, 92, 97–8, 100, 102, 104, 106; iv. 50, 77, 115, 128, 130, 133, 135, 139, 143, 156, 162, 166–8, 175, 183–4, 222, 234; vii. 2, 281; ix. 1, 14, 38, 62, 67, 145
Henry II, i. 490–1; ii. 6, 53, 89, 99, 103, 110, 121, 129, 171, 294, 296, 330*; iii. 81, 84–5, 90, 92, 100; iv. 1, 21, 25 *n*, 73, 77, 120, 122, 135, 145, 162, 192, 217; vii. 208, 258; ix. 2, 9, 14–15, 34–8, 49, 117
his s. (the Young King), *see* Henry son of Henry II
Henry III, i. 494–502, 507; ii. 10, 66, 92, 95, 99, 101, 130, 132, 171, 294, 304, 324; iii. 75, 81, 85, 100, 104, 165; iv. 51, 109 *n*, 154, 183–4, 237; vii. 2, 271, 286; ix. 2, 10, 17, 37, 39–40, 117, 123, 134, 168, 217
Henry IV, ii. 76, 78, 95, 141, 323; iii. 96; ix. 3, 15, 169
as earl of Lancaster, i. 512
Henry V, i. 513–14; ii. 120–1, 123, 131, 141, 331; iii. 96, 114, 153; ix. 70, 133, 150
as prince of Wales, iv. 123, 163
Henry VI, ii. 95, 107, 113, 117, 121, 242, 305, 324; iii. 94, 96; iv. 162; ix. 3, 117, 133, 244
Henry VII, i. 515; ii. 143, 150, 416; iii. 96; iv. 77; vii. 5–6, 15
Henry VIII, i. 515; ii. 20, 59, 75, 80, 96, 101, 109, 117, 131, 143–5, 147, 267, 305, 395, 402, 435; iii. 112, 134; iv. 31, 56, 73, 143, 149, 153, 159, 165, 223, 230–1, 234, 238; vii. 219, 224, 239, 257, 262; ix. 27, 94, 154, 177, 263

arms, iv. 50
Henry VI, emperor, ii. 72
Henry IV, king of France, i. 519
Henry, abbot of Battle, ii. 53, 55
Henry, abbot of Durford, ii. 91
Henry, abbot of Fécamp, ix. 49
Henry, count of Eu (d. 1140), ii. 112–13, 409; ix. 1, 14, 67, 118, 139–40, 145, 148, 155–7, 161–2, 195, 244
Henry, count of Eu (d. 1183), ii. 71, 76, 324; ix. 2, 14, 81, 140, 145, 230, 244, 257, 278
Henry, prior of Christ Church, Cant., ii. 53
Henry, prior of Hardham, ii. 75
Henry, prior of Pynham, ii. 81
Henry, prior of Shulbred, ii. 82
Henry, prince of Wales, son of James I, iv. 223
Henry, warden of St. Mary's hosp., Chich., ii. 102
Henry fitz John, see FitzJohn
Henry, son of Henry II, ix. 2, 14
Henry, schoolmaster at Battle, ii. 397
his dau., see Alice
Henry Frederick, duke of Cumberland, ii. 449, 456; vii. 19, 249
his w., ii. 456
Henry, Rob., ii. 78
Henshaw (Henshawe):
Jane, see May
Jos., prebendary of Bishopshurst, dean and precentor of Chich., bp. of Peterborough, ii. 51; iv. 103, 213; ix. 107
Mary, m. Jn. Sherer, iii. 147
Phil., iv. 213; ix. 107
Rog., iv. 213
Thos. (fl. before 1717), ix. 107
Thos. (fl. 1779), iv. 213
Tobias, vicar of Cuckfield, archdeacon of Lewes, vii. 163
Wm., iv. 213
Henslow (Hensley), Edm., ii. 317–18
Henty, Edwin, i. 340
Henworthe, Wm., i. 518
Hepburn:
G., ix. 195
Harriet, see Poole
Herald, iv. 135
herbage, right of, ii. 116, 293, 307–9, 312–13, 325; vii. 58
Herbard (Herberd), see Herbert
Herbert, dean of Bramber, ii. 60
Herbert, rector of Stoughton, iv. 117
Herbert (fl. 1086), iv. 218–19
Herbert (Herbard, Herberd):
Anne, see Sackville
Geo., iii. 1 n, 24, 51
Hen., earl of Pembroke, ii. 443
Jn., vii. 229
(or Finch), Jn., see Finch
Mary, ii. 438
Phil., earl of Pembroke, vii. 48
Sir Wm., ix. 75
Wm., ix. 15, 17–18
Herbetinges (Herbeting), fam., see Harpetynge
Herbertinges (Herbeting), see Piddinghoe: Harpeting
Hercez, Nichola de, prioress of Lyminster, ii. 121
Herchaia (unidentified), ii. 302
Hercules, i. 324; iii. 17, 63
Herdman, Arthur Widdrington, ix. 268
Hereford, Jn., iii. 154
Hereford, earls of, see Bohun, Humph.
Hereford, bp., see Braose, Giles de
Herefordshire, i. 68, 304; ii. 255–6
and see Moccas; Staunton on Wye
Heringaud (Heringot):
Ralph, i. 500
Wm., ix. 202
fam., ix. 202
Heringdales, see Waldron: Heronsdale
heriot, iv. 184; vii. 266; ix. 71
Heritage, Thos., dean of South Malling coll., ii. 119

Heriton, Thos. de, prior of Shulbred, ii. 82
Herkestede:
Agnes, see Knolle
Wm., iv. 161
Herling, rector of Easebourne, iv. 53
Herluin, iv. 175
hermit, Peter the, see Peter
Hermitage, see Westbourne
hermits, ii. 11, 46–7, 97
Hermon, S.A., iv. 480
Herolf (? two of this name), ix. 107, 168
Heron:
Eliz., see Say
Sir Wm., Ld. Say, ii. 99; vii. 114, 206–7, 255
Heron-Allan, E., iii. 66
Heronsdale, see Waldron
Herpes (Charente, France), i. 345, 347
Herris, see Harris
Herste:
Idonea, m. 2 Guy de Mortimer, ix. 133, 149, 206
(or Monceaux), Waleran de, see Monceaux
(or Monceaux), Wm. de, see Monceaux
fam., ix. 133
and see Hurst
Herstmonceux (Hurstmonceux), ii. 43; ix. 125, **131–7**
adv., ix. 137
agric., ii. 289; ix. 131, 133
Blackford, i. 156, 163
Bodle Street Green, q.v.
cast., ii. 78, 197, 198 n; ix. 131–4, *130–2*
archit., ii. 253, 334, 394–5; ix. 131–2
chap., ii. 338; ix. 132
earthworks, i. 477
char., ix. 137
ch., ix. 134–7, *135*
accessories, ii. 356, 361; ix. 137
archit., ii. 336, 340, 348, 370; ix. 134–6
Cowbeech (Cowbeach), ii. 452; ix. 125, 131
Flowers Green, ix. 131
Gardner Street, ix. 131
hunting, ii. 452
man., ix. 118, 120, 132–3, 139, 206, 248, 266–7, 274
natural history, i. 231*, 272
nonconf., ix. 131, 137
pk., ii. 297; ix. 131, 133–4
pop., ii. 222
rectors, ix. 209; and see Echingham, Sim.; Hare, Julius; Pencell
royal visits, i. 496, 505
Stunt's Green, ix. 131
trades and ind., ii. 236, 257, 260; ix. 131
Windmill Hill, q.v.
Place, ii. 447, 471; ix. 137
woods, ii. 299; ix. 131
Hertford College, Oxford, ii. 433; and see Hart Hall, Oxford; Magdalen Hall, Oxford
Hertfordshire, i. 169, 290; ix. 32
South Herts. militia, i. 534
and see Bishop's Stortford; Elstree; Hatfield; Offley; St. Albans; Sandridge; Theobalds
Hertley, see Hartley
Hervey (Hervy):
Fred. Wm., marquess of Bristol, vii. 261
Jn., Ld. Hervey of Ickworth, ii. 441, 443
Steph., iv. 152
Wm., and his w. Joan, ix. 98
and see Harvey
Hese, Ralph atte, ii. 108
Heselwode, see Ashdown forest
Heskett, Jn., ii. 305
Hesmon, Francis, ii. 319
Hesse, Eugène, i. 261

Hessell, Phoebe, vii. 259
Hesset, Hen. de, iv. 44
Hester, Chas., ii. 238
Heth, see Heath
Heuere, see Hevere
Heuerwyk, Jn., abbot of Durford, ii. 91
Heuster, Humph., iii. 142
Hevere (Hever, Heuere):
Alice, w. of Sir Thos. de, iv. 168
Hawise, w. of Ralph de, iv. 168
Joan de, m. —— St. John, iv. 168
Jn., and his w. Joan, vii. 159
Marg. de, m. Oliver Brocas, iv. 168
Ralph de, iv. 168
Ric., vii. 159
Sir Thos. de, ii. 304; iv. 168
Thos., vii. 159
——, ii. 320
Hewen Street, see Hamsey
Hewett (Hewitt, Huett):
Edw., ii. 471
Eliz., w. of Jn., ? m. 2 Sir Gilb. Wakering, ix. 146
Francis, ix. 191
Jn. (d. 1602), ix. 146
Sir Jn. (d. 1657), ix. 146
Jn. (d. 1684), ix. 146
Jn. (fl. 1696), ix. 146
Kath., see Bevill
Wm. (d. 1599), ix. 146
Wm. (fl. 1709), and his w. Mary, iv. 83
Hewitt Smith, Chas., see Smith
Hewson, Jn., iv. 112–13
Hexham, Jn., and his w. Joan, iv. 195
Heydon, Geo., vii. 37
Heyshott, ii. 43 n; iv. 40, 52, 58, **60–3**
adv., iv. 63, 84
ch., ii. 372; iv. *61–2*, 62–3
Cobden Club, iv. 60
dom. archit., iv. 60
earthworks, i. 466, 480
Heyshott Down, iii. 58; iv. 60, 118
insects, i. 116, 119, 121, 166
man., iv. 44, 60–2
mill, iv. 61–2, *61*
pop., ii. 221
prehist., iv. 60
sch., iv. 60
woodland, iv. 61
Heyworth (Hayworthe):
Jn. de, vii. 159
Phil. de, vii. 159
Hiberden (Huberden):
Eliz. Cath., see Miller
Humph., iv. 145
Jn., iv. 145
Rob., iv. 234
Thos., iv. 145
Wm., iv. 230
Hichcock, Rob., ii. 299
Hicket, Nic., rector of Pulborough, ii. 25
Hickey, T., iii. 145
Hicks, Wm., canon of Chich., ii. 32
Hickstead, see Twineham
Hide, see Hyde
Hidney, see Willingdon: Hydneye
Higden, Jn., iv. 117
Higford:
Jas., ix. 207
Marg., see Keyt
Higgins, Wm., ii. 165
Higgons (Hygons):
Edw., master of Arundel coll., ii. 109
Edw., i. 522
Thos., iv. 82
High Beeches warren, see Worth forest
High Down, see Ferring
High Hurst, see Newick
High Wood, see Battle
Higham (in Salehurst), see Salehurst
Higham (in Winchelsea), see Winchelsea
Highbrook, see Hoathly, West
Highden, see Washington
Highgate, see Forest Row
Highlands, see Hailsham
Highleigh, see Sidlesham

Highley, see Balcombe
Highley, prebend, see Sidlesham: High-
leigh
Hikke, Hen., master of hosp. of St. Jas.
and St. Mary, Chich., ii. 100
Hilary, bp. of Chich., ii. 6–7, 47–8, 53,
56, 89, 105, 332 n; iii. 125, 146; iv.
106, 120, 153–4*; ix. 1, 117
his bro., see Robert
Hilder:
Geo., ix. 61–2
T.P., ii. 476
Thos., ix. 197
fam., vii. 59
Hilditch, Ralph, iv. 29
Hildrop, Wm., iv. 129
Hill (Hille):
Aaron, ii. 324
Caroline Francis, mchnss. of Down-
shire, vii. 33
H.R., iv. 33
Jn., vii. 261
Margaretta, ix. 124
Ric. (fl. 1419), and his w. Philippa, iv.
238
Ric. (fl. c. 1420–40, another), vii. 144
Wm., vicar of Felpham, ii. 33
Hillary, w. of Alan, ix. 180
Hille, see Hill
Hillman, Aubrey, i. 339
Hills:
Eliz., w. of Wm., ix. 198
Fred., ii. 448
Gordon, iii. 12, 111, 144
Wm., ix. 198
Hilly, Jn., mayor of Chich., iii. 80 n, 92,
98
Hilton:
Eleanor, see Poynings
F.K., ii. 434*, 476
Sir Geof., iv. 199 n
Hindall, see Buxted: Hendall
Hindhead (Surr.), i. 290
Hindleap, see Forest Row
Hindover, see Alfriston
Hinkman, Wm., ix. 12
Hinksey (Berks.), ii. 421
Hiorne's Tower, see Arundel: pk.
Hipperholme (Yorks. W.R.), ii. 423
Hiscock:
Geo., iii. 133
Percy, iii. 133
Hitchman, R., iii. 164
Hive, see Wyndham Hive
Hlothere (Lothere), king of Kent, i. 482
Hoad:
Jas., ii. 235
——, ii. 198
Hoadley, see Ticehurst
Hoathly, East (Easthothly), i. 56; ii. 44,
297, 313, 416
ch., ii. 351, 378; iii. 114; vii. 245
Halland, ii. 197–8, 443
Ho., ii. 245, 387
Pk., ii. 386
Hawkhurst Common, i. 56
pop., ii. 227
prehist. rem., i. 329
rector, see Pickering, Benj.
Hoathly (? East or West), ii. 190
rector, see Walter
Hoathly, West, i. 55; ii. 43–4, 419; vii.
2, 92, 125, 164–72, 200
adv., vii. 106, 171
char., vii. 171–2
ch., ii. 48, 68; vii. 169–71, 170
accessories, ii. 352, 354, 374
archit., ii. 336, 340, 374–5
dom. archit., vii. 133, 164–8
earthworks, i. 478
fair, i. 523
Gravetye, ii. 249, 387; vii. 168, 197
Highbrook, ii. 44; vii. 164, 168, 171–2
man., vii. 168–9
ho., ii. 387
poor relief, vii. 172
pop., ii. 223
rly., vii. 164

roads to, iii. 42–3
Selsfield common, iii. 42–3
Selsfield Place, iii. 42
Hobart:
Jn., earl of Buckinghamshire, ix. 187
Maria Anne, m. Jn. Hen. Fraser, iii.
145
Hobgen:
E., ii. 284
F.N., ii. 284
Messrs., ii. 282
Hobson:
Jas., ix. 92
Thos. (? two of this name), ix. 92
Hoddinott, Chas., iii. 164
Hodge:
Jn., iii. 161
Rob., i. 512
Thos., iv. 29
Hodges:
H., ix. 148
J., ii. 166
Hodgkin, Jn., vii. 42
Hodgkinson, W., ii. 454
Hodlee, Wm. de, ii. 315
Hodson, see Hudson
Hoese, see Hussey
Hogarth, Arthur, ii. 470
Hogge, Ralph, ii. 246, 248
Hogue, La (Manche, France), battle, ii.
164–5
Holand, see Holland
Holbech, Mr., ii. 454
Holbeme, Thos., prior of Michelham, ii.
79
Holborn, see London
Holbourne, Jas., ii. 166
Holcombe, see Anstye
Holcote (Northants.), ix. 138
Holden:
Agnes, m. 1 Edw. Fynes, 2 Jn.
Threele, vii. 176; ix. 56*
Anne, w. of Ric., vii. 176
Joan, m. Thos. Culpeper, vii. 176; ix.
56*
Mary, vii. 176
Ric., vii. 176
——, ii. 22
Holderness (Yorks. E.R.), ii. 447
Hole:
Adam atte, and his w. Agnes, ii. 180
Wm. atte, ii. 179–80
Holinshed, Raphael, ii. 246
Holland (Holand):
Alice, w. of Thos., earl of Kent, ix.
153
Eliz., m. —— Nevill, ix. 153
Frances, m. Sir Jn. Ashburnham, iv.
212, 216; ix. 130
Hen., vii. 249
Joan, m. Edw., duke of York, ix. 153
Joan, m. Jn. de Montfort, duke of
Brittany, ix. 3
Joan, w. of Thos. de, see Joan, 'Fair
Maid of Kent'
Jn. de, duke of Exeter, vii. 3
Marg., m. Jn. Beaufort, marquess of
Somerset, ix. 153
Marg. de, m. Sir Jn. la Warre, iv. 159
Maud de, m. Sir Jn. Lovell, iv. 159
Maud, w. of Rob. de, see Zouche
Rob. (fl. before 1352), iv. 159 n
Rob. (another), iv. 159 n
Rob. (fl. 1600), iv. 200
Swinton, iii. 145
Sir Thos. de (fl. 1346), iv. 159
Thos. de, earl of Kent (d. 1360), iii.
85; ix. 153
Thos. de, earl of Kent (d. 1397), iii.
85; ix. 153
Thos. de, earl of Kent (d. 1400), iii.
85; ix. 153
Thos. Erskine, ii. 431
Wm. (fl. 1597), mayor of Chich., iii.
75 n, 76
Wm. (fl. 1614, ? another), alderman of
Chich., ii. 424
Wm. (fl. c. 1630, ? another), iv. 212

Wm. Woollams, rector of St. Andrew
and St. Martin, Chich., iv. 202
arms, iii. 85
Holland, see Netherlands
Holles, see Hollis; Pelham-Holles
Hollest (or Williams), Jn. Leigh, see
Williams
Hollier, Till, iii. 78
Hollingbury, see Brighton
Hollingsworth, J.H., iv. 63 n
Hollington, i. 57; ii. 43, 301; ix. 76,
81–6, 107
adv., ix. 28, 85–6
batrachians, i. 272
Beauport, see Battle
brickmaking, ii. 253
char., ix. 86
ch., ix. 26, 81, 85–6
Cortesley, ix. 3, 76, 84, 93, 138, 254
cts., ix. 82, 86
dom. archit., ix. 81–2
Filsham, ii. 5; ix. 76, 82, 254
man., ix. 3, 82–4, 92, 181
mill, ix. 83
fossils, i. 36, 38
Grove, the, ix. 20, 81, 84–6
insects, i. 115–17, 119–20, 123, 125–9,
131–5, 138, 140, 142–4, 147–50,
153–63, 167, 175, 177, 179, 194,
199, 213–19, 221–2, 225, 227–37
mammals, i. 302–3, 305
man., ix. 82–6, 88
Morley, ix. 3, 84
pop., ii. 222
prebend, ii. 113; ix. 85, 264, 268
rector, see Cotterill, Jn.
reptiles, i. 271
roads, ix. 81
vicar, see Carr, Jn.
Wilting (Wiltingham), ix. 76, 82, 84,
92, 128
chap., ii. 113; ix. 84
pk., ii. 294, 324
Hollis (Holles):
Denzil, vii. 146
Hannah, see Legay
Jane, see Shirley
Thos., iv. 193
Hollist:
Edw. O., ix. 255
Ellen, see Wetherell
Gerald, ix. 255
Ric., ix. 255
Col., iv. 53
Hollist, see Easebourne
Hollomby:
C.J., ii. 452
W., ii. 452
Holloway:
Jn., ix. 229
Jn. (another), ix. 229
Sarah, see Meryon
Wm. ix. 46, 60–1
Hollycombe, see Linch
Holm Bush, see Kingston-by-Sea
Holman:
Jn., ix. 202
Ric., ix. 148
fam., ix. 148
Holmborn, Jn., ii. 73
Holmbush, see Beeding
Holmdale, Jn. de, ii. 316
Holme:
Jn. atte, vii. 158
Thos., ii. 256
Holmes:
A.K., ix. 174
Alfred, ix. 174
Martha, ix. 31
Reg. T.H., ix. 174
Ric., iii. 101
Rob., ix. 31
Holmestrow (Holmestre, Holmstrow,
Homestreu) hund., i. 537; ii. 224;
vii. 1, 3 n, 53 n, 61
Holmewood, see Holmwood
Holmshurst, see Burwash
Holmsted, Wm., vii. 158

Holmstreet, *see* Wiggonholt
Holmstrow, *see* Holmestrow
Holmwood (Holmewood):
 Edw., vii. 96
 Jas., ii. 451–2
 Jn., vii. 96
 Mr., ii. 199
Holmwood (Surr.), Anstie Grange, iii. 33, 39
Holney, Jn., iv. 145
Holroyd:
 Geo. Augustus, earl of Sheffield, ii. 209 *n*; vii. 67, 96
 Hen. North, earl of Sheffield, vii. 64, 96
 Jn. Baker, earl of Sheffield, ii. 300; vii. 32, 35, 64
 arms, vii. *64*
Holstock, Steph., i. 512
Holt:
 Jn., ii. 404–5
 Steph., iv. 168
 Wm., vii. 183–4
 Mr., i. 320
Holter:
 Alice, vii. 31
 Jn., vii. 40
Holtye, *see* Hartfield
Holwell, Jas., ii. 166
Holyndale, Wm. de, vii. 229
Holyngbourne, Jn., master of St. Jas.'s hosp., Seaford, ii. 105
Holyngrove, Jn. de, ix. 229
Holywell, *see* Eastbourne
Homestall, *see* Forest Row
Homestreu, *see* Holmestrow
Homewood:
 Hen., vii. 159
 Jn., vii. 159
 Lawr., vii. 159
 Mic., vii. 159
 Ric., vii. 159
Homewood (in Lewes rape), ii. 297–8, 310–11
and see Hamoda, la
Honey:
 G.J., ii. 167
 Jn., vii. 106
Honeywood, Phil., ii. 442–3
Honfleur (Calvados, France), ix. 69
Honneywell, *see* Ashdown forest
Honorius IV, pope, ii. 57
Honorius Augustus Andria, iii. 8
Honourable Artillery Company, ii. 460
Hoo:
 Alice, w. of Sir Thos., *see* Urry
 Alice, w. of Sir Wm., *see* St. Omer
 Anne, m. —— Boleyn, ix. 138
 Anne, m. —— Copley, ix. 138
 Eleanor, m. Sir Jn. Carew, ix. 138, 229
 Eleanor, w. of Thos. Ld. Hoo, ix. 138
 Eleanor, w. of Sir Thos., *see* Felton
 Eliz., m. 1 Sir Thos. Massingberd, 2 Sir Jn. Devenish, ix. 119–20, 138, 229, 233, 248
 Eliz., w. of Sir Thos., *see* Echingham
 Isabel, w. of Sir Thos., *see* St. Leger
 Jn., ix. 138
 Marg., ix. 138
 Sir Thos. (d. 1380), ix. 138, 233
 Sir Thos. (d. 1420), ix. 138
 Sir Thos., Ld. Hoo and Hastings, ii. 113, 117; ix. 3, 79–80, 125, 133, 135, 138, 196, 229, 233, 248*
 Sir Thos. (d. 1486), ii. 325, 361*, 378*; iv. 15; ix. 3, 135, 138, 176, 196, 202, 248*
 Sir Wm. (fl. 1360), iv. 230
 Sir Wm. (d. 1410), and his w., ix. 138
 Wm., vicar of Eastbourne, ii. 19
 fam., ii. 325; vii. 213 *n*
Hoo (Essex), ii. 52
Hood, Russell, ii. 471 *n*
Hooe, ii. 43*, 46, 196, 223 *n*; ix. 120, 123, 239, **244–7**
 adv., ix. 246–7

agric., ix. 244
char., ix. 247
ch., ii. 112, 410; ix. 122, 141, 244–6, *245*
 accessories, ii. 353–4; ix. 246
 archit., ii. 339, 377; ix. 245–6
Haven, ix. 139
man., ii. 232; ix. 139, 244–5, 247
mill, ix. 244
pop., ii. 223
prebend, ii. 113, 410; ix. 141, 246
trades and ind., ii. 232, 238; ix. 244
vicar, ii. 30
Hook (Hooke, Houke):
 Eliz., m. Rob. Ottringham, iv. 231
 Francis, iv. 231
 Hen. atte (fl. 1309), iv. 184
 Hen. (fl. 1635), iv. 64
 Isabel atte, *see* Clare
 Jn., iv. 64
 Mary, iv. 231
 Ric., vii. 34
 Rob. de la, iv. 184
 Secunda, w. of Francis, m. 2 Ric. Olwin, iv. 231
 Wal., dean of Chich., ii. 51; iii. 126, 160
 Wm., vii. 258
Hook, the, (Netherlands), iii. 102
Hooke, *see* Hook
Hooker:
 Geo., ii. 469–71
 Thos., vii. 234
 Wm., ii. 475
Hookers Farm, (? in Horsham or Warnham), ii. 389
Hoone, Wm., ii. 405
hoop making, ii. 236–7, 300
Hooper (Hoper):
 Anne, *see* Tidcombe
 Eliz., ix. 148
 Jn., vii. 19
 Odiarne, and his w. Anne, ix. 148 *n*
 Rob., attorney general of Barbados, vii. 169
 Thos., ix. 148
 fam., ix. 148
Hoore, Wm., iii. 142
Hoorne, *see* Horn
hop pole making, ii. 234, 298, 300
Hope:
 Chas., ii. 166
 R., i. 71
Hope, St. John, *see* St. John Hope
Hope, tithing, ix. 55, 142
Hoper, *see* Hooper
Hopkins:
 Anne, w. of Rog., iv. 83
 Francis, vii. 38
 Fred. Russell, ix. 30
 Geo. Toppell, ix. 30
 Mary, w. of Rog., m. 2 Jn. Jenman, iv. 83
 Rog. (d. by 1686), iv. 83
 Rog. (fl. 1686), iv. 83
 Steph., ii. 25
hops, *see* crops
Hopton:
 Ralph, Ld. Hopton, i. 523–4; iii. 88; iv. 16, 50
 fam., ix. 170
Horace, ii. 419
Horam, *see* Waldron
Horcombe (Horecumba):
 Beatrice de, vii. 12 *n*
 Gerard de, vii. 68
 Isabel de, vii. 12 *n*
 Wal. de, vii. 68
Hordern, Hugh, iii. 130
Hore:
 Dorcas, m. Sir Ric. Ashfield, iv. 224
 Hen., ii. 257
 Jas., iv. 224
 Wm., mayor of Chich., iii. 92
Horecumba, *see* Horcombe
Horeham, *see* Waldron: Horam
Horemouth, *see* Chich.: harbour
Horley, Edw., ix. 156

Horley (Surr.), ii. 328 *n*
Horlockescrouch (unidentified), ii. 311
Hormer, Jn., prior of Pynham, ii. 81
Hormouth, *see* Chich.: harbour: Horemouth
Horn (Hoorne, Horne):
 Geo., bp. of Norwich, ix. 171
 J., ii. 477
 Rob., ix. 56
 Wm., ii. 104
Horna (unidentified), ii. 113
Hornby (Horneby):
 Geof. Stanley Phipps, iv. 91–2
 Sir Geof. T. Phipps, iv. 91–2, 111, 114
 Hen., vii. 281
 Sir Phipps, iv. 92–3, 112, 116
 R.S. Phipps, iv. 116
 Wm. de, iv. 28
 —— Phipps, ii. 461
Hornchurch (Essex), vicar, *see* Levett, Hen.
Horndean (Hants), i. 120, 167 *n*
Horne, *see* Horn
Horne (Surr.), ii. 328 *n*; vii. 199
Horneby, *see* Hornby
Horney common, *see* Maresfield
Horse Eye, *see* Pevensey
horse racing, *see* sport
horse stealing, ii. 201
Horselunges, *see* Hellingly
Horseman:
 Thos. (fl. 1540), iv. 231
 Thos. (fl. 1551, ? another), and his w. Eliz., vii. 228
horses, *see* livestock
Horsey, *see* Pevensey; Horse Eye
Horsfield:
 Marg., ix. 61
 Thos., iii. 46, 112; ix. 253
Horsham, Godfrey de, ii. 98
Horsham, i. 110, 290, 514; ii. 43, 310, 461; iii. 86
 ale-hos., ii. 196
 assizes, vii. 16 *n*
 Bell Ho., ii. 250
 birds, i. 284, 290–1, 293
 botany, i. 67
 chant., ii. 13, 20
 Chesworth (Chelsworth), ii. 307, 309
  dom. archit., ii. 230, 389
  earthworks, i. 477
  insects, i. 176
  man., ii. 309–10
  pk., ii. 297, 306–10
  textile ind., ii. 257
 Christ's Hosp., i. 536; ii. 434, **435–7**, 480
  ch., ii. 63
  accessories, ii. 250, 354, 358–9, 361–2, 375, 378
  archit., ii. 336, 339–40, 344, 346, 348–9, 368, 370, 374–5, 378
  ch. wardens, ii. 250
 Civil War, i. 524, 526
 Colstaple, ii. 310
 Coolhurst, i. 289
 Crockhurst, ii. 60
 Denne Pk., i. 273 *n*; ii. 310; ix. 84
  natural history, i. 164, 173, 179, 275–6, 279–80, 303, 306
 dom archit., ii. 230, 337, 386, 389–92
 earthworks, i. 477
 fossils, i. 36–8
 Friday Street, ii. 389
 gaol, ii. 28, 39
 geology, i. 4; ii. 336
 guild, ii. 20
 Hawksbourne, i. 36*
 insects, i. 115–16, 132–3, 136, 139, 144, 156, 163, 165–173, 175–90, 199–200, 205, 209
 Lanaways (Lenaways) Fm., ii. 389
 lecturer, *see* Chatfield, Jn.
 Lenaways, *see* Horsham: Lanaways
 local govt., ii. 423
 mammals, i. 300–1, 304
 Marlpost (Marlepast), ii. 113

Horsham (cont.):
  militia, i. 507
  museum, iii. 49
  nonconf., ii. 38
  pk., i. 282; ii. 310
  parl. rep., i. 504, 532
    M.P., see Middleton, Thos.
  pop., ii. 219
  prehist. rem., i. 330
  roads, ii. 240, 422–3; vii. 144
  Roffey (Roughey) Street, i. 53, 58; ii. 43
    birds, i. 278
    iron ind., ii. 242
    King's Farm, ii. 389–90
  royal visits, i. 505; ii. 307
  sch., ii. 198 n
    Christ's Hosp., see Horsham: Christ's Hosp.
    grammar (Collyer's), ii. 397, 399, 421–3
  smuggling, ii. 200
  Southwater, i. 173, 304; ii. 43
  sport, ii. 445–9, 480
  trades and ind., ii. 230, 242, 250–1, 254, 260, 263–4
  union, i. 539
  vicarage, ii. 8, 36
  vicars, ii. 421, 423; and see Hutchinson, Thos.; Simon, master of Bidlington hosp.
  and see Plumtree Cross
Horsham stone and roofing slabs, ii. 230, 337, 342, 380, 392; vii. 39, 45, 84–5, 95, 106, 111, 119–20, 127, 131–2, 137–8, 141–2, 145, 148–9, 152–4, 160, 164, 169, 175, 182, 187–8, 192–4, 214, 285
Horsley, Gilb., ii. 148
Horsley, see Wadhurst
Horsmonden (Kent), ii. 95, 217 n
  hund., see Brenchley and Horsmonden hund.
Horsted Keynes, ii. 44, 225
  angling, ii. 465
  Broadhurst, ii. 389
    chant., ii. 20
  ch., ii. 48, 68
    accessories, ii. 353, 356
    archit., ii. 336, 340, 366, 374
  Danehill Horsted hund., q.v.
  geology, ii. 336
  Hazelwood, ii. 303
  natural history, i. 109, 267
  Piplye, i. 109
  rector, ii. 202 n
  rectory, ii. 91
  sch., ii. 438
  trades and ind., ii. 229
  Treemaines (Trimmins), ii. 382
Horsted, Little, i. 505; ii. 44, 227
  ch., ii. 250, 336, 351, 360–1, 366, 374–5, 378
  Little Horsted Place, iii. 59
  Moat park, ii. 323
  rector, ii. 35
Hort, Ethel, see Gordon
horticulture, see market gardening
Horton-Smith, Mr., i. 346
Horton (Kent), priory, ii. 68
Hoskins (Hoskyns):
  B.G., archdeacon of Chich., iii. 130
  Ben., ii. 165
Hospitallers, see Knights Hospitaller
hospitals, ii. 45, 97–108; and see Aldingbourne: sanatorium; Arundel; Battle; Bexhill; Bramber; Bidlington; Brede; Brighton; Buxted; Chich.; Harting; Hastings; Lambeth: St. Thomas's; Lewes; Petworth: Thompson's; Playden; Rumboldswyke; Rye; Seaford; Shermanbury: Windham; Shoreham; Southover; Tarring, West; Udimore; Westham; Westhampnett: Loddesdown; Winchelsea
Hoth, Jn. atte, i. 512
Hotham, Sir Ric., ii. 204; iv. 225–6, 230

Hotherope, Jn., ix. 214
Hoton, Jn., master of Playden hosp., ii. 105
Hotot:
  Emma de, see Hareng
  Hawise, w. of Rob. de, iv. 168
  Peter de (fl. c. 1230), iv. 168
  Peter de (d. by 1306), iv. 168
  Rob. de, iv. 168
Hotspur, Harry, see Percy, Sir Hen.
Houghton:
  Eliz., m. Wm. Westbrook, ix. 214
  Thos., ix. 214
Houghton, i. 31–2; ii. 42–3
  anchorite, ii. 47
  bridge, i. 524; ii. 394
  ch., ii. 305, 339, 347, 374
  Downs, i. 60
  forest (or pk.), ii. 297, 301, 303, 305
    insects, i. 197, 200, 204, 207, 210
  foxhunting, ii. 443
  insects, i. 190, 198–200, 208
  man., ii. 109
  pk., see Houghton: forest
  pop., ii. 217
  Rom. rem., iii. 58
Houke, see Hook
Houndean, see Lewes
Hounds Mere Pit, see Rottingdean
Hounslow Heath (Mdx.), i. 513 n
Hounsom:
  Hen., and his w. Sarah, iv. 52
  Hen. (another), iv. 52
house-breaking, ii. 201
housebote, ii. 294, 302–3, 310, 315; vii. 105
Housman, A.V., iii. 17
Hova Ecclesia, see Hove: prebends
Hova Villa, see Hove: prebends
Hovar, Goodwife, ii. 198
Hove, ii. 43–4*, 162; vii. 216, 241–2, 258, 264, 265–8, 271
  adv., vii. 268
  chant., vii. 268
  ch., ii. 370; vii. 267–8, 268
  cts., vii. 266
  earthworks, i. 480
  fishery, ii. 265
  fossils, i. 128
  man., vii. 265–7
  museum, iii. 28, 50, 58–9, 61
  natural history, i. 131, 144, 193, 198, 229, 277, 287, 295
  parl. rep., vii. 265, 269
  poor relief, vii. 266
  pop., ii. 224
  prebends:
    Hova Ecclesia, ii. 48; vii. 265, 268, 273
    Hova Villa, ii. 48; vii. 140, 265; prebendary, see Vaughan, Jas.
  prehist. rem., i. 317–19, 318, 321, 330; vii. 265
  Rom. rem., iii. 51
  ship service, ii. 134
  sport, ii. 450, 470, 478; vii. 265
  tithes, ii. 265
  town hall, ii. 254; vii. 265
  Upwick, vii. 266–7, 270–1
  vicarage, vii. 273
Hovell, Wm., i. 514; iii. 86
Howard:
  Anne, dchss. of Norfolk, see Dacre
  Bernard Edw., duke of Norfolk, ii. 209 n
  Charity, see Leache
  Chas., earl of Nottingham (d. 1624), Ld. High Admiral, i. 520; ii. 236, 266; iv. 139
  Chas., earl of Nottingham (d. 1642), vii. 111, 113
  Chas., earl of Surrey, duke of Norfolk, i. 532; ii. 305
  Chas., ii. 475
  Diana Harriet, see Ponsonby
  Edw. Granville Geo., Ld. Laverton, iv. 86
  Eliz., ctss. of Arundel, see Stuart

  Gwendolin Mary, dchss. of Norfolk, vii. 30
  Hen., earl of Surrey, vii. 6
  Hen., duke of Norfolk, vii. 254
  Hen. Chas., earl of Surrey, duke of Norfolk, i. 535; ii. 209 n
  Sir Jn., vii. 54
  Jn., duke of Norfolk, Earl Marshal, iv. 184*, 193; vii. 5, 26 n, 35, 254
  Kath., see Katherine
  Marg., see Plaiz
  Mary, w. of Chas., earl of Nottingham, see Cokayne
  Mary, w. of Thos., duke of Norfolk, see FitzAlan
  Philip, earl of Arundel, iv. 66, 111, 124, 129; vii. 6, 35, 134, 156, 195
  Thos., earl of Surrey, duke of Norfolk (d. 1524), ii. 308; iv. 122; vii. 5–6, 254
  Thos., duke of Norfolk (d. 1554), ii. 20, 308, 312; iv. 122, 193; vii. 6; ix. 54
  Thos., duke of Norfolk (d. 1572), i. 519; ii. 309; iv. 143; vii. 6, 33, 134, 179
  Thos., Ld. Howard, ii. 154
  Thos., earl of Arundel and Surrey, duke of Norfolk (d. 1646), iii. 99; vii. 6, 64, 179, 254, 279
  Thos., earl of Arundel, duke of Norfolk (d. 1677), ii. 271
  Thos., ii. 165
  Wm., Ld. Howard of Effingham, iv. 139; vii. 12
  Ld. Wm., vii. 6, 74 n, 238
  Mr., ii. 468
  fam., iv. 122, 193; vii. 59, 141
  arms, vii. 5
Howard, Molyneux, see Molyneux Howard
Howard de Walden, Ld., see Ellis, Fred. Geo.
Howe, Ric., ii. 162
Howell, Sir Jn., iv. 185
Howes:
  A.E., ii. 474
  Edw., iv. 202
  Jn., ii. 436
  Marg., w. of Edw., iv. 202
Howick (Howyke):
  Ric., iii. 80 n
  fam., iv. 80 n
Howis, E.O., ii. 474
Howland, fam., ix. 209
Howley, Wm., abp. of Cant., iv. 233
Howyke, see Howick
Hramnesleagh, see Rameslie
Huberden, see Hiberden
Hübner, ——, iii. 47
Hudiham (or Waliland), Ric. de, see Waliland
Hudson (Hodson):
  E.H., ii. 450
  Edw., vii. 109
  J., ii. 167
  Jas., ii. 468
  Jn., ii. 249, 251
  W.H., vii. 57
  Mr., iii. 50
  Mrs., vii. 243
Huett, see Hewett
Hugaborg (? in East Dean), iv. 94
Hugessen:
  Dorothea, m. Sir Jos. Banks, ix. 273
  Mary, m. Edw. Knatchbull, ix. 273
  Sarah, ix. 273
  Wm. Western, ix. 273
Hugh, dean of Hastings coll., ii. 113, 117
Hugh, prior of Lewes, abbot of Reading, abp. of Rouen, ii. 65, 69
Hugh, prior of Lewes, abbot of Reading, abbot of Cluny (another), ii. 65, 70
Hugh, prior of Lewes (another), ii. 70
Hugh the sheriff (fl. c. 1100), ii. 5; vii. 1, 60
Hugh the sheriff (fl. c. 1145), vii. 1

Hugh, warden of Franciscan friary, Chich., ii. 95
Hugh son of Gold (Golda, Golde), vii. 33, 53, 56, 101, 183, 226, 234
his s., see Ralph
his w., see Basilia
Hugh son of Hugh, vii. 53, 234
Hugh son of Reyner (Ranulph), vii. 110, 213, 226
his dau., see Fredesend
Hugh son of Robert son of Tetbald, iii. 84
Hugh the clerk, iv. 135
Hugh (fl. 1086), iv. 171, 234
Hugh (fl. 1086, another), ix. 82, 84, 128, 267
Hugh, Osbern fitz, see Osbern
Hugh, Ric., master of hosp. of St. Jas. and St Mary, Chich., ii. 100
Hugham:
Beatrice, w. of Rob. de, ix. 92
Rob. de (d. by 1258), ix. 92
Rob. de (d. 1273), ix. 92
Rob. de (fl. 1273), ix. 92
Wm. de, ix. 92, 127
Hughes:
Ric., ii. 166
Sarah, m. 1 Jn. Billingsley, 2 Ric. Crichett, iv. 168
Huguenots, ii. 27, 148, 258, 260; ix. 60–1
Hull:
Jn., ii. 251
Wm., ii. 249, 251; vii. 40, 87; ix. 136, 189
Hull (Yorks. E.R.), ii. 149; vii. 10
Hulme, see Hume
Hulse, Ric., vii. 158
Humbert, prior of Lewes, ii. 70
Humbert, R. Jardine, ii. 457
Hume (Hulme):
Edw., ii. 470 n, 471
Ric. de, dean of Lewes, vii. 236
Humez, Wm. de, iv. 166
Humfrey, see Humphrey
Humphrey (Humfrey), anchorite of Pagham, iv. 233
Humphrey (fl. 1086), iv. 142
Humphrey (Humfrey):
Cornelius, ii. 236
Eliz., see Gale
Hen., vii. 111, 145, 195
Rob., ix. 106
hundred courts, see courts
Hundred of Manhood and Selsey Tramway, iii. 71; iv. 207
Hundred Years war, see wars
Hundresteddle Farm, see Wittering, East
Hungary, king, see Lajos
Hungerford, Jn., vicar of Selsey, iv. 210
Hungershall (unidentified), i. 65
Hunlaf (Hunlabe), vii. 196, 226, 239
Hunneman, Wm., iv. 201
Hunns Mere Pit, see Rottingdean: Hounds Mere Pit
Hunston:
Alice, m. 1 Thos. de Bradbridge, 2 Jn. Styllefeld, iv. 157
Godfrey de, iv. 157, 162
Joan, w. of Wm. de, iv. 157
Sybil, w. of Sir Wm. de, m. 2 Phil. Wychard, iv. 157
Thos. de (fl. 1365), iv. 157 n, 200
Thos. de (fl. 1428), iv. 157
Sir Wm. de (fl. 1329), iv. 157, 200
Wm. de (fl. 1343), iv. 157
Hunston, ii. 43, 295 n; iii. 71; iv. 133, 156–8
adv., iv. 156, 157 n, 158
angling, ii. 466
char., iv. 158
ch., ii. 7, 56; iv. 157–8
dom. archit., iv. 156
earthworks, i. 477
guild, iv. 158
inc., iv. 156
Kipson (Kipston), ii. 56; iv. 156–7

man., iv. 156–7, 167, 216
mill, iv. 156–7
pop., ii. 220
salt pans, iv. 156
tithes, iv. 156
vicar, see Covert, Chas. Randall
Hunt:
Chas., ii. 423
Jn., i. 512
Hunter, Ric., vii. 109
hunter, Norman the, see Norman; and see Chetel the huntsman
hunting, see sport
hunting rights, iv. 45, 61, 94, 118, 217; vii. 3, 105, 175–7, 235, 271
Huntingdon, earls of, see Hastings: Francis, Geo., Hen.
Huntingdon, Ctss. of, see Countess of Huntingdon's Connexion
Huntingdonshire, see Buckworth; Woolley
Huntington, Wm., ii. 41
Huntyre, Jn. ('French John'), ii. 147
Huntsland, see Worth
huntsman, Chetel the, see Chetel; and see Norman the hunter
Huraunt, Gerard, iv. 98
Hurdis:
Eliz., iii. 145
Jas., ii. 239
Naomi, w. of Thos., iii. 145, 147
Thos., canon of Chich., warden of St. Mary's hosp., Chich., ii. 102; iii. 145, 147
Hurlingham polo club, ii. 461
Hurlonde:
Alice, w. of Ric. atte, m. 2 Jn. atte Seton, iv. 135
Ric. atte, iv. 135
Hurly:
Hen., vii. 54, 57
Louisa, w. of Hen., vii. 57
Mary Eliz., m. Rob. Rosseter, vii. 54
Ric., vii. 54
Ruth, vii. 56
Hurrell, H.S., ix. 152, 163
Hurst:
A.S., ii. 474
Hen. de, iv. 24
J.W., ii. 280
Joan de, see Peplesham
Marg. de, m. 1 Jn. Hall, 2 Jn. Devenish, ix. 119
Margery, w. of Ric. de, ix. 119
Mary, iv. 191
Parnel de, see Peplesham
Philippe de, ix. 119
Ric. de, ix. 119
Rob. de, iv. 24
Thos., iv. 191
Wm. de, ix. 119
Wm. (another), ii. 262
fam., ii. 262
and see Herste
Hurst (unspecified), 1. 60, 143, 145, 156, 198
Hurst, see Hurstpierpoint
Hurst, prebendary, see Henshaw, Jos.
Hurst Green, see Salehurst
Hurstbourne Priors (Hants), ix. 165
Hurstmonceux, see Herstmonceux
Hurston Warren, see Storrington
Hurstpierpoint (formerly Hurst), i. 43; ii. 43–4, 208 n, 419; vii. 2, 14, 125, 172–8
adv., vii. 178
agric., vii. 172
char., vii. 178
ch., ii. 40, 361; vii. 171, 177–8
Court Bushes, vii. 6, 157 n
Danny (Daneghithe):
archit., ii. 387; vii. 171, 172–4
botany, i. 60
pk., ii. 297; vii. 176
dom. archit., vii. 172–5
fair, vii. 176
Ham Farm, iii. 47, 58
inc., vii. 176

man., vii. 9, 14, 36, 114, 116–17, 120, 126, 175–6, 213, 266 n
mkt., vii. 176
mills, vii. 175
natural history, i. 48, 150, 163, 167, 191, 204, 208, 282, 305
pks., ii. 297, 310; vii. 176; and see Hurstpierpoint: Danny
pop., ii. 223
prehist. rem., i. 330
rly., ii. 223 n
rector, see Letchford, Leonard
roads, ii. 240; iii. 58
Rom. rem., iii. 58
St. John's Coll., i. 536; ii. 409, 432–4, 476; vii. 172
trades and ind., ii. 236, 256–7, 260
Huscarl, Roland, and his w. Marg., iv. 168
Husee, see Hussey
Husiere, Rob. le, and his w. Denise, vii. 34
Huskisson:
Eliza, w. of Wm., iii. 134; iv. 152
Wm., M.P. for Chich., iii. 134, 145; iv. 152
Huson, Mr., ix. 154
Hussey (Hoese, Husee, Hussee):
Adam, iv. 66, 98
Ankarette, w. of Sir Hen., m. 2 Sir And. Hake, iv. 14, 64
Bridget, see Spring
Cath., m. Reynold Bray, iv. 11, 15
Cecily, iv. 27
Chas. Hubert, vii. 111
Constance, m. 1 Hen. Lovell, 2 Sir Rog. Lewknor, iv. 11, 13, 15, 64
Constance, w. of Sir Hen., iv. 14
Eleanor, vii. 158
Eliz., see Bohun
Geof., iv. 109
Geo., vii. 158
Hen. (fl. 1154), iv. 14
Hen. (d. c. 1174), ii. 89, 103, 330; iv. 13–14, 25, 109
Hen. (d. c. 1213), ii. 89, 302; iv. 14, 20–1, 25, 27
Hen. (d. by 1235), iv. 14
Hen., his s., iv. 14
Sir Hen. (d. 1290), i. 497, 500, 504; iv. 3, 8, 10, 14, 20 n, 21, 25, 36
Sir Hen., Ld. Husee, i. 507; iv. 14, 24, 105
Sir Hen. (d. 1349), i. 509; iv. 5, 10, 14, 20 n, 24, 63, 105
Sir Hen. (d. 1383), iv. 10, 14, 64
Hen. (fl. to 1393), iv. 14
Sir Hen. (d. 1409), iv. 14
Sir Hen. (d. 1450), iv. 5, 14–15, 64
Sir Hen. (d. c. 1460), ii. 90; iv. 15
Sir Hen. (fl. 1524), iv. 15
Hen. (fl. 1524, another), iv. 15
Hen. (fl. 1540, ? another), vii. 158
Sir Hen. (d. by 1556, ? another), iv. 157
Hubert, iv. 14
Isabel, w. of Sir Hen., iv. 14, 24
Jane, iv. 15 n
Jn. (fl. 1451), iv. 14 n, 15
Jn. (fl. 1560), iv. 15
Jn. (d. 1572, ? another), ii. 24; vii. 152 n, 158
Jn. (d. 1600), vii. 158, 163
Kath., w. of Sir Hen., m. 2 Sir And. Peverel, iv. 10–11, 14; ix. 202
Marg., w. of Sir Hen., m. 2 Ric. Buterley, iv. 14, 64
Mark, vi. 14
Mary, vii. 152 n, 158
Mary, w. of Nat., vii. 158
Mat., iv. 14
Maud, m. Wm. Paynel, iv. 14, 176
Nat., vii. 158
Nic., sheriff of Surr. and Suss., ii. 90; iv. 11, 15, 64
Ric., iv. 15 n
Rog., i. 509
Thos., iv. 15

Hussey (cont.):
Wal., ii. 90
Wm., iv. 14 n, 17
——, i. 280
——, ii. 84
fam., i. 513; iv. 3–4, 17, 25
arms, iv. 14; vii. 152, 158
Hutchins (Hutchings):
Geo., vicar of Telscombe, vii. 78
Geo., mayor of Hastings, ix. 30
Jas., vii. 78
Jas., vicar of Telscombe and Pidding-hoe, vii. 78
Martha, see Michell
Mrs., ix. 30
Hutchinson:
Chas., iv. 10
Chas. Edw., warden of St. Mary's hosp., Chich., ii. 102
Ezekiel, vii. 74
Thos., vicar of Horsham, ii. 423
Mr., iv. 10
Hutchinson, Messrs., ii. 235
Huth, Edw., vii. 140, 190–1
Hutton, ——, ii. 420*
Hutzell, Baron, vii. 271
Huy (Belgium), i. 536
Huysshe, see Whysh
Hwiccas, king of, see Eanfrid
Hyde (Hide):
Edw., earl of Clarendon, iii. 88
Hen., earl of Clarendon, i. 530
Jesse, ii. 476
Marg., iv. 149
Ric. de la, vii. 59
Sir Rog. de la, ii. 108
Sim. de la, vii. 59
Thos., iv. 216
Mr., ii. 456
Hyde abbey, see Winchester
Hydeneye, Jn. de, i. 507
Hydneye, see Willingdon
Hyenok park, see Midhurst
Hygons, see Higgons
Hyland, Wm., ix. 192
Hyndale, Jn. de, vii. 257
Hyndman's Trustees, ix. 27–8
Hythe (Kent), ii. 127, 235; iii. 102; ix. 10, 34–8

Iacobus, iv. 215
Iceland, i. 278, 281, 288, 292, 295
Iceni, iii. 1, 15
Ichington, Jn., ix. 187 n
Icklesham:
Ralph de, ix. 187
Rob. de, ix. 187
Sybil de, m. Nic. Harengod, ix. 187, 189
Sybil de (? another), ii. 86
Icklesham, ii. 43; ix. 34, 63, 184–90
adv., ii. 52; ix. 189
brickworks, ix. 184
Camber, ix. 69, 184
birds, i. 280
botany, i. 49, 65
cast., i. 516, 518; ii. 144, 149–50, 152, 155, 157, 159, 394–5; ix. 183–6, 185–6
golf, ii. 479; ix. 184
hermitage, ii. 47
insects, i. 111, 116, 120, 126, 128, 131–2, 134, 137–53, 155–6, 158–63, 176, 178, 199, 201–2, 216, 226–35, 237
Point, ix. 151
chant., ix. 189
char., ix. 189–90
ch., ix. 122, 187–9, 187
accessories, ii. 351–2, 354, 360; ix. 189
archit., ii. 332, 340, 342, 344, 347–9, 366–8, 370; ix. 89 n, 187–8
dom. archit., ix. 184
insects, i. 213
man., ii. 71 n, 88, 181 n, 186–7, 279
mill, ix. 184
nonconf., ix. 190

pop., ii. 222
vicar, ii. 40; and see Burrell, Wm.
vicarage, ii. 8
Ida, dau. of Jn., count of Eu, m. Wm. de Hastings, ix. 1
Iden:
Alex., sheriff of Kent, i. 514
Ric., vii. 143
Rob., ii. 437
Iden, ii. 43, 169; ix. 142, 145–6, 151, 152–7, 180
adv., ix. 156–7
chap., ix. 156–7
char., ix. 157
ch., ii. 113, 350, 352; ix. 155, 155–6
cts., ix. 153
dom. archit., ix. 152
earthworks, i. 477
ferry, ii. 169
man., ii. 173, 178, 186; ix. 56, 152–5
Moat, ix. 56, 153–5, 157, 176, 254
mills, ix. 154, 157 n
nonconf., ix. 152
pk., ix. 152–3
pop., ii. 222
rectors, ix. 62, 156; and see Lamb, Geo. Augustus
trades and ind., ii. 252, 260
Idonea, dau. of Osbert the white, m. Rob. de Glottingham, ix. 80
Idsworth (Hants), iv. 123
Ifield (Ifeld), Sir Jn. de, i. 507; ii. 295, 307
Ifield, ii. 7, 43–4; vii. 144, 147
ch., ii. 63, 118
accessories, ii. 250, 356, 358, 372
archit., ii. 342, 346, 348, 372, 375
earthworks, i. 477
Ewhurst Place, i. 477
nonconf., ii. 38
pop., ii. 219
trades and ind., ii. 38, 248, 257
vicarage, ii. 8–9
Iford, ii. 43–4; vii. 3–4, 45, 51, 52–7, 71, 217
adv., vii. 56–7
agric., vii. 52
Bird Brow, vii. 52
ch., vii. 55–6, 55, 56
accessories, ii. 250, 354, 356, 373; vii. 56
archit., ii. 328, 367–8; vii. 55–6, 237
dom. archit., vii. 52–3
earthworks, i. 480; vii. 52
fishing, ii. 264
inc., vii. 52
insects, i. 215
man., ii. 190; vii. 2, 53–5, 96, 101, 194
mill, vii. 55
pop., ii. 225
prehist. rem., i. 330
rector, see Delap
Swanborough:
chap., ii. 7, 377
man., ii. 69, 104; vii. 55, 68; ho., ii. 381–2; vii. 52–3, 53
tithes, ii. 7
vicarage, ii. 7
iguanodon, i. 5, 36
Igulden, Jn., ii. 24
Iham, see Winchelsea: Higham
Iles, Jn. Cyril, ii. 432
Ilkhurst (unidentified in Staple hund.), ix. 95
Ilsham, see Climping
image holders, see architecture: ecclesiastical
imparking (vol. ii. only), ii. 295–6, 302, 304, 306–7, 316, 320
Imperial yeomanry, i. 535
Impey, Sir Elijah, vii. 88
impressment of seamen, ii. 136–7, 140, 150, 153–8, 160–2
inclosure, ii. 189–91, 295, 299, 313, 322; and see parish names
Independents, see Congregationalists

Independents, Society of (Cokelers), ii. 41
India, see Ganges, riv.; Jagdespore
Indian mutiny, see wars
Indies, East, i. 15
Indies, West, i. 264, 535; ii. 148, 158, 164–7, 236, 256
industries, crafts, and trades, ii. 229–71; and see bellfounding; bent-wood making; brewing; brickmaking; cask making; cement ind.; charcoal burning; cider making; clockmaking; fence and wattle making; fisheries; flint mining; glass blowing; gunpowder making; hoop making; hop pole making; iron ind.; ladder making; lead mining; lime burning; needle making; paper making; plaster of Paris making; pottery; printing; rope making; sack making; salt ind.; sand quarrying; shingle making; shipbuilding; stone quarrying; tanning; textile inds.; tile making; timber ind.; trug making; wages; wool trade
Ine (Ini), king of Wessex, i. 482
infangthief, ix. 37, 68
Infield:
Agnes, m. Hen. Falconer, vii. 165, 168, 171
Bridget, m. Jn. Saunders, vii. 168
Cath., w. of Ric. (d. 1619), see Compton
Cath., w. of Ric. (d. 1625), see Culpeper
Cordell, m. Jn. Watson, vii. 168
H.J., ii. 453
Jas., vii. 168
Mary, w. of Jas., m. 2 Jn. Killingworth, vii. 168
Ric. (d. 1571), vii. 165–6, 168
Ric. (d. 1619), ii. 387; vii. 168, 171, 197
Ric. (d. 1625), vii. 168–9, 197
Mrs., vii. 164
fam., vii. 164
arms, vii. 168
Inge:
Sir Jn., iv. 144
Jn. (? another), iv. 144
Ingelare, see Ingler
Ingelram, Reinger s. of, see Reinger
Ingelram the sheriff, see Hastings, Ingelram de
Ingeram, see Ingram
Ingelby:
Arthur, vii. 232
C.N., vii. 232
Ingler (Ingelare, Inglere):
Geof., iv. 52
Jn., iv. 202
Wm., iv. 202 n
Ingolsted, Ludolph, ii. 248
Ingram (Ingeram):
And., ix. 248
Chas. Jas., vii. 105
Hen. Manning, vii. 276
Hugh, vii. 275
Jas., ii. 421
Jn. (fl. 1376), and his w. Marg., ix. 248
Jn. (fl. 1788), vii. 105
Rob. (fl. 1264), ix. 248
Rob. (fl. 1327), ix. 248
Steph., ix. 248
Wm. (fl. 1327), ix. 248
Wm. (fl. 1458), ix. 248
arms, vii. 105
Ingram's Green, see Iping
Ini, see Ine
Inlegh, see Westfield
Innis (Innes):
Chas., vii. 111
Jas., ii. 166
Thos., vii. 111
Thos. (another), vii. 111
Inniskilling Dragoons, ii.. 461
Innocent III, pope, i. 493; ii. 65, 72,

359; ix. 171
Innocent IV, pope, ii. 10, 411
Innocent VI, pope, ii. 63
Inold, Wm., ii. 18
Ins, Thos., ii. 421
insects, i. **110–237**
Inskipp (later Lade), Sir Jn., *see* Lade
Insula, *see* Lisle
interments, *see* burials
International Exhibition (London, 1885), ii. 236
Iohan (John), moneyer, iii. 83
Ionian Islands (Greece), i. 536
Iping, ii. 43; iv. 31, 40, **63–5**, 82
  adv., iv. 6, 64–5
  bridge, ii. 394; iv. 63, *66*
  ch., ii. 333; iv. 6, 64–5
  dom. archit., iv. 63
  Fitzhall, iv. 5, 63
  Hammer Pond, *q.v.*
  hare hunting, ii. 452
  inc., iv. 63
  Ingram's Green, iv. 32
  Kingsham, *see* Chithurst
  man., iv. 63–4
  marsh, iii. 58; iv. 63
  mills, ii. 394; iv. 63–4
  pop., ii. 221
  Rom. rem., iii. 2, 58
  trades and ind., ii. 230, 238; iv. 63
  Wardley, iv. 63, 64 *n*
Ipswich (Suff.), ii. 88; iii. 101 *n*
Irby, Leonard, vii. 74
Ireland, i. 168 *n*, 518; ii. 141, 148, 161, 165, 167; iv. 16; ix. 144
  Annadown (Enaghdun), bp., *see* O'Tigernach
  Athlone, rector, *see* Jones, Wm.
  linen, ii. 258
  ld. lieutenant, *see* Lennox, Chas. (d. 1819)
  militia, i. 527, 535
  shipping, ii. 132, 134
  trade with, ii. 262, 279–80; iii. 102
  and see Dublin; Londonderry; Lough Neagh; Tullamore; Waterford
Iremonger, ——, ii. 164
Irham, *see* Ertham
Iridge, *see* Salehurst
iron ind., i. 6, 50, 305, 322; ii. 170, 192, 194, 199, 229–30, 233–4, 237, 240, **241–9**, 296, 298–9, 310, 313, 319–20, 325, 336, 338, 397; iv. 21, 25, 44 *n*, 54, 63, 67; vii. 32, 95, 104; ix. 55, 78, 90, 101–2, 116, 120, 126, 143, 168, 172, 195, 201, 206–7, 211, 217, 220, 227–8, 232, 237, 247, 252;
  and see architecture: ecclesiastical: grave-slabs, cast iron; architecture: ecclesiastical: ironwork; Romano-British Suss.: ironworks
Ironmongers' Company, *see* London: guilds
Isaacs, Sir Rufus Daniel, earl of Reading, vii. 173
Isaacson, Fred. Wootton, iv. 235
Isabel, prioress of Rusper, ii. 64
Isabel, dau. of Thos., duke of Gloucester, ix. 87
Isabella (of Angoulême), queen of John, m. 2 Hugh of Lusignan, count of La Marche, ii. 307; iii. 84–5; ix. 2
Isabella, queen of Edw. II, i. 508; ii. 120; iv. 143; ix. 2, 15 *n*
Isfield, ii. 44; iv. 59
  angling, ii. 464–5
  ch., i. 477; vii. 49
    accessories, ii. 352–3, 360, 362
    archit., ii. 333, 349–51, 375
  earthworks, i. 477
  insects, i. 154–5, 168, 172, 179, 188, 190, 196, 221, 224
  Isfield Place, ii. 386
  pop., ii. 226
  rector, *see* Newton, Geo.
  Rom. rem., iii. 2, 59
  trug making, ii. 236

Isham:
  Euseby, iv. 224
  Frances, *see* Ashfield
  Jn., iv. 224
  Sir Justinian, iv. 224
  Margery, *see* Thatcher
Isle, *see* Lisle
Isle of Man, *see* Man, Isle of
Isle of Wight, *see* Wight, Isle of
Islesham, *see* Climping: Ilsham
Isleworth (Mdx.), *see* Syon
Islip:
  Rob., iv. 10
  Sim., rector of Pagham, abp. of Cant., ii. 80, 304; iv. 90, 233
  Wal., and his w. Mary, iv. 10
Issounden, *see* Exouden
Isted:
  Ric., vii. 35–6, 81 *n*
  Sam., vii. 37
Istria (Yugoslavia), i. 35
Italy, ii. 66, 255; iii. 34; iv. 70; *and see* Emia; Florence; Genoa; Messina; Milan; Naples; Rome; Siena; Ticinum; Turin; Viterbo
Itchenor (unspecified), i. 111, 117, 212, 217, 224, 229, 232–4, 236
Itchenor, East, *see* Birdham
Itchenor (Itchenore), West, ii. 43; iii. 100, 102; iv. 157, 198, **204–5**
  adv., iv. 205
  boundary, iv. 199, 204
  ch., ii. 56; iv. 204–5, *205*
    accessories, ii. 250, 356, 372
    archit., ii. 372
  dom. archit., iv. 204
  ferry, iv. 204
  guild, iv. 205
  insects, i. 174
  man., iv. 204
  pop., ii. 221
  roads, iv. 204
  shipbuilding, ii. 164, 166–7
  shipping, ii. 151
Itchingfield, ii. 43
  Bashurst, i. 53
  ch., ii. 339–40, 342, 358, 366
  pop., ii. 219
  and see Plumtree Cross
Ive, Denys, ix. 182
Iveagh, earl of, *see* Guinness
Ivelchestre, Steph. de, master of hosp. of St. Jas. and St. Mary, Chich., ii. 100
Ives, *see* Ivo
Ives:
  Billy, ii. 442–3
  Nim, ii. 442–3
Ivet, man. (? in Pett), ix. 175, 190
Ivo (Ives), prior of Pynham, ii. 80; iv. 80
Ivo (fl. 1086), iv. 104, 114
Iwonesmere, *see* Younsmere
Iwood, *see* Warbleton
Izard:
  Arthur, iv. 237
  Jane, iv. 237
  Wm. Chauntler, iv. 237
  Misses, iv. 237

Jackman:
  Edw., iv. 144
  Hen., ix. 146
Jackson (Jacson):
  C. Ward, ii. 451
  Geo., ii. 167
  Henrietta, *see* Collier
  Hen., ix. 86
  J.G., ii. 431
  Jn. Starkie, and his w. Eliz., vii. 57
  Rob., ii. 262
  T.G., iv. 236
  Thos., ii. 408
  Wm., ii. 426
Jacob, Wm., mayor of Chich., ii. 401–2; iii. 92, 128 *n*
Jacobites, ii. 159–60
Jacobs, Hen., ii. 432

Jacobson, Phil., ii. 248
Jacourt, *see* Jancourt
Jacson, *see* Jackson
Jaff, Herr, ii. 465
Jagdespore (India), i. 536
Jakes, Nic., iii. 86
James I, ii. 37, 163, 318, 320; iii. 95–6, 99; vii. 239, 262, 270; ix. 132, 134, 254
  his s., *see* Henry, prince of Wales
  arms, iv. 67; ix. 249
James II, i. 529 *n*, 530; ii. 40, 164; iii. 88, 96–7, 99; iv. 16–17, 144
  as duke of York, ii. 158; iv. 155, 172 *n*; vii. 36 *n*
'James III', *see* Stuart, Jas., the Old Pretender
James, duke of Monmouth, i. 529; ii. 305, 441; iii. 73, 88–9
James, thatcher, iv. 77 *n*
James son of William, ix. 120
  his s., *see* Northeye, Sir Wm. de
  his w. Rose, ix. 120
James:
  Arthur, ii. 455, 459
  Edw., ii. 28
  Edw. Frank Willis, iv. 90, 97
  G.P.R., ii. 431
  Wm. Dodge, iv. 31, 97
Jameson (Jamieson):
  Capt. Wm., ii. 165
  Revd. Wm., ii. 423
Jamyn, Jn., i. 512
Janaway, *see* Jannaway
Jancourt (Jacourt, Janicuria), Jn. de, prior of Lewes, ii. 68, 70
Jannaway (Janaway), Thos., vii. 186; ix. 256
Japan, i. 31, 254
  Tokyo, South, bp., *see* Awdry
Jarbarde, *see* Garbard
Jardyn (Jardine):
  Anne, w. of Jn., iv. 163
  Beatrice, m. Jas. Knottesford, iv. 163
  Jn., iv. 163
  Mabel, iv. 163
  Marg., m. Jn. Sopere, iv. 163
  Sara, iv. 163
  Thos. (d. by 1327), iv. 163
  Thos. (d. by 1411), iv. 163
  Mr., ii. 459
  and see Gardin
Jarvis, *see* Jervis
Jay, Ric. le, iv. 21
Jeake (Jeakes):
  Eliz., *see* Hartshorn
  Sam. (sr.), ix. 61
  Sam. (jr.), ix. 48, 61
Jeferye, *see* Jeffrey
Jeff, Nic., ii. 420
Jefferay (Jefferey), *see* Jeffrey
Jefferies, *see* Jeffreys
Jefferson, *see* Sergison
Jefferyes, *see* Jeffreys
Jeffrey (Jeferye, Jefferay, Jefferey, Jeffery, Jeffry):
  Bart., ix. 116
  Dorothy, *see* Carter
  Eliz., m. Edw. Montagu, Ld. Montagu of Boughton, vii. 117
  Sir Jn. (? two of this name), ii. 361; vii. 117
  Revd. Jn., ii. 424
  Marg., *see* Kyme
  Ric., vii. 42
  Ric., 'and his w., Eliz., iv. 163
  Mr., ii. 24
  ——, i. 277
Jeffreys (Jefferies, Jefferyes):
  David, vii. 54, 82, 101
  Geo., Ld. Jeffreys, ld. chancellor, i. 532; iv. 144
  Isam (Izan, Jevisham), *see* Wallcot
  Marg., vii. 82
  Morgan, iv. 35; vii. 54, 82, 101
Jeffry, *see* Jeffrey
Jelly, Miss, i. 71
Jenison, Ralph, ii. 442

Jenkin:
 Barbara, *see* Stapley
 Jn., ix. 224
 Meyrick, vii. 217
 Palacia, m. Edw. Frewen, ix. 224
Jenkins:
 Jn., ix. 191
 Jn. Molyneux, mayor of Rye, ii. 426; ix. 54
 Mary, ii. 414–15; vii. 12, 42
 Thos., ix. 197
Jenkinson:
 Chas. Cecil Cope, earl of Liverpool, vii. 33–4, 81; ix. 180, 191
 Julia Evelyn, *see* Shuckburgh
 Kath. Julia, m. Francis Vernon Harcourt, vii. 34
 Louisa Harriet, m. Jn. Cotes, vii. 34
 Selina, m. 1 Wm. Chas. Wentworth-FitzWilliam, Vct. Milton, 2 Geo. Saville Foljambe, vii. 34
Jenman:
 Jn. (fl. 1584), and his w. Alice, iv. 109
 Jn. (fl. 1689), iv. 83
 Marg., m. Wm. Fairmanner, iv. 109
 Marg., w. of Thos., iv. 109
 Mary, *see* Hopkins
 Nic., iv. 109
 Rob., iv. 109
 Thos. (fl. 1544), iv. 109
 Thos. (d. 1584), iv. 109
 Thos. (d. 1668), iv. 109–10
 Thos. (fl. 1668), iv. 109
 Wm. (d. 1578), iv. 109
 Wm. (fl. 1591), iv. 109
 Wm. (fl. 1613), iv. 109 *n*
 fam., iv. 109
Jenner:
 E., i. 43, 61
 Edw., vii. 159
 Hen., vii. 262
 J.H.A., i. 43, 55, 108, 119, 136
 Mary, vii. 159
 Thos., vii. 160
 Wm. Caleb, ix. 30, 179, 184
 fam., ix. 206
Jenney (Jenny):
 Agnes, w. of Nic., vii. 256
 Nic., vii. 48, 58, 224, 256
Jennings (Jenyns):
 Jn., iv. 143
 Sir Steph., ii. 416, 421
 ——, ii. 33
Jenny, *see* Jenney
Jenour, Geo., ix. 139–40
Jenyns, *see* Jennings
Jeppe, Geof., ii. 266
Jermyn (German, Germon, Jerman, Jermin):
 Alex., iv. 116, 128
 Anne, *see* Stoughton
 Eleanor, iv. 193
 Frances, m. 1 Francis More, 2 Jn. Shuckburgh, iv. 116
 Julia, *see* Lumley
 Peter, iv. 193
 Phil., iv. 116, 128
 Susan, iv. 193
 Thos., iv. 193
 ——, iv. 116 *n*
 and see Germayn
Jermyn Street museum, *see* Westminster
Jersey:
 ctss. of, *see* Villiers, Frances
 earl of, *see* Villiers, Geo. Child-
Jersey, ii. 147, 247
Jerusalem, ii. 11; iv. 77
 king, *see* Luis
Jervis (Jarvis):
 Fred., ii. 452
 Jn., earl of St. Vincent, ii. 162
Jervoise:
 Jervoise Clarke, iv. 109
 Sir Sam. Clarke, iv. 109
Jesson, Jas., ii. 165
Jessop, G.L., ii. 474
Jesus College, Cambridge, ii. 435
Jeudewyne, Ric., iv. 128, 195

Jevington, ii. 44, 122; ix. 251
 chap., ii. 77
 ch.:
  accessories, ii. 352, 356, 362, *363*, 364
  archit., ii. 337, 339, 351, *363*, 364, 368, 372, 374–5
 earthworks, i. 480
 Filching, i. 210
 horse training, ii. 461
 lime burning, ii. 231
 man., ii. 123
 pop., ii. 227
 rector, ii. 40
 roads to, iii. 48
 Rom. rem., iii. 48, 59
 Wannock, ii. 386, 394
Jewhurst, Steph., ix. 152
Jews, i. 505–6; iii. 80; iv. 31, 121
 synagogue, vii. 263
Joan, queen of Hen. IV, iv. 61 *n*
Joan, 'Fair Maid of Kent', m. 1 Thos. de Holland, earl of Kent, iii. 85; ix. 153
Joan (Lame Joan) (fl. 1281), iv. 77 *n*
Joce:
 Alice, ix. 153
 Sim., ix. 153
Joceaux, Peter de, prior of Lewes, ii. 67, 70
Jocelin (Joscelin), dean of Lewes, ii. 42 *n*
Jocelin (Joslen) the constable, vii. 67
Jocelin (of Louvain), iv. 56, 60–1
 his daus., *see* Alice; Eleanor
Jocelin (Gozelin) (fl. 1086), vii. 226
Jocelin (Joscelin) (fl. *c*. 1250), ii. 74
Jocelin, bp. of Salisbury, *see* Bohun, Jocelin de
Jockey Club, ii. 455
John, king, i. 490–4, 504; ii. 53, 110, 127, 129–30, 294, 296, 307; iii. 73, 79, 85, 91 *n*, 104, 107; iv. 73, 122, 192–3, 229, 237; vii. 2, 3 *n*, 105; ix. 2, 9–10, 15, 34, 37, 49, 67, 139
John XXI, pope, ii. 57
John XXII, pope, ii. 57, 67
John XXIII, pope, ii. 57
John, abbot of Bayham (fl. 1256), ii. 88
John, abbot of Bayham (fl. 1272), ii. 88
John, abbot of Durford (fl. 1258–86), ii. 91; iv. 17
John, abbot of Durford (fl. 1321), ii. 91
John, abbot of Durford (fl. 1400), ii. 91
John, abbot of Robertsbridge (fl. to 1230), ii. 73
John, abbot of Robertsbridge (fl. 1324), ii. 73
John, abbot of Robertsbridge (fl. 1345), ii. 73
John, abbot of Robertsbridge (fl. 1435), ii. 74
John, count of Eu, ii. 71, 113–14; ix. 2, 14, 84, 117, 122, 187, 212, 221, 235, 244
 his dau., *see* Ida
 his w., *see* Adelize
John, earl of Kent, ix. 153
John, prior of Boxgrove (fl. 1323), ii. 59
John, prior of Boxgrove (fl. 1421), ii. 59
John, prior of Hardham, ii. 75
John, prior of Hastings, ii. 76–7
John, prior of Pynham, ii. 80–1
John, prior of Shulbred, ii. 81–2
John, prior of Tortington, ii. 83
John, prior of Wilmington, ii. 123
John, sacrist of Bosham coll., ii. 112
John (moneyer), *see* Iohan
John the marshal, ii. 6; iv. 162–3, 183
John the pewterer, iii. 95
John fitz Geoffrey (fl. 1243), vii. 189, 258 *n*
John fitz Geoffrey (d. 1274), vii. 189
John fitz John, vii. 258
John, Hen. fitz, *see* FitzJohn
John, Jn. fitz, *see* John fitz John
John, Ric. fitz, *see* Richard
John of Gaunt, *see* Gaunt

Johnson:
 Anna, iii. 147
 Chris., ii. 405
 Edw. (fl. *c*. 1550), vii. 263
 Edw. (d. 1807), iii. 147
 Edw. (d. 1875), iii. 147
 Edw. Wm., iii. 147
 Jas., ix. 160
 Jane, w. of Edw., iii. 147
 Jn., iii. 147
 Marcon, ix. 171
 Mary, iii. 147
 Mary, w. of Wm., iii. 147
 Mary Jane, iii. 147
 Ric. (fl. 1570), ii. 405
 Ric. (fl. 1937), ix. 195
 Dr. Sam., ii. 450; vii. 249
 Tom, ii. 442–3; iv. 118 *n*
 Wm., iii. 147
 Mr., ii. 442
 ——, i. 283
Johnson, Price, and Freeland, Messrs., iv. 212
Johnston (Johnstone):
 Eliz., iii. 168
 Frances, ix. 112
 Geo., ii. 166
 H.S., ii. 472–4
 Jn., vii. 13
 Mary, ix. 112
 Phil., iii. 20, 130
 Thos., ii. 238
Jolliffe:
 Jn., iv. 17
 Thos. Sam., iv. 25, 36
Jonas, prior of Hastings, ii. 77
Jones:
 A., ix. 246
 Herb., bp. of Lewes, iii. 132
 Jn., ix. 137
 Sir Sam., vii. 71
 Sim., and his w. Eliz., vii. 78
 T.R., ix. 246
 Thos., ix. 207
 Capt. Wm., ii. 165
 Wm., rector of Athlone, vii. 226
 ——, ii. 420
 and see Ridge-Jones
Jonson, *see* Haskyn
Jordan, abbot of Durford, ii. 91
Jordan, abbot of Otham, abbot of Bayham, ii. 86, 88
Jordan (Jorden, Jurdan):
 Anne, *see* Burdett
 Hannah, m. Thos. Luxford, iii. 126
 Hen., vii. 144
 Marg., ix. 74, 174
 Martha, ix. 174
 Mary, m. Adrian Stoughton, iv. 193–4, 212
 Thos., and his w. Anne, ix. 241
 Wm., iv. 193
 Mr., ix. 199
Joscelin, *see* Jocelin, dean of Lewes; Jocelin (fl. *c*. 1250)
Joscelyn:
 Anne, *see* Torrell
 Hen., iv. 42
 Sir Thos., iv. 42
Jose, Moses s. of, *see* Moses
Joslen, *see* Jocelin the constable
Joye, Jn., prior of Boxgrove, ii. 59
Joynson-Hicks:
 Grace, Vctss. Brentford, vii. 88–9
 Sir Wm., Vct. Brentford, vii. 89, 91
Juckes, F.A., iv. 480
Juglet, Jn., ii. 147
Julia (fl. 1380), ii. 121
Juliana, iii. 77
Junnys, Jeremiah, vii. 78
Jupiter Serapis, statuette of, iii. 66
Jurdan, *see* Jordan
Jutes, ii. 126
Juxon:
 Jn., vii. 117
 Thos., iv. 175
 Wm., abp. of Cant., ii. 407

Sir Wm., vii. 117, 176
fam., iv. 107

Kailly, *see* Cailli
Kainsham, Wm. de, canon of Chich., ii. 56, 103
Kanc, Jormin de, i. 506
Kant, R. de, rector of Brighton, vii. 262
Kardun, Ric., vii. 280 *n*
Katherine, prioress of Rusper, ii. 64
Katherine (Howard), queen of Hen. VIII, ix. 255
Kaye (Kaye):
Ⓗ.G., ii. 449
Jos., ix. 25
Rob. Benj., ix. 28, 183
Kaynes, Ric. de, ii. 48
Kays, Wm., ii. 259
Keate:
Anne, *see* Gratwick
Hugh, vii. 235
and see Keyt
Keble College, Oxford, ii. 432–3
Kechenham, *see* Kitchenham
Kechenore (Chekenora, Cuchenovere, Kichenour, Kichinore, Kychenere):
Hugh de, ix. 145
Jn. de, ix. 145
Marietta de, ii. 261
Maud de, m. Edm. de Passeley, ix. 145
Rob. de, ix. 273
Wal. de, ix. 145
Wm. de (fl. 1210), ix. 145
Wm. de (fl. 1220), ix. 273
Wm. de (fl. 1304), ix. 155
fam., ix. 273
keepers of the coast, ii. 131, 135 *n*, 141, 147
Keith, ——, ii. 128
Kelleway (Kelway, Keyelweye):
Francis, and his w. Anne, vii. 34–5
Rob., vii. 55
Thos., iii. 90, 145
Kelley, nurse, ii. 198 *n*
Kelly:
Jas. Cullum, and his w. Mary, ix. 220
Ric., vii. 59
Wal., vicar of Hove and Preston, vii. 273
Wal. Wm., iv. 138
Kelsale, Jn., vii. 36, 58
Kelvedon Hatch (Essex), iv. 175
Kelway, *see* Kelleway
Keme, *see* Kyme
Kemp (Kempe):
Ant. (d. 1597), iv. 234–5
Ant. (fl. 1675), iv. 144
Ant. (d. 1753), iv. 153, 235
Barbara, m. Jas. Bart. Radcliffe, Ld. Kenaird, earl of Newburgh, iv. 153, 226, 235
Chas., iii. 124, 132
Sir Garret, iv. 153, 234, 238
Garret, iv. 234–5
Jn., abp. of York, ix. 150
Jn., vii. 19, 255
Kath., m. Thos. Eyre, iv. 234–5
Nat., vii. 217, 248, 257, 259
Phil., iv. 235
Phil. (grds. of last), iv. 234
Thos., vii. 19, 249, 255–7, 262
Thos. Read, M.P. for Lewes, vii. 19, 248, 250, 253, 255, 262; ix. 134, 137
(formerly Russell), Wm., vii. 105
fam., iv. 153, 226, 237; vii. 21
arms, iv. *235*
Kemp Town, *see* Brighton
Kempe, *see* Kemp
Kempsey (Worcs.), iii. 68
Kempthorne, Jn., ii. 165
Kenaird, Ld., *see* Radcliffe, Jas.
Kendall:
Dorcas, *see* Ashfield
Francis, ii. 420
H., vii. 268

Maur., iv. 224
Wm., iv. 135
Keneward, Reynold, vii. 266
Kenilworth (Warws.), Dictum of, i. 501–2
Kenmure, Vct., *see* Gordon, Rob.
Kenn (Kenne):
Chris., ix. 130
Eliz., m. 1 Jn. Paulet, Ld. Paulet, 2 Sir Jn. Ashburnham, ix. 130
Ric., ix. 213
Kennard:
Steph., ix. 192
T., ii. 474
Kenne, *see* Kenn
Kennington (Surr.), *see* Lambeth
Kenrick:
Frances, *see* Mascall
Wm., ix. 157
Kensington (London, formerly Mdx.), i. 74, 302; iii. 93 *n*, 115
Kent:
Jn. de, prior of Hardham, ii. 75
Jn. de, canon of Hardham, ii. 75
Jn. (fl. 1416), vii. 225
Jn. (fl. 1480), ii. 412
Jn. (fl. 1840), ii. 458
Kent and Ransome, ii. 164
Kent, Fair Maid of, *see* Joan
Kent:
ctss. of, *see* Holland, Alice; Joan, 'Fair Maid of Kent'
dchss. of, *see* Mary
earls of, *see* Burgh, Hubert de; Edmund; Holland, Thos.; John
Kent, i. 305, 347, 483, 485–6, 493, 503, 512; ii. 86, 170 *n*, 195, 463; iii. 1–2, 4; ix. 1, 142
agric., ii. 211
A.-S. rem., i. 343–5
archit., ii. 333
boundary, i. 536
ch. bells, ii. 250
Civil War, i. 526
coins, iii. 15
fortifications, i. 520
fossils, i. 30, 33, 35, 39
geology, i. 13, 16, 59
kings, *see* Baldred; Edric; Ethelbert; Hlothere
lands in, ii. 426; ix. 130, 209
maritime hist., ii. 125–7, 131, 133, 137–40, 144, 146–8, 151, 156, 158, 160–2
Martello towers, i. 534
militia, i. 507, 515
natural history, i. 47–8, 50, 55, 67, 110–11, 130, 164, 167 *n*, 170, 183, 278
prehist. rem., i. 309, 311
rebellions, i. 511–14, 516
roads, ii. 240
sheriff, i. 516; *and see* Iden, Alex.
smuggling, ii. 199
sport, i. 305; ii. 453, 467–76
trades and ind., ii. 194, 238, 248, 256, 263
woodland, ii. 291
and see individual place names
Kentish, Ric., vii. 121
Kenwards, *see* Lindfield
Keppel, Geo., Vct. Bury, earl of Albemarle, ii. 443
Kepston, Thos. de, iv. 58
Kerr, Phil., vii. 173
kerseys, *see* textile ind.: wool
Kerwood:
Eliz., w. of Jas., iii. 161
Jas., iii. 161
Keston (Kent), i. 314
Ketchenham, *see* Kitchenham
Ketel, *see* Kettel
Ketere (fl. 1196), vii. 256 *n*
Kettel (Ketel):
Hen., ix. 257
Peter, vii. 279
Kew (Surr.), ii. 236
Keyelweye, *see* Kelleway

Keyme, *see* Kyme
Keymer, ii. 313; vii. 2, 105, 125, **179–81**
adv., vii. 181
agric., vii. 181
brickmaking, ii. 254; vii. 179
Burgess Hill, *q.v.*
char., vii. 181
ch., vii. 144, 180, *180*
accessories, ii. 250, 354
archit., ii. 342, 366
cts., vii. 180
dom. archit., vii. 179
Hassocks, i. 7; vii. 179
A.-S. rem., i. 342
Butting Hill, iii. 43
insects, i. 167, 171, 175, 178–80, 183, 195–7 200–1, 208–10
roads to, iii. 43
Rom. rem., iii. 4, 42–3, 57–8
Stonepound, iii. 57–8
inc., ii. 313
insects, i. 165, 168 *n*
man., vii. 3–4, 6, 141, 179–80
mills, vii. 179–80
nonconf., vii. 179
pk., ii. 297, 310
pop., ii. 224
rly., ii. 224 *n*; vii. 179
Keyne, Nic. del, iv. 21 *n*
Keynor, *see* Sidlesham
Keyt:
Agnes, ix. 207
Eliz., m. Thos. Tracy, Vct. Tracy, ix. 207
Eliz., w. of Sir Wm., *see* Coventry
Marg., m. Jas. Higford, ix. 207
Sir Wm., ix. 207
Sir Wm. (another), ix. 207
and see Keate
Khartoum (Sudan), battle, i. 536
Kichenour (Kichinore), *see* Kechenore
Kidder, fam., ii. 317
Kidsbrooke gate, *see* Forest Row
Kighley, fam., ix. 209
Kilburn (in Willesden, Mdx.), nunnery, iv. 171
Kilburne, Ric., ix. 168
Kildare, earl of, *see* Fitzgerald
Kilgour, Alex., vicar of Terwick, iv. 29
Killingbeck (Killingbecke), Francis, rector of Poynings, vicar of Heathfield, ii. 420; vii. 211
Killingworth:
Jn., vii. 168
Mary, *see* Infield
Thos., ii. 164–5
Kilwardby, Rob., abp. of Cant., ii. 49, 57, 122; iii. 104
Kinahan, ——, i. 529
King (Kinge, Kyng):
Ant. Montague, iv. 5
Chas., ii. 238
Dan., iii. 113 *n*, 128
Dan. (another), ii. 475
E.T., ix. 255
G.W., ii. 475
H.J., ii. 474
Hen., bp. of Chich., i. 522–3; ii. 427; iii. 87–8, 112, 126, 133–4
Hen., his s., iii. 133
Capt. Hen., iv. 5
J. Godwin, vii. 165, 169
Jn. (fl. *c.* 1440), iii. 104
Jn. (fl. 1669), iii. 134
Philippa, ii. 85
Rob., master of Playden hosp., ii. 105
Thos., rector of Stanmer, ii. 26
Thos. (fl. 1825), vii. 59
Thos. (fl. 1935), iii. 13, 16
Mr., ii. 456
——, ii. 474
fam., i. 522
arms, iii. 112
King & Sons, ii. 263
King-Harman, Sir Chas. A., vii. 132
King-Noel, Lady Anne Isabella, Baroness Wentworth, m. Wilfred Scawen Blunt, vii. 195

Kinge, *see* King
Kingesfold, Joan de, prioress of Rusper, ii. 63–4
Kingley, *see* Stoke, West
King's College, Cambridge, ii. 124, 408; ix. 268
King's Farm, *see* Horsham: Roffey
Kingsbury, T.J., ii. 260
Kingscote (Kingscott):
  Chris., iv. 231
  Jn., dean of Hastings coll., ii. 117
Kingsfold, *see* Warnham
Kingsham (in Chich.), *see* Chich.
Kingsham (in Chithurst), *see* Chithurst
Kingsland:
  Jas., ii. 319
  R., ii. 448
Kingsley, Hen., vii. 148
Kingsmill, Constance, m. Thos. Baker, ix. 120
Kingston:
  Anne, *see* Oxenbridge
  Mat., iv. 224
  and see Kyngeston
Kingston:
  duke of, *see* Pierpoint, Evelyn
  earl of, *see* Pierpoint, Hen.
Kingston (by Ferring), i. 506 *n*; ii. 37, 43, 163, 217
Kingston by Sea (Kingston Buci), ii. 43–4
  ch., ii. 251, 340, 346–7, 358, 361, 365, 372
  coastguards, i. 506 *n*
  earthworks, i. 480
  Holm Bush, i. 68, 136, 139, 141–6, 148, 150–2, 154–9, 161–3, 165, 168–71, 175–6, 178, 180–1, 184–5, 188–9, 195, 198, 208, 227, 237
  man., vii. 279
  pop., ii. 219
  Rom. rem., iii. 28, 47, 59
  trades and ind., ii. 232, 269
Kingston near Lewes, i. 11*; ii. 43–4; vii. 15, 51, **57–60**, 225
  adv., vii. 60
  agric., vii. 58
  A.-S. rem., i. 339
  ch., ii. 5, 377; vii. 1, 59–60, *60*
  ch. ho., ii. 7
  cts., vii. 58–9
  dom. archit., vii. 57–8
  glebe, ii. 5
  hunting, ii. 451
  inc., vii. 52, 58
  insects, i. 115–16, 215
  man., vii. 34, 36, 58–9
  mills, vii. 58
  Newmarket:
    Hill, i. 55; iii. 61; vii. 57
    insects, i. 210
  pop., ii. 225
  rector, *see* Delap
  rectory, vii. 56
  tithes, ii. 7
  vicarage, ii. 7; vii. 60
Kingston Seymour (Som.), iv. 153
Kingston upon Thames (Surr.), ii. 306
  council of, ii. 3, 118
Kington, Thos., iv. 162
Kipling:
  Joshua, iv. 84, 117
  Rudyard, vii. 234; ix. 167, 195
Kipson (Kipston), *see* Hunston
Kirdford, i. 52; ii. 43; iv. 191
  adv., ii. 108, 119
  birds, i. 290
  ch., ii. 351–2, 354, 356, 359, 366, 372
  Ebernoe, ii. 43
  nonconf., ii. 41
  pop., ii. 218
  Shillinglee, i. 52
    birds, i. 284*
    Pk., ii. 276, 296–7, 305
  Shuerwode, ii. 254
  trades and ind., ii. 229, 247, 254
Kirkby (Kirkeby, Kyrkeby):
  Jn. de, ii. 78

Jn. of, bp. of Ely, ix. 67
Jn. de, dean of South Malling coll., ii. 119
Kirkpatrick, R., i. 74
Kitchenham (Kechenham, Ketchenham, Kychynhamme):
  Agnes de, ix. 158
  Eleanor de, ix. 128
  Elias de, ix. 128
  Godwin de, ix. 128
  Jn. de, ix. 158
  Ralph, ix. 128
  Wm. de, ix. 158
Kitchenham, *see* Peasmarsh
Kitchingham, *see* Etchingham
Kite, Hen., ix. 56
Kitelbere, Hen., mayor of Chich., iii. 91
Kithurst Hill, *see* Storrington
Kitson (Kytson):
  Ric., warden of St. Mary's hosp., Chich., ii. 102
  Thos., ix. 139
Kleinwort:
  Sir Alex. Drake, vii. 158
  Cyril H., vii. 158
Knap, *see* Shipley: Knepp
Knapp, J.W., ii. 472 *n*
Knapp, *see* Shipley: Knepp
Knatchbull:
  Edw. (sr.), ix. 273
  Edw. (jr.), ix. 273
  Mary, *see* Hugessen
  Sir Norton, ix. 160
  Norton Jos., ix. 273
Knell, *see* Beckley: Knelle
Knelle:
  Agnes, ix. 144
  Edm. de, ix. 144
  Edm. de, his s., ix. 144, 267
  Geof. de (d. by 1255), ix. 144
  Geof. de (d. 1295), ix. 144
  Geof. de (fl. 1332), ix. 144
  Marg. de, m. Wm. de Wells, ix. 144
  Mat. de (fl. 1255), ix. 144, 267
  Mat. de (fl. 1319), ix. 144
  Steph. de, ix. 144, 278
  fam., ix. 144
Knelle (Knell), *see* Beckley
Knellstone, *see* Udimore
Knepp, *see* Shipley
Knight:
  A.E., ii. 473
  Anne, w. of Kempster, iii. 162
  Anne, *see* Cragg
  (formerly Peachey), Bulstrode, *see* Peachey
  Edw., vii. 144
  Eliz., *see* Page
  Eliz. Woodward, m. 2 Bulstrode Peachey, iv. 97, 129*
  Geo., ix. 92
  Gilb., i. 292
  Jas., iii. 162
  Jn. (fl. 1561), iv. 223
  Jn. (fl. 1587, ? another), iv. 52
  Jn. (fl. 1788), and his w. Susan, iv. 83
  Kempster, iii. 162
  Mary, w. of Jas., iii. 162
  Ric. (fl. 1536), iv. 224
  Ric. (d. 1584, ? another), iv. 52
  Sam., vii. 97, 118, 123, 144
  Thos. (fl. 1584), iv. 224
  Thos. (fl. 1592, ? another), iv. 153
  Thos. May, iv. 104
  (formerly Brodnax), Thos. May, *see* Brodnax
Knights Hospitaller, ii. 45, 93; vii. 186–7, 205, 207
  arms, iii. *79*; vii. *207*
  estates, iii. 79; iv. 56, 61, 76, 78, 111, 172; ix. 278
  liberties, i. 502, 538; iv. 78
  patronage, ix. 278–9
  preceptory, *see* Poling
  prior, vii. 207–8; *and see* Docwra
Knights Templar, i. 502; ii. 45, 92–3; vii. 14 *n*, 40, 205, 207
  arms, vii. *207*

  estates, ii. 331*, 344 *n*
  preceptories, *see* Saddlescombe; Shipley
Knill, fam., arms, iii. 151
Knivet, *see* Knyvett
Knole (Kent):
  Ho., iv. 114
  Pk., ix. 117
Knolle (Knoll):
  Agnes de la, m. Wm. Herkestede, iv. 161
  Hen. de la, iv. 161
  Jn. de la, iv. 161
  Mat. de, ii. 104
  Wm. at, ix. 266 *n*
Knollys (Knolles), Sir Rob., i. 512; ix. 261
Knott:
  Jn., iii. 80
  Rob. Rowse, ii. 426
Knottesford:
  Beatrice, *see* Jardyn
  Frances, m. 1 Thos. Ford, 2 Thos. Kyrll, iv. 11, 24
  Jas., iv. 163
  Joan, m. Wm. Darrell, iv. 163
  Jn., iv. 24
  Wm., iv. 163
Knowles:
  Ric., and his w. Frances, vii. 190
  W.L., ii. 476
Knox, Arthur E., i. 274, 282, 284–6, 293; iv. 33
Knyvett (Knivet, Knyvet):
  Anne, *see* Pickering
  Eliz., *see* Clifton
  Sir Hen., vii. 54 *n*, 258; ix. 263
  Hen., iv. 16
  Sir Jn., iv. 123
  Magdalen, *see* Ford
Kocfeld, Ric. de, ii. 93
Kudenn, *see* Coudenne
Kychenere, *see* Kechenore
Kychynhamme, *see* Kitchenham
Kyffin, Marg., *see* Thatcher
Kyggesforde, Jn., ii. 360
Kyme (Cayme, Keme, Keyme):
  Eliz., m. Jn. Shirley, vii. 37
  Joan, m. Sir Geo. Paulet, vii. 37, 42, 45
  Jn. (d. 1582), vii. 73, 76; ix. 86
  Jn., M.P. for Lewes, vii. 16–17, 27 *n*, 31, 42, 75; ix. 86
  Marg., w. of Ric., m. 2 Ric. Jeffrey, vii. 42
  Ric., vii. 37 *n*, 42
  ——, m. —— Colte, ix. 86
Kymere, Maud de, *see* Peytevin
Kynaston, Mr., ii. 468
Kyng, *see* King
Kyngeston (Kyngestone):
  Gilb. de, vii. 59
  Isabel de, *see* Sykelfot
  Jn. de, vii. 59, 106
  Phil., vii. 59
  Rob., de, warden of St. Mary's hosp., Chich., ii. 102
  Warin de, vii. 59
  and see Kingston
Kynore, Jn. de, and his w. Isabel, iv. 213
Kyppyng, Rob., abbot of Durford, vicar of Rogate, ii. 90–1
Kyriel:
  Eliz., w. of Nic., ix. 146
  Jn. (fl. 1366), ix. 145
  Jn. (fl. 1470), ix. 146
  Nic., ix. 146
  Sir Thos., ix. 146
  arms, ix. *146*
Kyrkeby, *see* Kirkby
Kyrll:
  Frances, *see* Knottesford
  Thos., iv. 24
Kytson, *see* Kitson

La Denne hund., i. 537
La Hogue, *see* Hogue

La Lippe, count, ii. 443
La Marche, count of, *see* Lusignan, Hugh of
La Tille, *see* Dill
La Touche, W.H., ii. 411
Lacy:
  Alice, *see* Oxenbridge
  Edm., bp. of Exeter, iv. 140; ix. 169
  Hen., ix. 181
ladder making, ii. 300
Lade:
  Anne, w. of Sir Jn., ix. 212
  Sir Jn. (d. 1740), ix. 206–7, 209
  Sir Jn. (d. 1759), ix. 91, 212, 214
  Sir Jn. (d. 1838), ii. 449, 456; vii. 249; ix. 91, 212, 214, 266
  (formerly Inskipp), Sir Jn., ix. 207
  Letitia, w. of Sir Jn., ix. 212
  arms, ix. *207*
Ladyholt, *see* Harting
Lagenersh (Lageners):
  Jn. de, iv. 230
  Thos. de (fl. 1242), iv. 230
  Thos. de (fl. *c.* 1340), iv. 230
  Wm. de (fl. 1296), iv. 230
  Wm. de (fl. 1340), iv. 230
Lagness, *see* Pagham
Laigle (Aigle, Aquila):
  Gilb. de, i. 491, 493–4; ii. 76–8, 87, 313–14, 332; vii. 71
  Isabel de, *see* Warenne
  Nic. de, dean and bp. of Chich., dean of Avranches, ii. 9, 50
  Richer de, i. 490; ii. 122
  fam., ii. 313
Laigle (Aquila, Eagle, Pevensey), honor of, i. 503, 509; ii. 78, 123, 171–2, 182, 314, 317, 320; iv. 168 *n*; ix. 2
Lajes, Tallarte de, *see* Alard, ——
Lajos (Louis) I, king of Hungary, ii. 68
Lake:
  Jn., bp. of Chich., ii. 40; iii. 88, 133
  Thos. (fl. 1596), ii. 154
  Thos. (fl. 1724), ix. 56
Lamb:
  Sir Archibald, i. 302–3; ix. 91, 101
  Chas., ix. 8
  Sir Chas., ix. 101
  Sir Chas. Ant., ix. 91
  (formerly Burges), Sir Chas. Montolieu, ix. 91
  Eliz., *see* Davies
  Geo. Augustus, rector of Iden, ix. 91, 153, 156, 163
  Rob., vii. 227
  Thos., ix. 152, 156, 163
  Thos. Phillips, vii. 258, 284
  Thos. Wm., ix. 91
  fam., ix. 53, 60, 156
  arms, ix. *91*
Lamball, Edw., iv. 152
Lambdown Hill, *see* Binderton
Lamberhurst, Jn. de, abbot of Robertsbridge, ii. 73
Lamberhurst (Kent, formerly Suss.), i. 536; ii. 226, 292; ix. 251, 257
  ch., ii. 336, 346, 359–60
  iron ind., ii. 249, 296
  Scotney (Stackney) cast., i. 477; ii. 24, 29, 394–5
Lambert, Wal. fitz, *see* FitzLambert
Lambert:
  E.T., ii. 472 *n*
  Jas., ix. 131–2
  W., ii. 468
  ——, ii. 475
Lambeth (London, formerly Surr.), ii. 72, 242, 292 *n*, 300; iv. 110
  Kennington, iii. 42, 43 *n*
  Oval cricket ground, ii. 469
  St. Thomas's hosp., ii. 435–6
Lamburn, Jn., sacrist of Bosham coll., ii. 112
Laming, Agnes, ix. 32
Lampool (Lampol), *see* Maresfield
Lamport, Jn., ii. 61
Lamporte, *see* Lewes: Landport

Lampson:
  Sir Curtis Miranda, vii. 192 *n*, 199
  Godfrey L.T. Locker, vii. 199
  Hannah Jane Locker, vii. 199
  Jane Walter, vii. 199
Lanaway, C.F., ii. 453
Lanaways Farm, *see* Horsham
Lancashire, O.P., ii. 476
Lancashire, i. 168 *n*; ii. 473, 476
  Fencibles, i. 534
  and see Liverpool; Manchester; Sefton
Lancaster (Lancastre):
  Hen. of, earl of Lancaster, iv. 45; vii. 3*
    his dau., *see* Eleanor
  Jn. de, iv. 66
  Jn. of, duke of Bedford, ix. 244
  Jn., ix. 141
  Mabel de, *see* Moyne
  Thos. of, earl of Lancaster, i. 508
  Thos. of, duke of Clarence, ii. 141; ix. 127
  Thos., vii. 20, 24
  Mr., ix. 134
Lancaster:
  duke of, *see* Gaunt
  earls of, *see* Henry IV; Lancaster
Lancaster, duchy, ii. 78, 124, 230, 245, 320
  cts., ii. 317–18
Lancaster Great Park, *see* Ashdown forest
Lancastre, *see* Lancaster
Lancing (Launcing):
  Agnes de, ii. 106
  Bertha de, iv. 202
  Maud, w. of Wm. de, iv. 202
  Mic. de, ii. 106
  Wm. de, iv. 202
  Wm. de (another), iv. 202
Lancing, ii. 43, 74; vii. 34
  birds, i. 277, 279, 281, 292, 297
  ch., ii. 332, 337, 340, 342, 344, 346, 352, 356, 365–6, 370, 376
  coastguards, i. 506 *n*
  coins, i. 330
  Coll., i. 536; ii. 231, 432–3, 476
  crustaceans, i. 257, 263
  dom. archit., ii. 386
  Downs, i. 326; iii. 3, 59–60
  geology, i. 13
  inc., ii. 190
  insects, i. 137, 152, 173, 177, 187, 192–3, 195–9, 202, 205–9
  Pende, ii. 234
  pop., ii. 218
  prehist. rem., i. 330
  roads to, iii. 47
  Rom. rem., iii. 3, 47, 59–60
  shipping, ii. 151
  spiders, i. 241
  tithes, ii. 9
  trades and ind., ii. 232, 234
  vicarage, ii. 9
Land, Revd. Dr., and his w., ix. 198
land measures, Sussex, ii. 170–1
land reclamation, *see* Rye; Thorney, West
Land Settlement Association, iv. 211
Landen, Rog., iv. 46, 53
Landport, *see* Lewes
Landsell, Isaac, ix. 248
Landwelheade, *see* Ashdown forest
Lane:
  Anne, w. of Thos., iii. 144
  Dorothy, w. of Wm., iii. 147
  Eliz., m. Jn. Smith, vii. 81
  Eliz., w. of Wm., vii. 35, 54, 64
  Hen., vii. 254
  Hen. Chas., vii. 115
  Hen. Thos., vii. 115
  Jn., mayor of Chich., iii. 104
  Jn., ix. 197
  Kath., w. of Hen. Chas., m. 2 Hen. Bottomley, vii. 115
  Mary, *see* Dobell
  Mary Dorothy, iv. 27

  Thos. (fl. 1540), iv. 155
  Thos. (fl. 1730), ix. 197
  Thos. (fl. *c.* 1735, ? another), iii. 144
  Thos. (d. 1779), vii. 115
  Thos. (d. 1805), ix. 89, 115, 119
  Wm., clerk, iii. 95
  Wm., mayor of Chich., iii. 95
  Wm. (d. 1688), vii. 35, 54, 64
  Wm. (d. 1702), vii. 67, 81
  Wm. (fl. 1730), vii. 35, 54, 64, 67
  Mr., ii. 469
  Mrs., iv. 29
  arms, vii. *114*
Lane Fox (later Pitt-Rivers), A.H., i. 314, 322, 455, 457, 459–60, 463–5, 467, 481; iii. 53, 65
Lanfranc, abp. of Cant., ii. 5, 42
Langdale:
  Geo. Augustus, vicar of Compton, iv. 93–4
  Horace Marmaduke, vicar of Compton, i. 272, 282; iv. 93
    his w., iv. 93
  Marmaduke Rob., vicar of Compton, iv. 93
  Wm. Jn., vii. 43
Langdon:
  A.H., i. 71
  G.H., iv. 170
  H., i. 247–8
Langdon (Kent), abbey, ix. 75
Langebregge, *see* Longbridge
Langeford, *see* Langford
Langeton, *see* Langton
Langford (Langeford):
  Benj. Cooper, ix. 181
  Chas., vii. 159
  Isabel, *see* Beche
  Jn. de (fl. 1349), ix. 139, 153
  Jn. (fl. 1845), ix. 173
  Thos. (fl. 1360), ix. 139
  Thos. (fl. 1791), ix. 181
  Thos. Cooper, ix. 61, 173, 181
  Thos. Fred., ix. 173
  fam., ix. 153
Langham:
  F.G., ii. 474
  Jas. H., ix. 213
  Jn. (fl. *c.* 1650), ix. 213
  Jn. (fl. 1722), ix. 141
  Sarah, *see* Hay
  Toby, iv. 179
  Wm. (fl. 1630), ix. 196
  Wm. (fl. 1666), and his w. Martha, ix. 141
  fam., ix. 141
Langhurst:
  Geof. de, ix. 92
  Jn. (fl. 1354), and his w. Alice, ix. 92
  Jn. (fl. 1428), ix. 92
  Rob. de (fl. 1296), ix. 92
  Rob. de (fl. 1339, ? another), ix. 92
Langley:
  Thos., ix. 101 *n*
  W.F., ii. 472 *n*
Langley (in Rogate), *see* Rogate
Langley (in Westham), *see* Westham: Langney
Langmane, Rob., sacrist of Bosham coll., ii. 112
Langmead:
  Jn., ii. 453
  Wal., ii. 453
  Wm., iv. 159
Langney, *see* Westham
Langport, *see* Eastbourne
Langport hund. (Kent), ii. 222 *n*
Langridge, G.T., ii. 477
Langrish:
  Eliz., iv. 129
  Jn., iv. 129
  Mary, iv. 129
  Ric., iv. 129
Langstone (Hants), ii. 269; iv. 183
Langton (Langeton):
  Eliz., ii. 440
  Jn. de, bp. of Chich., ii. 13, *16*, 57, 90, 98; iii. 110, 121 *n*, 130–1,

Langton
Jn. de, bp of Chich. (*cont.*):
132 *n*, 133, 135, 139, 148; iv.
154; ix. 201
Steph., abp. of Cant., iv. 234
Wm. de, ii. 57
arms, iii. *110*
Lanzo, prior of Lewes, ii. 64–5, 69
Laprimaudaye, Francis, vii. 57
Large, Jn., rector of Rotherfield, ii. 35–6
Larnach-Nevill:
Guy, marquess of Abergavenny, vii.
104, 243
Temple Montacute, marquess of
Abergavenny, vii. 4, 35, 43
Lascelles:
(or Lasie), Chas., master of hosp. of
St. Jas. and St. Mary, Chich., ii.
99–100
Edw. Chas. Ponsonby, iv. 86
Hen., iv. 66
Hen. Arthur, iv. 86
Lasham, Frank, i. 310, 328
Lasher, Thos., ix. 31
Lasie, Chas., *see* Lascelles
lastage, iv. 183; ix. 9, 37, 49, 68
Latham:
Jn., ii. 414
Sir Paul, ix. 132, 134
Lathe, le, *see* Hastings: honor of: ct.
Latille hund., *see* Dill hund.
Latouche-Tréville, admiral, ii. 162
Laud, Wm., abp. of Cant., ii. 32, 34, 50,
407; iii. 87; vii. 87
Laughton, ii. 44, 77, 197, 277, 416; ix.
251
assarts, ii. 189
Broyle, *see* Ringmer
ch., ii. 249, 334, 376, 379
earthworks, i. 477
inc., ii. 190
insects, i. 119–22, 140–1, 146–8, 150–
1, 153–64, 166, 170–4, 178–9,
181, 183–9, 199, 212–13, 215–23,
225, 227
Laughton Place, ii. 252, 334, 386
man., ii. 175, 180 *n*, 181, 186 *n*, 187;
ix. 193
pop., ii. 227
rectory, ii. 77
sport, ii. 446, 452
Stone Cross, i. 56
Vert Woods, i. 56
woods, ii. 297, 313
and see Lewes and Laughton Levels
Launcel, Wm. de, ? prior of Tortington,
ii. 83
Launcing, *see* Lancing
Laurence, abbot of Bayham, ii. 87–9
Laurence (Lawrence), abbot of Robertsbridge, ii. 73
Laurence, rector of Brede, ix. 171
Laurence, son of William the clerk, iv.
162
Lauzun, duc de, ii. 456
Lavant, ii. 43; iv. 5, **101–6**
earthworks, i. 480
Hayes Down, i. 326–7, *326*; iii. 60; iv.
101
insects, i. 120, 224
Lavant, East, iv. 88, **101–4**, 144, 222
adv., iv. 101, 103–4
char., iv. 104, 149
ch., ii. 349, 359–60, 366; iv. 101–3,
103
curate, iv. 91
dom. archit., iv. 101
fair, iv. 101
man. iv. 101–3
pop., ii. 220
rector, ii. 62
roads to, iii. 46
Lavant, Mid, ii. 81; iv. 88, 101, **104–
6**, 222
adv., iv. 104, 106
ch., ii. 81, 351, 354, 366, 372; iv.
104–6, *106*
man., iv. 104–6, 114

mill, iv. 104
pop., ii. 221
rly. station, iv. 101
Raughmere (Rawmere), i. 65; ii.
81; iv. 101, 104–5
Rom. rem., iii. 60
tithes, iv. 106
vicarage, ii. 9
Lavant, West, iv. 101–2, 105
prehist. rem., iv. 101
rly., iv. 101
roads, iv. 101
Lavant, riv., i. 52; ii. 466; iii. 10, 35, 72,
82, 95, 102–3, 164; iv. 89, 94, 97,
101, 138, 154
Lavender, C., ii. 473
Lavenham (Suff.), iv. 157, 216
Laver, Wm., iii. 147
Laverton, Ld., *see* Howard, Edw.
Lavington, East, *see* Woolavington
Lavington, West, iv. 40, 44, 47 *n*, **65**, 79
Lawcock, Thos., ii. 38
Lawes, Wm., master of hosp. of St. Jas.
and St. Mary, Chich., ii. 100; iii. 90
Lawley:
Anne, *see* Manning
Esther, m. Rob. Palmer, ix. 207
Sir Francis, ix. 207
Sir Thos., ix. 207
Thos., ix. 207
Lawrence, *see* Laurence
Lawrence:
C.T., ii. 470
Thos., ii. 250; vii. 286
Capt. Thos., ii. 165
Lawson:
Reg. L., ix. 134
Thos., ii. 38
Lawton:
Hen., ix. 83
Mary, *see* Weekes
Laxman:
Joan, iv. 135
Ric., iv. 135
Wm., ii. 69
Layton, Ric., ii. 17, 54, 58, 69, 82, 91,
115
Le Clerk, Henrietta, m. Jn. Dorrien, ii.
444, 458; iv. 104, 106
Le Havre, *see* Havre
Lea, R.J., and his w., vii. 109; *and see*
Lee
Leache:
Charity, w. of Ric., m. 2 Chas.
Howard, earl of Nottingham, vii.
67, 111, 113
Ric., vii. 67, 111, 113
and see Leech; Lecche
Leachford, Sir Ric., i. 522
lead mining, iii. 63
Leadbeater, ——, i. 302
Leake, And., ii. 164–5
Lear, Upperton, ii. 477
leather ind., *see* tanning
Lebanon, i. 34
Lebaundy, R., ii. 459
Lecche, Jn., iv. 213; *and see* Leache
Lechford, *see* Letchford
Lechmere, Edm., ii. 166
Leconfield, Lds., *see* Wyndham
lectern, *see* architecture: ecclesiastical
Ledes (Ledys), *see* Leedes
Lee:
Chas., vii. 180
Eliz., m. Sir Phil. Harcourt, ix.
222
Jn., ix. 222
Mary, iii. 144
Mary, m. O.H.A. Nicholls, iii. 146
Sir Ric., iv. 31, 99, 124, 153, 199; vii.
58, 85
Rob. atte, prior of Tortington, ii. 83
Rob. atte, prior of Tortington
(another), ii. 83
Wm. (? two of this name), ii. 239; vii.
26 *n*, 28
and see Lea; Leigh; Ley
Lee, *see* Fittleworth

Lee, riv. (Kent), i. 161 *n*
Leech, ——, i. 247–50, 252–3, 256, 258,
260
Leechpool, *see* Sompting: Lychpole
Leedes (Ledes, Ledys, Leeds):
Agnes, vii. 100
Anne, w. of Wm., m. 2 Hen. Roberts,
vii. 100
Edw., vii. 70
Geof. de, iv. 177
Jn. (fl. 1449), vii. 67, 100
Jn. (d. 1606), ii. 25; vii. 67, 70, 100
Sir Jn. (fl. 1612), vii. 67
Mary, w. of Sir Thos., vii. 67
Sir Thos. (fl. 1612), i. 519; ii. 29; vii.
67
Thos. (fl. 1642), i. 522
Wm., vii. 67, 100
fam., ii. 27; vii. 71
arms, vii. *67*
Leeds, dukes of, iv. 146
Leeds (Kent):
cast., i. 505, 508
prior, ii. 72
Leefe:
Jn., ii. 302; iv. 124
Wm., iv. 124
Leem, Jn., prior of Michelham, ii. 78–
80, 123
leet court, *see* courts
Leetham, W., ii. 472 *n*
Leeves, Rob., and his w. Eliz., vii. 235
Leeward Islands, governor, *see* Shirley,
Thos.
Lefsi (Leofsige) (fl. 1066), iv. 111; ix.
278
Legas:
Jn. (fl. 1742), and his w. Judith, vii.
105
Jn. (d. 1752, ? another), ii. 249
Legay:
Eliz., m. Jn. Tutte, iv. 193
Hannah, m. Thos. Hollis, iv. 193
Isaac, iv. 193 *n*
Kath., w. of Issac, iv. 193
Martha, m. Jn. Solly, iv. 193
Mary, m. Thos. Phillips, iv. 193 *n*,
212
Peter, iv. 193
Sam., iv. 193 *n*
Legg, *see* Legge
Leggatt:
Rob., dean of Hastings coll., ii. 117
Thos., ii. 257
Legge (Legg):
Alfred, iv. 26
Anna, ix. 162
Augustus Geo., iv. 26
Frances Kath., *see* Nicholl
Hen., iv. 149
Hen. Bilson, iv. 26
Hen. Bilson, Ld. Stawell, iv. 22, 26
Jas. Hen., iv. 208
Thos., ii. 165
Wm., earl of Dartmouth, iv. 115
Revd. Wm., iv. 26
arms, iv. *26, 115*
Leggesheath gate, *see* Forest Row
Legh (Leghe), *see* Leigh
Leicester:
ctss. of, *see* Eleanor
earls of, *see* Montfort, Sim. de;
Sidney
Leicester, i. 496
Leicestershire, i. 68; ii. 472–3, 476; *and
see* Belvoir; Bosworth; Burton
Lazars; Glen, Gt.
Leigh (Legh, Leghe):
Bart. de, iii. 105
Edw., iv. 102
Egerton, iii. 133
Emma, m. Jn. Abel Smith, iii. 133
Emma, w. of Bart. de, *see* Ruffus
Jn., vii. 158
Nichola de, m. Rog. de Cauz, iii. 105
Ric., ix. 235
S.A., ii. 470
S. Austen, ii. 277

Steph. atte, ix. 155
Thos. de, ix. 235
Wm. de, vii. 158
fam., ix. 235
and see Lea; Lee; Ley
Leigh Green, *see* Withyham: Lye Green
Leigh-Smith, W., ii. 472 *n*
Leinster, duke of, *see* Fitzgerald
Leith Hill, *see* Dorking
Leland, Jn., ii. 136
Lemanae (Lemanis), *see* Lympne
Lemyng, Wm., ix. 140
Lenaways Farm, *see* Horsham: Lanaways
Lenham (Kent), i. 18
Lennard:
  Anne, w. of Thos., Ld. Dacre, *see* FitzRoy
  Francis, Ld. Dacre, ii. 299
  Hen., Ld. Dacre, ix. 134
  Laur., ix. 172
  Marg., *see* Fiennes
  Ric., ix. 172
  Sampson, ix. 133, 266
  Thos., Ld. Dacre, earl of Sussex, ix. 132, 134
  arms, ix. *133*
  and see Leonard
Lenne (Lynn), Wm. de, dean and bp. of Chich., ii. 51, 99; iii. 121 *n*
Lennox:
  Amy Gordon-, ctss. of March, iii. 115
  Ld. Arthur Gordon, iii. 116
  Chas., earl of March, duke of Richmond, i. 523; iii. 100; iv. 102, 142, 144
  Chas., duke of Richmond, Lennox, and Aubigny (d. 1750), ii. 442–3, 454, 467; iii. 13, 73, 90, 99, 113; iv. 118, 142, 144
  Chas., duke of Richmond, Lennox, and Aubigny (d. 1806), i. 535; ii. 301, 442–3, 454–5, 457–8, 467; iv. 17, 95, 101, 104, 122, 142, 144, 177, 180, 193
  Chas., duke of Richmond, Lennox, and Aubigny (d. 1819), ld. lieutenant of Ireland, ii. 444, 457
  Chas. Gordon-, ii. 455, 457–9; iii. 14, 80, 105, 116; iv. 120, 216
  Chas. Gordon-, duke of Richmond, Lennox, and Aubigny (d. 1903), ii. 409, 444–5; iii. 126; iv. 104
  Chas. Gordon-, duke of Richmond, Lennox, and Aubigny (d. 1928), ii. 277, 284, 444, 480; iii. 116
  Fred. Chas. Gordon-, duke of Richmond, Lennox, and Aubigny, iv. 95, 102, 104, 106, 144, 149, 238–9
  Ld. Geo. (d. 1805), iii. 100
  Ld. Geo. (fl. 1815), iv. 104
  Ld. Hen. Gordon-, ii. 409; iii. 100
  Mary Louisa, iii. 126
  Sarah, dchss. of Richmond, ii. 442
  Ld. Wal., iii. 100
  fam., iii. 99
  arms, iii. 73, *99*
Lennox, dukes of, *see* Lennox; Stuart, Jas.
Lenny, G.J., ii. 280
Lenox-Tindal, H.C., ii. 472 *n*, 474
Lenthall (Lenthale):
  Edm., ii. 69; vii. 3–5, 19, 35, 59, 71, 80, 84, 99, 110, 114, 156–7, 179–80, 195, 203, 206, 236, 280, 283
  Marg., w. of Edm., m. 2 Sir Thos. Tresham, vii. 3–4, 6–7, 35, 157, 180
  Marg., w. of Sir Rowland, *see* FitzAlan
  Sir Rowland, vii. 3–4
  ——, i. 523
  arms, vii. *4*
Leo, a Jew, i. 506; iii. 80
Leofnoth (Levenot) (fl. 1066), ix. 119
Leofnoth (Levenot) (fl. 1086), vii. 204

Leofric, abbot of Peterborough, i. 487
Leofric, moneyer, iii. 83
Leofsige, *see* Lefsi
Leofstan, iv. 166
Leofwine, earl, i. 487–8; vii. 114
Leofwine, moneyer, iii. 83
Leofwine, *see* Lewin
Leom, Jn. de, iv. 168
Leon (Spain), ii. 130
Leonard, Ric., ii. *242; and see* Lennard
Leonardslee, *see* Beeding
Leopold, prince of Coburg, vii. 250
Leppard, Philadelphia, m. Jn. Hen. Lintott, vii. 138
Leseur, ——, i. 265
Leslie:
  Chas. (d. 1870), iv. 153, 235, 237
  Chas. (d. 1930), iv. 235
  Chas. Steph., iv. 153, 235
  Dorothea (Dorothy), *see* Eyre
  J.E.C., ii. 472 *n*
Lessay (Manche, France), abbey, ii. 56–7; iv. 51, 142, 149, 156, 158, 179, 201
Lessingham, Wm. de, ix. 91, 119 *n*
Lester, Thos., vii. 146, 208; ix. 111
Lester and Pack, iv. 78, 131; vii. 123, 132; ix. 141, 264, 268, 276
L'Estrange, *see* Strange
Lestrange, Ld., *see* Stanley, Sir Geo.
Letchford (Lechford):
  Hen., vii. 196
  Leonard, rector of Hurstpierpoint, ii. 38
Letice, Ric., master of hosp. of St. Jas. and St. Mary, Chich., ii. 100
Lett, Francis, ix. 29
leucata de Pevense, *see* Pevensey: lowey
Leuelesham, *see* Leuesham
Leuelorde, Adam, ix. 56
Leuesham (Leuelesham):
  Agatha de, m. Jn. de Orlaston, ix. 56
  Agnes de, m. Rog. de Pagham, ix. 56
  Gerard de, ix. 56
  Maud, w. of Samson de, ix. 56
  Samson de (d. by 1260), ix. 56
  Samson de (fl. 1304), ix. 56
Leukenor (Leukenore, Leuknore), *see* Lewknor
Leven, Loch (Scot.), i. 288
Levenot, *see* Leofnoth
Leventhorp:
  Alice, m. Humph. Torrell, iv. 42
  Nic., vii. 276 *n*
  Thos., iv. 42
Leverton, Alan de, warden of St. Mary's hosp., Chich., ii. 102
Leveson-Gower:
  Jn., Vct. Trentham, Earl Gower, ii. 442
  Mary, Lady Gower, *see* Tufton
Levessunt, ii. 189
Levett (Levitt, Lyvet, Lyvett):
  Eliz., m. Wm. Gilderigge, ix. 120
  Everard, ii. 428; iv. 79; ix. 192
  Hen., vicar of Hornchurch, ii. 428
  Jn. (fl. before 1347), ix. 241, 244
  Jn. (d. 1534), ix. 20
  Jn. (d. 1556), ix. 20, 82*
  Jn. (d. 1606), ix. 242, 246, 263
  Jn. (fl. 1623), ix. 242, 246, 263
  Lawr., ix. 20, 82
  Marg., w. of Thos., ix. 242
  Mary, m. Thos. Eversfield, ix. 20, 241
  Ric., ix. 20, 120, 241
  Thos. (fl. 1376), ix. 240–1, 244
  Thos. (fl. 1446), ix. 241
  Thos. (fl. 1606), ix. 242, 263
  Wm., vii. 218
  ——, w. of Jn., m. 2 Lawr. Ashburnham, ix. 20
  fam., ix. 20, 81, 84, 241, 246
  arms, ix. *241*
Levfel (fl. 1066), vii. 213
levies, *see* militia
Levin Down, *see* Singleton

Levinge:
  Eliz., m. Delme Vanheythmpson, vii. 227
  Sam., vii. 227
Levitt, *see* Levett
Levret (fl. 1066), ix. 190
Lewes (Lews):
  Bridget, m. Thos. Lewknor, iv. 24, 208
  Hen. of, vii. 32
  Jn. de (d. 1330), ii. 361
  Jn. (d. 1537), and his w. Agnes, iv. 209
  Jn., parson of Elsted, iv. 10
  Jn. (d. 1567), and his w. Mary, iv. 208
  Martha, vii. 247
  Peter de, master of hosp. of St. Jas. and St. Mary, Chich., ii. 100
  Steph., prior of Hastings, ii. 77
  Wm. of dean of Hastings coll., ii. 114, 117
  Wm., abbot of Robertsbridge, ii. 73
  (or Sherman, or Baker), Wm., prior of Sele, ii. 61–2*
  and see Lewis
Lewes, earl of, *see* Nevill, Wm.
Lewes, i. 495; ii. 10, 169, 187, 195, 251, 289, 299; iii. 2, 16, 86; vii. 1–2, 6, **7–43**, 45
  ale hos., ii. 193, 196
  Allington, *q.v.*
  almshos., ii. 104; vii. 9, 43
  anchorite, ii. 47
  A.-S. rem., i. 336–8, 345; vii. 7, 12, 14, 37
  archdeacons, ii. 23, 76, 78; vii. 262; *and see* Hare, Julius; Henshaw, Tobias; Lyndrigge; More, Edw.; Passelewe
  arms, vii. 13, *24*, 32
  Ashcombe, *q.v.*
  Barbican ho., vii. 12
    museum, i. 349 *n*; vii. 40, 46, 234
  barony, vii. 1–7, 55, 109, 125, 141, 157–8, 180, 189, 194, 201, 203, 209, 213, 217, 225–6, 234, 242, 251, 253, 255, 258, 279–80, 283
  cts., vii. 3, 12 *n*, 19, 29–31, 81
  barracks, ii. 224 *n*
  battle, i. *496*, 497–500; ii. 73; iv. 183; vii. 2, 7, 15, 175
  birds, i. 275, 285–6
  bishops, *see* Cook, Thos. Wm.; Jones, Herb.; Streatfield, Wm.
  botany, i. 43, 48, 59, 66
  Brack Mount, i. 475; vii. 20–1, 30
  bridge, vii. 7–9, 27 *n*
  Bull Ho., vii. *9*, 10–11
  cast., i. 493, 496, 499–500, 503, 509, 511; ii. 393; iii. 60; vii. 2–3, 6, 12, 16, **19–24**, *20*, *24*, 30, 36 *n* 106
    archit., ii. 334, 394–5; vii. 21–3
    bailiff, vii. 20, 24
    cast. precincts (extra-par.), ii. 224
    constable, vii. 20
    earthworks, i. 475, *475*
    gaol, i. 512
    keepers, vii. 2, 20
    porters, vii. 20, 24
    steward, vii. 20
  chant., vii. 12, 41–2
  char., vii. 42–3
  chs., ii. 65
    All Saints, vii. 37–8, *38*, 41; adv., vii. 40–1; rector, *see* Snatt, Wm.
    Holy Trinity, vii. 40–1
    St. Andrew, vii. 10, 40
    St. Anne (formerly St. Mary Westout), vii. 8, 11, 31, *39*, 39–40, 42–3; accessories, ii. 356, 361; archit., ii. 344, 347–8, 368, 370, *370*; vii. 72, 77
    St. John-sub-Castro, ii. 3–4, 40; vii. 33, 37–8, 113; accessories, ii. 47, 249, 360; adv., vii. 40–1; archit., ii. 364; earthworks, iii. 60; vii. 7, 14, 37; rector, *see* Walter

Lewes
chs. (*cont.*):
St. Martin, vii. 40–1
St. Mary-in-Foro, ii. 95; vii. 9, 31, 40–1
St. Mary Westout, vii. 34, 41, 51; *and see* Lewes: chs.: St. Anne
St. Michael, ii. 22 *n*, 34; vii. 12, 38–9, *39*, 41; accessories, ii. 21; archit., ii. 334, 339–40, 366, 376–7, 379; rectors, *see* Bradford, Jn.; Postlethwaite, Wal.
St. Nicholas, vii. 13, 27, 40–1
St. Pancras, *see* Lewes: priory
St. Peter-the-Less, vii. 40–1
St. Peter Westout, vii. 16, 34, 41
St. Sepulchre, vii. 40–1
St. Thomas-at-Cliffe, ii. 351, 378; vii. 31, 41–2
Civil War in, i. 522, 524; vii. 16–17
Cliffe, *q.v.*
coaching, ii. 204; vii. 8–9
County Hall, vii. 13, 19
cts., ii. 248; vii. 14, 29–31, 34–6
county, i. 504; iii. 95
dean, *see* Hume, Ric.; Jocelin
deanery, ii. 42–4
defences, ii. 242; *and see* Lewes: walls
dom. archit., ii. 337, 372, 384, *385*, 386–7, 390, 392; vii. 9–14
earthworks, i. 480
fairs, ii. 282; vii. 3, 32
fishery, vii. 3
fossils, i. 10, 28, 30–5
friary, ii. 45, **95–6**; vii. 7, 9, 15–16, 36, 42
archit., ii. 331
warden, *see* Parker, Jn.
geology, i. 11–12
guilds, trade, ii. 69 *n*, 188; vii. 1, 24
Hangmans Acre, vii. 8, 27, 42
haws, vii. 14, 68, 228, 253
hosps.:
St. Jas., ii. 45, **103**, 191, 331, 378; vii. 16, 45
St. Nic., ii. 45, **104**, 191, 331; vii. 16, 224
Houndean, vii. 2–4, 6–7, 13, 15, 35–6, 236
hund., ii. 224
inns, i. 533; vii. 18, 32, 51
insects, i. 115–16, 119–21, 133–4, 136–7, 147, 149, 169–94, 196–9, 201, 203, 205, 211–26, 230–1
Jews, i. 506
Knights Templar estates, ii. 92
Landport (Lamporte), ii. 322; iii. 60; vii. 2
insects, i. 116, 121, 142, 145–6, 148–50, 155, 191, 212–19
libraries, vii. 17, 19
local govt., vii. 24–9
bailiff, vii. 24; *and see* Young, Jn.
constable, vii. 24–7, 29
Council of Twenty-four, vii. 24–6, 29
Fellowship of the Twelve, vii. 24–7, 30–1
headborough, vii. 24–6
Jury, vii. 18, 26
mayor, vii. 29; *and see* Baxter, Wynne E.
reeve, vii. 24
trustees, vii. 30, 42
lds., vii. 21, 29–30, 32, 34
Malling Without, South, *q.v.*
mammals, i. 302
man., vii. 25, 33–7
mkts., vii. 3, 31–2
militia, i. 507, 528, 534–5
mill, vii. 28
mint, i. 348–9; vii. 14, 32–3
molluscs, i. 108–9
museums, i. 309, 316, 320–1, 328–31, 339–40, 348 *n*; ii. 242; iii. 18, 31, 41, 55–7, 60, 68, 70; *and see* Lewes: Barbican ho.
nonconf., i. 528; ii. 22, 32–4, 38; vii. 17–18, 42–3
parishes, vii. 33, 41
All Saints, ii. 224
St. Anne (formerly St. Mary Westout), ii. 104, 193, 224, 415; vii. 51
St. Andrew, vii. 41
St. John-sub-Castro, ii. 206 *n*, 224; vii. 9, 15, 31, 33, 79 *n*
St. Mary Westout, *see* Lewes: parishes: St. Anne
St. Michael, ii. 224
St. Thomas-at-Cliffe, ii. 224
parl. rep., i. 504, 531; vii. 31
M.P.s, *see* Devenish, Wm.; Fitzroy, Hen.; Gravesend; Kemp, Thos. Read; Kyme, Jn.; Morley, Herb.; Spicer, Rob.; Walwer
Pells, the, ii. 238, 259
pest ho., vii. 16, 28
pillory, ii. 23
poor relief, vii. 28, 42, 266
pop., ii. 224
port, ii. 247–9, 256; vii. 14, 32
prehist. rem., i. 315, 317, 320–1, 330, 337
priory of St. Pancras, i. 496, 499–500, 539; ii. 4, 6, 16, 53, **64–71**, 103–4, 123 *n*, 252, 294, 311; iii. 125 *n*, 144 *n*; iv.30; vii. 2, 4, 8, 15, 31, 33, 43, *45*, 45–8, *46*, *47*, 263, 279; ix. 85
accessories, ii. 353–4, 360
archit., ii. 5, 328, 342, 347, 365, *366*, 372, 382; vii. 13, 46–9, 57
char., ii. 191
chartulary, vii. 1
ch., iv. 237 *n*
clerks, *see* Lucas
estates, ii. 65, 169, 189, 298, 381, 411; iv. 59–60, 63–4, 102, 168; vii. 55, 58, 67–8, 89, 95, 101, 105, 117, 169, 177, 183, 217–18, 224–6, 228, 234–5, 253, 255, 257–8, 275–6, 280; ix. 84, 201–2, 241
hunting rights, ii. 311
patronage, ii. 7, 9, 45, 48, 64–5, 68, 74, 78, 81–2, 84, 328; iv. 59, 65, 84, 91, 93, 104, 106, 111, 113,117, 122, 125, 237, 239; vii. 40–1, 56, 60, 65, 69, 73, 83, 91, 108, 123, 132, 135, 144, 163, 171, 179, 181, 211, 214, 219, 227, 237–8, 244, 262, 281, 286; ix. 241
priors, i. 514; ii. 14, 69–70, 139, 312, 413–14; vii. 15–16, 30, 55, 87, 101, 204, 223, 231, 233, 274, 286; *and see* Alexander; Ashdown; Aucher; Avignon; Caroloco; Chyntriaco; Crowham; Daniel, Jn.; Foville; Hugh; Jancourt; Joceaux; Lanzo; Monte Martini; Nelond, Thos.; Newcastle; Oke; Osaye; Russhelin; Stephen; Thyenges; William; Winchester, Adam
seal, ii. *74*
prisons, i. 503; ii. 224 *n*; vii. 2, 13, 19–21, 37
quarter sessions, ii. 170
rly., ii. 241; vii. 8–9
rape, i. 490, 504; ii. 64, 171, 175, 219 *n*, 223–5; iv. 185; vii. **1–7**, 104, 110, 125, 194, 201, 203, 206, 209, 212–13, 216, 241–2, 274–5, 279
coastguards, i. 507 *n*
famine, ii. 194
militia, i. 533, 535
sheriffs, vii. 1, 60
vagrancy, ii. 196
rebellions, i. 514
Reformation in, ii. 26
roads, iii. 47, 69; vii. 8
Rom. Cath., vii. 17
Rom. rem., iii. 60; vii. 14
royal visits, i. 491–2, 505; ii. 96
sch., vii. 15, 18, 91
grammar, ii. 397, 408, 411–15; vii. 12, 16, 42, 85
ship service, ii. 138, 153
shipping, ii. 155
smuggling, vii. 18
Southover, *q.v.*
sport:
angling, ii. 465
cricket, ii. 467, 469, 475
golf, ii. 479
horse racing, ii. 454–5, 461; vii. 18–19
hunting, ii. 296
shooting, ii. 462
stag hunting, ii. 449
taxation, ii. 189; vii. 27–8
theatre, vii. 19
timber, ii. 294
tithes, ii. 65
town bell, ii. 250; vii. 13, 19, 32
Town Brook, vii. 8, 27, 42
town lands, vii. 27
trades and ind., ii. 188; vii. 32
bellfounding, ii. 249–50
brewing, ii. 262–3; vii. 32
brickmaking, ii. 253
cement ind., ii. 231
charcoal, ii. 242
cider, ii. 264
iron ind., ii. 250; vii. 32
paper, ii. 238
printing, ii. 238–9
shipbuilding, ii. 235; vii. 32
tanning, ii. 259–60
textiles, ii. 256–8
wool, ii. 188, 284; vii. 32
union, i. 539
wages, agric., ii. 209
Wallands, i. 330, 497; vii. 2
walls, vii. 7, 12, 73
warren, ii. 312
Westgate, i. 499; vii. 7, 10–11
Westout, ii. 43–4, 47; vii. 16, 34, 51
Winterbourne, vii. 51
insects, i. 140, 142–3, 150, 157
man., vii. 36–7
river, *q.v.*
Lewes and East Suss. Natural History Society, i. 43, 66
Lewes and Laughton Levels, ii. 279
Lewes Journal, see Sussex Weekly Advertiser
Lewes Portland Cement Co., ii. 231
Lewin (Leofwine) (fl. 1066, ? two of this name), iv. 204; vii. 189; *and see* Leofwine, earl
Lewin (Leofwine) (fl. 1086), ix. 152
Lewinna, St., ii. 2
Lewis:
Fuller Wenham, vii. 76
Geo. Wenham, vii. 85
Jn., i. 326–7, 478
Jn. Wenham, ix. 91
W.A., ii. 474
Wm., iii. 162
Wm., master of hosp. of St. Jas. and St. Mary, Chich., iii. 167 *n*
——, w. of Jn. Wenham, *see* Lutman
and see Lewes
Lewisham (London, formerly Kent), *see* Sydenham
Lewknor (Leukenor, Leukenore, Leuknore, Lewkener, Lewkenor, Lewkenore, Lewkenour):
Anne, *see* Fraye
Beatrice, ix. 158
Bridget, *see* Lewes
Chris., recorder and M.P. for Chich., i. 523; iii. 86–7
Constance, m. 1 Thos. Foster, 2 Edw. Glemham, iv. 7, 28, 33 *n*, 35–6; vii. 54, 81–2, 97, 101; ix. 242, 263
Constance, w. of Sir Rog., *see* Hussey
Dorothy, w. of Edw., vii. 85
Edm., iv. 24
Edw. (d. 1528), vii. 85

Edw. (d. 1556), vii. 85
Edw. (another), vii. 85
Edw. (fl. 1594), vii. 85
Eleanor, w. of Sir Rog., *see* Audley
Eleanor, w. of Rog., *see* Camoys
Eliz., prioress of Rusper, ii. 64
Eliz., w. 1 of Sir Rog., 2 of Ric., *see* Meffant
Eliz., w. of Sir Thos., *see* Echingham
Fraye, ix. 187
Humph., ix. 181
Jane, m. —— Middleton, vii. 96 n
Jane, w. of Jn., ix. 158
Joan, m. 1 Sir Arthur Poole, 2 Sir Chris. Pickering, 3 Sir Wm. Barrington, iv. 35; vii. 194, 258; ix. 153, 242, 263
Joan, w. of Sir Jn., ix. 196, 255
Joan, w. of Ric., ix. 242
Joan, w. of ——, iv. 123
Sir Jn. (fl. 1463), ix. 196, 255
Jn. (d. by 1472), ix. 158
Jn. (fl. 1647), ii. 36; iv. 7, 101, 199
Jn. (fl. c. 1652, another), i. 527 n
Jn. (d. 1706, ? another), iv. 97
Kath., m. 1 Jn. Mill, 2 Wm. Morgan, iv. 7, 35; vii. 54, 81, 101, 226; ix. 242, 263
Sir Lewis, iv. 208
Mabel, m. Ant. Stapley, iv. 35; vii. 54, 81, 226; ix. 242, 263
Marg., m. Jn. Cowper, ix. 176
Mary, *see* Bennett
Mat., ix. 158
Nic., ii. 422*
Phil., ix. 158
Philippa (Philippe), *see* Dalingridge
Reynold, vii. 258
Ric. (fl. 1480), ix. 138 n
Ric. (fl. 1483, ? another), i. 515
Ric. (? fl. c. 1500), ix. 181
Ric. (fl. 1507, ? another), ix. 242
Ric. (fl. 1543), iv. 7*, 35
Ric. (? fl. c. 1550), vii. 96 n
Ric. (fl. 1564), ii. 24
Ric. (fl. 1588, ? two of this name), ii. 28; vii. 54
Ric. (fl. to 1592, ? another), recorder and M.P. for Chich., iii. 99
Ric. (d. 1602), iv. 100
Sir Ric. (d. 1616), iv. 100, 129, 199–200
Ric. (d. 1621), iv. 90, 97, 110 n
Sir Ric. (d. 1635), iv. 90, 97*, 100, 122, 199
Rob., ix. 181
Rog. (fl. 1351), ii. 316
Rog. (fl. before 1404), iv. 123
Sir Rog. (d. 1478), iv. 24, 35, 38; vii. 54, 81, 226, 258; ix. 263
Sir Rog. (fl. 1478), iv. 13, 15
Sir Rog. (fl. c. 1520), iv. 24 n
Sir Rog. (d. 1543), iv. 6–7*, 9, 35–6, 39; vii. 54, 81, 95–6, 101, 194, 226, 257; ix. 153, 242, 263, 267
Sir Rog. (fl. 1635), vii. 97
Thos. (fl. 1404), iv. 123
Sir Thos. (fl. 1420), ix. 138, 196 n
Sir Thos. (fl. c. 1450), ix. 153, 263
Sir Thos. (d. by 1453, another), ix. 118
Sir Thos. (d. 1484), i. 515; iv. 35; vii. 81; ix. 263
Thos. (fl. 1564), ii. 24
Thos. (fl. 1572, ? another), iv. 24, 208
Thos. (fl. 1588), i. 518
Mr. (fl. 1569), ii. 25
Mr. (fl. 1646), iv. 118
——, ii. 149
fam., i. 513; ii. 27, 63; iv. 24, 56, 76, 96–7, 123, 129; vii. 97; ix. 156, 209, 242
arms, iv. 35, 100; vii. 81; ix. 263
Lews, *see* Lewes
Lexden (Essex), iii. 19
Ley:
Jas., earl of Marlborough, ix. 130
Jane, *see* Butler

Tim., ix. 23, 25
and see Lea; Lee; Leigh
Leyburne:
Juliana de, m. Jn. de Hastings, ix. 146
Juliana de, w. of Wm., ix. 146
Wm. de, ix. 146
Leyden, Lucas van, ix. 126
Leyman, Jn., sacrist of Bosham coll., ii. 112
Leyntwardyn, Ric., ii. 123 n
Leythorne, *see* Mundham, North
Lezoux (Puy-de-Dôme, France), iii. 12, 17, 25, 28, 31–2, 41, 49, 51, 57, 64, 68–9
Libbard (Liberde):
Ric., and his w. Dorothy, iii. 145
Thos., ii. 257
lichens, i. **64–6**
Lichfield, Thos. de, dean of Chich., ii. 51, 100; iii. 114, 137, 139
Lichfield (Litchfield) (Staffs.), ii. 96, 432
Lickfold (in Lodsworth), *see* Lodsworth
Lickfold (in Wiggonholt), *see* Wiggonholt
Liddell:
Chas., rector of Ardingly and Worth, vii. 129
Dennis, vii. 129, 196
Sir Harry, ii. 442–3
Hen., Ld. Ravensworth, ii. 443
Ric., vii. 129
Lidgiter, Mr., ii. 460
Lidsey (in Aldingbourne), iv. 134, 136, 224 n
adv., iv. 138
chap., iv. 134, 138
dom. archit., iv. 134
Lidsey Ho., iv. 134*
man., iv. 135–6
Lifford, Ld., *see* Rochefoucauld
lighthouses, *see* lights
Lightmaker, Edw., ii. 438
lights and lighthouses, ii. 155, 163, 269; ix. 13
Lilford, Ld., *see* Powys, Thos. Littleton
Lilley (Lilly, Lylye):
Jn. (fl. 1419), iv. 5
Jn. (fl. 1700), vii. 217, 266
Lilljeborg, ——, i. 264
Lilly, *see* Lilley
Lillywhite:
Fred. Wm., ii. 468, 469 n; iv. 179
Jas., ii. 470–1, 475
Jas. (jr.), ii. 469–70
Jn., ii. 469–70
lime burning, ii. 198, 231; ix. 13; *and see* manures: lime
Limekiln wood, *see* Mountfield
Limerick, earl of, *see* Percy, Edm. Colquhoun
Limesy (Lymesy):
Marg., w. of Nic. de, *see* Murdac
Nic. de (d. by 1200), iv. 108, 145, 180
Nic. de (fl. 1246), iv. 108, 110
Wal. de, iv. 108, 145, 180
Limowart, lathe, *see* Shepway
Limpsfield (Surr.), ii. 52; iii. 45
Linces, *see* Lynche
Linch (Lynch), ii. 43; iv. 40–1, **65–7**, 82, 84, 109
adv., ii. 81; iv. 66–7
ch., ii. 81, 353; iv. 65–6
dom. archit., iv. 65
Hollycombe, i. 284; iv. 65
Linch Down, i. 224–5, 228, 231
man., iv. 65–6
pop., ii. 221
rector, iv. 65–6
tithes, ii. 263
Woodman's Green, iv. 5 n, 65–6
Linchmere, ii. 43, 81; iv. 40–1, 54, **67–70**
adv., iv. 70, 106
Brookham, *see* Bepton: Brookham
ch., iv. 67, 69–70
accessories, ii. 352, 356, 374
archit., ii. 330, 336, 339, 348–9,

366, 373–4, 379
dom. archit., iv. 67, 69
Hammer, iv. 67
man., iv. 44, 69
natural history, i. 68, 182, 184–6, 188, 194, 198, 200
pop., ii. 221
Rom rem., iii. 2, 4, 60
Shottermill, i. 68
Shulbred priory, *q.v.*
tithes, iv. 70
trades and ind., ii. 249; iv. 67, 69
Lincoln, Alfred de, iv. 108
Lincoln, earl of, *see* Clinton, Hen. Fiennes
Lincoln, ii. 87, 402, 404
battle, i. 495
bp., *see* Bloet, Rob.
cath., ii. 400
canon, *see* Courtenay, Ric.
prebendary, *see* Crowham
Lincoln College, Oxford, ii. 408, 428, 432, 434; iv. 224
Lincolnshire, ix. 1; *and see* Bardney; Belton; Boston; Grantham; Grimsby; Navenby; Newhouse; Spalding
Lind, Jn. de la, i. 498
Lindfield, i. 533; ii. 3, 44, 117, 311; vii. 92, 125, 148, 225–6
Benevolent Soc., ii. 207
ch., ii. 250, 340, 346, 354, 356, 374, 376–7
dom. archit., ii. 384, 386, 389–91
fair, sheep, ii. 281–2
Gravelye, ii. 207–8
Kenwards, ii. 389
Lindfield Arches, vii. 92, 239
Lindfield Bardolf, vii. 92
mammals, i. 301
man., vii. 129
Mascalls, East, ii. 389
Paxhill, ii. 382, 389
poor relief, ii. 208
pop., ii. 225
rly., ii. 225 n
rector, *see* Stonestreet, Jn.
Reformation in, ii. 25
riots, ii. 206 n
sch., ii. 207
sport, ii. 318, 464–5
trades and ind., ii. 237, 242, 252
Lindsay, Ludovic, earl of Crawford, i. 522–3, 525
Lindsey, earl of, *see* Bertie, Rob.
linen, *see* textile ind.
Lingfield (Surr.), ix. 81
Dry Hill, iii. 2
New Chapel, iii. 42–3
Linnaean Society, i. 290
Lintott:
Hen., vii. 190
Jn., vii. ·138
Jn. Hen., vii. 138
Philadelphia, *see* Leppard
Susannah, *see* Dennett
Thos., vii. 159
Liphook (Hants), i. 115–16
Lisbon (Portugal), ii. 129
bp., *see* Hastings, Gilb. of
Lisieux (Calvados, France), i. 488; ii. 110
Lisle (Insula, Isle, L'Isle):
Alice de, iv. 34
Amabil de, m. Ralph de Stopham, iv. 34, 65
Baldwin de (fl. 1279), iv. 91
Baldwin de (d. by 1307), iv. 92
Brian de, iv. 34, 65–6
Constance de, m. —— de Glamorgan, iv. 34
Eliz., m. Jn. Bramshott, iv. 115
Geof. de, and his w. Isoult, iv. 91–2
Godfrey de, iv. 115
Joan del, prioress of Lyminster, ii. 121
Joan, w. of Baldwin de, iv. 92
Joan, w. of Jn. de, m. 2 Hen. Romayn, iv. 92, 112, 115, 124
Joan de, *see* Bohun

Lisle (*cont.*):
  Jn. de (fl. 1282), iv. 115
  Jn. de (d. by 1347), iv. 92, 115
  Jn. de (d. 1370), iv. 92, 115
  Kath. de, prioress of Lyminster, ii. 121
  Maud de, *see* Estur
  Sibyl de, w. of Brian, m. 2 Wm. del Meinild, iv. 34 *n*
  Wal. de, iv. 115
  fam., iv. 115
Lisle, Vcts., *see* Dudley, Sir Jn.; Plantagenet; Sidney, Rob.
Liss (Hants), i. 169 *n*
Lister, J.J., i. 264
Litchfield, *see* Lichfield
Litlington (Littlington), ii. 44
  A.-S. rem., i. 336
  ch., ii. 250, 337, 339, 346, 350–2, 356, 358, 367–8
  earthworks, i. 480
  natural history, i. 136, 143–52, 154, 157–63, 282
  pop., ii. 226
  textiles, ii. 258
Little, T., ix. 178
Little Green, *see* Compton
Little Park, *see* St. Leonard's forest
Littleboys:
  Geo., ix. 130
  Jn., ix. 130
Littlehampton, ii. 42–3, 125, 148; iv. 190
  adv., ii. 108, 119
  batteries, ii. 152, 161
  botany, i. 60
  ch., ii. 340, 355, 376
  crustaceans, i. 257, 263
  geology, i. 11
  harbour lights, ii. 163
  insects, i. 112, 124–5, 128, 131–5, 142, 145, 149, 160, 162, 173, 221–3, 226, 228–32, 234
  man., ii. 230
  militia, i. 535
  museum, iii. 20, 58–61, 65
  pop., ii. 218
  roads to, iii. 47
  Rom. Cath., ii. 28
  Rom. rem., iii. 2, 47, 60
  sport, ii. 466, 477, 481
  trades and ind., ii. 164, 167, 235, 254, 271
Littlehampton Natural History Circle, iii. 49
Littleton, Sir Chas., iv. 172–3
Littlington, *see* Litlington
litus saxonicum, *see* Saxon shore
Liverpool, earl of, *see* Jenkinson, Chas.
Liverpool, ii. 285
liverworts, i. **61**
Livesay, Sir Mic., i. 526–7
livestock (vol. ii. only):
  cattle, ii. 274–9, 281, 289–90, 293, 298, 302–3, 307–8, 312–15, 319-21, 324–5
    Aberdeen Angus, ii. 277, 290
    Dexter Kerrys, ii. 277
    Irish, ii. 277
    Jersey, ii. 276, 290
    oxen, ii. 281
    shorthorns, ii. 276, 290
    Sussex, ii. 274, 276, 290
    Welsh Runts, ii. 277
  deer, ii. 291–6, 298–9, 302, 304–8, 310–12, 315–25
  horses, ii. 278, 281, 290, 293, 303, 306–8, 315, 319–21, 324
    Clydesdale, ii. 278
    shire, ii. 278
    Suffolk, ii. 278
  pigs, ii. 169, 180–1, 273–4, 276–8, 292–4, 296, 302–4, 306–8, 313–16, 320–1, 323–5
    Berkshire, ii. 278
    Sussex, ii. 277–8
    Tamworth, ii. 278
  poultry, ii. 212–13, 279–80, 288, 290

rabbits, ii. 292, 296, 305, 309, 311–12, 316, 321, 325
sheep, ii. 189–91, 211–12, 274, 276, 278–85, 289–90, 298, 300, 307–8, 324
  Dorsetshire, ii. 282–3
  Hampshire, ii. 282, 285
  Kent, ii. 274, 279
  Romney Marsh, ii. 279, 290
  Southdown, ii. 211, 274, 280–5, 290
Llewellyn, ——, ii. 474
Lloyd:
  David, ii. 164–5
  J., ii. 166
  Jn., iv. 61
  Nat., ix. 270, 273
    his w., ix. 273
  Sir Ric., ix. 187
  Wm., vii. 255
Lloyd George, David, vii. 173
Loader, *see* Loder
Locke:
  Jn., iv. 43
  Sam., ix. 89
Locker Lampson, *see* Lampson
Loddesdown (Loddesdune), *see* Westhampnett
lodemanage, *see* courts
Loder (Loader):
  G.W.E., Ld. Wakehurst, vii. 127, 129
  Jas., iii. 168
  R., ii. 447
  Sir Rob., vii. 185
Lodesdon, *see* Westhampnett: Loddesdown
Lodge, Mary, iv. 113
Lodsworth, i. 536; ii. 43; iv. 40, **71–3**, 76, 80
  adv., iv. 73
  Blackdown, iv. 71
    woods, i. 174–5, 177, 193
  ch., ii. 350, 355; iv. 53, 71, 73
  dom. archit., iv. 71–3
  insects, i. 182
  liberty, i. 502, 538; ii. 42; iv. 71, 73
  Lickfold, iv. 71–2
  man., iv. 71, 73
  mill, iv. 73
  pop., ii. 221
  tithes, iv. 73
  trades and ind., ii. 257; iv. 71
Lofeld (Lofilde), *see* Lotfield
Loft, Capel, ix. 229
Loges, Ric. de, i. 500
Loggebrok, la, *see* Ashdown forest
Loghteburgh, Jn., iv. 171 *n*
Logie-Pirie, Mrs., ix. 201
Lohareng, Jonas le, iv. 45
Lokesfeld, *see* Loxfield
Lokeswode, *see* Wisborough Green: Loxwood
Lollards, i. 513–14; ii. 14–15; iv. 79 *n*
Londa, Jn. de, prior of Boxgrove, ii. 59
Londnes (Lumnes):
  Edw., ix. 167 *n*
  Ric., ix. 167 *n*
  Rob., ix. 167 *n*
London:
  David of, vii. 217
  Edm. de, dean of Hastings coll., ii. 114, 117
  Wm., prior of Michelham, ii. 78–9
London, i. 302, 305, 483, 493, 496, 500; ii. 52, 125, 137, 145, 149, 160, 200, 289, 397, 400; iii. 9–10, 90–1, 97–8; iv. 10, 39; ix. 5, 102
  aldermen, *see* Bennett, Thos.; Bowyer, Francis; Garraway, Hen.; Stone, David Hen.
  archdeacon, *see* William
  Artillery Ground, ii. 467
  bp., i. 496; ii. 12, 42; iv. 76; *and see* Belmeis; Bonner; Sudbury
    arms, iv. *73*
    estates, i. 502, 538; iv. 71, 73
    patronage, iv. 125, 203, 217
  Bishopsgate, ii. 249
  Bridge, ii. 242
  chamberlain, *see* Cuddon, Sir Thos.
  Chancery Lane, ii. 10
  Cheapside, i. 321; ii. 422
  chs.:
    Christ Church, Newgate Street, ii. 435
    Holy Trinity Minories, vii. 239
    St. Antholin, ix. 198
    St. Martin le Grand, ii. 121
    St. Martin Outwich, ii. 416
    St. Swithin, London Stone, ii. 82
  City of, iv. 208
  Clement's Inn, iv. 161
  coaches from, ii. 204
  Cornhill, vii. 11
  Council of, iii. 105
  Finsbury Court, ii. 435
  Fire of, ii. 422
  fishermen, i. 267
  Fleet prison, ii. 22, 27
  geology, i. 8
  Grays Inn, iv. 24
  Grey Friars, ii. 435
  guilds, iii. 97
    Fishmongers, ii. 267; ix. 257
    Girdlers, ix. 199
    Ironmongers, ii. 242
    Mercers, ii. 404, 422–3
    Merchant Taylors, ii. 416; iv. 226
  Holborn, ix. 127 *n*
  Huguenots, ii. 27
  Inner Temple, ii. 434; iv. 162
  Lincolns Inn, ix. 134
  London House prison, iv. 16
  lord mayors, *see* Bromfield, Edw.; Dobbs; FitzAilwin, Hen.; Garraway, Hen.; Gurney, Sir Ric.; Perceval, Sir Jn.; Sheldon, Sir Jas.
  militia, i. 507
  mint, i. 349; iii. 60, 84
  Newgate, ii. 435
    prison, ii. 138
  persons from, i. 267, 497–9; ii. 133, 407, 461
  port, ii. 151, 154–6
  rly., ii. 205, 240; ix. 40
  rebellions, i. 514, 516
  roads to, i. 486; ii. 239–40, 266; iii. 2, 30, 32–3, 42–3, *44*, 46–7, 69–71; vii. 8; ix. 4; *and see* Stane Street
  St. Paul's cath., ii. 115 *n*, 249, 399; iv. 73
    deans, ix. 111; *and see* Colet; Gregory, Rob.; Nowell, Alex.
    St. Paul's Cross, ii. 15
  Savoy, the, i. 511; ii. 39
  schs.:
    Charterhouse, ii. 432
    Christ's Hosp., ii. 435–6
    City of London, ii. 431
    Merchant Taylors, ii. 407, 428
    and see Westminster
  sport, i. 305; ii. 467, 481
  synod, ii. 399
  Tower, i. 531; ii. 19, 233, 246, 302, 312; iv. 16, 184; vii. 85, 246
    constable, *see* Gage, Sir Jn.
    lieutenant, *see* Morley, Herb.
    Wharf, vii. 63
  trade with Suss., ii. 195, 211, 246–7, 276–7, 279–80, 285; iii. 30; ix. 13
  trades and ind.:
    bellfounding, ii. 249–51
    fish trade, ii. 266–8, 271
    hoops, ii. 236
    iron, ii. 242
    shipbuilding, ii. 132, 154, 157, 159 *n*, 164
    textiles, ii. 256
  Trinity Ho., *q.v.*
  Tyburn, ii. 28
  university, ii. 425, 429–30
  water supply, iv. 16
  and see Addington; Barking; Beckenham; Bermondsey; Blackheath; British Museum; Chelsea; Coulsdon; Croydon; Deptford;

Edmonton; Great Exhibition; Greenwich; Hackney; Hampton Court; Harmondsworth; Hounslow; Hurlingham; International Exhibition; Kensington; Kew; Kilburn; Kingston upon Thames; Lambeth; Marylebone Cricket Club; Merton; Morden; Putney; Richmond Park; Rotherhithe; Southwark; Staines; Stratford le Bow; Strawberry Hill; Streatham; Sunbury; Sydenham; Syon; Westminster; Wimbledon; Woolwich
London and Brighton Rly., ii. 223 n, 225 n, 240; vii. 37
London and Croydon Rly., ii. 240
London, Brighton, and South Coast Rly., i. 44; ii. 240
Londonderry (Irel.), ii. 164
Long (Longe):
  Joan, see Pyke
  Jn., prior of Hastings, ii. 77
  Ric., iv. 109
  Rob., master of Playden hosp., ii. 105
  Thos., ix. 61
  Wm. (fl. 1420), ix. 61
  Wm. (fl. 1773), ii. 166
  ——, ii. 96
Long Down, see Eartham
Long Man of Wilmington, see Wilmington
Longbridge (Langebregge) hund., i. 537; ii. 182 n, 226
Longcroft:
  Edw. Roy, iv. 128
  Hen., iv. 159 n
  Thos., iv. 159
  fam., iv. 107
Longdown (unidentified), ii. 467
Longe, see Long
Longley:
  Chas., vii. 124
  Jn., vii. 89
Longney (Glos.), ix. 209
Longstock estate, iv. 121, 132
Lons (Lonys), Jn., vii. 121 n
Lonsford, see Lunsford
Lonys, see Lons
Loppedelle, Wm. de, rector of Selsey, ix. 123
Lord:
  Jas. W., ii. 276
  Jn., vicar of Salehurst, ix. 224
  Priscilla, see Norman
  Thos., vicar of Salehurst, ix. 224
  W.E., ix. 276
  fam., ix. 274, 276
Lord's cricket ground, see Marylebone Cricket Club
Lordington, see Racton
Loring, T., ii. 166
Lorkyn:
  (formerly Mulstone), And., see Mulstone
  Thos., and his w. Marg., vii. 229–30
Lorraine (France), ii. 254–5
Losecroft, Jn., prior of Tortington, ii. 83
Loseley House (in Artington, Surr.), ii. 387
Lotfield (Lofeld, Lofilde) (in Streat hund.), vii. 92; and see Loxfield
Lothere, see Hlothere
Lotte, H.F., ii. 473
Lough Neagh (Irel.), i. 316
Louis VIII, as dauphin of France, i. 493–5; ii. 130; iii. 79; vii. 2; ix. 37, 49
Louis XIII, king of France, ii. 268
Louis XIV, king of France, ii. 158
Louis Philippe, king of France, vii. 64; ix. 5
Louis I, see Lajos; Luis
Louisberg (Canada), ii. 166
Louvain, Jocelin of, see Jocelin
Love, H., ii. 473
Lovel (fl. 1086), iv. 135; vii. 271

Lovel, see Lovell
Lovelace, Wm., ix. 150
Lovell (Lovel):
  Agnes, m. Jn. Empson, iv. 15
  Alice, m. —— Dawtrey, iv. 144
  Christiane, ? m. —— de Argenteyn, iv. 144
  Constance, see Hussey
  Eliz., m. 1 Sir Edw. Bray, 2 Sir Ant. Windsor, iv. 15, 129
  Eliz., w. of Wm., see St. Clare
  Francis, Ld. Lovell, vii. 110
  Hen. (fl. 1259), iv. 51, 144
  Hen., dean of Chich., ii. 51
  Hen. (d. 1506), iv. 11, 15, 64, 129
  Hugh, iv. 144
  Sir Jn., iv. 159
  Maud, see Holland
  Olive, m. Jn. de Gurney, iv. 144
  Ric., iv. 144
  Thos., ii. 250
  Wm., iv. 129
  fam., iv. 25, 144
Loveys, J., ii. 453
Lovintone, Jn. de, iv. 102
Low Countries, see Netherlands
Lowe:
  Edw. Clarke, canon of Ely, ii. 431 n, 433–4
  Geo., vii. 239
  Jn. (d. 1426), ix. 102, 110–11
  Jn. (fl. 1671), and his w. Mary, ix. 120
  Marg., w. of Jn., ix. 103
Lower, Mark Ant., i. 472 n; iii. 6, 54, 60
Lowestoft (Suff.), ii. 235
Lowther, Claude, ix. 132, 134
Loxfield (Framelle, Lokesfeld, Mellinges) hund., i. 537–8; ii. 226, 228; vii. 92 n, 93
Loxlye:
  Hen. de, and his w. Alice, iv. 230
  Rog. de, iv. 230
Loxwood, see Wisborough Green
Loyola, St. Ignatius, iv. 22
Lucas, clerk, ii. 411
Lucas:
  Ann, vii. 82
  Chas. J., i. 306; ii. 276, 480
  Edw., vii. 82
  Faith, ii. 83
  Francis, vii. 82
  J.C., i. 348
  Jn., warden of Windham hosp., ii. 108
  Jn. (fl. 1706), vii. 82
  Jn. (d. 1769), vii. 82
  Lucy, vii. 82
  Mary, m. Wm. Shadwell, vii. 82
  Sarah, vii. 82
  Wal., vii. 106, 109, 124
  Mr., ix. 198
Lucas Shadwell, see Shadwell
Luci, see Lucy
Lucian (classical author), ii. 406
Lucius III, pope, ii. 53
Lucke (Luke), Thos., ix. 28
Lucretius, ii. 414
Lucullus, C. Sallustius, iii. 15
Lucullus, son of Amminius, iii. 14–15
Lucuman, reeve, i. 483
Lucy (Luci):
  Geof. de, ii. 131; ix. 39
  Ric. de, ii. 53
  Wal. de, abbot of Battle, ii. 42, 53, 55–6; ix. 103
Ludd, Mr., ii. 245
Ludgater, Thos., iii. 162
Ludley, see Beckley
Ludlow (Ludlowe):
  Edm., vii. 17
  Thos. de, abbot of Battle, ii. 55; iv. 234
Ludwick, see Slinfold: Lydwicke
Luffa, Ralph, bp. of Chich., ii. 5–6, 47, 53, 332, 335, 342, 360, 366; iii. 82, 90, 97, 106, 116, 118, 121, 131, 146; iv. 30 n, 106, 166; vii. 69, 226, 237, 275, 281, 286

Luis, king of Jerusalem and Sicily, ii. 68*
Luke, son of William, ix. 180
Luke, see Lucke
Lukin, Jn. M., ix. 183
Lulham:
  Jn., ii. 250
  Wm., ii. 259
Lullingden, Wm., and his w. Joan, vii. 67 n
Lullington (Lullyngton), Wm., dean of Chich., ii. 48, 51
Lullington, ii. 44, 187
  adv., ii. 52
  ch., ii. 339, 372, 375
  earthworks, i. 480
  hare hunting, ii. 452
  pop., ii. 225
  vicarage, ii. 9
Lumley:
  Eliz., w. of Sir Jn., iv. 95
  Hen., iv. 116
  Jas., iii. 75; iv. 93, 122, 127
  Jane (or Joan), see FitzAlan
  Jn., Ld. Lumley, i. 519; ii. 302–3; iii. 75; iv. 23, 31, 36, 45, 59, 85, 89–90, 95, 97, 111, 118, 122, 127–8, 143–4, 153, 176–7, 203
  Julia, m. Alex. Jermyn, iv. 116 n
  Ric., Vct. Lumley, ii. 298; iii. 75; iv. 116 n, 118, 122, 128
  Ric., earl of Scarborough (d. 1721), ii. 305; iii. 75; iv. 93, 121–2, 127, 172, 189, 212
  his w., iv. 131
  Ric., earl of Scarborough (fl. 1730), iv. 118
  fam., ii. 303, 305; iv. 118, 122, 127, 133, 172
  arms, iii. 75; iv. 122
Lumnes, see Londnes
Lundsford family, see Lunsford
Lundsford (in Etchingham), see Etchingham
Lundy, A.C., iv. 195
Lunnesford, see Lunsford
Luns:
  Alice le, vii. 121
  Osbert le, vii. 121
Lunsford (Lonsford, Lundsford, Lunnesford):
  Agatha, w. of Hugh de, ix. 214 n
  Alice, w. of Ric. de, ix. 214 n
  Bart. de, ix. 214
  Cecily, ix. 198
  Eliz., see Echingham
  Hugh de, ix. 197, 214
  Joan, w. of Jn. de, see Somery
  Joan, w. of Wm., see Woknolle
  Jn. de (fl. 1214), ix. 214
  Jn. de (fl. 1287), ix. 214
  Jn. de (fl. 1289, ? another), ix. 240–1
  Jn. de (fl. 1339), ix. 241
  Jn. de (fl. 1360), ix. 145
  Jn. (fl. 1361, ? another), ix. 241
  Jn. (fl. 1372, another), ix. 214
  Jn., abbot of Robertsbridge, ii. 74
  Jn. de (fl. 1411), ix. 198, 214
  Jn. (fl. 1437), ix. 198
  Jn. (fl. 1467), iv. 202
  Jn. (fl. 1545), ix. 198, 214
  Jn. (fl. 1564), ii. 24
  Jn. (fl. 1606), ix. 254
  Sir Jn. (d. after 1615), ix. 198, 214
  Marg., see Ernele
  Margery, w. of Jn., ix. 214
  Margery, w. of ——, see Passeley
  Maud de, m. Wm. Gulafre, ix. 197, 214 n
  Ric. de, ix. 214
  Sim. de (fl. 1296), ix. 214
  Sim. de (fl. 1431), ix. 241
  Sir Thos., i. 529; ii. 197; ix. 198, 214
  Thomasine, w. of Wm., ix. 198
  Wm. de (fl. 1332), ix. 214
  Wm. de (fl. c. 1340, ? another), ix. 145
  Wm. de (d. 1352), ix. 214
  Wm. (fl. 1437), ix. 198

Lunsford (*cont.*):
 Wm. (d. *c.* 1469, another), ix. 214
 Wm. (fl. 1480), ix. 214
 Wm. (fl. 1488, ? another), ix. 106
 Wm. (d. 1531), ix. 214
 ——, i. 514
 fam., i. 529; ix. 137, 197, 214
 arms, ix. *214*
Luntley:
 Cath., *see* Barttelot
 Wm., iv. 161
Lurdingstrete, fam., ix. 266 *n*
Lurgashall, ii. 43; iv. 201
 Black Down, i. 49, 59–61
 ch., iv. 56
  accessories, ii. 352, 354, 356, 360
  archit., ii. 334, 340, 346, 348–9,
   364, 372–4, 376
 man., iv. 56
 pop., ii. 218
 tithe, ii. 263
Lusher, Nic., ix. 229
Lusignan:
 Alice of, m. Jn. de Warenne, earl of
  Surrey, vii. 2
 Guy de, i. 499
 Hugh of, count of La Marche, iii. 85;
  vii. 2
 Isabella, *q.v.*
 Ralph de, *see* Exoudun
 fam., ix. 2
Luther:
 Edw., iv. 175
 Jn., iv. 175
 Sarah, *see* Dawtrey
Lutman:
 Anne, m. Wm. Gordon, ix. 91
 Wm., ix. 91
 ——, m. Jn. Wenham Lewis, ix. 91
Lutudarum, *see* Matlock
Lutyens, Sir Edwin, iv. 152; vii. 109
Luxford:
 Anne, m. 1 —— Watson, 2 Laur.
  Price, vii. 144
 Anne, w. of Geo., ix. 229
 Anne, w. of Jn., *see* Dunk
 Cath. Sarah, *see* Curteis
 Edw., vii. 144, 180
 Geo. (d. 1631), vii. 100, 180, 190
 Geo. (fl. 1635), ix. 237
 Geo. (d. *c.* 1680), vii. 180, 190
 Geo. (fl. 1688), ix. 241
 Geo. (d. by 1759), ix. 229
 Hannah, *see* Jordan
 Hen., ix. 241
 Jn. (fl. 1668), ix. 248
 Jn. (d. 1673, another), vii. 100, 144,
  180
 Jn. (fl. 1806), ix. 151
 Mary, m. Wm. Hassell, vii. 101
 Ric. (d. 1653), vii. 180, 190
 Ric. (fl. 1668), ix. 248
 Thos. (fl. 1578), vii. 176
 Thos. (fl. 1655), vii. 121
 Thos. (fl. 1764), ix. 229
 Thos. (d. 1778, ? another), iii. 126
 Wm., vii. 190
 fam., vii. 100–1; ix. 248
 arms, vii. *101*
Luyde, Wm., iii. 93
Luzerne, la (Manche, France), abbey,
 iv. 162
lych gates, *see* architecture: ecclesiastical
Lychpole, *see* Sompting
Lydbury, Jn., abbot of Battle, ii. 54–5
Lydd (Kent), i. 135; ii. 142, 235, 473;
 ix. 34 *n*, 35–6
Lydwicke, *see* Slinfold
Lye Green, *see* Withyham
Lylye, *see* Lilley
Lylyott, Rob., iv. 138
Lyme Regis (Dors.), ix. 12
Lymesy, *see* Limesy
Lyminster, i. 483; ii. 42–3
 Batworth (Badworth) pk., ii. 297
 ch., ii. 121
  accessories, ii. 350–1, 354, 356,
   359–60, 372

archit., ii. 327, 332, 336–7, 342,
 346, 348–9, 351, 364–6, 370–2,
 374, 380 *n*
Crossbush, ii. 388
 pop., ii. 218
priory (Nunminster), ii. 4, 46, **121**,
 331, 365
Pynham (Calceto) priory, ii. 16–17,
 80–1, *92*, 304, 306; iv. 80, 93, 130
 archit., ii. 330, 348–9
 priors, ii. 80–1; iv. 6; *and see* Ivo;
  Parker, Ellis
 roads to, iii. 20, 46
 Rom. rem., iii. 60
Toddington, ii. 384, 388, *388*
 vicar, *see* Cartwright, Edm.
Lympne (Lemanae, Lemanis) (Kent),
 iii. 5–6, 8, 10, 30*; ix. 38
Lynberg, Tideman de, ii. 123
Lynch, *see* Linch
Lynche (Linces):
 Rog. de, iv. 108
 Urse de, iv. 66
Lyndon, Wm. de, rector of St. Cle-
 ments, Hastings, ix. 23
Lyndrigge, Wal. de, dean of Hastings
 coll., archdeacon of Lewes, ii. 116–
 17
Lyne:
 Phil., iv. 197
 Ric., iii. 77
Lynn, Wm., *see* Lenne
Lynton, Ant., rector of Worth, vii. 199
Lyon (Rhône, France), iii. 60, 69
Lyons:
 Hen. de, iv. 91
 Jn. de, iv. 91–2
 Ric. de, iv. 91
 fam., iv. 91
Lytton:
 Barbara, m. Wm. Warburton, ix. 212
 Eliz., m. Laur. Williams, ix. 212
 (formerly Strode), Sir Wm., *see*
  Strode
 Wm. Robinson, ix. 212
Lytton, Ld., *see* Bulwer-Lytton
Lytton, the, *see* Chich.
Lyvet (Lyvett), *see* Levett
Lywood, Leonard, ii. 447

Mabbott (Mabbot):
 Eliz., *see* Newton
 Thos., ii. 165
 Wm. Courthope, vii. 230–1
Mabel, prioress of Lyminster, ii. 121
Mabel, iv. 193
 her s., *see* Alexander
Maberley, Leonora Emily, vii. 163
Mabuse (Jan Gossaert), ix. 126*
Macartney:
 Jn., ii. 166
 Mervyn, iv. 234
MacCarthy, Rob., Ld. Clancarty, iv. 20
Macclesfield (Ches.), ii. 416, 421
McCleverty, Wm., ii. 166
McCormick:
 E.J., ii. 472
 G., ii. 473
MacDermott, K.H., iii. 50
MacDonald (Macdonald):
 Geo., ix. 8
 Jas. Ramsay, iii. 130
Macdonald-Buchanan, Mrs., iv. 60
Macedon, Phil. of, i. 324
Macedonia, iii. 30
McElderry, Prof. ——, iii. 30
McEwan, Douglas, ii. 478
McFarland, Jn., and his w. Eliz., iv. 189
Mackenzie (McKenzie):
 Harry Ward, ii. 432–3
 Jack, iii. 146
McKergrow, R.W., ii. 446
Mackie, Jn., iii. 145
Mackintosh, Dr., ii. 477
Maclean (Macleane):
 Arthur Jn., ii. 430–1
 Jn. L., ix. 214
Macro, Thos., ix. 56

Madden, Edw., iii. 145
Madehurst (Medlers), ii. 42–3, 443; iv.
 59
 ch., ii. 82; iv. 59
 Dale Pk., *q.v.*
 insects, i. 226, 228
 man., iv. 114, 123
 pop., ii. 217
 vicar, ii. 37
 vicarage, ii. 8
 and see Mehers
Madeira, i. 112
Madgewick (Madgwick):
 Edw. (fl. 1645), and his w. Mary, iv.
  129
 Edw. (fl. 1695), iv. 124
 Edw. (fl. 1793), iv. 124
 Eleanor, ix. 234
 Eliz., iv. 124
 Jn. (fl. 1684), iv. 93, 230
 Jn. (fl. 1713), iv. 124
 Kath., *see* Comber
 Mary, iv. 124
 Wm., iv. 124
 fam., iv. 124
Madingley (Cambs.), ix. 132
Magdala (Ethiopia), vii. 40
Magdalen College, Oxford, ii. 61–2, 81,
 97, 309, 404, 414, 420; iii. 137
Magdalen Hall, Oxford, ii. 408–9, 420;
 iv. 10; *and see* Hart Hall, Oxford;
 Hertford College, Oxford
Magdalene College, Cambridge, vii. 276
Magnentius, Rom. emperor, iii. 4, 64
Magnus, anchorite, ii. 47
Maher, J.H., rector of Brede, ix. 171
Maiden Bradley (Wilts.), priory, iv.
 108–10
Maidstone and Winchilsea:
 ctss. of, *see* Heneage, Eliz.
 earls of, *see* Finch: Heneage, Thos.
Maidstone (Kent), i. 503; ii. 156, 231,
 245
Mainard, abbot of Robertsbridge, ii. 73
Mainers, *see* Meyners
Mainz (Germany), iii. 61
Maitland:
 Ann, vii. 59
 Eliz., vii. 59
 Jn., vii. 59
 Rob. (fl. 1779), and his w. Eliz., vii.
  58–9
 Rob. (fl. 1829), vii. 59
 fam., vii. 58
Makenade, Wm., ii. 78
Malaga (Spain), battle, ii. 165
Malaya, i. 16
Malden, Mr., i. 538
Malemayns (Malemeins, Malmains,
 Malmayns):
 Agnes, w. of Nic., ii. 241–2
 Beatrice, m. Sir Otto de Grauntson,
  iv. 229
 Nic. (fl. before 1220), ii. 98
 Nic. (fl. 1263), ii. 241
 Nic. (d. 1291), iv. 229
 Nic. (d. 1349), iv. 229
 Ric. (? Nic.) de, iv. 230
 Wm., ii. 98
Malet:
 Marg., w. of Wal., vii. 236
 Rob., vii. 236
 Wal. (sr.), vii. 236
 Wal. (jr.), vii. 236
Malevile, Gilb. de, ix. 266
Malherbe, Wm., prior of Sele, ii. 62
Malim:
 Frances Eliz., iv. 212
 Mary Charlotte, iv. 212
Malling (Kent), i. 33
Malling Without, South, ii. 7, 44, 53,
 299; vii. 8, 14
 A.-S. rem., i. 336, 339
 bellfounding, ii. 251
 Bible Bottom, i. 171–2
 botany, i. 60
 ch., ii. 118, 230, 379, 412; vii. 18
 Clares chase, *q.v.*

Cliffe, *q.v.*
coll., ii. 3–4, 12, 20, 46, **117–19**, 311; vii. 196–7, 226, 235, 239
deans, ii. 61, 118–19, 311; vii. 197; *and see* Brent, Thos.
deanery, ii. 42, 44, 118
dean, ii. 118
earthworks, i. 480
insects, i. 138, 142–3, 146, 149, 152, 158, 161, 212–15, 217–18, 222
Malling Down, iii. 46, 69
man., ii. 3, 63, 117–18, 179, 186 *n*, 292, 296, 322; vii. 14, 129, 196; ix. 1
man. ho., ii. 333, 380
molluscs, i. 109
Oxsettle, i. 121
peculiar, ii. 3, 42
pop., ii. 227
Ranscombe:
  camp, iii. 64
  earthworks, i. **459–60**, *460*
  insects, i. 142, 156, 212, 214, 216
  prehist. rem., i. 460
  and see Ramestede
reeves, vii. 235
royal visit, i. 491
Southerham (Southeram), iii. 66; vii. 8
  ch., ii. 118
  fossils, i. 30–1, 33–5
  insects, i. 153, 156, 216
  quarrying, ii. 231
  Stoneham, i. 140, 220; iii. 2, 47, 69; vii. 50
vicar, ii. 468
Mallinges, *see* Mallyng
Mallory, And., ii. 422
Mallyng (Mallinges, Mallynge):
  Jn. de (fl. before 1272), vii. 24 *n*
  Jn. (fl. 1480), ii. 412
  Wm. de, and his w. Marg., vii. 81
Malmains (Malmayns), *see* Malemayns
Malmesbury, Wm. of, i. 481; iii. 83, 105
Malmesbury (Wilts.), ii. 394
Malta, i. 535
Maltby:
  Edw., bp. of Chich., iv. 198
  Wm., ii. 166
Maltby (Yorks. W.R.), *see* Roche abbey
malting, *see* brewing
maltode tax, ii. 233; ix. 50, 55
Maltravers, fam., arms, iii. 151, 154; iv. 131; ix. 216
Maltravers, Ld., *see* Arundel, Jn.; Fitz-Alan; Lady, *see* FitzAlan, Anne; FitzAlan, Eleanor
mammals, i. **299–307**
  prehist. rem., i. 312
Man, *see* Mann
Man, Isle of, ii. 167
Manasses, count of Guines, ix. 149
  his w., *see* Arques, Emma de
Manchester, ii. 254, 285, 408, 469
Mandeville, fam., arms, ix. 135
Manewode, *see* Manhood
Manfeld, Reynold, iv. 270
mangolds, *see* crops
Manhood (Manewode, Manwood, Man-woode, Sumerlege, Westringes), hund., i. 538; ii. 221; iii. 103; iv. 1, **198**; vii. 264
Manhood and Selsey Tramway, *see* Hundred of Manhood
Manhood End, *see* Birdham
Manhood peninsula, i. 45, 52, 168
Maning, *see* Manning
Mann (Man):
  Sir Horace, ix. 20
  Thos., ii. 96
  fam., ix. 20 *n*
Manners:
  Lady Bridget, m. Rob. Tyrwhitt, ix. 212
  Geo., earl of Rutland, iii. 87
  Hen., earl of Rutland, i. 516
  Herb., iii. 163
  Jas., iii. 160

Ld. Rob., ii. 443
  Rog., earl of Rutland, ix. 212
Manning (Maning):
  Anne, m. 1 Sir Thos. Lawley, 2 Sir Jn. Glynn, ix. 207
  Edw., iv. 223
  Eliz., m. 1 Rob. Carson, 2 Francis Coventry, ix. 207
  Hen., rector of Graffham and Wool-avington, cardinal, ii. 41; iii. 122; iv. 60, 65; vii. 234
  Jn., ix. 207
Manningham:
  Eliz., w. of Thos., iii. 126
  Thos., bp. of Chich., ii. 438; iii. 126
Mannock:
  Eliz., *see* Aylwin
  Sir Wm., iv. 31
manor houses, *see* architecture: civil and dom.
Mansell (Mansel, Maunsel):
  Bussy, Ld. Mansell, vii. 89, 101
  Chris., Ld. Mansell, vii. 89, 101
  Francis, vii. 247
  Jn., i. 495; vii. 283
  Louisa Barbara, m. Geo. Venables Vernon, Ld. Vernon, ii. 440; vii. 89, 91
  Nic., iv. 98
  Sir Rob., ii. 155
  Thos., Ld. Mansell, vii. 101
  Thos., ii. 167
Mansfield:
  Eliz., *see* Thatcher
  Hen., ix. 191
Mansfield, Ld., *see* Murray, Wm.
mansion houses, *see* architecture: civil and dom.
Mantell:
  Gideon, i. 27, 32, 36–8, 260, 339; iii. 60; vii. 12, 19
  H.K., ii. 453
  Joshua, ix. 253
  Thos., vii. 42
manures, ii. 273, 282, 286, 289
  lime, ii. 274–5
  marling, ii. 273
Manwaring, Wm., ii. 166
Manwood (Manwoode), *see* Manhood
Mapledurham (Hants), iv. 24
Maplehurst, *see* Ore
Maplesden (in Ticehurst), *see* Ticehurst
Marazion (Cornw.), iii. 68
March bros., vii. 13
March:
  ctss. of, *see* Lennox, Amy; Mortimer, Anne
  earls of, *see* Edward IV; Lennox, Chas.; Mortimer, Edm.; Mor-timer, Rog.
Marchant (Marchand, Marchaunt):
  Jn. (fl. 1362), ix. 157 *n*
  Jn. (d. before 1873), vii. 176
  Joshua le, iii. 144
  Ric., ii. 132
  Rob., ix. 157 *n*
  Steph., ix. 157 *n*
  Thos., vii. 176
  Wm., ix. 154, 157
  fam., vii. 176
Marci:
  Ela de, *see* Dene
  Wm. de, ii. 86
Marden, Jn., and his w. Rose, iv. 112
Marden (united parish), iv. 107–8
Marden, East, ii. 43; iv. 88, 91, **107–8**, 109
  adv., iv. 108, 110
  ch., ii. 339, 349; iv. 107–8, *107*
  dom. archit., iv. 107
  East Marden Down, iv. 107
  insects, i. 169
  man., iv. 107, 109
  pop., ii. 221
  prebend (Mardon), ii. 48; iv. 107–8
  roads, iv. 107
  Rom. rem., iii. 61
Marden, North, i. 524; ii. 43, 303*; iv.

88, 107, **108–10**
  adv., iv. 108, 110
  char., iv. 94
  ch., ii. 339, 342, 366; iv. 109–10, *110*
  curate, iv. 110
  man., iv. 107–11
  North Marden Down, iv. 108
  pop., ii. 221
  prehist. rem., iv. 108
  roads, iv. 108
Marden, Up, ii. 43, 93, 283; iv. 80, 88, 91, **110–13**, 121
  adv., ii. 81; iv. 93, 111, 113, 125
  char., iv. 94
  ch., ii. 9, 15–16, 84; iv. 110, 112–13, *112–13*
    accessories, ii. 250, 355
    archit., 339, 348, 365
  dom. archit., iv. 110
  earthworks, iv. 110
  insects, i. 169, 173
  man., iv. 109–12, 114, 122, 128
  Marden, West, iv. 88, 94, 110
    adv., iv. 113
    chap., ii. 15; iv. 112
    insects, i. 183
    man., iv. 111–12
    Rom. rem., iii. 28
  mill, iv. 111
  pop., ii. 221
  prehist. rem., iv. 110
  roads, iv. 110
  Rom. rem., iii. 61
  tithes, iv. 111 *n*
  vicarage, ii. 9
  Watergate Hanger, iii. 20, 61
Marden, vale of, iv. 8
Marden, West, *see* Marden, Up: Mar-den, West
Mardon, prebend, *see* Marden, East: prebend
Mare, Jn. de la, vii. 204
Mareschall, *see* Marshal
Maresfield, ii. 44, 291, 313–19, 322; vii. 94
  botany, i. 60, 65
  Braby's (Braberry) Hatch, ii. 322
  Buntisgrove (Bunchgrove), ii. 319
  Butcher's Cross, i. 57
  Camp Hill, iii. 44, 46
  chant., ii. 20
  ch., ii. 314, 316, 336, 352, 354–6, 366, 370, 377
  Coldharbour, i. 55
  Cophall, i. 207
  Duddleswell, iii. 44, 46
    Gate, i. 55
    lodge, ii. 317, 319
    man., ii. 318, 322
    walk, ii. 318–19
  Fairwarp, ii. 44; iii. 31, 44
  Horney (Harney) common, ii. 319
  Lampool (Lampol), ii. 314; iii. 44
  man., ii. 175, 181, 322
  Milbrook, ii. 319
  Nutley, ii. 44, 200
    Hill, i. 55
  Oldlands, iii. 29, 31
  pk., ii. 297, 315–16
  Pippingford (Pippinford, Pipp-yngworth):
    lodge, ii. 317, 319
    walk, ii. 319
  pop., ii. 227
  prehist. rem., i. 330
  Pressrtdge Warren, i. 60
  Prickett Hatch, ii. 322
  rector, ii. 314, 316; *and see* Taylor, Ric.
  roads to, iii. 43–4, 46, 69–70
  Rom. rem., iii. 29, 31, 43–4, 69–70
  Stumblewood, *see* Stomlett
  Sweet Mine Pits, i. 55
  tithes, ii. 315
  trades and ind., ii. 238, 241, 248, 257, 296
  White House, ii. 319, 321
  Wych Cross (Wichecross, Witch-

Maresfield
Wych Cross (cont.):
cross), i. 55; ii. 319
botany, i. 60
insects, i. 166, 179, 188
quarrying, ii. 230
Margaret (of France), queen of Edw. I,
iv. 95
Margaret, queen of Hen. VI, ii. 113
Margaret, dchss. of Norfolk, dau. of
Thos. de Brotherton, iv. 184
Margaret (fl. 1380), ii. 121
Margary, Ivan, iii. 31, 44, 69
Margerison, Rob., ix. 152
Margery, prioress of Easebourne, see
Pygon
Marie, princess of Roumania, ix. 167
marine algae, i. **62–4**
marine zoology, i. **71–107**
Marini, Chris., cardinal priest of St.
Cyriacus, dean of Chich., ii. 48
Marinis, Aubrey de, and his w. Eleanor,
vii. 67
Marinus, iii. 9
Mariteau, ——, ii. 258
maritime history, i. 492; ii. **125–67**; iii.
87, 102; and see coast, defence of
Mark Cross, see Rotherfield
Markely:
Agatha, w. of Jn. de, iv. 161
Alice de, iv. 161
Jn. de, iv. 161
market gardening, ii. 285–6; iv. 188; vii.
87, 98, 116, 119, 172
markets, see Arundel; Battle; Bodiam;
Bognor Regis; Bosham; Brighton;
Bulverhythe; Burwash; Chich.;
Cocking; Crawley; Cuckfield;
Ditchling; Grinstead, East; Hail-
sham; Harting; Hastings; Hurst-
pierpoint; Lewes; Midhurst;
Northiam; Pagham; Petworth;
Pevensey; Preston; Robertsbridge;
Rye; Shoreham; Wartling; West-
bourne; Winchelsea
Markewyk, see Markwick
Markham:
Sir Clements, ii. 143
Gervase, ii. 273
Sir Jn., i. 516
Markly, see Warbleton
Markwick (Markewyk):
Edw., vii. 87, 236
Jas., ix. 20
Mary, see Eversfield
Wm., ix. 107
(later Eversfield), Wm., see Eversfield
——, i. 273 n, 279, 282–4, 290, 293
Marlborough:
ctss. of, see Butler, Jane
duke of, see Churchill, Jn.; Spencer,
Geo.
earl of, see Ley, Jas.
Marlborough (Wilts.), ii. 3, 316
Coll., ii. 471–2
Marlebergh, Jn. de, and his w. Agnes,
iv. 98
Marlepast, see Horsham: Marlpost
Marlett, Wm., i. 527
Marley, Edw., prior of Michelham,
ii. 79
marling, see manures
Marlott:
Jn., iv. 213
Jos., iv. 213
Ric., iv. 213
Marlpost, see Horsham
Marmion:
Isabel, see Plaiz
Jn., vii. 54
Rob., i. 495
Rog., ii. 122
arms, ix. 135
Marmoutier (Bas-Rhin, France), abbey,
ii. 46, 52, 65, 123
Marne ware, see Romano-British Suss.:
pottery
Marney, Wm., ix. 154

Marsden:
R.G., ii. 154
Mrs., ix. 148
Marsh (Marshe, Mersh, Merssh):
J.W., ii. 474
Jn. (fl. 1400), ii. 124
Jn. (fl. 1574), ii. 106
Jn. (fl. 1656), ii. 321
Letitia, vii. 183
Wm., abbot of Battle, ii. 55
Wm. (fl. 1524), ii. 97
Wm. (fl. 1574), ii. 106
marshal, see Gilbert the marshal; John
the marshal; Ralph the marshal
Marshal (Mareschall, Marshall):
Anselm, iv. 183
Cecily, see Thorney
Chas., vii. 266
Eleanor, see Eleanor, dau. of King
John
Gilb., iv. 145, 163, 195
Hen., vicar of Wilmington, ii. 106
Isabel, m. Gilb. de Clare, earl of
Gloucester, iv. 230
Jn., sheriff of Suss., iv. 183
Jn., rector of Ovingdean, iv. 183
Mary, w. of Wal., iv. 183
Maud, m. 1 Hugh Bigod, 2 Wm. de
Warenne, earl of Surrey, iii.
125 n; iv. 163, 183; vii. 2, 194
Maud, m. Hugh d'Aubigny, earl of
Arundel, iv. 59, 98 .
Ric., Earl Marshal, iv. 183
Rog., iv. 42
Sam., vii. 54
Steph., vii. 203 n
T.A., i. 124
Wal., earl of Pembroke, Earl Marshal,
iv. 163, 183
Wal., prior of Boxgrove, ii. 59
Wm., earl of Pembroke (d. 1219),
sheriff of Suss., iii. 79; iv. 183,
230
Wm., earl of Pembroke (d. 1231), iv.
163; vii. 2
Wm. (fl. 1250), iii. 91
Wm. (fl. 1835), vii. 139, 232, 266
Capt., i. 528
fam., iv. 163
Marshal, Earl, see Earl Marshal
Marshalsea prison, see Southwark
Marshe, see Marsh
Martel:
Alan, iv. 159
Amice, w. of Rog., iv. 158
Ela, m. Peter FitzReynold, iv. 158–9
Eliz., m. 1 Jn. Bonville, 2 Ric.
Stukeley, iv. 159
Eliz., w. of Herb., iv. 159
(or FitzRoger), Hen., iv. 159
Herb., iv. 159
Joan, m. Reynold FitzReynold, iv.
158–9
Joan, w. of Rog., iv. 158
(or FitzRoger), Jn., iv. 159
Marg., w. of Wm., iv. 158
Rog. (fl. c. 1240), iv. 158
Rog. (d. 1280), iv. 158
Rog. (d. 1334), iv. 159
Thos., iv. 159
Wm., iv. 158
Martello towers, i. 534; ii. 162–3; ix. 123
Marten, see Martin
Martin IV, pope, ii. 57
Martin, and his w. Julian, ii. 101
Martin (Marten, Martyn):
Ann, w. of Mic., vii. 100
Anne, w. of Jn., ix. 177
Denny, vii. 259
Edw., iii. 161
Geo., ii. 166
Hen., vii. 111 n
Joan, iv. 171
Joan, m. —— Wykes, ix. 128
Jn. (fl. 1700), vii. 239, 259
Jn. (d. 1741), vii. 100
Jn. (fl. 1760), ix. 177
Jn. (d. 1797), vii. 100

Mary, ix. 177
Mic., vii. 100
Peter, iii. 32, 35, 53, 63
Ric., and his w. Joan, vii. 96
Rob., ii. 164
Sarah, ix. 177
Sim., ix. 128
Sybil, see Michelborne
Thos. (fl. 1593), iv. 111
Thos. (d. 1684), ix. 207
——, ii. 475
Martindale, Mr., ii. 454
Martinsgrove, see Oving
Martyn, see Martin
Martyrs Memorial Trust, vii. 124, 220;
ix. 28, 276
Mary I, i. 305; ii. 21–2, 48, 150; iv. 223,
230; vii. 85, 220, 227, 238, 284; ix.
153
Mary, queen of Jas. II, iv. 16–17
Mary, queen of Scots, i. 519; vii. 6
Mary, dchss. of Kent, ii. 204
Mary, prioress of Easebourne, ii. 85
Maryland (U.S.A.), ii. 201
Marylebone Cricket Club (M.C.C.), ii.
467–71, 475–6
Lord's cricket ground, ii. 468–70,
473–5
Mascall:
Anne, ix. 157
Caroline, m. Herb. Curteis, ix. 157
Edw., vii. 111
Frances, m. Wm. Kenrick, ix. 157
Jn. (d. 1571), vii. 109–11, 121, 159
Jn. (d. 1769), ix. 157
Leonard, ii. 299
Martha, see Curteis
Nic., and his w. Agatha, vii. 159
Ric. (fl. 1528), ii. 260
Ric. (fl. before 1540), vii. 121
Ric. (fl. 1620), vii. 111, 123
Rob. (fl. 1740), ix. 157
Rob. (d. by 1777), ix. 157
Rob. (d. by 1821), ix. 157
fam., vii. 110; ix. 161
arms, vii. 111
Mascalls, East, see Lindfield
Masher Wood (unidentified), i. 138
Mason:
Chris., ii. 165
Eliz., w. of Thos., ix. 25
Thos., ix. 25
Wm., iii. 73
Massines, see Beckley
Massingberd:
Ann, ix. 248
Eliz., see Hoo
Sir Thos., ix. 233, 248
Massyngham, Hugh, ii. 412
Masters, Jas. Hoare, warden of St.
Mary's hosp., Chich., ii. 102
Mather, Wm., ii. 167
Matlock (Lutudarum) (Derb.), iii. 163
Matsys, Quentin, ix. 126
Matthew, dean of Chich., ii. 50; iii. 103
his s., see Simon
Matthew, prior of Tortington, ii. 83
Matthews (Matthew):
Geo., ii. 238
Hen., vii. 275
Jas., iii. 126
Ric., ii. 166
Sarah, w. of Jas., iii. 126
Thos., vii. 43
Maud, queen of Hen. I, ii. 99
Maud, Empress, i. 490
Maud, m. Robert of Mortain, ii. 122
Mauden, Gunnor de, m. Brian Fitz-
Ralph, iv. 44–5, 47, 69, 80
Maufe:
Brunna, see St. Sampson
Joan, m. Alan de Chartres, iv. 111 n
Sim., vii. 111 n
Wm., i. 498, 500; ii. 316
Mauger (fl. 1086), iv. 195
Maunsel, see Mansell
Mauny, Sir Wal. de, ii. 138
Maurice, ct. of Nassau, prince of

Orange, i. 518
Mavesyn:
  Hen., ix. 241
  Jn. (fl. 1339), ix. 241
  Jn. (fl. 1446), ix. 241
  Philippe, m. Jn. Engehame, ix. 241
Maw, Mr., vii. 260
Mawle, H., ii. 473
Mawrynge, Thos., ii. 99
Mawtalye, Peter, iv. 120
Maxfield, see Guestling
Maximian, Rom. emperor, iii. 4
Maximus, Rom. emperor, iii. 7
Maxstoke (Warws.), ix. 259
Maxwell, Dr., ii. 160
May (Maye):
  Ant. (d. by 1614), ix. 230
  Sir Ant. (d. 1636), sheriff of Suss.,
    vii. 217; ix. 214, 221 n, 255
  Ant. (fl. 1670), ix. 233
  Audrey, see Wildgose
  Barbara, w. of Thos., ix. 197
  Caroline, m. Ric. Wetherell, ix. 255
  Edw. (fl. 1624), ix. 255
  Edw. (d. 1693), ix. 255
  Francis, ix. 255
  Geo., ix. 197, 230
  Hen., ix. 255
  Jane, m. Jos. Henshaw, iv. 103
  Joan, w. of Ant., m. 2 Jn. Giles, 3 Jn.
    Busbridge, ix. 230, 233, 237
  Jn. (fl. 1545), iv. 106
  Jn. (d. 1631), iv. 104, 106
  Sir Jn. (d. 1672), i. 529; iv. 104, 163
  Jn. (d. 1677), iv. 104
  Mary, w. of Sir Jn., see Morley
  Mary, w. of Ric., iv. 104
  Mary, w. of Thos., ix. 254
  Mary (? another), ix. 256
  Ric. (d. 1588), iv. 64, 104
  Ric. (fl. 1590), iv. 104
  Sir Ric. (fl. 1674), iii. 80
  Ric. (fl. 1681, ? another), iv. 161
  Sir Ric. (fl. c. 1700, ? another), ix. 255
  Rob., ii. 83
  Susannah, m. Sir Ric. May, ix. 255
  Thos., prior of Tortington, ii. 83
  Thos. (d. 1552), ix. 255
  Thos. (d. 1610), ix. 214, 255
  Thos. (fl. 1623), iv. 106
  Thos. (fl. 1642), M.P. for Midhurst,
    i. 523
  Thos. (fl. 1686), iv. 106
  Thos. (d. c. 1690, another), ix. 255
  Sir Thos. (d. 1718), iv. 101, 104
  (formerly Brodnax), Thos., see
    Brodnax
  Thos. (fl. 1795), ix. 254–5
  fam., iv. 104; ix. 256
  arms, iv. 104; ix. 256
Maydenhithe, Jn. de, dean of Chich., ii.
  48, 51; iii. 111 n
Maydeston, Wm., abbot of Bayham, ii.
  89
Maye, see May
Mayer (or Fyner), Harry, ii. 242
Mayeslond, see Ashdown forest
Mayfield, i. 505; ii. 2–3, 43–4; ix. 1, 193,
  195, 209
  assarts, ii. 189
  Bibleham (Bevilham), ix. 79, 193, 196
  man., ii. 173 n, 178–9; ix. 3, 79
  ch., ii. 2, 18
    accessories, ii. 242 n, 249–50, 355–
      6, 358–60, 362, 378
    archit., ii. 336, 340, 344, 346, 350–
      1, 374, 378
  ct., ii. 189, 292
  dom archit., ii. 389–91
  farmers' club, ii. 289
  Frankham pk., ii. 295, 297, 316
  heretics burnt at, ii. 22
  natural history, i. 41, 285
  palace of abp. of Cant., ii. 333, 346,
    383
  pk., ii. 297
  pop., ii. 226
  prebend, ii. 118

prehist. rem., i. 330
rectory, ii. 12
roads, ii. 240
sch., ii. 439
trades and ind., ii. 252, 259–60, 296
vicarage, ii. 8
vicars, ii. 439; and see Maynard, Jn.
woodland, ii. 300
Mayhew:
  Hubert Edgar, ix. 124
  Nic., iv. 136
Mayn, see Mayne
Maynard (Maynerde):
  Sir Hen., iv. 115
  Jn., ix. 157, 178
  Jn., vicar of Mayfield, ii. 35
  Kath., see Gunter
  Ric., ii. 408
  Wm., iv. 115
  ——, ii. 33
Mayne (Mayn):
  Ric., vii. 171; ix. 183
  Wm., rector of Mid Lavant, iv.
    106
Maynerde, see Maynard
Maytham (Kent), ix. 144
Meade:
  (later Meade Fetherstonhaugh), Sir
    Herb., iv. 16
  Sir Jn., iv. 64
Meade-Waldo, ——, i. 277, 280, 284
Meadhome, see Petworth: Medhone
Mears & Co., bellfounders (including
  C. & G., Thos., W. & T., Wm.),
  iii. 162–4; iv. 187, 210, 217, 225,
  233; vii. 97, 132; ix. 111, 148, 156,
  171, 223, 231, 246, 264
Mears & Stainbank, ix. 203
Mears, and see Chapman & Mears
measurage, ix. 84
Meching, see Newhaven
Mecklenburg-Strelitz, prince of, see
  Ernest
mede panes, ix. 80
Medehei (unidentified), ix. 239
Medeley, see Medley
Medhone, see Petworth
Mediterranean Sea, i. 258; ii. 144, 155,
  164–7
Medlers, see Madehurst
Medley (Medeley):
  Adam de, iv. 61 n
  Annabella, m. Jn. Evelyn, vii. 33; ix.
    191
  Edw., vii. 81; ix. 191
  Geo., vii. 32, 218; ix. 180, 191
  Jane, ix. 191
  Susan, see Raynes
  Thos. (d. 1728), vii. 33, 35, 82, 218;
    ix. 180, 191
  Thos. (d. 1796), vii. 33
  fam., ix. 191–2
  arms, vii. 33; ix. 191
Medmerry, see Selsey
Medstede (Medsted):
  And. de, sheriff of Suss., vii. 225
  Sir Phil., i. 512; vii. 225
  Phil. (another), vii. 225
  arms, vii. 225
Medusa, iii. 22–3
Medwall, Hen., master of hosp. of Holy
  Cross, Winchelsea, ii. 107
Medway, riv., i. 42, 58, 61; ii. 153, 158,
  453, 463; iii. 45
Meeching, see Newhaven
Meffant:
  Eliz., m. 1 Sir Rog. Lewknor (d.
    1543), 2 Ric. Lewknor, iv. 7, 35;
    vii. 226; ix. 263
  Thos., iv. 35
Mehers (? Midhurst or Madehurst), iv.
  80
Meinert, ——, i. 261
Meinieres, see Meyners
Meinild:
  Sibyl del, see Lisle
  Wm. del, iv. 34 n
Melbourne (Australia), ii. 433

Meleburn, Jordan de, dean of Chich., ii.
  50
Melgrave, see Hellingly
Melkhurst:
  Adam de, ix. 229
  Alice de, ix. 229
  Rob. de, ix. 229
Mellinges, see Loxfield hund.
Menchecurt, Guy de, vii. 55
Mendham, Sophia, ix. 29
Mene, Wal., abbot of Durford, ii. 90–1
Meon, East, hund. (Hants), ii. 221 n
Meonwaras, i. 482
Mercer:
  Jn., prior of Arundel, ii. 120
  Thos., ix. 237
Mercers' Company, see London: guilds
Merchant Taylors' Company, see Lon-
  don: guilds
Merchant Taylors school, see London:
  schs.
Mercia, i. 347
  kings, see Coenwulf; Offa; Wulfhere
Mercredesburn (Mercroedsburn), riv.,
  battle, i. 334, 481
Meresey (unidentified), iii. 102
Mereworth:
  Christiane de, see Wykes
  (or Wykes), Wal. de, iv. 171
Merfeld:
  Jn., i. 514
  Wm., i. 514
Meri:
  Lucy de, see Bohun
  (or Bohun), Muriel de, see Bohun
  Ric. de, iv. 77
Merley, fam., arms, ix. 135
Merrick (Meyrick):
  Geo., ix. 232
  Ric., iv. 160
Merricks:
  Ric., mayor of Chich., iv. 230
  Wal., ix. 187
Merrifield, Mrs., i. 72
Merriman (Meryman):
  Edw., ii. 415
  ——, ii. 28
Merrow (Surr.), ii. 56
Merry, Mr., ii. 459
Mersey, Steph., abbot of Durford, ii.
  90–1
Mersey, Vct., see Bigham
Mersh, see Marsh
Mershe Green, see Withyham: Lye
  Green
Mershurst, Herb. de, iv. 56
Merssh, see Marsh
Merston, ii. 43; iv. 133, **158–60**, 165
  adv., iv. 159–60, 170
  char., iv. 160
  ch., ii. 339, 374; iv. 158–60, 160
  dom. archit., iv. 158
  man., iv. 158–60, 167
  mills, iv. 158
  pop., ii. 220
  tithes, iv. 158
Merstone, Emeline de, iii. 72
Mertens, F.M.D., ii. 434
Merton, Wal. de, ix. 52
Merton (Surr.), ix. 38
Merton College, Oxford, ii. 420
Mervyn (Mervin):
  Anne, see Harleston
  Edith, see Windsor
  Sir Edm. (fl. 1544), iv. 17*, 25–6, 28,
    92, 116
  Edm. (fl. 1606), iv. 230
  Eliz., m. Peter Bettesworth, iv. 28
  Eliz., w. of Sir Edm., see Pakenham
  Hen., ii. 24; iv. 15, 17, 21, 25–6, 28,
    92
Meryman, see Merriman
Meryon, Sarah, m. Wm. Holloway, ix.
  61
Messel, L., ii. 480
Messier, Jn., prior of Arundel, ii. 120
Messina (Sicily), iv. 145; ix. 49
Meteyard, Mr., iv. 54

Metham, Jordan, ix. 191
Metherall, R., iv. 195
Methodists, iv. 77, 227; vii. 42, 62,
147–8, 172, 181, 192; ix. 7, 61–2,
123–4, 144, 148, 152, 157, 160, 168,
171–2, 190, 224–5, 247, 249, 257,
265, 272
Mewet, Ellis, iv. 35
Mewy, Wm., sacrist of Bosham coll., ii.
112
Meynell, Mic. de, ix. 50
Meyners (Mainers, Meinieres):
Agnes de, m. Wm. de Benfield, vii.
68, 189, 280
Isabel de, m. Phil. de Neubaud, vii.
68, 280
Maud de, see Freschville
Ralph de, vii. 68, 280
Reynold de, ix. 221, 278
Meyrick, see Fuller-Meyrick; Merrick
Michael, bailiff of Atherington, ii. 120
Miche, Oliver, bailiff of Atherington, ii.
120
Michel park, see Northchapel: Mitchell
pk.
Michelborne (Michelbourne):
Abraham, vii. 179
Anne, see Ashburnham
Arthur, ix. 197
Bridget, vii. 239, 259
Cordelia, w. of Sir Ric., vii. 239
Dorothy, see Shoyswell
Edw. (fl. c. 1570), ix. 235
Edw. (d. 1609, ? another), ix. 237
Edw. (fl. 1614), vii. 141, 144
Edw. (fl. 1617, ? another), ix. 237
Edw. (d. 1701), vii. 117, 239, 259
Francis, vii. 179
Geo., vii. 239
Jn. (fl. 1541), ix. 235
Jn. (fl. 1552, another), vii. 259; ix.
155
Jn. (fl. c. 1570, another), vii. 116–17;
ix. 235
Jn. (d. by 1604), ix. 235
Jn. (fl. 1653), vii. 117, 239
Lawr., vii. 259; ix. 155
Mary, m. —— Bethell, ix. 197
Nic., ix. 235
Ric. (d. 1588), vii. 196–7, 259
Ric. (d. 1607), vii. 106, 144 n, 197 n
Sir Ric. (d. 1638), vii. 106, 109, 179,
239, 259
Sybil, m. Jn. Martin, vii. 239, 259
Thos. (d. 1582), ix. 155
Thos. (d. 1582, another), iv. 42
Thos. (d. 1584), vii. 196, 259
Thos. (d. by 1656), ix. 197
Thomasine, m. —— Thorpe, ix. 197
Wm., vii. 106, 117, 179, 239, 259
——, i. 529
——, m. Launcelot Davis, ix. 235
——, m. Ric. Dunk, ix. 235
fam., ix. 155
arms, vii. 117
Michelgrove (Michellgrove):
Eliz., m. Jn. Shelley, iii. 105; iv. 185
Hen., ii. 25 n
Joan, see Whelton
Jn. (d. by 1439), iii. 105; iv. 185, 202
Jn. (d. by 1459), iii. 105; iv. 185
Jn. (fl. 1459), iv. 185
Mary, see Sidney
fam., i. 513; ii. 63
arms, iv. 23
Michelgrove, see Clapham
Michelham (in Arlington):
man., ii. 296
Michelham (or Peverse) pk., ii. 77,
313
priory, ii. 13–14, 58, 77–80, 83, 242,
464
accessories, ii. 353
archit., ii. 330, 337, 374, 383, 395
earthworks, i. 477
estates, ii. 77, 305, 313–14; iv. 153;
vii. 71, 257
patronage, ii. 87

priors, ii. 78–9, 87, 183 n, 184; vii.
256; ix. 139; and see Leem
royal visits, i. 505; ii. 78
sub-prior, see Parker, Ellis
Michell (Mitchell):
Davy, ii. 25
Edm., vii. 160, 194
Fred., ii. 253
G.S., iii. 52
Hen., vii. 123
Jas. Chas., vii. 78
Jane, see Chambre
Jn. (d. 1525), vii. 121, 160
Jn. (d. 1546), vii. 121, 160
Jn. (fl. 1567), vii. 157
Jn. (fl. 1825), vii. 78
Martha, m. Jas. Hutchins, vii. 78
Mary, vii. 59
Milicent, vii. 162
Ric., vii. 36
Rob. Wm., ix. 30
Thos. (fl. before 1528), ii. 416–17,
419–20
Thos. (fl. 1548), ii. 312
Thos. (d. 1551), vii. 169, 194
Thos. (fl. 1597), vii. 36
Thos. (d. 1624), vii. 59, 157, 160,
169, 196
W., i. 278
Wm., ii. 253
Mr., vicar of Brighton, rector of West
Blatchington, vii. 262
Michellgrove, see Michelgrove
Mickleham (Micklam) (Surr.), ii. 468
Micklethwait (Micklethwaite):
Eliz., see Peckham
Geo. Nat., ix. 221
Jn., ix. 212, 221
Sir Sotherton Branthwayt Peckham,
ix. 212–13, 221, 224
fam., ix. 222
Mid Lavant, see Lavant, Mid
Middle Saxons, see Saxons: Middle
Middleborgh, see Barcombe
Middleborough (Middelborch, Middle-
bourgh) (in Holmestrow hund.),
vii. 61
Middleburgh (Netherlands), iii. 101 n,
102
Middlesex, earls of, see Cranfield; Sack-
ville, Chas.; Sackville, Lionel
Middlesex, i. 534–5; ii. 467, 472–3, 475
and see Chelsea; Edmonton; Hamp-
ton Court; Harmondsworth;
Hounslow; Kensington; Kil-
burn; Staines; Stratford le Bow;
Strawberry Hill; Sunbury; Syon;
Westminster; Whitechapel
Middleton (Midelton, Myddelton):
Anne, see Fawkenor
Arthur, vii. 34
David, ix. 95 n, 96–7
Edm., and his w. Anne, vii. 183
Edw., vii. 37, 220
Elliott, see More
Everard de, and his w. Agatha, iv. 157
Frances, m. Rob. Day, vii. 34, 124
Frances, w. of Jn., vii. 134
Francis, vii. 344
Hen., ii. 165
Jane, see Lewknor
Jn. de, iv. 157 n
Jn., ii. 312; vii. 34, 124, 134
Lewknor, vii. 96–7
Ric., vii. 134 n
Rob., vii. 163
Thos. (fl. 1560), vii. 220
Thos. (fl. 1630), and his w. Barbara,
vii. 134
Thos. (fl. 1643, ? another), M.P. for
Horsham, i. 524, 529; ii. 312
Thos. (fl. 1732), vii. 124
fam., ii. 310, 312
Middleton, ii. 42–3, 152
Elmer, i. 225–6, 234; iv. 41
insects, i. 115–16, 220, 222, 234
pop., ii. 217
Rom. rem., iii. 61

Midelton, see Middleton
Midewinde fishery, see Hamsey
Midhurst, Steph. de, iii. 75
Midhurst, i. 52; ii. 43; iv. 40–1, 52,
74–80; vii. 15
adv., iv. 78–9
ale hos., ii. 196
birds, i. 292
bridge, ii. 394; iv. 76
cast., iv. 49, 74
chap. (St. Denis), iv. 74, 79
chant., iv. 78–9
chaps.:
St. Denis, see Midhurst: cast.:
chap.
St. Mary Magdalene, see Midhurst:
ch.
St. Thos., see Midhurst: Knights
Hospitaller: chap.
chaplain, see Nicholas
char., ii. 429; iv. 79–80
ch. (St. Mary Magdalene, formerly
chap.), ii. 84; iv. 53, 74, 75,
78–80
accessories, ii. 355–6, 358–9
archit., ii. 340, 370–2, 378
Civil War, i. 526
curate, ii. 428
deanery, ii. 42–3; iv. 78
dom. archit., ii. 386, 388–90; iv. 74–5
fairs, iv. 76
Hyenok pk., ii. 295
insects, i. 115–16, 118–19, 164–5,
167–8, 171, 181, 184, 187
Knights Hospitaller:
chap. (St. Thos.), iv. 76, 79
estates (Liberty of St. John), i. 502,
508; ii. 93, 221 n, 428; iv. 78
local govt., ii. 429–30; iv. 75–6
bailiff, ii. 429; iv. 75–6
constables, i. 503
cts., ii. 301; iv. 76
potteresgavel, ii. 251; iv. 76
mammals, i. 301
man., ii. 295; iv. 34, 75, 77–8
mkt., iv. 73–4, 74, 76, 79
militia, i. 507, 535
mills, iv. 76
molluscs, i. 109
nonconf., iv. 77
parl. rep., i. 504, 532; iv. 76
M.P.s, see Bageley, Mic.; Burgoyne; Cawley, Wm.; Fox, Chas.
Jas.; Fox, Hen.; May, Thos. (fl.
1642); Walpole, Spencer
pop., ii. 221
prehist. rem., i. 310, 312, 330
rly., ii. 240
Red Lion Street, iv. 74, 74–5
Rom. Cath., iv. 76–7
Rom. rem., iii. 2, 46
royal visit, i. 505
St. Anne's Hill, i. 479; iv. 49, 74
schs., ii. 429
grammar, ii. 257, 427–30; iv. 74, 79
sport, ii. 460, 466, 468, 475
trades and ind., ii. 251, 256–7, 259,
427; iv. 76
union, i. 539
vagrancy, ii. 210
vicarage, ii. 62
vicars, ii. 429–30; iv. 79
waterways, ii. 241; iv. 74
and see Mehers
Midlothian, see Musselburgh
Midmer, Thos., vii. 105
Midwinter, Wm., vii. 263
Miers, see Myers
Milan (Italy), ii. 11
Milane the recluse, ii. 74
Milbanke, Sir Jn. Ralph, iv. 152
Milbrook, see Maresfield
Mildeby (Mildebi):
Jn. de, iv. 102
Jn. de (another), iv. 102
Lucy de, iv. 103
Mildmay, F., ii. 461
Miles, see Myles

military architecture, see architecture: military
militia, musters and levies, i. 491–2, 506–10, 515–21, 530, 532–6; iii. 87–8, 97, 102
Mill (Mille, Myll):
  Alice, m. —— Dawtrey, iv. 157
  Amy, vii. 101
  Anne, m. Wm. Apsley, iv. 123
  Anne, w. of Sir Jn., iv. 7
  Sir Chas., iv. 7, 56, 85–6
  Edm., iv. 123, 157; ix. 263
  Hen., rector of Woolbeding, iv. 87
  Jn. (d. by 1587), iv. 7, 35; vii. 81, 101
  Sir Jn. (d. 1648), sheriff of Hants, iv. 7, 35; vii. 54, 81, 101
  Jn., his s., iv. 7
  Sir Jn. (d. 1670), iv. 7, 35, 85; vii. 54*
  Jn. (d. c. 1697), iv. 7
  Sir Jn. (d. 1706), iv. 7
  Kath., see Lewknor
  Lewknor, iv. 35; vii. 54, 81*
  Marg., m. Thos. Ball, iii. 145
  Marg., w. of Sir Jn., see Sandys
  Mary, m. Jn. Backshell, iii. 126
  Ric. (d. 1476), iv. 41, 123; ix. 263
  Sir Ric. (d. 1760), iv. 7, 86
  Thos., master of hosp. of Holy Cross, Winchelsea, ii. 107
  Thos., iii. 95
  Wm. (fl. 1476), iv. 123
  Wm. (fl. 1494, another), iv. 157
  fam., iv. 9, 36, 56, 85, 87; vii. 81
    arms, iv. 7
  and see Mills
Millais, J.G., i. 301
Milland, see Trotton
Millard:
  Alice, see Smith
  Sir Wm., iv. 90
Mille, see Mill
miller, Reynold the, see Reynold
Miller:
  Ann, see Elson
  Challen, iv. 169
  Chas., iv. 230
  Combe, dean of Chich., warden of St. Mary's hosp., Chich., ii. 51, 102; iv. 230
  Eliz. Cath., m. Wm. Hiberden, iv. 230
  Emblem, iii. 125
  F.P., ii. 469
  Hannah, m. Thos. Gooch, iii. 147
  Hannah, w. of Sir Thos., iii. 125
  Sir Hugh, iii. 120
  Sir Jn., M.P. for Chich., iii. 89, 99, 125–6; iv. 102
  Sir Jn. (another), iv. 230
  Marg., w. of Sir Jn., see Peachey
  Mary, m. Jn. Backshell, iii. 126
  Mary, m. Hen. Cheynell, iii. 147
  Susannah, iv. 155
  Sir Thos. (d. 1705), M.P. for Chich., iii. 125; iv. 124, 144 n, 155, 213, 230
  Thos. (another), iii. 125
  Sir Thos. (fl. 1788), iv. 155
  Sir Thos. Combe, iv. 155
  fam., iv. 155
Miller's Tomb, see Ferring: High Down
Milles, see Mills
Milliers:
  Constance de, iv. 237
  Wm. de, iv. 237
Millington, Francis, vii. 89, 91
Mills (Milles):
  E., ii. 273
  Edw., ix. 221
  Frances, m. Jn. Brooke, ix. 177
  Jas., and his w. Eliz., vii. 78
  Jn., ix. 263
  Rachel, see Glydd
  Ric. (fl. 1623), i. 521
  Ric. (fl. 1727), vii. 78
  Rob. (fl. 1577), vii. 169
  Rob. (fl. 1622), vii. 169
  Thos., ix. 273

Maj., ix. 222
fam., ix. 222
and see Mill
mills:
  fulling, ii. 257; iv. 127, 185; vii. 82; ix. 168
  paper, see paper making
  powder, see gunpowder making
  tide, iv. 127, 155, 199, 206, 210, 229; vii. 63–4; ix. 244
  and see parish names; architecture: civil and domestic
Millyard, G., ii. 469
Milne-Edwards, Alfonse, i. 249, 252, 258
Milner:
  Alfred, Vct. Milner, vii. 173; ix. 167
  Thos., vicar of Bexhill, ix. 122
  Violet Georgina, w. of Alfred, Vct. Milner, ix. 217, 222
Milton:
  Anne, w. of Wm., iii. 161
  Frances, w. of Wm., iii. 161
  Wm., dean of Chich., ii. 51; iii. 144
  Wm. (d. 1752), iii. 161
  Wm. (d. 1783), iii. 161
Milton, Vctss., see Jenkinson, Selina
Milton, see Arlington
Milward:
  Clem., ii. 167
  Edw. (d. 1811), mayor of Hastings, ix. 11, 20, 28, 86
  Edw. (fl. 1827), mayor of Hastings, ix. 11, 28, 86
  (formerly Sayer), Hen. Collier, see Sayer
  J. Spencer, ix. 28
  Mary, see Collier
  Sarah, w. of Edw., m. 2 earl of Waldegrave, ix. 32, 86
  Thos., vii. 183
  Wm. Carlisle Sayer, ix. 30–1
  Mr., ii. 271
  fam., ix. 20
Minerva, iii. 12–14
Mingaye, Capt., ii. 163
mining, see flint mining; lead mining
Minshull:
  Eliz., see Sutton
  Sir Ric., iv. 224
Minstead (Minsted), see Stedham
mints, i. 349; and see Chich.; Hastings; Lewes; London; Rye; Selsey; Winchelsea
miracles, ii. 2, 7, 11, 87
Mirlees, Eliz., ix. 171
misericords, see architecture: ecclesiastical
Mitchell, see Michell
Mitchell park, see Northchapel
Mitford (Mitforde):
  Charlotte, iii. 134
  Francis, iii. 134
  Jn. de, canon of Chich., iii. 86
  Ric., bp. of Chich., iii. 92, 157
  Wm., iii. 134
Mittell, Jos., ii. 249
Mitten, W., i. 43
Mixen (Mixon), see Selsey
Moat, see Iden: man.
Moat park, see Horsted, Little
Moberly, Chas. Edw., ii. 432
Moccas (Herefs.), iv. 212
Mockford, Jn., ii. 449
Mockfords, see Henfield
Moffatt, J.A.S.P., rector of Elsted, and his w., iv. 212
Mohaut (Monhaut, Montalt, Muhaut):
  Cecily de, iv. 123
  Sir Rob de, ii. 120; iv. 2, 143, 158
  Rog. de, iv. 171
Mohun (Moun):
  Hen. de, iv. 91
  Jn. de, iv. 91
Moin (Moine), see Moyne
Mole, riv., i. 58
Molecombe, see Westhampnett

Moleyns (Molyns):
  Adam, bp. of Chich., ii. 378; iii. 132; iv. 217; ix. 116 n, 117, 197
  Sir Jn. de, vii. 203
molluscs, i. 71, 108–9
Molton, Mr., ix. 185
Molyneux, Edm., ii. 419
Molyneux Howard, Eliz., Lady Molyneux Howard, iv. 134
Molyns, see Moleyns
Monaco, prince of, see Charles Honore
Monboucher:
  Bertram de (d. 1331), ix. 3, 83–4, 254
  Bertram (d. 1387), ix. 83
  Bertram (d. 1400), ix. 83
  Bertram (d. 1415), ix. 83
  Eliz., w. of Bertram, ix. 83
  Isabel de, m. —— Harbotell, ix. 83
  Joan, w. of Bertram de, ix. 3, 83–4, 254
  Reynold, ix. 83
  ——, ix. 83
  arms, ix. 83
Monceaux (Monceux, Mounceaux, Munceaus, Munceaux, Munceus):
  Dru de, ix. 133 n
  Edith de, see Warenne
  Jn. de (fl. 1296), i. 506; ix. 133, 137
  Jn. de (d. 1316), ix. 133, 137
  Jn. de (d. by 1331), ix. 133
  Maud de, m. Jn. de Fiennes, ix. 133
  Olympia, w. of Jn., ix. 137
  (or Herste), Waleran de (d. by 1217), ix. 133–4, 149, 206
  Waleran de (d. by 1296), i. 498, 501; ix. 133–4
  (or Herste), Wm. de, vii. 2, 20, 213; ix. 133, 149
  Wm. de, rector of Herstmonceux, ix. 137
  fam., ix. 133, 267
  arms, ix. 133
Monchesney, Wm. de, i. 497
moneyers, iii. 83, 84 n; vii. 32
Mongomerie, see Montgomery
Mongre, Wm., vii. 121
Monhaut, see Mohaut
monk, Eustace the, see Eustace
Monk (Monke):
  Jn., ii. 260
  Rob., ii. 312
  T.G., i. 281
  T.J., i. 275, 278, 283, 285, 293
Monk Bretton, Lds., see Dodson
Monke, see Monk
Monk's Gate, see Beeding
Monkton Farleigh (Farley) (Wilts.), priory, ii. 68–9
Monmouth, duke of, see James
Monmouthshire, see Caerwent
Mont, see Du Mont
Montacute, Wm. de, iii. 85
Montacute, Ld., see Poole, Hen.
Montagu (Montague):
  Anna Maria, dau. of Geo. Montague Dunk, earl of Halifax, m. 1 —— Donaldson, 2 Ric. Archdall, iv. 122, 127
  Anne, see Dunk
  Edw., Ld. Montagu of Boughton, vii. 117
  Sir Edw., earl of Sandwich, ii. 310
  Eliz., m. Rob Bertie, earl of Lindsey, vii. 117
  Eliz., w. of Edw., see Jeffrey
  Frances, m. Jn. Blomer, ix. 121
  Geo., earl of Halifax, ii. 441, 443, 454; iii. 75
  (later Dunk), Geo., earl of Halifax, see Dunk
  Hen. (fl. 1669), and his w. Mary, ix. 137 n
  Hen. (fl. 1737), ix. 155
  Jn., earl of Salisbury, i. 510; ix. 220, 229
  Jn., duke of Montagu, ii. 443
  Ric., bp. of Chich., ii. 32, 34; iv. 208; ix. 117

Montagu (cont.):
Wm., ii. 77
Mr., i. 249
——, w. of Jn., earl of Salisbury, see Bugsell
fam., ii. 122; vii. 70
Montagu (Montague):
duke of, see Montagu, Jn.
Ld. Montague of Boughton, see Montagu, Edw.
marquess of, see Nevill, Geo.
Vcts., see Browne
Montalt, see Mohaut
Monte Martini, Jn. de, prior of Lewes, ii. 67, 70–1
Montefiore:
Sir Francis, vii. 146, 196
Mrs. H.F., vii. 146
Montfort:
Eleanor de, dau. of King John, see Eleanor
Guy de, i. 497
Hen. de (d. 1265), i. 497, 500–1
Hen. de (fl. 1324), ix. 139
Isabel de, prioress of Easebourne, ii. 84–5
Joan de, m. Ralph Basset, Ld. Basset, ix. 3
Joan, w. of Jn., duke of Brittany, see Holland
Jn. de, duke of Brittany, ? earl of Richmond (d. 1345), ix. 3, 212, 216
Jn. de, duke of Brittany, earl of Richmond (d. 1399), ii. 325; ix. 3, 119, 221
Pernel de, see Dunstanville
Ric. de, i. 501
Rob. de, iv. 41
Sim. de, earl of Leicester, i. 496–501; ii. 66, 131; ix. 37, 50
Sim. de, i. 495 n, 501, 502 n
Wm. de, iv. 41
Montgomery (Mongomerie):
Archibald, earl of Eglinton, ii. 458–9
Hugh de, earl of Arundel and Shrewsbury, iii. 84
Mabel, w. of Rog., ii. 121; iv. 20
Rob. de, see Belleme
Rog. de, earl of Arundel and Shrewsbury, i. 487; ii. 119, 121, 294, 302–3, 332, 398; iii. 79, 83–4, 90; iv. 1, 3–4, 13, 17, 20, 27, 30, 34, 40–1, 44, 47, 50–1, 58, 63, 65, 77, 80, 83, 85, 89, 91, 104, 108–9, 111, 114–115, 118, 120, 122, 127, 142, 155–6, 158, 161–2, 171, 174, 176, 198–9, 204, 216, 222, 234; vii. 84 n
his dau., ii. 121
Montgomeryshire:
Carreghova, castellan, see Strange, Ralph le
Montreal:
Hubert de, i. 500
Imbert de, i. 502
Montrose, duke of, see Graham, Jas.
Monyn:
Jn., ix. 61
Nic., and his w. Alice, ix. 61
Moody:
M., iii. 126
Sam., iv. 25
Moore, see More
Moorey:
Jn. (d. 1606), iv. 129
Jn. (d. 1613), iv. 129
Moorsom, Rob., ix. 168 n
Morand, Wm., iv. 144
Morayshire, see Duffus
Morden, Rob., ii. 297–8
Morden (Surr.), iii. 41
More (Moore, Moure):
Adrian, vii. 195
Agnes, w. of Jn., vii. 195
Agnes, w. of Thos. atte (d. 1374), iv. 238
Agnes, w. of Thos. atte (fl. after

1474), iv. 231
Anne, see Parker
Edw. (Edm.), archdeacon of Lewes, canon of Chich., ii. 405; iii. 124, 154, 159
Edw. (d. by 1565), vii. 195
Sir Edw. (d. 1623), vii. 134, 195
Edw. (fl. 1657), vii. 195
Eliz., w. of Jn., iv. 136
Elliott, m. Jn. Middleton, vii. 124
Frances, vii. 124
Frances, w. of Francis, see Jermyn
Francis (d. 1617), vii. 124, 213
Francis (fl. 1665), iv. 116
G.H., ii. 473
Hen., iii. 133
Jn. atte (fl. 1374), iv. 145
Jn., master of Playden hosp., ii. 105
Jn. (d. by 1557), vii. 109, 123, 194
Jn. (d. 1559), iv. 136
Jn. (fl. 1571), vii. 195
Mary, see Hendley
Nic., iv. 136
Ralph atte, iv. 105, 145, 238; ix. 118
Sarah atte, see Passeley
Thos. atte (d. 1374), iv. 105, 145, 238; ix. 145
Thos. atte (fl. 1474), iv. 231
Thos. (fl. 1617), vii. 213
Thos. (d. 1732), vii. 124
Wm. atte (fl. 1416), iv. 238
Wm. (fl. 1569), ii. 255
Sir Wm. (fl. 1581, ? another), iv. 95
Wm. (d. by 1623), vii. 195
Sir Wm. (d. 1684), vii. 156, 196
arms, iii. 124, 159; vii. 195
More park (? in Glynde), ii. 297, 301
Morell, Thos., iv. 233
Mores, Jn., ii. 59
Moreton, see Mortain; Morton
Morewood, Jn., iv. 110
Morford, Thos., iv. 102
Morfote, Wm., ii. 142
Morgan:
Sir Ant., ix. 191
David Wal., and his w. Mary, vii. 57
Eliz., m. Hen. Bosvile, ix. 242, 262
Eliz., w. of Sir Ant., see Fromond
Geo., ii. 447
J., ii. 166
Kath., see Lewknor
Mary, m. Peter Farmor, ix. 191
Roffey, ii. 447
Wm. (or Wyndham), vii. 81, 101, 226; ix. 242
Dr., ii. 424
Morice, see Morris
Morin (fl. 1086), iv. 4
Morland:
Thos., ix. 161
Wm. (fl. to 1774), ix. 161
Wm. (fl. 1937), ix. 161
Wm. Alex., ix. 161
Wm. Courtenay, sheriff of Suss., ix. 161
fam., ix. 161
Morley (Morlay, Morleye, Morly):
Agnes, ii. 411–15; vii. 16
Anne, see Bowyer
Ant., and his w. Bridget, vii. 96
Sir Edw., iv. 21; vii. 238
H., ii. 468, 470
Herb., M.P. for Lewes, lieutenant of Tower of London, i. 523–5, 529; ii. 268; vii. 17, 18 n
Jn. (fl. to 1606), iv. 36, 101–2, 143, 238
Jn. (fl. 1620), iv. 21; vii. 58, 238
Sir Jn. (d. 1622), iv. 101–2, 143–4
Sir Jn. (fl. 1642), i. 522; iii. 87; iv. 163
Sir Jn. (fl. 1662), iv. 104
Sir Jn. (d. by 1675), iv. 161
Kath., iv. 104
Mary, m. Jas. Stanley, earl of Derby, ii. 439; iv. 101, 104, 143, 149–50, 239

Mary, m. Sir Jn. May, iv. 104, 106, 163
Mary, w. of Sir Jn., see Smith
Rob. de (fl. 1323), ii. 304
Rob. de (fl. 1335, ? another), ii. 120; iv. 143
Rob. (fl. 1614), ix. 83 n, 254
Sim., master of hosp. of Holy Cross, Winchelsea, ii. 107
Wm. (d. 1505), ii. 412
Wm. (fl. 1564), ii. 24
Sir Wm. (fl. to 1650), i. 522; iv. 102 n, 103, 146, 208
Sir Wm. (d. 1701), iv. 92, 103, 143, 163, 208
Capt., i. 526–7
fam., iv. 76, 163
arms, iv. 143
Morley, see Hollington: man.
Morly, see Morley
Morocco, see Tangier
Morris (Morice, Morryce):
A., vii. 9
David, ix. 56
F.D., i. 119, 130
Salmon, ii. 165
Thos., ii. 474
Wm., and his w. Mary, ix. 177
Wm., vii. 237, 262
——, ii. 148
Morrison, Emma, ix. 33
Morryce, see Morris
Morshead, Angela, ix. 200
Mortain (Moreton):
Rob. of, count of Mortain, i. 487–8; ii. 122–3, 313, 381, 441; iii. 6; iv. 143; vii. 1, 53, 70, 80, 104, 196, 225, 234; ix. 266
his w., see Maud
Wm., count of Mortain, i. 490; ii. 122–3, 313
Mortain, counts of, see Mortain; William
Mortain (Manche, France), priory, ii. 46, 76, 123
Mortain, honor of, i. 491
Mortimer:
Agnes, see Bardolf
Anne, ctss. of March, iv. 167
Beatrice, m. 1 Edw., s. of Thos. de Brotherton, 2 Thos. de Braose, iv. 184
Chas. S., ix. 181
Edm., earl of March, vii. 110
Eliz., m. 1 Sir Hen. Percy, 2 Sir Thos. Camoys, iv. 35, 37
Eliz., w. of Chas., see French
Eliz., w. of ——, see Badlesmere
Guy, ix. 149
Idonea, see Herste
Isabel de, m. Jn. FitzAlan, earl of Arundel, ii. 190; iv. 97, 118, 122, 168
Jn. Hamilton, ix. 25
Keith, ix. 204
Nic., ii. 123; iii. 114
Rob., iv. 85
Rog., earl of March (d. 1330), warden of Cinque Ports, i. 508–9; iv. 184; ix. 35, 138
Rog., earl of March (d. 1360), iv. 167
Rog., ix. 24–5
Sir Thos., vii. 110
——, iv. 167
fam., iv. 167
arms, iii. 151; iv. 38
Mortlock, E., canon of Chich., iii, 130
Morton (Moreton):
Anne, see Covert
Eliz., see Boyce
Sir Jas., vii. 145, 156*, 183
Jas., vii. 156*
Jane, see Weekes
Jn., vii. 254
Mercy, w. of Jas., m. 2 Chas. Goodwin, vii. 156*
Rob. de, see Mortain
Sir Wm., vii. 159, 183

Wm., ix. 83
Mory:
  Steph., ix. 113 *n*
  Valentine, ix. 113
Moseley:
  Rob. (d. 1789), ix. 92
  Rob. (d. 1798), ix. 92
  Rob. (fl. 1798), ix. 92
Moses son of Jose, i. 506
Moses, friar of Chich., ii. 26
Moses (fl. *c.* 1200), iii. 80
Mosewell:
  Joan de, *see* Farley
  Rog. de, ix. 190, 192
Mosse, H.R., iv. 227
mosses, i. **58–60**
Mote (Mot):
  Rob. de la, iv. 89
  Rob., vii. 140; ix. 279
  Wm. de la, iv. 89
Mottisfont (Hants), priory, ii. 353; iv. 87
Mottle, Ric., ii. 99
Motyn:
  Jn., ix. 198
  Lawr., ix. 198
  fam., ix. 198
Moulescombe (Moulescoomb), *see* Patcham
Moun, *see* Mohun
Mounceaux, *see* Monceaux
Mounsher, Jn., iv. 129
Mount Caburn, *see* Glynde
Mount Harry, *see* Hamsey
Mountfield, ii. 43; ix. 210, 224, 226, **234–6**, 258
  adv., ii. 72; ix. 224, 236
  ch., ii. 112; ix. 223, *235*, 236
    accessories, ii. 352, 356, 360, 374
    archit., ii. 329, 351, 374
  Derfold (Darwell), ix. 1
  dom. archit., ix. 234–5
  Eatendon (Eatonden), ix. 107, 146, 235–6
  Glottenham, *see* Etchingham
  gypsum, ii. 232; ix. 235
  insects, i. 125
  Limekiln wood, i. 4
  man., ix. 235–6
  pk., ii. 297
  pop., ii. 223
  prehist. rem., i. 320–1, *322*, 330; ii. 291
  rly., ii. 222 *n*
  woodland, ii. 324–5; ix. 234
Mountjoy, Ld., *see* Blount, Edw.
Mountjoy tithing, ix. 95
Moure, *see* More
Mournour, Jn., i. 512
Mowatt, Frank, iv. 36
Mowbray:
  Aline de, *see* Braose
  Anne, m. Ric., duke of York (d. 1483), iv. 122, 184; vii. 5, 24, 35, 71, 212, 253–4*
  Blanche de, m. Sir Thos. de Poynings, vii. 183 *n*, 203–4, 209
  Eleanor, m. 1 Sir Rog. de la Warr, 2 Sir Lewis Clifford, vii. 283
  Eleanor, w. of Jn., duke of Norfolk, vii. 36
  Eliz., w. of Jn., duke of Norfolk, iv. 98, 122, 168, 184; vii. 5, 64, 203, 206, 212
  Eliz., w. of Jn., *see* Talbot
  Eliz., w. of Thos., duke of Norfolk, *see* FitzAlan
  Hen., Ld. Mowbray, vii. 64
  Isabel, vii. 5
  Sir Jn. de, ii. 97, 307
  Jn., duke of Norfolk (d. 1432), iv. 122, 184; vii. 64
  Jn., duke of Norfolk (d. 1461), ii. 61, 99; iv. 184; vii. 3–4, 19, 33, 36, 64*, 71, 80–1, 84, 114, 141, 175, 195, 212–13, 231, 253, 279
  Jn., duke of Norfolk (d. 1476), ii. 61, 69, 312; iv. 98, 122, 168, 184; vii.

5, 64, 71*, 134, 195
  Kath., *see* Nevill
  Marg., vii. 5
  Sir Thos. de, duke of Norfolk, ii. 308, 312; iv. 184; vii. 3, 21, 58, 196
  Thos., earl of Norfolk and Nottingham, Earl Marshal, iv. 163, 184
  fam., iv. 163, 193; vii. 4, 7
  arms, iii. 151; vii. *5*
Mowyn, *see* Moyne
Moyle:
  Cath., m. Thos. Finch, ix. 107
  Sir Thos., ix. 107
Moyne (Moin, Moine, Mowyn):
  Geof. le, iv. 168 *n*
  Heceline, w. of Jn., ix. 84
  Jn. (fl. after 1200), ix. 92
  Sir Jn. (d. by 1285), ix. 84
  Sir Jn. (fl. 1285), ix. 84
  Jn. (fl. 1361), and his w. Cecily, iv. 168
  Mabel, w. of Sir Jn., ix. 84
  Mabel, w. of Sir Wm. le, m. 2 Jn. de Lancaster, iv. 66
  Reynold le, iv. 168
  Rog. de (? two of this name), ix. 92 *n*, 95
  Wm. de (fl. 1210), ix. 84
  Sir Wm. le (fl. 1326), iv. 66
Moyses, Jn., ii. 24
Mucegros:
  Jn., i. 498; vii. 257
  Ric. de, iii. 79
Muckleston (Mucklingtone), Ric., ii. 420
Mudbrooke Gate, *see* Forest Row
Muddiman, Mr., vii. 18
Muggridge, Emma, iii. 168
Muhaut, *see* Mohaut
Mullagh, Johny, ii. 472 *n*
Mullelond, *see* Trotton: Milland
Mullens, *see* Mullins
Müller, O.F., i. 264
Mullinger, J. Bass, ii. 435
Mullins (Mullens):
  Eliz., iii. 147
  Geo., iv. 52
  Hen., iii. 147
  Maria, ii. 29
  Sarah, iii. 147
  Sarah, w. of Hen., iii. 147
  W.H., ix. 29
Mulssh, And., ii. 316
Mulstone (Mulston):
  (later Lorkyn), And., vii. 229–30
  Margery, vii. 36, 229
  Rob. de, vii. 106
  Thos., vii. 229
  Wm. de, vii. 106
Multon, fam., arms, ix. 135
Mumford, Jn., mayor of Chich., iii. 91
Mun, *see* Munn
Munceaus (Munceaux, Munceus), *see* Monceaux
Mundeville, Ric. de, ii. 171
Mundham, North, ii. 43, 57, 270; iv. 133, 145, **160–5**
  adv., iv. 158, 165
  Bowley, iv. 184*
    farm, ii. 338*
    manor, iv. 163, 183, 218 *n*
  Bramber Rife, *see* Bremere Rife
  chant., iv. 149, 165
  char., iv. 165
  ch., ii. 56; iv. 161, 164–5, *164*
    accessories, ii. 351, 355, 361
    archit., ii. 339, 342, 350, 372, 374, 377–8
  dom. archit., ii. 382*; iv. 160–1
  glebe, ii. 5
  insects, i. 186, 191, 194, 198, 202, 205–7, 209
  Leythorne, iv. 160–3, 167
  man., ii. 109; iv. 161–5, 229, 231
Mundham, South, iv. 160, 227
  adv., iv. 165
  Bowley, *see* Mundham, North: Bowley

dom. archit., iv. 160
man., iv. 161–3, 229
Rom. rem., iii. 61
mills, iv. 161–2
pop., ii. 220
roads, iv. 160
Runcton, i. 526; iv. 62 *n*, 133, 162
  adv., iv. 165
  chap., iv. 165
  dom. archit., iv. 160
  man., ii. 121; iv. 162–3, 165, 167, 175
  mills, iv. 160, 162
  priory, ii. 46, **121**; iv. 162, 165
  tithes, iv. 162, 165
Unredisditch, *see* Bremere Rife
vicar, iv. 165
Mundy:
  Cath., *see* Barwell
  Edw. Miller, iv. 172, 189 *n*, 195
Munfichet, Phillipa de, m. Hugh de Plaiz, vii. 54
Munn (Mun):
  Geo. (? two of this name), ii. 238; ix. 224
  Thos., and his w. Frances, ix. 181
Munro, J.C., ii. 447
Munt, E.J., vii. 37
murage, vii. 7, 24 *n*; ix. 40, 63·
Murdac (fl. 1086), iv. 135
Murdac:
  Denise, iv. 108
  Florence, iv. 108
  Marg., m. Nic. de Limesy, iv. 108, 145, 180
  Ric., iv. 108, 145
  ——, w. of Ric., *see* Gundeville
Murietta, Messrs., ii. 461
Murray:
  Alex., Ld. Elibank, ix. 86
  Alicia, w. of Geo., iii. 145
  Ann, w. of Sir Geo., iii. 145
  Ann, w. of Jas., ix. 88
  Cecilia, *see* Collier
  G.R., ii. 472 *n*
  Sir Geo., iii. 145
  Jas., governor of Quebec, jurat of Hastings, ix. 7, 86, 88, 101
  Jas. Patrick, ix. 88
  Wm., Ld. Mansfield, Solicitor-General, ii. 423
  Mrs., ix. 137
Musard:
  Joan, w. of Wm., iv. 63
  Ric., iv. 63–5
  Wm. (fl. 1212), iv. 63
  Wm., his s., iv. 63
  Wm. (d. 1330), iv. 63
  Wm. (fl. 1339), iv. 63
  fam., iv. 63
museums, *see* Brighton; British Museum; Cambridge; Chich.; Eastbourne; Hastings; Horsham; Hove; Lewes; Lewes: Barbican ho.; Littlehampton; Oxford; Preston: Thomas-Stanford museum; Worthing
Musgrave, Thos., iv. 51
Musgrove, C., ii. 470 *n*
Musselburgh (Midlothian), ii. 478
mustard, *see* crops
musters, *see* militia
Mutton, David, iii. 277
Myddelton, *see* Middleton
Myers (Miers, Myeres):
  E.J., i. 252
  Jn. Simpson, ii. 426 *n*
  Mat., ii. 407
Myles (Miles):
  Jn., ii. 308
  Jn. (another), iv. 138
  Thos., prior of Boxgrove, ii. 58–9; iv. 147, 149
Myll, *see* Mill
Myllers, Phil., vii. 258
Myllet (Myllett):
  Cecily, iii. 77
  Edw., ii. 263; iii. 77

Myllet (*cont*):
Phil., ii. 263; iii. 77 *n*
Mylsent, Mr., ii. 104
Mynn:
Alfred, ii. 468, 470
Thos., ii. 246

Nabynaux, Peter de, prior of Sele, ii. 60, 62
Nailand:
Eliz. Ward, *see* Cooke
Hen., vii. 158, 180
Jn., vii. 180
Nanefield, *see* Ninfield
Napier, Chas., ii. 166
Naples (Italy), iv. 139
Napoleon, *see* Bonaparte
Napoleonic wars, *see* wars
Napper:
Edwin, ii. 468–9
Wm., ii. 469
Narbonne (Salsulae) (Aude, France), iii. 28
Nash (Nasch, Nasshe):
Eliz., ii. 439; iv. 149, 188
Isabel atte, *see* Ferring
Jn. atte, vii. 100
Jn. (fl. 1687), ix. 121
Jn. (fl. 1732), ii. 439
Jn., architect, iv. 65
Peter atte, preceptor of Poling, ii. 93
Rob., abbot of Bayham, ii. 88–9
T., iii. 77
and see Ashe
Nassau, counts of, *see* Maurice; William
Nasshe, *see* Nash
Nat wood, *see* Folkington: Gnat wood
Nathley (Nathilay):
Edw., ix. 249
Thos., ix. 81
National Church League, vii. 91
National Coursing club, ii. 453
National Trust, iv. 80, 235; ix. 264
Nauberg, Hen. de, ii. 304
Nauchal:
Mic., bailiff of Atherington, ii. 120
Mic. de, prior of Arundel (? another), ii. 120
naval recruitment, *see* impressment of seamen
Navenby (Lincs.), ix. 50
Naylor:
Bethia, m. Francis Hare, bp. of Chich., ix. 134
(formerly Hare), Francis, *see* Hare
Geo., ix. 134, 137
Grace, *see* Pelham
fam., ix. 137
Naylor, Vickers & Co., ix. 25
Nedeler (Nedler):
Jn. le, ii. 229
Ric. le, ii. 229
—— le, iii. 97
Nederfeld, *see* Netherfield
Nedler, *see* Nedeler
needle making, ii. 199, 229; iii. 97
Neel (Neele):
Jn., master of Arundel coll., ii. 109
Wm., mayor of Chich., ii. 47; iii. 91–2, 97; iv. 177
Nelond:
Jn., and his w. Mary, ii. 69; vii. 225, 256
Thos., prior of Lewes, ii. 68–70, 361
Nelson:
Horatio, Vct. Nelson, ii. 128, 162; iv. 76
——, a jockey, ii. 458
Nembhard, Wm., iii. 145, 147
Nenefeud, *see* Ninfield
Neptune, iii. 12–14
Nerford (Nereford):
Alice, w. of Sir Thos. de, vii. 207–8
Maud de, vii. 3
Rob., ix. 37
Sir Thos. de, vii. 207–8
Nero, Rom. emperor, iii. 1, 14

Nesbit:
Arnold, ix. 69, 187
Jn., ix. 187
Netherfield (Nederfeld) (in Battle), ii. 43; ix. 97, 106
earthworks, i. 477
(formerly Hailesaltede) hund., i. 537; ii. 223; ix. 3, 95, **226**, 239, 242
insects, i. 126, 137, 142–6, 149–50, 155, 157, 159, 162–3, 227–9, 232, 234–5
man., ii. 324; ix. 92, 107, 187, 235, 240, 242
Netherfield Green, i. 57
Netherlands (Holland, Low Countries), ii. 136, 141–2, 148, 156; ix. 52
trade with, ii. 232, 261, 332, 397; ix. 55
wars with, *see* wars: Dutch
and see Alkmaar; Bergen op Zoom; Breda; Camperdown; Hague, the; Hook, the; Middleburgh; Sluys; Utrecht; Walcheren; Zeeland; Zierikzee
Netley (Hants), priory, iv. 148 *n*
Netter, Thos., ii. 19
Nettleship, Hen., ii. 432
Neubaud (Newbaud):
Isabel de, *see* Meyners
Phil. de, vii. 68, 280
Neuport, *see* Newport
Nevers, count of, *see* Donzy
Nevill (Neville):
Alan de, iv. 98
Anne, w. of Geo., Ld. Bergavenny, m. 2 Jn. West, Earl de la Warr, vii. 96, 217
Cecily, m. Ric., duke of York, iii. 14
Chas. Wm., vii. 77
Dorothy, w. of Reg. Hen., iv. 28, 36
Edw., Ld. Bergavenny (d. 1476), ii. 69; vii. 4, 162, 195
Edw., Ld. Bergavenny (d. 1589), vii. 4, 195–6
Edw., Ld. Bergavenny (d. 1622), vii. 4, 70, 114, 234, 279
Eliz., m. Ric. Covert, vii. 185
Eliz., w. of Edw., Ld. Bergavenny, *see* Beauchamp
Eliz., w. of ——, *see* Holland
Frances, vii. 179
Geof. de, iv. 98
Geof. de (another), iv. 98
Geo., marquess of Montagu, iv. 80, 130
Geo., Ld. Bergavenny (d. 1492), vii. 4, 35–6
Geo., Ld. Bergavenny (d. 1535), ii. 324; iv. 129; vii. 4, 7, 36, 70, 185, 230, 242, 254, 280
Geo., iv. 102
Geo., Ld. Abergavenny (fl. 1717), vii. 71, 96
Ld. Geo., ii. 448
Hawise de, *see* Savage
Hen., earl of Westmorland, ix. 153
Hen., Ld. Bergavenny (d. 1587), vii. 4, 26 *n*, 105, 156, 179, 204, 280
Hen., Ld. Bergavenny (d. 1641), ii. 244; vii. 179
Hen., earl of Abergavenny, ii. 207; vii. 35, 70
Ld. Hen., ii. 448
Hugh de, ii. 121; iv. 58, 115
Jane, *see* Ashburnham
Joan, w. of Hugh, iv. 115
Joan, w. of Ralph, earl of Westmorland, ix. 3
Jn. de (fl. 1244, ? two of this name), iv. 58, 98, 174; vii. 81
Jn. de (fl. 1357), iv. 58
Kath., m. Jn. Mowbray, duke of Norfolk, vii. 64*
Lucy, m. Sir Ant. Browne, iv. 80, 130
Marg., m. Hen. Poole, vii. 105
Marg., m. Sir Rob. Southwell, vii. 145, 183, 189
Marg., w. of Ralph, earl of Westmor-

land, *see* Cobham
Mary, m. Thos. Fiennes, Ld. Dacre, vii. 175 *n*
Mary, baroness Despenser, m. Sir Thos. Fane, vii. 4; ix. 195
Ralph de, bp. of Chich., chancellor of Eng., ii. 9–10, 13, 76, 81, 87, 98, 332, 373, 399, 404; iii. 81–2, 108–10, 114, 124–5, 131; iv. 47, 58 *n*, 70, 135, 138, 217, 239; ix. 27, 81, 130, 234
Ralph, earl of Westmorland (d. 1425), ix. 3, 15, 79–80
Ralph, earl of Westmorland (d. 1484), ix. 120, 153
Reg. Hen., iv. 29, 36
Reg. Wm., marquess of Abergavenny, vii. 20, 30, 70
Ric., earl of Warwick, ii. 143
Ric. Plantagenet, vii. 30
Sir Thos. (fl. 1535), vii. 4, 117, 183, 189
Sir Thos. (d. 1628), vii. 179
Wm., chancellor of Chich., iv. 110
Wm., earl of Lewes, marquess of Abergavenny, i. 306; ii. 448, 461, 465, 480; vii. 4, 156
Mr., vii. 97
fam., ii. 247, 324; iv. 174; vii. 101
arms, vii. *4*
Nevitt, Thos., ix. 199
New, ii. 46
New Brighton Guide, ii. 204
New Chapel, *see* Lingfield
New College, Oxford, i. 529; ii. 405, 407, 409, 428; iii. 146; ix. 27, 86
warden, *see* Young, Jn.
New Cross, *see* Deptford
New Forest (Hants), i. 165, 169 *n*, 172 *n*; iv. 217; *and see* Romano-British Suss.: pottery
New Haven (in Sidlesham), *see* Sidlesham
New Lodge (in Beeding), *see* Beeding
New Lodge (in Hartfield), *see* Hartfield
New Place (in Angmering), *see* Angmering
New Place (in Pulborough), *see* Pulborough
New Town, *see* Chich.: suburbs
New Zealand, i. 297; ii. 481
Newbaud, *see* Neubaud
Newbery, *see* Newbury
Newbridge, *see* Hartfield
Newbridge, riv., ii. 319
Newburgh:
ctss. of, *see* Eyre, Dorothea; Kemp, Barbara; Radcliffe, Anne
earls of, *see* Radcliffe, Ant. Jas.; Radcliffe, Jas. Bart.
Newbury (Newbery, Nubery):
Jn., iv. 231
Jn. (another), ix. 200
Francis, ix. 200
Ric. de, iii. 93
Col., i. 534
Mr., ii. 457
Newbury (Berks.), battle, i. 525
Newcastle, Jn. of, prior of Lewes, ii. 66–7, 70
Newcastle, dukes of, *see* Clinton, Hen.; Pelham-Holles
Newcastle (Northumb.), i. 507; ii. 140, 143, 155, 429
Newdigate (Newdegate, Nudygatt), Thos., vii. 123, 213
Newdigate (Surr.), ii. 328 *n*
Newe Hous, *see* Newhouse
Newehavene, Cyprian de la, iv. 210
Newells, *see* Beeding
Newenden (Kent), ix. 144, 276
Newenden park, *see* Buxted: Newnham pk.
Neweton, *see* Nonyngton
Newey:
Frances, m. Edw. Waddington, iii. 126
Jn., dean of Chich., ii. 51

Newfoundland (Canada), ii. 165–7
Newgate, *see* London
Newham, W., ii. 470, 476
Newhaven (Meching, Meeching), ii. 43–4, 209, 322; iii. 102; vii. 1, **62–5**, 66, 255
  adv., vii. 65
  battery, ii. 152, 161
  birds, i. 286, 294–5
  botany, i. 45, 59
  Castle Hill, iii. 61; vii. 62, 64
  ch., vii. 64–5, *65*, *68*
    archit., ii. 328, 332, 340, 342, 348, 366
  coastguards, i. 507 *n*
  cts., vii. 64
  Denton Island, iii. 61
  dom. archit., vii. 62
  earthworks, i. **457**, 470
  ferry, vii. 62, 64
  fossils, i. 13, 29
  geology, i. 2, 7
  harbour and port, ii. 125, 159, 163, 247–8; vii. 62–3
  insects, i. 112, 134, 137–52, 155, 161, 173, 181, 216, 220
  man., vii. 2–4, 6–7, 35, 64
  militia, i. 519, 534–5
  mills, vii. 63
  molluscs, i. 109
  naval recruitment, ii. 161
  pop., ii. 224
  port, *see* Newhaven: harbour
  prehist. rem., i. 330; vii. 62
  Red Nore (Redware), ii. 146
  Rom. Cath., vii. 62
  Rom. rem., iii. 4, 61; vii. 62
  R.D., vii. 31
  shipping, ii. 151, 153, 155
  spiders, i. 242–3
  sport, ii. 446, 449, 451, 465, 467, 479
  trades and ind., ii. 146, 164, 231, 235, 269–70; vii. 63–4
  union, i. 539
  U.D., vii. 31, 62
Newhouse (Newe Hous) (Lincs.), abbey, ii. 88, 90
Newhurst (unidentified), i. 159
Newick (Northborgh), ii. 43–4; vii. 79, **87–91**, 94
  adv., vii. 91
  agric., vii. 87
  angling, ii. 464
  char., ii. 440; vii. 91
  ch., vii. *87*, 89–91, *90*
    accessories, ii. 353*, 355–6, 376
    archit., ii. 346, 366, 376, 378; vii. 85
  cts., vii. 89
  dom. archit., vii. 87–9
  High Hurst, ii. 44
  man., ii. 440; vii. 89, 101
  natural history, i. 68, 116, 169
  Newick Place, ii. 440
  pop., ii. 223
  sch., ii. 440; vii. 91
  tanning, ii. 259
Newington:
  Alice, w. of Jas., ix. 196
  Mrs. Campbell, ix. 252
  Jos., ix. 196, 224
  Thos., ix. 220 *n*
  Zabulon, ix. 224
Newington, Messrs., ii. 231
Newington (Kent), ix. 149–50
Newland:
  Hen. Garrett, iv. 131
  Jn., mayor of Chich., ii. 257; iv. 163–4
  Martha, iv. 129
  Ric. (? two of this name), ii. 467; iv. 129
  Maj., iv. 131
  Mr., iv. 160
Newman:
  Eliz., ix. 233, 237
  Sir. Geo., ix. 215
  Jn. (fl. 1560), iv. 123

Jn. (fl. 1593), iv. 41, 123
Jn. (? another), iv. 152
Ric., vii. 270
Sybil, *see* Shoyswell
Wm., iv. 123
Wm. Jas. Hermann, vicar of East Dean, iv. 96
——, i. 254
Newmarket, *see* Kingston near Lewes
Newmarket Plantation, *see* Falmer
Newmouth (unidentified), ii. 139
Newnham:
  Emma, iv. 163
  Geo. Lewis, vii. 207
  Jn., vii. 134
  Jn. Lewis, vii. 207
  Nat., iv. 163; vii. 207, 208 *n*
  fam., vii. 128
Newnham park, *see* Buxted
Newport (Neuport):
  G., i. 265
  Luke de, ii. 114
Newport (I.W.), i. 108; ii. 427
Newson, Alice A., ix. 32
Newtimber, ii. 43–4; vii. 1, 201, **204–8**, 214
  adv., vii. 208
  agric., vii. 204–5
  ch., ii. 344, 358–9; vii. 208, *208*
  dom. archit., vii. 205–6
  earthworks, i. 478, 480
  fossils, i. 31, 33, 35
  man., vii. 206–7
  natural history, i. 60, 166, 170
  Newtimber Hill, iii. 61, 66
  Newtimber Ho., ii. 444
  Newtimber Place, ii. 387; iii. 47; iv. 163; vii. 206
  pop., ii. 224
  rectory, vii. 208, 214
  roads, iii. 47; vii. 204
  Rom. rem., iii. 47, 61
  Saddlescombe, *q.v.*
  tanning, ii. 259–60
Newton:
  Apsley, vii. 37 *n*
  Edw., vii. 17
  Eliz., m. Wm. Courthope Mabbot, vii. 230
  Geo., rector of Isfield, vii. 230
  Geo., and his w. Mary, vii. 256
  Grace, m. Wm. Pellatt, vii. 37 *n*
  Jane, *see* Erley
  Jn., abbot of Battle, ii. 55
  Jn., ix. 26
  Mary Dorothy, iv. 10
  Sir Mic., ii. 454
  Nic., vii. 256
  Wm. (fl. 1572), vii. 45, 256
  Wm. (fl. 1654), vii. 35, 144
  Col., ii. 415
  Mr., ix. 197
Newykestreet, *see* Rumboldswyke: hosp.
Neyr, Mabel, *see* Felde
Nicholas III, pope, ii. 57
Nicholas IV, pope, taxation of, ii. 8, 11–12, 60, 72, 77; iii. 166
Nicholas, abbot of Durford, ii. 91
Nicholas, abbot of Robertsbridge, ii. 73
Nicholas, chaplain of Midhurst, iv. 78 *n*
Nicholas, prior of Boxgrove, ii. 59; iv. 162, 199
Nicholas, prior of Hastings, ii. 77
Nicholas, prior of Shoreham friary, ii. 97
Nicholas son of Ruffus, iv. 24
Nicholas (Nicolas) (fl. 14th cent.), iv. 201
Nicholas (Nicolas):
  Cath., *see* Pounde
  Sir Harris, ii. 137
  Wm. (sr.), ix. 82 *n*
  Wm. (jr.), ix. 82
Nicholl (Nichole, Nicol, Nicoll):
  Sir Chas. Gunter, iv. 115
  Frances Kath., m. Wm. Legge, earl of Dartmouth, iv. 115
  Hen. J., i. 306

Jn., master of hosp. of St. Jas. and St. Mary, Chich., ii. 100
Jn. (fl. 1362), ix. 213
Jn. (fl. 1662), ix. 235
Jn. (fl. 1786), ix. 235
Judith, m. Geo. Gunter, iv. 115
Kath., *see* Felde
M.J., i. 284, 287
Sam., ix. 235
——, w. of Jn., m. 2 Ric. Rideout, ix. 235
fam., ix. 235
Nicholls (Nicolls):
  Anne, iii. 146
  G. Green, iii. 146
  Geo., and his w. Philippa, vii. 106
  Georgina, iii. 146
  Guy, iii. 146
  Harriet, iii. 146
  Harriet, w. of O.H.A., *see* Crawley
  Henrietta, iii. 146
  J.E. Tannatt, iii. 146
  Sir Jasper, iii. 146
  Louisa, iii. 146
  Louisa, w. of J.E.T., iii. 146
  Mary, w. of O.H.A., *see* Lee
  Miriam, iii. 146
  Miriam, w. of Oliver, iii. 146
  O.H.A., iii. 146
  Oliver, iii. 146
  Rob. Cradock, vii. 134
Nicholson, Wm. Edw., vii. 30
nicknames, medieval, ii. 185
Nickson, Geo. Bernard, vii. 213; *and see* Nixon
Nicol, *see* Nicholl
Nicolas, *see* Nicholas
Nicoll, *see* Nicholl
Nicolls, *see* Nicholls
Niel (Nigel) (fl. 1086), iv. 51, 142, 144, 199
Niel (Nigel) (fl. 1086, another), vii. 33, 68, 101, 280
Niel, Ralph s. of, *see* Ralph
Nigel, *see* Niel
Nigh woods, *see* Harting: Nyewoods
Nimrod, *see* Apperley
Nineveh, *see* Arundel
Ninfield (Nanefield, Nenefeud, Nymensfeud), ii. 43, 324; ix. 126, 239, **247–50**
  adv., ix. 249
  char., ix. 249–50
  ch. (chap.), ii. 112, 249, 410; ix. 141, 246, 248–50, *249*
  dom. archit., ii. 393; ix. 247
  hund., i. 537; ii. 223; ix. 3, **239**
  man., ix. 247–8*
  natural history, i. 121–2, 162, 216, 277, 303
  nonconf., ix. 247, 249
  pop., ii. 223
  prebend, ii. 113, 410; ix. 249
  trades and ind., ii. 260; ix. 247
Nix:
  Chas. Geo. Ashburner, vii. 196
  Jn., vii. 196
Nixon:
  Frances, m. Jn. Blagden, iii. 147
  Ruth, *see* Geere
  and see Nickson
Noakes (Nokes):
  Eliz., m. Wm. Burrell, ix. 228
  Hen., ix. 160, 171
  Thos., ii. 262
  and see Oke
Noble, Mark, ii. 165
Noel:
  Marg., *see* Strange
  Thos., vii. 229
  and see King-Noel
Nogon, *see* Nugon
Nokes, *see* Noakes
Nomansland, *see* Waltham, Up
nonconformity, *see* Baptists; Calvinists; Congregationalists; Countess of Huntingdon's Connexion; Dependents; Family of Love; Indepen-

nonconformity (*cont.*):
  dents, Society of; Methodists;
  Plymouth Brethren; Presbyterians;
  puritanism; Quakers; Roman
  Catholicism; Salvation Army; Unitarians
Nonyngton (Neweton, Noveton, Novynton) (unidentified), prioress, ii. 46
Norbury, Jn., iv. 61; ix. 3, 79
Norden:
  Jas. (fl. 1705), vii. 158–9
  Jas. (another), vii. 159
  Jane, *see* Plumer
  Jn., ii. 247, 297
  Rob., ii. 421; vii. 158–9
  Mr., ix. 198 *n*
  ——, ii. 31
Norfolk, Martha, *see* Rootes
Norfolk:
  dchss. of, *see* FitzAlan, Eliz.; Fitz-Alan, Mary; Howard, Gwendolin Margaret
  dukes, of, ii. 300; iv. 163, 203; *and see* FitzAlan-Howard; Howard; Mowbray
  earls of, *see* Bigod; Brotherton, Thos. de; Mowbray, Thos.
Norfolk, i. 30, 516; ii. 147, 161, 454; vii. 1, *2 n*
  Broads, i. 164
  Jews, i. 506
  lands in, ii. 52, 65; ix. 2
  natural history, i. 110, 176, 274, 287–8, 290
  sport, ii. 461, 475
  and see Bromholm; Castle Acre; Crabhouse; Deopham; Feltwell; Fincham; Hardingham; Norwich; Pensthorpe; Postwick; Rougham; Rungeton; Sandringham; Thetford; Walsingham; Walton; Weeting; Yarmouth, Great
Noricum (Rom. province), iii. 30
Norman the hunter, vii. 67
Norman (fl. 1066–86), ix. 128, 233
Norman (fl. 1086, another), vii. 70
Norman:
  Cecil, iii. 130
  Francis, ix. 222
  Priscilla, m. Jn. Lord, ix. 224
  fam., ii. 253; vii. 94
Normandy (France), i. 484, 490–1; ii. 129, 140, 161, 254, 397, 400; iv. 162; ix. 9, 37, 40
  A.-S. rem., i. 343, 347
  archit., ii. 327–8, 382
  birds, i. 283
  dukes of, *see* Robert; William I
  earthworks, i. 473, 475
  fishing, ii. 142 *n*
  governor, ii. 143
  hunting, i. 305
  lands in, ix. 2, 262 *n*
  marshal, iv. 77
  Normans, i. 264, 349; ii. 132, 138–9; iii. 83
  ports, ii. 128–9, 263
Normanhurst, *see* Catsfield
Normanville, Gerald (Gerold) de, ix. 145, 244
Norris (Norreys):
  Sir Edw., ii. 153
  Sir Jn. (fl. 1592), i. 518 *n*; vii. 63
  Sir Jn. (fl. 1727), ix. 53
Nortburne, Jn. de, abbot of Battle, ii. 55
North:
  Eliz., *see* Uridge
  Fred., Ld. North, i. 532
  Jn., vii. 20
  Jn. (another), vii. 59 *n*
  M.K., ix. 172
  Col., ii. 459
North Sea, i. 268–9
Northampton, earls of, *see* Bohun, Wm. de; Compton, Chas.; Compton, Geo.

Northampton, i. 496; ii. 54, 78, 88
  council of, ii. 6
Northamptonshire, iii. 93 *n*; ix. 263
  Peterborough:
    abbot, *see* Leofric
    bps., *see* Dee; Henshaw, Jos.
  and see Delapré; Grafton; Holcote; Northampton; Sywell
Northborgh, *see* Newick
Northburgh, Mic., canon of Chich., ii. 93; iii. 116 *n*
Northchapel, ii. 41, 43, 237, 475
  ch., ii. 356
  Mitchell (Michel) pk., ii. 297
  pop., ii. 218
Northcliffe, Wm., vii. 280
Northease, *see* Rodmell
Northedone, Thos., sacrist of Bosham coll., ii. 112
Northeton, *see* Norton
Northeye (Northey, Northye):
  Berenger, *see* Northeye, Reinger
  (or Becchenridere), Ingelram de, ix. 118, 120, 230
  Jn. de (fl. before 1200), ix. 120 *n*, 230
  Jn. de (fl. 1203), ix. 118, 120, 161
  Jn. de (d. by 1269), ix. 120, 146
  Margery de, m. Wm. de Stokes, ix. 118, 120, 190
  Reinger (or Berenger) de, ix. 118, 120, 230
  Sir Wm. de, i. 498; ix. 118, 120, 123, 146
Northeye, *see* Bexhill
Northiam, ii. 43, 206, 276; ix. 91, 156, 258, **268–76**
  adv., ix. 276
  Brickwall, ii. 334, 387, 389; ix. 269, *269*
    Pk., i. 306
  char., ix. 276
  ch., ii. 30; ix. 274–6, *275*
    archit., ii. 340, 344, 365, 374
  Dixter:
    Great, ix. 270–1, *270–1*
    Little, ii. 389; ix. 271
    man., ix. 273–4
  dom. archit., ii. 389; ix. 269–72
  Gatecourt, ix. 144, 273–4
  Goatley (Goteley), ix. 169, 266–7, 273–4
  insects, i. 167, 179
  man., ix. 155, 272–4
  mkt., ix. 272
  mills, ix. 273
  nonconf., ix. 272
  pk., ix. 273
  pop., ii. 223
  roads, ix. 268, 276
  sch., ii. 437; ix. 269
  sport, ii. 463, 470–1
  Strawberry Hole, ii. 389; ix. *269*, 271–2
  trades and ind., ii. 255, 260
Northmareys marsh, ix. 50
Northmore:
  Thos., vii. 179–80
  Wm., vii. 144, 180
Northo (Northoo):
  Denise de, w. of Wm., vii. 147
  Olive de, *see* Hautentoft
  Wm. de (? two of this name), i. 507, 509; vii. 147
Northon, *see* Norton
Northoo, *see* Northo
Northstok, Jas. de, iv. 188
Northumberland:
  duke of, *see* Dudley, Sir Jn.
  earls of, *see* Percy
Northumberland, i. 295; ii. 452; iv. 211; *and see* Berwick; Corbridge; Farne Islands; Newcastle
Northwode:
  Agnes, vii. 209 *n*
  Dering de, ix. 180
  Juliana de, ix. 180
  Sir Rob., vii. 209 *n*
  arms, ix. 216
Northwood, *see* Stoughton

Northye, *see* Northeye
Norton (Northeton, Northon):
  Ann, m. —— Corbett, vii. 96
  Ant., i. 527
  Cath., ix. 155
  Cath., m. Thos. Owens, ix. 153
  Denise de, i. 500
  F.C., vii. 109
  Geo., vii. 109
  Sir Greg., iv. 185, 191, 195
  Hen., vii. 96
  Joan, *see* Queeche
  Jn. (fl. 1402), vii. 230
  (formerly Bradbury), Jn., ix. 56, 153, 155
  Jn. (fl. 1881), vii. 261
  Martha, *see* Drew
  Mary, vii. 96
  Mary, w. of Jn., ix. 153
  Ralph, ix. 153
  Ric., vii. 230
  Sarah, m. —— Vernetty, vii. 96
  Steph., ix. 187
  Thos. Herb., vii. 109
  W.S., ii. 472
  Col., i. 523, 526
  ——, ii. 29
Norton (in Aldingbourne), *see* Aldingbourne
Norton (in Bishopstone), *see* Bishopstone
Norton, Church, *see* Selsey
Norton, East, *see* Selsey
Norway, i. 263, 276, 298; ii. 234
  king, *see* Harold; Olaf
Norwich, Alex. of, ix. 14
Norwich, earl of, *see* Goring, Chas.; Goring, Geo.
Norwich (Norf.), i. 24; ii. 258; ix. 67
  bps., *see* Gooch, Sir Thos.; Horn, Geo.
Norwood, Upper, *see* Croydon
Nothelm (Nunna, Nunne), king of South Saxons, i. 482; iv. 94, 134–6, 161, 211, 215 *n*
Nothgithe (fl. 692), iv. 134–5, 161
Notley, Harold, iv. 210
Nottingham, earls of, *see* Berkeley, Wm.; Howard, Chas.; Mowbray, Thos.
Nottingham, i. 496; ii. 468
Nottinghamshire, ii. 468, 470, 473–4; *and see* Nottingham; Southwell; Welbeck
Notyngham, Jn., dean of Hastings coll., ii. 117
Novaille, P., ii. 258
Noveton (Novynton), *see* Nonyngton
Noviomagus Regnum, *see* Chich.
Nowell:
  Alex., dean of St. Paul's, iv. 161
  Joan, *see* Bowyer
Noyes, Wm., iv. 35
Nubery, *see* Newbury
Nucella, Timothy, ii. 166
Nudygatt, *see* Newdigate
Nugon (Nogon), Nic. de, vii. 180
Nunminster priory, *see* Lyminster
Nunna (Nunne), king of South Saxons, *see* Nothelm
Nutbourne (in Pulborough), *see* Pulborough
Nutbourne (in Westbourne), *see* Westbourne
Nuthurst, ii. 43, 208
  ch., ii. 42, 355, 357, 377
  insects, i. 154
  pop., ii. 219
  Sedgewick, ii. 230
    cast., ii. 394
    Lodge, ii. 309
  man., i. 495; ii. 307, 309
  pk., ii. 297, 306–10
Nutley, *see* Maresfield
Nuttall, R.H., ii. 473–4
Nyanser, Thos., iv. 231
Nye:
  Allen, ii. 408

C.W., ii. 452
Hen., rector of Clapham, ii. 33, 35
Nyetimber, see Pagham
Nyewoods, see Harting
Nymensfeud, see Ninfield
Nysell, ——, ii. 245
Nytimber, see Pagham: Nyetimber
Nyton:
  Phil. de, iv. 136 n
  Thos. de, iv. 136 n
Nyton, see Aldingbourne

Oakeley (Ockley, Ocle, Okeleye, Okerlee):
  C.J., ii. 473
  Isabel, w. of Wal. de, vii. 180
  Jn., vii. 180
  Julian, see Blundell
  Rob., iv. 231
  Thos. de, vii. 180
  Thos., dean of South Malling coll., ii. 119
  Wal. de, vii. 180
Oaklands, see Westfield
Oakwood, see Funtington
Oakwood Hill, see Ockley
Oates:
  Sam., ix. 8
  Titus, i. 529; ii. 39; ix. 8
  Capt., ii. 472
oats, see crops
O'Brien Wyndham, Geo., see Wyndham
Ockenden:
  Barbara, w. of Ric., vii. 233
  Hugh, vii. 234–5, 238
  Ric., vii. 183, 233, 235
  Thomasine, m. 2 Geo. Boord, 3 Rog. Aderton, vii. 159, 183, 235
Ockley, see Oakeley
Ockley (Surr.), ii. 448; iii. 33
  Oakwood Hill, iii. 33, 42
Ocklynge, see Eastbourne
Ocle, see Oakeley
O'Clery, Kath., Ctss. O'Clery, ix. 33
Oddingsells, fam., arms, ix. 135
Ode, Ric. fitz, see Richard
Odeby, Ric., master of hosp. of St. Jas. and St. Mary, Chich., ii. 100; iii. 167 n
Odiarne, Wm., ix. 167 n
Odiham (Hants), ix. 244
Odo, bp. of Bayeux, i. 487–90; ii. 294, 323
Odo, dean of Chich., ii. 50
Odo, prior of Christ Church, Cant., abbot of Battle, ii. 53, 55–6
Offa, king of Mercia, i. 349; ii. 127; ix. 1, 8, 117
Offa (fl. 1066), iv. 30
Offham (in Hamsey), see Hamsey
Offham (in South Stoke), see Stoke, South
Offington (Offynton), Hamo de, abbot of Battle, ii. 54–5; ix. 67
Offington, see Durrington
Offley:
  Thos., ii. 163
  Urith, m. Sam. Shore, ix. 181
  fam., ix. 181
Offley (Herts.), ix. 138
Offynton, see Offiington
Ogbourne (Wilts.), ix. 244
Oghir, Steph. le, ii. 256
Oglander:
  Geo., iii. 105
  Mary, w. of Geo., iii. 105
  Wm., ii. 149
Ogle:
  Sir Chas., vii. 218
  his w., see Roe
  E.V.M., m. —— Curwen, vii. 218
Ognell, Geo., iv. 79
Oismelin (fl. 1086), iv. 158, 160
Oke (Ok):
  Jn., prior of Castle Acre and Lewes, ii. 70; vii. 219, 224
  Ralph atte, vii. 34

Ric. atte, vii. 34
and see Noakes
Okehurst:
  Cecily, w. of Jn., m. 2 Wm. Walton, iii. 142; iv. 212
  Jn., iii. 142; iv. 212
  Wm., iii. 142; iv. 129, 212; vii. 217, 231
  ——, m. Thos. Barttelot, iv. 212
  fam., ii. 63; vii. 217
Okeleye, see Oakeley
O'Kelly, Mr., ii. 455
Okerlee, see Oakeley
Okes, Jn., ii. 255
Olaf (Olave), king of Norway, i. 483; iii. 166
Old Court, see Wartling: Oldcourt
Old House warren, see Worth forest
Old Park, see Bosham
Old Pretender, see Stuart, Jas.
Oldbury, see Boxgrove
Oldcourt, see Wartling
Older, Wm., ii. 437
Oldfield, Hen. J., ix. 30
Olding, Jn., ii. 445
Oldlands, see Maresfield
Olecumbe, Rob. de, ix. 180
Oliver (Olliver, Olyver):
  C., vii. 199
  Edw., ii. 427
  Geo., and his w. Mary, ix. 221
  J.J., ii. 474
  Jn., i. 467 n
  Ric., canon of Wells, rector of Chilbolton (Hants), archdeacon of Winchester, ii. 428
  Thos., ii. 437
  Wm., bailiff of Atherington, ii. 120
  Wm., ii. 437
  Mr., ii. 207 n
  and see Edwardes, Brown and Oliver
Olsson, ——, i. 265
Olwin:
  Ric., iv. 231
  Secunda, see Hook
Olyver, see Oliver
Omelina, prioress of Lyminster, ii. 121
Omerod brothers, ii. 476
Onewyne, see Unwin
Onley:
  Jn., iv. 56
  Thos., iv. 56
Onslow:
  Anne, m. Ant. Shirley, vii. 254, 270
  Ric. (fl. 1569), ii. 255
  Sir Ric. (fl. 1653), ii. 271; vii. 64, 270
  Ric., Ld. Onslow, vii. 254, 270
Onwyn, see Unwin
Opton (or Eye):
  Maud de, see Paynel
  Nic. de, iv. 176, 213
Orange, princes of, see Maurice; William, count of Nassau
ordeal by water, ii. 52; ix. 94
Ore:
  Agatha de, see Guestling
  Amice de, m. Jn. Hall, ix. 19, 87*, 89, 92, 190
  Amice, w. of Jn. de, ix. 87, 180, 183
  Cecily, w. of Ric., ix. 192
  (or Pett) Gilb. de, ix. 190
  Hen. de, ix. 87, 180
  Joan de, see Read
  Jn. de (d. by 1307), ix. 87, 180, 183
  Jn. de (d. 1361), ix. 87
  Jn. (d. 1422), see Hall
  Nic. de, ix. 87
  Ric. de (d. by 1274), ix. 87, 180, 192
  Ric. de (d. 1361), ix. 19, 87
  Rob. de (fl. before 1200), ix. 87
  Rob. de (fl. to 1405), i. 510; ix. 87, 192, 213
  Wm. de (fl. c. 1220), ix. 87, 278 n
  Wm. de (fl. 1332), ix. 87, 254, 278 n
  fam., ix. 190
  arms, ix. 88, 170–1
  Ore, ii. 43, 173, 178, 410; ix. 4, 6, 76, **87–90**

adv., ix. 89
Baldslow, ix. 88
batrachians, i. 272
brickmaking, ix. 87
char., ix. 30, 89–90, 179
ch., i. 533; ii. 361, 376; ix. 25, 88, 88–9
crustaceans, i. 265
insects, i. 112, 114, 116, 119, 121–2, 126–7, 129, 132, 135, 138, 140–1, 144, 146–8, 150–1, 154, 158, 162–3, 196–7, 201, 211–12, 221–2, 224, 226, 237
man., ix. 87–8, 92, 190, 221, 254
Maplehurst, ix. 88
  wood, i. 148
Ore Place, ix. 87
pop., ii. 222, 228
rly., ii. 222 n
roads, ix. 87
Rom. Cath., ix. 87
St. Helen's, i. 122–3, 126, 265, 276, 302
Orfevre, Ric. le, warden of St. Mary's hosp., Chich., ii. 102
Orford (Suff.), ii. 133
  Orford Ness, ii. 141, 162
Orgericus, Peter de, bailiff of Atherington, ii. 120
Oriel College, Oxford, ii. 420–1
Orival:
  Mabel d', m. Adam de Port, iv. 143
  Muriel d', see St. John
  Rainald d', iv. 143
Orkney Islands, i. 296–7
Orlanden (Orlandini), Sebastian, ii. 255
Orlaston (Orlauston):
  Agatha de, see Leuesham
  Agnes, see Salerne
  Joan, m. Wm. Scott, ix. 177
  Jn. de, ix. 56
  Marg., m. Wm. Parker, ix. 177
  Ric., ix. 177
  Wm., ix. 177
Orleans:
  Ferdinand Philippe, duc d'Orleans (d. 1842), ii. 458
  Louis Philippe, duc d'Orleans (d. 1793), ii. 456
Orleans Cricket Club, ii. 472
Orlebar, Mrs., vii. 177
Orleswick, see Piddinghoe
Orme:
  Alice, w. of Garton, iv. 95
  Charlotte, m. Ric. Bettesworth, iv. 59
  Garton, ii. 442; iv. 59, 95
  Mary, see Garton
  Rob., iv. 59, 95
  fam., iv. 96
Ormerod, E.O., ii. 476
Orreby:
  Isabel de, see Tattersall
  Jn. de, iv. 41, 123, 168
  Thos. de, iv. 41
Orvis, C., ii. 447
Orwell Haven (Suff.), ii. 136
Osaye, Guichard (Guigardus) de la, prior of Lewes, ii. 70, 411
Osbaldeston, Mr., ii. 468
Osbarn, see Osborne
Osbern, bp. of Exeter, i. 485; ii. 3–4, 109; iv. 3, 8, 90, 183, 185
Osbern fitz Hugh, ix. 262
Osbern the clerk, iv. 8
Osbern (fl. 1086), ix. 117–18
Osbern (fl. 1086, ? another), ix. 128, 237
Osbern (fl. 1086, ? another), ix. 267
Osbern, see Sbern
Osbert, abbot of Durford, ii. 91
Osbert, prior of Lewes, ii. 69
Osbert the white, ix. 80
  his dau., see Idonea
Osborne (Osbarn, Osborn, Usbornes):
  Alice, w. of Geo., m. 2 —— Smith, iv. 90
  Geo., iv. 90
  J., ii. 477
  Jane, iii. 164

Osborne (*cont.*):
Jn. (fl. 1456), and his w. Alice, vii. 235
Jn. (d. 1593), iv. 219
Jn. (d. 1740), iii. 164
Jn. (fl. 1835), ix. 268
Leighton, and his w. Eliz., vii. 207
Ric., and his w. Jane, iii. 164
Sidney Godolphin, vii. 42
Thos. (d. 1710), vii. 207
Thos. (d. 1727), vii. 207
Wm., iv. 219
fam., iv. 219
Oscroft, Wm., ii. 474
Oseburnham, *see* Ashburnham
Osferth, i. 483; vii. 104; ix. 144
Osgood, Francis, ii. 423*
Oslac, ealdorman of the South Saxons, iv. 202*
Osmund, king of South Saxons, i. 482
Osmund (fl. 1086), vii. 33
Osp', Gervase de, ix. 146
Ospringe (Kent), iii. 51
Ossory, earl of, *see* Butler, Chas.
Ossulstone, Lds., *see* Bennett, Chas.
Ostend (Belgium), ii. 157
Oswald, bp. of Selsey, ix. 79
Oswald, *see* Oswol
Oswald, Felix, iii. 28, 56
Osward (fl. 1066–1086), vii. 202, 204, 213, 282; ix. 266*
Oswol (Oswald, fl. 1066), vii. 194
Oswold, moneyer, vii. 33
Otehale, *see* Ottehale
Otham (in Hailsham):
abbey, ii. 7, 45, **86**, 232, 314, 330
abbot, *see* Jordan
accessories, ii. 352, 376
archit., ii. 330, 376
estates, ii. 232
chap., ii. 86
man., ii. 86–7
O'Tigernach, Gilb., bp. of Annadown (Enaghdun), ii. 61
Otley (Ottley):
Thos., rector of Ripe, vicar of Burwash, ii. 414
Wm., iv. 200
Ottehale (Otehale):
Joan de, vii. 121 *n*
(or Donne), Jn. de (fl. 1292), vii. 121
Jn. de (fl. 1292, another), vii. 121
Jn. de (fl. 1348), vii. 121
Maud de, *see* Donne
Ric. de (fl. before 1300), vii. 121
Ric. de (fl. 1370), vii. 121
Thos. de, vii. 121
Wal. de, vii. 121
Wm. de, vii. 121
Otten:
Dorothy de, *see* Drew
Harpocrates de, iv. 191 *n*
Otter, Wm., bp. of Chich., ii. 41–2; iii. 126
arms, iv. 233
otter hunting, *see* sport: hunting
Ottley, *see* Otley
Ottobon, Cardinal, ii. 12
Ottringham:
Eliz., *see* Hook
Rob., iv. 231
Otway:
Eliz., w. of Humph., iv. 87
Humph., rector of Woolbeding, iv. 33, 87
Thos., iv. 33, 87 *n*
Oualet, iv. 63
Oulele, *see* Ashdown forest: Uleley
Ouse, riv., i. 18, 25, 43, 55–6, 267, 475, 481 *n*, 498–9; ii. 139; iii. 2, 4, 10, 30, 46, 69; vii. 9, 15, 62–4, 66, 69, 73, 76, 83, 94, 127
as a boundary, i. 58, 503, 539; vii. 80, 87, 132, 147
raids, i. 510
salt, ii. 232
sport, ii. 453, 464–5
Ouse Preservation Society, i. 267; ii.

464–5
outfangthief, ix. 37, 39, 68
outlaws, i. 503
Oval cricket ground, *see* Lambeth
Oven, Jn., ii. 28
Ovenden, Jn., vii. 178
Overman, Thos., ix. 127
Overton:
E.P., i. 292
Ric., iii. 77
Wm. (? two of this name), ii. 102; iii. 77
Overy:
R., ii. 451
Wm., vii. 105
Ovid, ii. 406, 419
Oving, Wal., mayor of Chich., iii. 91
Oving, ii. 43; iii. 71; iv. 133, 158, **165–70**
adv., iv. 156, 170, 173
almshos., iv. 170
char., iv. 170
ch., iv. 169–70, *169*, *172*
accessories, ii. 250, 351, 356, 372
archit., ii. *345*, 349–50, 371–2
Colworth, iv. 170
chap., iv. 170
forest, i. 50
man., iv. 166
prebend, iv. 166
tithes, ii. 99
dom. archit., iv. 165–6
Drayton, iii. 71, 104; iv. 166
man., iv. 166–7
rly. station, iv. 165
tithes, iv. 170 *n*
Egley, iii. 71, 104–5; iv. 168
man., iv. 105, 166–9
Martinsgrove, iii. 71, 104; iv. 2, 167–8, 170 *n*
pop., ii. 220
Portfield, *see* Chich.: suburbs
prebend, iv. 166, 170
prehist. rem., i. 330
roads, iii. 46; iv. 165
Shopwyke, ii. 452–3; iii. 46, 71, 104; iv. 166, 168–9
tithes, iv. 170
vicarage, ii. 8; iv. 170
Woodhorn, prebend, iv. 166
Ovingdean, Mary, m. Guy le Strange, vii. 228–9
Ovingdean, ii. 43–4, 296; vii. 14, 221, **227–32**, 244, 253
adv., vii. 229, 232
agric., vii. 227, 230
chap., vii. 228
ch., ii. 40; vii. 231–2, *231*
accessories, ii. 352, 358
archit., ii. 334, 339, 349, 365, 372
earthworks, ii. 480; vii. 228
insects, i. 182, 186
man., vii. 2, 226, 228–31, 276
pop., ii. 225
rector, *see* Code; Marshal, Jn.
rectory, ii. 37; vii. 262
Roedean sch., vii. 228
Woodingdean, vii. 227–8, 234
Ow, Hen. de, *see* Eu
Owen:
Alice, *see* Blount
Sir David, ii. 85; iv. 49, 51, 53, 77, 79; vii. 207; ix. 273
E.L., ii. 471
H., ii. 473
H.G., ii. 471
Sir Hen., iv. 77; vii. 207
Jn. (fl. 1557), iv. 51
Jn. (another), ii. 420
Mary, *see* Bohun
Ric., and his w. Patience, vii. 57
Owens:
Cath., *see* Norton
Jane, w. of Ric., iii. 115
Ric., iii. 115
Thos., ix. 153
Owers, the, *see* Cymenesore
Owing, Rob., ii. 407

oxen, *see* livestock: cattle
Oxenbridge (Oxenbrigge):
Agnes, ix. 216
Alice, w. of Jn., ix. 169
Alice, w. of Rob., m. 2 —— Blount, 3 Hen. Lacy, ix. 181
Alice, w. of Sir Rob., ix. 220, 274
And., ix. 197
Anne, m. 1 Hen. Stokes, 2 Oliver St. John, ix. 181
Anne, m. —— Kingston, ix. 92
Anne, w. of Sir Goddard, *see* Fiennes
Anne, w. of Rob., ix. 171, 220
Anne, w. of Sir Thos., *see* Blount
Eliz., m. Sir Rob. Tyrwhitt, ix. 212
Eliz., w. of Sir Goddard, *see* Echingham
Sir Goddard (Godard), ix. 165, 169, 171, 181, 197, 212, 220
Jn. (d. by 1405, ? more than one of this name), ix. 144, 169, 169 *n*
Jn. (fl. 1450), i. 514
Jn. (d. 1493), ix. 169 *n*
Jn. (another), ix. 92
Jn. (fl. 1498), ix. 92
Kath., ix. 171
Margery (d. *c.* 1500), ix. 171
Margery, w. of Thos. (? another), ix. 92
Pernel, w. of Wm., m. 2 Seth Standishe, ix. 145
Rob. (fl. 1398), vii. 142
Rob. (fl. 1405, ? another), ix. 165, 169
Rob. (s. of the last), ix. 169
Rob. (fl. 1421, ? one of the above), vii. 106
Rob. (d. 1487), ix. 164, 169, 171, 181, 220
Rob., his s., ix. 181
Rob. (fl. after 1498), ix. 92
Rob. (fl. 1538), ix. 92
Sir Rob. (d. 1574), ix. 165, 169, 220, 274
Rob. (d. 1591), ix. 169
Rob. (d. 1616), ix. 169
Sir Rob. (d. 1645), ix. 165, 169
Thos. (fl. mid 15th cent.), ix. 145
Thos. (d. 1497, another), i. 515; ix. 133, 169, 169 *n*
Thos. (fl. 1498), ix. 92
Sir Thos. (d. 1540), ix. 169, 181 *n*, 197, 212
Wm. (fl. mid 15th cent.), ix. 145
Wm. (fl. after 1498), ix. 92
Wm. (fl. 1543), i. 516 *n*; ix. 185
fam., ii. 379; ix. 74, 92 *n*, 169–71, 274
Oxenden, Sir Hen., ix. 83
Oxenel, Jn. de, ix. 27
Oxford:
ctss. of, *see* Scrope, Eliz.
earl of, *see* Vere, Jn. de
Oxford, i. 112, 527; ii. 130; iii. 87
bp., iv. 47; vii. 109*; ix. 189; *and see* Wilberforce, Sam.
Hope museum, i. 112, 261
Magdalen Coll. sch., ii. 404, 406
militia, i. 534
Univ., ii. 54, 399, 406–7, 419–20, 427, 430–1, 433
Bodleian library, iii. 12
chancellor, *see* Chase
colleges and halls, *see* All Souls; Balliol; Brasenose; Canterbury; Cardinal; Christ Church; Corpus Christi; Exeter; Hart Hall; Hertford; Keble; Lincoln; Magdalen; Magdalen Hall; Merton; New College; Oriel; Pembroke; Queen's; St. Alban Hall; St. Bernard's; St. John's; St. Mary Hall; Trinity; University; Wadham
cricket, ii. 471–2, 476
Oxfordshire:
militia, vii. 64
and see Banbury; Cogges; Crowmarsh; Eynsham; Oxford; Radley; Shirburn; Woodstock
Oxleys Green, *see* Brightling

Oxney, Isle of (Kent), ii. 410–11
Oxsettle, see Malling Without, South

Pacchyng, see Patching
Pacific Ocean, i. 269
Pack, Wm., ix. 111
Pack and Chapman, ix. 60, 156, 223
Pack, see Lester and Pack
Packham, Jn., ii. 475
Paddockhurst, see Worth
Padwick:
  Fred., iv. 172, 195, 197
  Hen., iv. 172
  Wm., iv. 127, 172, 189
  ——, i. 290
  fam., iv. 195
Page:
  Agnes, m. Jn. Watersfield, iv. 153
  Cath., iv. 173
  Eliz., m. Thos. Knight, iv. 153
  Frances, m. Geo. White, iv. 150
  Jane, m. Edw. Rose, iv. 153
  Jn., prior of Tortington, ii. 83
  Jn. (d. 1551), iv. 153
  Jn. (fl. 1560), vii. 89
  Jn. (d. 1779), M.P. for Chich., iii. 77;
    iv. 150, 152, 173
  Thos., ii. 257
  Wm., iv. 153
  Mrs., ii. 123
  fam., iv. 150
Pageham, see Pagham
Pagen, see Payn
Paget:
  Hen. Wm., earl of Uxbridge, ii. 458
  T. Guy, ii. 452
  fam., i. 519
Pagham (Pageham):
  Agnes de, see Leuesham
  Jn. de, iv. 239
  Ric. de, iv. 237
  Ric. de, chancellor of Chich., ii. 77;
    iv. 229
  Rog. de, ix. 56
  Wm. de, iv. 239
Pagham, ii. 43, 295; iii. 102; iv. 160,
  205–6, 222–3, 226, **227–33**
  adv., iv. 225, 233
  Aldwick, q.v.
  anchorite, ii. 47; and see Humphrey
  bailiwick, iii. 104
  beacons, ii. 152
  birds, i. 288, 292–3
  boundary, iv. 2, 227
  Bowley, see Mundham, North
  chant., ii. 16; iv. 226, 229–30, 233
  chap., iv. 227, 233
  ch., ii. 347, 356, 370; iv. 226–7, 228,
    231–3, 232
  coins, i. 326, 330
  cts., iii. 104
  Crimsham (Cremesham), iii. 92; iv.
    227, 229–31
  deanery, ii. 42, 118; iv. 101
    dean, ii. 16
  defences, ii. 152, 163
  dom. archit., ii. 333; iv. 227–9
  earthworks, i. 479
  erosion, iv. 227
  fair, iv. 229
  guilds, iv. 233
  (or Selsey) harbour (formerly Wyther-
    ing Haven), i. 14, 25; ii. 125,
    140, 144, 152; iii. 65, 100–1; iv.
    198, 205–6, 210–11, 227, 229,
    237
  hund., see Aldwick: hund.
  insects, i. 111, 117, 178, 181–2, 190,
    193, 197, 206, 212, 214, 217–20,
    224, 226–30, 234–7
  Lagness, i. 233; iv. 227, 231
    man., iv. 230–1
  man., ii. 6, 292; iii. 92, 100, 103; iv.
    161–2, 183, 222–4, 229–31, 237
  mkt., iv. 229
  Marsh, i. 112–13, 117
  mills, iv. 229, 233
  Mundham, South, see Mundham,

  North
  Nyetimber (Nytimber), iv. 20, 227–8
    Barton, man. ho., ii. 334, 380; iv.
      227–8, 228; chap., ii. 338, 372,
      380; iv. 228, 228
    man., iv. 229, 231
    mill, iv. 229
  Pagham Point, iii. 100
  peculiar, ii. 1, 3, 42
  pop., ii. 220
  rectors, ii. 37; iii. 93; iv. 233; and see
    Bar, Theobald de; Duèse; Islip,
    Sim.
  rectory, ii. 12; iv. 233
    ho., iv. 227
  roads, iv. 227
  Rom. rem., iii. 62
  ship service, ii. 130
  shipping, ii. 151
  tithes, iv. 229, 233
  trades and ind., ii. 145, 263; iv.
    229
  vicar, iv. 227
  woods, ii. 292
  Wythering (Wodering), ii. 131*,
    138*; iv. 231, 233; and see
    Pagham: harbour
Pagham Harbour Company, ii. 284
Paice:
  Thos., iv. 25
  ——, iv. 25
Paine (Payn, Payne):
  Alan, ii. 98
  Alex., iv. 193
  Anne (Anna), m. Gibbs Crawford,
    vii. 169, 197
  Chas., vii. 169, 197
  Edw. (d. 1660), 168–9, 197
  Edw. (fl. 1871), iv. 208
  Eliza, vii. 42
  Eliz., see Alcock
  Grace, vii. 217
  Harriett, ix. 62
  Hen. (fl. 1290), ii. 86
  Hen. (fl. 1676), vii. 197
  Hen. E., ix. 173
  Joan, see Baseville
  Jn. (fl. 1252), iv. 193
  Jn. (fl. 1586), ii. 28
  Jn. (d. 1768), vii. 217
  Jn. (d. 1803), vii. 217
  Jn. (fl. 1812), vii. 217
  Mabel, iv. 193
  Mary, vii. 230
  Mary, w. of Ric., see Pellatt
  Ric. (d. by 1693), vii. 168–9, 230
  Ric. (d. 1725), vii. 168, 230
  Ric. (d. 1733), vii. 168, 230, 232
  Rob. (fl. 1676), vii. 197
  Rob. (fl. 1708), ii. 430
  Sim., ii. 86
  Thos. (fl. 1498), and his w. Marg., iv.
    216
  Thos. (d. 1763), vii. 168
  Thos. (d. 1809), vii. 10, 18
  Thos. Holles, vii. 168, 230, 232
  Wm. (fl. 1276), iv. 42
  Wm. (fl. 1560), ii. 407
  Wm. (fl. 1760), ix. 177
  Mr., vii. 228
  arms, vii. 168
Pakenham:
  Constance, m. Sir Geof. Poole, ii. 25;
    iv. 92, 116
  Sir Edm., iv. 28
  Sir Edw., iv. 92, 116
  Eliz., m. Sir Edm. Mervyn, iv. 25–6,
    28, 92, 116
  Jn. (fl. 1385), and his w. Justina, ii.
    263
  Sir Jn. (fl. 1479), iv. 28, 92, 116
  Marg., see Bramshott
Pakyn:
  Rog., vii. 176
  Wal., vii. 176
palaeontology, i. **27–39**
palebote, ii. 310; vii. 105
Palestine, ii. 53

Palgrave:
  Diana, see Covert
  Jn., vii. 280
Pallant, see Chich.
Pallingfeud, Jn. de, ii. 184
Pallingham, Humph. de, rector of Cock-
  ing, iv. 47
Pallingham, see Wisborough Green
Palmer (Palmere):
  Anne, see Stephens
  Blanche, see Reynolds
  Brice, ix. 61
  Denise, ii. 397
  Edw., iv. 42
  Eliz., iv. 99
  Eliz., m. Jn. Cheney, ix. 183
  Esther, see Lawley
  Frances, see Wyndham
  J., ii. 167
  Jn., prior of Tortington, ii. 82–3
  Jn. (fl. c. 1540), ii. 190
  Jn. (fl. 1623), iii. 95
  Jn. (fl. 1649), vii. 77
  Jn. (fl. c. 1650, another), ii. 319
  Mary, m. Francis Goater, iii. 126
  Nat., iv. 150
  Peregrine (fl. 1654), iv. 99, 150
  Peregrine (fl. 1723), iv. 150
  Ric., ix. 207
  Rob., ix. 139
  Thos. (fl. 1527), ix. 139
  Sir Thos. (fl. 1547), ii. 118; vii. 235
  Sir Thos. (d. 1553, ? another), iv.
    234
  Sir Thos. (d. 1582), iv. 95, 150
  Sir Thos. (fl. 1588), i. 518; ii. 24–8,
    152
  Sir Thos. (fl. 1597, ? another), iv.
    234 n
  Thos. (fl. 1723), iv. 150
  Wm., iv. 98, 150
  Misses, ix. 89
  ——, ii. 83
  fam., ii. 386
  arms, iv. 150
Palmer-Acland, see Fuller-Palmer-
  Acland
Palosius, Steph., cardinal priest of St.
  Marcellus, dean of Chich., ii. 48
Palyng:
  Amice de, vii. 99 n
  (or Ferring), Jn. de, iv. 24, 135; vii.
    99
  Sim. de, vii. 99 n
Pangdean, see Pyecombe
Pankhurst (Penkhurst):
  Steph., vii. 76
  T., ii. 253
pannage, right of, ii. 63, 293–4, 303–4,
  306–8, 310, 312–17, 320–5; iv. 10,
  135, 142; vii. 176; ix. 80, 123
  cts., see courts
Pannell, Jn., iv. 237
Panningridge, see Ashburnham
Panton:
  Jn., ix. 242
  Nehemia, ix. 242
paper making, ii. 238; iv. 63, 190 n
Papillon:
  Anne, see Pelham
  D., ii. 470 n
  G.K., ii. 472 n, 474
  H.G., ii. 472 n, 474
  Hen., iv. 184
  Mabel, iv. 184
  Pelham Rawstorn, ix. 80–2, 241
  Phil. Oxenden, ix. 80
  Rog., iv. 184
  Thos. (sr.), ix. 80
  Thos. (jr.), ix. 80
  Wm., iv. 184
  fam., ix. 240
  arms, ix. 80
Paplesbury (? Bury), ii. 303
parage, vii. 228
parapet walls, see architecture: ecclesias-
  tical
Parentin, Rob. de, ix. 80

Pargitter:
Marg., *see* Fuller
Sam., iv. 83
(later Fuller), Sam., *see* Fuller
Parham, i. 8, 502, 524; ii. 43, 301; iv. 99, 150
ch., ii. 378
man., ii. 3
militia, i. 535
natural history, i. 47, 208–9, 282, 286
Parham Ho., ii. 387–8; iii. 63
pk., ii. 306
pop., ii. 218
Rackham, *q.v.*
Rom. rem., iii. 62
Paris (Parys):
Hen., ix. 63
Jn. (fl. *c.* 1280), ix. 63
Jn. de (fl. 1340), vii. 34, 70
Marg. de, *see* Radmylde
Mat., ix. 63
Paris (France), i. 536; ii. 236, 399; iv. 17 *n*
abbey of St. Denis, ii. 3, 331; ix. 8
peace of, ii. 125
Parish:
W.D., ii. 470 *n*
Capt., ii. 470 *n*
Park, Willie, ii. 480
Park Bottom, *see* Brighton
Park Brow, *see* Sompting
park keeper, *see* Walter
Park Mount, *see* Pulborough
Parkehurst, *see* Parkhurst
Parker:
Alex., ii. 38
Ambrose, vii. 199
Anne, m. 1 Adrian More, 2 Sir Jn. Smith, vii. 195
Anne, m. Jas. Clayton, iii. 160
Dorothy, *see* Whitson
Ellis, sacrist of Tortington, sub-prior of Michelham, prior of Pynham, ii. 79, 81, 83
Geo., iii. 160
J., ii. 167
Jane, iii. 161
Jn., warden of Lewes friary, ii. 96
Jn. (d. *c.* 1558), ix. 202
Jn. (fl. 1564), ii. 256–7
Marg., *see* Orlaston
Mary (d. 1757), iii. 161
Mary (fl. 1887), ix. 265
Mat., abp. of Cant., ii. 23–4
Nic. (fl. 1588), ix. 202, 206
Sir Nic. (fl. 1603), i. 519–20; ii. 31; vii. 195
Ric. (fl. 1552), and his w. Anne, iv. 162
Ric. (fl. 1676), ix. 165, 169
Thos. (fl. 1563), ix. 202, 206
Thos. (fl. 1564, ? another), ii. 24
Thos. (fl. 1608), vii. 239
Sir Thos. (fl. 1653), ix. 155
Thos., and his w. Susannah, iii. 161
Thos. (d. 1740), iii. 161
Timothy, vii. 135
Sir Wal., ii. 460
Wm., master of Playden hosp., ii. 104–5
Wm., ii. 410–11
——, i. 514
——, iii. 75
fam., iv. 135
Parkhurst (Parkehurst):
Edw., iv. 51
Jn., iv. 51
Ric., vii. 43
Rob., vicar of Washington, ii. 25
Parkin:
J.S., ii. 471 *n*
Jn., ix. 32
T., ii. 472–3
Parkminster, *see* Cowfold
parliamentary representation:
boroughs. *see* Arundel; Bramber; Brighton; Chich.; Eastbourne; Grinstead, East; Hastings;

Horsham; Hove; Lewes; Midhurst; Rye; Seaford; Shoreham; Winchelsea
county, i. 504, 532
elections, i. 530–2
M.P.s, i. 522–4
Parma, duke of, *see* Farnese
Parr:
Geo., ii. 469
Jn., ii. 165
Parratt, B., i. 272
parrocks, ii. 311, 322
Parrok:
Jn. de, ix. 266
Maud de, *see* Wacelyn
Parshaw, Ric., ii. 99
parson, *see* David the parson; Robert the parson
Parson (Parsons):
(formerly Freake), Jas., iv. 70
Ric., vii. 102
Wm. Hen., rector of Linchmere, iv. 70
——, iii. 130
Partington:
Edw., vii. 85
Jessie, vii. 85
Thos., vicar of Netherfield, vii. 85
Thos. Whalley, vii. 85
Partridge Green, *see* Grinstead, West
Partrych, Geo., ii. 257
parvise chambers, *see* architecture: ecclesiastical
Parvishe, Jewell, ii. 191
Parys, *see* Paris
Pasch, Jn., ix. 230
Pashley, *see* Passeley
Pashley (in Ticehurst), *see* Ticehurst
passage, right of, ix. 37, 49, 68
Passele, *see* Passeley
Passelewe, Rob., archdeacon of Lewes, ii. 10; iv. 163 *n*; vii. 283
Passeley (Pashley, Passele):
Sir Edm. de (d. 1327), ii. 325; iv. 230; ix. 144 *n*, 145–6, 153–4, 156, 176, 178, 254, 257
Edm. de, his s., ix. 154
Elias de, ix. 254
Giles de, ix. 254
Idonia de, m. —— Chalfhunte, ix. 145
Joan, w. of Edm. de, iv. 230
Jn. de (fl. 1340), iv. 230; ix. 145, 154, 254
Sir Jn. (d. by 1453), ix. 154, 176
Jn. (fl. 1460), ix. 154, 157, 176, 254–5
Marg. de, *see* Basyng
Margery de, m. —— de Lunsford, ix. 145
Maud de, *see* Kechenore
Philippe, w. of Rob., m. 2 Wm. Swynbourne, ix. 154
Rob. de (fl. 1272), ix. 145, 153, 254
Rob. de (fl. 1327), ix. 154, 254
Rob. (fl. 1366), ix. 254–5
Rob. (fl. *c.* 1400), ix. 154
Sarah, w. of Rob. de, ix. 254
(? or Farndon), Sarah de, m. 1 Jn. de Stoke, 2 Ralph atte More, iv. 105, 238; ix. 118, 145
Thos. de, ix. 154, 176, 254
Wm. de, ix. 145
fam., ix. 146
arms, ix. *154*
Passenger, Wm., ii. 165
Passingworth, *see* Waldron: Possingworth
Paston, Rob., ii. 165
pastoral husbandry (vol. ii only), ii. 189–91, 274–85
pasture, right of (vol. ii. only), ii. 302–3, 307–8, 314, 316, 320–5
Patch:
J., ix. 75
Jn., ix. 75
Patcham, i. 54; ii. 43–4; vii. 103. 109, **216–20**, 223, 225, 244, 253, 264–5
adv., vii. 219–20
ch., ii. 68; vii. *215*, 218–19, *219*

accessories, ii. 355, 358
archit., ii. 346, 349, 351, 366, 372, 377
cts., vii. 218
dom. archit., ii. 382; vii. 216
earthworks, vii. 216
fossils, i. 28
French raids, ii. 138
geology, i. 11
inc., ii. 190–1
man., vii. 1–2, 4, 216–17, 279
mill, vii. 216
Moulescombe (Moulescoomb), i. 172, 190, 200; iii. 24, 61
natural history, i. 170, 284
pop., ii. 224
rly., ii. 224 *n*
Rom. rem., iii. 3, 51, 62
royal visits, i. 505; vii. 216
stag hunting, ii. 449
Sweet Hill, iii. 62
truffles, i. 66
vicar, ii. 37
Withdean, i. 180, 186, 188, 198, 207; ii. 277
man., vii. 120–1, 217, 241
Patching (Pacchyng, Patchinge):
Agnes, ii. 99
E.C., ii. 478
Thos., mayor of Chich., ii. 91, 98, 111
Thos., ii. 39
Patching, i. 66; ii. 13, 43, 61, 292
ch., ii. 25, 118, 333, 340, 349, 356–7, 371–2
hund., ii. 219; *and see* Poling: hund.
peculiar, ii. 3
pop., ii. 219
rector, *see* Whetston, Wal.
rectory, ii. 37
Pateney, Jn., dean of South Malling coll., ii. 119
Paterson, A.G., ii. 478
Patey, Chas. Rob., iv. 39
Patiala, maharaja of, ix. 250
Patmore, Coventry, ix. 7–8
Patrington, Steph., bp. of Chich., ii. 15
Patten (or Waynflete), Jn., dean of Chich., *see* Waynflete
Pattison, Mr., ii. 455
Pauethorn:
Juliana de, vii. 204
Wm. de, and his w. Alice, vii. 204
Wm. de (another), and his w. Isabel, vii. 204
Paul II, pope, ix. 157
Paul, Rob., ii. 167
Paulet (Paulett, Powlatt, Powlett):
Chas., duke of Bolton (d. 1722), ii. 441–2
Chas., duke of Bolton (d. 1754), ii. 454
Eliz., w. of Jn., Ld. Paulet, *see* Kenn
Eliz., w. of Wm., *see* Ward
Sir Geo., vii. 37, 42, 75
Henrietta, w. of Chas., duke of Bolton, ii. 441
Joan, *see* Kyme
Jn., Ld. Paulet, ix. 130
Ld. Nassau, ii. 441
Wm., marquess of Winchester, iv. 213
Wm., iii. 163; vii. 157
Paulin (Paulyn):
Hen., bailiff of Rye, ix. 51
Rob., bailiff of Winchelsea, ix. 50, 68, 144, 152–3
Pauncefort, Edw., ii. 442–3
Paveley:
Maud de, *see* Burghersh
Wal. de (d. 1327), ix. 196
Sir Wal. (fl. 1365), ix. 196
Pawnefold, Sir Wal., vii. 190, 280
Paxhill, *see* Lindfield
Paxton:
Jn., canon of Chich., iii. 153
Wentworth, ii. 165
Pay (Paye):
Hen. (fl. 1407), ii. 141
Hen. (fl. 1598), iv. 111

Jn., iv. 111
Ric., and his w. Anne, iv. 111
Susan, w. of Jn., iv. 111
Thos., iv. 92, 189
Wm., iv. 111
Payn (Pagen) (fl. 1086), iv. 118, 127–8
Payne (fl. 1200), vii. 1
Payn (Payne), fam., *see* Paine
Paynel (Peynell):
  Eve, *see* Dawtrey
  Godeheuda, m. Wm. de St. John, iv. 162, 176
  Hasculf, iv. 59
  Jn., ii. 74; iv. 85, 176
  Marg., *see* Gatesden
  Maud, m. Nic. de Opton, ii. 74; iv. 85, 176, 213
  Maud, w. of Wm., *see* Hussey
  Nic., iv. 176
  Sir Thos. (fl. 1270), iv. 25
  Thos. (? another), ii. 316
  Thos. (fl. 1308, ? another), iv. 199 n
  Wm. (fl. 1268), iv. 14, 176
  Wm. (d. c. 1316), ii. 74; iv. 8, 34, 36, 59, 85, 108, 176, 213; vii. 81
  fam., iv. 176
Peacehaven, *see* Piddinghoe
Peachey (Peachie, Peachy, Pecche, Peche):
  (later Knight), Bulstrode, iv. 97–8, 100, 129
  Caroline Mary, m. Leveson Vernon Harcourt, iv. 31, 97, 122, 208
  Eliz., *see* Knight
  Godeheuda, w. of Jn., iv. 161
  Hen. (fl. 1637), iv. 167
  Sir Hen. (d. 1737), iv. 75, 208
  Sir Hen. Jn., Ld. Selsey, iv. 10, 31, 97, 122, 208
  Jas., iv. 5, 31
  Sir Jas., Ld. Selsey, iv. 5, 10, 31, 83–4, 90, 97, 208
  Jn. de (fl. 1288), iii. 92, 103; iv. 161, 199 n, 230
  Jn. (fl. 1545), and his w. Anne, iv. 83
  Jn. (d. 1636), iv. 238
  Jn. (fl. 1663), iii. 125
  Sir Jn. (fl. 1741), iv. 76, 83, 97, 208
  Sir Jn. (d. by 1794), iv. 208
  Sir Jn., Ld. Selsey, iv. 5, 98, 129
  Marg., iv. 195
  Marg., m. Sir Jn. Miller, iii. 125
  Marg., w. of Jn. de, *see* Greyly
  Susan, iv. 195
  Wm. (fl. 1637), iv. 167
  Wm. (fl. 1674), and his w. Anne, iv. 219
  Wm. (fl. 1693), iv. 98
  fam., iv. 76, 129
  arms, iv. 97, 208
Peacock, Thos., ii. 425; *and see* Pecocke
Pearce (Pearse, Perse, Pierce):
  Brice, ix. 178
  Chas., ix. 225
  Jeffrey, ii. 165
  Jn., ix. 86
  Thos. (d. 1606), ix. 24
  Thos. (fl. 1772), ix. 89
  Mr., ii. 414
  and see Piers
Pearson (Peirson):
  Cecilia Harriet, ix. 29
  F.L., iii. 112
  Jn. L., iii. 112–13, 143; vii. 267; ix. 26
  Sir Weetman, Vct. Cowdray, iv. 49, 69, 76–7
  Sir Weetman Jn. Churchill, Vct. Cowdray, iv. 43, 45, 73, 77, 80, 82
  Gen., i. 533
  ——, ii. 31
  arms, iv. 78
peas, *see* crops
Peasants' Revolt, *see* rebellions
Pease Pottage, *see* Slaugham
Peasmarsh, ii. 43; ix. 40, 142, 145, **157–60**
  adv., ix. 159–60

Barline (Berelynde), ix. 146
basket making, ii. 236
char., ix. 160
ch., ii. 113; ix. *158*, 158–9, *160*
  archit., ii. 349, 351, 366, 370, 374
Combe, ix. 142
cts., ix. 157
insects, i. 134*, 162*
Kitchenham (Checeham), ix. 158, 164
man., ix. 157–8, 161
mills, ix. 157
nonconf., ix. 157, 160
Peasmarsh Place, ii. 447, 471
pop., ii. 222
prebend, ii. 113; ix. 148, 156, 162
rectory, ix. 160
roads, ix. 157
vicar, ix. 159
Wivelridge (Wevilrigge), ix. 55, 142
Peat:
  A.E., ii. 461
  J.E., ii. 461
Pebsham, *see* Bexhill
Peccam (Peccham), *see* Peckham
Pecche, *see* Peachey
Pechall:
  Sir Geo. Brooke, iv. 157
  Kath. Annabella, *see* Bishop
Pecham, *see* Peckham
Pechard, Rob., ix. 139
Peche, *see* Peachey
Peck:
  Hen., ix. 160
  S., ii. 479
Peckham (Peccam, Peccham, Pecham):
  Anne, iv. 93, 111
  (formerly Smith), Chas., iv. 136
  Edw., and his w. Grace, iv. 144
  Eliz., m. Jn. Micklethwait, ix. 221
  Eliz., w. of Hen., *see* Greenfield
  Eliz., w. of Jn., iii. 126
  Eliz., w. of Thos., *see* Dobell
  Geo. (d. 1617), ix. 220
  Geo. (d. 1788), ix. 221
  H., iii. 126
  Harry, iii. 126
  Harry, Jn., iv. 136
  Hen. (d. 1616), iv. 144
  Hen. (fl. 1620), iv. 134
  Hen. (fl. 1648), iv. 200
  Hen. (fl. 1668), iv. 109
  Sir Hen. (d. 1673, ? another), iii. 76
  Hen. (d. 1764), iii. 76
  Hen. (fl. to 1768), iv. 104, 120, 237
  Jn., abp. of Cant., ii. 12, 57, 61, 66, 76, 78, 84, 94–5, 122, 323, 412; iii. 93, 104; iv. 234; vii. 15, 216
  Jn., prior of Boxgrove, ii. 59
  Jn. (fl. 1673), iii. 76
  Jn. (fl. 1674, ? another), iv. 144
  Jn. (fl. 1782), iii. 126; iv. 136, 200
  Mary, ix. 248
  Mary, m. Chas. Hewitt Smith, iv. 136, 200
  Mary, m. Ric. Cooper, iv. 80
  Mary, w. of Wm., iv. 112
  Ric. (fl. 1609), iv. 111
  Ric. (fl. 1658), iv. 123
  Ric. (d. 1718), iv. 80, 110–11, 116
  Ric. (d. 1734), iv. 92, 116
  Rob., iv. 92
  Rob., his s., iv. 92
  Sarah, m. Geo. Farhill, iii. 162
  Sarah, m. Thos. Phipps, iv. 92–3
  Sarah, w. of H., iii. 126
  Thos. (fl. 1648), iv. 200
  Thos. (fl. 1683), iv. 80, 136
  Thos. (fl. 1715), iv. 200 n
  W.D., iii. 110 n, 148 n, 166
  Wm. (fl. 1620), iv. 134
  Wm. (fl. to 1681), iv. 162
  Wm. (fl. 1693), iv. 112
  Wm. (fl. 1699, ? another), iv. 221–2
  Wm. (fl. 1717), ix. 221
  Wm. (d. 1737), ix. 221
  Mr., i. 526
  fam., iv. 91, 109, 111, 136, 185, 200; ix. 223

arms, iii. *76*; iv. *92*, 93
Peckham Phipps, Thos., *see* Phipps
Peckham, West (Kent), ii. 323
Pecocke, Reg., bp. of Chich., ii. 15; *and see* Peacock
peculiar jurisdictions, i. 502–3; iii. 104, 164; *and see* Canterbury: abps.: peculiars
Pedley:
  C.H., ii. 476
  W.E., ii. 476
Peel, Col., ii. 458
Peerman, Mr., ii. 442
Peirson, *see* Pearson
Pelham:
  Agnes, ix. 19
  Agnes, m. Jn. Colbrand, ix. 133
  Anne, m. T. Papillon, ix. 80
  Anne, w. of Sir Nic., *see* Sackville
  Anne, w. of Thos., earl of Chichester, ix. 197
  Ant., ii. 24; ix. 120, 123, 138 n, 207, 233
  Cath., m. Hen. Clinton, earl of Lincoln, ix. 139, 196
  Edm., ix. 241
  Edw., and his w. Eliz., iv. 179
  Eliz., w. of Herb., ix. 120
  Frances, ix. 139, 196
  Frances, m. Geo. Augustus Thursby, ix. 80
  Frances, w. of Hen., *see* Heath
  Francis Godolphin, earl of Chichester, ix. 4
  Francis Godolphin Hen., earl of Chichester, ix. 4
  Gilb., ix. 4
  Grace, m. Geo. Naylor, ix. 134
  Grace, m. Lewis, Ld. Sondes, ix. 139, 196
  Hen. (fl. 1709), ii. 414
  Hen. (fl. 1709, another), ii. 414
  Hen. (d. 1754), i. 531; vii. 101, 239; ix. 121, 139, 196–7
  (later Cresset), Hen., ix. 79–80, 82
  Hen. Thos., earl of Chichester, ii. 209 n, 430; vii. 67; ix. 4, 25, 27
  Herb. (fl. to 1598), ix. 120, 206–7, 233
  Sir Herb. (fl. 1599), vii. 284
  Herb. (fl. 1610), ii. 34; ix. 244
  Herb. (fl. 1612, ? another), ix. 241
  Herb. (fl. 1613, another), ix. 120
  Isabel, m. Jn. Covert, ix. 171
  Jas. (? two of this name), vii. 111; ix. 82
  Joan, *see* Zouche
  Jocelyn Brudenell, earl of Chichester, ii. 284, 420; ix. 4
  Sir Jn. (d. 1429), i. 513; ii. 76, 78; iv. 158, 171, 184; ix. 3, 19, 79, 125, 133–4, 217 n
  Sir Jn. (d. 1466), ii. 325; ix. 3, 79–80, 125, 133, 209
  his chaplain, i. 514
  Jn. (d. by 1503), ii. 325; ix. 19, 79
  Sir Jn. (d. 1580), ii. 24, 149 n, 318; vii. 239; ix. 78 n, 79, 139, 196
  Sir Jn. (d. 1702), ix. 4, 79, 139, 197, 246
  Jn. (d. 1786), ix. 79, 82
  Jn. Buxton, earl of Chichester, vii. 111, 227, 240; ix. 4, 226, 239
  Jn. Cresset, ix. 80
  Judith, w. of Sir Jn., ix. 76 n, 79
  Kath., m. Jn. de Bramshott, iv. 28
  Lucy, *see* Sidney
  Marg., w. of Sir Thos., ix. 79, 241
  Mary, ix. 139, 196
  Mary, w. of Sir Thos., vii. 270
  Mary, w. of Thos., *see* Wilbraham
  Sir Nic. (d. 1560), i. 518; ii. 145; vii. 39; ix. 79, 139, 207, 237
  Sir Nic. (fl. 1596), i. 518
  Sir Nic. (d. 1739), ix. 79
  Oliver, vii. 239; ix. 79
  Thos. (d. 1516), ix. 79
  Sir Thos. (d. 1624), ii. 197, 420; vii. 270, 284; ix. 3–4, 21, 79, 120,

Pelham:
Sir Thos. (*cont.*):
139, 197, 233, 252
Sir Thos. (d. 1654), i. 523; ix. 4, 79,
82, 120, 139, 241
Thos. (fl. 1686), ix. 4
Thos. (fl. 1708–56), ix. 79
Thos. (fl. 1709, ? another), ii. 415
Sir Thos., Ld. Pelham, ii. 414; ix. 4,
139
Thos. (fl. 1734), i. 531
Thos. (d. 1737, another), i. 531
Thos., duke of Newcastle, *see*
Pelham-Holles
Thos., earl of Chichester (d. 1805), i.
534; vii. 224, 227, 239; ix. 4, 197
Thos., earl of Chichester (d. 1826), ii.
415; ix. 4, 15
Wal. Jn., earl of Chichester, ix. 4
Wm. (d. 1503), ix. 79
Wm. (fl. 1516), ix. 79
Sir Wm. (fl. 1548), ii. 197
Sir Wm. (d. 1587, ? another), i. 518
fam., ii. 193, 247, 317, 325, 378, 386;
vii. 9, 31, 39, 101, 239; ix. 81,
113, 121, 199, 209, 217, 229, 238,
241
arms, vii. 10; ix. *79*
Pelham-Holles, Thos., Ld. Pelham, earl
of Clare, duke of Newcastle, i. 530–
1; ii. 160, 443; vii. 31, 101, 111; ix.
4, 53, 139, 196–7, 199
Pell (Pelle):
Jn., ii. 424
Ralph, iii. 101
Pelland:
Edw., iv. 179
Jn., iv. 179; vii. 85
Mary, w. of Jn., vii. 85
Thos., vii. 12
Pellard, Jn., ii. 99
Pellatt (Pellett):
Apsley, vii. 37
Sir Benj., vii. 138
Grace, *see* Newton
Hannah, *see* Alcock
Jane, m. Sir Wm. Culpeper, vii. 138
Jn., ii. 38
Mary, m. Ric. Paine, vii. 230
Thos., vii. 37, 230
Wm. (fl. 1650), vii. 230
Wm. (d. 1725), vii. 37, 230
Mr., ii. 26
arms, vii. *37*
Pelle, *see* Pell
Pellett, *see* Pellatt
Pells, the, *see* Lewes
Pelock's wood (unidentified), ii. 298
Pembroke:
ctss. of, *see* Sackville, Anne; St. Pol,
Mary de
earls of, *see* Clare, Gilb. de; Hastings,
Jn. de; Hastings, Laur. de; Her-
bert, Hen.; Herbert, Phil.; Mar-
shal; Valence
Pembroke College, Cambridge, ii. 402,
409
Pembroke College, Oxford, ii. 415, 433
Pembrokeshire, i. 191, 318 *n*
Pembury (Kent), ii. 88
Pencell (Pensell):
Jn., dean of Hastings coll., ii. 117
Jn. (? another), rector of Herstmon-
ceux, ii. 136
Pencestre, Steph. de, warden of Cinque
Ports, ix. 37, 50, 63
Pende, *see* Lancing
Penenden Heath (Kent), council of, ii. 3
Penfold:
F.E., ii. 479
Kath., iii. 162
Penhalls, Jn., and his w. Cecily, ix. 150
Penhurst:
Alice de, ix. 237
Eliz. de, m. Ninian Burrell, ix. 237
Hen. de (d. by 1290), and his w.
Aubrey, ix. 237–8
Hen. (fl. 1336), and his w. Kath., ix.

237
Isabel, w. of Hen., ix. 237
Jn. (fl. 1479), ix. 237
Jn. (another), ix. 237
Ric., ix. 237
Sim., ix. 238
Wm. (fl. 1210), ix. 237
Wm. (fl. 1327), ix. 237–8
fam., ix. 237
arms, ix. *237*
Penhurst, ii. 43, 324; ix. 226, 234, **237–8**
adv., ix. 238
Broomham, ix. 226
char., ix. 238
ch., ix. *236*, 237–8, *238*
accessories, ii. 353, 357, 360
archit., ii. 336, 339, 346, 348, 351
dom. archit., ix. 237
iron ind., ix. 237
man., ix. 128, 236–7
ho., ii. 387
mills, ix. 237
pop., ii. 223
rector, *see* Giles, Jn.
woodland, ix. 237
Penistone:
Mary, *see* Sommer
Thos. (fl. 1598), ix. 154
Sir Thos. (fl. 1617), ix. 154
Penkhurst, *see* Pankhurst
Penn:
Gulielma, *see* Springett
Springett, ix. 187
Springett, his s., ix. 187
Thos., iv. 94
Wm., ii. 39 *n*; ix. 187, 245
arms, ix. *187*
Pennant:
Wm., vii. 74
——, i. 247–8
Pennington:
Isaac, ix. 187
Mary, *see* Springett
Pensell, *see* Pencell
Penshurst (Kent), ii. *242*
Fordcombe, ii. 452
Pensthorpe, (Norf.), i. 337
Penven, Jn., ii. 407
Penycoke:
Jn., sacrist of Bosham coll., ii. 112
Jn. (another), ii. 308
Penysfold, *see* Slinfold
Peperynge, *see* Battle: Peppering
Peplesham:
Hugh de, ix. 1, 91, 119 *n*
Isabel de, m. Steph. Playsted, ix. 139
Isabel, w. of Jn. de, *see* Coudenne
Joan de, m. Ric. de Hurst, ix. 119
Jn. de (fl. before 1254), ix. 119
Jn. de (fl. 1254), ix. 119
Jn. de (fl. 1296), ix. 119
Marg. (Margery) de, m. 1 Wm. Bats-
ford, 2 Rob. Cralle, ix. 91, 92 *n*
Parnel de, m. Wm. de Hurst, ix. 119
Ralph de, ix. 91 *n*
Rob. de, and his w. Joan, ix. 119
Sim. de (fl. before 1338), ix. 119
Sim. de (fl. 1338), ix. 119
Sim. de (d. by 1384), ix. 138–9
Sim. de (fl. *c.* 1400), ix. 91
Wm. de, ix. 119
fam., ix. 91
Peplesham, *see* Bexhill: Pebsham
Pepper, Messrs., ii. 231
Peppering (in Battle), *see* Battle
Peppering (in Burpham), *see* Burpham
Pepys, Mr., vii. 249
Perceval (Percival, Percyvale):
Augustus, earl of Egmont, i. 306; iv.
77
Chas. Geo., Ld. Arden, iv. 67
Chas. Geo., earl of Egmont, ii. 429;
iv. 53
Geo. Chas., earl of Egmont, iv. 67, 77
Sir Jn., ld. mayor of London, ii. 416,
421
Jn., earl of Egmont, iv. 67

fam., iv. 67
Perching (in Edburton and Fulking), i.
477; ii. 256, 294; vii. 2, 14
cast., i. 498
man., vii. 202–4
mills, vii. 204
Percival, *see* Perceval
Percy:
Agnes de, ? m. 1 Lambert le Taylor, 2
Rob. Bon Johan, iv. 61
Alan, master of Arundel coll., ii. 109
Algernon, earl of Northumberland, iv.
144
Alice de, m. Phil. de Thetford, iv. 61
Edm. Colquhoun, earl of Limerick,
vii. 159
Eleanor, w. of Hen., earl of North-
umberland, *see* Poynings
Eleanor, w. of Thos., *see* Harbotell
Eliz., m. Chas. Seymour, duke of
Somerset, iii. 99
Eliz., w. of Sir Hen., *see* Mortimer
Eliz., w. of Jn. de, *see* Hartridge
Geo. de, vii. 147
Hen. de (fl. 1195), iv. 44–5, 69, 80
Hen. de (d. 1245), iv. 60–2
Hen. (d. 1272), i. 498–9
Sir Hen. de (d. 1314), iv. 61–2, 77,
98, 104
Sir Hen. (fl. 1347), iv. 61–2
Hen. (fl. 1347, another), iv. 61
Hen., earl of Northumberland (d.
1408), i. 510; iv. 61
Sir Hen. (Harry Hotspur) (d. 1403),
iv. 35, 61
Hen., earl of Northumberland (d.
1461), ii. 81; vii. 117, 189, 209
Hen., earl of Northumberland (d.
1489), vii. 117, 183, 189, 203,
209
Hen., earl of Northumberland (d.
1537), ii. 82; vii. 117, 189, 209,
211, 279
Hen., earl of Northumberland (d.
1585), i. 519
Hen. Algernon, earl of Northumber-
land, i. 515; vii. 189
Isabel de, m. Ric. de Buslingthorpe,
iv. 61
Isabel, w. of Hen., iv. 61
Jn. de (fl. 1239), iv. 61
Jn. de (d. by 1288), iv. 61
Jn. de (d. 1339), vii. 147
Jn. de, his s., vii. 147
Jocelin, vii. 209
Jocelin, earl of Northumberland, iii.
99
Kath., w. of Hen., earl of North-
umberland, vii. 209
Marg. de, vii. 147
Mary de, *see* Filliol
Ric. de, iv. 98
T., ii. 446
Thos. (fl. 1428), iv. 61
Thos. (d. 1537), ix. 83
Wm. de (fl. before 1239), iv. 61
Sir Wm. (fl. 1239), ii. 81; iv. 60–2,
104
Wm. de (fl. 1339), ii. 116; ix. 15
Wm. de (fl. before 1347, ? another),
iv. 61
Wm. (fl. 1377), i. 510
Sir Wm. (d. 1407, ? another), vii. 147
fam., ii. 81, 441; iii. 99; iv. 44, 60–1,
65, 83
arms, iv. *61*; vii. *209*
Percyng, Phil. de, vii. 203
Percyvale, *see* Perceval
Perigord, Sim. de, dean of Chich., ii.
51; iii. 103, 166
Perkins:
Mr., ii. 459
——, ii. 448
Peronius, ii. 402
Perrin, Hugh, warden of St. Mary's
hosp., Chich., ii. 102
Perris, Jn., i. 272
Perrott, Dame Gertrude Louisa Grace,

iv. 192
Perschute, *see* Pershete
Perse, *see* Pearce
Persehouse, F., i. 295
Pershete (Perschute, Sperschute, Spershute):
 Peter de, iv. 129
 Nic. de (d. 1327), iv. 128–9
 Nic. de (fl. 1363), and his w. Joan, iv. 129
Pesson, Ralph, iv. 136
Peter, prior of Michelham, ii. 79
Peter, prior of Sele, ii. 62
Peter fitz Reynold, *see* FitzReynold
Peter son of Reimer, vii. 89
Peter the clerk, ix. 51
Peter the hermit, ii. 46–7
Peter the sheriff, ii. 5; vii. 1, 60
Peterborough (Northants.):
 abbot, *see* Leofric
 bps., *see* Dee: Henshaw, Jos.
Petersfield (Hants), i. 7, 50, 169 *n*, 182–3, 272; ii. 240; iii. 47; iv. 10, 13, 17
 Sheet, *q.v.*
Peterson:
 Jn., ii. 102
 Rob., dean of South Malling coll., ii. 119
Peterston, Jn., warden of St. Mary's hosp., Chich., ii. 102
Petevyne, *see* Peytevin
Petit Iham, *see* Winchelsea: Higham
Petley wood, *see* Battle
Petraponte, *see* Pierpoint
Petre:
 Cath., m. Jn. Caryll, iv. 16
 Wm., Ld. Petre, iv. 16
Pett:
 Alfred Hen., ix. 30
 Gilb. de, *see* Ore
 Sam., iv. 129
 Ursula, ix. 160
 Wm., ix. 160
Pett (Pette), ii. 43; ix. 34, 92, 175, **190–2**
 adv., ix. 192
 birds, i. 286–7, 291
 botany, i. 61, 65, 67
 char., ix. 183, 192
 ch., ix. 191–2
 Cliff End (Cliveshend, Clyveshend), i. 57, 247, 261, 507 *n*; ii. 71
 crustaceans, i. 261
 dom. archit., ii. 382; ix. 190
 insects, i. 113, 116–17, 122, 127–8, 135, 139–41, 145, 152, 159, 162, 174, 176, 178, 187, 195–6, 198–9, 203–4, 206, 215, 217–20, 222–6, 228–35
 Level, ii. 159, 162
 mammals, i. 303–4
 man., ix. 71, 177, 190
 nonconf., ix. 190
 pop., ii. 222
 and see Ivet
Pettar, Thos., ix. 157
Pette, *see* Pett
Pettewin, vii. 1
Petworth, Tetbald of, iv. 30
Petworth, i. 52; ii. 43; iii. 95; iv. 56, 61, 83
 ale-hos., iii. 196
 birds, i. 282, 287
 Byworth, ii. 386
 ch., ii. 352, 361, 366, 374
 Civil War in, i. 524, 526
 constables, i. 503
 dom. archit., ii. 382, 386, 388–90
 earthworks, i. 480
 geology, i. 49
 guild, ii. 21
 honor, i. 491; ii. 297; iii. 104; iv. 30, 44, 50, 58, 60, 65, 69, 80, 83, 98, 104, 115, 122, 150, 155, 159, 193
 ho. of correction, ii. 195
 inc., ii. 190
 insects, i. 142, 176, 191, 198, 200
 lands in, ii. 75, 81

mammals, i. 305
man., iv. 56, 183–4
mkt., ii. 194
Medhone (Meadhome) pk., ii. 296–7, 305
militia, i. 535
pk., i. 306–7; ii. 247, 297, 306, 462
Petworth Ho., ii. 229, 338, 392
poor law, ii. 196 *n*, 206–7, 238
pop., ii. 218
rectors, ii. 439; *and see* Cheynell, Francis
rectory, ii. 12
roads, i. 239–40
royal visits, i. 505, 515
sch., ii. 439; iv. 83
sport, ii. 444–6, 448–9, 475
studs, ii. 461
Thompson's hosp., ii. 196 *n*
trades and ind., ii. 229, 231, 238, 253, 256–7, 264
union, i. 539
waterways, ii. 241
Petworth (or Sussex) marble, ii. 229, 337–8, 353, 356; vii. 146, 163, 171
Pevensey (Pevense):
 Drew of, ix. 212
 Jn. de, abbot of Battle, ii. 55
 Ric. of, ii. 188
Pevensey (Anderida, Andredsceaster), i. 56, 334, 348, 484–6, 500–1, 503; ii. 7, 44, 187, 315; iv. 183
 bailiff, ii. 78
 barons, i. 494; ix. 36
 Bay, i. 38; ii. 125, 158–60
 botany, i. 46, 49
 cast., i. 489–90, 492–6, 499–501, 503, 507, 509, 511–12, 516; ii. 131, 152, 174, 183, 251, 314; ix. 15, 133
 archit., ii. 230–1, 394–5
 chap., ii. 316, 395
 prehist. rem., i. 313, 330
 repairs, ii. 315, 325
 Rom. rem., i. 472, *472*
 serjeant, ii. 171
 signal post, i. 533
 ch., ii. 30, 160, 250, 351, 355
 archit., ii. 332, 337, 340, 344, 349, 374, *374*
 coins, i. 330
 constable, *see* Witsand
 cts., ii. 185; vii. 29
 deanery, ii. 42, 44
 defences, ii. 160, 163; ix. 8
 dom. archit., ii. 386, 393
 forest, *see* Ashdown forest
 geology, i. 45
 harbour, i. 26; ii. 125–9, 132, 144, 150, 159, 169
 hare hunting, ii. 452
 honor, *see* Laigle
 Horse Eye (Horsey), ii. 77
 hosp., *see* Westham: hosp.
 hund., i. 537; ix. 1
 insects, i. 124, 126, 128, 140, 162, 208, 215–16, 219–22, 224, 226, 229–36
 keeper of the coast, ii. 131
 lands in, ii. 77, 122–3; ix. 8
 Levels (marshes), i. 274; ii. 77–8, 96, 169, 274, 278, 280, 291, 447–8
 natural history, i. 42, 45, 108–9, 287, 291, 294–5
 sport, ii. 446, 451–2
 statutes, ii. 78
 trades and ind., ii. 231–2
 lowey (leucata), i. 503; ii. 106, 226; ix. 36
 mammals, i. 302–3, 305
 man., i. 490, 495, ii. 170
 mkt., ii. 278
 militia, i. 509, 534
 peculiar jurisdiction, i. 503
 piracy, ii. 149
 pop., ii. 226
 port, ii. 3, 154, 247
 rly. station, ix. 137, 244

rape, i. 490, 507 *n*, 511; ii. 194–6, 199, 225–7, 247; iv. 133; vii. 1, 2 *n*, 7–8, 14, 84 *n*, 99, 101, 175, 221 *n*, 224; ix. 38, 193, 210, 251
 militia, i. 535
 rebellion, i. 514
 roads to, iii. 42, 47
 Rom. rem., ii. 264; iii. 3–10, *5–8*; 12, 15, 30, 42, 47, 55
 ship money, ii. 157
 ship service, ii. 130, 131 *n*, 134–5, 138, 142
 shipping, ii. 137–8, 151
 siege, i. 481–2; ii. 291; iii. 82; vii. 2
 trades and ind., ii. 146, 231, 251, 270–1
 wreck, right of, ii. 146
Peverel (Peveral):
 Alice, m. —— Brocas, ix. 202
 And. (d. 1273), ix. 202
 Sir And. (d. 1375), i. 509; ii. 295; iv. 14 *n*; ix. 202
 Geof., iv. 171, 173, 177
 Godeheude, *see* Planchis
 Kath., *see* Hussey
 Lucy, m. —— Fitzherbert, ix. 202
 Thos., ix. 202
Peverse park, *see* Michelham: Michelham pk.
pewterer, Jn., the, *see* John
Peynell, *see* Paynel
Peytevin (Petevyne, Peytevyn):
 Jn., ix. 61
 Maud, m. —— de Kymere, vii. 226
 Ric., ii. 46
Peyton:
 A., ii. 461
 Sir Chas., iv. 64
 Jn. East Hunter, vii. 129, 132
 Jn. Ritson, vii. 129
 Jos. (d. 1804), vii. 129
 Jos. (d. 1816), vii. 129, 196
 Jos. Jn., vii. 129
 Ruth, *see* Box
Phelip, *see* Phillips
Phelphs, Nic., *see* Phippes
Phelps, Ric., iii. 160; iv. 84, 187; vii. 65, 171; ix. 74, 148, 162, 276
Phené, J.S., i. 324
Philcox:
 Cath., ix. 111
 Jas., ix. 200
Philip II Augustus, king of France, i. 491, 493
Philip II, king of Spain, ii. 143, 150
Philip, prior of Hastings, ii. 77
Philippa, queen of Edw. III, i. 509; ii. 78, 353; ix. 133, 172
Philipson-Stow:
 Sir Elliot, iv. 72 *n*
 Sir Fred., iv. 72
Phillipps, *see* Phillips
Phillips (Phillipps, Phelip):
 Albert, ii. 471, 473
 Ann, ix. 31–2
 Anne, m. —— Styant, iv. 193
 Arthur, iv. 13
 Eliz., m. Jn., Vct. Beaumont, vii. 110
 Francis, iv. 21
 H.G., ii. 473
 Hen., ii. 471–3
 Jas., ii. 471–3
 Joan, *see* Bardolf
 Jn., ix. 249
 Mary, ix. 249
 Mary, w. of Thos., *see* Legay
 Peter, ii. 471
 Thos., iv. 193, 212
 Sir Wm. (d. 1441), vii. 110
 Wm. (fl. before 1644), iv. 193
 Wm. (fl. 1874), ii. 471
 Col., i. 527
Philpott:
 Jn., vii. 78
 ——, iii. 89
Phippes (or Phelphs, or Smith), Nic., ii. 28

Phipps:
Barré, iv. 210
Harriet, iv. 94
Rob., ix. 246
Sarah, *see* Peckham
Thos., iv. 92, 110, 116
(later Peckham Phipps), Thos., iv. 92, 94, 111, 116
arms, iv. *92*
and see Hornby
Phisicon, Jn., iii. 86
Phripp, Amelia, iii. 144
Phymer, Sir Jas., vii. 71
Picheford (Pycheford):
Alice, w. of Geof. de, m. 2 Rob. le Butler, iv. 167, 168 *n*, 171
Geof. de (d. by 1300), iv. 167, 171
Geof. de (fl. 1317), iv. 171
Jn. de, iv. 167
Mary, w. of Geof. de, iv. 171
Ric. de, iv. 168, 171
Thos. de, iv. 167
Wm. de, iv. 2, 167
Pickard-Cambridge, O., i. 238
Pickering:
(or Poole?), Anne, m. 2 Sir Hen. Knyvett, 3 Jn. Vaughan, vii. 194, 258*; ix. 263
Benj., rector of East Hoathly, ii. 35
Sir Chris., vii. 194
E.H.U., ii. 474
Joan, *see* Lewknor
Jn., ix. 89
Picknell:
Geo., ii. 469–70, 475
R., ii. 475
Picot, *see* Pycot
Piddinghoe, ii. 43–4; vii. 3–4, 61–2, 64, **66–9**, 73
adv., vii. 69
agric., vii. 66
birds, i. 287
ch., ii. 356; vii. *68*, 68–9
architt., ii. 339–40, 367, 372; vii. 77
dom. archit., vii. 66
earthworks, i. 480; vii. 66
Harpeting (Herbertinges, Herbeting), vii. 61, 67–8
man., vii. 2, 7, 66–8
ho., vii. 66
mill, vii. 67
Orleswick, vii. 61
Peacehaven, iii. 62; vii. 66, 69
pop., ii. 224
prehist. rem., i. 330
trades and ind., ii. 256; vii. 66
vicar, *see* Hutchins, Jas.
vicarage, ii. 8
Piddingworth, *see* Ditchling: man.
Pidelingeworth:
Joan, w. of Nic. de, vii. 106
Martin de, vii. 106
Nic. de, vii. 106
pie-powder court, *see* courts
Piecombe, *see* Pyecombe
Pieram, Peregrine, ii. 427–8
Pierce, *see* Pearce
Pieres, moneyer, iii. 84 *n*
Pierpoint (Petraponte, Pierrepoint, Pierrepoint):
Beatrice, m. Wm. de Warenne, vii. 99, 228–9
Evelyn, duke of Kingston, ii. 443
Geo., vii. 71
Godfrey de, vii. 67, 99, 175, 228, 275–6, 283
Hen., Ld. Pierpoint, earl of Kingston, vii. 64
Hugh de, vii. 175, 228, 234
Jn. de, vii. 175
Maud de, w. of Rob., vii. 117
Ralph de, vii. 81
Rob. de (fl. 1086), vii. 99, 116, 175
Rob. de (fl. 1264), i. 498; vii. 100, 117, 175, 177, 266
Sim. de (fl. 1166), vii. 266
Sim. de (d. by 1240), vii. 99 *n*, 175–7, 266

Sim. de (fl. 1280), ii. 185
Sim. de (d. 1354), vii. 117, 119, 175–7, 266
Sybil de, m. Edm. de Ufford, vii. 175
T., ii. 468
Wal. de, vii. 266
Wm. de (fl. 1090), vii. 67, 175, 226, 234
Wm. de (fl. 1213), vii. 81, 175
fam., vii. 229
arms, vii. *175*
Pierre, Graunt, *see* Roberd, Pieter
Pierrepoint (Pierrepont), *see* Pierpoint
Piers, Geof. fitz, *see* Geoffrey
Piers:
Anne, *see* Gotele
Edw., ix. 91, 266–7
Eliz., m. Thos. Scott, ix. 274
Geo. (fl. 1516), ix. 91–2
Sir Geo. (d. 1720), ix. 91, 274
Jn. (fl. 1440), ix. 91, 274
Jn., dean of South Malling coll., ii. 119
Laur., ix. 91–2, 267, 274
Marg., w. of Edw., ix. 91, 266
Thos. (d. 1606), ix. 91–2, 266–7, 274
Sir Thos. (d. 1680), ix. 91–2, 274
Sir Thos. (d. 1693), ix. 91, 274
Wm., dean of South Malling coll., ii. 119
Capt., ii. 149
fam., ix. 266
arms, ix. *91*
and see Pearce
pigeon-cotes, *see* architecture: civil and dom.: dovecots
Pigg, Herb., ii. 472 *n*, 473
Piggott (Piggot, Pigott):
Jas. (d. 1815), iv. 5, 63 *n*, 212
Jas. (d. 1822), iv. 5
Jane, m. Sim. Frazer Cooke, iv. 5
Nat., ix. 191
Sim., *see* Frazer Cooke
Miss, i. 279
Pigou, Francis, dean of Chich., ii. 51; iii. 113, 121
pigs, *see* livestock
Pilch, Fuller, ii. 468, 470, 475
pilgrimages, ii. 11, 50, 54, 64, 95, 115, 142
Pilkington:
Sir And., ix. 242
his w., ix. 242
Ann, iii. 147
Chas., canon of Chich., and his w. Harriet, iii. 147
Chas., warden of St. Mary's hosp., Chich., ii. 102
Geo., iii. 147
Theophania, iii. 147
——, m. Burrell Hayley, ix. 242, 244
pillory, vii. 2; ix. 196, 201
Pilsey (Pilsea), *see* Thorney, West
Piltdown, *see* Fletching
Pilton, Jn., ii. 308
Pinckney, Wm. Jn., ix. 30
Pine, Hen., ii. 167
Pinger, R. Broome, rector of Whichford, iv. 190
Pinnix, Atwick, ii. 283
Pipard, Hugh, master of Playden hosp., ii. 105
Piper, J.T., ii. 474
Pipering, *see* Burpham: Peppering
Piplye, *see* Horsted Keynes
Pipon, Phil., ii. 167
Pippingford (Pippinford, Pippyngworth), *see* Maresfield
piracy and privateering, ii. 134, 139, 141–2, 144–50, 152, 154–60, 165–6, 268; *and see* Brighton; Cinque Ports; Hastings; Rye; Winchelsea
Pirie, Wm., ii. 423*
Pironis, *see* Valle Pironis
piscinas, *see* architecture: ecclesiastical
Pitcher, Algernon, ii. 451
Pitsham, *see* Cocking
Pitt, Wm., iii. 100

Pitt-Rivers, *see* Lane Fox
Pius II, pope, ii. 61; ix. 171
Pix:
Thos., ix. 155, 266, 273
Thos. Smith, ix. 155, 266
Wm., ix. 274
Plagh Chase, *see* Forest Row: Plaw Chase
plague, *see* epidemics
Plaiz:
Alice de, w. of Hugh, vii. 54, 59, 80, 89, 95
Giles de (d. 1302), vii. 54, 95
Giles de (d. 1334), vii. 54
Hugh de (fl. 1150), vii. 54–5
Hugh de (d. 1244), vii. 54, 80, 95, 175, 194
Isabel de, w. of Ralph, m. 2 Jn. Marmion, vii. 54
Jn. de, vii. 54
Marg. de, m. Sir Jn. Howard, vii. 54
Phillipa de, *see* Munfichet
Ralph de (fl. 1140), vii. 54–5
Ralph de (fl. 1177), vii. 54
Ralph de (fl. 1177, another), vii. 54
Ralph de (d. c. 1194), vii. 54, 96
Ralph de (d. c. 1204), vii. 54
Ralph de (d. 1283), vii. 54
Ric. de (d. 1269), ii. 310–11; vii. 54, 59, 89, 95
Ric. de (d. 1327), vii. 54
Ric. de (d. 1360), vii. 54
fam., vii. 53, 96–7, 101, 183
arms, vii. *54*
Planchis:
Eustache de, m. Hubert de Warham (or de Wykes), iv. 171
Godeheude, w. of Wm., m. 2 Geof. Peverel, iv. 171
Ric. de, iv. 171
Wm. de, iv. 171
Plancus, ——, i. 247
Plantagenet, Arthur, Vct. Lisle, iv. 93
Plashett, *see* Ringmer
plaster of Paris making, ix. 235
plate, *see* architecture: ecclesiastical
Plaw Chase, *see* Forest Row
Plaw Hatch, *see* Forest Row
Playden, ii. 43; ix. 40, 142, 151–2, **160–3**
adv., ix. 162
char., ix. 163
ch. (or chap.), ii. 104, 113; ix. 152 *n*, *161*, 161–2
accessories, ii. 261, 358, 360; ix. 162
archit., ii. 340, 342, 344, 346, 348, 370; ix. 162
fair, ii. 104; ix. 161
glebe, ii. 5
hosp. of St. Bart., ii. 45, **104–5**, 331; ix. 39, 49, 160–1
master, *see* Brent, Thos.
lands in, ii, 72; ix. 83, 157 *n*
man., ix. 146, 158, 160–1
military camp, ii. 161
mills, ix. 160–1
pop., ii. 222
roads, ix. 160
trades and ind., ii. 238, 261; ix. 161
Player, Thos., iv. 135–6
Playsted:
Eliz., w. of Thos., m. 2 Rog. Shoyswell, ix. 255
Isabel, *see* Peplesham
Ralph, ix. 139, 255
Ric. (? two of this name), ix. 139
Rob., ix. 139
Steph., ix. 139
Thos., ix. 139 *n*
Playters, Sir Wm., vii. 64
Pleshey (Essex), vii. 3
honor, ix. 87, 221
Pleydell-Bouverie, Jacob, earl of Radnor, ii. 444
Plompton, *see* Plumpton
Plottesbridge park, *see* Framfield
Plow Chase, *see* Forest Row: Plaw Chase

plowbote, ii. 294, 309–10
Pluket:
Rob., mayor of Chich., iii. 91
Rog., mayor of Chich., iii. 91
Plumer:
Hen., vii. 158
Jas., vii. 76, 158
Jane, m. Rob. Norden, vii. 158
Jane, w. of Hen., *see* Ward
Jn., vii. 158
Rob., vii. 76, 158
Plummer's Plain, *see* Beeding
Plumpton (Plompton):
Hugh de, vii. 1
Nic. de, ii. 122
Plumpton, ii. 43–4; vii. 2, 66, 92, 94, **109–13**
adv., vii. 113
agric., ii. 277; vii. 109
birds, i. 276
char., vii. 113
ch., ii. 328, 354 *n*, 355; vii. 111–13, *111, 112*
County Agric. Coll., vii. 109
cts., vii. 111
dom. archit., vii. 109–10
earthworks, i. 478, 480
inc., ii. 190
man., iv. 185; vii. 11, 14 *n*, 67, 80, 110–11, 129, 158–9, 168, 203, 226, 283
mills, vii. 110
natural history, i. 214–15, 217–20, 276
Plumpton Place, ii. 387; vii. *108*, 109–10
pop., ii. 225
prehist. rem., i. 330
rly., vii. 98, 109
sport, ii. 453–4, 461; vii. 109
textile ind., ii. 257
Plumtree Cross (in Horsham or Itchingfield), i. 53
Plymouth:
ctss. of, *see* Sackville, Mary
earl of, *see* Archer, Other
Plymouth (Devon), i. 535; ii. 135, 140, 143, 153, 155, 159, 165–6, 231
Plymouth Brethren, ii. 41; iii. 164; iv. 227; vii. 179
poaching, ii. 63, 75, 186, 197, 201, 293–4, 296, 302, 304, 306, 311–12, 315–17, 323; ix. 133, 213
Poate:
Judith, iv. 109 *n*
Ric., iv. 109
Pococke, Ric., iv. 208 *n*
Podmore:
Thompson, ii. 434
fam., ii. 476
Poggesley (Puggislee):
Agnes, *see* Erley
And., ii. 412
Clement (? two of this name), ii. 412; vii. 256
Rog., ii. 412
Thos. (sr.), ii. 412–13
Thos. (jr.), ii. 412
point-to-point racing, *see* sport
Poitou (France), ii. 131
Poitevins, i. 495
Poland, *see* Gdansk
Poley, *see* Poole
Polegate (in Hailsham):
botany, i. 61
brickmaking, ii. 254
coins, i. 330
insects, i. 111, 113, 116, 121, 126, 165–6, 168 *n*, 178, 186, 188, 197–8, 201, 210, 221, 224
rly., i. 348
roads, iii. 47, 62
Rom. rem., iii. 47, 62
stud, ii. 461
Poley, *see* Weller-Poley
Polhill:
Edw., ix. 196
fam., ix. 197
Poling, ii. 42–3; iv. 78 *n*

bailiwick, iv. 172
ch., ii. 121, 339, 351, 353, 355, 358, 361, 370
dom. archit., ii. 386, 388, 390
hund., i. 538; ii. 217–18; iv. 1; *and see* Patching: hund.
insects, i. 180, 189, 198, 203, 207, 210
man., ii. 121
pop., ii. 218
preceptory of Knights Hospitaller, ii. 45, **93**; iv. 78, 145, 172
archit., ii. 331, 348, 382–3
chap., ii. 352
prehist. rem., i. 330
roads, iii. 20, 46
Rom. rem., iii. 20, 46
political history, i. **481–539**
Poll Bay, riv., *see* Bay
poll tax, i. 511; ii. 182, 256–7, 259; iii. 98
Pollard (Pollerd):
Mr., ii. 104
——, ii. 230
Pollock, Mrs., iv. 92, 111
polo, *see* sport
Polsted:
Francis, and his w. Audrey, vii. 217
Hen., iv. 20, 188, 229, 233; vii. 217
Ric., vii. 217
Pomeriis, Jn. de, prior of Sele, ii. 62
Ponet:
Jn., bp. of Winchester, ix. 94
Rog., vicar of Ashford, bp. of Rochester, ix. 245
Poninges (Ponninges), *see* Poynings
Ponsonby:
Arthur, Ld. Ponsonby, iv. 69
his w., iv. 69
Diana Harriet, m. Edw. Granville Geo. Howard, Ld. Laverton, iv. 86
Geo., and his w. Diana Juliana, iv. 86
Vere Brabazon, earl of Bessborough, iv. 122, 126
fam., iv. 121
Ponsonby Lascelles, Edw. Chas., *see* Lascelles
Pont-des-Rèmes (? Marne, France), iii. 17
pontage, ix. 67
Pontarche (Ponte Arche):
Wm. de (fl. 1130), iv. 131
Wm. de (fl. 1217), i. 495
Ponthieu (France), i. 485
Pontifex, Fanny, ix. 32
Pontigny (Yonne, France), ii. 10
Ponynges (Ponyngs), *see* Poynings
Pooke:
Jn., ix. 222
Steph., ix. 222
Poole (Pole, Powle):
(or Pickering), Anne, *see* Pickering
Sir Arthur, iv. 35; ix. 153
Chas., ii. 165
Charlotte Eliz., m. —— Blencowe, vii. 98
Constance, *see* Pakenham
Sir Ferdinand, vii. 37
Frances, *see* Sackville
Sir Francis, vii. 37
Francis, vii. 105
Sir Fred., ii. 454, 456
Sir Geof. (fl. 1528), ii. 405; iv. 92, 116
Geof. (fl. 1573), and his w. Kath., vii. 256
Geof. (fl. 1609), iv. 116
Harriet, m. —— Hepburn, vii. 97–8
Hen., Ld. Montacute, iv. 13
Hen. (d. 1580), ii. 24, 361; vii. 105, 108
Hen. (fl. 1687), ix. 117
Sir Hen., rector of Chailey, vii. 97
Joan, *see* Lewknor
Jn., vii. 105
Marg., *see* Nevill
R.L., iii. 84
Reynold, rector of Harting, abp. of Cant., iv. 13, 113, 116, 223, 230–

1, 238; vii. 109, 163, 227
Thos., mayor of Chich., iii. 92
Thos., ii. 25; iv. *116*
Wm. de la, iii. 101
fam., iv. 116
arms, iv. *116*
Poor (Poore), Ric., bp. of Chich., bp. of Salisbury, ii. 9, 48; iv. 27, 221; vii. 265
poor relief, i. 539; ii. 193–6, 205–11, 238; *and see* Chich.; Ditchling; Hoathly, West; Hove; Lewes; Southover; Streat; Worth
Pope:
Alex., ii. 301; iv. 17
Edm., vii. 121
Jn. (fl. before 1409), and his w. Joan, vii. 169
Jn. (fl. 1527), ix. 56
Jn. (fl. before 1536, ? another), vii. 169
Jn. (fl. 1536), vii. 169
Nic., vii. 121
Ralph, vii. 121
Ric. Brazier, and his w. Mary, iii. 147
Sackville, vii. 121
Thos. (fl. 1454), and his w. Kath., ix. 56
Thos., his s., ix. 56
arms, vii. *121*
popes, *see* Adrian V; Alexander III; Alexander IV; Boniface VIII; Boniface IX; Celestine V; Clement VI; Clement VII; Eugenius III; Gregory IX; Gregory XI; Honorius IV; Innocent III; Innocent IV; Innocent VI; John XXI; John XXII; John XXIII; Lucius III; Martin IV; Nicholas III; Nicholas IV; Paul II; Pius II; Sixtus IV; Urban V; Urban VI
Popish Plot, *see* rebellions
population, i. 311–12, 317; ii. **215–28**
porches, *see* architecture: ecclesiastical
Port:
Adam de, iv. 143
Mabel, *see* Orival
Port Egmont (Falkland Islands), ii. 166
Portchester (Hants), i. 501; ii. 137; iii. 5
Porter:
Cath., *see* Pounde
Diana, *see* Goring
Eliz., vii. 97
Endymion, vii. 280
Geo., vii. 71, 280
J.H., ii. 166
Jn. (d. 1599), vii. 158
Jn. (fl. 1616), ix. 161
Jn. (fl. 1624, ? another), ix. 169
Ric., ix. 161
Rog., ii. 185
Sackville, vii. 158
Sim., ii. 185
Thos. (fl. 1713), vii. 97
Thos. (fl. 1733), ix. 82
Thos. (fl. 1762), vii. 97
fam., ix. 169
Portesmouth, Joan, ii. 85
Portfield, *see* Chich.: suburbs
Portinari, Jn., vii. 46
Portland, duke of, *see* Cavendish-Bentinck
Portland stone, ii. 335
Portman, Ld., *see* Berkeley, Wm. Hen.
Portmore, earl of, *see* Colyear
Portslade, i. 13; ii. 43–4; vii. 2, 274*, **282–6**
adv., vii. 286
A.-S. rem., i. 340
ch., vii. 243, *283*, 284–6, *285*
accessories, ii. 250, 351–2, 355–6, 372
archit., ii. 344, 346, 349, 368, 370, 372, 374
dom. archit., ii. *385*, 393; vii. 282
earthworks, i. 480; vii. 282
fair, vii. 284
fossils, i. 28

Portslade (*cont.*):
hunting, ii. 295
man., vii. 14, 67, 99, 100, 204, 228, 258, 276, 281–4
ho., ii. 381; vii. 282, *282*
natural history, i. 47, 165, 171, 180, 198, 209
pop., ii. 224
prehist. rem., i. 330
roads to, iii. 47
Rom. rem., iii. 28, 62; vii. 282
U.D., vii. 31, 275
vicar, *see* Cooper, C.E.
vicarage, ii. 8
Portslade Atlingworth, half hund., vii. 274
Portsmouth (Hants), ii. 133–4, 158, 165; iii. 87; iv. 127; vii. 246; ix. 10, 34
cath., iv. 146 *n*
ch. of St. Thos. of Canterbury, ii. 329, 371
Civil War, i. 522–3, 528
God's Ho., prior, iv. 83
harbour, ii. 126, 129–30, 132, 135, 140, 144–5, 152–3; iii. 101
mail coaches, ii. 201, 204
port, *see* Portsmouth: harbour
Rom. Cath., ii. 28
royal visits, i. 492; ii. 302
shipbuilding, ii. 234
waterways, ii. 241
Portugal, ii. 129, 153
Lisbon, bp., *see* Hastings, Gilb. of
Portus Adurni, iii. 5, 62; vii. 275
Portus Petri, *see* St. Pierre en Port
Possingworth, *see* Waldron
postal service, ii. 154
Postlethwaite (Postlethwayt):
Jos., iv. 189
Susan, m. Jn. Rickman, iv. 13
Wal., rector of St. Michael's, Lewes, ii. 39; vii. 17
Postwick (Norf.), vii. 236
Potel, Wm., ii. 47
Pott (Potte, Potts, Putte):
Gervase de la, iv. 109 *n*
Isabel de la, iv. 104
Jn., iv. 224
Wm., iv. 224
(or St. George), Wm. de la, *see* St. George
Mr., ii. 414; vii. 18
pottery:
A.-S., *see* Anglo-Saxon remains
manufacture, ii. **251–3**; iv. 58, 76; vii. 94; ix. 13, 56, 79, 168
prehist., i. 312–13, 317
Rom., *see* Romano-British Sussex
Potts, *see* Pott
Poulton (Kent), *see* Bradsole
poultry, *see* livestock
Pound Gate, *see* Buxted
Pounde:
Ant., ix. 82
Cath., m. 1 Wm. Nicholas, 2 —— Porter, ix. 82
Eliz., w. of Jn., ix. 82
Hen., ix. 82
Jn., ix. 82
Thos. (d. 1476), and his w. Maria, ix. 82
Thos. (fl. 1559), vii. 266
Thos. (fl. 1642), ix. 82
Wm. (d. 1525), ix. 82
Wm. (d. 1559), ix. 82
arms, ix. *82*
Pountfreyt, Hen., ii. 123 *n*
Powell:
Barnham, ix. 154, 178, 264
Sir Chris., ix. 154–5, 242, 263–4
Jas., vii. 89, 91
Jn., ii. 164
Jn. Cotton, vii. 169
Sir Nat., ix. 154, 242, 263, 266, 268
Thos. Baden, vii. 91
Wm., vii. 91
fam., ix. 266
arms, ix. *154*

Powell Edwards:
H., vii. 100
H.J., vii. 100
and see Edwards
Power (Powers):
Mary L., ix. 32
Capt., i. 519
Powlatt, *see* Paulet
Powle, *see* Poole
Powlett, *see* Paulet
Pownall:
H.H., ii. 277
Philemon, ii. 166
Powys:
Henrietta, *see* Spence
Thos., iv. 193; vii. 36
Thos. Littleton, Ld. Lilford, i. 285 *n*
Poynings (Ponynges, Ponyngs, Poyninges):
Adam de (sr.), and his w. Beatrice, vii. 209, 211, 214
Adam de (jr.), vii. 209, 211, 214
Blanche de, *see* Mowbray
Edw., master of Arundel coll., ii. 109
Sir Edw., vii. 5, 35
Eleanor de, m. Hen. Percy, earl of Northumberland, vii. 117, 183, 189, 209, 279
Eleanor, w. of Sir Hugh, m. 2 Sir Geof. Hilton, iv. 199 *n*
Hawise de, vii. 189 *n*
Sir Hugh, iv. 143, 199 *n*
Isabel, w. of Sir Luke de, *see* St. John
Isabel, w. of Sir Ric. de, vii. 209, 212
Joan, m. —— Bonville, iv. 143
Joan, w. of Mic. de, Ld. Poynings, vii. 209
Luke de (d. 1294), vii. 145, 183, 189, 209, 212, 214, 279
Sir Luke de (d. 1376), iv. 91–2*, 143, 145, 177
Margery de, m. 1 Edm. Bacon, 2 Nic. de la Beche, 3 Sir Jn. Dalton, ix. 139, 153
Margery, w. of Mic. de, vii. 209, 212, 213 *n*
Maud, w. of Sir Thos., m. 2 Hugh Halsham, iv. 143
Mic. de (fl. 1203), vii. 145
Mic. de (d. 1316), vii. 183, 189, 209, 212, 213 *n*, 279
Sir Mic., Ld. Poynings, ii. 97, 317; vii. 117, 147, 189, 204; ix. 139
Rainald de, vii. 209
Reiner de, vii. 209
Sir Ric., Ld. Poynings, i. 512; ii. 115 *n*, 317; vii. 117, 203, 209–10, 281 *n*
Rob., Ld. Poynings, i. 513; vii. 117, 183, 204, 209–10, 279
Thos. de (fl. 1243), vii. 209, 212
Thos. de, Ld. Poynings (d. 1339), vii. 183, 186, 189, 209, 213
Thos. de, Ld. Poynings (d. 1375), vii. 34, 203–4, 209–10
Sir Thos. de, Ld. St. John, iv. 143, 177
Sir Thos. (fl. c. 1441), iv. 201
fam., iv. 91, 156, 176; vii. 34, 145; ix. 202
arms, vii. *209*
Poynings (Poninges, Ponninges), ii. 43–4; vii. 2, 201, **208–12**
adv., vii. 211–12
agric., vii. 208
chant., vii. 212
ch., vii. 201, *209, 210*, 210–11
accessories, ii. 352–3, 355–6, 358–60
archit., ii. 334, 340, 346, 349–50, 377–8
Devil's Dyke, i. 49; ii. 478; iii. 43, 54; vii. 208
earthworks, i. **461–3**, *462*, 464, 468, 470, 479; vii. 208–9
insects, i. 156, 169
prehist. rem., i. 313, 321, 463
hund., i. 537; ii. 219 *n*, 224; vii. 1,

3 *n*, **201**
hunting, ii. 295
man., vii. 34, 183, 203–4, 209–10, 212–13, 279
mills, vii. 210
natural history, i. 42, 165 *n*, 166, 171, 183, 188, 204, 285, 301
Pk., vii. 210
pop., ii. 224
prehist. rem., i. 330
rector, *see* Killingbeck
Rom. road, vii. 209
Poynte, Agatha de la, prioress of Lyminster, ii. 121
Poyntz:
Eliz. Mary, *see* Browne
H.S., ii. 476
Wm. Steph., ii. 444, 459; iv. 50, 56, 77; vii. 142, 204, 208, 210, 213
Praetorius, C.J., iii. 25
Pranke, Jn., ii. 319
Pratt (Pratte):
Clementina, w. of Jn. Chas., earl of Camden, m. 2 Philip Green, ii. 461
Ralph, ii. 85
Mr., i. 278, 281
——, ii. 142
Pratt Barlow:
Edw., iv. 70
Francis, iv. 70
Rob., iv. 70
Pratte, *see* Pratt
Praty, Ric., bp. of Chich., ii. 9, 15, 61, 82, 104; iii. 144 *n*; iv. 57–8, 201
prehistoric Sussex, i. *308–9*, **309–31**
Prémonstré (Aisne, France), abbey, ii. 87–8
Presbyterians, ii. 35–6, 39; vii. 42, 263; ix. 61, 123
Press, Jn., ii. 446, 450
Pressridge Warren, *see* Maresfield
Presteton family, *see* Preston
Prestetune, *see* Preston
Preston (Presteton):
Jn., master of Playden hosp., ii. 105
Jn., iv. 201
Ric. de (fl. 1242), iv. 90
Ric. (fl. 1292), iv. 90
Preston (Prestetune), i. 13, 54; ii. 43; vii. 244, 252, 264–6, **268–73**
adv., vii. 273
ch., vii. *268*, *271*, 271–3
accessories, ii. 250, 352, 355, 361, 374
archit., ii. 339, *339*, 349–50, 372–4, 376
cts., vii. 270
fair, vii. 271
(or Preston and Dean) hund., i. 537–8; ii. 224; vii. 1, 215, **264**
inc., ii. 190–1
man., ii. 185; iv. 152, 202; vii. 1, 14, 138, 216, 265, 269–71
ho., ii. 381; vii. 268–9, 269
mkt., vii. 271
natural history, i. 197, 200, 205, 210, 301
Pk., ii. 475, vii. 271
polo, ii. 461
pop., ii. 224
Prestonville, ii. 43; vii. 273
Radynden, vii. 4
Rom. rem., iii. 3–4, 20, *23*, 23–4, 43, 51; vii. 268
textile ind., ii. 256
Thomas-Stanford museum, vii. 268
vicar, *see* Douglas, Jas.
Preston, East, ii. 43, 210
ch., ii. 37, 332, 337, 339–40, 350–1, 359, 368, 378
dom. archit., ii. 388
man., ii. 121
pop., ii. 218
union, i. 539; ii. 205–7, 210
Prestonville, *see* Preston: Prestonville

Prestwick (Prestwyk):
  Joan, ix. 209
  Jn., ix. 209
  Wm., dean of Hastings coll., ii. 117, 361; ix. 209
  Wm., ix. 209
Pretender, Old, see Stuart, Jas.
Price (Prise):
  Anne, see Luxford
  Harry, iii. 25, 63
  Hen., iv. 212
  Sir Hen., vii. 127
  J.E., iii. 65
  Jn., iv. 212
  Laur., vii. 144
  Wm., vii. 101
  and see Johnson, Price and Freeland
prices, ii. 188, 194–5, 197–8, 206, 214
Prickett, Thos., ii. 249
Prickett Hatch, see Maresfield
priest, see Beorhthelm the priest; Godfrey the priest; Godwin the priest; Ralph the priest; Richoard the priest; Tetbald the priest
Prikelowe, Hen., mayor of Chich., iii. 91
Primer, Rog., sacrist of Bosham coll., ii. 112
Primrose, Archibald Phil., earl of Rosebery, ii. 457, 460
Prince, Wm., ii. 141
Prince of Wales corps, i. 535
Prinsted, see Westbourne
printing, ii. **238–9**
Prior (Pryor):
  F., ii. 459
  Jn., vii. 67
  W.H., ii. 411
  Messrs., iii. 75
Prior John, see Bidoux
Priors Dean (Hants), ii. 466
Prise, see Price
prisons (gaols, hos. of correction), i. 503; and see Battle; Chich.; Chich.: rape; Guildford; Horsham; Lewes; London: Fleet; London: Newgate; Petworth; Rye: defences: Ypres Tower; Seaford; Southwark: Marshalsea; Winchelsea
Pritchard (Prychard):
  Anne, see Sergison
  Jn., dean of Chich., ii. 51
  W.S., vii. 156
Prittlewell (Essex), priory, ii. 68
  prior, see Cusancia, Jas. de
privateering, see Piracy
Privy Council, ii. 21, 23, 145, 148–50, 153–6, 194–5, 255, 423, 426, 436; iii. 96
Proctor, Thos., and his w. Charlotte, ix. 181
Promhelle, see Broomhill
Prosser, Rob., ii. 421
Provence, Eleanor of, see Eleanor
Pruett, Wm., iv. 83
Prychard, see Pritchard
Pryclove, Rob., prior of Hardham, ii. 75
Pryor, see Prior
Ptolemy, iii. 9
Pubhurst wood (unidentified), ii. 298
Puckering, Eliz., iv. 215
Puckhurst, Goodwife, ii. 198
Pudentinus, Clemens s. of, see Clemens
Pudsey:
  Philippa, see Thatcher
  Thos., ix. 191
Puggislee, see Poggesley
Pugin, Augustus N., iii. 164
Pulborough, i. 8, 52, 264, 476; ii. 43; 212; ix. 84
  bridge, ii. 394
  Broomer's Hill, iii. 63
  ch., ii. 63, 351–2, 356–7, 361
    archit., ii. 336–7, 339, 344, 346, 348, 374, 377–8
  Codmore Hill, iii. 32, 39, 48, 63–4
  Coldharbour, iii. 63
  dom. archit., ii. 384, 386, 391
  geology, ii. 335, 366, 393

lands in, ii. 75
man., ii. 173 n, 176, 244
natural history, i. 164 n, 192, 208, 277, 293, 304
New Place, ii. 386
Nutbourne, iii. 64
  man., iv. 112, 158
Park Mount, i. 472–3, 473
  pop., ii. 218
prehist. rem., i. 310, 330
rectors, see Apsley, Randall; Hicket Redfold, iii. 4*, 64*
roads, ii. 240; iii. 32–3, 36, 39, 48, 64
Rom. rem., iii. 2, 4, 20, 25, 26, 32–3, 38, 63, 63–4
sport, ii. 448–9, 466
trades and ind., ii. 229, 231, 244, 260
Pulford, Hen., see Pylfold
Pullen-Burry, Messrs., iii. 62
pulpits, see architecture: ecclesiastical
Pulteney:
  Sir Jas., i. 534
  Jn. (fl. 1688), iv. 179
  Jn. (fl. 1823), ix. 5
  Sir Wm., iv. 179
Punchardon (Punchardun):
  Hugh, iv. 31
  Oliver de, and his w. Asceline, vii. 255
Punfold:
  Geof. atte, iv. 184
  Jn. atte, iv. 184
Punnett's Town, see Heathfield
Punning, Mic. de, ii. 307
Pupe, Goodwife, ii. 185
Purbeck, Isle of (Dors.), i. 19; iii. 107
Purbeck marble, ii. 329, 337, 351, 355–6, 371; vii. 151, 171
Purchase:
  Geo., ix. 204
  Ric., ii. 475
Purchyn, Wm., and his w. Susan, vii. 235
Purdue, Wm., iii. 160
puritanism, i. 522, 528; ii. 23, 29–36, 39, 183; iii. 87–8
Purling, Jn., i. 531
Putlegh, Juliana de, vii. 280
Putney (London, formerly Surr.), ix. 207
Putron:
  Geof. (or Godfrey) de, vii. 78
  Pierre de, vii. 78
Putte, see Pott
Puttenham:
  Eliz., see Windsor
  Sir Geo. (d. 1533), ix. 206
  Geo. (fl. 1560), ix. 145, 181, 273 n
  Hen., ix. 206
  Marg., see Warbleton
  Ric., ix. 145, 206
  Rob., ix. 206
  Wm., ix. 206
Pycheford, see Picheford
Pycombe, fam., vii. 188 n
Pycot (Picot, Pykot):
  Jn., and his w. Lucy, vii. 203
  Jn., prior of Wilmington, ii. 123
  Nic., sacrist of Bosham coll., ii. 112
  Peter, iv. 59
Pye:
  Thos. (d. 1592), ix. 231
  Thos., rector of Brightling, vicar of Bexhill, ix. 228
  Thos. (fl. 1741), ii. 166
  Wm., dean of Chich., warden of St. Mary's hosp., Chich., ii. 51, 102
  ——, ii. 420
Pyecombe (Piecombe), ii. 43–4; vii. 2, 201, 208, 212–14
  adv., vii. 214
  Brookside Harriers, ii. 450–1
  ch., vii. 213–14, 214
    accessories, ii. 250, 352, 356, 370, 377
    archit., ii. 367
  dom. archit., vii. 212
  earthworks, i. 480; vii. 212
  man., vii. 3–4, 212–13

natural history, i. 48, 60, 166, 169
Pangdean, vii. 157, 201, 212–13
pop., ii. 224
prehist. rem., i. 330
roads, iii. 43; vii. 212
Rom. rem., iii. 62; vii. 212
sport, ii. 450, 479
Wolstonbury, iii. 68
  earthworks, i. 461, 463–4
Hill, i. 59, 320, 331; vii. 212
  natural history, i. 187, 190, 195, 200, 203–5, 282
  prehist. rem., i. 320, 331, 461, 469–70
Pygon, Margery, prioress of Easebourne, ii. 85; iv. 78 n
Pyke:
  Edw., iv. 109
  Joan, m. —— Long, iv. 109
Pykot, see Pycot
Pylfold (Pulford), Hen., ii. 422
Pynde, Nic., iv. 10
Pynham prior, see Lyminster
Pynson, Ric., ii. 405
Pype, Ric., iv. 172
Pyryman:
  Joan, see Queeche
  Wm., vii. 230
Pysing, Jn. de, ix. 127 n

Quabrook, see Hartfield
Quakeland, Laur., ii. 133
Quakers (Society of Friends), ii. 37–9; iii. 88, 164; vii. 14 n, 18, 21, 42, 234, 263; ix. 61, 131, 245
Quantock:
  Jn., iii. 145; iv. 163
  Mary, see Heather
  Mat. Heather, iii. 145
  fam., iv. 163
Quarr abbey (I.W.), iii. 107
quarrying:
  right of, ii. 230
  and see sand quarrying; stone quarrying
quarter sessions, see courts
quayage, ix. 10, 37, 49
Quebec (Canada), ii. 166
  governor, see Murray, Jas.
Queeche:
  Hugh, and his w. Eliz., vii. 230
  Joan, m. 1 Jn. Norton, 2 ? Wm. Pyryman, vii. 230
Queen Anne's Bounty, iii. 168–9
Queens' College, Cambridge, ii. 408
Queen's College, Oxford, ii. 420, 431–3
Queensberry, duke of, see Douglas, Wm.
Queneby:
  Agnes de, see Wappenbury
  Ralph de, vii. 229
Quennell, Wal., iv. 28–9
Quickhoppes, Dr., ii. 96
Quivil (Wyville), Peter, bp. of Exeter, ii. 110

rabbits, see livestock
Rackele, Hen. de, mayor of Rye, ix. 50
Rackham (in Amberley, later Parham):
  earthworks, i. 479
  insects, i. 185–6, 188, 190, 194, 199–200, 203–5, 207
  pop., ii. 218
Rackham Hill, iii. 3, 62
Racton (Rackton), ii. 16, 43, 302; iv. 88, **113–18**, 121, 138
  adv., iv. 117–18, 125
  botany, i. 48
  char., iv. 118
  ch., ii. 348, 358, 361; iv. 104, 113, 116, 116–17
  dom. archit., iv. 113–14
  Lordington, ii. 16, 43; iv. 88, 111, 113
    adv., iv. 115, 117–18
    chap., ii. 70 n
    dom. archit., ii. 387*, 396; iv. 113–14, 116, 118
  inc., ii. 190

Racton
Lordington (*cont.*):
man., iv. 92, 115–16, 123, 128
mills, iv. 115
priest, *see* William
man., iv. 104, 113–16, 122–3, 128
mill, iv. 114
pop., ii. 221
royal visit, i. 527
woodland, ii. 302
Radcliffe (Radclyffe, Ratcliffe):
Anne, ctss. of Newburgh, iii. 167
Ant. Jas., earl of Newburgh, iv. 153*, 235
Arthur, iv. 36
Barbara, *see* Kemp
Edw., iv. 36
Humph., vii. 279
Jas. Bart., Ld. Kenaird, earl of Newburgh, iv. 153, 235
Jane, m. Ant. Browne, Vct. Montagu, iv. 52
Jane, w. of Jn., *see* Alcock
Jn., iv. 35, 163
Jn., his s., iv. 36
Mary, w. of Wm., iv. 92
Wm., iv. 92
Rademelde, *see* Radmylde
Radford, *see* Woolbeding
Radimall, fam., arms, vii. 10
Radley (Oxon.), ii. 431
Radmylde (Rademelde, Radmelde, Radmyld, Radmylle):
Agatha de, m. 1 Ric. Wyville, 2 Jn. Broke, vii. 70–1, 73 *n*, 229, 232
Jn. de, vii. 34, 85
Marg., w. of Jn. de, m. 2 Jn. de Paris, vii. 34, 70
Marg., w. of Ralph, *see* Camoys
Ralph de (fl. 1203), vii. 70
Ralph de (fl. 1279), vii. 34, 59, 231
Ralph (fl. 1426), iv. 35, 202; vii. 81, 226
Ric., iv. 202
Rob., iv. 35; vii. 81
Wm. (fl. 1341), vii. 34, 70, 85
Wm. (fl. 1457), iv. 35, 202; vii. 81, 226
fam., iv. 202
Radnor, earl of, *see* Pleydell-Bouverie
Radynden, fam., arms, ix. 259 *n*
Radynden, *see* Preston
railways, ii. 240–1; *and see* Aldingbourne; Aldrington; Balcombe; Barcombe; Battle; Binderton; Bodiam; Bognor Regis; Bosham; Brighton; Chailey; Chich.; Clayton; Cocking; Crawley; Crowhurst; Cuckfield; Dean, West; Eastbourne; Elsted; Etchingham; Ewhurst; Falmer; Guestling; Hailsham; Hardham; Harting; Hastings; Hellingly; Hoathly, West; Hurstpierpoint; Keymer; Lavant: Lavant, Mid; Lewes; Lindfield; London; London and Brighton; London and Croydon; London, Brighton, and South Coast; Midhurst; Mountfield; Ore; Oving; Drayton; Patcham; Pevensey; Plumpton; Polegate; Robertsbridge; Rogate; Rye; Salehurst; Seaford; Selham; Selsey; Singleton; South Eastern and Chatham; South Western; Southease; Southern; Stedham; Ticehurst; Tunbridge Wells; Wadhurst; West Sussex; Westbourne; Whatlington; Wivelsfield; Worth; Worthing
Rainald, *see* Reynold
Rainer, *see* Reyner
Rainstorp, Wal., iv. 10
Rake, Hen., vii. 20, 24
Rake, *see* Rogate
Rakeley, ——, i. 514
Rakinton (Rakindon):
Ilbert (Imbert) de, iv. 104, 114, 123
Wm. de, iv. 104, 114, 123

Raleigh (Ralegh):
Jn. de, iv. 157
Mabel, w. of Ralph de, iv. 157
Philippa, m. Oliver Weekes, vii. 235
Ralph de, iv. 157
Rob. de, iv. 157
Sir Wal., vii. 235 *n*
Ralf, *see* Ralph
Ralfe, Wm., ix. 241
Ralph, abbot of Fécamp, ii. 104; ix. 160
Ralph, prior of Boxgrove, ii. 59
Ralph, prior of Boxgrove (another), ii. 59
Ralph, prior of Rochester, abbot of Battle, ii. 53, 55; ix. 111, 118
Ralph the marshal, ii. 315
Ralph son of Alan of Woodhorne, iv. 162
Ralph son of Gernagan (or Ralph Gernagan), iv. 24
Ralph son of Hugh, vii. 33
Ralph son of Niel, vii. 68, 280
Ralph son of Richard, vii. 234
Ralph son of Savaric fitz Cane, iv. 23, 34, 77, 78 *n*, 117; vii. 208
Ralph the king's falconer, iv. 122
Ralph the priest, iv. 8, 10
Ralph (fl. 1086, three or more of this name), iv. 101, 216, 218–19; ix. 84, 128, 137, 262
Ralph, Brian s. of, *see* FitzRalph
Ralph, moneyer, *see* Rauf
Ralph, Rob. s. of, *see* Robert
Rameslie (Hramnesleagh, Rameslege), man., ii. 127; ix. 8, 34, 49, 56, 61–2, 107, 168, 171, 175
Ramestede (? Ranscombe), nunnery, ii. 45, **63**, 331
Ramsgate (Kent), ii. 235
Ramsyn, Agatha, *see* Blundell
Ramus (Raymus):
Bertram, ix. 163
C.M., ix. 163
Clement, ix. 154
Rance, Goody, ii. 185
Randall (Randyll):
Alice, vii. 217
Jos., iii. 105, 164
Mat., iii. 164
Ric., dean of Chich., ii. 51; iii. 113
Sarah, w. of Jos., iii. 164
Randals (near Horsham), ii. 389
Randolph (Randolf):
Barnard (Bernard), ix. 83, 254, 257
Herb., ix. 83
Jn. (fl. 1549), iv. 10
Jn. (fl. 1558, ? another), ix. 83
Judith, m. Ant. Apsley, ix. 83, 254
Judith, w. of Herb., *see* Shirley
Rands, Ric., rector and vicar of Hartfield, ii. 427, 437
Randyll, *see* Randall
Ranjitsinhji, K.S., ii. 470, 472, 474
Rannulf, *see* Ranulph
Ranscombe, *see* Malling Without, South
Ransom:
F., ii. 472
W.J., ii. 473
Ransome, *see* Kent and Ransome
Ranulph, steward of count of Mortain, iv. 143
Ranulph, vicar of Udimore, ix. 26
Ranulph, Hugh s. of, *see* Hugh son of Rainer
rape, *see* crops
Raper, Rob., iii. 168
rapes, i. 506, 537; ii. 171; iv. 1
militia, i. 520, 534
and see Arundel; Bramber; Chich.; Lewes; Pevensey
Raphael, ix. 126
Raphael, Mr., ii. 460
Raphson, Jn., iv. 101
Rapley:
Edw., iv. 70
fam., iv. 70
Ratcliffe, *see* Radcliffe
Ratenden:
Agatha, vii. 257

Alice de, m. Rog. Dalingridge, vii. 257
Jn. de, vii. 257
Maud de, vii. 257
Wal. de, vii. 257
Wm. de, vii. 257
arms, vii. *257*
rates, ii. 287; vii. 201
poor rates, ii. 205–6
Ratham, *see* Funtington
Rathbun, M.J., i. 251
Ratingdene, Jn. de, i. 507
Ratton, *see* Willingdon
Rauf (Ralph), moneyer, iii. 84 *n*
Raughmere, *see* Lavant, Mid
Raven, J.E., ii. 471 *n*
Ravensworth, Ld., *see* Liddell, Hen.
Rawlings, ——, ii. 478
Rawmere, *see* Lavant, Mid: Raughmere
Ray (Raye):
Anne, *see* Dunk
Jn., i. 41
Jn. E., iii. 31–2; ix. 169, 173, 270
Thos., ix. 248
W., ii. 474
Raymus, *see* Ramus
Raynes:
Edm., vii. 40
Edw., vii. 228
Jn., vii. 218
Susan, vii. 40
Susan, m. Thos. Medley, vii. 218
——, ii. 475
Re, Jn. atte, abbot of Durford, ii. 91
Rea, fam., vii. 59
Read (Reade, Rede, Reed, Reid):
A.B., ii. 474
Chas. H., i. 340–1, 343, 346
Clement, i. 43
Fred., iii. 133
Hen. le, ii. 302
Hen., master of Holy Trinity hosp., Arundel, ii. 98
Joan, m. Ric. de Ore, ix. 19
Joan, w. of Jn. de la, vii. 280
Jn. de la (d. by 1272), vii. 280
Jn. de la (fl. 1275), i. 500; ii. 259
Jn. (fl. 1343), ix. 19, 180
Jn. (another), ix. 208
Parnel, *see* Gensing
Rob., bp. of Chich., ii. 58, 78, 101, 109; iii. 98, 124; iv. 134–5, 225
Rob., ix. 12
T., ii. 431
Thos., ix. 208
Wm., bp. of Chich., ii. 14–15, *16*, 298, 395, 401; iii. 72 *n*, 111, 124, 125 *n*; iv. 208 *n*
Reader:
Eliz., *see* Glydd
Hilkiah, ix. 273
Reading, Mr., ii. 414
Reading, earl of, *see* Isaacs
Reading (Berks.), i. 292; ii. 52, 250; iv. 10, 139
abbey, ii. 53; iv. 56
abbots, ii. 54; *and see* Aucher, prior of Lewes; Hugh, prior of Lewes
Reason:
Anne, *see* Sheldon
Hugh, iv. 177, 179
rebellions, i. 490, 508, 515–16, 519
Gunpowder Plot, i. 530; iii. 89
Jack Cade's, i. 513–14; ii. 230, 236, 257, 259; iii. 86; vii. 16; ix. 241, 252
Peasants' Revolt, ii. 186–7; vii. 16
Popish Plot, i. 529
and see riots
Reckitt:
Harold Jas., iv. 91
Jas., iv. 111
Sir Phil., iv. 110
Sir Phil. Bealby, iv. 91, 109
Record, Rob., ix. 245
recusants, *see* Roman Catholicism
Red Nore, *see* Newhaven
Red Sea, i. 254

Rede, *see* Read
Redee, la, *see* Ashdown forest
Redfold, *see* Pulborough
Redhill (Surr.), vii. 132
Redinghurst, fam., ix. 209
Redmond (Redman), Ric., abbot of Shap, bp. of St. Asaph, ii. 88, 90–1
Redrebruge, *see* Rotherbridge hund.
Redstone, *see* Reigate: man.
Redvers:
  Amice de, *see* Clare
  Baldwin de, earl of Devon, iv. 230
Redware, *see* Newhaven: Red Nore
Reed, *see* Read
Reedpond (unidentified), i. 214
reeve, Thurstan the, *see* Thurstan
Reeves (Reeve, Reve, Rieves, Ryves):
  Bruno, dean of Chich., warden of St. Mary's hosp., Chich., ii. 51, 102; iii. 88, 112
  Fred., ii. 447
  Jas., iii. 144
  Jn., iv. 23, 64
  Kingsnorth, ix. 160
  Mary, iv. 64
  Thos. (? two of this name), iv. 10; vii. 109, 169
  Thos. (another), ix. 160
Reformation, i. 515; ii. 16–29; iii. 86, 112, 121, 146, 154; ix. 57
Reginald, *see* Reynold
Regni (Regnenses), i. 326; iii. 1, 9
  kings, *see* Cogidubnus; Tincommios
Regnum, *see* Chich.
Reid, *see* Read
Reigate (Surr.), ii. 240, 306; vii. 1
  bailiff, ii. 67
  cast., vii. 1–2, 189
  ch., ii. 328 *n*, 332 *n*, 371
  hund., vii. 125, 129
  man., vii. 6
  Redstone, ii. 416–17, 419–20
  priory, ii. 75
Reimer, Peter s. of, *see* Peter
Reinbert the sheriff, ii. 112; ix. 82, 84, 112, 117, 140, 172, 174, 212, 220, 223, 235, 244, 253
Reinfrid, Rog. fitz, *see* Roger
Reinger, son of Ingelram, ix. 118
Reinir, *see* Reyner
Relfe:
  Anne, iv. 212
  Anne (another), iv. 212
  Edw., vii. 89
  Jas., ix. 92
  Jn., vii. 89
  Ric., ix. 92
  Wm. (fl. 1634), ix. 126–7, 232, 246
  Wm. (fl. 1637, another), ix. 127
Relhan, Ant., ii. 203; vii. 247
religious houses, ii. 42, 45–124
reliquary, *see* architecture: ecclesiastical
Remi (fl. 1284), iv. 58
rents, ii. 173, 178–9, 183, 189–90, 286–7
  agric., ii. 206–7, 211–13
  arrows, vii. 180, 266
  bacon, ix. 157
  beans, vii. 203
  capons, iv. 104–5, 114, 184–5; ix. 157
  cumin, iv. 28 *n*, 168; ix. 92
  deer, ix. 118
  fox, ix. 118
  gloves, iv. 98
  goshawk, vii. 145
  herrings, vii. 253, 270
  horse, ix. 91, 106
  hunting spear, iv. 128
  pepper, vii. 190
  pigs and trees, iv. 143
  rose, iv. 25; ix. 153
  salt, ix. 161, 244
  sparrowhawk, vii. 67
  spurs, gilt, iv. 61; vii. 189
  wheat, iv. 163 *n*; vii. 203–4
  wine for mass, iv. 144
Repoun:
  Joan, *see* Charles
  Wm., ix. 187

reptiles, i. **271–2**
Repton Down (unidentified), i. 169
Repyngdon, Ralf de, master of Playden hosp., ii. 105
Reredfelle, *see* Rotherfield
reredoses, *see* architecture: ecclesiastical
Restold (fl. 1086), iv. 176
Restone, Jn., sacrist of Bosham coll., ii. 112
Retherfeld (Retherfeud), *see* Rotherfield
Retlyng, Alan de, abbot of Battle, ii. 54–5; ix. 102
Reve, *see* Reeves
Reveby, Willey, ix. 137
Revell (Ryvel):
  Alice, vii. 229
  Sir Jn., vii. 229
  Nic., vii. 229
  Rob., vii. 229
  fam., vii. 229
  arms, vii. *229*
Rewell (Rewel), *see* Arundel
Reynberd, Hildebrand, ii. 185; vii. 266
Reyner, prior of Tortington, ii. 83
Reyner (Rainer, Reinir) (fl. 1086), ix. 158, 160
Reyner (Rainer), Hugh s. of, *see* Hugh
Reynold (Reginald), abbot of Battle, ii. 55–6, 397
Reynold (Reginald), abbot of Bayham (two or three of this name), ii. 87–9
Reynold, prior of Wilmington, ii. 123
Reynold the miller, vii. 203 *n*
Reynold (Rainald) (fl. 1086), iv. 216
Reynold fitz Reynold, *see* FitzReynold
Reynold, Peter fitz, *see* FitzReynold
Reynold, Thos. s. of, *see* Thomas
Reynold (Rainald), Wm. s. of, *see* William
Reynolds:
  Blanche, w. of Ric., m. 2 Rob. Palmer, 3 Sir Wm. Forman, ix. 139
  Jn., ii. 166
  Jn. Clifford, vii. 168 *n*
  Ric., ix. 139
  Rob., iv. 129
Rheinzabern (Germany), iii. 41, 57, 68
Rhine, riv., i. 18; iv. 77
Rhodes:
  H.A., ii. 434
  Wilfred, ii. 474
Riburghe, Ralph de, sacrist of Bosham coll., ii. 112
Rice, R. Garraway, i. 310, 312, 328–9; iii. 37, 63
Rich:
  Sir Chas., ii. 165
  St. Edm., abp. of Cant., ii. 10–11, 19, 63, 87; iii. 109
Richard, St., *see* Wych
Richard I, ii. 53, 72, 122, 129, 302; iii. 79, 84, 104; iv. 77, 120, 145, 192; ix. 9, 34, 36–8, 49, 51, 230
Richard II, i. 510, 513; ii. 14, 57, 60, 78, 94–5, 123; iii. 92, 96, 157; iv. 52, 143 *n*, 168; vii. 3, 20, 195
Richard III, i. 515; iv. 168, 184; vii. 6
Richard, abbot of Battle, ii. 55–6; ix. 106
Richard, abbot of Bayham, ii. 87, 89
Richard, bailiff of Atherington, ii. 120
Richard, canon of Chich. (? two of this name), ii. 7; iv. 153
Richard, dean of Battle, ii. 397
Richard, dean of Chich. (fl. 1115), ii. 50
Richard, dean of Chich. (fl. 1144), ii. 50
Richard, duke of York (d. 1460), ii. 143; iii. 114; iv. 167
  his w. Cecily, *see* Nevill
Richard, duke of York (d. 1483), iv. 122, 184; vii. 5–6, 71, 253–4
  his w. Anne, *see* Mowbray
Richard, earl of Cornwall, king of the Romans, i. 496, 498–9; ii. 95; iii. 71–2, 80, 85, 91, 98
  his s., *see* Edward
Richard, prior of Hardham, ii. 75
Richard fitz John, vii. 189, 258

Richard fitz Ode, iv. 152 *n*
Richard son of Haming, ii. 122
Richard, friar of Lewes, ii. 96
Richard the archdeacon, vii. 217–18, 243
Richard the chaplain, iv. 153
Richard the king's falconer, iv. 122
Richard the robber, iii. 103
  his w., iii. 103
Richard (fl. 1086), iv. 8
Richard (fl. 1086, another), iv. 176
Richard (fl. 1086, another), vii. 216, 242
Richard (fl. 1302), ii. 398
Richard, Ralph s. of, *see* Ralph
Richard, Jules, i. 264
Richardes, *see* Richards
Richardeville, Wal. de, ii. 123
Richards (Richardes):
  Joan, ix. 150
  Jn., i. 256
  Mary Eliz., iv. 53
  Steph., ix. 150
  T., ix. 189
  T.A., iv. 29
  Wm., ix. 264
Richardson:
  A.H., ii. 474
  Eliz., *see* Ashburnham
  Mary, w. of Wm., iv. 64
  Thos., vii. 82
  Wm., iv. 23, 64
Richborough (Ritupis) (Kent), iii. 2, 5, 10, 52
Richiardi, ——, i. 265
Richmond:
  dchss. of, *see* Lennox, Sarah
  dukes of, ii. 457, 460–1; iii. 114, 125; iv. 96, 101, 104, 162 *n*, 193; *and see* Lennox; Stuart, Jas.
  earldom, ix. 2
  earls of, *see* Brittany; Gaunt; Montfort, Jn.
Richmond Park (Surr.), ii. 442
Richoard the priest, vii. 40
Rickingale, Jn., bp. of Chich., iii. 124 *n*
Rickling Green (Essex), ii. 472
Rickman (Rykeman):
  Jn., prior of Boxgrove, ii. 58–9
  Jn., iv. 13
  Nic., and his w., ii. 39
  Susan, *see* Postlethwaite
  Thos., ii. 342; iv. 13 *n*
Rickson, Thos., and his w. Mary, vii. 96
Ricz, *see* Ritz
Riddlesdown (Surr.), i. 315
Rideout:
  Eliz., *see* Alcock
  Jn. (fl. 1751), vii. 232
  Jn. (fl. 1780), vii. 232
  Ric. (d. 1732), vii. 40, 232
  Ric. (d. 1765), iv. 40, 232
  Ric. (fl. after 1786), ix. 235
  his w., *see* Nicholl
Rider, ——, ii. 475
Ridge:
  Anne, iii. 147
  Hannah, *see* Boys
  Humph., iv. 23, 64
  Jane, *see* Chambre
  Lacy W., vii. 199, 272
  Louisa, *see* Eames
  Ric., iv. 25, 29
  Sam., vii. 36
  Steph., vii. 59
  Thos. (fl. 1723), iv. 23
  Sir Thos. (fl. 1757), iv. 23, 25, 64 *n*
  Thos. (fl. 1834), iv. 29
  Thos. (fl. 1875), iv. 29
  Thos. Jn., iv. 25
  Thos. Rog., iv. 25
  Wm., and his w. Sarah, iii. 147
Ridge-Jones, Mrs., vii. 55
Ridge Hill, *see* Grinstead, East
Ridgeway, Chas., bp. of Chich., iii. 145, 150
Ridley:
  Louisa, vii. 57
  Thos. Glyn, vii. 57
  Ursula, vii. 169

Rieves, see Reeves
Rigby, Nic., ix. 263
Riggs (Rigge):
　Ambrose, ii. 38
　Ann, see Bettesworth
　Anne, iv. 51
　Eliz., w. of Ogle, iv. 51
　Ogle (fl. 1725), iv. 51
　Ogle (fl. 1762), iv. 51
　Thos., iv. 51
　Thos. (another), iv. 63 n
Righton:
　Benj., ix. 213
　Ric., ix. 213
　Sarah, see Austen
　Wm. Austen, ix. 213
　Mrs., ix. 213
Ringmer, i. 8, 512; ii. 44, 206 n
　A.-S. rem., i. 338
　barracks, ii. 446
　Broyle (la Broile) pk., ii. 251, 292,
　　297, 313–14, 317–18, 322
　ch., ii. 118, 344, 348–9, 353, 378–9
　foxhunting, ii. 446
　hund., ii. 227; vii. 221 n
　insects, i. 147, 166, 171–6, 179–80,
　　182–4, 212–13, 220
　man., ii. 292 n
　pk., ii. 292, 297
　Plashett:
　　insects, i. 142, 154, 156, 161–3,
　　　167, 170, 173, 175, 183–5, 190,
　　　192, 198, 212–14, 216–25
　　pk., ii. 297, 301, 324, 465
　　pop., ii. 227
　trades and ind., i. 253; ii. 231, 251–2
　vicar, ii. 118
riots, ii. 13–14, 23, 136, 190, 206; and
　see rebellions
Ripe, ii. 44; ix. 244, 251
　adv., ii. 78
　bellfounding, ii. 249
　ch., ii. 249, 339, 349, 352, 378
　Eckington, ii. 44; ix. 193, 251
　man., ix. 193
　rector, ii. 312; and see Otley, Thos.
ripereeve, iv. 189
Rishton:
　Cath., m. Ric. Taylor, iv. 203
　Rob., iv. 203
　Wm., iv. 203
　　his w., see Tyll
Rising, Mr., i. 295
Risso, ——, i. 249, 258, 260
Riston (Ristone), hund., i. 537
Ritch, riv., i. 55
Ritupis, see Richborough
Ritz (Ricz), Ant., ix. 3, 79–80
rivage, ix. 9, 37, 49
Rivallis:
　Emery de, iv. 89
　Peter de, i. 495
River, see Tillington
Riverhill, see Sevenoaks
Rivers:
　Sir Geo., vii. 31, 238
　Jas., vii. 85, 87
　Jn., vii. 73, 75
　Mary, m. Jn. Bridger, vii. 85 n
　——, ii. 35
rivers, i. 18–19; and see Adur; Arun;
　Ashburn; Asten; Bay; Blackbrook;
　Brede; Combe Haven; Cuckmere;
　Cut; Darwell; Eden; Ems; Lavant;
　Medway; Mercredesburn; Mole;
　Newbridge; Ouse; Ritch; Rother;
　Stor; Thames; Tillingham; Uck-
　field; Wellesbourne; Wey; Winter-
　bourne
Rixman, Jn., sacrist of Bosham coll., ii.
　112
roads (selected references), ii. 204–5,
　240, 243, 306, 310, 322, 422–3
　ancient, ii. 239; iii. 3, 42, 62, 64, 68
　medieval, iii. 71
　Roman, see Romano-British Sussex;
　　Stane Street
　turnpike, ii. 239–40, 266

Robardes, see Roberts
robber, Richard the see Richard
Roberd, Pieter (or Graunt Pierre), ii.
　242
Roberdes, see Roberts
Robert, abbot of Durford, ii. 91
Robert, abbot of Durford (another), ii.
　91
Robert, abbot of Durford (another), ii.
　91
Robert, abbot of Grestain, ii. 123
Robert, abbot of Robertsbridge, ii. 73
Robert, count of Eu, ii. 112, 189, 264,
　294, 409–10; ix. 1, 14–15, 76, 79–
　80, 82, 84, 88, 91, 107, 112, 117,
　123, 127–8, 132, 137, 145, 148–9,
　152, 155–7, 160, 162, 172, 175–6,
　180, 190, 195, 220, 228, 233, 235,
　237, 240, 242, 244, 246–7, 249, 253,
　262, 266–7, 272, 278–9
Robert (Curthose), duke of Normandy,
　i. 489–90; ii. 129; vii. 2; ix. 1, 9
　his s., see William
Robert, earl of Gloucester, i. 490
Robert, master of Playden hosp., ii. 105
Robert, prior of Boxgrove, ii. 59; iv. 51,
　167
Robert, prior of Boxgrove (another), ii.
　57, 59
Robert, prior of Hardham, ii. 75
Robert, prior of Pynham, ii. 81
Robert, prior of Sele, ii. 62
Robert, prior of Sele (another), ii. 62–3
Robert, bro. of Bp. Hilary of Chich., iv.
　154
Robert son of Edgar, iv. 192
　his dau., see Alice
Robert son of Ralph, ii. 264
Robert son of Tetbald, sheriff of Arun-
　del, iii. 84, 96 n; iv. 30, 44, 50, 58,
　65, 69, 80, 83–4, 108, 216
　his granddau., see Aveline
　his s., see Hugh
Robert son of Walter, iv. 24
Robert the clerk, iv. 135
Robert the cook (fl. 1086), ix. 247
Robert (? the cook) (fl. 1086), ix. 228
Robert the parson, vii. 286
Robert the Scot, iv. 112
Robert the smith, ix. 199
Robert the vicar, vii. 286
Robert (fl. 1086), ix. 82, 84
Robert (fl. 1533), ii. 96
Roberts (Robardes, Roberdes):
　A.J., rector of Harting, iv. 21
　Albert Jn., ix. 148
　Anne, see Leedes
　Avery, vii. 178
　G., ii. 473
　Sir Gabriel, iv. 223
　Hen., vii. 100
　Hugh, i. 531–2
　Jn. (fl 1554), vii. 159
　Jn. (fl. 1610), vii. 177
　Jn. (d. 1639), ix. 254
　Jn. (d. 1728), ix. 254
　Jn. (d. 1732), ix. 254
　Jn. (d. 1741), ix. 254
　Jn. (fl. after 1783), ix. 254
　Jn. (fl. after 1783, another), ix. 254
　Sir Jn. Reynolds, ix. 124
　Lucy, see Fowle
　Ric., rector of Elsted, iv. 10
　Sam., ix. 254
　Thos. (fl. 1557), ix. 254
　Thos. (fl. 1563, ? another), ix. 213
　Thos. (d. 1638), ix. 209
　Wal. (fl. 1488), ix. 254
　Wal. (fl. 1504, ? another), ix. 241
　Wal. (d. 1632), ix. 254
　Wal. (d. 1684), ix. 221
　Wal. (d. 1700, ? another), ix. 254
　Wm., ii. 254
　Mr., ii. 24
　fam., ix. 205, 209, 254
　arms, ix. 254
Robertsbridge (Rotherbridge) (in Sale-
　hurst), i. 514; ix. 210, 213 n, 217–

20
　abbey, i. 496; ii. 16, 45, 49, **71–4**, 105,
　　246; ix. 174, *219*, 224
　abbots, ii. 72–4, 113, 115–16; ix.
　　119, 146, 148–9, 151, 175, 221–2,
　　224, 258; and see Denis; William
　accessories, ii. 353
　archit., ii. 330, 347, 372; ix. 217,
　　218; 219–20
　estates, ix. 1, 83, 119, 127, 140,
　　146, 149, 158, 161, 176–7, 187,
　　190, 221, 230, 253, 255, 267,
　　278–9
　liberty, ix. 210
　royal visits, ii. 73; ix. 217
　seals, ii. *74*
　woodland, ii. 324–5
　wool trade, ii. 188, 255
　bridge, ix. 221
　cts., ix. 221
　dom. archit., ii. 386; ix. 218
　fair, ix. 221
　hund., see Henhurst and Robertsbrige
　insects, i. 115, 140–1, 224, 231
　iron and steel ind., ii. 246; ix. 211, 217
　man., ix. 119, 221, 224
　mkt., ix. 221
　nonconf., ix. 225
　rly., ii. 240; ix. 217
　roads, ix. 217
　sch., ix. 224
　smuggling, ii. 200
　sport, ii. 463, 470
Robertson:
　F.W., iii. 260
　Patrick F., M.P. for Hastings, ix. 12
　Mr., ix. 5
Robertson-Luxford, J.S.O., ix. 151
Robilliard, Mary, A., ix. 33
Robins, E., & Son Ltd., ii. 263
Robinson:
　Ernest, vii. 208
　Hen., ix. 178
　J., ii. 455, 458
　J.C., vii. 71
　Jn. (fl. 1562), ii. 260
　Jn. (d. by 1895), iv. 79
　Thos., ii. 38
　Wm., vii. 165, 168
　——, i. 532
Robroke, Wm., iv. 238
Roche (Rupe):
　Cecily de la, m. Jn. Dawtrey, iv. 128
　Ralph de la, iv. 128
　Ric. de la, iv. 128
　Rob. de la, iv. 128
Roche abbey (in Maltby, Yorks. W.R.),
　vii. 235
Rochefoucauld, Fred. de la, earl of Lif-
　ford, ii. 443
Rochelle, La (Charente-Maritime,
　France), ii. 139; ix. 55
Rochester:
　Philadelphia, see Bateman
　Rob., iv. 35; vii. 82, 101
　Wm., iv. 35
Rochester (Durobrivae) (Kent), i. 496,
　514; ii. 54, 156, 323; iii. 10
　bp., see Ponet, Rog.
　prior, see Ralph
Rock, Jas., iii. 32
Rockingham, marquess of, see Watson-
　Wentworth
Rockland, see Wartling
Rodd, J.T., ii. 167
Rodmell, ii. 43–4; vii. 2–4, 53 n, 61,
　69–73
　adv., vii. 73
　agric., vii. 69, 71
　ch., vii. 71–3, *71*
　　accessories, ii. 356–7, *358*, 376
　　archit., ii. 344, 351, 367–8, 370,
　　　370, 371; vii. 77
　dom. archit., vii. *68*, 69–70, *70*
　earthworks, i. 480; vii. 69
　man., vii. 2, 48, 70–1
　mill, vii. 69
　nonconf., vii. 70

Northease:
chap., vii. 69–70, *69*
man., ii. 77, 190; vii. 2–4, 53, 61,
71
pop., ii. 224
Rom. rem., iii. 64
trades and ind., ii. 256, 264
Roe:
Wm., vii. 217–18
Wm. Thos., vii. 218
——, m. Sir Chas. Ogle, vii. 218
Roedean, *see* Ovingdean
Roemer, C.H. von, ii. 472 *n*
Roffey, Delamere B., ii. 452
Roffey Street, *see* Horsham
Rogate:
Edm. de, iv. 28
Eliz. de, m. Ralph de Camoys, iv.
24–5, 28 *n*, 34
Isabel de, iv. 28
Mary de, *see* Taylecortays
Rob. de (fl. 1202), iv. 25
Rob. de (fl. 1273), iv. 21, 25, 28
Rob. (d. 1310), iv. 25, 28
Wm. de, iv. 24–5, 28, 34
Rogate, ii. 43; iv. 3, 10, 13, 21–7, 30, 32
adv., iv. 20, 27
bridge, ii. 394; iv. 21–2
char., iv. 27
ch., ii. 89; iv. 24, *26*, 26–7, *28*
accessories, ii. 351–2, 355–6, 359–
60, 362
archit., ii. 328 *n*, 330, 340, 342, 344
dom. archit., ii. 388; iv. 22–3
Durford abbey, *q.v.*
fair, iv. 25
Fyning, iv. 5, 24–5, 28
dom. archit., iv. 22–3
man., iv. 24–7, 29
Haben, iv. 394; iv. 21–2
inc., iv. 21–2
iron ind., iv. 21
Langley, iv. 21, 23, 33
mammals, i. 301
man., iv. 15, 20 *n*, 23–6, 32, 36, 114
mills, iv. 13, 21, 25
pop., ii. 221
rly. station, iv. 10, 22
Rake, iv. 11 *n*, 21, 33
roads, iv. 21
Rom. rem., iii. 47
tithes, iv. 24
vicar, *see* Kyppyng
Wenham, iv. 12 *n*, 22, 24
man., iv. 15, 21, 24
woodland, iv. 21–2, 25
Roger, abbot of Robertsbridge, ii. 73
Roger, prior of Michelham, ii. 79
Roger, prior of Michelham (another), ii.
79
Roger, prior of Michelham (another), ii.
79
Roger, prior of Shulbred, ii. 82
Roger, reeve of Bosham, iv. 183
Roger fitz Reinfrid, iv. 85
Roger (fl. 1086), ix. 123
Roger (fl. 1086, another), ix. 262, 267
Roger (fl. *c.* 1200), ii. 110
Rogers (Roger):
Dan., ii. 320
Eliz., m. Wm. Essex, iv. 172
Marg., w. of Thos., m. 2 Thos. Fety-
place, iv. 172
Sir Ric., iv. 224
Sam., vii. 249
Thos. (d. 1488), iv. 172
Thos. (fl. 1660), vii. 54, 59
Thos. Attree, and his w. Mary Eliz.,
vii. 59
W., ii. 472 *n*
Wm., ii. 308
——, m. Sir Ric. Ashfield, iv. 224
Rokeland, *see* Wartling: Rockland
Rokenham, Wm., ii. 242
Rokesle, Jn. de, and his w. Lora, iv. 157
Roksbye, *see* Brokysby
Roland (Rolland) (fl. 1086), iv. 58
Rolf, Hugh, warden of Windham hosp.,

ii. 108
Rolland, *see* Roland
Rolland, Douglas, ii. 477
Rolleston (Staffs.), iv. 163
Rollo, Wm. Chas. Wordsworth, Master
of Rollo, ii. 479
Rolt:
Cecily, *see* Bellingham
Hen., vii. 6 *n*, 157, 230
Roman Catholicism, i. 519; ii. 23–9, 37,
40; iii. 88, 164, 167; iv. 16, 43 *n*,
50, 65 *n*, 70, 76–7, 109 *n*, 188, 227,
231, 237; vii. 17, 42, 62, 66, 144,
148, 179, 263, 282; ix. 6, 26, 28, 33,
61, 87, 106, 112–13, 123, 200, 212
Roman Gate, *see* Slinfold
Roman Wood, *see* Rudgwick
Romano-British Sussex, ii. 328, 362,
374–5; iii. **1–70**, *2*
agric., iii. 3–4, 54, 70
buildings, iii. 5–8, *6*–7, 10, 12–13, 24,
37–9, 49–54, 56, 58–63, 66–8;
and see Romano-British Suss.:
villas
burials, i. 470; iii. 2–4, 9–10, 13,
15–18, 20, 23–4, 31, 33, 37–8, 46,
49–68, 82
camps, *see* Romano-British Suss.:
roads and camps
coins, i. 338; iii. 1, 4–5, 7–9, 10,
12–13, 15–16, *16*, 18, 23–5, 28,
31–2, 37–8, 40–2, 47, 49–69
country hos., *see* Romano-British
Suss.: villas
glass making, ii. 254 *n*
govt., iii. 9–10
inscriptions, iii. 1, 4–5, 7, 8–15, 23,
59, 63, 68
ironworks, ii. 241, 291; iii. 2–3, 7,
29–32, 43, 46
livestock, i. 306
maritime hist., ii. 125–6
milestones, iii. 12, *50*
occupation, i. 481
pottery, i. 335, 343; ii. 251; iii. 4, 8,
10, 12–13, 16–18, *17*, 20, 24–5,
27, 32, 35, 37–42, 47, 49–70
Belgic, iii. 31, 37, *38*, 55, 57, 64, 69
Castor, iii. 8, 17, 38, 52, 55, 57, 59,
62, 64, 69
Gaulish, iii. 57
Marne, iii. 8
New Forest, iii. 8, 17, 38, 56–7, 59,
62, 69
Samian, iii. 4, 8, 10, 12–13, 16–18,
17, 24–5, 28–9, 31–2, 37–8, 40–1,
49, 51–9, 61–70
Upchurch, iii. 52
roads and camps, i. 470–2; ii. 291; iii.
2–3, 10, 16, 20, 32–48, *44*, 55,
57–8, 60–4, 68–70, 146; iv. 133,
210; vii. 14, 127, 204, 209; *and
see* Stane Street
temples, iii. 1, 9, 12, 51–3, 59–60, 63
tesselated pavements, iii. 10, 12–13,
20, 22–5, *22–3*, 40, 49–50, 52–9,
61–2, 68, 70
topographical index, iii. 49–68
trade and commerce, iii. 3, 7, 10, 50
tribes, British, *see* Belgae; Dobunni;
Iceni; Regni
villas, i. 340; iii. 4, 20–9, *21–3*, *26–8*,
35, 50, 68, 70
and see parish names
Romans, king of, *see* Richard, earl of
Cornwall
Romayn (Romeyn, Romyn, Rumyn):
Edm., iv. 112, 124
Hen., iv. 92, 112, 115, 124
Joan, *see* Lisle
Jn. (fl. 1244), iv. 123
Jn. (fl. 1300), iv. 112 *n*, 124
Wm., iv. 124
Rome, J.W., ii. 473–4
Rome (Italy), ii. 73, 95, 144, 411; iii. 1,
10, 60; iv. 13
army, iii. 6, 9
emperors, iii. 48; *and see* Anthemius;

Augustus; Caesar; Carausius;
Claudius; Constantine; Constan-
tius II; Diocletian; Domitian;
Hadrian; Magnentius; Maxi-
mian; Maximus; Nero; Trajan;
Valentinian; Vespasian
empire, iii. 1, 30
Romene (Romeney), *see* Romney
Romesey, *see* Romsey
Romeyn, *see* Romayn
Romney (Romene, Romeney):
Geo., iv. 152
Jn. de, ii. 107
Steph. de, ix. 148
Romney (Kent), i. 491; ii. 136, 154,
235; ix. 10, 34–6, 38–40, 50, 149
Romney Marsh, i. 333, 486; ii. 162,
447, 452; ix. 150
Romsey (Romesey, Rumsey):
Edw., ii. 165
Thos., ii. 401, 403
Romyn, *see* Romayn
Roos (Roose):
Ann, vii. 87
Jn., ii. 308
Rootes (Roots):
Ann, *see* Thatcher
Eliz., m. —— Wharton, ix. 191
Eliz., w. of Thos., *see* Thatcher
Hen., ix. 181, 191
Jas. (fl. 1608), ix. 181, 191
Jas. (fl. 1659), ix. 181, 191
Joan, w. of Thos., ix. 181
Jn., ii. 318
Martha, m. —— Norfolk, ix. 191
Thos., ix. 181
Wm., vii. 97–101
roots, *see* crops
rope making, ii. 238; ix. 13
Roper:
F.C.S., i. 43, 64
Mr., ii. 441–2
Rosam, Rob., ix. 141
Rose:
Edw. (fl. 1591), vii. 75
Edw. (fl. 1615, another), iv. 150 *n*,
153, 157
Eliz., m. Jn. Fuller, ix. 227
Geo., iv. 52
Hen., vii. 122
Jane, *see* Page
Judith, m. 1 Sir Maur. Digges, 2 Dan.
Sheldon, iv. 52
Kath., *see* Rowe
Marg., m. Sir Jas. Sheldon, iv. 52,
179–80
Marg., w. of Wm., *see* Dennis
Seth, vii. 73 *n*, 75
Thos., iv. 157
Wal., vii. 262
Wm., iv. 52, 157, 204 *n*
Mr., ix. 227
Rosebery, earl of, *see* Primrose
Roses, wars of the, *see* wars
Roset, *see* Rosey
Rosewell, Mary, iii. 146
Rosey (Drosey, Roset):
Geof. de, vii. 36, 59
Lucy de, vii. 59
Saer de, vii. 36, 59
Wm. de, vii. 59
Ross, Thos., ix. 29
Rosseter:
Jas., vii. 54
Jas. Hurly, vii. 57
Jas. Marmaduke, vii. 57
Mary Eliz., *see* Hurly
Rob., vii. 54
Rote, Nic., ix. 145
Roteham, Peter de, iv. 190 *n*
Rother, Eastern, riv., i. 18, 55–6, 58,
227, 477; ii. 324, 463; ix. 54, 211,
263
as a boundary, ix. 143, 150, 184, 252,
259
botany, i. 43, 57–8, 61
estuary, i. 536; ix. 34, *34*, 185
Fishery Assoc., ii. 464

Rother, Eastern (*cont.*):
Fishery dist., board of conservancy, ii. 464
sport, ii. 448, 453, 463–4
Rother, Western, riv., i. 19, 310; iii. 35–8; iv. 12–13, 22, 28, 32–3, 68, 71, 74, 82, 84
as a boundary, iv. 10, 12, 21, 28, 32, 47, 74, 80, 84
botany, i. 42, 52–3
sport, ii. 453, 466–7
Rother Navigation, ii. 241*, 466
Rotherbridge, *see* Robertsbridge
Rotherbridge (Redrebruge, Rotherbrige) hund., i. 538; ii. 171–2, 218; iv. 1
Rotherfield (Reredfelle, Retherfeld, Retherfeud, Rytherfeud), i. 57, 483, 539; ii. 44, 207; ix. 8
Blackthorn Hill, *q.v.*
Castle Hill, i. 55
char., ii. 438
chase, ii. 323
ch., ii. 3, 12, 323
accessories, ii. 21, 250, 352–3, 355–6, 358–60
archit., ii. 336, 340, 374, 378
Colegrove, iii. 29, 31
Crowborough, *q.v.*
Eridge, *q.v.*
horse racing, ii. 460–1
hund., i. 537; ii. 227, 323
man., ii. 3, 173 *n*, 323–4
Mark Cross, i. 61; ii. 44
natural history, i. 62, 154–6, 159, 164, 212–20, 223
pk., ii. 294, 297, 323
pop., ii. 227
rector, *see* Large
rectory, ii. 12, 324
Sand Hill, i. 55
Saxonbury, i. 343, 479; iii. 31
trug making, ii. 236
woodland, ii. 323
Rotherhithe (London, formerly Surr.), iii. 45
Rothonis, Gerald, prior of Lewes, ii. 70
Rothschild:
L. de, ii. 457
Lionel Nathan de, Baron Rothschild, ii. 459
Rottingdean, i. 54–5; ii. 43–4, 142, 206; vii. 58, 221, 225, **232–8**, 253
adv., vii. 237–8
agric., vii. 234
Balsdean, i. 285; ii. 311; vii. 221, 232–4, 238
chap., ii. 7, 338, 366; vii. 232–4, *233*, 237–8
man., vii. 229, 235
ch., vii. 231, *232*, 236, 236–7
accessories, ii. 356, 372–3
archit., ii. 332, 340, 344, 349, 365, 372
coastguards, i. 507 *n*
cts., vii. 235
earthworks, i. 480; vii. 234
fishing, ii. 265 *n*
French raids, i. 510–11; ii. 68, 139; vii. 15, 233
headborough, vii. 221
Hounds (Hunns) Mere Pit, vii. 221–2
light, ii. 163
man., vii. 2–4, 234–6
mill, vii. 233
natural history, i. 47, 59–60, 145, 165, 215, 278, 281, 286, 304
poor relief, ii. 209
pop., ii. 225
prehist. rem., i. 321, 330
Rom. rem., iii. 4, 51–2, 64–5
Saltdean, iii. 51, 65
sport, ii. 449, 451
taxation, vii. 221
vicarage, ii. 7
Rottingeham, *see* Ashdown forest
Rouen, Emery de, mayor of Chich., iii. 91, 101, 103

Rouen (Seine-Maritime, France), ii. 27, 162
abp., *see* Hugh, prior of Lewes
St. Amand's abbey, ii. 264
St. Katherine's abbey, ix. 27, 178
St. Mary de Pré abbey, iv. 184
Rougham (Norf.), vii. 4
Roughey Street, *see* Horsham: Roffey Street
Roumania, princess of, *see* Marie
Roundean, Jane, *see* Goodwin
Rouse:
Ant., ix. 196
Jas., ii. 420
Ric. le, ii. 266
Capt., ii. 457
Routh (Routhe):
Cuthbert, ix, 247
Dan., rector of Balcombe, ii. 420
O.F., ix. 247
Misses, ix. 247
Rover, riv., ii. 453
Rowe:
J., ii. 477–8, 480
Jn. (fl. 1586), iv. 112–13
Jn. (d. 1639), vii. 11–12, 16, 25 *n*, 26–7, 29, 37, 40, 42, 64, 122, 203 *n*
Kath., m. Hen. Rose, vii. 122
Kath., w. of Jn., *see* Adeane
Thos., vii. 40
Rowhook, *see* Rudgwick
Rowlands:
Alan, ii. 260
David, ix. 160
Rowley:
Joshua, ii. 166
Mr., i. 278, 283
Royal Ashdown Forest (Royal Ashdown and Forest Row) golf club, ii. 477, 480
Royal (Grand) Military Canal, ii. 162, 463; ix. 152, 160, 190
Royal Munster Fusiliers, ii. 472
Royal Navy, ii. 299–300, 322; iv. 127
Royal Oak, Order of, i. 529
Royal Sovereign lightship, ii. 163
Royden, Alice de, vii. 280
Royse, Wm., iv. 138
Rozelin (fl. 1086), iv. 211
Rubie, Geo. C., ix. 62
Rude, Jn. de la, ii. 316
Rudefin, Gilb., ii. 397
Rudgwick, ii. 43, 276
botany, i. 68
ch., ii. 339, 352, 358, 372, 377
fair, ii. 218 *n*
pop., ii. 218
roads to, iii. 33, 41–2
Rom. rem., iii. 41
Roman Wood, iii. 41
Rowhook, iii. 33, 42
Rudhall:
Jn., vii. 237
Thos., vii. 259
Rudwell, riv., ii. 453
Ruell (Ruelle), *see* Arundel: Rewell
Rufford, P., i. 247
Ruffus, Nic. s. of, *see* Nicholas
Ruffus:
Emma, m. Bart. de Leigh, iii. 105
Gilb., iv. 58
Ric., iv. 23–4
Wm., iii. 105; iv. 168
Wm. (another), ii. 404
Rugby (Warws.), ii. 428, 432, 435
Ruisselun, *see* Russhelin
Ruiter, Mic. de, ii. 158
Rumbold, Thos., i. 531–2
Rumbold's Hill, *see* Frant
Rumboldswyke (Wyke), ii. 43, 229; iii. 71, 88, 168; iv. 133, 165, **171–4**
adv., iv. 173
char., iv. 173–4
ch., ii. 48, 334, 338, 351, 364; iii. 65, 165; iv. 172–3, *173*
cts., iv. 172
fields, iv. 172–3

guilds, iv. 173
hosp. (? Newykestreet hosp.), ii. **103**
Knights Hospitallers' estates, ii. 93
man., iv. 171–3, 204
mill, iv. 171
pop., ii. 220
Rom. rem., iii. 65
tithes, iv. 171–2
Rumbregger:
Agnes, *see* Almodington
Ric., iv. 202
Rumsey, *see* Romsey
Rumworth, Hen., dean of Hastings coll., ii. 117
Rumyn, *see* Romayn
Runcton, *see* Mundham, North
Rungeton (Norf.), vii. 229
Runtinton:
Jn. de, and his w. Margery, ix. 202
Maud de, ix. 202
Ric. de (fl. 1253), ix. 202
Ric. de (fl. after 1312), ix. 202
Rupe, *see* Roche
Rupert, Prince, i. 522
Rusbridge, Wm., iv. 215
Rush (Rushe):
Ant., canon of Windsor, rector of Brightling, dean of Chich., ii. 51; ix. 228
Mr., ii. 458
Rushlake Green, *see* Warbleton
Rushmonden (Rustonden) hund., i. 537; ii. 182 *n*, 227
Rushook, Thos., bp. of Chich., ii. 14
Rushout, Sir Jas., ix. 245
Ruskin, Jn., ii. 301
Rusper, i. 58; ii. 43
ch., ii. 358, 360, 362, 376, 378
earthworks, i. 478
Faygate, i. 145, 156, 160–4, 175, 181, 206, 214, 217–18, 222–4, 230, 234
natural history, i. 137, 139, 142, 148, 150–1, 155–6, 159–64, 230, 233, 235, 277, 304
pop., ii. 219
priory, ii. 14, 45, **63–4**, 331; iv. 42, 80–2
prioress, ii. 63–4
Russell (Russel):
Agnes A.E., ix. 124
Alice, *see* Aguillon
Eliz., iii. 105
Eliz., w. of Sir Wm., *see* Wheatley
Francis, earl of Bedford, iv. 61
Francis, marquess of Tavistock, ii. 458
Francis (fl. 1640), ix. 241
Francis, duke of Bedford, ii. 455, 457
Jn., Ld. Russell, ii. 144
Jn. (fl. 1664), ii. 163; vii. 63
Jn. (fl. 1713), and his w. Eliz., ix. 181
Kath., *see* Wheatley
Nat., vii. 247
Ric. (fl. 1539), ix. 214, 220
Ric. (d. 1757), ii. 203; vii. 105, 247, 265
St. John, ix. 181
Wm. (fl. 1236), iv. 89, 111
Wm. (fl. 1664), ii. 163
(later Kemp), Wm., *see* Kemp
Wm. C., ix. 216
Misses, iii. 90
Mr., ix. 185
——, ii. 33
——, ii. 245
fam., ix. 241
Russell, E. & H., ii. 280
Russhelin (Ruisselun), Wm., prior of Lewes, ii. 70, 74
Russia, i. 278 *n*; ii. 236
Rusthall (unidentified), i. 61
Rustington, ii. 37, 42–3
adv., ii. 108, 119
ch., ii. 121
accessories, ii. 351, 353, 355–6, 358–61, 376
archit., ii. 332, 339, 342, 344, *345*,

346–51, 367–8, 370–4, *374*, 376, 378
dom. archit., ii. 388
man., ii. 121, 171, 182–3
pop., ii. 218
Rom. rem., iii. 47, 65
vicar, ii. 40
vicarage, ii. 9
Rustiton, Laur. de, iv. 188
Rustonden, *see* Rushmonden
Rutherford, Mark, *see* White, Wm. Hale
Rutland, earls of, *see* Manners
Ruxey's gang, ii. 160; ix. 13
Rye:
    Elias de, ix. 149
    Wm. atte, vii. 236
    Wm., and his w. Sara, vii. 236
Rye, i. 72, 247, 494; ii. 43, 46, 113, 188, 192, 197, 255; iii. 102; vii. 64; ix. **39–62**, *40*, 67, 164, 175
    adv., ix. 50, 61
    agric., ii. 289; ix. 40
    almsho., ix. 61
    bailiffs, ii. 130, 265; ix. 49–51, 153; *and see* Gare; Hastings, Sir Mat. de; Paulin, Hen.
    barons, i. 494; ii. 104; ix. 50, 52
    bay, i. 96, 101; ii. 125, 137, 145, 157–8; ix. 34
    birds, i. 289, 292–3, 295, 297
    botany, i. 41, 46
    boundaries, ix. 39
    Cadborough, *see* Rye: Gateborough
    Camber, *see* Rye: harbour
    cast., ix. 2, 40; *and see* Rye: defences
    chant., ix. 61
    char., ii. 425–6; ix. 61–2
    charters, ii. 129; ix. 9, 34, 37–9, 49
    ch., ii. 9, 36, 160, 267; ix. 40, *56*, 57–61, *58*, *59*, 62, 189
      accessories, ii. 351, 353, 357–9, 378
      archit., ii. 332, 340, 344, 347, 349, 367–8, 370, 374, 377–8
    ch. wardens, ii. 253
    Civil War, i. 527
    coastal erosion, ii. 143; ix. 40
    cts., ii. 146, 193; ix. 51
    curate, ii. 18, 34, 36
    custumal, ix. 51, 67
    defences, i. 512, 516; ii. 138–40, 144, 152–3, 155–61; ix. 40–2, 50, 80
      Land Gate, ii. 396; ix. 40–1, *41*
      Ypres Tower, ii. 394, 396; ix. 40–2, *41*, *42*
    dom. archit., ii. 253, 384, 386, 389–91; ix. 42–9
    Dutch War, ii. 158
    earthworks, i. 478
    epidemics, ii. 199
    erosion, ix. 40
    fairs, ix. 49
    famine, ii. 193
    fortification, *see* Rye: defences
    French raids, i. 510, 513; ii. 138–40, 143; ix. 66–7
    friaries:
      Augustinian, ii. 45, **96–7**; ix. 40, *40*, *42*, 61; archit., ii. 331, 377; ix. 42–3
      of the Sack, ix. 43
    Gateborough (Cadborough), ix. 56–7, 164
    geology, i. 274
    golf, ii. 479
    guilds, trade, ii. 192; ix. 55–6
    Haltone, le, ii. 97; ix. 40
    harbour (Camber), i. 26, 485; ii. 125, 137, 142–4, 149–50, 152, 154, 157, 159, 229; ix. 34, 39, 52, 70, 74 *n*
    lights, ii. 163
    marine zoology, i. 97, 99–100
    hosp., ix. 48
      St. Bartholomew's, *see* Playden: hosp.
    Huguenots, ii. 27; ix. 61
    inns, ii. 196, 262, 384, 386, 393; ix. *44*, 44–8

insects, i. 115–16, 125, 131, 135, 137–49, 152–8, 161–3, 174, 176, 185, 187, 190, 198, 206, 215, 220, 228–33, 236
Jews, i. 506
Land Gate, *see* Rye: defences
land reclamation, ix. 40, 52, 54
levels, ii. 159
liberties, ix. 49, 52
local govt., ii. 24; ix. 49–54
    bailiffs, *see* Rye: bailiffs
    corporation, ii. 107, 266, 426; ix. 52–4
    freemen, ix. 35–6, 52–4
    jurats, ii. 104, 149–50, 153–5, 233–4, 267–8, 425–6; ix. 36, 52–3, 55, 90
    mayors, ii. 30, 96, 104, 107, 144, 147–50, 153–4, 233–4, 236, 258, 262, 266–8, 425–6; ix. 50–5, 90, 153, 157; *and see* Hamon
    regalia, ix. 54
    seals, ix. 54
    wards, ix. 52
mammals, i. 301–2
man., ii. 3, 181; ix. 49, 56–7; *and see* Rameslie
marine zoology, i. 98, 100, 106
mkt., ix. 40
Martello towers, ii. 162
militia, i. 519–20, 528, 535
mills, ix. 40, 50
mint, ix. 49
naval recruitment, ii. 161
nonconf., ii. 18, 30, 34, 41; ix. 61–2
parl. rep., i. 504, 532; ix. 52–4
    M.P., *see* Hay, Jn.
persons from, ii. 7
piracy, ii. 136, 147–9
poor relief, ii. 193, 205, 238
pop., ii. 228
port, ii. 3, 169, 247–8; ix. 54–5, 70, 151
prison, *see* Rye: defences: Ypres Tower
privateering, ii. 144, 148 *n*, 150, 153–4, 156, 159
rly., ix. 40
    station, ix. 150, 152, 157
Rameslie man., *q.v.*
roads, ix. 40
Rom. Cath., ix. 61
Rom. rem., iii. 2, 65
royal visits, i. 492; ix. 49, 269
Rye Foreign, ix. 56, 142, 153 *n*, 172
Rye Hill, ix. 39–40, 56
sch., ii. 398, 426; ix. *45*, 46, 61–2
    grammar, ii. 390–1, 425–6
sea defences, ix. 157
Sea Fencibles, ii. 162
ship money, ii. 157
ship service, ii. 129–30, 131 *n*, 134–5, 138, 140–2, 144, 150, 152–4; ix. 9–10, 36, 49–50, 54
shipping, ii. 129–30, 132, 134 *n*, 136–9, 144–5, 149 *n*, 151–8, 162; ix. 40, 54
streets, ix. 40–8
taxation, ix. 50, 52, 55
Town Hall, ix. 40, 45, *45*, 53
trades and ind., ix. 55–6, 70, 211
    baking, ii. 262; ix. 56
    brewing, ii. 261–2; ix. 56
    charcoal, ix. 55
    chemical works, ii. 232
    fisheries, ii. 130, 140, 145–6, 151, 154, 156–7, 160, 236, 265–70; ix. 13, 49–50, 52, 55, 70
    goldsmith, ii. 229
    gunpowder, ii. 237
    iron, ix. 55, 168
    lime burning, ii. 231
    oil, ix. 55
    pottery, ii. 252–3; ix. 56
    printing, ii. 239
    rope making, ii. 238
    sacking, ii. 238
    salt, ii. 113, 232–3; ix. 55

    shipbuilding, ii. 130, 141, 145, 164, 234–5; ix. 55–6
    shoemaking, ix. 56
    spices, ix. 55
    tanning, ii. 260
    textiles, ii. 256; ix. 55
    timber, ii. 233–4; ix. 55
    wine, ix. 55
    wool, ii. 145
union, i. 539
vicarage, ii. 9, 333; ix. 61
vicars, ii. 37; ix. 62; *and see* Twyne, Brian; Wells, Mr.
witchcraft, ii. 31
Ypres Tower, *see* Rye: defences
rye, *see* crops
Rykeman, *see* Rickman
Rykhill, Joan, m. Ric. Bruyn, ix. 118
Ryman:
    Cicely, m. Brune Bickley, iv. 189
    Cox, iv. 204
    Eliz., w. of Wm., iv. 238
    Joan, *see* Tawke
    Jn., iv. 204
    Ric., iv. 51, 177, 204, 230
    Wm. (fl. 1410), iv. 138, 238
    Wm. (fl. 1569), ii. 25
    Wm. (fl. 1616), iv. 139
    Wm. (fl. *c.* 1654), iv. 204
Rymans, *see* Appledram
Rynghede, Harold, ii. 83
Ryslee:
    Alice de, m. Rob. de Beyvill, vii. 229
    Jn. de, vii. 229
Ryth (Rythe):
    Constance, *see* Windsor
    Geo., iv. 17 *n*
    Thos., iv. 15
Rytherfeud, *see* Rotherfield
Ryvel, *see* Revell
Ryves, *see* Reeves

sac and soc, ix. 9, 34, 37
Sacheverell, fam., arms, iii. 155
sack making, ii. 238
Sackville (Sackvile):
    And. de, ix. 139
    Anne, m. Gregory Fiennes, Ld. Dacre, vii. 89, 175 *n*; ix. 33
    Anne, m. Sir Nic. Pelham, vii. 39; ix. 139
    Anne, w. of Ric., earl of Dorset, m. 2 Phil. Herbert, earl of Pembroke, vii. 36, 48, 232
    Arabella Diana, *see* Cope
    Chas., earl of Dorset and Middlesex, i. 536; ix. 117
    Cicely, ctss. of Dorset, vii. 74 *n*
    Edw., earl of Dorset, ii. 319–20; vii. 35–6, 64, 89, 105, 255; ix. 53, 117
    Edw. (fl. 1678), ix. 88
    Ela de, *see* Dene
    Eliz., Baroness Buckhurst, m. Geo. Jn. Sackville-West, Earl de la Warr, vii. 7, 35, 257, 279; ix. 117
    Eliz., w. of Ric., iv. 178
    Frances, w. of Ric., earl of Dorset, m. 2 Hen. Poole, ix. 117
    Ld. Geo., ix. 117
    Geo., duke of Dorset, vii. 7, 35; ix. 117
    Hen., ix. 117, 119
    Herbrand Edw. Dundonald Brassey, Earl de la Warr, vii. 30; ix. 114, 278–9
    Isabel, vii. 105, 227
    Joan, ii. 85
    Jn. (fl. 1532), ix. 177
    Jn. (fl. *c.* 1540, ? another), ii. 317
    Jn. (fl. 1544), iv. 231; vii. 144, 228
    Jn. (fl. 1617), ix. 92
    Jn. (d. 1619, another), ix. 168
    Sir Jn. (fl. 1628), ix. 88, 92
    Jn. (fl. 1712), ix. 278
    Ld. Jn., ii. 468
    Jn. Fred., duke of Dorset, vii. 257; ix. 117
    Jordan de (fl. *c.* 1208) ii. 86

Sackville (*cont.*):
Jordan de (fl. 1264), i. 497; ii. 317 *n*
Lionel Cranfield, earl of Dorset and
Middlesex, duke of Dorset, ii.
322; ix. 82 *n*, 114, 117
Marg., prioress of Easebourne, ii. 84–
5
Marg., m. Jn. Tufton, earl of Thanet,
vii. 33, 48, 105, 227, 255; ix. 61
Mary, m. 1 Other Archer, earl of
Plymouth, 2 Wm. Pitt Amherst,
earl of Amherst, vii. 20, 35, 257,
276, 286; ix. 117
Mary, m. Wm. White, ix. 146, 269 *n*
Sir Ric., ii. 312; iv. 101, 103, 145,
178, 185, 199, 201, 230–1, 238;
vii. 33, 41, 60, 76, 109, 135,
179 *n*, 228, 238, 257; ix. 19, 21,
88, 92, 94, 119, 123, 177–8
Ric., earl of Dorset (d. 1624), vii.
33–5, 41, 48, 58, 64, 74 *n*, 76, 91,
105, 135, 224, 227, 232, 238, 255;
ix. 94, 117, 154, 245
Ric., earl of Dorset (d. 1677), ii. 39 *n*,
249, 320–2; vii. 41, 135, 232; ix.
117, 278
Ric., ix. 117, 278
Rob., earl of Dorset, ii. 193, 318; vii.
7, 34, 36 *n*; ix. 117, 245
Sir Thos. (fl. 1381), i. 512
Thos., Ld. Buckhurst, earl of Dorset,
i. 517, 519; ii. 20, 149 *n*, 233,
318; iv. 101, 238; vii. 7, 33–4, 36
n, 48, 55, 57–8, 60, 64, 69, 74 *n*,
76, 78, 85, 224, 231, 252, 279,
281; ix. 19, 53, 55, 88, 92, 115,
117, 138, 177, 248
Thos. (fl. 1614), ix. 88, 92, 177, 180
Thos. (fl. 1619, another), ix. 168
Thos. (fl. 1677), ix. 168
Thos. (d. 1692, another), ix. 279
Wm., iv. 231; vii. 144
Winifred, w. of Sir Ric., ix. 119
fam., ii. 362; vii. 26 *n*, 35, 48, 64, 74,
257; ix. 19, 61, 94, 172, 278–9
arms, iv. 178; vii. 7; ix. *117*, *278*
Sackville, Lds., *see* Sackville-West
Sackville college, *see* Grinstead, East
Sackville-Germain, Chas., duke of
Dorset, ix. 117
Sackville-West:
Chas., Ld. Sackville, vii. 280
Chas. Ric., Earl de la Warr, vii. 279–
80
Eliz., *see* Sackville
(formerly West), Geo. Jn., Earl de la
Warr, vii. 7, 19–20
Gilbert Geo. Reg., Earl de la Warr, i.
306; ii. 477–8
Herbrand Edw., Earl de la Warr, ix.
115, 117
Lionel, Ld. Sackville, vii. 280
Lionel Edw., Ld. Sackville, vii. 280
Mortimer, Ld. Sackville, vii. 279
Reg. Windsor, Earl de la Warr, ii.
451; vii. 55, 280
and see West
sacristies, *see* architecture: ecclesiastical
Saddlescombe (in Newtimber), i. 31*;
ii. 263; iii. 43, 65; vii. 201, 204–5;
ix. 279 *n*
man., ii. 92–3; iv. 185; vii. 14 *n*, 190,
207–8, 213
ho., vii. 205, *205*
preceptory of Knights Templar, ii. 45,
92, 263, 331*; vii. 205, 207
Sadler (Sadleir):
Jn., vii. 216
R., ii. 453
Sir Ralph (? two of this name), iv. 56;
ix. 221
Saffron Walden (Essex), ii. 405, 417
Saham, Jn. de, i. 509
Sahara, i. 253
St. Alban Hall, Oxford, ii. 421
St. Albans (St. Alban):
Jn., ii. 500
Reynold of, ii. 82

St. Albans, duke of, *see* Beauclerk,
Chas.
St. Albans (Verulamium) (Herts.), iii.
10
abbot, i. 511
battle, iv. 159; ix. 146
cath., ii. 50
St. Amand, abbey, *see* Rouen
St. Andrews Bay (Scot.), i. 289
St. Anne's Hill, *see* Midhurst
St. Anthony's Hill, *see* Eastbourne
St. Asaph, Vct., *see* Ashburnham, Geo.
St. Asaph (Flints.), bp., *see* Redmond,
Ric.
St. Abuyn, W.M., ii. 470 *n*
St. Bernard's College, Oxford, ii. 406
St. Carileff (Sarthe, France), abbey, ii.
53
St. Catharine's College, Cambridge, ii.
411, 416–17
St. Clare (St. Clere):
Edith, m. Sir Ric. Harcourt, vii. 256
Eliz., m. Wm. Lovell, iv. 129
Joan, w. of Rob., iv. 129
Jn. de (d. 1336), iv. 129
Sir Jn. (fl. 1370), i. 509–10; ii. 315
Jn. (d. 1418), vii. 256
Sir Phil. (d. 1408), vii. 256, 258
Sir Phil. (d. 1422), iv. 129
Rob. de, iv. 129
Thos. (d. 1434), iv. 129
Thos. (d. 1435), vii. 256, 258
fam., vii. 256
arms, iv. *129*; vii. *256*; ix. 216
St. Clement's caves, *see* Hastings
St. Clere, *see* St. Clare
St. Cyriacus, cardinal, *see* Marini
St. David's, bp. *see* Burgess, Thos.
St. Denis abbey, *see* Paris
St. Dominic's Press, *see* Ditchling
St. Ermine, Wm. de, iv. 51
St. Evroul (Orne, France), monk of, iv.
118
St. Florent (in Saumur, Maine-et-Loire,
France), abbey, ii. 60, 329, 331
St. George:
Agatha de (fl. 1231), iv. 34, 36
Agatha de (fl. *c.* 1330), iv. 177
Alan de (fl. *c.* 1190), iv. 34, 36
Alan de (fl. *c.* 1220), iv. 7, 34, 39
Amy de, m. Jn. de Wytham, iv. 105
Amy, w. of Thos. de, iv. 105
Elias de, iv. 51, 53
Isabel de, ? m. Wm. Tawke, iv. 177
Joan de, iv. 177
Jn. de (fl. 1248), iv. 34, 51, 53, 56,
177
(or Thadeham), Jn. de, iv. 105
Jn. de (fl. 1316), iv. 177
(or Thadeham), Peter de, iv. 105
Ralph de, iv. 177
Ric. de, iv. 34, 36, 177
Rog. de, iv. 177
Sarra, w. of Wm., iv. 51, 177
(or Thadeham), Thos. de, iv. 34, 51,
105, 177
Wm. de (d. by 1278), iv. 177
(or Thadeham, or Tadeham or Pott),
Wm. de (d. 1316), iv. 34, 51, 53,
61, 105, 177
Wm. de (d. 1334), iv. 34, 51, 105, 177
Wm. de (d. by 1368), iv. 52, 105, 177
fam., iv. 51, 105
St. George's Channel, i. 344
St. Germain-en-Laye (Seine-et-Oise,
France), ii. 164; iv. 17
St. Giles (unidentified), iii. 102
St. Helen's, *see* Ore
Saint Hill, *see* Grinstead, East
St. John:
Agatha de, iv. 157 *n*
Agnes, w. of Rob. de, m. 2 Jn. de
Turevylle, iv. 199
Alice, w. of Edw., iv. 123
Anne, *see* Oxenbridge
Cecily de, *see* Hay
Edm. de, iv. 51, 91, 143, 177, 199–
200, 212–13

Edw. de (d. 1346), i. 509; iv. 35, 56,
85, 108, 110, 145, 176–7, 213
Sir Edw. (fl. 1367), ii. 120; iv. 66,
106, 123, 202
Sir Edw. (fl. 1377), iv. 168
Edw. (d. 1400), i. 512; iv. 123
Eliz., m. Hen. Dyke, iv. 108
Eliz., w. of Edm. de, iv. 91, 143, 177
Eve, *see* Dawtrey
Fred., vii. 134 *n*
Godeheuda, *see* Paynel
Hugh de (d. 1337), iv. 143, 162, 177,
199
Hugh de (fl. 1404), iv. 144
Isabel de, m. 1 Hen. de Burghersh, 2
Sir Luke de Poynings, 3 Sir
Thos. Worting, iv. 91, 143, 177
Isabel, w. of Jn. de, *see* Courtenay
Joan, m. Giles de Chanceus, iv. 199
(or Arundel), Joan, w. of Edw., iv.
66, 202
Joan, w. of Sir Edw., *see* Tregoz
Joan, w. of ——, *see* Hevere
Jn. de (d. 1301), ii. 190, 295; iv. 25,
143, 177, 199
Sir Jn. de (d. 1329), iv. 51, 143,
144 *n*, 161, 176–7, 199–200
Jn. (fl. 1354), iv. 108
Jn. de (fl. 1379), ii. 294
Marg., m. Jn. de St. Philibert, iv. 51,
91, 143, 177, 212–13
Muriel de, m. Rainald d'Orival, iv.
143
Olive, w. of Wm., iv. 162
Oliver, iv. 42; ix. 181
Ric. de, ii. 121
Rob. de (fl. to 1187), ii. 56; iv. 91 *n*,
143, 162, 201
Rob. de (d. by 1269), i. 501; ii. 294;
iv. 143–4, 199
Rog. de, ii. 56, 303; iv. 91, 93, 143
Thos. de, Ld. St. John, iv. 144
Wm. de (fl. 1187), ii. 56; iv. 51, 91,
93, 136, 143, 145, 149, 156–7,
162, 165, 176, 179, 201
Wm. de (fl. 1230), i. 494; ii. 296; iv.
43, 156, 177, 199
Wm. de (d. by 1329), iv. 143
Wm. (fl. 1428), iv. 108
——, w. of Wm., *see* Hay
fam., ii. 63, 303; iv. 91, 156, 161, 165,
176, 199, 213
arms, iv. *143*
St. John, Ld., *see* Poynings, Sir Thos.
de; St. John, Thos. de
St. John Hope, Sir Wm., iv. 49; vii. 46
St. John of Jerusalem, Knights of, *see*
Knights Hospitaller
St. John of Jerusalem, liberty of, *see*
Midhurst: Knights Hospitaller
St. John's College, Cambridge, ii. 408,
414, 422–3, 426, 429–31; iv. 233
St. John's College, Oxford, ii. 420, 428;
433–4
St. John's Common, *see* Burgess Hill
St. Just, Alan, vii. 256
St. Katherine, abbey, *see* Rouen
St. Laurence in Lucina, cardinal, *see*
Tolet
St. Leger (Seyntleger):
Agnes, w. of Geof., *see* Warbleton
Agnes, w. of Jn., *see* Salerne
Alice, m. Rob. de Beauchamp, ix. 176
Ant., iv. 236
Biset de, ix. 138
Clarembald de, ix. 138, 149
Geof. de (d. by 1166), ix. 84, 138, 149
Geof. (d. by 1225), i. 495; ix. 84, 138,
176
Geof. (fl. 1239), ix. 138
Geof. (another), ix. 180
Geof. (d. by 1296), i. 498 *n*, 500; ix.
138, 207, 233
Helisend, w. of Reynold de, ix. 84
Heudiart, w. of Jn. de, ix. 84
Isabel, m. Sir Thos. Hoo, ix. 138, 233
Isabel, w. of Jn., m. 2 Giles de Braun-
son, ii. 180; ix. 138

Joan, w. of Geof., ix. 138
Jn. (d. *c.* 1205), ix. 84, 138
Jn. (d. by 1312), ii. 180, 324; ix. 138, 207, 233
Jn. (d. 1326), ix. 138
Jn. (fl. 1328), ix. 138 *n*
Marg., m. Jn. Ld. Clinton, vii. 84, 87
Reynold, ix. 84, 138
Ric. de, ix. 138
Rob., ix. 117, 176
Sybil, w. of Wm. de, ix. 197
Thos. (fl. 1166), ix. 84, 138, 176
Sir Thos. (fl. 1481), iv. 216
Wal. (fl. 1217), i. 494
Wal. (fl. 1264), ii. 324
Wm. de (fl. 1086), ix. 82, 84, 137–8, 149, 233
Wm. de (fl. before 1195, another), ix. 229
   his s., *see* Socknersh, Rog. de
Wm. (d. by 1265), ii. 324; ix. 138, 176, 197, 237
———, w. of Wm., *see* Echingham
fam., ix. 138, 228
arms, vii. 140; ix. *84, 138, 176*
St. Leofard (Sancto Leofardo):
Gilb. de, bp. of Chich., ii. 13, 72, 75, 98, 305, 332; iii. 110, 113, 115–16, 125; iv. 117; ix. 118
Jn. de, dean of Chich., ii. 51
arms, iii. *110*
St. Leonards (in Hastings), i. 57, 71, 247, 292, 304–5; ii. 43; ix. 4, 6, 76
batrachians, i. 272
Beaulieu, ii. 276
birds, i. 276–7, 279, 281, 283, 289, 295–6
Bohemia:
   ch., ix. 26, 28
   pottery, ii. 251; ix. 13
Bopeep, i. 115, 126, 138–42, 145, 147–8, 151–2, 154, 156–60, 162–3, 224, 265, 272; ii. 470–2; ix. 8
botany, i. 43, 61–2, 67–8
ch., ix. 25, 27–8
   Christ Ch., ix. 25–6, 28, 33
   St. John's, ix. 28
crustaceans, i. 261–2
fossils, i. 35–6
Gensing, ix. 8, 19, 21
insects, i. 114, 116, 119–21, 125–30, 132, 134–6, 138–44, 147, 149–55, 157, 159–60, 163, 171–2, 176–7, 180–1, 183, 185, 189–93, 212, 216, 218–21, 224
mammals, i. 302–3, 307
man., ix. 20
militia, i. 536
pier light, ii. 163
pop., ii. 222, 228
prehist. rem., i. 327, 330, *330*
reptiles, i. 271
resort, ii. 204
sport, ii. 460, 469–74, 479
St. Leonard's forest, i. 49, 110, 305; ii. 189, 253, 293, 296–7, 299, **306–10**, 313, 318, 466
assarting, ii. 306
birds, i. 276–7, 280, 290, 292
botany, i. 50, 53–4, 68
chap., ii. 20, 306, 308
deer, i. 306
fair, ii. 308
insects, i. 148, 150, 155–7, 159, 161–6, 168–9, 170, 173–8, 181, 183–7, 196–9, 203–4, 228–30, 234
iron ind., ii. 230, 247–8, 310
Little Pk., ii. 307–8, 310
mammals, i. 301, 303
molluscs, i. 109
ponds and fisheries, ii. 308
prehist. rem., i. 330
sport, ii. 307, 309, 448, 462
tithes, ii. 306
wards, ii. 308
St. Lo, Edw., ii. 166
St. Lucy in Silice, cardinal, precentor of Chich., ii. 12

St. Malo (Ille-et-Vilaine, France), ii. 165
St. Marcellus, cardinal, *see* Palosius
St. Martin:
   Adelize, w. of Alfred de, *see* Adelize
   Alfred (Alured) de, sheriff of Hastings, ii. 71, 330*; ix. 14, 120, 146, 149, 235, 255, 267
   Geof. de, ix. 267
   Rob. de, ix. 221
   Wm. de, ix. 146
St. Martin du Bosc (Eure, France), abbey, ix. 139, 244
St. Mary de Pré, abbey, *see* Rouen
St. Mary Hall, Oxford, ii. 407, 421
St. Noet, Wm. de, abbot of Robertsbridge, ii. 73
St. Omer (Seyntomer):
   Alice de, m. Sir Wm. de Hoo, iv. 230
   Eliz. de, iv. 229
   Pernel de, *see* Grauntson
   Thos. de, iv. 229
St. Osyth, priory (Essex), iv. 73
St. Owen (St. Oweyn):
   Godehuda, *see* Aguillon
   Ralph de (fl. 1236), iv. 89, 111
   Ralph (fl. 1337), iv. 145
St. Pancras, Wm. de, vii. 224
St. Pancras, *see* Chich.: suburbs
St. Pancras, Corporation of, *see* Chich.: clubs
St. Pancras, priory, *see* Lewes: priory
St. Paul, W.F., ii. 442
St. Peter:
   Marg. de, *see* Somery
   Urian de, iv. 166–7
St. Philibert:
   Jn. de, iv. 51, 91, 143, 177, 212–13
   Marg. de, *see* St. John
St. Pierre en Port (Portus Petri) (Seine-Maritime, France), ii. 140
St. Pol, Mary de, m. Aymer de Valence, earl of Pembroke, ix. 2
St. Quintin, Herb. de, iv 63
St. Radegund's abbey, *see* Bradsole
St. Radegund's priory, *see* Cambridge
St. Roche's Hill, *see* Singleton: Trundle
St. Sampson:
   Brunna de, m. Sim. Maufe, iv. 111 *n*
   Ralph de, iv. 111 *n*
St. Saviour's school, *see* Ardingly
St. Sepulcre, ch. of (unidentified), ii. 113
St. Thomas's hospital, *see* Lambeth
St. Valery sur Somme (Somme, France), i. 485; ii. 128
St. Victor, (? comte de), ii. 442
St. Vincent, earl of, *see* Jervis, Jn.
St. Vincent, battle, ii. 162
Sait, Jas., and his w. Fanny, iv. 129
Sale, Wm., ii. 407
Salehurst, ii. 43; ix. 209–10, 212–13, **217–25**, 258
   adv., ii. 72; ix. 221–4
   Bexwesell (Becketwesell), ix. 220 *n*
   Bugsell, ix. 213, 220
   chap., ix. 72; ix. 224
   char., ix. 224
   ch., ii. 112; ix. 22–3, 222, *223*
      accessories, ii. 351–2, 356, 358, 360; ix. *224*
      archit., ii. 330, 344, 346, 374
   dom. archit., ix. *217*, 217–18
   Drigsell, ix. 210
   earthworks, i. 478
   Higham, ix. 258 *n*
   Hurst Green, ii. 391; ix. 211–12, 217
   insects, i. 129, 144–9, 155–6, 159, 161, 227–37
   Iridge, ix. 103, 210, 220–2, 224
   man., ix. 210, 220–2
   mills, ix. 220
   nonconf., ix. 217, 224–5
   pop., ii. 223
   prebend, ii. 113; ix. 174, 223–4
   rly., ii. 222 *n*
   rectory, ix. 221–2, 224
   Robertsbridge, *q.v.*
   Silverhill, ix. 217

trades and ind., ii. 257, 259; ix. 220
Wigsell, ix. 221–2
   Gt. Wigsell, ii. 387, 390; ix. 217–18
Salerne:
   Agnes, m. 1 Jn. Orlaston, 2 Jn. St. Leger, ix. 177
   Sim., ix. 177
Salisbury, ———, ii. 33
Salisbury, earl of, *see* Montagu, Jn.
Salisbury (Wilts.), ii. 394
   bp., *see* Aiscough; Bohun, Jocelin de; Poor
   cath., ii. 9, 340, 400
   prebendary, *see* Seager, Jn.
Salkeld, Frances, *see* Wildgose
Sallust, ii. 406, 419
Salman:
   Rog., and his w. Alice, vii. 231
   Thos., vii. 231
Salmonsbury hund. (Glos.), ix. 50
Salnervill (Sandrevill):
   Agnes de, m. Wm. Bernehus, iv. 98
   Gilb. de, iv. 98
   Itaria (Italia) de, m. Hen. de Cheney, iv. 98
   Itarius de, iv. 97–8
   Sara de, iv. 98
Salomon, iii. 80
Salsulae, *see* Narbonne
Salt, Sampson, ii. 166
salt industry, ii. 89, 112, 232–3; iv. 139, 156 *n*; ix. 55, 63, 120, 161, 244
Saltdean, *see* Rottingdean
Salter:
   Anne, m. 1 Hen. Bowyer, 2 ——— Harris, iv. 155, 172
   Nic., iv. 155, 172
Salvation Army, iii. 164; vii. 144; ix. 247
Salvington, *see* Durrington
Salwey, Arthur, iv. 54
Salye, Thos., ix. 119
Saman, Hen., vii. 37
Sambrook, Jn., ix. 221
Samian ware, *see* Romano-British Suss.: pottery
Sampson, a Jew, i. 506
Sampson:
   Ric., bp. of Chich., ii. 18–19, 186
   Ric. King, ii. 450–1
   Thos., dean of Chich., ii. 48, 51
Samuel, Mr., ii. 455
Sancroft, Wm., abp. of Cant., ii. 101; iii. 88
Sancto Leofardo, *see* St. Leofard
Sancto Romano, Steph. de, prior of Lewes, ii. 70
Sand Hill, *see* Rotherfield
sand quarrying, ix. 6
Sanden, Thos., iii. 160
Sanders, *see* Saunders
Sanderson (Saunderson):
   Bridget, m. Wm. Speed, iv. 231
   Rob. Edw., canon of Chich., ii. 432
Sandes, *see* Sandys
Sandford, Jn., ii. 407
Sandgate (Kent), ix. 185
Sandham:
   Cath., iii. 147
   Rob. (fl. 1542), iv. 231
   Rob. (d. 1776), iii. 130
   Wm., iv. 51
Sandhurst (Kent), ii. 449, 451
Sanditon, iv. 226
Sandlake, *see* Battle
Sandown castle, *see* Deal
Sandreville, *see* Salnervill
Sandridge (Herts.), ii. 431
Sandringham (Norf.), ii. 284
Sands, Harold, i. 477; *and see* Sandys
Sandwich, Ralph de, ii. 304
Sandwich, earl of, *see* Montagu, Sir Edw.
Sandwich (Kent), i. 483–4, 495, 501; ii. 126–7, 129, 136, 142, 154, 155 *n*, 247; ix. 34, 38
   fishing, ii. 235
   liberties, ix. 35, 37
   local govt., ix. 10, 35

Sandwich (*cont.*):
ship (or sea) service, ix. 3b
shipping, ii. 144; ix. 50
Sandy, Rob., iii. 161
Sandys (Sandes):
Hen., iv. 7
Marg., m. Sir Jn. Mill, iv. 7, 35, 85
Margery, *see* Bray
Wm., Ld. Sandes, iv. 15
and see Sands
Sanglake, *see* Battle: Sandlake
Sankey, Percy E., ix. 179
Sanzaver (Saunzaver):
Eve, w. of Hugh, iv. 114
Hugh (d. *c.* 1250), iv. 23, 114
Hugh (d. 1284), iv. 114, 152
Maud, *see* Cheney
Ralph (Ralf) (d. by 1229), iv. 23, 56, 114, 123
Ralph (fl. 1284), iv. 23, 58, 152
Ralph (d. 1314, another), iv. 58, 152-3
Ralph (fl. 1316), iv. 114
Ralph (? another), iv. 51
Thos., iv. 114
Wm., iv. 23
fam., iv. 58, 114, 152 *n*, 153
Saracen, Peter, iv. 115
Sarah, dau. of Brian FitzRalph, m. Rog. de Bavent, iv. 45
Sarcrino, Nic. de, ii. 397
Sardene, *see* Shernedene
Sargent:
Charlotte, *see* Bettesworth
Emily, m. Sam. Wilberforce, iv. 59
Jn., M.P. for Seaford, iv. 59
Jn., rector of Graffham, iv. 59
Sarre (Kent), i. 337, 344
Sars, G.O., i. 262-4
Sartilli (Sortell'):
Clarice de, ? m. —— de Craucumbe, iv. 144
Emma de, *see* Falaise
Geof. de, iv. 199
Gilb. de, iv. 144, 179
Rob. de, iv. 199
fam., iv. 144, 199
Saulf (fl. 1170-8), iv. 183
Saumur, *see* St. Florent
Saunders (Sanders):
Ant., ii. 438
Bridget, *see* Infield
Chas., ii. 166
Eliz., m. Jn. Courthope, ix. 255
Geo., ii. 165
Howard, i. 277, 288
J.J.G., ii. 475
Jas., ii. 410-11, 426
Jn. (fl. 1450), ii. 236
Jn. (fl. 1647), vii. 168
Jn. (fl. 1709), iv. 83
Mary A., ix. 32
Rob., ii. 164
Sarah, vii. 115
Wm. (fl. 1501), ix. 255
Wm. (fl. *c.* 1546), ii. 246
Mr., ii. 475
——, vii. 261
Saunderson, *see* Sanderson
Saunzaver, *see* Sanzaver
Sauvage, *see* Savage
Sauz, Steph. de, prior of Sele, ii. 61-2
Savage (Sauvage):
Hawise, m. 1 Jn. de Nevill, 2 Jn. de Gatesden, iv. 8, 34, 59; vii. 81, 226
Hen., ii. 238
Jn., i. 495 *n*
Ric. le, iv. 51
Rob. (? two of this name), i. 495; iv. 51
Thos., ii. 238
fam., ii. 307; iv. 51
Savaric fitz Cane, iv. 23, 50, 53, 77, 104, 106, 111, 113-14, 117, 122, 125
his sons, *see* Geldwin; Ralph; Savaric
his w. Muriel, *see* Bohun

Savaric son of Savaric fitz Cane, iv. 23, 77
Savary, Wm., ii. 314
Savigny, ——, i. 252
Savoy:
Amadeus of, iv. 95; ix. 2
Bernard of, iv. 89; ix. 133
Lewis of, ix. 2
Peter of, ii. 146, 295, 314, 325; vii. 2, 20; ix. 2, 15, 37, 40, 79
Thos. of, ix. 2
Savoy, the, *see* London
Sawkyn, Jn., iv. 212
Sawyer:
Edw., vii. 239
Geo., ix. 211
Jn., i. 339
——, ii. 470
Saxby, Chas., vii. 70
Saxe, Marshal Maur., ii. 125
Saxham (Suff.), iv. 143
Saxon remains, *see* Anglo-Saxon
Saxon shore (litus saxonicum), i. 481; ii. 127; iii. 4-7, 62
Saxonbury, *see* Rotherfield
Saxons, i. 305; iii. 3-4, 12, 19-20, 58-9, 83-4
Middle, i. 333
South, i. 333-4, 347, 481-3; ii. 1, 47, 109, 126, 128, 241, 264, 291, 328, 362; iv. 187, 205, 207
ealdormen, *see* Berhtwald (fl. 795); Oslac
kings, iii. 83; *and see* Aelle; Aldulf; Cissa; Ealweald; Ethelbert; Ethelwold; Nothelm; Osmund
sub-king, *see* Athelstan
West, *see* Wessex
Saxony, Peter of, i. 495-6, 500-1, 503
Saxton, Chris., ii. 150, 297-8*
Say (Sey):
Alice de, *see* Cheney
Aveline de, *see* Aveline
Eliz. de, m. 1 Sir Jn. de Falvesley, 2 Sir Wm. Heron, vii. 114, 206, 255
Geof. de (d. 1214), vii. 114, 203, 207, 255
Geof. de (d. 1230), i. 495; ii. 92; vii. 114
Geof. de (d. 1322), vii. 85, 114
Geof. de (d. 1359), ii. 314 *n*; vii. 114
Idonea de, vii. 114
Joan de, m. 1 Jn. de Fiennes, 2 Steph. de Valence, vii. 114; ix. 133
Jn. (fl. 1260), iv. 45
Jn. le (fl. 1331), iv. 129
Jn. de (d. 1382), vii. 114
Thos. de, vii. 114
Sir Wm. de (d. 1272), ii. 311; vii. 84-5, 114
Wm. de (d. 1295), vii. 114, 203, 206
Wm. de (d. 1375), ii. 312; vii. 114, 255
fam., iv. 129; vii. 203, 206-7
arms, vii. *84*
Say, Ld., *see* Clinton, Edw.; Heron, Sir Wm.
Saye and Sele, Ld., *see* Fiennes, Sir Jas.
Sayer:
A.L., ii. 472 *n*; ix. 26
Cordelia, ix. 192
Edw., ix. 86
(later Milward), Hen. Collier, ix. 86
Maria, ix. 26
Sarah, *see* Collier
Mrs., ix. 26
Sayer-Milward, *see* Milward, Wm. Carlisle Sayer
Sayers, Bernard, ii. 480
Sbern (? Osbern) (fl. 1066), iv. 91
Scalariis, Jn. de, and his w. Alice, vii. 203
Scale, ——, iii. 97
Scandinavia, i. 278
Scapula, Ostorius, iii. 1
Scarborough, earls of, *see* Lumley, Ric.
Scarborough (Scarborow) (Yorks.

N.R.), ii. 145, 266-8; ix. 55
Scardevile (Scardevyle, Skardevyle):
Jn., iii. 105; iv. 128, 185
Marg., *see* Whelton
Peter, iv. 185
Wm. (d. 1453), iv. 185, 192
Wm. (fl. 1453), iv. 185
Wm. (fl. 1498), iv. 123, 185
fam., iv. 185
Scarlett:
Benj., vii. 111; ix. 120, 233
Francis, ix. 233
Thos., ix. 233
Scawen:
Rob., vii. 195
Winifred, m. Sam. Blunt, vii. 195
Scherren, Hen., i. 261
Schiedame, Jn. de, ii. 233
Schiödte, ——, i. 261
schools, ii. **397-440**; *and see parish names*
Scilly Isles, i. 44, 295; ii. 165
Sclater:
Eliz. Rebecca, iv. 29
Francis Saunderson, vii. 89
G.E., vii. 89, 101
Jas. Hen., vii. 89
fam., vii. 88
and see Slater
Scobell:
Jn., vii. 50
Sandford G.T., vii. 50
Scolland (fl. 1086), vii. 189
Scory, Jn., bp. of Chich., ii. 22; iii. 93 *n*
Scot, Rob. the, *see* Robert
Scot, *see* Scott
scot and lot, iv. 78; vii. 27; ix. 8, 51-3, 68, 193
Scote, *see* Scott
Scotland, i. 307, 506-7, 509; ii. 129, 192, 267, 401; iv. 162
Church of, vii. 63
Covenanters, ii. 35
king, *see* Alexander III
natural history, i. 44, 168 *n*, 279, 282, 285, 287-90, 292
wars, *q.v.*
and see Aberdeenshire; Berwick, North; Duffus; Dumfries; Edinburgh; Forth, riv.; Glasgow; Grampian mountains; Leven, Loch; Musselburgh; Orkney Islands; St. Andrews Bay; Shetland Islands
Scotney:
Maud, w. of Peter de, ix. 81
Peter de, ii. 76; ix. 19, 79, 81, 118, 146 *n*, 180, 220, 253-4, 257, 278
Ralph de, ix. 79 *n*
Wal. de (fl. before 1200), ii. 75-6; ix. 79, 81, 253, 257, 278
Wal. de (d. 1259), i. 495; ix. 77, 79, 83, 118
fam., ix. 253, 278
Scotney castle, *see* Lamberhurst
Scott (Scot, Scote):
Dorothy, m. Jn. Frewen, ix. 274
Edm., vii. 180, 260-1
Eliz., w. of Thos., *see* Piers
Eliz., w. of Wm., ix. 154
Francis, earl of Dalkeith, ii. 443
Fred. H., ix. 232
Sir Gilb., ii. 431; iii. 113, 126, 146, 158 *n*
H. von E., ii. 472 *n*
J. Oldrid, vii. 261
Joan, *see* Orlaston
Sir Jn., ix. 154, 157
Kath., m. Steph. Frewen, ix. 274
Marg., m. Sir Edw. Bedingfield, ix. 146 *n*
Mary, w. of Wm., ix. 154
Thos. (fl. 1547), ix. 28
Thos. (fl. *c.* 1600), ix. 274
Thos. (fl. 1792), ii. 475
Wal., ix. 14
Wm., sacrist of Bosham coll., ii. 112
Wm. (fl. *c.* 1420), ix. 177

Wm. (fl. 1486), ix. 154
Wm. (d. 1585), ii. 24; ix. 154, 160
Wm. (d. 1589), ix. 154
Wm. (fl. 1646), ix. 154
fam., vii. 217; ix. 156
arms, ix. *154*
Scott and Cawthorn, vii. 273
Scovill, Jos., master of Playden hosp.,
    ii. 105
Scrase:
    Chas., vii. 218, 254
    Edith, m. Geo. Bedford, vii. 85 *n*,
        87
    Edw., vii. 243, 285
    Eliz., *see* Chambre
    Hen., vii. 243
    Joan, w. of Hen., vii. 243
    Jn., vii. 218, 229
    Mary, m. —— Whitpaine, vii. 177
    Ric. (d. 1499), vii. 243, 285
    Ric. (d. 1519), vii. 243, 285
    Ric. (fl. 1534), ii. 75
    Ric. (d. 1549, ? another), and his w.
        Mary, vii. 243
    Ric. (d. 1625), vii. 96, 233, 235, 243
    Ric. (d. 1634), vii. 243
    Ric. (d. 1733), vii. 177
    Tuppin, vii. 85, 87, 96, 106, 243, 266
    Wm. (fl. 1641), vii. 266
    Wm. (fl. 1704), vii. 262
    fam., vii. 243
    arms, vii. *243*
Scrase Dickins:
    (formerly Dickins), Chas., vii. 248,
        254
    Chas., vii. 254
    Chas. Rob., vii. 254
    Chas. Spencer, vii. 254
    fam., vii. 59
screens, *see* architecture: ecclesiastical
Scrimgeour:
    Mrs. J.A., iv. 83–4
    Mrs., iv. 83–4
Scrimshire, Jn., vii. 71
Scrope:
    Sir Adrian, iv. 213
    Eliz., m. 1 Wm., Vct. Beaumont, 2
        Jn. de Vere, earl of Oxford, vii.
        67, 110
    Ralph, iv. 213
    Ric. le, dean of Chich., ii. 51, 401
Scull, Maur., iv. 135 *n*
sculptors, *see* Adley; Burns Brown;
    Bushnell; Harman, Jonathan;
    March; Westmacott, Sir Ric.
scutage, vii. 177; ix. 198
Scutt:
    Benj., vii. 266
    Jn. (d. 1725), vii. 266
    Jn. (d. 1744), vii. 266
    Thos., vii. 266–7
    Thos. (another), vii. 266–7
sea defences, *see* Broomhill; Guldeford,
    East; Rye; Winchelsea
Sea Fencibles, i. 535; ii. 161–2
Sea Houses, *see* Eastbourne
Seabeach, *see* Boxgrove
Seaford (Seaford, Seford), i. 31, 483,
    492, 539; ii. 44, 175, 251, 443; iii.
    101; vii. 64; ix. 36
    bay, ii. 159
    birds, i. 286
    botany, i. 63–4
    ch., ii. 2, 332, 351, 367, 370
    coastguards, i. 507 *n*
    coins, i. 330
    cts., ii. 185, 188
    crustaceans, i. 261, 264
    Cuckmere Haven, i. 56, 287, 291, 329,
        507 *n*; ii. 125, 152
    defences, ii. 142, 152, 159, 161, 163
    dom. archit., ii. 383–4, 392
    earthworks, i. 457, *457*, 470, 480
    French raids, ii. 138–9
    Green Street, iii. 65
    harbour, ii. 2, 125, 129, 144, 169; iii.
        301; vii. 63
    hermitage, ii. 47

hosps.:
    St. Jas., ii. 16, 45, **105**, 331
    St. Leonard, ii. 45, **105–6**, 331
insects, i. 133–7, 141, 146, 149–53,
    159–61, 163, 166, 168, 170, 207,
    212, 214–20, 223–4, 228, 234
Jews, i. 506
man., ii. 77, 188; vii. 2–4, 6–7
Martello Towers, i. 534
militia, i. 534–5
parl. rep., i. 504, 532
    M.P., *see* Sargent, Jn.
piracy, ii. 149
pop., ii. 226
prebend, *see* Seaford: Sutton
prehist. rem., i. 311, *322*, 323, 330,
    457
prison, ii. 160
privateering, ii. 159
rly., ii. 241
rebellion, i. 514
roads to, iii. 69
Rom. rem., i. 457; iii. 65
royal visits, i. 491, 493–4
sch., ii. 398
sea bathing, ii. 204
ship money, ii. 157
ship service, ii. 130, 131 *n*, 134–5,
    138–9, 144, 154
shipping, ii. 137–8
Spittelland, ii. 105
sport, ii. 452, 479
Sutton, ii. 122; iii. 65
    man., ii. 77, 105
    prebend, ii. 48, 263
    tithes, ii. 265
trades and ind., ii. 145, 231, 261, 265
U.D., ii. 228; vii. 31
vicar, ii. 40
Whasbetel rock, ii. 146
wreck, right of, ii. 146
Seager (Segar):
    Jn., vicar of Preston, vii. 273
    Jn., prebendary of Salisbury, rector of
        Harting, iv. 20
    Mr., vii. 30 *n*
Seagrave, *see* Segrave
Searles, *see* Fletching
Sears, S., vii. 139
seating, church, *see* architecture: eccle-
    siastical
Seavington (Som.), ii. 108*
Secretan:
    Douglas Liston, vii. 136
    P., vii. 136
Seculer, Alex. le, iv. 31
Sedbergh (Yorks. N.R.), ii. 433
Sedgemoor (Som.), battle, ii. 441
Sedgewick, *see* Nuthurst
Sedgwick (Sedgewick):
    Geo., ii. 438
    ——, iii. 167
sedilia, *see* architecture: ecclesiastical
Sedlescombe, ii. 43, 324; ix. 95, 258,
    276–9
    adv., ix. 114, 279
    A.-S. rem., i. 349
    batrachians, i. 272
    birds, i. 281
    botany, i. 60*
    ch., ii. 34; ix. 279
        accessories, ii. 242 *n*, 352, 357, 359–
            60
        archit., ii. 336, 378
    cts., ix. 1
    dom. archit., ii. 386, 389–91; ix. *276*,
        276–8
    Footlands, iii. 29, 31; ix. 278–9
    insects, i. 116, 129*, 156, 157 *n*, 229
    iron ind., ii. 241
    mammals, i. 303
    man., ii. 254, 278–9
    mill, ix. 278
    pop., ii. 223
    rectors, *see* Thorpe, Edm.; Warner,
        Jn.
    roads, ix. 276
    Robertsbridge abbey estates, ii. 71

Rom. rem., iii. 29, 31–2
sch., ii. 438
Sedlescombe Street, ix. 276
See:
    Joan atte, *see* Stopham
    Jn. atte, iv. 66
Seebohm, Hen., i. 280, 288
Séez (Sées) (Orne, France), abbey, ii.
    81–2, 89, 108, 119–20, 331, 398; iv.
    20, 27, 47, 53, 70, 170 *n*
    abbot, ii. 108, 120; iii. 80, 82; iv. 14
    bailiff, ii. 338 *n*
    estates, ii. 46; iv. 155–6
    patronage, ii. 48; iv. 120, 157
Seffrid I, abbot of Glastonbury, bp. of
    Chich., ii. 6, 53, 57, 298; iii. 90, 98,
    106
Seffrid II, archdeacon, dean, and bp. of
    Chich., ii. 5, 7, 47–8, 50, 57, 63, 65,
    70 *n*, 71, 76, 99, 121, 123, 294, 329,
    332, 334, 337, 368; iii. 106–8, 116,
    144, 146, 148; iv. 25 *n*, 27, 30, 65,
    81, 106, 117, 125, 205, 237, 239;
    vii. 33, 52 *n*, 60, 69, 237, 263, 281,
    286; ix. 81, 257
Seffrid, dean of Chich. (another), ii. 51
Seffrid the falconer, iv. 109
Seffrid the treasurer, prebendary of Wit-
    tering, iv. 205
Seford, *see* Seaford
Sefton (Lancs.), ii. 419
Segar, *see* Seager
Segrave (Seagrave):
    Emma de, *see* Cauz
    Jn. de, iii. 105
    Jos., ii. 239
    Nic. de, i. 497–8
    Wal. de, dean of Chich., ii. 51
Seinliz (Seintlyz, Senliz):
    Sim. de (fl. before 1200), ii. 56
    Sim. de (fl. 1225, ? another), steward
        of bp. of Chich., ii. 241; iv. 135
Selborne (Hants), iv. 13
Selby-Bigge, Sir Amherst, vii. 59
Selda, Hen. de, mayor of Chich., iii. 91
Selden, Jn., ii. 407; iii. 92
Sele priory (in Beeding), ii. 4, 17, 45,
    54, **60–3**, 74, 92, 122, 306; iii. 137
    archit., ii. 329
    estates, ii. 294; vii. 235
    priors, ii. 60–3
    royal visits, i. 505; ii. 61
    suppression, ii. 17, 62
Selebourne, Wm. de, warden of St.
    Mary's hosp., Chich., ii. 102
Selham (Seleham):
    Phil. de, iv. 80
    Phil. de (another), iv. 80
    Sir Ralph de, iv. 80–1
Selham, ii. 43; iv. 40, 58, **80–2**
    adv., iv. 80–2
    ch., ii. 63, 355; iv. 80–1, *81*
        archit., ii. 327, 334, 338, 349, 351,
            364, 380 *n*
    man., iv. 44, 80–1
    mills, iv. 80–1
    pop., ii. 221
    rly. station, iv. 80
    sport, ii. 442, 466–7
    tithes, iv. 82
Selhurst, Hen., ix. 144
Selhurst park, *see* Dean, East
Selkedene, Wm. de, iv. 212
Seller, Wal., vicar of Iden, ix. 156
Selme (Selmes):
    Chas., ix. 54
    Ric., vii. 235
Selmeston, i. 8; ii. 44
    adv., ix. 203
    ch., ii. 48, 339, 342, 351, 361, 377
    dean, ii. 42
    pop., ii. 225
    roads to, iii. 47
    Sherrington, ii. 122; ix. 251
    Tilton, *q.v.*
    tithes, ii. 122; ix. 203
Selsey, Lds., *see* Peachey
Selsey, ii. 1, 43, 126, 291 *n*, 362, 408; iii.

Selsey (*cont.*):
  83; iv. 198, **205–10**
  adv., iv. 210
  battery, iii. 102
  birds, i. 295
  bps., ii. 333; iii. 102, 166; iv. 135,
    198; *and see* Alfred; Alric;
    Beorhthelm; Beornheah;
    Edberht; Eolla; Ethelgar; Ethel-
    ric; Grimketel; Hecca; Oswald;
    Sigga; Stigand; Wilfrid; Wulf-
    hun
  botany, i. 43
  bridge, iv. 205
  cath., ii. 2, 46–7, 332, 334; iii. 105–6,
    112, 124; iv. 127, 202, 205
  char., iv. 210
  ch., ii. 14, 361, 374; iii. 65–6; iv.
    117 *n*, 147, 205–6, 208–10, *208*,
    209
  Church Norton, *see* Selsey: Norton,
    Church
  coastguards, i. 506 *n*
  coins, i. 326, 330
  dom. archit., iv. 206–7, 208 *n*
  earthworks, iv. 207
  East Norton, *see* Selsey: Norton, East
  fair, iii. 98
  ferry, iv. 205
  fields, iv. 206, 208
  fossils, i. 15, 27*
  geology, i. 1, 14, 19–21; ii. 335, 380
  golf, ii. 480
  guild, ii. 21; iv. 210
  Halton, iii. 69
  harbour, *see* Pagham: harbour
  inc., iv. 206
  insects, i. 111–12*, 120, 199, 204,
    215, 224, 227–9, 231, 234–5
  island, ii. 125; iv. 205
  man., iv. 175, 206–8
  Medmerry, ii. 164; iii. 82; iv. 202,
    205 *n*
  militia, i. 535
  mills, iii. 66; iv. 206
  mint, iv. 205 *n*
  Mixen (Mixon) rocks, i. 15; ii. 164;
    iv. 206–7
  mon., ii. 4; iv. 135–6, 198–9, 207,
    211, 215
  nonconf., iv. 210
  Norton, Church, iii. 66; iv. 205, 208–
    10
  Norton, East, ii. 152
  pk., iv. 207–8
  pop., ii. 221
  prebend, iv. 208, 210
  rly., ii. 240; iv. 207
  rectors, ii. 37; iv. 210; *and see* Lop-
    pedelle
  rectory, iii. 66; iv. 210
  resort, iv. 206
  roads, iv. 205–6
  Rom. rem., iii. 4, 9, 65–6, 69; iv. 207
  see, ii. 1–4; 328; iii. 84, 133; iv. 161,
    166, 207, 218; vii. 269; ix. 201
  Selsey Bill, i. 15, *21*, 21–2, 254, 256,
    265; ii. 125–6, 163–4; iii. 100; iv.
    205; vii. 244
  shipping, ii. 151; iii. 101
  tithes, iv. 208
  trades and ind., ii. 145, 263, 270–1
  tramway, *see* Hundred of Manhood
    and Selsey Tramway
  woodland, ii. 291
  Wythering, *see* Pagham: harbour
Selsfield, *see* Hoathly, West
Selwyn:
  Agnes, *see* Bates
  Eliz., w. of Thos., iv. 64 *n*
  Jn., ii. 24; iv. 64
  Thos. (fl. after 1437), ix. 229
  Thos. (fl. *c.* 1490), ix. 229
  Thos. (fl. 1575), iv. 64 *n*
  ——, i. 514
  fam., ii. 362
Seman, Jn., ii. 105
Semen (fl. *c.* 1150), iv. 128

Sempill:
  Anne, w. of Hugh, *see* Collins
  Hugh, iii. 90, 161
Sengelton, *see* Singleton
Senlac, *see* Battle: Sandlake; Hastings:
  battle
Senliz, *see* Seinliz
Sennicots, *see* Funtington
Sentlache, *see* Battle: Sandlake
Sepelake, *see* Shiplake
Sephton, Thos., master of hosp. of St.
  Jas., Chich., iii. 167 *n*
Septmuels, Wm. de, ix. 190
Septvans (Sevauns):
  Rob. de, ix. 247
  Wm. de (d. 1323), ix. 148, 247
  Wm. de (d. 1351), ix. 247–8
  Wm. de (d. 1407), ix. 248
  Wm. de (fl. 1407), ix. 248
  fam., ix. 247
  arms, ix. *248*
Sere:
  Giles, ix. 144
  Thos., ix. 144
Sergison:
  Anne, m. Francis Jefferson (later Ser-
    gison), vii. 156
  Anne, m. W.S. Pritchard, vii. 156
  Chas., vii. 156–8, 162, 183
  Chas. Warden, i. 306; ii. 480; vii. 156
  Cynthia, m. Sir Basil Stanlake
    Brooke, vii. 156
  (formerly Jefferson), Francis, vii. 156
  Francis, vii. 156
  Francis Warden, vii. 121
  (formerly Warden), Mic., vii. 156
  Prudence, m. Sir Bertram Sergison-
    Brooke, vii. 156, 183 *n*
  Prudence, m. Thos. Warden, vii. 156
  (formerly Warden), Thos., i. 533; vii.
    39, 156, 183
  Warden, vii. 156
  Warden Geo., vii. 156
  Warden Jefferson, vii. 156
  fam., vii. 159–60, 162–3, 196
  arms, vii. 149–50, *156*
Sergison-Brooke:
  Sir Bertram, vii. 183
  Prudence, *see* Sergison
serjeanty, i. 492; iv. 85, 104–5, 184–5;
  ix. 1, 106
Serreys Farm, *see* Grinstead, East
Servat, Wm., iii. 101
Sessely:
  Jn., ix. 213
  Kath., *see* Haremere
Sessingham, *see* Arlington
Seton (Setene):
  Alice atte, *see* Hurlonde
  Jn. atte, iv. 135
  Jn., rector of Harting, iv. 13, 20
Seuebech (Seuebeche):
  Hugh de, iv. 145
  Ric. de, iv. 145
  Thos. de, iv. 145, 153
Sevauns, *see* Septvans
Seven Years War, *see* wars
Sevenoaks (Kent), ii. 467
  Riverhill, ix. 276
Seward (fl. 1086), ix. 127
Sexteyn, Rob., iii. 92
Sey, *see* Say
Seymour (Seymor):
  Alice, w. of Thos., m. 2 Rog. Daling-
    ridge, vii. 257
  Chas., duke of Somerset, i. 532; ii.
    441, 444; iii. 96, 99
  Dan., iii. 127
  Sir Edw., duke of Somerset, vii. 209;
    ix. 133
  Eliz., *see* Percy
  Sir Rob., iv. 64
  Thos., vii. 257
  Thos., Ld. High Admiral, ii. 147,
    246, 308–10, 312; vii. 33
Seynt, Ric., i. 514; iii. 86
Seyntleger, *see* St. Leger
Seyntomer, *see* St. Omer

Shaa, Sir Edm., *see* Shaw
Shadforth-Boger, W., ii. 470 *n*
Shadwell:
  Mary, *see* Lucas
  Wm., vii. 82; ix. 177, 220
  (formerly Stent), Wm. Drew Lucas,
    vii. 82; ix. 178
  Wm. Lucas, i. 300; vii. 82; ix. 88 *n*
Shaftesbury (Dors.), abbess, iii. 84
Shakespeare, Wm., ii. 419; iv. 35
Shakespeare's Cliff, *see* Dover
Shales:
  Hen., rector of Hangleton, vii. 279
  Hen., iv. 112
  Isabel, w. of Jn., m. 2 Geo. Atkins, iv.
    112
  Jn., iv. 112
Shand:
  Ellen, iv. 237
  Jas., iv. 237
Shap (Westmld.), abbot, *see* Redmond,
  Ric.
Sharp (Sharpe):
  Joan, *see* Strode
  Jn., master of Playden hosp., ii. 105
  Jn. (fl. 1567), ii. 246
  Jn. (d. 1583), ix. 276
  R. Bowdler, i. 278
  Ric., ix. 276
  Rob., iii. 146
  Thos., ix. 274
  Thos., rector of Beckley, and his w.
    Anne, ix. 143
  Mr., ii. 255
Shaves wood (unidentified), i. 204
Shaw:
  Alex., ix. 31
  (or Shaa), Sir Edm., ii. 421
  Geo., vicar of Hartfield, ii. 427
  Sir Jn. (d. 1680), vii. 176
  Sir Jn. (d. 1721), vii. 176
  Sir Jn. (d. 1739), vii. 176
  Sir Jn. (d. 1779), vii. 176, 178
  Sir Jn. Gregory, vii. 176, 178
  Rob., vii. 178
  W.F., iv. 195
  fam., vii. 125
  arms, vii. *176*
sheep, *see* livestock
Sheet (in Petersfield, Hants), bridge
  (Shetebrugge, Stretebridge), ii.
  174; iv. 85
Sheffield, T., ii. 446
Sheffield, earls of, *see* Holroyd
Sheffield (Yorks. W.R.), ii. 469
Sheffield (in Fletching), *see* Fletching
Shefford, East (Berks.), i. 344 *n*
Sheldon:
  Anne, m. Hugh Reason, iv. 179–80
  Dan., iv. 52; vii. 227
  Sir Jas., Ld. mayor of London, iv. 52
  Judith, vii. 227
  Judith, w. of Dan., *see* Rose
  Marg., *see* Rose
  Mary, vii. 227
  ——, and his w., iii. 87
Shelley:
  Alice, *see* Belknap
  Bysshe, vii. 134
  Sir Chas., iii. 105; ix. 85–6, 145
  Cordelia, vii. 77, 220
  Edw., ii. 28
  Eleanor, m. Geo. Jn. Dalbiac, vii. 77
  Eliz., vii. 77, 216
  Eliz., w. of Jn., *see* Michelgrove
  Hen. (fl. 1580), iii. 105
  Hen. (fl. 1594, another), vii. 216–17,
    279
  Hen. (d. 1691), vii. 18, 67–8, 76, 134
    n, 220
  Hen. (d. 1735), vii. 76
  Hen. (d. 1805), vii. 36, 76, 160
  Hen. (d. 1811), vii. 36, 76, 160
  Jn. (fl. 1511), iii. 105; iv. 185
  Sir Jn. (d. 1550), vii. 217; ix. 144
  Jn. (d. 1587), vii. 204, 217
  Jn. (d. 1592), iii. 105
  Sir Jn. (d. 1642), iii. 105; ix. 144–5

Jn. (fl. 1648), i. 527
Sir Jn. (d. 1703), iii. 105
Jn. (d. 1739), vii. 134
Sir Jn. (d. 1771), iii. 105
Sir Jn. (d. 1790), ii. 454–5; vii. 134, 224
Sir Jn. (fl. 1792), ii. 467 n
Martha, see Heath
Mary, vii. 204
Percy Bysshe, vii. 134
Sir Percy Florence, i. 286; vii. 134
Ric. (d. 1594), ii. 27, 149 n; vii. 217, 219, 230, 252
Ric. (fl. 1634), iv. 76; vii. 160
Ric. (d. 1716), vii. 76, 160
Thos. (fl. 1562), iii. 105; iv. 199
Thos. (fl. 1670), vii. 239
Timothy (fl. 1669), vii. 134
Timothy (fl. 1739), vii. 134
Sir Timothy (fl. 1814), vii. 134
Sir Wm. (d. c. 1549), ii. 96; iii. 105; iv. 163, 185; ix. 144
Wm. (d. 1597), ii. 24, 27–8; iii. 105; ix. 144
Wm. (fl. 1640), vii. 68
Mr. (fl. 1564), ii. 24
Mr. (fl. 1830), ii. 458
fam., ii. 27, 297, 361; vii. 199, 217
arms, iii. 105; vii. 12, 77, 134; ix. 145
Shelley park, see Beeding
Shelton, Peter, iii. 111, 159 n
Shelvestrode:
    Eve de, see Dawtrey
    Joan de, m. Jn. Aske, iv. 56
    Jn. de, iv. 56, 145
    Rog. de (d. by 1317), iv. 56, 108
    Sir Rog. de (fl. 1360), iv. 56, 154
    Wm. de, prior of Michelham, ii. 79
Sheparde, see Shepherd
Shepelake, see Shiplake
Shepherd (Sheparde, Sheppard):
    Alex., ix. 157, 160
    Chas., ii. 445
    Edw., ix. 157
    Giles, ix. 106
    Jn., master of hosp. of St. Jas. and St. Mary, Chich., ii. 100
    Kath., w. of Wm., ix. 217
    Marg., ix. 157
    Ric., ix. 157
    Rob., ix. 157, 161
    Sam., M.P. for Bramber, i. 531
    Thos., iv. 206 n
    Wm. (d. 1634), ix. 157
    Wm. (fl. 1895), ix. 217
    Mr., ix. 175
    fam., ix. 160
    arms, ix. 157
Shepherds Field forest, ii. 307
Shepherd's Hill, see Buxted
Sheppard, see Shepherd
Sheppey (Kent), i. 29–30; ii. 126
Shepway (Kent):
    ct. of, see Cinque Ports: cts.
    (or Limowart), lathe, ix. 38
Sherborn, see Sherburne
Sherborne (Dors.), ii. 437
Sherburne (Sherborn), Rob., bp. of Chich., ii. 16, 16–17, 49, 58, 80, 82, 105, 108, 333, 352, 359, 361, 379, 386, 395, 405, 407; iii. 86, 93, 112–14, 116, 123–4, 133–4, 135, 146, 148–9, 151, 154; iv. 134, 146, 153 n, 154, 162–3, 165, 206, 208, 217; vii. 270
    arms, iii. 112, 124, 149
Shere (Surr.), vii. 189, 238
Sherer:
    Eliz., iii. 147
    Jn. (fl. 1394), iii. 98
    Jn. (fl. 1438), mayor of Chich., iii. 92
    Jn. (d. 1707), iii. 147
    Jn. (d. c. 1730), mayor of Chich., iii. 147
    Marg., iii. 147
    Mary, iii. 147
    Mary, w. of Jn., see Henshaw

Ric., iii. 147
Thos., iii. 147
Wm., iii. 147
Sheridan:
    R. Brinsley, ix. 165 n, 169
    Ric. (statesman and dramatist), vii. 249
sheriff, see Hugh the sheriff; Peter the sheriff; Reinbert the sheriff
Sherley, see Shirley
Sherlock, Thos., dean of Chich., warden of St. Mary's hosp., Chich., ii. 51, 101–2; iii. 90, 155
Sherman:
    Jn., vii. 41–2
    Marg., vii. 35
    Susan, w. of Thos., vii. 280
    (or Baker), Thos., see Baker
    Thos. (fl. 1494), vii. 42
    Thos. (fl. 1569), vii. 35
    Thos. (fl. 1701), vii. 280
    (or Lewes), Wm., see Lewes
Shermanbury, ii. 43–4
    ch., ii. 40, 337, 353, 356
    Ewhurst, i. 478; ii. 384, 388, 395
    pop., ii. 220
    Windham:
        hosp., ii. 16, 108
        prebend, iii. 146
Shernedene (Sardene):
    Hen. de, ix. 266
    Nichola de, see Wacelyn
Sherrington:
    Eliz., m. Geo. Gunter, iv. 115
    Wm. (sr.), iv. 115
    Wm. (jr.), iv. 115
Sherrington, see Selmeston
Sherwin, Wm., warden of St. Mary's hosp., Chich., ii. 102
Shetebrugge, see Sheet
Shetland Islands, i. 297
Shields, South (Co. Dur.), i. 534; ii. 233
Shiffner:
    Sir Geo. (fl. 1795), i. 535
    Sir Geo. (d. 1842, ? another), vii. 85
    Sir Geo. (fl. 1859), vii. 34
    Geo., prebendary of Eartham and warden of St. Mary's hosp., Chich., ii. 102; iv. 154
    Sir Hen., vii. 34, 85
    Sir Hen. Burrows, vii. 34, 85
    Mary, see Bridger
    Thos., iii. 67
    fam., vii. 84
Shiffness (unidentified), i. 121
Shilfox:
    Anne, see Cuddon
    Dan., iv. 212
Shillinglee, see Kirdford
Shindler, Eliz., ix. 221
shingle making, ii. 300
ship money, ii. 156–7; and see parish names
ship service, ii. 126, 129–30, 133, 142–3, 153, 156; and see parish names
shipbuilding, ii. 124, 130, 132, 136, 138, 141, 145, 152, 155, 157, 159–60, 164–7, 234–5, 298–9; iii. 90, 102; vii. 32, 63; ix. 13, 50, 55–6, 69
Shipden, Thos., ix. 150
Shiplake (Edivestone, Sepelake, Shepelake), hund., i. 537; ii. 172 n, 227
Shipley, ii. 43; iv. 16
    ch., ii. 60, 92
    accessories, ii. 352, 355, 362, 367
    archit., ii. 331, 337, 340, 346, 349, 367–8
    coins, i. 330
    insects, i. 125, 133–4, 137–9, 141–3, 145–6, 148–50, 152–6, 158–61, 164, 223, 225
    Knepp (Cnapp, Cnep, Cnepp, Knap, Knapp), i. 491, 494
        cast., i. 493; ii. 278, 306–7, 394, 462, 465; earthworks, i. 472, 472–3, 476
    chap., ii. 92

natural history, i. 219, 288, 297, 303
    pk., 293 n, 296–7, 301, 306–8, 310
man., ii. 92
pop., ii. 220
preceptory of Knights Templar, ii. 45, 92–3, 109, 331
shipping, see maritime history; and see Chich.; Hastings; Rye; Selsey; Shoreham; Winchelsea
Shipweye, see Cinque Ports: cts.: Shepway
Shirburn (Oxon.), ix. 259
Shireforde, Wal. de, sacrist of Bosham coll., ii. 112
Shirley (Sherley, Shurley):
    Anne, vii. 270–1
    Anne, w. of Ant., see Onslow
    Ant. (d. 1624), vii. 258, 270; ix. 83
    Sir Ant. (d. c. 1635), i. 518
    Sir Ant. (d. 1683), vii. 235, 254
    Edw. (? two of this name), vii. 49, 145
    Eliz., m. Wm. Boyce, vii. 254
    Eliz., w. of Jn., see Kyme
    Eliz., w. of Thos., see Stapley
    Eliz., w. of ——, see Godman
    Frances, vii. 87
    Frances, w. of Jn., see Capel
    Isabel, m. Sir Jn. Dawtrey, iv. 157
    Jane, m. 1 Wal. Covert, 2 Jn. Freake, 3 Denzil Hollis, vii. 145–6, 190
    Jn. (d. 1616), ii. 28; iv. 89; vii. 37*, 87
    Jn. (d. 1631), ii. 362; vii. 37, 87, 145
    Jn. (d. 1637), vii. 37, 87
    Judith, vii. 270
    Judith, m. Herb. Randolph, ix. 83
    Judith, m. Sir Peter Garton, iv. 59, 95
    Judith, w. of Sir Ric., m. 2 Sir Hen. Hatzell, vii. 270
    Mary, m. Thos. Western, vii. 218, 258, 270–1
    Mary, w. of Wm., m. 2 Ric. Elrington, vii. 258, 270
    Ralph, iv. 157
    Sir Ric. (fl. 1539), ii. 144 n
    Sir Ric. (d. 1692), vii. 270
    Sir Ric. (d. 1705), vii. 254, 258, 270
    Thos. (d. 1579), vii. 145
    Sir Thos. (d. 1612), i. 518; ii. 149 n, 309; iv. 59; vii. 134, 252
    Thos. (d. 1637), vii. 196, 270
    Thos. (d. 1641), vii. 270
    Sir Thos., governor of Leeward Islands, vii. 121
    Wm., vii. 258, 270
    Wm., governor of Bahamas, vii. 121
    Sir Wm. Warden, vii. 121
    fam., ii. 361*, 386
    arms, vii. 270, 272
Shoesmith, Geo., ii. 474
Shoesmiths, see Wadhurst
Shoeswell hund., see Shoyswell
shooting, see sport
Shopwyke, see Oving
Shore:
    Eliz., w. of Jn., see Briggs
    Jane, w. of Jn., iii. 147
    Jn. (fl. c. 1690), ii. 420
    Jn. (d. 1721), iii. 147; iv. 36
    Jn. (d. 1773), iii. 147
    Phil. (fl. 1674), vii. 41
    Phil. (fl. 1712), vii. 41
    Phil., vicar of Wartling, rector of Woodmancote, ii. 420*
    Sam., ix. 181
    Urith, see Offley
Shoreham (Shorham):
    Thos., abbot of Bayham, ii. 89
    Wm. de, iii. 94
Shoreham (Old Shoreham, New Shoreham), i. 55; ii. 7, 43–4, 169, 189, 291 n; vii. 247
    barons, i. 494
    birds, i. 278, 282, 290, 292, 294, 297
    botany, i. 42, 46, 60, 63–4
    chant., ii. 20
    chap., ii. 92

Shoreham (*cont.*):
ch., ii. 60
  accessories, ii. 350–3, 356–7, *358*,
    359, 367–8, 376
  archit., ii. 327, 332, 334, 337, 340,
    342, 347–50, 364–8, *366*, 370–2,
    374–6
Civil War in, i. 524
clubs:
  Christian Society, i. 531–2
  golf, ii. 480
coastguards, i. 506 *n*
coins, i. 326, 330
county ct., i. 504; iii. 95
curate, *see* Woodard, Nat.
defences, ii. 152, 157, 163
earthworks, i. 480
Erringham, i. 209; ii. 152*, 380–1
ferry, ii. 74
fossils, i. 22
French raids, ii. 156
friary, ii. 45, 61, 92, **97**, 331, 334
geology, i. 45
harbour, i. 55; ii. 125, 129, 132, 140,
  142, 144, 157, 159, 163
hosps., ii. 45, 331
  St. Jas., ii. **106**
  St. Kath., ii. *92*, **106**
insects, i. 116, 137–9, 141–2, 144–7,
  149–50, 152–3, 160–1, 167 *n*,
  169, 171–3, 176–8, 180–7, 189–
  90, 201–9, 229
lands in, ii. 92, 97
mammals, i. 304
marine zoology, i. 94
mkt., ii. 188
molluscs, i. 109
naval recruitment, ii. 161; vii. 64
Old Shoreham man., iv. 51–2, 123;
  vii. 252
parl. rep., i. 504, 531–2; ii. 160
pop., ii. 219
port, ii. 248; iii. 101–2; vii. 246
privateering, ii. 156
riv., *see* Adur
roads to, iii. 47
Rom. rem., iii. 47, 66
royal visits, i. 491, 494, 508
sch., ii. 397–8, 432–4
ship money, ii. 156
ship service, ii. 130, 131 *n*, 134–5,
  138–9, 141, 153; vii. 246
shipping, ii. 129, 137–8, 140, 142,
  151, 155–6
spiders, i. 239–42
sport, ii. 446, 460, 465, 480
taxation, ii. 189; vii. 15
Thundersbarrow Hill, iii. 47, 66
tithes, ii. 60, 265
trades and ind.:
  brewing, ii. 261
  fisheries, ii. 146, 160, 265, 269–70
  iron, ii. 242
  quarrying, ii. 230
  salt, ii. 233
  shipbuilding, ii. 124, 130, 152, 155,
    157, 159–60, 164–7, 234–5
  timber, ii. 233
U.D., ii. 228
vagrancy, ii. 210
vicar, ii. 37
vicarage, ii. 8
workho., ii. 210
wrecking, ii. 148
Shorham, *see* Shoreham
Short:
  Hugh, iv. 129
  Jane, *see* Burrell
  Peter (sr.), vii. 158
  Peter (jr.), vii. 158
  Thos., vii. 158, 177; ix. 56
  fam., ix. 56
Shortnose, Hugh, iv. 80
Shoswelle, *see* Shoyswell
Shotter:
  Jn., iv. 69
  Rog., iv. 69
  Wm., iv. 67

Shottermill, *see* Linchmere
Shovell, Sir Cloudesley (Clowdisley), ii.
  164–5; ix. 7
shows, agricultural:
  Arundel, ii. 290
  Royal, ii. 280
  Smithfield, ii. 276
  Sussex Agricultural Soc., ii. 289–90
  Tunbridge Wells, ii. 290
Shoyswell (Shoswelle):
  Ann, w. of Benj., ix. 215
  Benj., ix. 197, 215
  Dorothy, m. Thos. Michelborne, ix.
    197
  Eliz., *see* Playsted
  Jn. (fl. 1469), ix. 215
  Jn. (fl. 1614), ix. 197, 215
  Judith, w. of Jn., ix. 215
  Ralph, ix. 255
  Rog. (fl. 1501), ix. 255
  Rog. (fl. 1656), vii. 218
  Rog. (d. 1697), ix. 215
  Sybil, w. of Thos., m. 2 Sir Geo.
    Newman, ix. 215
  Thos. (fl. 1549), ix. 215
  Thos. (fl. 1596), ix. 215
  Wm., ix. 215
  arms, ix. *215*, 216
Shoyswell, *see* Etchingham
Shoyswell (Esseswelle, Shoeswell)
  hund., i. 537; ii. 222 *n*, 223, 261;
  ix. 3, 210, **251**
Shrewsbury, earls of, *see* Belleme;
  Montgomery, Hugh de; Montgom-
  ery, Rog. de
Shrewsbury (Salop.), ii. 434
Shripney, *see* Bersted
Shropshire, *see* Bridgnorth; Shrews-
  bury; Wenlock
Shrubb:
  Alfred, ii. 481
  Chas., ix. 163
Shuckburgh (Shuckborgh):
  Frances, *see* Jermyn
  Sir Geo., ix. 180
  Jn., iv. 116
  Julia Evelyn, m. Chas. Cecil Cope
    Jenkinson, earl of Liverpool, vii.
    33, 81; ix. 180, 191
  Julia Medley, *see* Evelyn
Shuerwode, *see* Kirdford
Shulbred (Wlenchemere, Woolyn-
  chmere), priory (in Linchmere), ii.
  17, 58, 80, **81–2**, 295; iv. 56–7,
  104–6, 113
  accessories, ii. 355
  archit., ii. 330, 347, 371–2, 381; iv.
    66, 67–9, *68*
  priors, ii. 82, 295; iii. 95; iv. 66; *and
    see* Bury, Wm.; Glottyngs;
    Young, Jn.
Shullegh park, *see* Beeding: Shelley pk.
Shurley, *see* Shirley
Shute, Capt., ii. 153
Shuttleworth, Nic., bp. of Chich., iii.
  126
Shypwright:
  Joan, *see* Almodington
  Thos., iv. 202
Siberia, i. 278 *n*
Sibertswold (Kent), iv. 153
Sibton (Suff.), abbey, vii. 236
Sicily:
  king, *see* Luis
  and see Messina
Sicklemore, Jas., ii. 420*
Sidlesham, ii. 43; iii. 100–2; iv. 188,
  198, 201, 205, **210–15**
  adv., iv. 212, 215
  Almodington Green, iv. 211
  chant., iv. 215
  char., iv. 215
  ch., iv. 210, 213–15, *214*, *219*
    accessories, ii. 352, 355–6, 358–9,
      372
    archit., ii. 340, 342, 348, 372, 374,
      379
  common, iv. 210–11

dom. archit., iv. 211
Easton, iv. 213
  chap., iv. 215
  Farm, iv. 210–12
ferry, iv. 210
guild, iv. 215
Highleigh (Highley), iv. 210–11
  prebend, ii. 48, 402–9; iv. 213
  tithes, iv. 213
inc., iv. 211
Keyner, ii. 291 *n**; iv. 177, 210–11
  man., iv. 212–13
  tithes, iv. 213
man., iv. 202, 211–13
mills, iv. 206, 210, 212
natural history, i. 285, 307
New Haven, iv. 210–11
pop., ii. 221
prebend, iv. 203, 213, 215
roads, iv. 210
Rom. rem., iii. 66
shipping, ii. 151–2
streams, iv. 210
Streetend, iv. 198 *n*, 210
tithes, iv. 213
vicar, *see* Taylor, Jn.
Wardur, iv. 210–11
Sidney (Sydney):
  Agnes, w. of Sir Wm., ix. 119, 146,
    161, 221, 267
  Algernon, i. 525; iii. 88
  Eliz., prioress of Rusper, ii. 64
  Sir Hen., ii. 246; vii. 135; ix. 174
  Jn., earl of Leicester, ix. 221*
  Lucy, m. Sir Jn. Pelham, ix. 197
  Mary de, m. Jn. Michelgrove, iii. 105
  Sir Phil., vii. 58 *n*
  Rob., Vct. Lisle, earl of Leicester, ix.
    161, 221, 224, 230
  Sir Rob., earl of Leicester, ix. 197,
    230
  Wm. de (fl. 1325), iii. 105
  Wm. de (fl. 1428), iii. 105
  Wm. de (fl. 1445), iii. 105 *n*
  Wm. de, his s., iii. 105 *n*
  Wm. (fl. 1448, ? another), iv. 157
  Sir Wm. (fl. 1539), ix. 119, 146, 161,
    174, 221, 224, 267, 279
  fam., ii. 63; ix. 221
  arms, ix. *221*
Sidonham, Jos., ix. 152
Siena (Italy), iv. 131, 177
Sigebert, king of Wessex, ii. 292
Sigga, bp. of Selsey, ii. 2
signalling, i. 470, 533; ii. 131, 158, 160,
  162–3
Silchester (Calleva Atrebatum) (Hants),
  iii. 10, 47, 68
silk, *see* textile inds.
Silletone hund., *see* Westbourne and
  Singleton hund.
Silver Hill (in Hastings), *see* Hastings
Silverhill (in Salehurst), *see* Salehurst
Silvester, archdeacon of Chich., iv. 117
Silvester the king's falconer, iv. 122
Simeon Trustees, iii. 166; ix. 89
Simes (Symes):
  Edw., ix. 152
  N.P., iv. 84
Simmons:
  Chas., ii. 474
  Thos., vii. 58
  and see Symonds
Simon, abbot of Bayham, ii. 89
Simon, abbot of Robertsbridge, ii. 73
Simon, bp. of Chich., *see* FitzRobert
Simon, master of Bidlington hosp., vicar
  of Horsham, ii. 98
Simon, master of hosp. of St. Jas., Sea-
  ford, ii. 105
Simon, master of Playden hosp., ii. 104–
  5
Simon, prior of Boxgrove, ii. 59
Simon, rector of West Tarring, ii. 10–11
Simon, reeve of Bosham, iv. 183
Simon son of Matthew the dean, iii. 103
  his dau. ——, m. Richard the robber,
    iii. 103

Simon the draper, iv. 85
Simon, moneyer, iii. 84 *n*
Simpson (Sympson, Symson):
  Geof., dean of Chich., ii. 51
  Jn., abbot of Durford, abbot of Titch-
    field, ii. 91–2
  Marg., iv. 27
  W.S., ii. 478
Singer, Dan., iii. 126
Singlecross hund., i. 538; ii. 219
Singleton (Sengelton), i. 11; ii. 43, 206,
    305; iv. 58, 88, *118*, **118–21**
  adv., iv. 96, 100, 120
  chap., iv. 120
  char., iv. 121
  Charlton, *q.v.*
  ch., ii. 4, 442; iv. 53, 118–20, *119*
    accessories, ii. 352–3, 355–6, 358–9,
      361, 378
    archit., ii. 335, 339, 346, 348, 350,
      363, 364, 371, 378, 380
  Civil War in, ii. 36
  cricket, ii. 467
  dom. archit., iv. 118
  Downley, ii. 303, 441*
  Drove, ii. 445
  forest, iv. 43, 118
  guild, iv. 120
  hund., *see* Westbourne and Singleton
    hund.
  Levin Down, i. 186; ii. 441*
  man., ii. 176; iv. 94–5, 97, 118, 120
  mills, iv. 118
  natural history, i. 108–9, 114, 117,
    231, 233
  pop., ii. 221
  prebend, ii. 48; iv. 90, 120
  prehist., iv. 118
  rly., iv. 118
    station, iv. 97
  rector, ii. 37
  roads, iii. 46; iv. 118
  Rom. rem., iii. 46, 66
  St. Roche's Hill, *see* Singleton:
    Trundle
  tithes, iv. 120
  Trundle, the (or St. Roche's Hill), i.
    48, *466*, *466*, 470; iii. 19, 46, 65;
    iv. 97, 118, 120
  valley, iv. 118
Sion, *see* Syon
Sirgood, Jn., ii. 41
Siscia (Sisak, Yugoslavia), iii. 60
Sisk, *see* Gausden & Sisk
Sissinghurst (Kent), ii. 160
Sisteleberg (Sistaleberga) (? Tilbury,
  Essex), ii. 113, 410
Siulf (fl. 1066), ix. 160
Sivier:
  Steph., ix. 264
  ——, m. —— Davies, ix. 264
Siward, son of Sigar of Hastings, ix. 118
Siward (fl. 1086), ii. 311; vii. 194
Siward (another), iv. 200
Siwell:
  Hen. de, ix. 262
  Isabel de, *see* Bodiham
  Wm. de, ix. 262
Sixtus IV, pope, ii. 68
Skardevyle, *see* Scardevile
Skelton:
  Eliz. Mary, vii. 57
  Martha, m. Thos. Sanden Dupuis, iv.
    202
  Mary, iv. 202
  Sarah, iv. 202
  fam., iv. 202
Skipsey, Wm., ii. 167
Skipwith:
  Eliz., m. Wm., Ld. Craven, vii. 224
  Sir Fulwar, vii. 224
Skiret (Skyret), Thos., ix. 113
Skoterall, Wm., ii. 308
Skynner:
  Hen., abbot of Durford, ii. 91
  Melmoth, vicar of Cocking, iv. 47
  Thos., i. 514
Skyret, *see* Skiret

Slade:
  Jn., and his w. Eliz., iv. 202
  Sam., dean of Chich., ii. 51; iii. 126
  Wm., and his w. Eliz., iv. 202
  fam., iv. 202; ix. 53
Slater:
  Joan, *see* Syteler
  Jn., iv. 191
  W., iii. 123
  and see Sclater
Slater & Carpenter, vii. 262
Slaterford, Jn., iii. 145
Slaugham, ii. 34, 43–4, 236, 311–12; vii.
  2, 125, **181–6**, 271 *n*
  adv., vii. 186
  angling, ii. 465
  ch., vii. *181*, *184*, 184–6
    accessories, ii. 355–6, 361–2
    archit., ii. 344, 349, 365, 379
  cts., vii. 183
  dom. archit., vii. 181–3
  earthworks, i. 478
  Eastland's Fm., i. 55
  Handcross, i. 53, 55, 58; vii. 181–3
  golf, ii. 479–80
  insects, i. 213–14, 225, 227–32, 234,
    236–7
  prehist. rem., i. 330
  insects, i. 177, 190
  man., vii. 145, 157, 183–4, 196
  nonconf., vii. 181
  pk., ii. 297, 312
  Pease Pottage, i. 53; vii. 144, 181
  pop., ii. 224
  Slaugham Place, ii. 387; vii. 182
  Slut Ho. Fm., i. 55
  Warninglid, i. 55; ii. 447; vii. 181–4
Slaughter, Wm., ix. 156
Slaughter, Lower (Glos.), ix. 50
Slee, Jn., ii. 38
Slefhurst:
  Jn. de, iv. 5
  Ric. de, iv. 4–5
  Rob. de, iv. 5
Slindon, ii. 43; iv. 2, 222, 226, **234–7**
  adv., iv. 237
  char., iv. 237
  ch., iv. 235–7, *236*
    accessories, ii. 351, 355–6, 359, 361
    archit., ii. 345, 371, 373
  Dale Pk., *q.v.*
  dom. archit., ii. 392; iv. 234
  Fairmile Bottom, i. 199, 205
  foxhunting, ii. 443
  guild, ii. 21
  Gumber, the, ii. 220; iii. 34; iv. 234;
    and see Bignor: Gumber Corner
  insects, i. 111, 113–14, 116–17, 119–
    21, 131, 134–5, 165–71, 173–6,
    181, 183, 187–8, 190, 192–5,
    197–9, 203–5, 207–10, 215–17,
    227–36
  man., ii. 303–5; iv. 234–5
  mill, iv. 234
  pk., ii. 295, 297, 304–5; iv. 234–5
  pop., ii. 220
  rector, *see* Wyflise
  roads, iii. 34; iv. 234
  Rom. rem., iv. 234
  royal visit, i. 505
  Slindon Common, iv. 234
  Slindon Ho., ii. 29, 333, 383; iv. 234
  wood, iv. 234
Slinfold, ii. 43
  Alfoldean, iii. 33, 37–41, *40*, 70
  ch., ii. 42, 250, 340, 359, 361
  Clemsfold (Climpsfold) man., ii. 109
  dom. archit., ii. 230, 389
  Lydwicke (Ludwick), i. 53
  natural history, i. 169, 304
  Penysfold, ii. 398
  pop., ii. 218
  Roman Gate, iii. 39
  Rom. rem., iii. 39
  Strowde, ii. 398
  vicarage, ii. 9
Sloane:
  Sir Hans, iv. 217

——, m. Geo. Stanley, iv. 217
Slough Green, *see* Cuckfield
Sluice, *see* Hastings: Liberty of the
  Sluice
Slut House Farm, *see* Slaugham
Sluys (Netherlands), ii. 47, 132–3, 138,
  140; ix. 70
Slyhand, Wm., ii. 106
Small:
  Jn., ii. 467
  ——, ii. 475
  —— (another), ii. 475
Smallam, Ric., vii. 147
smallholdings, *see* allotments and small-
  holdings
Smallhythe (Kent), ii. 145
smallpox, *see* epidemics
Smalpage:
  Mic., iii. 147
  Percival, iii. 147
Smart (Smarte):
  Hen., iii. 147
  Martha, w. of Hen., *see* Carter
  Rob., iii. 147
  Wm., vicar of Wilmington, ii. 420
Smeaton, Jn., ix. 55
Smegle, *see* Brede
Smelt:
  Margery, w. of Ric., ix. 120
  Maur., iv. 237
  Ric., ii. 130 *n*; ix. 120
Smirke, Sidney, ix. 274
smith, *see* Giles the smith; Robert the
  smith; William the smith
Smith (Smyth, Smythe):
  A.F., ii. 472 *n*
  Abigail, vii. 82
  Alfred, ii. 475
  Alice, w. of Thos., m. 2 Sir Wm.
    Millard, iv. 90
  Alice, w. of ——, *see* Osborne
  Ann (fl. 1572), vii. 42
  Ann (fl. 1709), vii. 82
  Anna Abel, iii. 131
  Anne, w. of Sir Jn., *see* Parker
  Anne, w. of Thos., m. 2 Thos. Darby,
    vii. 266
  Ant., vii. 247
  Archibald Seth, iv. 227
  Barbara, m. Wal. Bartlett, iv. 90
  Benj., ix. 92
  C.J., ii. 472 *n*
  C.L.A., ii. 475–6
  C.P., i. 59
  C. Roach, iii. 6–7, 9, 12, 59
  Cath., w. of Sir Jn., m. 2 Sir Wm.
    Courtenay, vii. 111, 195 *n*
  Cecil, i. 295
  Chas. (fl. 1564), ii. 257
  Chas. (fl. 1795), iv. 212
  (later Peckham), Chas., *see* Peckham
  Chas. H., ii. 475
  Chas. Hewitt, iv. 136, 200
  Edw., iv. 136
  Eliz., w. of Jn., iv. 231
  Eliz., w. of Jn., *see* Lane
  Eliz., w. of Sir Thos., iv. 89
  Emma, *see* Leigh
  F.P., i. 238
  Frances, vii. 190
  Francis, and his w. Marg., vii. 35
  Geo. (fl. 1595), vii. 6
  Geo. (fl. 1711), iv. 90, 139
  Geo. (d. 1776), iv. 90
  Geo. (fl. *c.* 1800), iv. 76
  Geo. (fl. 1867), vii. 134
  Gerald Dudley, iv. 76
  Hannah, iv. 90
  Hannah, m. Thos. Woodward, iii. 147
  Hen. (fl. *c.* 1620), ix. 81, 117, 206,
    209
  Hen. (fl. 1634), iv. 5 *n*
  Hen. (d. 1725), iii. 126
  Hen. (fl. 1739), iv. 95
  Hen. (fl. *c.* 1900), iv. 121, 132
  J., ix. 157, 160
  Jane, iii. 146
  Jane, w. of Jn., iii. 145

Smith (*cont.*):
Jane, w. of Thos., iv. 163
Jeremiah, ix. 56
Jn. (fl. 1474), iv. 231
Jn., prior of Hastings, ii. 77
(or Waterman), Jn., vii. 257
Jn. (fl. 1551), iv. 56, 89, 135
Jn. (fl. 1579), ii. 255
Jn. (d. 1635), iv. 135–6
Jn. (fl. 1635), iv. 136
Jn. (fl. 1637), iv. 184
Sir Jn. (d. 1662), vii. 111, 195
Jn. (fl. 1697), vii. 35, 81–2, 111, 134, 195, 199
Jn. (d. 1743), iii. 145
Jn. (fl. 1759), vii. 190
Jn. (d. 1764), iii. 90
Jn., rector of Rumboldswyke, iv. 173
Jn. (fl. *c.* 1800), iv. 76
Jn., M.P. for Chich., ii. 207
Jn. Abel, iii. 133
Mary, m. Sir Jn. Morley, iv. 163
Mary, m. Wm. Hamilton, iv. 90, 139
Mary, w. of Chas. Hewitt, *see* Peckham
Mary, w. of Thos., iv. 191
Nehemiah, ii. 427
Nic., *see* Phippes
Reg., iii. 31, 65
Ric. (fl. *c.* 1500), vii. 271
Ric. (fl. 1584), vii. 35
Ric. (fl. 1666), iv. 191
Ric. (fl. 1687), iv. 144
Ric. (d. 1767), iii. 147
Ric. (fl. 1795), iv. 29
Rob. (fl. 1695), iv. 202
Rob. (d. 1721), iii. 126
Rob., Ld. Carrington, iv. 76
Thos. (d. by 1559), vii. 266
Sir Thos. (d. 1577), ii. 229; iv. 89; vii. 132
Thos. (d. 1658), iv. 89–90, 99, 139, 204
Thos. (fl. 1677), iv. 191
Thos. (d. 1688), iv. 89–90
Thos. (fl. 1704), ii. 166
Thos. (d. 1721), iv. 90
Thos. (fl. 1756), iv. 163
Thos. (fl. *c.* 1790), ii. 236
Tilden (fl. 1814), ix. 235
Tilden (another), ix. 235
W.H., ii. 453
(formerly Bartlett), Wal., *see* Bartlett
Wm. (d. 1620), iv. 89, 163
Wm. (d. *c.* 1623), iv. 89, 99, 106, 139, 163
Wm. (d. 1634), ii. 437
Wm. (fl. 1635), iv. 136
Wm. (fl. 1707), iii. 90
Wm. (fl. 1709), vii. 82
Wm. (d. 1764), iii. 90
Wm. Leigh, ix. 92
Gen., ii. 160
Mr., i. 293
fam., iv. 76, 89 *n*, 90, 135
arms, iv. *90*
and see Bassett Smith
Smith, Messrs. G. & T., ii. 235
Smith, Messrs. Geo. & Thos. (? another firm), ii. 236
Smithewic (Smythewic):
Jn. de, vii. 36 *n*
Maud de, w. of Ralph, vii. 36
Ralph de, vii. 36
Smithwick, *see* Southover
Smolyng, Jn., mayor of Chich., iii. 91–2
smuggling, ii. 158, 160, 199–201, 268, 313; vii. 18, 76, 224, 246; ix. 13, 47, 211, 217, 244
Smyth (Smythe), *see* Smith
Smythewic, *see* Smithewic
Snailham, *see* Guestling
Snapper, Susan, ii. 31
Snashall:
Jn., vii. 13
Mary, w. of Jn., vii. 13
Sam., vii. 54
Mrs., vii. 54

Snatt:
Edw., ii. 414
Jn., ix. 202
Ric., ix. 202
Thos., ix. 202
Wm., rector of All Saints, Lewes, canon of Chich., ii. 38, 414
Snaylham (Sneilhamme, Sneylham):
Hen. de, ix. 181
Jn. de, ix. 181
Maud de, *see* Somery
Thos. de, ix. 56
Wm. de, ix. 240
Snelling:
Cecily, w. of Sir Geo., vii. 284
Sir Geo., vii. 258, 284
Joan, vii. 284
Joan, w. of Thos., m. 2 —— Wetley, vii. 284
Marg., w. of Ric., vii. 284
Peter, vii. 258
Ric., vii. 258, 284
Thos., vii. 284
Snepp:
Hannah, w. of Jn., ix. 220
Jn. (? two of this name), ix. 214, 220
Mr. (? another), ix. 211
Sneylham, *see* Snaylham
Snoad, Geo., ix. 177
Snokeshall, Agnes, prioress of Rusper, ii. 64
Snooke, Eliz., iii. 163
Snow, Edw., ix. 92
Soale, Phil., vii. 177
Soames:
A.W., ii. 472 *n*
Arthur Gilstrap, vii. 96
his w., vii. 96
Capt., vii. 96
socage, ii. 173; iv. 52, 129, 184; vii. 2, 48, 58, 100, 132, 197; ix. 11, 79, 157, 214
social and economic history, ii. **169–228**; *and see* agriculture; industries, crafts, and trades
Society for the Maintenance of the Faith, vii. 41, 232
Society of Antiquaries, i. 310, 320, 338, 455, 466; iii. 14, 22, 113
Society of Friends, *see* Quakers
Sockett, T., ii. 207 *n*
Socknersh (Sokenerse):
Christine, w. of Wm., m. 2 Jn. de Burne, ix. 229 *n*
Isabel de, ix. 229
Margery de, m. Rob. de Echingham, ix. 229, 235
Maud, w. of Rog. m. 2 Rog. Doget, ix. 229 *n*
(or St. Leger), Rog., ix. 229
Rog., ix. 229, 235
Wm. de (fl. 1235), ix. 229
Wm. de (fl. 1287), ix. 229, 235
fam., ix. 235
Socknersh, *see* Brightling
Sokenerse, *see* Socknersh
soilage, ix. 84
Solace, Geof., ix. 144
Solent, the, ii. 271
Solicitor-General, *see* Murray, Wm.
Solihull (Warws.), ii. 375
Solly:
Jn., iv. 193
Martha, *see* Legay
Ric., iv. 193
Solomon, abbot of Bayham, ii. 89
Solomon, a Jew, i. 506
Soltykoff, Prince Dmitri, ii. 455, 459
Somer, Chris., ii. 312
Somerley, *see* Wittering, East
Somers-Clarke, *see* Clarke
Somerset:
dukes of, *see* Beaufort; Seymour
mchnss. of, *see* Holland, Marg.
Somerset, i. 68; ii. 241, 286, 473–4, 476; iii. 1; iv. 36; ix. 52
Winford, rector, *see* Cotterill, Jn.
and see Bath; Bristol; Bruton; Castle

Cary; Glastonbury; Kingston Seymour; Seavington; Sedgemoor; Spargrove; Wedmore; Wellington; Wells
Somerville, Jn., i. 519; ii. 29 *n*
Somery (Sumeri, Sumery):
Agnes de, ix. 240
Alice de, ix. 240, 242
Isabel de, m. —— de Chilleye, ix. 240
Joan de, m. Jn. de Lunsford, ix. 240–1
Jn., iv. 166
Mabel, iv. 123
Marg. de, m. 1 Urian de St. Peter, 2 Ralph Basset, iv. 166–7
Maud, m. Wm. de Snaylham, ix. 240
Nichole de, *see* Aubigny
Pernel, w. of Sim., ix. 240
Rog. de, iv. 58, 115, 124, 166–7
Sim. de (fl. *c.* 1200), ix. 240
Sim. de (d. *c.* 1289), ix. 240–1
fam., ix. 241
Sommer:
Frances, m. Jas. Cromer, ix. 154
Jn., and his w. Marten, ix. 154
Mary, m. Thos. Penistone, ix. 154
Sompting, ii. 43
ch., ii. 92; iii. 66
accessories, ii. 351–2, 356–8, 361, *363*, 376
archit., ii. 331, 334–5, 337, 339–40, 342, 344, 346–9, 351, 362, *363*, 364, 368, 371, 376, 378, 380
Cokeham:
chap., ii. 92
hosp., ii. 74, **106**
man., ii. 74–5, 106
earthworks, i. 479
insects, i. 166, 168, 187, 190, 195, 198, 200–1, 204–8, 210
Knights Templars' estate, ii. 331*, 344 *n*
Lychpole (Leechpool), i. 208, 313
Park Brow, iii. 3, 62
pop., ii. 218
roads to, iii. 47
Rom. rem., iii. 66
vicar, ii. 40
Sond (Sonde), *see* Fittleworth
Sondes:
Grace, *see* Pelham
Lewis, Ld. Sondes, ix. 196
Sone:
Bart., iv. 123
Francis, iv. 123
Jn. (fl. 1510), iv. 123
Jn. (fl. 1544), iv. 111
Thos. (d. 1557), iv. 111
Thos. (d. 1633), iv. 123
Wal., iv. 111
Wm., iv. 111
Wood, iv. 123
Sopere:
Jn., iv. 163
Marg., *see* Jardyn
Sophia, princess, dau. of Geo. III, ii. 204
Sorrell, Thos., i. 276
Sortell', *see* Sartilli
Sotheran, Hen. Cecil, vii. 43
Sotton, *see* Sutton
Souter (Suter):
Francis, ii. 235
Jn., iv. 27
South Africa, ii. 473–4
Grahamstown, bp., *see* Cotterill, Hen.
and see Cape of Good Hope; wars
South Coast Harriers, ii. 453
South Coast Staghounds, ii. 449
South Down hunt, ii. 444, 446–8, 452, 460
South Eastern and Chatham Rly., ii. 240; ix. 61
South Lodge (near Horsham), i. 289
South Saxons cricket club, ii. 472–3
South Sea Bubble, iii. 89
South Western Rly., ii. 240

Southampton:
  ctss. of, *see* Fitzwilliam, Mabel
  earls of, *see* Fitzwilliam, Sir Wm.;
    Wriothesley
Southampton (Hants), i. 491, 523; ii.
    133, 135–6, 143, 247; iii. 101–2; iv.
    7; ix. 40
  God's Ho. (Domus Dei), ii. 294; iv.
    208
Southampton Water, ii. 126
Southborough (Southborgh), *see*
    Hamsey
Southbourne, *see* Westbourne
Southdown and East Grinstead
    Breweries Ltd., ii. 263
Southease, ii. 43–4; vii. 14, 66, **73–6**
  adv., vii. 75–6
  ch., ii. 356; vii. *74*, 74–5
    archit., ii. 337, 339–40, 367, 371
  cts., vii. 74, 371
  dom. archit., vii. 73
  man., ii. 179 *n*; iv. 150; vii. 7, 14,
    73–4
  pop., ii. 224
  rly., vii. 73
  trades and ind., ii. 256, 264
Southeram, *see* Malling Without, South:
    Southerham
Southerden, Holland, ii. 451–2
Southerham, *see* Malling Without,
    South
Southern Rly., iii. 37 *n*, 71; vii. 8–9, 46,
    49, 94, 98, 103, 116, 127, 132, 140,
    147–8, 164, 179, 192, 223, 265, 269,
    275
Southerton, Jas., ii. 469
Southey, Rob., iv. 152
Southover, ii. 43–4; vii. 1, 8, 12, 16, 31,
    45–50
  adv., vii. 50
  Anne of Cleves Ho., vii. 12, *44–5*,
    45–6
  char., vii. 50
  ch., ii. 40, 412–13; vii. 46, 48–50, *49*
    accessories, ii. 354, 356, 360–1, 378
    archit., ii. 366, 378
  ch. wardens, ii. 413
  Crane Down, vii. *27 n*
  dom. archit., ii. 387; vii. *44*, 45–6
  Dripping Pan, vii. 8, 48
  hosp., vii. 16, 48
  hund., i. 537; vii. 1, 16, **44**
  insects, i. 167 *n*
  man., vii. 15, 45 *n*, 48
  mills, ii. 259; vii. 27 *n*, 48
  nonconf., ii. 38
  poor relief, vii. 50
  pop., ii. 224
  priory, *see* Lewes: priory
  sch., *see* Lewes: sch., grammar
  Smithwick, vii. 3, 36
  trades and ind., ii. 256, 259, 262
  Watergate, ii. 412–13, 259
Southwark (London, formerly Surr.) ii.
    22, 28, 83, 145, 246; iii. 45
  archdeacon, ii. 87
  bp., iv. 188; ix. 200; *and see* Amigo
  cath., ii. 371
  ch. of St. Olave, ii. 65, 69
  dioc., ix. 33
  Marshalsea prison, ii. 27, 147
  mill, ii. 306
  priory of St. Mary, vii. 113
Southwater, *see* Horsham
Southwell:
  Edw., vii. 280
  H.K., iii. 130
  Hen., vii. 280
  Jane, m. Sir Clement Boehm Traf-
    ford, vii. 281
  Marg., w. of Rob., iv. 82
  Marg., w. of Sir Rob., *see* Nevill
  Sir Rob. (fl. *c.* 1500), iv. 77; vii. 207
  Rob. (fl. 1539), iv. 82, 123
  Sir Rob. (fl. 1542, ? another), vii. 117,
    145, 183, 189
  Ursula, *see* Bohun
Southwell (Notts.), ii. 402, 404

Southwick, ii. 43–4; vii. 277
  adv., ii. 92
  ch., ii. 331, 339, 348, 359, 367–8, 371
  guild, ii. 21
  harbour, ii. 219 *n*
  insects, i. 113, 190, 193, 195, 198–9,
    202
  pop., ii. 219
  rector, ii. 40
  roads to, iii. 43, 47
  Rom. rem., iii. 4, 20, 25–8, *27–8*, 47,
    52, 70
  shipbuilding, ii. 235
  tithes, ii. 60
  U.D., ii. 228
Southwick (Hants), priory, iv. 185
Southwood, Ebenezer P., vii. 65
Southwood, *see* Bosham
Souvigny (Allier, France), vii. 47
Sowton, Jas., vii. 284
Spade, Wm., sacrist of Bosham coll., ii.
    112
Spain, i. 250, 517; ii. 150, 163; iii. 30, 88
  ambassador, ii. 147
  Armada, i. 518–20; ii. 28–9, 152–3;
    iii. 102; iv. 50, 207
  king, *see* Philip
  privateers, ii. 148
  ships from, ii. 136, 140, 166
  trade with, ii. 242, 247; ix. 55, 70
  wars with, *see* wars
  and see Cadiz; Cape Finisterre; Cas-
    tile; Compostella; Estapona; Fla-
    viobriga; Leon; Malaga; Vigo;
    Vipasca
Spalding, Eliz., ix. 29
Spalding (Lincs.), ii. 425
Spanish Armada, *see* Spain: Armada
Spanish Succession, war of, *see* wars
Spann, Jonathan, ii. 165
Spargrove (Som.), iv. 114
Sparke (Sparkes):
  Hen., iv. 216
  Rob., ii. 427
Sparkford (in Compton by Winchester,
    Hants), iv. 85
Sparling, W.A.S., ii. 474
Sparrow:
  Bodychen, high sheriff of Anglesey,
    vii. 254
  Eliz., *see* Boyce
  Hen., high sheriff of Anglesey, vii.
    254
  Jn., vii. 254
Speed:
  Bridget, *see* Sanderson
  Geo., iv. 231
  Jn., ii. 293, 297–8
  Jos., iv. 231
  Wm., rector of St. Pancras, Chich., ii.
    33, 37; iii. 87
  Wm. (fl. 1657, ? another), iv. 231
  Wm. (fl. 1666, another), iv. 231
Speer, Wal., canon of Torre abbey
    (Devon), ii. 90
Speke, Hugh, iv. 116, 123
Spence:
  Anne, vii. 36
  Anne, w. of Jn., vii. 36
  Anne, w. of Thos., *see* Barrett
  Eliz., vii. 36
  Henrietta, m. Thos. Powys, iv. 193 *n*
  Hen., vii. 35–6
  Jn. (fl. 1682), vii. 35
  Jn. (d. 1713), vii. 35–6, 228
  Mary, *see* Fagge
  Rob., vii. 35–6
  Ruth, vii. 36
  Ruth, w. of Jn., vii. 35
  Thos., iv. 193 *n*
  Wm., vii. 6, 35
  Mrs., ii. 443
  arms, vii. *35*
Spencer:
  David (Davy), rector of Clapham, ii.
    25–6
  Eliz., m. Wm., Ld. Compton, vii. 217
  Geo., duke of Marlborough, ii. 442

Harriet, *see* Fawkenor
Herb., ix. 8
Sir Jn., vii. 217
M., ii. 442
Rob., earl of Sunderland, ii. 443
Ld. Rob., ii. 444; iv. 7, 9, 50, 56, 64,
    86
Sperling, J.H., vicar of Westbourne, iv.
    131
Sperschute, *see* Pershete
Spershott, Jas., ii. 199, 201–3; iii. 89–90
Spershute, *see* Pershete
Spicer (Spyser):
  Jn., and his w. Joan, ii. 417
  Rob., M.P. for Lewes, vii. 13
  Wm., rector of Balcombe, ii. 416–17,
    419
spiders, i. **238–44**
Spilman, Francis, ii. 24
spires, *see* architecture: ecclesiastical
Spithurst, *see* Barcombe
Spittelland, *see* Seaford
Spokes, Sidney, iii. 59
sponsage, ix. 9, 37, 49
sport, ii. **441–81**
  angling, ii. 463–7
  athletics, ii. 480–1
  badger baiting, ii. 202
  bowls, ii. 197
  bull baiting, ii. 202
  cock fighting, ii. 202
  cock scailing, ii. 202
  coursing, ii. 453–4
  cricket, ii. 467–76; vii. 265; ix. 8, 29,
    178
  cudgeling, ii. 202
  dog fighting, ii. 202
  football, ii. 197, 202
  golf, ii. 477–80, ix. 184
  hawking, ii. 197
  horse racing, ii. 454–61; vii. 18–19,
    109; ix. 8; *and see* sport: point-
    to-point
  hunting, i. 305–6, 512; ii. 294–6, 299,
    302, 304–7, 309–11, 314, 316,
    318, 322–5; vii. 175–6, 235; ix.
    80
    beagling, ii. 452–3
    fox, i. 302; ii. 441–8
    hare, ii. 307, 322, 449–52; iv. 150 *n*;
      ix. 157
    otter, ii. 453; vii. 192
    stag, ii. 296, 448–9
  point-to-point racing, ii. 452
  polo, ii. 461
  shooting, ii. 322, 461–3
  wrestling, ii. 202
Spray, Adrian, ix. 90 *n*
Spring (Springe):
  Bridget, m. 1 Wm. Ernele, 2 Sir Hen.
    Hussey, iv. 157, 216
  Thos., iv. 157, 216
Springett:
  Ant. (d. 1695), vii. 67, 111, 228
  Ant. (d. 1735), vii. 111
  Ant. (fl. 1740), ii. 439; vii. 247
  Barbara, m. Wm. Campion, vii. 111
  Barbara, w. of Sir Herb., vii. 74
  Edm., ix. 273
  Eliz., m. Jn. Whalley, vii. 74
  Eliz., m. Sim. Stone, vii. 228
  Geo., ix. 273
  Gulielma, m. Wm. Penn, ix. 187, 245
  Herb. (d. 1622), ix. 187
  Sir Herb. (d. 1662), vii. 16, 40, 74
  Herb. (d. by 1691), vii. 228
  Herb. (fl. 1691), vii. 228
  Mary, w. of Sir Wm., m. 2 Isaac
    Pennington, ix. 187
  Sir Thos. (d. 1639), vii. 74, 111; ix.
    245
  Thos. (fl. 1639), vii. 111
  Sir Wm., i. 524; vii. 228; ix. 187
  fam., vii. 16; ix. 273
  arms, vii. *111*
Springham, Thos. de, iv. 25
Sprott (Sprot):
  Ant., ix. 147

Sprott (*cont.*):
Jeremiah, ix. 147
Steph., and his w. Mary, ii. 397
——, vii. 109
Spurrell, Herb., i. 335
Spyney, Rog. de, iv. 235
Spyser, *see* Spicer
squints, *see* architecture: ecclesiastical
Stackney castle, *see* Lamberhurst: Scotney
Staffele, *see* Harvey and Staffele
Staffer, Thos., rector of Guestling, ix. 183
Stafford:
Anne, w. of Edm. de, earl of Stafford, ix. 87
Cecily, *see* Bonville
Edm., earl of Stafford, ix. 87
Hen., duke of Buckingham, ix. 87
Hen., earl of Wiltshire, iv. 159
Jn., abp. of Cant., ii. 118
Rob., and his w. Denise, vii. 230
arms, ix. *87*
Stafford, ii. 407
Staffordshire, i. 168 *n*; *and see* Denstone; Lichfield; Rolleston; Stafford; Wolverhampton
stag hunting, *see* sport: hunting
Stahlschmidt, Mr., ii. 250
Stainbank, *see* Mears & Stainbank
Staines (Mdx.), ii. 407; iii. 47
Stainton, Mr., i. 165
stakebote, ii. 309
Staker:
Eliz., *see* Ewen
Jn., iv. 231
stallage, ix. 68
Stamford Bridge (Yorks. E.R.), battle, i. 485–6
Stamper:
Anne, iv. 163
Gertrude, iv. 163
Wm. (sr.), iv. 163
Wm. (jr.), iv. 163
Stanbridge, Jn., ii. 406, 417–18
Standard, Wm. atte, ix. 247
Standen (Standon, Staundon):
Geo., ii. 470
Hugh de, *see* Wallace
Jn., iv. 106
R., ii. 472
Rob. de, iv. 167
Sam., ix. 155
Mr., ii. 450
Standen (? in East Grinstead), chap., ii. 89
Standishe (Standyssh):
Pernel, *see* Oxenbridge
Seth, ix. 145
——, ii. 28
Standon, *see* Standen
Standyssh, *see* Standishe
Stane Street, i. 479; ii. 239, 306; iii. 1–2, 4, 9–10, 16, 23–4, 32–42, *33*, *40*, 46, 48, 50, 56–7, 63–4, 71, 82–3; iv. 140, 152, 174–6, 234
Stanesgate priory (in Steeple, Essex), ii. 68–9
Stanfield, Jn., vii. 38, 235
Stanford:
(formerly Thomas), Sir Chas. Thomas-, vii. 20, 271
Edw., iv. 155
Ellen, m. 1 Vere Fane-Benett, 2 Chas. Thomas, vii. 271
J.M. Benett-, vii. 271
(formerly Fane-Bennett), Vere, vii. 271
Wm. (d. 1841), vii. 177, 258, 266–7, 271
Wm. (d. 1853), vii. 271
Mr., ii. 447
arms, vii. *270*
Stanhope:
Chas. Augustus, earl of Harrington, ii. 461
Geo., earl of Chesterfield, ii. 457–8
Staninges, *see* Steyning

Stanley (Stanlygh):
Anne, w. of Thos., *see* Dawtrey
Anne, w. of Thos., earl of Derby, vii. 24 *n*, 26 *n*
Edw., earl of Derby (d. 1572), vii. 7, 179
Edw., Ld. Stanley, earl of Derby (d. 1869), ii. 459
Edw. Lyulph, Ld. Stanley, vii. 96
Fred. Arthur, earl of Derby, ii. 457, 460
Sir Geo., Ld. Lestrange, vii. 7
Geo., iv. 217
Hans, iv. 217
Hen., earl of Derby, vii. 7, 33, 35, 55, 85, 117, 134, 141, 156, 195, 231
Jas., earl of Derby, iv. 103, 143
Jn., iv. 128
Mary, ctss. of Derby, *see* Morley
Nic. de, prior of Boxgrove, ii. 59
Sir Thos., earl of Derby (d. 1504), vii. 5–7, 254–5
Thos., earl of Derby (d. 1521), vii. 7, 157
Thos., iv. 128
Wm., iv. 217
——, w. of Geo., *see* Sloane
fam., vii. 141, 195
arms, vii. 7
Stanley (Wilts.), abbey, ix. 61
Stanlygh, *see* Stanley
Stanmer, ii. 3, 44, 284; vii. 103, 221 *n*, 223, 226–7, **238–40**
adv., vii. 239–40
ch., ii. 118; vii. 239, *240*
earthworks, i. 480; vii. 238
hunting, ii. 311, 446, 449–51
man., vii. 14, 239
militia, i. 535
pop., ii. 227
rector, *see* King, Thos.
Rom. rem., iii. 67; vii. 238
South Malling coll. land, ii. 117–18
Stanmer Pk., i. 59*, 65, 219, 276*; vii. 238
Stanmer Place, vii. 238–9
Stanney:
Jn. (fl. 1470), iv. 195, 213
Jn. (fl. 1545), and his w. Mary, iv. 195
Rob., iv. 212
Wm., ii. 24; iv. 213
fam., iv. 212–13
Stansted (Stanstead) (in Stoughton), ii. 43; iv. 112, 121, 124–7, 130, 223
angling, ii. 467
botany, i. 49, 66
forest, i. 50; ii. 293, 297–8, 301–3, 305; iv. 121–3
cts., ii. 302
Lodge, ii. 25
man., iv. 114–15, 121–3, 127–8
pk., ii. 297, 302–3; iv. 122–3
ho., ii. 302–3; iv. 11, *119*, 121–2, 126
royal visits, i. 505; ii. 302
sch., ii. 25, 397
warren, ii. 298
Stanton (Staunton):
Jn. de, vii. 117
Ric., vii. 78
Thos. (fl. 1699), vii. 136
Thos. (fl. 1857), iv. 39
Wm., iv. 173
Stapele, *see* Staple
Stapeley (Stapely), *see* Stapley
Staple Cross, *see* Ewhurst
Staple (Stapele) hund., i. 537; ii. 223; ix. 3, 95, 213, **258**
Staplefield, *see* Cuckfield
Staplehurst (Kent), i. 140
Stapleton:
Thos., prebendary of Chich., ii. 25
Wal., bp. of Exeter, ii. 111
Wm., ii. 24; iv. 231
Stapley (Stapeley, Stapely):
Anne, *see* Thatcher
Ant. (fl. 1564), ii. 24
Ant. (d. 1583 × 1588, ? another), iv.

35; vii. 81, 226; ix. 242, 263
Ant. (d. 1606), vii. 105, 217, 266
Ant. (d. 1655), i. 525, 529; ii. 198 *n*, 299; vii. 17, 31, 35, 36 *n*, 217, 266
Ant. (fl. 1661), ix. 107, 235
Ant. (d. 1667, ? another), vii. 189
Ant. (d. 1733), vii. 189
Barbara, m. Meyrick Jenkin, vii. 217
Dougles, w. of Ant., ix. 107
Drew, vii. 196
Eliz., m. Thos. Briggs, vii. 217
Eliz., m. Thos. Shirley, vii. 196
Herb., vii. 219
Jn. (fl. 1538), and his w. Joan, ix. 201
Jn. (d. 1568), vii. 189
Jn. (d. 1606 × 1608), vii. 189–90
Jn. (d. 1639), vii. 158, 189
Sir Jn. (fl. 1691), vii. 6, 17, 36, 105, 217, 220, 266
Jn. (d. 1737), vii. 189
Mabel, *see* Lewknor
Martha, m. Jas. Wood, vii. 189
Mary, m. —— Dobell, vii. 217
Mary, w. of Sir Jn., vii. 217
Philadelphia, m. Peter Courthope, vii. 36 *n*
Ric. (d. 1546), vii. 189
Ric. (fl. 1692), vii. 190 *n*
Ric. (d. 1762), vii. 189
Wm. (d. 1602), vii. 189–90
——, ii. 35
fam., ii. 389; vii. 189
arms, vii. *189*
Starkey (Starky):
Jn., sacrist of Bosham coll., ii. 112
Thos., iv. 5 *n*
Startin, Alex. Chas., ix. 257
Starvecrow wood (unidentified), i. 68
Starye, Thos., and his w. Eliz., ix. 228 *n*
Staundon, *see* Standen
Staunton, *see* Stanton
Staunton on Wye (Herefs.), ii. 409
Stawell, Ld., *see* Legge, Hen. Bilson
Stead, Alfred, vii. 232
Stebbing, Revd., i. 263
Stedall, A., ii. 457
Stedham, ii. 43; iv. 4, 40, 64–5, **82–4**
adv., iv. 63, 65, 84
anchorite, ii. 47
bridge, iv. 82
ch., ii. 340, 355–6, 360, 365, 379; iv. 63, 83–4, *84*
dom. archit., ii. 388; iv. 82–3
insects, i. 184
man., iv. 83–4
mills, ii. 394; iv. 83
Minstead (Minsted), iv. 44, 82
pop., ii. 221
quarrying, ii. 230; iv. 83
rly., iv. 82
rector, *see* Garrett
Steele (Steel, Stele):
Ann, iii. 144
Jane, vii. 190
Thos. (fl. 1754), recorder of Chich., iii. 95
Thos. (d. by 1777, ? another), iv. 159 *n*
Thos., M.P. for Chich., iii. 90
Wm. (fl. 1371), ix. 127
Wm., bailiff of Chich., ii. 401
Wm. (fl. 1651), ii. 408
Steep (Hants), iv. 4, 40, 54, 56, 80; *and see* Ambersham
Steere:
Geo., ii. 415
H.C. Lee, ii. 449
Stele, *see* Steele
Stempe, Jn., and his w. Anne, vii. 48
Stent:
Agnes, *see* Beche
Bridger, ii. 450
Hen., ix. 178
Wm., vii. 34
Wm. Drew Lucas, *see* Shadwell
Stephen, king, i. 490; ii. 53, 113; iii. 90–1, 102; iv. 168, 239; vii. 263; ix.

2, 14, 36, 117
his s., *see* William, count of Mortain
Stephen, dean of Hastings, ii. 42 *n*
Stephen, prior of Hardham, ii. 75
Stephen, prior of Lewes, ii. 70–1; vii. 89
Stephen, prior of Pynham, ii. 80
Stephen, vicar of Fairlight, ix. 150
Stephen the clerk, vii. 286
Stephens (Stephen):
  Anne, m. Peregrine Palmer, iv. 150
  Jn., ii. 401
  Jonathan, ix. 177
  W., vii. 48–9
  and see Stevens
Stephenson, Thos., vii. 41
Stevens:
  Jn., ii. 409
  Jos., ix. 266
  Wm., vii. 163
  and see Stephens
Stewart (Steward):
  Abigail, iv. 23
  Humph., iv. 23, 64
  Jas., ii. 165
  Jn., iv. 23
  Ric., dean of Chich., ii. 51
  Thos., iv. 23, 64
  Wm., iv. 64
  Wm. (another), iv. 64
  and see Stuart
Stewart-Brown, Egerton, ix. 179
Steyning (Staninges), i. 483; ii. 43, 187, 197, 328; iv. 237 *n*; vii. 15
  ale hos., ii. 196
  Brotherhood Hall, ii. 390–1, 424–5
  ch., ii. 2, 26, 94, 124
    accessories, ii. 355, 357–8, 360
    archit., ii. 230, 327, 332, 334, 339, 346, 349, 365, 367, 378–9
  coins, i. 326, 331
  collegiate ch., ii. 42, **121–2**; canon, *see* Fawkham, Wm. de
  cts., ii. 184
  dom. archit., ii. 384, 386, 390–2
  Fécamp abbey lands, ii. 46
  fossils, i. 31, 35
  guild, ii. 20
  harbour, i. 485
  hund., i. 538; ii. 219
  insects, i. 166, 178, 191, 195, 197–8, 201, 203, 205–10
  local govt., ii. 425
  man., ii. 3–4, 122, 124, 306
  mint, i. 349
  nonconf., ii. 22, 38
  parl. rep., i. 504, 532
  peculiar, ii. 42
  pop., ii. 219
  port, ii. 3
  roads to, iii. 47
  Rom. rem., iii. 2, 67
  sch., ii. 397, 424–5
  sport, ii. 460, 465
  trades and ind., ii. 259, 262
  union, i. 539; ii. 210
  watchmen, ii. 184–5
  Wickham (Wyckham), iii. 47
  woodland, ii. 306
Stigand, abp. of Cant., ii. 3
Stigand, bp. of Selsey, bp. of Chich., ii. 4–6, 42, 47, 52; iii. 105
Stileman:
  R.C., ii. 470 *n*
  Rob. Jn., vii. 169
Stock, *see* Stocks
Stockbridge hospital, *see* Chich.: hosps.
Stockbridge hund., *see* Box and Stockbridge hund.
Stocker, Wm., iv. 224
Stocks (Stock):
  F.W., ii. 476
  Wm., iv. 168
  Wm. Stone, ii. 426
Stoghton, *see* Stoughton
Stoke, *see* Stokes
Stoke Down, *see* Stoke, West
Stoke Guildford (Surr.), ii. 69
Stoke, North, i. 32; ii. 42–3, 466

ch., ii. 82, 340, 352, 372–4, 376
insects, i. 189, 209
pop., ii. 218
prehist. rem., i. 327; ii. 291
Stoke, South, ii. 42–3
  ch., ii. 346, 351, 365, 367, 372
  insects, i. 187
  man., ii. 109; iv. 58, 145, 174
  Offham, ii. 121
  pop., ii. 217
  rector, ii. 121
  Rom. rem., iii. 2, 66
  sport, ii. 443, 466
Stoke, West, ii. 43; iv. 181, **192–5**
  adv., iv. 193, 195
  ch., ii. 340, 352; iv. 192–5, *194*
  earthworks, i. 480
  Kingley (Bottom and Vale), i. 170, 466; ii. 301; iv. 192
  man., iv. 183, 185, 192–3, 195
  ho., iv. 193
  natural history, i. 65, 170, 179
  nonconf., iv. 193 *n*
  pop., ii. 220
  prehist. rem., i. 331; iv. 192
  Stoke Down, iii. 67
Stokes (Stoke):
  Anne, *see* Oxenbridge
  Ant., ix. 162
  G., ii. 452
  Hen., ix. 181
  Jn. de, iv. 102, 105; ix. 118, 240
  Margery de, m. Ric. Haket, ix. 118
  Margery, w. of Wm. de, *see* Northeye
  Sarah de, *see* Passeley
  Wm. de, i. 506; ii. 131 *n*; ix. 118, 176, 190, 240
Stollion (Stolyon):
  Thos. (fl. 1598), ix. 206–7
  Thos. (fl. 1679), ix. 209
  fam., ix. 206, 208
Stomlett common (? Stumblewood in Maresfield), ii. 246
Stonam, Jn., iv. 39
Stonard, Hugh, prior of Winchelsea Dominican friary, ii. 95
Stone:
  Agnes atte, *see* Ferring
  David Hen., alderman of London, ix. 85
  Eliz., *see* Springett
  Gilb. de, dean of Hastings coll., ii. 117
  Sir Ric., ix. 198
  Sim., vii. 228, ix. 245
  Thos. atte (fl. 1356), vii. 100
  Thos. atte (fl. 1440), vii. 100
  Thos. H., ix. 200
  W.O., ix. 198
  fam., vii. 100
Stone and Bartlett, ii. 164
Stone, *see* Hastings
Stone Cross (in Crowborough), *see* Crowborough
Stone Cross (in Laughton), *see* Laughton
Stone gate, *see* Amberley
Stone Lodge, *see* Beeding
stone quarrying, ii. 229–32; iii. 3; vii. 132; ix. 168, 259
Stonegate, *see* Ticehurst
Stoneham, *see* Malling Without, South
Stoneham, North (Hants), iv. 93
Stoneland park, *see* Ashdown forest
Stoneleigh (Warws.), Cryfield, iv. 79*
Stoneley:
  Dorothy, m. Wm. Dawtrey, iv. 174
  Ric., iv. 174
Stoneling (Stonelink), Sir Jn., ix. 181
Stonelink, *see* Fairlight
Stonepound, *see* Keymer: Hassocks
Stonequarry Hill, *see* Grinstead, East
Stonestreet:
  Geo., vii. 36
  Jn., rector of Lindfield, ii. 39
  Jn. (? another), vii. 6, 36
  Martha, vii. 6, 36
Stonewall Farm, *see* Bosham

Stonkylle, Thos., and his w. Alice, vii. 106
Stopham (Stopeham):
  Amabil de, *see* Lisle
  Brian de, iv. 65–6
  Eve (Eva) de, m. Wm. de Echingham, ii. 72; iv. 66; vii. 70; ix. 212, 229
  Eve, w. of Ralph de, iv. 66
  Isabel, w. of Ralph de, ii. 270; iv. 66
  Joan de, m. —— atte See, iv. 66
  Ralph de (fl. *c.* 1194), iv. 65–6
  Ralph de (d. 1271), iv. 34, 65–6
  Ralph de (d. 1291), iv. 66; vii. 70; ix. 212
  arms, iv. 66
Stopham, ii. 43; iv. 136
  anchorite, ii. 47
  bridge, ii. 394
  ch., ii. 250, 337, 347, 349, 353, 364, 371
  insects, i. 133
  man., iv. 65
  pop., ii. 218
Stor, riv., iii. 48, 64
Storey (Storie), *see* Story
Storrington, ii. 43
  Chantry Hill, iii. 59
  ch., ii. 378
  Cootham, iii. 48, 64
  deanery, ii. 42–3
  earthworks, i. 480
  Hurston Warren, iii. 64
  insects, i. 166, 169, 172, 184–6, 192–3, 196, 199, 202–8, 210
  Kithurst Hill, iii. 3, 59
  natural history, i. 109, 119–22, 185, 190, 192, 209
  pop., ii. 218
  prehist. rem., i. 321, 331
  rector, ii. 35
  rectory, ii. 9
  roads to, iii. 48, 64
  Rom. rem., iii. 67
  sport, ii. 453, 475
  vicarage, ii. 9
Story (Storey, Storie):
  Bart., iv. 100
  Edw., bp. of Chich., ii. 16, 50, 58, 64, 82, 84–5, 394, 402, 404–5; iii. 73–4, 116 *n*, 120, 124–5; iv. 66, 134; vii. 147
  Thos., vicar of Findon, ii. 25
  arms, iii. *73*; iv. 147
Stoughton (Stoghton):
  Adrian, iv. 123, 129, 193–4, 212
  Anne, m. —— Bowyer, iv. 193
  Anne, m. Peter Jermyn, iv. 193
  Cecily, w. of Geo., iv. 129
  Eleanor, iv. 193
  Eliz., iv. 193
  Jane, *see* Garton
  Jn., iv. 129
  Geo., iv. 129, 167, 193, 195
  Geo. (another), iv. 129
  Mary, m. —— Gunter, iv. 193
  Mary, w. of Adrian, *see* Jordan
  Sara, m. Wm. Styant, iv. 193, 212
  Thos. (fl. 1448), ix. 53
  Thos. (fl. 1532), ix. 10
  Thos. (fl. 1559), iv. 167, 193, 195
  Thos. (fl. 1564, ? another), ii. 24–5, 397
  Thos. (d. 1626), iv. 193, 211–12
  arms, iv. *193*
Stoughton, ii. 43, 302; iii. 83; iv. 88, 91, 107, 113 *n*, 116, **121–6**
  adv., iv. 117, 125–6
  Bow Hill, i. 331; iii. 51; iv. 121
  ch., iv. 104, 122, 124–5, *125*
    accessories, ii. 351, 356
    archit., ii. 340, 346, 349, 364, 371
  dom. archit., iv. 121
  earthworks, i. 480
  glebe, ii. 5
  inc., iv. 121
  insects, i. 167–8, 174, 177–8, 184
  man., iv. 114, 121–4

Stoughton (cont.):
  Northwood:
    Farm, iv. 121
    man., iv. 111, 123–4
  pk., ii. 297
  pop., ii. 221
  prehist. rem., iv. 121
  rectors, see Godfrey; Herbert
  roads, iv. 121
  Stansted, q.v.
  tithes, iv. 122
  Walderton, iv. 121, 123, 126
    Down, iv. 121
    man., iv. 14, 41, 98, 123
stoups, water, see architecture: ecclesiastical
Stour, riv., ii. 453
Stow, Messrs. Thos. & Son, ii. 235
Stowe (Stow):
  Baldwin de (fl. before 1285), ix. 84
  Baldwin de (fl. 1291), ix. 84
  Kenyon, ii. 461
  Rose, w. of Baldwin de, ix. 84
  Wm. de, ix. 84
  and see Philipson-Stow
Stowting, see Stutinges
Stoyf, Heynrich, iv. 66
Strabo, ii. 291; iii. 30
Strachan, Mr., ix. 74
Stradling (Stradlyng):
  Geo., dean of Chich., ii. 51
  Sir Thos., iv. 89
Straker, Ernest, iii. 31
strand and den, ix. 9, 37
Strange (L'Estrange):
  Agatha le, see Freville
  Guy le, vii. 228–9
  Hamon le, vii. 231 n
  Juliana le, m. Ric. de Wappenbury, vii. 229
  Marg. le, m. Thos. Noel, vii. 229
  Mary le, see Ovingdean
  Maud le, m. Griffin of Wales, vii. 229
  Ralph le, castellan of Carreghofa, vii. 229, 232
  and see Gilbert the stranger
Stratford:
  Jn., abp. of Cant., iii. 85; iv. 235
  Marg., see Syteler
  Rob. de, bp. of Chich., ii. 13, 63, 81, 335, 361, 377; iii. 72, 85, 111, 113, 132, 133 n; iv. 106, 134, 170; vii. 108
  Rob., iv. 191
Stratford (Warws.), ii. 254
Stratford le Bow, (London, formerly Mdx.), ii. 22
Strawberry Hill (in Twickenham, Mdx.), ix. 122
Strawberry Hole, see Northiam
Streat (Estrat, Street, Strete), ii. 43–4; vii. 92, 109, **113–15**
  adv., vii. 115
  char., vii. 115
  ch., ii. 374; vii. 115, *115–16*
  hund., i. 537; ii. 225; vii. 1, 3 n, 51, **92–3**, 129
  man., ii. 173 n; vii. 100, 114–15, 129, 206
  poor relief, vii. 115
  pop., ii. 225
  Streat Place, ii. 387; vii. 113–14, *116*
Streater, an ensign, i. 523
Streatfield (Streatfeild):
  Eliz., see Beard
  G.E., vii. 272
  Hen., vii. 228, 236
  R.J., ii. 276, 446
  Wm., bp. of Lewes, iii. 126
Streatham (London, formerly Surr.), iii. 42
Streatham (in Henfield), see Henfield
Street (Strete):
  E.E., iii. 165
  Wm., ix. 187
Street, see Streat
Streetend, see Sidlesham
Streetin, Eliz., iv. 165

Strete, fam., see Street
Strete, see Streat
Stretebridge, see Sheet
Stretham (Cambs.), i. 322*
Strettington, see Boxgrove
Stride, Messrs., ii. 282
Stringer:
  Ant., iv. 109
  Geo., and his w. Lucy, ix. 150
  Ric. (sr.), iv. 83
  Ric. (jr.), iv. 83
Strode (Strowde):
  Sir Geo. (d. 1663), ix. 212
  Sir Geo. (d. 1707), ix. 212
  Jas., ix. 274
  Joan, m. Thos. Sharp, ix. 274
  Jn., iv. 52
  Ric. de la, vii. 196
  Ric. atte, vii. 196
  Rob. atte, prior of Boxgrove, ii. 59
  (later Lytton), Sir Wm., ix. 212
Stronghill:
  Jn. (d. 1619), ix. 160
  Jn. (fl. 1638), ix. 160
Strowde, see Strode
Strowde (in Slinfold), see Slinfold
Strudgate, see Worth
Stuart:
  Chas., vii. 57
  Eliz., m. Hen. Fred. Howard, earl of Arundel, ii. 271
  Jas., duke of Lennox and Richmond, ix. 53
  Jas. ('James III'), the Old Pretender, iii. 89; iv. 17
  Sarah, iv. 202
  and see Stewart
Stubbe:
  Jn., mayor of Chich., iii. 82, 91
  Mabel, w. of Jn., iii. 82
Stubberfield, Hen., ii. 469, 471
Stucle (Stucley), see Stukeley
Studley (Studeley):
  Jn., vii. 38
  Nat., vii. 17 n
  Rob., ii. 165
Stukeley (Stucle, Stucley):
  Eliz., see Martel
  Hugh, vii. 37
  Ric., iv. 159
  Rog., iv. 159
  Wm., iii. 46
Stumblewood, see Stomlett
Stunt, Joan, iv. 179
Stunt's Green, see Herstmonceux
Sturmi, see Sturmy
Sturminster Marshall (Dors.), ii. 84
Sturmy (Esterman, Esturmi, Sturmi):
  Alice, m. Thos. de Cheney, iv. 204
  Hugh, iv. 98, 204–5
  Jn. (? two of this name), iii. 73 n, 166; iv. 204
  Jn. (? another), and his w. Rose, ii. 121
  Ketel, iii. 82, 166
  Rog., iv. 204 n
  Sarah, m. Godfrey de Goudeswode, iv. 204
  Wm., iv. 204 n
  fam., iv. 204
Sturt, H.C., iii. 62
Stutinges (Stowting, Kent), ii. 112
Styant:
  Anne, see Phillips
  Geo., iv. 212
  Sara, see Stoughton
  Thos., iv. 193, 212
  Wm., iv. 193, 212
  Wm., his s., iv. 212
Styles:
  Ric. (fl. 1682), iv. 52; ix. 26
  Ric. (fl. 1713, ? another), ix. 264
Stylle, Wm., master of hosp. of St. Jas., Chich., iii. 167 n
Styllefeld:
  Alice, m. Wm. Whitney, iv. 157
  Alice, w. of Jn., see Hunston
  Jn., iv. 157

Styngel (unidentified), ii. 302
Stynt:
  Jane, m. Jn. Duncombe, iv. 24
  Jn., iv. 24
Suckling:
  Jn., vii. 227
  Sir Jn., i. 521
Sucton, Hen., ii. 95
Sudan, see Abu Klea; Khartoum
Sudbury, Sim., bp. of London, ii. 70 n
Suffolk, i. 176; ii. 52, 147, 461; vii. 1; ix. 2; and see Burgh Castle; Dunwich; Frostenden; Hardwick Hall; Ipswich; Lavenham; Lowestoft; Orford; Orwell; Saxham; Sibton; Wretham
Suggeworth, fam., vii. 159
Sullington, ii. 43, 264
  chant., ii. 20
  ch., ii. 250, 351, 356, 360–1
  Heath Common, q.v.
  insects, i. 199, 205
  pop., ii. 219
  rectory, ii. 9
Sulpicius, ii. 405–6
Sulyard, Jn., iv. 115
Sumeri, see Somery
Sumerlege, see Manhood
Sumery, see Somery
sumptuary laws, ii. 197
Sumter, Jn. le, vii. 20
Sunbury (Surr., formerly Mdx.), ii. 41
Sunderland, earl of, see Spencer, Rob.
Sunworth (in Buriton, Hants), ii. 89*
Surrey, earls of, ii. 65; and see FitzAlan, Thos.; Howard; Warenne; William, count of Mortain
Surrey, i. 53, 58, 348, 512; ii. 211, 311; iii. 42 n, 96; iv. 40; vii. 1–2
  birds, i. 278–9
  botany, i. 50, 67
  boundary, i. 536, 539; iv. 67
  ch., ii. 250, 328
  Civil War in, i. 523
  fossils, i. 39
  geology, ii. 333, 335, 337
  insects, i. 111, 130, 164 n, 169 n, 170, 183
  mkts., ii. 195
  militia, i. 508, 525
  outlaws, i. 503
  parishes, i. 538
  political history, i. 483
  roads, ii. 240
  sheriffs, i. 521; and see Fiennes, Sir Ric.; Hussey, Nic.
  sport, i. 306; ii. 453, 467–72, 474
  textile ind., ii. 256
  and see individual place names
Surrey Staghounds, ii. 449
Surrey Union hunt, ii. 448
Sussex:
  duke of, see Augustus Frederick
  earls of, see Aubigny, Wm. d'; Lennard, Thos.
Sussex:
  acreage, ii. 217
  East Sussex, iv. 1; vii. 12
    County Council, ii. 213, 277, 288–91; vii. 12
  Fencible Cavalry, i. 535
  Guides, i. 535
  Ld. Lieutenant, i. 516, 533
  M.P., see Hay, Jn.
  pop., ii. 217
  regiment, i. 535–6; iii. 142
  rifles, i. 536
  sheriffs, i. 492, 521; ii. 233, 241–2; iv. 183; ix. 3, 67; and see Borrer, Wm. (d. 1832); Dobell, Wal. (d. 1694); Eversfield, Nic.; Fiennes, Sir Ric.; Gage, Sir Edw.; Guldeford, Sir Jn.; Hastings, Sir Mat. de; Hussey, Nic.; Marshal, Jn.; Marshal, Wm.; May, Sir Ant.; Medstede, And. de; Morland, Wm. C.; Turner, Arthur
third penny, iv. 1

under sheriff, ii. 201
vice-admiral, ii. 151
West Sussex, ii. 148–9; iv. 1, 144
  County Council, ii. 430; iii. 73–4
and see Saxons, South
Sussex Amalgamated Newspapers Ltd., ii. 239
Sussex Archaeological Society, ii. 362; iii. 16, 25, 31, 39; vii. 12, 20–1, 39, 45–6
Sussex Archaeological Trust, iii. 25; vii. 10, 20, 152, 165, 179
Sussex Association for Improving the Condition of the Labouring Classes, ii. 208 *n*, 209
Sussex Basket Industry Ltd., ii. 236
Sussex Committee of Defence, i. 524
Sussex Congregational Union, ix. 29
Sussex County Coursing Club, ii. 453–4
Sussex Dairy Farmers' Assoc., ii. 289
Sussex marble, *see* Petworth marble
Sussex Piscatorial Society, ii. 464–5
Sussex Polo Club, ii. 461
Sussex Portland Cement Co., ii. 231
Sussex Royal Garrison Artillery, i. 536
Sussex Sea Fisheries District, ii. 269
Sussex stone, vii. 46, 94, 99, 140, 185, 199, 267
Sussex Weekly Advertiser or Lewes Journal, ii. 238–9
Suter, *see* Souter
Sutthery, A.M., ii. 472 *n*, 473
Sutton (Sotton):
  Chas. Manners, abp. of Cant., iv. 226
  Eliz., m. 1 Sir Jas. Altham, 2 Sir Jn. Ashfield, 3 Sir Ric. Minshull, iv. 224
  Eliz. Henrietta, *see* Cuddon
  Griffin de, *see* Griffin of Wales
  Sir Jn. de, vii. 54
  Jn. (fl. 1675), iii. 163
  Jn. (fl. 1786), iv. 212
  Ric., iv. 224
  Wal. de, and his w. Sarra, iv. 51
Sutton, i. 483; ii. 43–4; iv. 61
  botany, i. 48, 66
  ch.:
    accessories, ii. 352–3, 355–6, 359, 361
    archit., ii. 334–5, 348, 371, 376–7
  earthworks, i. 480
  poor law union, ii. 206–7, 209–10
  pop., ii. 218
  rector, *see* Cruso
  workho., ii. 210
Sutton (in Seaford), *see* Seaford
Sutton, East (Kent), vii. 180
Sutton, Long (Hants), iv. 70
swain-motes, *see* courts
Swainson, Chas. Ant., warden of St. Mary's hosp., Chich., ii. 102
Swallowfield (Berks.), *see* Beaumoys
Swanage (Dors.), i. 37
Swanborough (in Iford), *see* Iford
Swanborough hund., i. 537; ii. 172 *n*, 225; vii. 1, 3 *n*, 34–6, 44, **51**, 58, 92
Swanbourne, *see* Arundel
Swanbridge (? in Bury), ii. 303
Swanley, Capt., i. 522
Swanton, Wm. de, dean of South Malling coll., ii. 119
Swayne, Anne, vii. 176
Swaysland, Mr., i. 278, 281, 283, 293
Sweden, ii. 248
swedes, *see* crops
Sweet Hill, *see* Patcham
Sweet Mine Pits, *see* Maresfield
Swegen, king of Denmark, i. 483
Swegen (Sweyn), earl, i. 484; ii. 127; iv. 182; ix. 8
Swift, Jonathan, ix. 171
Swinham (Swynham):
  Alex. de, ix. 80
  Giles, *see* Giles the smith
  Luke de, ix. 80
  Luke de (another), ix. 80
  Thos. de, ix. 80
  Thos. (another), ix. 80

Switzerland, i. 328; iii. 88; *and see* Zurich
Swyn, the (Belgium), ii. 136
Swynbourne:
  Philippe, *see* Passeley
  Wm., ix. 154
Swynham, *see* Swinham
Sydenham, Sim., bp. of Chich., iii. 124; iv. 134
Sydenham, Lower (in Lewisham, London, formerly Kent), iii. 70
Sydney, *see* Sidney
Sydney Sussex College, Cambridge, ix. 160
Sykelfot:
  Gilb., vii. 106
  Isabel, m. Jn. de Kyngeston, vii. 59, 106
  Jn., vii. 106
Sylvester, Jn., ix. 197
Symes, *see* Simes
Symonds:
  Jn., ii. 404
  Sam., ix. 171
  T.E., ii. 167
  Thos., i. 527
  Wm., ii. 404
  and see Simmons
Sympson (Symson), *see* Simpson
synagogue, *see* Jews
Syon (Sion) abbey (in Isleworth, Mdx.), ii. 104, 120, 124, 230, 379; iv. 20, 155–6; ix. 26, 75, 160, 169, 171, 172 *n*
Syteler:
  Hen., iv. 191
  Joan, m. Jn. Slater, iv. 191
  Joan, w. of Ric., iv. 191
  Marg., m. Rob. Stratford, iv. 191
  Ric., iv. 191
  Ric. (another), iv. 191
  fam., iv. 191
Sywell (Northants.), ix. 262 *n*

tabernacles, *see* architecture: ecclesiastical
Tabor, Jn., iii. 24, 55
Tacitus, iii. 30
Tadeham, Wm. de, *see* St. George
Taiard (Taillard), *see* Tayard
Taillefer, ——, i. 487
Tailor (Taillour), *see* Taylor
tailors, *see* textile inds.
Talbot:
  Chas., iv. 31
  Eliz., m. Jn. Mowbray, iv. 184
  Mary, w. of Chas., *see* Aylwin
  Mary, w. of Wm., Ld. Talbot, *see* Cardonell
  Ric., dean of Chich., ii. 51
  Wm., Ld. Talbot, iv. 180
tallage, iv. 122, 167, 183; ix. 37, 49
Talmaco, Hugh de, precentor of Chich. cath., iv. 170
Talman, Wm., iv. 121
Tamplin & Sons, ii. 263
Tamworth:
  Jn. (fl. 1425), ix. 177
  Jn. (fl. 1532), ix. 10
Tandridge (Surr.), ii. 328 *n*
Taneto, Jn. de, abbot of Battle, ii. 55
Tanfield, Wm., dean of Hastings coll., ii. 117
Tangier (Morocco), ii. 165
Tangmere, ii. 43; iv. 133, 222, **237–9**, *238*
  adv., iv. 149, 239
  airfield, iv. 165, 237
  char., iv. 149, 239
  ch., ii. 37, 351–2, 355; iv. 235, 238–9, *238–9*
    archit., ii. 328 *n*, 333, 336, 339–40, 342, 350–1, 365–6, 371–4, 377
  man., iv. 237–9
  pk., ii. 295
  pop., ii. 220
  roads, iv. 237
  Rom. rem., iii. 16

tithes, iv. 239
Tankerville, earls of, *see* Bennett; Grey, Ford
Tanner:
  Ant., vii. 121–2, 124
  Hen., vii. 42
  Jane, vii. 121, 124
  Ric., vii. 124
  Wm. (d. 1831), vii. 121, 124
  Wm. (d. 1870), vii. 121
Tanners, *see* Waldron
tanning, ii. **259–60**; iii. 75; iv. 76; ix. 70, 247
Tapling, V.L., ii. 480
Taplow (Bucks.), iv. 62
Tapsell (Tapsil):
  Hen., ii. 250
  Rob., iv. 87
  Rog., ii. 250; iv. 60, 64; vii. 38, 91; ix. 23
Tarberry Hill, *see* Harting
tares, *see* crops
Tarrant (Dors.), abbey, iv. 89
Tarring:
  deanery, ii. 42
  hund., i. 538; ii. 219
Tarring (unspecified), i. 187, 195, 199, 201–2, 207, 331
Tarring Neville (or East Tarring), ii. 44; vii. 225
  ch., ii. 250, 351, 356, 371–2
  man., ii. 174
  pop., ii. 225
Tarring, West, i. 53; ii. 13, 43
  bellfounding, ii. 249–50
  chant., ii. 20
  ch., ii. 12, 22 *n*, 118
    accessories, ii. 325, 355, 358–9, 374, 378
    archit., ii. 334, 339–40, 344, 349, 374, 377–8
    dom. archit., ii. 384, *385*, 386, 390–1
  French raids, i. 513; ii. 142
  guild, ii. 21
  hosp., ii. **107**
  man., ii. 292
  palace, ii. 333, 381
  peculiar, ii. 3, 42
  pop., ii. 219
  rectors, *see* Borle; Bysshe, Thos.; Camilla; Flisco; Simon
  rectory, ii. 12
  Rom. rem., ii. 291
Tasciovannus, i. 326, 329
Tatchell, Frank, iv. 79
Tate, F.W., ii. 470
Tateshale, *see* Tattersall
Tateshale, honor (or barony), iv. 42, 123
Tateshall (Tateshull), *see* Tattersall
Tatsfield (Surr.), iii. 45
Tattersall (Tateshale, Tateshall, Tateshull, Teteroale, Tettersell):
  Emma de, m. Adam de Cailli, iv. 123
  Eve, w. of Rob. de, m. 2 Jn. de Cove, iv. 115 *n*
  Isabel de, m. Jn. Orreby, iv. 41, 123, 168*
  Joan de, m. Sim. de Driby, iv. 41, 98, 123, 168
  Jn., ii. 421
  Maud de, *see* Aubigny
  Nic., i. 527–9; vii. 247, 259
  Rob. de (fl. 1243), iv. 13, 41, 98, 111, 168
  Rob. de (d. 1272), iv. 13, 123
  Rob. de (d. 1303), iv. 13–14, 98, 112, 115, 128, 158
Tauk (Tauke), *see* Tawke
Taverner:
  Alice, w. of Jn., iii. 105
  Bart. le, iii. 94
  Eliz., iii. 105
  Isabella le, iii. 94
  Jn. le (fl. 1343), iv. 157
  Jn. (d. 1414), iii. 105
  Maud, w. of Wm. le, iv. 157
  Nic., sacrist of Bosham coll., ii. 112, 402

Taverner (*cont.*):
  Ric. le, iii. 94
  Wm. le, mayor of Chich., iii. 91
  Wm. le, iv. 157–8
Tavistock, marquess of, *see* Russell, Francis
Tavistock (Devon), abbey, ii. 67
Tawke (Tauk, Tauke, Tawk):
  Agnes, prioress of Easebourne, ii. 84–5
  Anne, m. Thos. Devenish, iv. 51, 177, 230; ix. 248
  Isabel, *see* St. George
  Joan, m. Ric. Ryman, iv. 51, 177, 204, 230
  Joan, w. of Wm., iv. 230
  Jn. (fl. 1368), iv. 51
  Jn. (fl. 1416), iv. 238
  Jn. (fl. 1587), iv. 129
  Rob. (d. 1400), iv. 51–2, 177
  Rob. (fl. 1428), iv. 52, 177
  Rob. (? another), iv. 230
  Thos. (d. 1419), iv. 51, 177
  Thos. (fl. 1428), iv. 52
  Thos. (d. 1493), iv. 51, 177, 230
  Sir Wm. (d. 1375), iii. 159 *n*; iv. 51, 105, 177, 230
  Wm. (d. 1505), iv. 51, 177, 230
  fam., iv. 129
  arms, iv. *51*, *177*, 179
taxes, i. 505, 512–13; ii. 140, 142, 144–5, 189; *and see* Chich.; gavel; Lewes; maltode; Nicholas IV, pope; poll tax; rates; Rottingdean; Rye; scot and lot; ship money; Shoreham; Winchelsea
Tayard (Taiard, Taillard):
  Ralph, ii. 113; ix, 84–5, 264, 268
  fam., iv. 56
Taylecortays, Mary, m. Rob. de Rogate, iv. 28
Taylor (Taillour, Tailor, Tayler, Tayllor, Taylur):
  Agnes le, *see* Percy
  Alice, ii. 99
  Ann, ii. 31
  Benj., iv. 163
  C.G., ii. 469
  Cath., *see* Rishton
  Sir Chas. (fl. 1841), iv. 23, 38, 65
  Sir Chas. (d. 1876), iv. 195
  Sir Chas. Wm., iv. 83
  Geo., iv. 211 *n*
  Hen. (fl. 1349), iv. 177
  Hen. (fl. *c.* 1643), iv. 35
  Isaac, ii. 292 *n*
  J.H., ii. 478, 480
  Jas., iii. 101
  Jn. (fl. 1615), ix. 192
  Jn., vicar of Sidlesham, ii. 420
  Jn. (d. 1653), ix. 8
  Jn. (fl. 1676), ix. 202
  Jn. (d. 1700), iv. 203
  Jn. (fl. 1775), ii. 439
  Lambert le, iv. 61
  Mat., ix. 121
  Myles, vii. 263
  Rebecka, *see* Bennett
  Ric., rector of Maresfield, ii. 420
  Ric. (d. 1613), iv. 82
  Ric. (d. 1633), iv. 202–3, 218 *n*
  Ric. (fl. 1633), iv. 202
  Ric. (fl. 1695), iv. 202
  Shadrack, iv. 163
  Susan, *see* Bateman
  Thos. (fl. 1378), ix. 153
  Thos., abbot of Robertsbridge, ii. 73–4
  Thos. (fl. 1616), ix. 202
  Thos. (fl. 1663), and his w. Mary, ix. 233, 237
  Wm. (fl. 1356), and his w. Eliz., iv. 177
  Wm. (fl. 1368), and his w. Agnes, ii. 96
  Wm. (fl. before 1371), ix. 153
  Wm. (fl. 1378), ix. 153, 156
  —— (fl. 1792), ii. 475

—— (fl. 1906), ix. 223
  fam., iv. 213
  arms, iv. 211
Taylors (of London), ii. 164
Tebbs, W.M., ii. 453
Teddington, Jn. de, warden of Windham hosp., ii. 108
Teesdale:
  Chris. (d. 1855), iv. 192
  Chris. (fl. 1892), iv. 192
  Chris. Baker, iv. 192
  Sir Geo., iii. 145
Telham, *see* Battle
Telscombe, ii. 43–4; vii. 61, 66, 73, **76–8**
  adv., vii. 78
  agric., vii. 76
  Brighton Industrial Sch., i. 8
  char., vii. 78
  ch., ii. 40, 352, 356, 368, 370–2; vii. 77–8, *77–8*
  cts., vii. 76
  dom. archit., vii. 76
  hare hunting, ii. 451
  inc., vii. 76
  man., iv. 150; vii. 7, 73, 76–7
  mill, vii. 74, 77
  pop., ii. 224
  racehorse training, vii. 76
  rectory, vii. 69
  smuggling, vii. 76
Templars, *see* Knights Templar
Temple:
  Sir Alex., i. 521; ix. 154
  Jas., M.P. for Bramber, i. 524, 528–9
  Jas. (? another), ix. 214
  Jn., vii. 281 *n*
  Mary, *see* Busbridge
  Purback, and his w. Sarah, vii. 105
  fam., ix. 214
Temse, Mr., ii. 25
tenancies, agricultural, ii. 286–7
Tenterden (Kent), ii. 143, 152–3, 240; ix. 34, 36, 54
tenures, ii. 171–83, 186–7; iii. 84, 92, 96; *and see* alodial; parage; scutage; serjeanty; socage
Terence, ii. 419
Terry, Steph., iv. 70
Terwick, ii. 43, 218 *n*; iv. 3–4, **28–30**, 32
  adv., iv. 27–30
  ch., ii. 334, 339, 349, 357, 367; iv. 29, *29*
  common, iv. 28
  Dangstein Ho., iv. 28, 36, 69
    pk., iv. 28
  dom. archit., iv. 28
  free warren, iv. 28
  inc., iv. 28
  man., iv. 28–9
  mill, iv. *frontispiece*, 28
  pop., ii. 221
Tetbald the priest, ix. 160
Tetbald, Rob. s. of, *see* Robert
Tetersoale (Tettersell), *see* Tattersall
Teuelby (Tylleby):
  Alice de, *see* Baseville
  Jn. de, iv. 42
Teulon:
  Josiah Sanders, warden of St. Mary's hosp., Chich., ii. 102
  S.S., ix. 25
  W.H., ix. 80
Tew, T.P., ix. 227
Tewkesbury (Glos.), abbey, iv. 148 *n*
textile inds., ii. **255–8**
  cotton, ii. 257–8
  dyeing, ii. 256–7; iii. 97
  fulling, ii. 256–7; iv. 63
  hemp, ii. 257
  linen, ii. 203, 257–8; iii. 89; ix. 67
    cambric, ii. 258
    flax, ii. 257–8
  silk, ii. 258; ix. 13
  tailors, iii. 97
  weaving, ii. 38; iii. 97
  wool, ii. 255–7, 427
    broadcloths, ii. 256–7; iv. 160
    fustian, ii. 257

  kerseys, ii. 256–7
  and see wool production
Tezelin (fl. 1086), vii. 202–4
  his s., *see* William
Thadeham, *see* St. George
Thakeham, i. 53; ii. 43
  ch.:
    accessories, ii. 351, 355–6, 358, 361
    archit., ii. 337, 339, 346, 348, 351, 371, 378
    dom. archit., ii. 386, 388
  Heath Common, *q.v.*
  pop., ii. 219
  tithes, ii. 60
  union, i. 539; ii. 205
Thames, riv., i. 13, 18–20, 54, 58, 306, 328, 333, 338 *n*; ii. 125, 130, 133, 144, 153, 158, 160, 306, 466; iii. 2, 10, 30, 46; iv. 16
Thanet, earls of, *see* Tufton
Thanet, Isle of (Kent), ii. 235; ix. 90
Thatcher (Thetcher):
  Agnes, ii. 103
  Ann, m. Jas. Rootes, ix. 181, 191
  Ann, w. of Wm., *see* Tresham
  Anne, m. —— Stapley, ix. 191
  Dorothy, m. Rob. Fromond, ix. 191
  Eliz., m. 1 Thos. Rootes, 2 Hen. Mansfield, ix. 191
  Jas., ix. 181, 191
  Jn. (fl. 1564), ii. 24
  Jn. (d. 1574), ix. 177, 191
  Jn. (d. by 1574, his s.), ix. 191
  Jn. (fl. 1589), vii. 132
  Jn. (fl. 1612), ix. 191
  Kath., ix. 191
  Marg., m. —— Kyffin, ix. 191
  Margery, m. —— Isham, ix. 191
  Mary, m. Wm. Eyston, ix. 191
  Philippa, m. Thos. Pudsey, ix. 191
  Susan, m. Bart. Fromond, ix. 191
  Wm., ix. 191
  fam., ii. 27
  arms, iv. 178
thatching, ii. 337
Theford, *see* Thetford
Themeus wood, *see* Thonicus
Theobald, St., abbot of Vaux de Cernay, iii. 139
Theobald (of Bec), abp. of Cant., ii. 53, 118; iv. 237
Theobald, prebendary of Hastings, ii. 113
Theobald:
  Edw., ix. 114
  Fred., ii. 453
  Geo., ix. 192
  Mr., ii. 458
Theobalds (in Waltham Cross, Herts.), ix. 132
Theodgar, moneyer, vii. 33
Theodore, abp. of Cant., ii. 1; iv. 229, 237; vii. 101
Thetcher, *see* Thatcher
Thetford (Theford):
  Alice de, *see* Percy
  (or Tyford), Phil. de, iv. 61
  Thos., ix. 146
Thetford (Norf.), ii. 397
Thickpeny, David, ii. 29
Thiers, Louis, ix. 5
Thiétry, fam., ii. 254
Thille hund., *see* Dill hund.
Thisac, fam., ii. 254
Thomas, St., *see* Becket
Thomas, abbot of Bayham, ii. 88–9
Thomas, abbot of Bayham (another), ii. 88
Thomas, abbot of Durford, ii. 91
Thomas, abbot of Robertsbridge (three of this name), ii. 73–4
Thomas, duke of Gloucester, ix. 87, 263
  Eleanor his w., *see* Bohun
  his dau., *see* Isabel
Thomas, master of hosp., of St. Jas. and St. Mary, Chich., ii. 100
Thomas, prior of Boxgrove, ii. 57, 59

Thomas, prior of Boxgrove (another), ii. 59
Thomas, prior of Pynham, ii. 81
Thomas, prior of Sele, ii. 62
Thomas, prior of Tortington, ii. 83
Thomas, reeve of Bosham, iv. 183
Thomas, warden of St. Mary's hosp., Chich., ii. 102
Thomas son of Geoffrey, ix. 149
Thomas son of Reynold, iv. 45
Thomas, clerk of Lordington, ii. 70 *n*
Thomas:
  Chas., ix. 62
  (later Thomas-Stanford), Chas., *see* Stanford
  Ellen, *see* Stanford
  F. Freeman, ii. 448, 473
  Frances, m. Jn. Gustavus Crosbie, iii. 77; iv. 150
  Freeman, ii. 446, 478
  Geo. White, *see* White
  Sir Geo., i. 535
  Sir Jn. Godfrey, vicar of Wartling and Bodiam, ix. 265
  Lambrook, dean of Chich., ii. 51*; iii. 126; iv. 39; ix. 242
  Marg., w. of Lambrook, m. 2 Thos. Briggs, ix. 242
  Sam. Webb, vii. 76
  W.W., vii. 76
  Sir Wm. (fl. 1551), vii. 76
  Sir Wm. (fl. 1676), ii. 441; iv. 62, 204
  Wm. (fl. 1835), ii. 238
  Wm. Geo. Jas., iii. 126
  ——, vii. 249
Thomas-Stanford museum, *see* Preston
Thompson:
  Geo., vii. 228
  Geo. Alfred, ii. 423
  Rob., ii. 165
  Thos., and his w. Agnes, iv. 52
  Thos., ii. 196 *n*
Thompson's hospital, *see* Petworth
Thomson (Tomson):
  Geo., iii. 145
  Harry Redmond, ii. 434
  Peter, ii. 103
  Mr., ii. 442
Thonicus (Themeus) wood, ii. 297
Thony (Toeni):
  Alice de, m. 1 Guy de Beauchamp, earl of Warwick, 2 Wm. la Zouche, iv. 171
  Ralph de, iv. 171
  Rob. de, iv. 171
  Rog. de, iv. 171
Thorglode, *see* Thurlwood
Thornbrigge, *see* Tonbridge
Thorne, Wm., dean of Chich., ii. 51; iv. 110; vii. 266
Thorneton, *see* Thornton
Thorney:
  Cecily de, m. 1 Wm. Gardin, 2 Gilb. Marshal, iv. 145, 163, 195–6
  Emma de, m. —— de Grenested, iv. 195
  Mabel, w. of Wm. de, iv. 195
  Margery de, m. —— Aguillon, iv. 195
  Maud, w. of Ric. de, iv. 195
  Ric. de, iv. 195
  Wm. de, iv. 195–6
Thorney (Cambs.), abbey, ii. 15
  abbot, *see* Gunter
Thorney, East, *see* Wittering, East
Thorney, West (or Thorney Island), i. 52; ii. 43, 84, 127; iv. 126, 181, **195–7**, *196*
  adv., iv. 195, 197
  causeway, iv. 195
  ch., iv. 93 *n*, *194*, 196–7
    accessories, ii. 352, 356, 358, 377
    archit., ii. 339, 350, 371, 374
  Civil War, i. 572
  land reclamation, ii. 220 *n*; iv. 195
  man., ii. 230; iv. 183–5, 195–7
  natural history, i. 45, 177–8, 181–2, 185, 191, 193, 197, 205, 286
  Pilsey (Pilsea), i. 52; ii. 467; iv. 195

pop., ii. 220
R.A.F. station, iv. 195
Thorney channel, *see* Chich.: harbour
Thornhill:
  Rob., iv. 136
  Mr., ii. 458
Thornton (Thorneton):
  Rob., iv. 42
  Sam., vii. 183
  W.A., iv. 208
Thornwell, Ric. de, and his w. Alice, vii. 34
Thoroughgood, Jn., ii. 408
Thorpe (Thorp):
  Edm., rector of Sedlescombe, ii. 39
  Jas., ii. 411
  Jn. (d. 1610), vii. 182
  Jn. (fl. 1631), vii. 59
  Jn. (fl. 1699), and his w. Mary, ix. 221
  Mary, *see* Chambre
  Thomasine, *see* Michelborne
Thorpe (Essex), i. 170
Thrale:
  Hen., and his w. Hester, ii. 450; vii. 249
  Wm., ii. 263
  and see Threele
Three Bridges, *see* Worth
Threele:
  Agnes, w. of Jn., *see* Holden
  Anne, w. of Jn., ix. 56
  Frances, w. of Laur., ix. 56
  Jn. (fl. 1591), vii. 176; ix. 56*
  Jn. (fl. 1655), vii. 177; ix. 56
  Laur., vii. 177; ix. 56
  Marg., vii. 177
  Nic., vii. 196
  Thos., vii. 176–7; ix. 56
  and see Thrale
Throckmorton:
  Baynham, ix. 83
  Clement, vii. 224
  Lucy, m. Wm. Bromley, vii. 224
  Mary, *see* Garton
  Sir Rob., ix. 145
Thumok:
  Joan de, *see* Tracy
  Jn. de, iv. 115
Thundersbarrow Hill, *see* Shoreham
Thurbarn, Jn., ix. 12
Thurlwood (Thorglode), tithing, iv. 218 *n*, 219
Thurnam, Hen., vii. 41
Thurrock (Turok), West (Essex), ii. 113, 410
  prebendary, *see* Cusancia, Wm. de
Thursby:
  Frances, *see* Pelham
  Geo. Augustus, ix. 80
Thursley (Surr.), ii. 328 *n*
Thurstan the reeve, iii. 91
Thurstan (or Awood), Thos., *see* Awood
Thurwell, Elias, and his w. Joan, iv. 216
Thwaytes (Thwaites):
  Edw., ii. 470
  Jn., vii. 280
  Margery, *see* Chauncy
Thyenges, Jn. de, prior of Lewes, ii. 66, 70–1
Thynne, Jas., ix. 198
Tiberius Claudius Trophinus, iii. 63
Ticehurst:
  Jn., ix. 130
  N.F., i. 277, 281
Ticehurst, ii. 43, 325; ix. 251, **252–7**
  adv., ix. 257
  Bardown, iii. 29, 31
  Boarzell, ii. 387; ix. *252*, 253–4
  boundaries, ix. 252
  Bricklehurst, ix. 251, 253–4, 278 *n*
  Cassingham, ix. 220 *n*
  chant., ix. 254
  char., ix. 257
  ch., ii. 30, 76; ix. *252*, 255–7, *256*
    accessories, ii. 353, 356–7
    archit., ii. 336, 346
  dom. archit., ii. 386–7; ix. 252–3

fair, ix. 252
Flimwell, ii. 43; ix. 252, 255
Hammerden (Hamerden), ii. 170 *n*, 173 *n*, 180 *n*; ix. 3, 253–4
Hastings priory estates, ii. 76
Hoadley, ix. 251, 253, 255
insects, i. 168, 179, 216
Institute, ix. 252, 257
iron ind., ix. 252
man., ix. 220 *n*, 253–5
Maplesden, vii. 4; ix. 254–5
nonconf., ix. 257
Pashley, ii. 266, 295, 387; ix. 214, 251, 254–5, 257
pop., ii. 223
prebend, ii. 113
rly., ii. 223 *n*
  station, ix. 252
roads, ix. 257
Rom. rem., iii. 29, 31
Stonegate, ii. 43; ix. 252
union, i. 539
vicars, ix. 257; *and see* Cowley, Thos.,
Whiligh, ix. 253–5
Witherenden, ix. 251, 253
Ticinum (Italy), iii. 60
Tickham (Kent), ii. 447
Tidcombe:
  Anne, w. of Sam., m. 2 Rob. Hooper, vii. 169
  Jn., vii. 169
  Sam., vii. 169 *n*
tide mills, *see* mills
Tidebrook, *see* Wadhurst
Tifeld hund., i. 538
Tilbury (Essex), iv. 50; *and see* Sisteleberg
Tilden, Jas., iv. 152
tile making, ii. 198, 253–4; iv. 69; ix. 13
Tilgate, *see* Worth
Tilgate forest, i. 49, 110, 305; ii. 297, 312; vii. 92
  deer, i. 306
  fossils i. 5, 35–8
  insects, i. 132, 138, 140–3, 145, 147–8, 150–1, 154–5, 157–8, 164–6, 167 *n*, 168–79, 181–2, 184–9, 191–210, 214, 219, 221, 231, 236
Tillard:
  A.E., ii. 472 *n*
  Col., vii. 94
  Mrs., vii. 98
Tilleul, Humph. of, ix. 14
Tilley (Tilly):
  Anne, *see* Young
  Jn., iv. 129
  Wm. Joshua, iv. 237
Tillingham, riv., i. 57; ii. 463–4; iii. 32; ix. 143, 172
Tillington, ii. 43, 81, 388
  ch., ii. 356, 371
  pk., ii. 297
  pop., ii. 218
  quarrying, ii. 232
  rectors, ii. 439
  River (Treve) man., iv. 73, 112, 158, 171
Tillstone, *see* Tilston
Tilly, *see* Tilley
Tilston (Tillstone):
  E.S., vii. 218
  (later Chowne), J.H., ix. 215 *n*
  fam., vii. 218
  arms, vii. *218*
Tilton (in Alciston and Selmeston), ii. 86, 122, 174; ix. 193
timber, *see* crops
timber-framed buildings, *see* architecture: civil and dom.
timber industry, ii. 233–4, 300
Tincommios, king of the Regni, i. 326, 328–9, 331; iii. 9
Tindall (Tyndall):
  H.C.L., *see* Lenox-Tindall
  ——, iii. 53
Tinling, Chas., ii. 167
Tinsley Green, *see* Worth

Tipnoak (Hamfelde, Typenhok), hund.,
i. 538; ii. 219
Tipper:
Wm., iii. 165; vii. 40; ix. 257
——, vii. 62
Tiptoft, Jn., earl of Worcester, iv. 15
Tipton, Edw., vii. 28 n
Tireman:
Cath., w. of Wm., iii. 160
Ric., prebendary of Gates, ii. 408; iii.
130
Wm., iii. 160
Titchfield (Hants), abbot, ii. 90; and see
Simpson, Jn.
Titherington, Arthur Fluitt, rector of
Bramshott (Hants), ii. 431
Titsey (Surr.), iii. 43, 45, 70
Coldharbour Green, iii. 43, 45
Titus, Silas, ii. 163
Toddington, see Lyminster
Toddingworth, see Heathfield: Totting-
worth
Todham, see Easebourne
Toeni, see Thony
Toftes, Thos., ii. 61
Toghill, Moses, warden of St. Mary's
hosp., Chich., ii. 102; vii. 70
Tokyo, South, bp. see Awdry
Tolet, Jn. de, cardinal priest of St. Laur-
ence in Lucina, ii. 411
Toll, Chas., ix. 241
Tollervey, Edw., iv. 127
Tolleshunt D'Arcy (Essex), vii. 50
Tolly, Hugh, rector of Etchingham, ix.
216
tombs, see architecture: ecclesiastical
Tomlinson, Jn., vii. 159
Tomlyng, Ric., vii. 74
Toms, Herbert S., i. 313, 478; iii. 24, 65
Tomson, see Thomson
Tonbridge (Tonebrig):
Gilb. of, ii. 323
Ric. of (de), ii. 311; vii. 194
Wm. de, ii. 87
Tonbridge (Thornbrigge, Tonebrige,
Tonebrigge) (Kent), i. 489*, 496;
ii. 323
Tonclerk, Sim. le, iii. 93
Tonebrig (Tonebrige, Tonebrigge), see
Tonbridge
Tonell, Peter, ii. 69
Tonne, Jn., ii. 250; vii. 191
Toogood, Clara, iv. 237
Tooke:
Edw., vii. 224
Jn. Horne, vii. 248
Toope:
Alice, see Weller
Ric., ix. 197
Topp (Tupp), Rob., ii. 408
Torbay (Devon), iii. 89
Torel, see Torrel
Torkesey, Jn. de, dean of Battle, ix. 111
Torkington, Lawr. Jn., vii. 76
Torquay (Devon), i. 44, 295
Torr, Thos. Jos., vii. 136
Torre (Devon), abbey, canon, see Speer
Torrell (Torel, Tyrrell):
Agnes, w. of Jn., iv. 42
Alice, w. of Humph., see Leventhorp
Alice, w. of Wm., see Baseville
Anne, m. Hen. Joscelyn, iv. 42
Hen. (d. 1480), iv. 42
Hen. (fl. 1502), iv. 42
Humph. (fl. 1480), iv. 42
Humph. (d. 1544), iv. 42
Jn. (d. 1282), iv. 42
Jn. (d. 1329), iv. 42
Jn. (d. 1355), iv. 42
Jn. (fl. 1405), iv. 42
Margery, see Abingdon
Ric., iv. 42
Thos. (fl. 1356), iv. 42
Thos. (fl. 1428), iv. 42
Sir Thos., iv. 42
Wal., iv. 42
Wm., iv. 42
arms, iv. 42

Torrington, Ld., see Byng
Tortington, ii. 42–3, 294, 303
ch., ii. 37, 82
accessories, ii. 356, 359, 368
archit., ii. 327, 330, 339–40, 348–9,
367–8, 372
insects, i. 200, 205–6
man., iv. 41
pop., ii. 217
priory, ii. 58, 75, 82–3, 108, 367
archit., ii. 330, 347, 372
as appropriator, ii. 82; iv. 204–5
canons, ii. 79; vii. 266
char. doles, ii. 191
estates, ii. 294, 330; iv. 42, 99, 123,
199–200
priors, ii. 83
sacrist, see Parker, Ellis
roads to, iii. 46
woods, ii. 184, 196, 199
Torumherd (fl. 12th cent.), iv. 128
Tosard (fl. 1086), vii. 53
Tosear (Toscar, Tosiar), Clement, iv.
96, 170, 187, 233
Tostig, earl, i. 485; ii. 128; iv. 155
Totnore (Totenore, Tottenore) hund., i.
537; ii. 182 n, 227
Tottingworth, see Heathfield
Touchenor, see Tychenor
Toulon (Var, France), ii. 166
Toures, Rob. de, ii. 259
Tourle, Jn., ix. 207
Tournay, Rog. de, ix. 134
Tourner, see Turner
Tourville, count de, see Costantin
Tovy, Ric., abbot of Battle, ii. 55
Tower, Bernard Hen., ii. 433
Towers, Thos., ii. 88
towers, see architecture: ecclesiastical
Towner, Jas., ii. 474
Townsend (Townesend, Townshend):
Hen., vii. 40
Horace, ii. 165–6
and see Farquhar
Towton (Yorks. W.R.), battle, vii. 189
Tracy:
Eliz., Vctss. Tracy, see Keyt
Joan, w. of Wm. de, m. 2 Jas. de
Hampton, 3 Jn. de Thumok, iv.
115
Sir Jn. de, iv. 115, 117
Thos., Vct. Tracy, ix. 207
Sir Wm. de, iv. 115, 117
Wm., master of Playden hosp., ii. 105
Trafford:
Sir Clement Boehm, vii. 281
Jane, m. —— Baker, vii. 281
Jane, w. of Sir Clement, see Southwell
Sigismund, vii. 281
Traheron, Bart., dean of Chich., ii. 48,
51
Trajan, Rom. emperor, ii. 241
Tranckmore, Rob., ii. 155
Tratington, see Trotton
Travers, Thos., vii. 113
Trayton:
Ambrose, i. 522
Edw., vii. 38, 48
Nat., vii. 48–9
treasure trove, ix. 9
treasurer, Seffrid the, see Seffrid
Tredcroft:
Eliz., w. of Nat., vii. 266
Jn., rector of West Grinstead, iv. 155
his w., see Biggs, ——
Nat. (fl. 1702), vii. 266
Nat. (fl. 1808), vii. 266
Tree, Ben Harry Went, ix. 30
Treemaines, see Horsted Keynes
trefoil, see crops
Tregoz (Tregosse, Tregoze):
Alice, w. of Rob., m. 2 Jn. Dewyas,
iv. 164
Hen. (fl. 1310), iv. 41, 167
Hen. (fl. 1331), ii. 82
Hen. (d. by 1387, ? another), iv. 123
Joan, w. of Hen., m. 2 Sir Edw. St.
John, iv. 123

Sir Jn. (fl. 1271), ix. 71 n, 152
Jn. (d. by 1280, ? another), iv.
167
Jn. (fl. 1280), iv. 167
Jn. (d. 1404), ii. 103; iv. 123
Jn. (fl. 1618), iv. 99
Mabel, w. of Jn., ix. 152
Marg., iv. 123
Rob. de (fl. 1196), iv. 167
Rob. (d. by 1280), iv. 167
Sybil, m. Wm. de Grandison, ix. 71,
152
Sybil, w. of Rob. de, iv. 167
Thos., i. 507; iv. 41, 123, 167
fam., iv. 99, 123
arms, iv. 123
Treiponters, Wm., iv. 102
his s., see Emfred
Tremylet, Rob., sacrist of Bosham coll.,
ii. 112
Trenchmere, Alan, ii. 92
Trentham, Vct., see Leveson-Gower
Tréport (Seine-Maritime, France), ii.
268
abbey, ii. 46, 113; ix. 83, 119, 161
abbot, ii. 72
Tresham:
Ann, m. Wm. Thatcher, ix. 191
Geo., iv. 25
Marg., see Lenthall
Sir Thos., iv. 25
Tresse:
Francis, ix. 274
Thos., ix. 274
fam., ix. 274
Trevanion:
Jn., iv. 20
Nic., ii. 165
Treve, see Tillington: River
Trèves, see Trier
Trevor:
A.H., ii. 472–3
Jn. Hampden, Vct. Hampden, ii. 415;
vii. 32
Trew (Trewe):
Jn. (fl. 1521), ii. 252
Jn. (fl. 1559), ii. 23
P.H., ii. 451
Treyford, ii. 16, 43; iv. 3, 6–10, 30–2
adv., iv. 7, 10, 32
chant., ii. 20
ch., iv. 28, 30–2, 32
accessories, ii. 351, 355, 358
archit., ii. 335, 339, 367
dom. archit., ii. 382, 388, 392; iv. 30
earthworks, i. 480; iv. 30
man., iv. 28, 30–2
mill, iv. 30
pk., iv. 31
pop., ii. 221
woodland, iv. 30
Trier (Trèves) (Germany), i. 344; iii. 57
Trimmins, see Horsted Keynes:
Treemaines
Tring (Bucks.), i. 277, 278 n, 293
Trinity College, Cambridge, ii. 424,
430; ix. 131
Trinity College, Dublin, ii. 431
Trinity College, Oxford, ii. 432
Trinity House, London, ii. 145–6, 159,
163
Tristram:
Guy, vii. 41
Wm., ii. 175
Canon, i. 278
Mrs., vii. 41
Troarn (Calvados, France), abbey, ii.
46, 121; iii. 75; iv. 145, 158, 160,
162, 165, 174–5, 179
Trobewyk, see Trubwyk
Troghton, Marg., m. Jn. Gunter, iv.
115
Trollope:
Ant., iv. 13
T., ii. 471 n
Thos., ix. 33
Tromp, Maarten H., ii. 157–8
Tronall, see Trunnell

Trotemenu (Trot):
Denise de, *see* Cauz
Rob., iv. 58
Wm., iv. 58 *n*
Trotton (Tratington), i. 505; ii. 43; iv. 3–4, 23, 25, **32–9**
adv., iv. 38–9
bridge, ii. 394; iv. *29*, 33
chant., iv. 39
chap., iv. 38
ch., iv. *29*, 35–8, *37*
accessories, ii. 350–3, 355, 357–8, *357*, 360–1, 376, 379
archit., ii. 330, 339, 346, 348–50, 375–6, 379
cts., iv. 33
dom. archit., ii. 382; iv. 33–4
Dumpford, iv. 3, 33
adv., iv. 39, 90, 100, 120
chap., iv. 7
hund., *see* Dumpford
man., ii. 173 *n*; iv. 32, 34 *n*, 36
pk., iv. 36
inc., iv. 8
man., ii. 173 *n*; iv. 6, 8–9, 24–5, 28, 33–6, 38
Milland (Mullelond, Tuxlith), ii. 43; iv. 23, 32–3
chap., ii. 379; iv. 39, *39*
ch., iii. 59; iv. 33, 39
man., iv. 36
mill, iv. 33–4
Milland Place, iv. 36
Rom. rem., iii. 3, 58–9
mills, iv. 33
pk., iv. 35
pop., ii. 221
Trotton Place, ii. 392; iv. 33
Tuxlith, *see* Trotton: Milland
woodland, iv. 32
Troup, F.G., iv. 227
Trowbrigge, Jn., ii. 412
Trower, Mr., ii. 454
Trubwyk (Trobewyk):
Jn. de, vii. 159
Maud de, vii. 159
Ric. de, vii. 159
truces, conservators of, ii. 131, 141, 147
truffles, i. 66; ii. 292
trug making, ii. 236; ix. 131
Trumbull, Ant., ix. 191
Trundle, the, *see* Singleton
Trunnell (Tronall):
Jn. (d. 1584), iv. 136
Jn. (d. 1595), iv. 136
Ric. (d. 1610), iv. 136
Ric. (fl. 1650), iv. 136
Sim., ix. 201
Trussel, Wm., iv. 199
Trygge, Thos., iv. 17 *n*
Tryser, Jn., and his w. Agnes, ix. 155
Tucker:
Thos., ix. 168
Wm., ii. 166
Tudor, Owen, iv. 77
Tue, Rob., and his w. Isabel, iv. 51
Tuechener, *see* Tychenor
Tufnell:
Chas., vii. 122
Edw., iv. 53
Mrs., iii. 77
Tufton:
Chas., ix. 61, 169
Hen., earl of Thanet, vii. 238
Jn. (fl. 1560), ix. 160–1
Sir Jn. (d. 1624), ix. 158, 161
Jn., earl of Thanet, i. 522–3; ii. 36; vii. 33, 64, 255; ix. 61, 158, 161, 242, 263
Kath., w. of Wm., vii. 48
Marg., w. of Jn., earl of Thanet, *see* Sackville
Mary, m. Jn. Leveson-Gower, Earl Gower, ii. 439; ix. 61, 146
Nic. (d. 1538), ix. 160, 276
Nic., earl of Thanet (d. 1631), ix. 158, 161, 242, 263
Nic., earl of Thanet (d. 1679), ix. 158,

161, 242, 263
Sackville, vii. 255
Sackville, earl of Thanet, vii. 255
Sarah, w. of Chas., m. 2 Wm. Cave, ix. 61, 169
Thos., earl of Thanet, ii. 437; vii. 33, 48; ix. 146
Thos., ix. 146
fam., ix. 158, 273
arms, vii. *33*
Tullamore (Irel.), i. 296
tumbrell, vii. 2; ix. 201
tumuli, *see* earthworks: barrows
Tunbridge Wells (Kent), i. 57–8; ii. 289–90; vii. 9
natural history, i. 43, 60–1, 65, 182, 213–15, 220
rly., ii. 223 *n*, 240
roads, ii. 266
sport, ii. 448, 452, 470
Tunisia, ii. 155
Tupp, *see* Topp
Tuppen, *see* Tuppin
Tupper:
Eliz., w. of Rog., iii. 162
Martin, i. 319 *n*; iii. 23
Mary, w. of Rog., *see* Doyly
Rog., iii. 162
Tuppin (Tuppen):
Annis, ii. 265 *n*
Hen., ix. 274
Wm., ii. 265 *n*
Turald (fl. 1086), iv. 44
Turbill, Wm., ix. 198
Turevylle:
Anges de, *see* St. John
Jn. de, iv. 199
Turgeys (Turgys):
Rob., iv. 153
Thos., iv. 106
Turgis (fl. 1226), ix. 37
Turgod (fl. 1066), vii. 189
Turgys, *see* Turgeys
Turin (Italy), ix. 215
Turmanowicz, Mr., i. 71
Turnbull, Hugh, dean of Chich., warden of St. Mary's hosp., Chich., ii. 51, 102
Turneham, *see* Turnham
Turner (Tourner, Turnour):
Agnes, w. of Sim., ix. 229
Arthur (fl. 1705), sheriff of Suss., i. 532
Arthur (fl. to 1721, ? another), iv. 144
Chatfield, vii. 28 *n*
Dawson, i. 64
Sir Edw., iv. 144 *n*, 203
Edw. (d. 1736), iv. 144
Edw., Earl Winterton (fl. 1766), iv. 144, 203
Revd. Edw., ii. 313, 316–17, 322; iii. 31
Edw., Earl Winterton (d. 1879), i. 284; ii. 468
Edw., Earl Winterton (fl. 1907), ii. 276
Hen., ix. 146
Jn., ix. 232
(later Turnour Fetherstonhaugh), Keith, iv. 16
Laton Frewen, ix. 146
Mary Ann, ix. 62, 89
Methuselah, ii. 39
Nic., and his w. Mary, iv. 52
Ric. (fl. 1673), ix. 207
Ric. (fl. 1762), and his w. Mary, vii. 190
Ric. And., vii. 235
Sarah, m. Jas. Garth, iv. 144
Sarah, w. of Sir Edw., *see* Grove
Sim. de, ix. 229
Steph., vicar of Arlington, ii. 30
Thos. (fl. 1637), vii. 109
Thos., dean of Cant., ix. 130
Thos. (fl. 1880), ix. 89
——, iv. 23
fam., iv. 144
Turner's Green, *see* Warbleton

Turner's Hill, *see* Worth
Turnham (Turneham):
Rob. de, ii. 86; ix. 139
Steph. of, ix. 14
Turnour, *see* Turner
turnpikes, *see* roads: turnpike
Turok, *see* Thurrock
Turpin:
Hen., iv. 145
Wm., iv. 145
Turstin, son of Engeler, iv. 185
Turton:
Thos., ix. 207
Thos. (another), ix. 207
Turvey, Jas., iv. 10
Tusculum, cardinal bp., *see* Ceccano
Tutte (Tut, Tutt, Tutté):
Eliz., *see* Legay
Francis, ix. 213
Geo., ii. 235
Jn., iv. 193
Randolph, iv. 193
Steph. le, ii. 180
——, ii. 470
Tuttenham, Zachariah, ix. 234
Tuxlith, *see* Trotton: Milland
Twickenham (Mdx.), *see* Strawberry Hill
Twine, *see* Twyne
Twineham, ii. 43–4; vii. 1, 125, **186–91**, 280
adv., vii. 191
ch., vii. *189*, 190–1, *191*
accessories, ii. 250, 359
archit., ii. 334, 337, 339, 346, 350, 379
cts., vii. 190
dom. archit., vii. 133, 186–9, *188*
earthworks, i. 478
Hickstead, ii. 299; iii. 3; vii. 186, 190
Place, ii. 389; iii. 67; vii. 186–7
man., vii. 145, 183, 189–90, 226, 258, 280
mill, vii. 189
nonconf., ii. 38
pop., ii. 224
Rom. rem., iii. 3, 67
Twisden (or Bede), Thos., ii. 55
Twychener, *see* Tychenor
Twyford:
Jn., prior of Sele, ii. 62
Sam. (fl. 1803), iv. 36, 38
Sam. (fl. 1851), iv. 36, 38
Twyne (Twine):
Brian, vicar of Rye, vii. 17
Thos., vii. 17, 40
Twysden:
Sir Wm., ix. 53
Wm. (? another), ix. 88 *n*
Tyacke, Humph., iii. 145
Tyburn, *see* London
Tychenor (Touchenor, Tuechener, Twychener):
Jn., ii. 405–6
Wm., ii. 64
Tye, Jn. atte, vii. 160
Tyes Cross, *see* Grinstead, East
Tyford, Phil. de, *see* Thetford
Tyll:
Rob., iv. 203
——, m. Wm. Rishton, iv. 203
Tylleby, *see* Teuelby
Tyndall, *see* Tindall
Tyneham (Dors.), ii. 82
Tyne's Cross, *see* Grinstead, East: Tyes Cross
Tyntuna (unidentified), ii. 113
Typenhok hund., *see* Tipnoak
Tyreshers:
Reynold de, ix. 197
Ric. de, i. 500
Rog. de, ix. 197
Thos. de, ix. 197
Tyrrell, *see* Torrell
Tyrwhitt:
Bridget, *see* Manners
Eliz., *see* Oxenbridge
Sir Rob. (fl. 1571), ix. 168, 211–12

Tyrwhitt (*cont.*):
  Rob. (d. 1620), ix. 212
  Wm. (d. 1591), ix. 212
  Wm. (fl. 1622), ix. 212–13, 235
Tyxale, Agnes, iv. 136

U.S.A., *see* America
Uckfield, ii. 44, 228, 277, 279; vii. 8
  agric. coll., ii. 288–9
  angling, ii. 464–5
  assarting, ii. 189, 292 *n*
  botany, i. 60, 65, 67
  Budlett's Common, i. 68
  chap., ii. 118, 242 *n*
  char., ii. 438
  Fairhazel Brocks, i. 68
  insects, i. 114, 116, 172, 177, 182–3,
    186, 188–9, 194–5, 197–8, 213,
    215, 218, 220, 224
  man., ii. 292 *n*
  pop., ii. 226
  royal visit, i. 505
  sch., ii. 438
  trades and ind., ii. 254, 256, 259–61
  union, i. 539
  U.D., ii. 228
Uckfield, riv., i. 55
Uckham, *see* Battle
Udimore, ii. 43; iv. 66; ix. 26, 40, 164,
  172–4
  adv., ii. 72; ix. 173–4, 224
  Brede, Little, *see* Brede: Brede, Little
  chap., ix. 223
  char., ix. 174
  ch., ii. 112, 355, 368, 371, 374; ix.
    170, 173, 173–4
  Cockmarling, ix. 165, 172
  dom. archit., ii. 384, 390; ix. 172
  Knellstone, ix. 164, 172
  half hund., ix. 164
  hosp., ix. 172
  land reclamation, ix. 172
  lands in, ii. 426
  mammals, i. 302–3
  man., ii. 173; ix. 172–3, 273
  mills, ix. 168, 173
  nonconf., ix. 172
  pk., ix. 173, 273
  pop., ii. 222
  roads, ix. 172
  royal visit, i. 505
  vicar, *see* Ranulph
  vicarage, ii. 9
Udny:
  Archbould, iii. 145
  Ernest, iii. 146
  Sarah, iii. 145
Uffington (Berks.), i. 324
Ufford:
  Edm. de, vii. 175
  Sybil, *see* Pierpoint
  arms, ix. 135
Ukfeld, Arnold de, ii. 261
Ulbald (fl. 1066), ix. 180
Ulbert (fl. 12th cent.), ii. 112
Uleley (Uleleye), *see* Ashdown forest
Ulf, iv. 211
Ulham, Siward de, iv. 237
Ulmer, ix. 82, 176
Ulnod, iv. 51
Ulstan, iv. 115
Ultyng, Jn., abbot of Durford, ii. 90–1
Ulvehola wood (unidentified), ii. 298
Ulveva, vii. 84 *n*
Ulvric, iv. 65
Ulward (fl. 1066), vii. 33, 253
Ulward (fl. 1086), ix. 82
Ulwin, ix. 279
Ul-, *and see* Wul-, Wulf-
Undersheld:
  Jn., ii. 259
  Sim., ii. 259
Underyng, *see* Chich.: harbour
Unitarians, iii. 168; vii. 42–3; ix. 112
United States *see* America
University College, Oxford, ii. 420, 434;
  ix. 148
Unredisditch, *see* Bremere Rife

Unwin (Onewyne, Onwyn):
  Jn., iv. 25, 29
  Rob., ix. 53, 56
  W.C., i. 43, 59
  and see Fisher Unwin
Upchurch ware, *see* Romano-British
  Sussex: pottery
Upcott, Arthur Wm., ii. 437
Upnatley (Hants), iv. 70
Uppark, *see* Harting: Up Park
Upperton, Jos., iv. 163
Upperton (in Eastbourne), *see* East-
  bourne
Upperton (in Harting), *see* Harting
Upton:
  Jn., ix. 246
  Rob. de, iv. 17
  Wal. de, iv. 17
Upton, *see* Harting: Upperton
Upwaltham, *see* Waltham, Up
Upwick, *see* Hove
Urban V, pope, iii. 92
Urban VI, pope, ii. 120, 398
Uridge:
  Eliz., m. Jn. North, vii. 59 *n*
  Nic., and his w. Anne, vii. 59 *n*
  Ric., vii. 59 *n*
Urry:
  Alice, m. Sir Thos. Hoo, ix. 196
  Jn., vii. 177
  Wal., ix. 196
  Willelme, *see* Burchester
Usbornes, *see* Osborne
Utrecht (Netherlands), peace of, ii. 164
Utterson:
  Edw. Vernon, iv. 83
  Jn., iv. 23, 64–5, 83–4
Uvedale:
  Sir Edm., iv. 80
  Eliz., vii. 196
  Eliz., w. of Thos., *see* Foxle
  Jn. de, iv. 168
  Mary, *see* Browne
  Rob., vii. 196
  Sybil de, *see* Brocas
  Thos. (fl. 1446), iv. 171
  Thos. (fl. 1547), iv. 163
Uxbridge, earl of, *see* Paget, Hen. Wm.

Vacher:
  Herb. Perkins, iv. 128
  Thos. Brittain, iv. 127–8, 224
vagrancy, ii. 194–6, 210–11
Vaisseler, Wm. le, ii. 230; *and see* Ves-
  seler
Valdoe, *see* Westhampnett
Vale Royal (Ches.), abbey, iv. 122
  abbot, iv. 127
Valence:
  Aymer de, bp. of Winchester, i. 495
  Aymer (Aylmer) de, earl of
    Pembroke, ix. 85; vii. 180
  Joan de, *see* Say
  Mary, *see* St. Pol
  Steph. de, ix. 133
  Wm. de, earl of Pembroke, i. 495;
    498–9; ii. 60
Valentine, abbot of Durford, ii. 91
Valentinian, Rom. emperor, i. 337
Vallance, Brooke, ii. 450
Valle, Jn. de, prior of Wilmington, ii.
  123
Valle Pironis:
  Eustace de, iv. 111
  Mary de, m. —— Aguillon, iv. 111
Valoynes (Valoignes):
  Ladereyna de, *see* Baseville
  Waresius de, ii. 136
  Wm. de, iv. 42, 171
Van Dyck, Sir Ant., ix. 126
Vane:
  Cath., dchss. of Cleveland, ix. 118
  Ld. Harry, duke of Cleveland, ix.
    105–6, 111, 273
  Oliver de, ix. 278
Vanheythmpson:
  Delme, vii. 227
  Eliz., *see* Levinge

Vardon, H., ii. 478
Varenne, *see* Warenne
Varndell, S.W., ii. 453
Vaughan:
  Anne, *see* Pickering
  Blanche, m. Ric. Covert, vii. 185
  Eleanor, *see* Arundel
  Geo., ii. 20
  Jas., prebendary of Hova Villa, iii. 123
  Jn. (? two of this name), i. 517–18;
    vii. 34, 258
  Thos., iv. 92, 112, 168
  ——, ii. 28
vaulting, *see* architecture: ecclesiastical
Vaux:
  Eliz., m. Hen. Bowyer, vii. 150, 162
  arms, vii. 150
Vaux de Cernay, abbot, *see* Theobald,
  St.
Vaver, fam., arms, vii. 186
Veal, Jos., ii. 166
Veautrey (Voytrer), Hugh, master of
  hosp. of St. Jas. and St. Mary,
  Chich., ii. 100
Veer, Rob., iv. 174 *n*
Vegierski, Mr., ii. 456
Velingham, *see* Belyncham
Velu, Harold le, ii. 174
Venables, Ric., ix. 157, 178
Venta Belgarum, *see* Winchester
Ventnor (I.W.), ii. 335; iv. 138
Venus, iii. 17, 20
Verdley (Verdly), *see* Fernhurst
Verdon, Lady Maud de, iv. 95
Vere:
  Eliz. de, *see* Scrope
  Sir Francis, i. 518
  Joan de, m. Wm. de Warenne, iv.
    144 *n*
  Jn. de, earl of Oxford, vii. 110
  arms, ix. 216
Veretot, Hugh de, ii. 234; ix. 169
Verica, i. 326, 328, 330–1
vernacular architecture, *see* architecture:
  civil and dom.
Vernetty, Sarah, *see* Norton
Verney:
  Jn., Ld. Willoughby de Broke, iv.
    101, 104
  Sir Thos., iii. 87–8
Vernon:
  Edw., ii. 160
  G.F., ii. 472
  Geo. Venables, Ld. Vernon, ii. 440;
    vii. 89
  Louisa Barbara, *see* Mansell
  Mr., ii. 454
  fam., vii. 88
  and see Chitty and Vernon
Vernon Harcourt, *see* Harcourt
Verrall (Verral):
  Araunah, vii. 24 *n*
  Edw., vii. 28 *n*
  Frank, vii. 45 *n*, 48
  G.H., i. 210
  Geo., vii. 37
  R.R., ii. 284
  Wm., vii. 48
  ——, ii. 415, 475
Vert woods, *see* Laughton
Verulamium, *see* St. Albans
Veselir, *see* Vesseler
Vespasian, Rom. emperor, i. 481; ii.
  241, 362; iii. 1, 19, 30, 50
Vesseler (Veselir):
  Alice le, m. Jn. de Elkham, iv. 4–5
  Jn. le, rector of Chithurst, iv. 4, 6
  Jn. le, iv. 4–5
  Juliana le, iv. 5
  Sir Rob., iv. 5
  Rob., his s., iv. 5
  Rob. (fl. 1320), iv. 4–5
  Wm. le (? two of this name), ii. 89; iv.
    4–5
  fam., iv. 4
  and see Vaisseler
Veulettes (Wylet) (Seine-Maritime,
  France), ii. 140

Veysey, Jn., bp. of Exeter, iv. 189
vicar, Rob. the, see Robert
Vicarye, ——, vii. 96 n
vice-admirals of counties, ii. 131, 141, 147–8
Vickers, Thos., vicar of Cuckfield, ii. 416 n, 420–1
Vickers, see Naylor, Vickers & Co.
Victoria, queen, ii. 204, 236, 423, 426, 436; vii. 250; ix. 5
Vidal, Emeric Essex, vii. 57
Vidler, L.A., ix. 56
Vienne (Vyenne):
    Jean de, ii. 139; ix. 10
    Luke de, ii. 185
Vigo (Spain), ii. 165
Vigor:
    Jane, see Goodwin
    Wm., iv. 62
Vilers (Vylers):
    Alan de, iv. 30
    Hawise de, m. Laur. Basset, iv. 41
    Joan de, m. —— de Berwick, iv. 31
    Joan de, w. of Nic., iv. 31
    Jn. de, iv. 31
    Nic. de (fl. to 1315), iv. 28, 31
    Nic. de (fl. 1344), iv. 31
    Pain de, iv. 30
    Ric. de, iv. 31
    Rob. de (d. c. 1223), iv. 28, 30–1, 167
    Rob. de (d. 1237), iv. 31
    Rob. de (fl. 1278), iv. 31
    Rob. de (fl. 1347), iv. 31
    Wm. de (fl. 1278), iv. 31
    Wm. de (fl. 1347), iv. 31
    fam., iv. 30
Vilesent (unidentified), chap., ii. 113
villas, see Romano-British Sussex: country hos.
Villiace, Peter de, prior of Lewes, ii. 70
Villiers:
    Barbara, dchss. of Cleveland, ix. 134
    Frances, Lady Jersey, vii. 249
    Geo., duke of Buckingham, ii. 155
    Geo. Child-, earl of Jersey, ii. 455, 458
    Wm., Ld. Grandison, i. 522
Vinall:
    Anne, w. of Wm., see Farrington
    Anne, w. of Wm. (another), vii. 60 n
    Eliz., vii. 58
    Eliz., w. of Wm., iv. 212
    Jn., vii. 55 n, 142, 226
    Thos. (d. 1630), vii. 226
    Thos. (fl. 1630), vii. 226
    Wm. (fl. after 1671), iv. 212
    Wm. (d. c. 1680, another), vii. 58, 60 n, 142
    Wm. (fl. 1717), vii. 58, 142, 256
Vincenesium, see Winchelsea
Vincent, dean of Hastings coll., ii. 114, 117
Vincent:
    Barbara, ix. 191
    Sir E., ii. 460
Vine, Steph., iii. 42–3
Viny:
    Eliz., ix. 154
    Jn., ix. 154
    Jos., ix. 154
    Thos., ix. 154
violin making, ii. 300
Vipasca (Spain), iii. 30
Virgil, ii. 406, 419
Virginia (U.S.A.), ii. 201
Virzilini, Jacomo, ii. 255
Visigoths, i. 347
Vistynden (Fistinden), Jn., ix. 113
Viterbo (Italy), ii. 11
Vody, Eliz., ii. 99
Voytrer, see Veautrey
Vyenne, see Vienne
Vylers, see Vilers

W., abbot of Durford, ii. 91
Wacelyn:
    Jn., ix. 266
    Maud, m. Jn. de Parrok, 2 Ric. de

Coding, ix. 266
Nichola, m. Hen. de Shernedene, ix. 266
Nic., ix. 266 n
Waddington:
    Edw., bp. of Chich., iii. 126, 148–9
    Frances, see Newey
    arms, iii. 148
Wade:
    Geo. Frank Graham Rochfort, iv. 188
    Jn., dean of Hastings coll., ii. 116–17
    Mary Rochfort, iv. 188
    Wm. (fl. 1231), ii. 234
    Wm. (fl. 1740), ii. 408
Wadeham:
    Jas. de, iv. 152 n
    Sarah de, iv. 152 n
Wader, Ralph of, i. 487
Wadeson, Ric., ix. 178
Wadham College, Oxford, ii. 431
Wadhurst, ii. 44, 197, 252, 252; ix. 1, 193, 251, 257
    assarting, ii. 189
    char., ii. 438
    ch., ii. 118, 242 n, 336, 346, 349, 357, 360
    farmers' club, ii. 289
    geology, ii. 243
    Horsley, i. 124, 127
    man., ii. 178
    natural history, i. 213–14, 302
    pop., ii. 226
    rly., ii. 226 n
    Shoesmiths, ii. 387
    Tidebrook, ii. 44
    trades and ind., ii. 259, 296; ix. 259
Wadman, E.J., ii. 280
wages:
    agricultural, ii. 181–3, 198–9, 206, 209, 213–14, 287
    industrial, ii. 214
Wagner, Hen., vii. 263
waifs and strays, right of, vii. 254, 271; ix. 68
Wailes of Newcastle, iii. 137
wainbote, ii. 294, 309–10
Wainway Creek, iv. 62–3, 69, 149
Wakefield:
    Ant., iv. 43, 63, 151
    Ric., ix. 28
    Thos., ii. 250; iv. 60, 84, 93, 113, 138, 165, 236; ix. 23
Wakefield (Yorks. W.R.), ii. 65, 67
Wakeford, Jn. (? two of this name), iii. 162; iv. 189
Wakeham, Sim., ix. 86
Wakehurst:
    Eliz. de, m. Nic. Culpeper, vii. 129, 131; ix. 235, 273
    Eliz., w. of Sir Ric. de, see Echingham
    Jn. de, vii. 129
    Marg. de, m. Ric. Culpeper, vii. 129, 131; ix. 273
    Ric. de (fl. 1309), vii. 129
    Sir Ric. de (d. 1454), ii. 361; vii. 129, 131; ix. 273
    Wm. de (fl. 1235), vii. 129
    Wm. de (fl. 1278), vii. 129
    Wm. de (another), vii. 129
    fam., ii. 387
Wakehurst, Ld., see Loder, G.W.E.
Wakehurst, see Ardingly
Wakeman, Jn., vii. 111
Wakering, Sir Gilb., ix. 146
    ? his w., see Hewett, Eliz.
Wakle, see Wykley
Walberton, ii. 42–3, 382; iv. 109 n
    Avisford, ii. 303; iii. 4, 15, 46, 49
    hund., q.v.
    insects, i. 117, 201, 215, 227–8, 231, 233
    char., ii. 439; iv. 188
    ch., ii. 7, 56
        accessories, ii. 351, 355, 360, 362
        archit., ii. 329, 334, 339, 346, 349, 365–7, 372
    Civil War, i. 526

glebe, ii. 5
insects, i. 114*, 119, 222, 237
lands in, ii. 56, 81
man., iv. 143
pk., ii. 294, 303
pop., ii. 217
roads to, iii. 46
Rom. rem., iii. 46, 67
sch., ii. 439
tithes, ii. 263
vicarage, ii. 9
Walcheren (Netherlands), i. 536
Walcott, Mackenzie, iii. 109–13, 115 n, 119, 128 n, 131, 132 n, 133 n, 142, 144, 158–9
Waldeby, Jn. de, master of Playden hosp., ii. 105
Waldegrave:
    Frances Eliz. Anne, Ctss. Waldegrave, ix. 178
    Sarah, Ctss. Waldegrave, see Milward
    fam., ix. 22
Walden, Geo., prior of Shulbred, ii. 82
Walden, Ld. Howard de, see Ellis, Fred. Geo.
Walderton, see Stoughton
Waldeshef, Wal., ii. 316
Waldron, i. 6; ii. 43–4, 313
    botany, i. 44
    ch., ii. 48, 339, 348, 351, 355, 376–8
    Claveridge forest, q.v.
    Cross-in-Hand, i. 55–7
    dom. archit., ii. 334, 387
    earthworks, i. 478
    (or Woodland) forest, ii. 297, 317
    Heronsdale (Heringdales), ii. 387
    Horam (Horeham), i. 48, 50; ii. 387
    inc., ii. 190
    man., ii. 317; ix. 193
    pop., ii. 227
    Possingworth (Passingworth), i. 56, 331; ii. 387
    prehist. rem., i. 331
    sport, ii. 447–8, 468
    Tanners, ii. 387
    trades and ind., ii. 229–30, 241 n, 244–5, 248–9, 253, 257
    Woodland, see Waldron: forest
Wale:
    Nichole, see Bardolf
    Sir Thos., vii. 203–4
Walerand (Waleraund), Rob., ii. 295; iv. 6 n, 58–9; vii. 81
Wales, i. 44, 168 n, 319; ii. 279, 291, 323; iv. 211; vii. 5–7
    princes of, see Edward II; Edward VII; George II; George IV; Henry V; Henry, prince of Wales
    wars with, see wars
Walesbeach (Walesbeech), see Grinstead, East
Waleys, see Wallace
Walford, Hen., ii. 432
Walheath, see Ashdown forest
Waliland:
    Geof. de, ix. 267
    Jn. de, ix. 267
    Mabel de, m. 1 Elias Folet, 2 Steph. de Barmling, ix. 267
    (or Hudiham), Ric. de, ix. 267
    Rob. de, ix. 267
    Wm. de, ix. 267
    Wimarc, w. of Ric., ix. 267
    fam., ix. 267
Walker:
    A.O., i. 259
    Geo. Alfred, iv. 190
    Hen. Fawre, vii. 134
    Hester, iv. 190
    Jn. Russell, warden of St. Mary's hosp., Chich., ii. 102
    R.W., ii. 460
    Wm., master of hosp. of St. Jas. and St. Mary, Chich., iii. 82
    W. Hall, ii. 455
Wall, Jos. B., mayor of Bexhill, ix. 124
wall paintings, see architecture: ecclesiastical

Wallace (Waleys):
Agatha, w. of Hugh le, iv. 105
Euan, iv. 59
(or Standen), Hugh le, iv. 104–5
Jn. le, iv. 105*
Thos. le, ii. 107
fam., i. 513
arms, ix. 216
and see Wallis
Wallands, *see* Lewes
Wallcott:
Beatrice, m. 1 Wal. Buckland, 2 Ant.
Brunning, iv. 35
Chas., iv. 35
Isam (Izan, Jevisham), m. Morgan
Jeffreys, iv. 35; vii. 82
Mary, *see* Foster
Waller:
Edm., M.P. for Hastings, ix. 12
Ric., ii. 309
Sir Thos., ii. 268
Wm., abbot of Battle, ii. 55
Sir Wm., i. 522–5; ii. 35, 50, 157,
248; iii. 87–8, 112; iv. 50; vii. 17
Waller-Bridge, *see* Bridge
Wallingford (Berks.), iii. 83
honor, iii. 85; iv. 123
Wallis:
Jn. (fl. 1583), iii. 160
Jn. (fl. 1643), ix. 273
Sir Provo, iv. 190
Susan, *see* Glydd
and see Wallace
Walloons, ii. 27
Wallop:
Hen., and his w. Eliz., iv. 102
Sir Jn., iv. 102
fam., iv. 102
Wallop, Nether (Hants), ii. 458
Wallyngfelde, Jn. de, abbot of Roberts-
bridge, ii. 73
Walmer (Kent), ii. 395; ix. 185
Walmesley, Bart., ix. 191
Walo (fl. 1086), ix. 79
Walpole:
Horace, ii. 200, 204; ix. 132 n, 217
Sir Rob., ii. 160, 199, 443
Spencer, M.P. for Midhurst, i. 245,
256; iv. 76
Walrond:
Eliz., w. of Hen., iv. 144
Hen., iv. 144, 177
Wm., iv. 177
Walsh (Walshe):
Eliz., w. of Rob., ix. 214
Goddard, ix. 214
Joan, w. of Thos., ix. 214, 220
Rob. (fl. 1539), ix. 214
Sir Rob. (fl. 1612), ix. 214, 220
Thos., ix. 213–14, 220
Walsh (Walshes), *see* Crowborough
Walsingham, Thos., vii. 226
Walsingham (Norf.), priory, ii. 50
Walter, abbot of Robertsbridge, ii. 73
Walter, dean of Chich., ii. 51
Walter, prior of Arundel, ii. 120
Walter, prior of Boxgrove (four of this
name), ii. 59
Walter, prior of Sele, ii. 62
Walter, prior of Tortington, ii. 82–3
Walter, rector of Hoathly, ii. 93
Walter, rector of St. John-sub-Castro,
Lewes, ii. 186
Walter, warden of St. Mary's hosp.,
Chich. (two of this name), ii. 102
Walter, warden of Windham hosp., ii.
108
Walter the park keeper, vii. 104
Walter (fl. 1086), vii. 225
Walter (fl. 1086, ? another), ix. 160
Walter, Rob. s. of, *see* Robert
Walter:
Abel, and his w. Jane, vii. 96
Dan., iii. 126
Hubert, abp. of Cant., ii. 63, 65, 72;
iii. 101 n; iv. 27, 230; ix. 149
Jacob, ii. 200
Walters, Ant., vii. 239

Waltham, Thos. de, iv. 174 n
Waltham (Essex), i. 489; ii. 72, 237
Waltham, Cold, *see* Coldwaltham
Waltham, Up, ii. 43, 121, 303; iv. 133,
174–5
adv., iv. 174–5
ch., iv. 175, *175*
accessories, ii. 351, 355, 367
archit., ii. 339, 342, 350, 367, 372
dom. archit., iv. 174
earthworks, i. 480
man., iv. 58, 145, 174–5
Nomansland, ii. 303*
pk., ii. 294; iv. 174
poor law, ii. 207
pop., ii. 220
prebend, iv. 175, 208
Walton:
Cecily, *see* Okehurst
Rog., i. 518
Wm., iv. 212
Walton (Norf.), ii. 64, 69
Walton (in Bosham), *see* Bosham
Walton-on-the-Naze (Essex), i. 170
Walwer:
Wm., M.P. for Lewes, vii. 9
fam., vii. 9
Wandelmestrei hund., i. 537
Wandle, riv., iii. 38
Wandsworth (London, formerly Surr.),
see Barking
Wane, Anne, m. 1 Jn. Batner, 2 Wm.
Chowne, 3 Magnus Byne, vii. 144
Wanningore, *see* Chiltington, East:
Warningore
Wannock, *see* Jevington
Wansdyke (Wilts.), iii. 34
Wantele, Jn. de, ii. 361
Wanton, Jn. de, ii. 304
Wappelade, Wm., iv. 200
Wappenbury:
Agnes de, m. 1 Ralph de Queneby, 2
(? Ric.) de Beyvill, vii. 229
Joan de, vii. 229
Jn. de, vii. 229
Juliana de, *see* Strange
Margery de, m. 1 Gerard Duredent, 2
(? Rob.) de Wassingle, vii. 229
Ric. de, vii. 229
Thos. de (fl. 1237), vii. 229
Thos. de (fl. after 1248), vii. 229
Thos. de (fl. 1295), vii. 229
Wapsbourne (Wapsburn), *see* Chailey
Warbeck, Perkin, ii. 143
Warbleton:
Agnes de, m. Geof. de St. Leger, ix.
207
Alice, w. of Jn., m. 2 Wal. de Burton,
ix. 206
Eleanor, w. of Thos., ix. 206
Jn. (d. 1332), ix. 206
Jn. (d. 1350), ix. 206
Jn. de (fl. 1368), ix. 206
Juliana, w. of Wm., ix. 206
Kath. de, w. of Jn., ix. 206
Mabel de, ix. 80
Marg., m. —— Puttenham, ix. 206
Margery, *see* Hannys
Maud, w. of Jn., ix. 207
Thos. (fl. 1242), ix. 206–7
Thos. (d. 1317), ix. 206
Thos. de (d. by 1384), ix. 206
Wm. de (d. by 1242), ix. 206
Wm. de (d. 1469), ix. 206, 244
arms, ix. *206*
Warbleton, ii. 7, 43; ix. 125, 193, **204–9**,
233
adv., ix. 209
agric., ix. 206
Bodle Street Green, *q.v.*
Bucksteep, ix. 95, 125, 197, 207, 209
chant., ix. 199, 209
char., ix. 206, 209
ch., ix. *204*, 206, *208*, 208–9
accessories, ii. 117 n, 353, 356, 361,
374
archit., ii. 331, 336, 339, 349, 374,
376–8

dom. archit., ix. 204–6, *205*
Dyll, *q.v.*
earthworks, i. 478
Iwood, ix. 208
man., ix. 91, 206–8, 244
Markly, ii. 41
mills, ix. 206–7
nonconf., ii. 38; ix. 206
pop., ii. 222
prehist. rem., i. 331
priory, ii. 76, 331; ix. 10, 27,
204
rector, ii. 22; ix. 209
rectory, ix. 209
Rushlake Green, ix. 204, 209
trades and ind., ii. 236, 246–7, 263;
ix. 206–7
Turner's Green, i. 57
ward, ix. 1
woodland, ix. 204
Warblington (Hants), iv. 127
Warblinton, Thos. de, ix. 133
Warburton:
Barbara, *see* Lytton
Wm., ix. 212
Ward (Warde):
Agnes, w. of Wm., ix. 255
C.R., iii. 54, 70
Dorothy Nelson, iv. 150
Eleanor, ix. 201
Eliz., m. Wm. Paulet, iii. 163; vii. 37,
157
Geo., vii. 157
Geo. (another), vii. 157
Hen. (d. 1634), vii. 158; ix. 201
Hen. (d. 1664), vii. 158; ix. 201
Jas. Cooke, vii. 158
Jane, m. Hen. Plumer, vii. 158
Jasper, vii. 157
Jn. (fl. 1532), iv. 5
Jn. (fl. 1590), vii. 158
Jn. (d. 1660), vii. 157
Jn. (d. by 1670), vii. 157–8
Jn. (fl. 1702), ii. 165
Jn. (d. 1718), vii. 157
Jn. Wm., earl of Dudley, ii. 203
Mary, *see* Davie
Mary Eliz., vii. 158
Nic., master of Holy Trinity hosp.,
Arundel, ii. 98
Ninian, vii. 132, 158; ix. 201
Ric., vii. 157
T., iii. *27*, 70
Thos. (fl. 1427), ix. 255
Thos. (fl. 1757), ii. 166
W., ii. 468–9
Wm. (fl. 1372), ix. 255
Wm. (fl. 1547), vii. 263
arms, vii. *157*; ix. 216
Wardedieu (Wardedyeu):
Alice, m. —— Harmer, ix. 263
Eliz., m. Sir Edw. Dalingridge, ix.
263
Sir Hen., ix. 127–8, 262
Hen. (another), ix. 263
Jn. (fl. 1347), ix. 82, 237, 263
Jn. (d. by 1378), ix. 263
Jn. (another), ix. 263 n
Nic., ix. 237, 262
Nic., dean of South Malling coll., ii.
119
Parnel, w. of Thos., ix. 119
Ric., ix. 237, 263
Thos., ix. 119
Wm., ix. 263
fam., ix. 259, 264
arms, ix. *262*
Warden:
Francis, vii. 121, 159
Jn. (fl. 1627), ii. 420
Jn. (d. 1650), vii. 159
Jn. (fl. 1662), vii. 159–60
(later Sergison), Mic., *see* Sergison
Prudence, *see* Sergison
(later Sergison), Thos., *see* Sergison
Wardley, *see* Iping
Wardroper, Chas, ix. 220
Wardur, *see* Sidlesham

Ware:
Hen., bp. of Chich., iii. 133 n
Rog. le, ii. 181
Wareham, Ranulf of, bp. of Chich., ii. 9; iii. 116; iv. 34; ix. 189
Warehead Farm, see Halnaker
Warelwast, Wm., bp. of Exeter, ii. 110
Warenge, Jn. de, prior of Boxgrove, ii. 59
Warenne:
Alice (Alesia), m. Edm. FitzAlan, earl of Arundel, iii. 144 n; vii. 3
Alice, w. of Jn. de, earl of Surrey, see Lusignan
Alice, w. of Rainald de, see Wormegay
Beatrice de, m. Doun Bardolf, vii. 80, 110
Beatrice, w. of Wm. de, see Pierpoint
Edith de, m. Dru de Monceaux, vii. 213; ix. 133 n
Ela de, m. Wm. Fitzwilliam, vii. 235
Gundrada de, see Gundrada
Hamelin de, earl of Surrey, ii. 65; vii. 2, 228, 235, 258, 279
Isabel de, m. 1 Wm., count of Mortain and Boulogne, 2 Hamelin, Earl Warenne, ii. 69 n; vii. 2
Isabel de, m. Gilb. de Laigle, vii. 71
Isabel de, m. Hugh d'Aubigny, earl of Arundel, ii. 93; iv. 122, 127
Joan, w. of Jn. de, earl of Surrey, see Bar
Joan, w. of Wm. de, see Vere
Jn. de, earl of Surrey (d. 1304), i. 496, 498–9, 501–4; ii. 66–7, 146, 171, 185, 190, 295, 311; vii. 2–3, 7, 21, 30 n, 36, 66, 73, 104–5, 133–4, 138, 189, 195–6, 226, 234, 253, 283; ix. 120, 133
Jn. de, earl of Surrey (d. 1347), i. 508; ii. 67–8, 92–3, 296, 312; vii. 3, 20 n, 23, 104, 115, 144, 156, 176, 195, 212, 253; ix. 15, 153
Maud de, see Marshal
Phil. de, ii. 69 n
Rainald (Reg.), de, ii. 69 n; vii. 1, 24, 80, 105, 110, 113, 234, 281, 283
Thos. de, vii. 3
Wm. de, earl of Surrey (d. 1088), ii. 4–5, 64–5, 191, 294, 360, 395; iv. 1, 185; vii. 1–2, 14–15, 19, 33–4, 36, 43, 45, 48–9, 51, 55, 67, 70, 80, 84, 104, 108, 110, 114, 116–17, 120, 141, 156, 175, 189, 201, 204, 206, 209, 213, 216–17, 224–6, 228, 253, 255, 274–5, 279–82
his w., see Gundrada
Wm. de, earl of Surrey (d. 1138), ii. 65, 104; vii. 2, 31, 40–1, 48, 58, 60, 65, 69, 71, 73, 83, 89, 91, 95, 99, 101, 105, 108, 123, 132, 135, 144, 163, 171, 194, 211, 214, 217–19, 225–6, 228, 234, 236, 244, 255, 262, 275, 279, 281, 283
Wm., earl of Surrey (d. 1149), vii. 1–2, 24, 55, 58, 214, 253
Wm. de (d. by 1178), vii. 34, 99, 110, 228, 255, 286
Wm. de, earl of Surrey (d. 1240), i. 491–4; ii. 66, 77, 92; iv. 183; vii. 2, 35–6, 64, 66, 71, 85, 175, 203; ix. 37
Wm. de (d. 1286), iii. 144 n; vii. 3
fam., ii. 103; vii. 1, 39, 179, 228–9
arms, vii. 2, 49, 131, 135, 199
and see Warren
Warenne, earls, ii. 7, 65, 311, 332; vii. 2, 242, 244, 251; and see Warenne, fam., William, count of Mortain
Warenne (Varenne, Seine-Inférieure, France), i. 504
Warham:
Eustache de, see Planchis
(or Wykes), Hubert de, iv. 171
Wm., abp. of Cant., ii. 54, 118
and see Wareham
Warin, iv. 171, 204
Warke, Ld. Grey of, see Grey, Ford;

Grey, Ralph
Warkenby, Hugh le, iv. 170
Warminghurst, i. 7; ii. 39 n, 43, 230, 235
ballivate, ii. 46, **124**
ch., ii. 351, 355, 358–9, 361
Heath Common, q.v.
pk., ii. 297
pop., ii. 219
Warneford:
Isabel de, iv. 196
Ric. de, iv. 196
Warner, abbot of Battle, ii. 53, 55
Warner, prior of Arundel, ii. 120
Warner (fl. 1086), vii. 33
Warner:
Jn., and his w. Isabel, ix. 154
Jn., rector of Sedlescombe, ix. 279 n
Ric., ii. 246
Warner, Jn. & Sons, iv. 151; vii. 132; ix. 113
Warnham, ii. 43; iv. 16
Bailinghill, ii. 389
Broomhall, ii. 389*
ch., ii. 63, 339–40, 356, 358, 362, 378–9
Court, i. 278, 306; ii. 276
dom. archit., ii. 389–90, 392–3
Ends Place, ii. 389
Graylands, i. 302
hunting, i. 306; ii. 299, 449
Kingsfold, i. 306
natural history, i. 180, 279, 286, 288, 290–1, 294–5, 297, 301, 303–4
nonconf., ii. 41
pk., ii. 299, 310
pop., ii. 219
vicarage, ii. 8
Warningcamp:
curate, ii. 33
dom. archit., ii. 388
insects, i. 172, 194, 209
man., ii. 109; iv. 58, 174
nonconf., ii. 33
pop., ii. 218
Warninglid, see Slaugham
Warningore, see Chiltington, East
Warr (Warre):
Eleanor de la, see Mowbray
Eliz., w. of Sir Jn. de la, vii. 283
Joan de la, m. Sir Thos. West, vii. 283
Joan, w. of Jn., Ld. de la Warr, see Greyly
Jn. la (d. c. 1274), i. 501; vii. 225
Jn., Ld. de la Warr (d. 1347), vii. 99, 283, 286
Sir Jn. la (d. by 1352), iv. 159
Sir Jn. de la (d. 1398), vii. 283
Marg. la, see Holland
Olimpia de la, see Fokington
Sir Rog. de la, vii. 225, 283
Thos., Ld. de la Warr, vii. 258, 276 n, 283
arms, vii. 187
Warr:
Lds. de la, see Warr; West
Earls de la, see Sackville; Sackville-West; West, Jn.
Warre, see Warr
Warren (Waryn):
Agnes, m. Wm. Bassano, vii. 106
E.P., vii. 272
Hen., vii. 106
Jn. Raymond, vii. 186
Laur., ii. 436
Ric., see Adeane
Rob., iii. 95
Thos., master of hosp. of St. Jas. and St. Mary, Chich., ii. 100
Thos., ii. 165
and see Warenne
Warren, Messrs. J.C., ii. 238
Warren furnace, see Worth
Warrengore, see Chiltington, East: Warningore
Warrington, P.E., vii. 124
wars:
American Independence, ii. 161; iv. 54

Anglo-Saxon, i. 482
Barons', ix. 133, 180, 197, 217, 252
Civil, i. 521–8; ii. 35–7, 39, 50, 157, 199, 229, 234, 248, 298, 305, 312, 318; iii. 99; iv. 16, 50, 121; vii. 2, 5, 16–17, 254; ix. 61, 214
Clubmen's rising, i. 525–6; iii. 88
Crimean, ix. 56
Dutch, i. 516–18; ii. 132, 153, 157–60, 248; iii. 88; ix. 10
Egypt, i. 536
First World War, iv. 210
French revolutionary, i. 533; ii. 161–3, 199, 211
Hundred Years, ix. 10, 15, 23, 40, 66–7, 69–70, 133, 144, 206, 259
Indian mutiny, i. 536
of the Roses, ii. 143; ix. 146, 263
of 1215, ix. 10
of 1340, iv. 162
Seven Years, ii. 160
South African, i. 535–6
Spanish Succession, ii. 159
with France, i. 510; ii. 54, 57, 60, 67–8, 104, 108, 116, 120–2, 130–2, 135, 138–45, 150, 156, 159–61, 242, 398; iii. 86; iv. 156, 162; ix. 2, 10, 15, 24, 26, 40, 49, 52, 54, 69, 71 n, 212, 244; and see wars: Hundred Years; wars: French revolutionary; wars: Seven Years; wars: Spanish Succession
with Scotland, ii. 87, 131–2, 134–8, 141, 144–5, 150; ix. 212
with Spain, ii. 152–5, 161; ix. 5, 10; and see Spain: Armada
with Wales, ii. 131; ix. 2
Wartling, ii. 43–4, 324; ix. 125, 131, **137–41**
adv., ix. 141
Boreham, ix. 125, 128, 140
Bridge, i. 478–9
Street, ii. 386, 452
chap., ii. 112, 410; ix. 140
char., ix. 141
ch., ii. 353; ix. *140*, 140–1
Cowden, ix. 138–9, 233
earthworks, i. 478
hare hunting, ii. 452
mans., ii. 174–5, 176 n, 179–80, 182–3, 187; ix. 84, 137–40, 177, 207, 228
mkt., ii. 187; ix. 138
nonconf., ix. 141
Oldcourt, ix. 139, 177
pop., ii. 222
prebend, ii. 113, 410; ix. 141, 246, 249
prehist. rem., i. 331
roads, ix. 137
Rockland (Rokeland), ix. 139
tithes, ii. 410
vicars, see Shore, Phil.; Thomas, Sir Jn. Godfrey
ward, ix. 1
Windmill Hill, q.v.
woodland, ix. 137
Warwick, Jas., vii. 57
Warwick, earls of, see Beauchamp; Dudley, Sir Jn.; Nevill, Ric.
Warwick, ii. 398
Warwickshire, i. 68; ii. 447; iv. 69
Fenny Compton, rector, see Bigg, Chas.
Whichford, rector, see Pininger
and see Birmingham; Kenilworth; Maxstoke; Rugby; Solihull; Stoneleigh; Stratford; Warwick
Waryn, see Warren
Washington:
Geo., vii. 155
Laur., vii. 155
Marg., see Butler
Washington, i. 53; ii. 43
Chanctonbury, i. 222*, 348; ii. 300
Ring, i. 458, *462*, 462–4, 470, 480; iii. 3, 52–3
ch., ii. 60, 250, 339, 378

Washington (*cont.*):
fossils, i. 30, 35
Heath Common, *q.v.*
Highden, i. 53, 479
insects, i. 199–200
pop., ii. 219
Rom. rem., iii. 3, 67
tithes, ii. 60
trades and ind., ii. 232, 250
vicar, *see* Parkhurst, Rob.
Washington Hill, iii. 67
Washington Ho., ii. 29
Washlingstone hund. (Kent), ii. 227 *n*
Wassingle:
Marg. de, vii. 230
Margery de, *see* Wappenbury
Rob. de, vii. 229
Watcombe, *see* Beckley
Watenhull, Jn. de, ii. 137
Waterdown forest, i. 49–50, 58, 61; ii. 323–4
Watere (Waterer):
Cecily atte, *see* Weston
Hen., ii. 263
Wm. atte, iv. 129 *n*
Waterford (Irel.), ii. 165
Watergate, Wm. de, iv. 114–15
Watergate (in Emsworth), *see* Emsworth
Watergate (in Southover), *see* Southover
Watergate Hanger, *see* Marden, Up
Waterloo (Belgium), battle, i. 536
Waterman (Watreman):
Emelyn, ii. 416
(or Smith), Jn., *see* Smith
Ralph, sacrist of Bosham coll., ii. 112
Waters, Wal., and his w. Eliz., ix. 143
Watersfield:
Agnes, *see* Page
Jn. (sr.), iv. 153
Jn. (jr.), iv. 153
Thos., iv. 153
Watersfield, *see* Coldwaltham
Watevile:
Maud de, m. Ralph de Cheney, vii. 203
Wm. de, vii. 80, 141–2, 179, 202–3, 253, 255, 262
Watkins (Watkin):
J., ii. 166
W.T., iii. 15, 17 *n*
Watkinson:
Eliz., *see* Bateman
Hen. (sr.), iv. 35
Hen. (jr.), iv. 35; vii. 82, 101
Watling Street, iii. 45
Watlynton, Godfrey, iv. 229
Watreman, *see* Waterman
Watson:
Anne, *see* Luxford
Ant., bp. of Chich., ii. 31
Cordell, *see* Infield
Eliz., m. Wm. Davies, vii. 284
Geo. (fl. 1735), vii. 74
Geo. (fl. *c.* 1770), ii. 166
H.C., i. 44
Jn. (fl. 1635), vii. 168
Jn. (fl. 1697), vii. 74
Jn. (d. 1722), vii. 74
Jn. (fl. 1735), and his w. Hannah, vii. 74
R.A., vii. 186
Thos., vii. 74
Wm. (fl. 1670), ix. 100
Wm. (fl. 1750), vii. 284
Watson-Wentworth, Chas., marquess of Rockingham, ii. 443
Watts:
Anna, iii. 145
Giles, ix. 111
Jn., iii. 147
Mary, w. of Whitwood
W.E.M., ii. 447, 470 *n*
Waukeford, Jn. de, ii. 316
Wauncy:
Felice de, *see* Hareng
Nic. de, iv. 168
Wm. de, iv. 58

Wauton:
Sir Jn. de, ii. 323
fam., ii. 323
Wavell:
Edith, m. Thos. Arnold, iv. 129
Edith, w. of Wm., iv. 129
Jane, m. Geo. Bowler, iv. 129
Ric., iv. 129
Wm., iv. 129
Waverley (Surr.), iv. 24 *n*, 25
abbey, iv. 25, 76, 98–9
abbot, *see* William
Way, Lewis, iv. 121–2, 127, 131
Wayflete (Woflet) (unidentified), iv. 198
Waylett, Jn., ii. 249; vii. 37; ix. 199
Waymark, Thos., ii. 467
Waynflete:
(or Patten), Jn., dean of Chich., ii. 51
Wm., bp. of Winchester, ii. 61–2, 81, 421
Wayte, Honour, iv. 190
Weald, i. *frontispiece*, 55, 333; iii. 1–2, 10, 46, 52
birds, i. 273, 281, 283, 285–6, 290, 292
botany, i. 49, 59–60
fossils, i. 27
geology, i. 1–2, 17, 25, 43, 52, 57
insects, i. 167, 188
iron ind., i. 322
weapons, Anglo-Saxon, *see* Anglo-Saxon remains
weatherboarding, *see* architecture: civil and dom.
weaving, *see* textile inds.
Webb (Webbe):
Sir Aston, ii. 436; vii. 199
Barbara, *see* Belasye
Sir Jn. (fl. 1692), ix. 121
Jn. (fl. 1715), and his w. Jane, vii. 78
Jn. (fl. 1724), ix. 121
Lucas, ii. 179
Mary, *see* Blomer
Percival, prebendary of Firle, iii. 116
Ric., vii. 105
Wm., vii. 123
fam., vii. 218
Webber:
Chas. (fl. 1756), ii. 166
Chas., warden of St. Mary's hosp., Chich., ii. 102, 403, 409
Chas. (another), warden of St. Mary's hosp., Chich., ii. 102
Webster:
Sir Augustus, ii. 447, 470 *n*; ix. 106
Sir Augustus F., ix. 106, 111
Sir Godfrey (d. 1780), ix. 106, 113, 264
Sir Godfrey (d. 1800), ii. 238; ix. 264
Sir Godfrey Vassal, ix. 106, 221, 264, 266
Lucy, ix. 106, 111
Nic., ix. 83
Sir Thos., ii. 238; ix. 20, 26, 106, 113, 141, 221, 246, 264
Sir Whistler, ix. 106, 113, 264
fam., ix. 20, 26, 109, 111, 246, 266
arms, ix. *106, 264*
Webster & Co., iii. 68
Wedmore (Som.), peace of, ii. 126
Weedon (Wedon, Widdon):
Edw., vii. 78
Wm. de, ii. 120, 398
Mrs., ix. 198
Weekes (Wekes):
Carew, M.P. for Arundel, iii. 163
Charity, *see* Hampton
Eliz., ix. 24
Eliz., m. Jn. Bromfield, ix. 83
Jane, m. 1 Edw. Cowper, 2 Wm. Morton, ix. 83
Jane, w. of ——, *see* Davis
Jn. (d. 1680), ix. 83
Jn. (d. 1702), ix. 83
Kath., w. of Carew, iii. 163
Mary, m. Hen. Lawton, ix. 83
Mary, w. of Jn., *see* Gilbert
Oliver, vii. 235

Philippa, *see* Raleigh
Ric. (fl. *c.* 1770), vii. 113
Ric. (fl. 1841), vii. 138
Susanna, ix. 83
Thos., and his w. Margery, ix. 24
fam., ix. 82 *n*
Weelkes, Thos., iii. 90, 134
Weeting (Norf.), Grimes Graves, i. 314, 316
Weghelton, *see* Whelton
Weir:
Archibald, ix. 247
Jenner, i. 165
Wekes, *see* Weekes
Weklintun (unidentified), ii. 113
Welbeck (Notts.), abbey, ii. 330
abbot, ii 90–1; *and see* Berengar
Welch, H. Vyse, ii. 451
Welesmere, *see* Whalesbone
Welewe, Wal. de, sacrist of Bosham coll., ii. 112
Welle, Jn. de, and his w. Idonea, vii. 229
Weller:
Alice, w. of Ric., ? m. 2 Ric. Toope, ix. 197
Jas., vii. 199
Jn., iii. 75 *n*
Jos., ix. 207
Ric., ix. 197
——, iii. 75
fam., ix. 207
Weller-Poley, Thos., iii. 147
Welles, *see* Wells
Wellesbourne, riv., i. 54; vii. 212, 216, 244–5, 268
Wellesley, Arthur, duke of Wellington, vii. 262; ix. 8, 231–2
Wellington (Som.), ii. 433
Wells (Welles):
Alex., ix. 61
Alice, m. Hen. Auchier, ix. 144
Dymoke, vii. 76
Geo., ii. 469, 471
H.G., iv. 13
Joan, m. Jn. Auchier, ix. 144
Jn., prior of Sele, ii. 62
Sir Jn., vii. 158
Jos., ii. 469
Marg., *see* Knelle
(or FitzRobert), Sim. de, *see* Fitz-Robert
W., i. 82
Wm. de, ix. 144
Mr., vicar of Rye, ii. 18
Mr., i. 276
——, ii. 455
Wells (Som.):
archdeacon, *see* FitzRobert
bp. of Bath and, *see* Barlow, Wm.
canons, ii. 121; *and see* Courtenay, Ric.; Oliver, Ric.
Welshe:
Rob., ix. 168
fam., ix. 168
Weltje, ——, vii. 249
Wemyll, Thos. de, i. 509
Weymss, Sir R., vii. 173
Wenden:
Ric. atte, iv. 98
Wm. atte, iv. 98
Wenenc (Wennenc) the priest, ix. 137, 242
Wenenc (fl. 1086, ? the same), ix. 128; *and see* Werenc
Wenestan (fl. 1066), ix. 91, 266, 278
Wenham:
Jn. (fl. 1549), ix. 248
Jn. (fl. *c.* 1620), and his w. Mary, ix. 248
Jn. (fl. 1668), ix. 248
Jn. (d. 1768), vii. 85
Jn., rector of Hamsey, ii. 449; vii. 85
O., ii. 474
Wm. (fl. 1547), ix. 248
Wm. (fl. 1627), ix. 177
fam., ix. 248
arms, ix. *248*
Wenham, *see* Rogate

Wening (fl. *c.* 1100), ii. 52; ix. 91, 94
Wenlock, Much (Salop.), priory, iv. 200
Wenman, J.G., ii. 470
Wennenc, *see* Wenenc
Wentworth, *see* Watson-Wentworth
Wentworth, Baroness, *see* Blunt, Judith Anne Dorothea; King-Noel
Wentworth-FitzWilliam, Selina, *see* Jenkinson
Wepham, Jn. de, sub-prior of Hastings, ii. 76
Wepham, *see* Burpham
Weps:
Jn., vii. 189
Rog. le, vii. 189
Wal., vii. 189
Werenc (fl. 1086), ix. 240; *and see* Wenenc
Werplesburn, *see* Chailey: Wapsbourne
Werth forest, *see* Dallington forest
Werthe, Wm., ix. 267
Wesley, Jn., ii. 41; ix. 61
Wessex (West Saxons), i. 333–4, 343, 346–8, 482; ii. 1, 126
earls, *see* Godwin; Harold
kings, *see* Alfred; Athelstan; Caedwalla; Ceawlin; Ceolwulf; Egbert; Ethelbert; Ethelwulf; Ine; Sigebert
see, ii. 2
West:
Alice, w. of Hen., vii. 6
Alice, w. of Sir Thos., *see* Fitzherbert
And., ix. 198
Anne, *see* Nevill
Ant., iii. 146
Cecily, *see* Bellingham
Eliz., *see* Bonville
Sir Geo. (fl. 1537), vii. 284; ix. 20, 233
Geo. (fl. 1764), vii. 217
(later Sackville-West), Geo. Jn., *see* Sackville-West
Hen., vii. 6, 230
Jas., and his w. Anne, vii. 190
Jas. E., ix. 75
Joan, *see* Warr
Jn., prior of Michelham, ii. 79
Jn., Earl de la Warr (d. 1766), ii. 442–3; vii. 96, 217
Jn., Earl de la Warr (d. 1777), ii. 430; vii. 96, 217
Mary, w. of And., ix. 198
Sir Owen, vii. 284
Sir Reynold, Ld. de la Warr, vii. 283; ix. 202
Ric., Ld. de la Warr, i. 514–15; vii. 283; ix. 202
Sarah, iii. 145
Sir Thos. (d. by 1395), ix. 202
Sir Thos. (d. 1405), ix. 202
Sir Thos. (d. 1417), i. 513; vii. 283; ix. 202
Thos., Ld. de la Warr (d. 1525), ii. 308; iv. 51, 143–4, 177; vii. 85, 87, 284
Thos., Ld. de la Warr (d. 1554), ii. 58–9, 144 *n*, 147, 361; iv. 141 *n*, 142–3, 147–8, 161–2, 165, 177, 199; vii. 284
Thos., Ld. de la Warr (d. 1602), vii. 284
Thos., Ld. de la Warr (d. 1618), ii. 31
Thos. (fl. 1637), vii. 6, 230, 232
Thos. (fl. 1718), vii. 140
Wal., vii. 6 *n*, 157
Wm., Ld. de la Warr, vii. 284
fam., iv. 176
arms, iii. 151; vii. *7*; ix. *117*
and see Sackville-West
West India Dock Co., ii. 166
West Kent hunt, ii. 448
West Sussex County Council, *see* Sussex
West Sussex Golf Club, iii. 64
West Sussex Rly., iii. 71 *n*; iv. 207
Westbece, *see* Battle: Beech
Westborne, Jn., and his w. Anne, ix. 88
Westbourne, ii. 43; iv. 23, 88, **126–32**

Adsdean, iv. 126, 128
adv., iv. 131
Aldsworth, i. 42; iv. 127
man., iv. 114–15, 128–9
botany, i. 67
char., iv. 132
ch., iv. *126*, *130*, 130–1
accessories, ii. 352, 355, 357–8
archit., ii. 339, 372, 378
dom. archit., iv. 113, 126–7
fair, iv. 127
Hermitage, i. 45; ii. 46
Bridge, iv. 126
chap., iv. 131
Hill, iv. 131
inc., iv. 126
man., iv. 115, 121–3, 127–31, 172, 189
mkt., iv. 126–7
ho., iv. 126 *n*
mills, iv. 127, 131
Nutbourne, iv. 126–7
chap., iv. 131
man., iv. 111, 128–9, 131
mill, iv. 127–9
pop., ii. 221
Prinsted, iii. 47, 63; iv. 5, 126–7
man., iv. 127–9
rly., iv. 126
roads, iii. 47; iv. 126
royal visit, ii. 302
Southbourne, i. *318*, 331; ii. 43; iv. 126
ch., iv. 126, 131
tithes, iv. 131
union, i. 539
vicar, *see* Sperling
watercourses, iv. 127, 129
Westbourne (Burne) and Singleton (Silletone), hund., i. 538; ii. 221; iv. 1, **88**, 222
Westbrook (Westbroke, Westbrooke):
Durban, vii. 106
Eliz., m. Thos. Andrews, vii. 284
Eliz., w. of Wm., *see* Houghton
Hen. de, iv. 23
Jn. (d. 1709), vii. 106
Jn. (d. 1788), vii. 106
Nic., iv. 130
Phoebe, m. Thos. Chowne, ix. 214
Ric., iv. 130
Wm. de (fl. 1280), iv. 23
Wm. (fl. 1680), ix. 214
Wm. (fl. 1694), iv. 99, 103, 130
Wm. (d. by 1704), vii. 284
Wm. (d. 1750), vii. 106
Westbrooke, prebendary, ii. 110
Westburton Hill, *see* Bignor
Westdean (E. Suss.), i. 483; ii. 15, 44; iv. 101; ix. 251
Charlston, ii. 122, 381–2, *385*
ch., ii. 122–3
accessories, ii. 352, 356, 361, 376–7
archit., ii. 332, 337, 365, 377
dom. archit., ii. 382–3, *385*
Exceit, *q.v.*
pop., ii. 227
Westdene:
Anne, w. of Jn., iv. 191
Jn., iv. 191
Wm., ii. 259
Westenton tithing (unidentified), ii. 184
Westergate, *see* Aldingbourne
Westerham (Kent), ii. 416
Western:
Anne, vii. 239
Chas. Callis, vii. 217–18, 258, 271
Mary, *see* Shirley
Maximilian, ix. 111, 168
Rob., vii. 239
Thos. (fl. 1693), ix. 111, 168
Thos. (d. 1763), vii. 218, 258, 269, 271
Thos. (fl. 1793), ii. 166
Thos. Walsingham, vii. 218, 258
Westerton, Jn. de, iv. 177
Westerton, *see* Westhampnett
Westfield, Wm., abbot of Battle, ii. 55

Westfield, ii. 43, 438; ix. 76, 89 *n*, **90–4**
adv., ii. 52; ix. 94
agric., ix. 90
birds, i. 281
ch., ix. *93*, 93–4
accessories, ii. 352, 355
archit., ii. 329, 336, 349, 367, 372
cricket, ii. 470
Crowham, ix. 1, 90, 207
dom. archit., ix. 90
Inlegh, ix. 76
insects, i. 126, 129, 140, 159, 176, 184, 231–2, 237
mammals, i. 303, 305
man., ix. 91–3, 274
Oaklands, iii. 29, 31–2
Pk., iii. 31–2, 49
pop., ii. 222
Rom. rem., iii. 29, 31
trades and ind., ii. 233, 236, 241; ix. 90
vicarage, ii. 8
Westgates, *see* Aldingbourne: Westergate
Westgrenestede, *see* Grinstead, West
Westham, ii. 34, 44, 122
ch., ii. 123, 337, 348, 351–3, 356, 358, 378
Hankham, ii. 452
hosp. (or Pevensey hosp.), ii. 45, **106–7**
Langney (Langley), i. 56; ii. 104, 122, 162–3, 384
pop., ii. 226
rector, *see* Citizen
Westhampnett, ii. 43; iv. 133, 139, **175–80**
adv., iv. 179–80
chap., iv. 180
ch., ii. 7, 56; iii. 33, 67; iv. 93 *n*, 117 *n*, *173*, 176–9, *178*
accessories, ii. 356
archit., ii. 334, 340, 344, 347 *n*, 349–50, 364, 370–1
dom. archit., ii. 392; iv. 176
Loddesdown (Loddesdune, Lodesdon), iv. 51
hosp., ii. **102–3**; iv. 143, 176
man., iv. 51, 105, 176–7, 179–80, 212
mills, iv. 176–7
Molecombe, i. 286; ii. 190
pop., ii. 220
roads to, iii. 33
Rom. rem., iii. 33, 67
R.D., iii. 76
tithes, iv. 179
union, i. 539; ii. 205, 207
Valdoe, i. 65
vicarage, ii. 9
vicars, ii. 37; iv. 145
Westerton, iv. 157, 176–7, 180
Woodcote, i. 65; iv. 51, 143, 177
Westlovinton, Wm. de, iv. 102
Westmacott:
Hen., iii. 146
Sir Ric., ix. 192
Westmeston, i. 55; ii. 43–4; vii. 92, 98, 109, **116–19**
adv., vii. 119
Chiltington, East, *q.v.*
ch., vii. 117–19, *118*
accessories, ii. 328, 354 *n*, 355
archit., ii. 340, 344, 347, 351, 367
dom. archit., vii. 116
earthworks, i. 480
fair, ʼvii. 117
Hailey (Hayley) pk., i. 295, 298; vii. 117
insects, i. 175
man., i. 370*; vii. 2–4, 100, 116–17, 177
nonconf., ii. 38
pop., ii. 225
rector, ii. 33
rectory, vii. 115, 119
tanning, ii. 259
Westwood, i. 55
and see Weston

Westminster, duke of, *see* Grosvenor,
  Hugh
Westminster (London, formerly Mdx.),
  ii. 138–9; iii. 84 *n*, 85
  abbey, ii. 3, 104–5, 340; ix. 103 *n*,
    155, 160, 255 *n*
  abbot, i. 502, ii. 96; iv. 193
  Assembly of Divines, ii. 35, 407
  Bridge, ii. 481; vii. 11
  councils of, ii. 6–7
  Hall, ii. 233
  Jermyn Street museum, i. 330
  St. Stephen's coll., ix. 119, 146
  Sch., ii. 409, 471
  Whitehall, ii. 237
Westmorland, earls of, ix. 195; *and see*
  Nevill, Hen.; Nevill, Ralph
Westmorland, i. 168 *n*
  Shap, abbot, *see* Redmond, Ric.
Weston:
  Agnes, iv. 224
  Cecily, m. —— atte Watere, iv. 129 *n*
  Edm., warden of St. Mary's hosp.,
    Chich., ii. 102
  R., vii. 124
  Ric. de, iv. 128, 129 *n*, 195
  Ric., prior of Hastings, ii. 76–7
  S.T., ii. 472
  Wm., ii. 427
  ——, ii. 473
  arms, iii. 155
Weston (in Buriton, Hants), ii. 91 *n*
Weston (? Westmeston), ii. 209
Westout, *see* Lewes
Westrate, Geof. de, mayor of Chich., iii.
  91
Westringes, *see* Manhood
Westwood, J.O., i. 255, 258–61
Westwood, *see* Westmeston
Wetherden, Wm., vicar of Bodiam, ix.
  264
Wetherell:
  Caroline, *see* May
  Chas., vii. 196
  Ellen, m. Edw. O. Hollist, ix. 255
  Harriet, ix. 255
  Nathan, ix. 255
  Ric., ix. 255
  Susan, m. —— Darby, ix. 255
Wetley, Joan, *see* Snelling
Wevilrigge, *see* Peasmarsh: Wivelridge
Wey, riv., ii. 241, 466*; iv. 67
Wey and Arun canal, ii. 241*, 466*
Weybridge (Surr.), i. 171 *n*
Weymouth (Dors.), ii. 154; iii. 101
Weyvile (Weyvyle), *see* Wyville
Whalesbone (Welesmore, Whalesbon)
  hund., i. 537; ii. 225; vii. 1, 3 *n*,
  215, **241**, 264
Whalley:
  Eliz., *see* Springett
  Herb., vii. 74
  Jn., vii. 74, 279
  Lucy, m. Thos. Harris, vii. 74
  Mary, m. 1 Ric. Bellingham, 2 Bar-
    nard Whitstone, vii. 279
  Ric., vii. 279
  Mr., ii. 414
Whaplode, Wm., and his w. Eliz., iv.
  200
Wharry:
  Ruth, *see* Covert
  Wm., iv. 162
Wharton:
  And., ix. 191
  Eliz., w. of Thos., ix. 191
  Eliz., w. of ——, *see* Rootes
  Thos., ix. 191
Whasbetel rock, *see* Seaford
Whateman:
  Sarah (Sarra), *see* Aguillon
  Wm., iv. 128
Whatenhull, Jn. de, sacrist of Bosham
  coll., ii. 112
Whatlington:
  Joce de, ix. 113, 242
  Jn. de, abbot of Battle, ii. 55
  Rog. de, ix. 113

Ric. de (d. 1339), ix. 113
Ric. de (fl. 1339), ix. 113
Wm. de, ix. 242
Wm. de (another), ix. 113
Whatlington, ii. 43; ix. 95, **112–14**, 226,
  258
  adv., ii. 52; ix. 113
  char., ix. 114
  ch., ii. 329, 367, 374; ix. 113
  lands in, ii. 324; ix. 19, 209
  man., ix. 112
  pk., ii. 297
  pop., ii. 222
  rly., ii. 222 *n*
  rector, *see* Doddridge
  rectory, ix. 279
  roads, ix. 112
wheat, *see* crops
Wheatley:
  Eliz., w. of Jn., m. 2 Sir Wm. Russell,
    ix. 241
  Jn., ix. 241
  Kath., m. Francis Russell, ix. 241
Wheatley Hall, *see* Doncaster
Wheeler:
  Sir Edw., iii. 145
  Jn. (d. 1643), vii. 106
  Jn. (fl. 1671), vii. 101, 106
  R.E.M., iii. 59
  Susanna, iii. 126
  Thos., iii. 126
  Sir Wm., vii. 97
Whelton (Weghelton):
  Eliz. de, iv. 184–5
  Isabel, w. of Thos. de, iv. 184
  Joan de, m. Jn. Michelgrove, iii. 105;
    iv. 185, 202
  Marg. de, m. 1 Jn. Scardevile, 2 Ric.
    Fust, iii. 105; iv. 184–5
  Ric. de, iv. 184–5
  Rose de, iv. 184
  Thos. de (fl. 1340), iv. 184
  Thos. de (d. 1361, another), iv. 184
Wherwell (Hants), abbey, iv. 94–5, 143
Whetham, Ric., iv. 163
Whetston (Whetstone):
  Thos., ix. 123
  Wal., rector of Patching, ii. 37
Whichford (Warws.), rector, *see*
  Pininger
Whight, Jn., ix. 28; *and see* White
Whiligh, *see* Ticehurst
Whissh, *see* Whysh
Whitaker:
  Edw., ii. 164–5
  G.C., iv. 122
  Laur., iv. 212
Whitby:
  Oliver, archdeacon of Chich., warden
    of St. Mary's hosp., Chich., ii.
    101–2; iii. 90, 147; iv. 219
  Oliver (d. 1702), ii. 437–8; iii. 74, 90,
    147; iv. 13, 20, 219
  Oliver (fl. 1815), iv. 218 *n*
Whitby (Yorks. N.R.), ii. 362
White (Whyte):
  Adam, i. 246–8, 254, 257–60, 265
  Edw., iv. 110
  Eliz. (fl. 1616), iv. 189
  Eliz. (fl. 1752), vii. 180
  Eliz., w. of Sir Ric., iv. 189
  Frances, *see* Page
  (later White Thomas), Geo., M.P. for
    Chich., iii. 77, 90; iv. 150
  Gilb., i. 46, 282, 291, 300; iv. 13
  Hen., ii. 181
  Jane, w. of Jn., ix. 269
  Jn. (fl. *c.* 1520), iv. 10
  Jn. (fl. 1589), ix. 269
  Mary, w. of Jn., ix. 269
  Mary, w. of Wm., *see* Sackville
  Mat., ii. 310
  Nic., ii. 18
  Ric., ii. 259
  Sir Ric., iv. 189
  Sam., ix. 202
  Sim., mayor of Chich., iii. 92
  Thos., ix. 269

Sir Thos., iv. 155
Wm., master of Arundel coll., ii. 109
Wm. (fl. 1564), ix. 146
Wm. (fl. 1654), vii. 218
Wm. (d. 1666), ix. 146, 269
Wm. Hale ('Mark Rutherford'), ix. 8
Mr., vii. 196
fam., ix. 146
and see Whight
white, Osbert the, *see* Osbert
White Hawk Hill, *see* Brighton
White House, *see* Maresfield
Whitechapel (London, formerly Mdx.),
  ii. 250–1
Whitegod, Jn., iii. 104
Whitehall, *see* Westminster
Whiteman's Green, *see* Cuckfield
Whiteway, Wm. de, ii. 302
Whitfield:
  Francis, vii. 235
  Geo., vii. 32
  Rob., vii. 192 *n*
  Thos., vii. 200
Whiting (Whitinge):
  Jn., vii. 144
  Thos. (fl. 1571), and his w. Joan, vii.
    196
  Thos. (d. 1599, ? another), vii. 144
Whitmore, Sir Geo., ix. 154
Whitney:
  Alice, *see* Styllefeld
  Wm., iv. 157
Whitpaine:
  Mary, *see* Scrase
  Ric., vii. 177
Whitson (Whitsond):
  Dorothy, m. 1 Timothy Parker, 2
    Wal. Gatland, vii. 135
  Eliz., vii. 135
  Jane, vii. 135
  Nic., vii. 135
  Wm. de, and his w. Margery, iv. 191
  Wm. de (? another), mayor of Chich.,
    iii. 91
Whitstone:
  Barnard, vii. 279
  Mary, *see* Whalley
Whittington:
  Ric., iii. 102
  Rob., ii. 418–19
Whitton, Jn., abbot of Robertsbridge, ii.
  74
Whitwood:
  Jas., iii. 147
  Mary, m. 1 Jn. Watts, 2 Jn. Bull, iii.
    147
Whitworth:
  Arabella Diana, *see* Cope
  Chas., Earl Whitworth, vii. 35, 257
Whysh (Huysshe, Whissh):
  Alice, w. of Hen., iv. 213
  Anne, iv. 213
  Hen. (d. 1347), iv. 162, 213
  Hen. (d. 1384), iv. 213
  Kath., w. of Hen., iv. 213
  fam., iv. 213
Whyte, *see* White
Wiatt, *see* Wyatt
Wibert (fl. 1086), ix. 91, 132, 206–7, 267
Wibert, Wm. s. of, *see* William
Wich, *see* Wych
Wichecross, *see* Maresfield: Wych Cross
Wichelo, Jn., vii. 248*
Wick Pond, *see* Albourne
Wicken Fen (Cambs.), i. 164 *n*
Wickham, Jn., *see* Wykeham
Wickham (in Clayton), *see* Clayton
Wickham (in Steyning), *see* Steyning
Wickham, West (Kent), i. 315; iii. 44,
  70
Wickliffe, *see* Wycliffe
Wicksted, Alex., iii. 76
Wiclif, *see* Wycliffe
Widard (fl. 1086), vii. 253
Widdon, *see* Weedon
Wideringe, Alan de, iv. 216
Widget, ——, vii. 249
Wido (fl. 1086), *see* Guy

Widville, fam., arms, iv. 131
Wigge, la, *see* Ashdown forest
Wiggonholt:
 ch., ii. 339, 356, 358
 Holmstreet, iii. 48
 insects, i. 200, 203, 205, 207–8, 210
 Lickfold, iii. 48, 64
 man., ix. 71
 pk., ii. 82
 pop., ii. 218
 prehist. rem., i. 309, *310*, 331
 roads to, iii. 48
 Rom. rem., iii. 38, 48, 64
Wight, Isle of, i. 333, 347, 466, 482–3, 485; ii. 1, 126, 136, 141; iii. 1, 19
 A.-S. rem., i. 343–4
 fossils, i. 36, 38
 French attacks, i. 510; ii. 145
 geology, i. 15–16, 20
 natural history, i. 68, 194, 286, 296–7
 quarrying, ii. 230
 stone from, ii. 334–5, 355, 380
 and see Atherfield; Bembridge; Binstead; Brading; Carisbrooke; Freshwater; Newport; Quarr abbey; Ventnor
Wightring, prebend, *see* Wittering, West
Wigot (fl. 1066), iv. 41
Wigsell:
 Lucy de, ix. 222
 Sim. de (d. by 1242), ix. 221–2
 Sim. de (fl. 1339), ix. 222
 Thos., ix. 222
 Wm. de, ix. 221
Wigsell, *see* Salehurst
Wihttringes, iv. 215
Wikham, *see* Wykeham
Wilbar, Jn., ii. 264
Wilberforce:
 Emily, *see* Sargent
 Ernest, bp. of Chich., iii. 126; iv. 179
 Reg. Wm., iv. 59
 Sam., bp. of Oxford, bp. of Winchester, i. 282; iv. 59, 152
 fam., iv. 59
 arms, iv. *59*
Wilbraham:
 Mary, m. Thos. Pelham, ix. 139
 Sir Rog., ix. 139
Wilcombe, *see* Wylcombe
Wild (Wylde):
 H.L., ix. 137
 Thos., and his w. Eliz., ix. 150
 Wm., ix. 137
Wild Brooks, *see* Amberley
Wildbore, Jn., vii. 228
Wildbridge, *see* Yapton
Wildegos, *see* Wildgose
Wilder:
 Augustina Ivens Mary, w. of ——, m. 2 Chas. Dixon, iv. 122
 Geo., iv. 122, 127
Wildgose (Wildegos, Wilgoose):
 Anne, m. Sir Jn. Fowle, vii. 218; ix. 221
 Sir Annesley, vii. 217
 Audrey, m. Sir Ant. May, vii. 217 *n*; ix. 221
 Cordelia, m. Sir Wm. Boys, vii. 218; ix. 221
 Frances, w. of Sir Rob., m. 2 —— Salkeld, ix. 222
 Grace, ix. 221
 Grace, w. of Sir Jn., *see* Annesley
 Jn. (d. 1606), ix. 220
 Sir Jn. (d. 1636), vii. 217–18; ix. 220–2
 Rob., vii. 218; ix. 221–2
 Mr., i. 519
Wilding, Rob., ix. 117
Wildman, Revd., ii. 420
Wilds, Mr., vii. 37
Wilds and Busby, vii. 261
Wilebald, moneyer, vii. 32
Wilford (Wylford):
 Jas., ix. 276
 Thos. de, prebendary of Hampstead (Hempsted), vii. 233

——, i. 519
Wilfrid, St., bp. of York, bp. of Selsey, i. 336; ii. 1–2*, 11, 109, 126, 264, 362, 380 *n*, 400; iii. 82, 103, 112, 133–4; iv. 135, 161–2, 187, 198, 207, 211, 215, 223, 229–30, 233, 237
Wilgoose, *see* Wildgose
Wilicheres, *see* Willicheres
Wilkason, Bryan, ii. 38–9
Wilkes, Jn., vii. 19
 his dau., vii. 19
Wilkynson, Edm., warden of Windham hosp., ii. 108
Willard (Willerd):
 Ralf, ii. 229
 Mr., ii. 450
Willbees, *see* Arlington
Wille, Mr., i. 294
Willehale, *see* Wylehale
Willelm, moneyer, iii. 84 *n*
Willerd, *see* Willard
Willesden (Mdx.), *see* Kilburn
Willett:
 Ernest H., i. 314, 326, 466; iii. 53, 62
 Hen., i. 326
 (formerly Catt), Wm., *see* Catt
 Revd., iv. 202
William I, i. 305, 472, 485–9; ii. 4, 52, 54–5, 64, 112, 122, 124, 128–9, 292, 301, 323, 328, 381; iii. 82–3; iv. 1, 30 *n*, 182–3, 185; vii. 1, 33, 104; ix. 1, 8, 14, 49, 62, 95, 117, 168
William II (Rufus), i. 489; ii. 5–6, 52–3; iii. 106; vii. 1, 33; ix. 9, 14
William III, i. 530, 535; ii. 40, 164, 441; iii. 89; iv. 17
William IV, vii. 19, 37, 250
William, abbot of Bayham, ii. 88–9
William, abbot of Durford, ii. 91
William, abbot of Robertsbridge (fl. to 1219), ii. 65, 72–3
William, abbot of Robertsbridge (fl. 1252), ii. 73
William, abbot of Robertsbridge (fl. 1483), ii. 74
William, abbot of Robertsbridge (fl. 1523), ii. 74
William, abbot of Waverley, iv. 25
William, archdeacon of London, iv. 120
William, bp. of Chich., ii. 5
William, count of Eu, ix. 14
William, count of Mortain and Boulogne, earl of Surrey, i. 490, 498 *n*; vii. 2, 224
 his w., *see* Warenne, Isabel de
William, count of Nassau, prince of Orange, ii. 148
William, dean of Chich., ii. 100
William, earl of Gloucester, and his w. Hawise, iv. 17
William, ? prebendary of Chich., iv. 208
William, prior of Boxgrove, ii. 57, 59
William, prior of Chich. Dominican friary, ii. 94
William, prior of Lewes, (fl. 1150), ii. 69
William, prior of Lewes, (fl. 1195), ii. 70; iv. 117
William, prior of Michelham, ii. 79
William, prior of Pynham, ii. 81
William, prior of Runcton, ii. 121
William, prior of Tortington, ii. 83
William, prior of Wilmington, ii. 123
William, sheriff of Lewes (fl. 1120), vii. 1
William, sheriff of Lewes (fl. 1150), vii. 1
William, vicar of Didling, iv. 7
William fitz Aucher, iv. 183
William son of Alan, iv. 166
William son of Alan of Clun, iv. 166 *n*
William son of Alfred, ii. 122
William son of Durand, iv. 183
Sir William, son of Emfred, iv. 102
William son of Ernulf, iv. 184
William son of Geoffrey at Felde, ii. 179
William son of Gervase, vii. 67
William son of Gilbert le Baker, master

of hosp. of St. Jas. and St. Mary, Chich., ii. 100
William son of Godwin, vii. 55
William son of Reynold, vii. 209, 212–13
William son of Robert (Curthose), duke of Normandy, ix. 1
William son of Tezelin, vii. 203
William son of Wibert, ii. 52; ix. 91, 94, 206–7
William le Chanoyn, ii. 302
William, priest of Lordington, iv. 118
William the clerk, iv. 162
 his s., *see* Laurence
William the dean, *see* Brackelsham, Wm. de
William the smith, ii. 52
William (fl. 1086), iv. 51, 142–5, 156, 176, 199
William (fl. 1086, ? one or two others), iv. 115, 118
William (fl. 1086, another), iv. 142
William (fl. 1086, another), iv. 176
William (fl. 1086, another), vii. 196
William (fl. 1086, another), ix. 213
William (fl. 1180), iv. 183
William, Jas. s. of, *see* James
William, Luke s. of, *see* Luke
William, Mr., ii. 398
Williams:
 Basil, i. 530
 Sir Booth, iii. 80
 Chas. Kevern, ii. 415
 Eliz., *see* Lytton
 Emily, w. of Jn. Leigh, iii. 74
 Emma, iii. 147
 F.S., ii. 435
 F.V., ii. 448
 Harry Montague, vii. 266
 Henrietta, w. of Wm. Peere, iv. 213
 Sir Hutchins, iii. 80, 160; iv. 176–7, 180, 213
 J., ii. 165
 Jas., ii. 423
 Jn. (fl. 1493), iv. 157; vii. 190 *n*, 280
 Sir Jn. (fl. 1543), iv. 109
 Jn. (fl. after 1671), iv. 185
 Jn., bp. of Chich., iv. 166
 Jn. (fl. after 1750), iii. 74
 (or Hollest), Jn. Leigh, iii. 74
 Judith, iii. 145
 Lawr., ix. 212
 Margery, *see* Chauncy
 Peckham, iii. 74
 Sir Pier, iii. 80
 Rupert, ii. 451–2
 Thos., ii. 423
 Wm., iii. 147
 Wm. Jn., vii. 266
 Sir Wm. Peare, iv. 177
 Wm. Peere (another), iv. 213
 Lady, iii. 123
 ——, iii. 93
Williams-Freeman, J., iii. 19
Williamson, Mary, m. Jas. Hargraves, iii. 126
Willicheres (Wilicheres):
 Humph. de, ix. 187, 235
 Wm. de, ix. 187, 235
Willingdon (Willindon, Willington), ii. 44, 77, 208, 227; ix. 251
 A.-S. rem., i. 335, 348, *348*
 Burgelstaltone, *q.v.*
 ch., ii. 8, 48, 123
  accessories, ii. 352, 356, 358
  archit., ii. 337, 340, 349–50, 372
  cross, ii. 25 *n*
 earthworks, i. 480
 golf, ii. 478
 hund., i. 537; ii. 182 *n*, 227
 Hydneye (Hidney), i. 335*; ii. 130; ix. 36
 lime-burning, ii. 231
 man., ix. 193
 natural history, i. 60, 209
 pop., ii. 122
 Ratton, ii. 277, 384, 478; ix. 193, 251
 Rom. rem., iii. 67
 sch., ii. 208

Willingdon (*cont.*):
  timber, ii. 315
  tithes, ii. 8
Willis:
  Browne, iii. 89, 160 *n*
  Jn., ii. 421
  R., iii. 106–7, 109–10, 113, 117, 121,
    129 *n*, 132 *n*, 133
  Wm., ix. 150
Willot, Thos., i. 512
Willoughby, Sir Hen., vii. 84; ix. 83
Willoughby de Broke, Ld., *see* Verney,
  Jn.
Willoughby d'Eresby, Lds., *see* Bertie
Willyard, Thos., vii. 171
Wilmer, Sam., rector of Clapham, ii. 37
Wilmington, earl of, *see* Compton, Sir
  Spencer
Wilmington, ii. 44, 301; ix. 226
  ch., ii. 48, 123
    accessories, ii. 356, 359
    archit., ii. 329, 337, 339–40, 350,
      365, 367
  earthworks, i. 480
  insects, i. 165–7, 175
  Long Man, i. 323–4, *325*
  man., ii. 122
  pop., ii. 226
  prehist. rem., i. 320, 331
  priory, i. 501; ii. 4, 46, **122–3**, 313–14
    archit., ii. 329, 395
    priors, ii. 122–3
  roads to, iii. 48
  Rom. rem., iii. 3, 67
  vicarage, ii. 8–9
  vicars, *see* Marshal, Hen.; Smart,
    Wm.
  wood, i. 56
Wilmot:
  Hen., Ld. Wilmot, i. 527; vii. 247
  Thos., vicar of Ashford, ix. 244
Wilner, Jn., ix. 171
Wilsham (Wylesham):
  Adam de, ix. 128 *n*
  Christine, w. of Jn. de, ix. 128, 248
  Jn. (fl. 1375), ix. 128, 248
  Jn. (fl. 1392), ix. 128
  Ric. de, ix. 128
  Rob. de (? two of this name), ix. 128
Wilson:
  Alex., iv. 191
  Ambrose Jn., ii. 433
  Ann, ix. 33
  Cath. D., ix. 33
  Sir Chas., i. 536
  Sir Edw., vii. 247
  Edw., ix. 61
  G.L., ii. 476
  Sir Hen., vii. 173
  J., ii. 166
  Mary, m. Steph. Comyn, ix. 229
  R.J., ii. 474
  Ric. (fl. 1549), ii. 154
  Ric. (fl. 1657), iv. 191
  Sir Rob., ii. 450
  Sir Spencer Maryon, ii. 464
  Thos., and his w. Martha, iv. 191
  W.P., iv. 192
  Wm., vii. 35–6
  Wm., vicar of Billingshurst, ii. 39
  Sir Wm., ii. 441
  Woodrow, president of U.S.A., vii.
    173
  Mr., vii. 97
Wilting (Wiltingham), *see* Hollington
Wilton:
  Jn., iv. 168
  Wm. de, i. 500
Wilton, earl of, *see* Egerton, Thos.
Wilton (Wilts.), abbey, vii. 224
  canon, *see* Courtenay, Ric.
Wiltsher, Geo., vii. 59
Wiltshire, earls of, *see* Boleyn, Thos.;
  Stafford, Hen.
Wiltshire, i. 19, 47, 280, 318; ii. 251 *n*;
  iv. 14; *and see* Amesbury; Bradford
  on Avon; Bromham; Fisherton;
  Maiden Bradley; Malmesbury;

Marlborough; Monkton Farleigh;
  Ogbourne; Salisbury; Stanley;
  Wansdyke; Wilton
Wimbis (Wymbissh):
  Jn., vii. 210
  Ric., vii. 211
  Wal., vii. 60
Wimble, Nehemiah, vii. 37
Wimbledon (Surr.), i, 348
Wimples, Rog. de, vii. 34
Wimund, Ric., ix. 50
Win, *see* Wyn
Winchcombe (Glos.), ix. 62 *n*
Winchelsea (Winchelse, Winchelsey,
  Wynchelse):
  Laur., prior of Michelham, ii. 78–9
  Manasses (Manasser) of, ix. 10, 67, 70
  Rob., abp. of Cant., ii. 8, 74–5, 82,
    87, 114, 295; iv. 233; vii. 105
  Wal. de, ix. 50
Winchelsea, Old and New (Vin-
  cenesium, Wynchelse), i. 501, 506,
  508; ii. 7, 41, 43, 46, 71, 96, 177,
  192–3; vii. 245; ix. 40, 53, 56,
  62–75, *64*, 168, 175, 184
  adv., ii. 333; ix. 50, 75
  battle of the Spaniards, ix. 69
  birds, i. 278, 281, 292, 295
  botany, i. 41, 46
  Camber, *see* Icklesham: Camber
  chant., ix. 75
  char., ix. 75
  charters, ii. 129; ix. 9, 34, 36–8, 49
  chs.:
    St. Giles, ix. 3, 63, 75
    St. Thos., ix. 3, 63, *72–3*; accessor-
      ies, ii. 352–3, 376–7; ix. 74–5;
      archit., ii. 14, 327, 340, 344, 346–
      9, 376–7, 379; ix. 71–4, 89 *n*
  coastguards, i. 507 *n*
  crustaceans, i. 261
  custumal, ix. 67, 69
  defences and fortifications, ii. 138,
    152, 395; ix. *62*, 63–4, 67
  dom. archit., ii. 384, *385*, 386; ix.
    63–6
  fair, ix. 70
  fortifications, *see* Winchelsea: de-
    fences
  French raids, i. 509–11, 513; ii. 54,
    139–40, 143; ix. 66–7
  friaries:
    Dominican (Black Friars), ii. 45,
      94–5, 331; ix. 63, 66; prior, ii. 95
    Franciscan (Grey Friars), ii. 45, **96**,
      358; ix. 63–4, *65*; archit., ii. 331,
      342, 376; ix. 64
  geology, i. 274
  harbour and port, i. 26, 485; ii. 3, 125,
    135, 137, 141–2, 144, 150, 154;
    iii. 101–2; ix. 9, 15, 34, 54, 63,
    69–71, 263
  hermitage, ix. 69–70
  Higham (Iham, Petit Iham), ii. 43; ix.
    4, 36, 49–50, 63, 71, 175, 273
    ch., ii. 113; ix. 3, 63, 75
    man., ii. 169, 173, 178; ix. 68, 71,
      75, 185
    shipping, ii. 130
  hosps., ii. 45; ix. 63
    Holy Cross, ii. **107**
    St. Ant., ix. 70
    St. Bart., ii. **107**
    St. Jn. ii. **107**
  Iham, *see* Winchelsea: Higham
  inns, ix. 66
  insects, i. 117–18, 137, 139–42, 147,
    149–50, 152–3, 155–6, 159, 161,
    183, 190, 220, 224, 229, 232–4,
    236–7
  Jews, i. 506
  local govt., ix. 10, 36, 67–9, 176
    bailiffs, ii. 265; ix. 66–7; *and see*
      Alard, Gervase; Alard, Rob.;
      Guldeford, Sir Ric.; Paulin,
      Rob.
    barons, i. 494; ix. 50, 63, 67
    corporation, ii. 107; ix. 67

    cts., ix. 39, 67
    jurats, ii. 107; ix. 67
    mayors, i. 521; ii. 107; ix. 50, 67–9;
      and see Alard, Gervase; Finch,
      Hen.; Helde
    other officers, ix. 68–9
  mammals, i. 303
  man., ii. 3; ix. 71
  mkt., ix. 70
  marshes, i. 116
  militia, i. 535
  mill, ix. 63
  mint, ii. 126; ix. 62
  nonconf., ii. 18; ix. 75
  parl. rep., i. 504, 532; ix. 68
  piracy, ii. 131, 136–7, 147
  pop., ii. 228; ix. 66, 71
  port, *see* Winchelsea: harbour
  prison, ix. 64 *n*
  privateering, ii. 144
  rector, ix. 62
  riots, ii. 136
  royal visits, i. 492–4, 496, 505; ix. 67
  sch., ii. 398
  sea defences, ix. 50, 63, 67
  Sea Fencibles, ii. 162
  ship money, ii. 157
  ship service, ii. 129–30, 131 *n*, 132–5,
    138, 140–4, 153–4; ix. 9–10, 36,
    69
  shipping, ii. 129–30, 132–8, 140, 142,
    144, 150–1; ix. 69
  storms, ii. 169, 188, 259; ix. 63, 149
  streets, ix. 65–6
  taxation, ix. 63, 67
  town hall, ii. 383; ix. 64
  trades and ind., ix. 67, 70
    brewing, ii. 261
    charcoal, ii. 237
    cider, ii. 263
    clock making, ix. 60
    fisheries, ii. 130, 145, 151, 265–7,
      269–70; ix. 63, 70
    iron, ii. 229, 242
    salt, ii. 232–3; ix. 63
    shipbuilding, ii. 130, 132, 136, 138,
      234–5; ix. 13, 69
    tanning, ii. 259–60; ix. 70
    textiles, ii. 256, 258; ix. 67, 70
    timber, ii. 233–4
    wine, ii. 134; ix. 70
  vicar, ix. 62
  Wainway Creek, *q.v.*
  workho., ix. 64
Winchelsey, Rob., *see* Winchelsea
Winchester (Winchestre):
  Adam of, prior of Lewes, ii. 67, 70
  Ailwin of, vii. 58
  Eldred of, iv. 63
  Hen., dean of South Malling coll., ii.
    119
  Hen., ix. 224
  Jn. of, prior of Boxgrove, ii. 57, 59
  Odo of, iv. 85
Winchester:
  earl of, *see* Despenser, Hugh le
  marquess of, *see* Paulet, Wm.
Winchester (Venta Belgarum) (Hants),
  i. 483, 493, 501; ii. 2, 126, 129; iii.
  10, 47; iv. 149, 184 *n*
  arms, iii. 159
  bps., ii. 15, 22; ix. 61, 94; *and see*
    Bilson, Thos.; Blois; Duppa;
    Edendon; Ethelwold; Gardiner;
    Ponet, Jn.; Valence, Aymer de;
    Waynflete, Wm.; Wilberforce,
    Sam.; Wykeham, Wm. of
  cast., i. 494; ix. 15
  Civil War in, i. 522, 526
  College, ii. 401, 405, 407, 409, 417,
    428–9, 433, 439, 472; iii. 90, 146
  dioc., ii. 6, 10, 306; iv. 2
    archdeacon, *see* Oliver, Ric.
  dom. archit., ii. 241
  fish trade, ii. 266
  Hyde abbey, ii. 179 *n*; iv. 30, 150,
    152; vii. 7, 14, 73–6, 78
    abbots, *see* Alfwig; Ethelgar

arms, iv. *150*; vii. *73*
residence of abbot of Battle, ii. 52
royal visit, ii. 302
Statute of, ii. 187
Winchestre, *see* Winchester
Winchfield (Hants), ii. 368
Winchilsea:
 ctss. of Maidstone and, *see* Heneage,
  Eliz.
 earls of Maidstone and, ix. 187; *and
  see* Finch
wind vane, *see* architecture: ecclesiastical
Winde:
 Burgunnia, *see* Folet
 Jn., ix. 267
Windeham, *see* Wyndham hund.
Winder, Jos., ii. 165
Windham, *see* Shermanbury
Windham hund., *see* Wyndham hund.
Winding Bottom (near Sompting), i. 200
Windmill Down, *see* Hambledon
  (Hants)
Windmill Hill (in Herstmonceux and
  Wartling), i. 286; ii. 447, 471; ix.
  125, 131, 137
Windover Hill, *see* Arlington
Windsor (Wyndesor, Wyndsor):
 And., Ld. Windsor, iv. 15; ix. 160,
  173, 181, 196–7, 273
 And., and his w. Anne, ix. 145
 Anne, w. of Sir Ant., iv. 15 *n*
 Sir Ant. (d. 1548), iv. 15, 129
 Ant. (fl. 1559), iv. 15
 Aveline de, *see* Aveline
 Constance, m. Thos. Ryth, iv. 15
 Edith, m. Hen. Mervyn, iv. 15, 92
 Edm. (fl. 1560), ix. 145, 181
 Edm. (fl. 1567, ? another), and his w.
  Agnes, iv. 200
 Edw., Ld. Windsor, ix. 145, 160, 173,
  181, 206*
 Eleanor, w. of Hen., iv. 15, 83, 129
 Eliz., w. of And., Ld. Windsor, *see*
  Blount
 Eliz., w. of Sir Ant., *see* Lovell
 Eliz., w. of Wm., Ld. Windsor, m. 2
  Geo. Puttenham, ix. 273 *n*
 Fred., Ld. Windsor, ix. 145, 173
 Hen., iv. 15, 83, 129
 Hen., Ld. Windsor, ix. 145, 173, 273–
  4
 Honora, iv. 15
 Joan, w. of Sir Ant., iv. 15
 Joan, w. of Ant., iv. 15
 Reynold de, iv. 84
 Thos., iv. 181
 Wal., vii. 36
 Wm., Ld. Windsor, ii. 20; ix. 160,
  173, 181, 206, 273
 ——, m. Sir Edm. Dudley, ix. 196
 fam., ix. 145, 274
  arms, ix. *273*
Windsor (Berks.), i. 473, 491; ii. 437
 forest, ii. 238
 St. George's chap., iv. 162; ix. 214,
  230
  canon, *see* Rush
Winford, Capt., i. 522
Winford (Som.), rector, *see* Cotterill,
  Jn.
Wingfield:
 Sir Ant., vii. 6
 Sir Jn., vii. 5–7, 35, 254
 fam., vii. 179
  arms, vii. *6*
Wingham (Kent), ii. 12
Winkins wood, *see* Dean, East: woodland
Winnington:
 Sir Edw., vii. 178
 Sir Thos. Edw., vii. 178
Winslow, Thos., ix. 248
Winter (Wynter):
 F.J., ii. 474
 Geo., vicar of Cowfold, ii. 35
 Jn., iv. 212
 Wm., ii. 256

Winterbourne, *see* Lewes
Winterbourne, riv., vii. 7, 45, 51
Winterselle, Jn. de, ii. 316
Winterton, earls, *see* Turner, Edw.
Winton:
 Ann, vii. 68
 Jn. E., ix. 112
 W.E. de, i. 302
Winton Street, *see* Alfriston
Wiohstan (fl. 935), iv. 110
Wisborough Green, i. 52; ii. 43, 314 *n*
 ch., ii. 19, 334, 346, 351–2, 355, 367,
  371–2
 earthworks, i. 478
 lands in, ii. 92, 408
 Loxwood (Lokeswode), ii. 41, 43, 92,
  254, 263
 Pallingham, i. 330; ii. 244
 pop., ii. 217
 tithes, ii. 263
 trades and ind., ii. 254, 263
 vicar, ii, 37
Wisden (Wysdon):
 Jn., abbot of Robertsbridge, ii. 73
 Jn., ii. 469
 Thos., vii. 255
 Capt., iii. 53
Wiseman (Wyseman):
 Jn., iv. 104
 Jn. (another), and his w. Margery, iv.
  104
 Thos., iv. 106
 Thos. (? another), and his w. Anne,
  iv. 70
Wish Tower, *see* Eastbourne
Wispillun, Rob., iv. 58
Wisshouse (unidentified in Staple
  hund.), ix. 95
Wiston, ii. 43
 Buncton, iii. 47, 52
  ch., ii. 339, 348, 352, 354, 366–7,
   376; iii. 52
 ch., ii. 353, 355, 361
 coins, i. 331
 fish trade, ii. 266
 pop., ii. 219
 rector, *see* Beaton
 Rom. rem., iii. 47, 67–8
 Wiston Ho., i. 524; ii. 387
 Wiston Pk., i. 306; ii. 297
witchcraft, ii. 31–2
Witchcross, *see* Maresfield: Wych Cross
Withdean, *see* Patcham
Witherden, Carey, ii. 451
Witherenden, *see* Ticehurst
withernam, ix. 10, 39
Withers:
 Bigg, ii, 444
 Thos., iii. 145
Withringes (Wyghtring, Wyghtryng,
  Wystringes, Wystryng):
 Jn. (fl. *c.* 1290), iv. 216
 Jn. de (fl. 1311), iv. 219
 Jn. de (fl. 1332), iv. 216
 Jn. (fl. 1428), iv. 216
 Oliver de, iv. 216–17
 Sim. de, iv. 216
 Steph. de, iv. 219
 Rob., iv. 216
 Wm. (fl. 1300), iv. 216
 Wm. (fl. 1481), and his w. Joan, iv.
  216
Withyham (Wythyham), ii. 44, 76, 313,
  319
 adv., ii. 123
 Blackham, ii. 123
 botany, i. 67
 Buckhurst:
  man., ii. 317 *n*
  pk., i. 306; ii. 297, 318–20, 322
  Tower, ii. 384
 ch., ii. 13, 40, 316
  accessories, ii. 249, 251, 353, 355,
   360, 362
  archit., ii. 336, 339, 379
 earthworks, i. 478
 Fishers (Fidges) Gate, ii. 319
 Friar's (Frayes) Gate, ii. 319

Groombridge, i. 175, 179; ii. 44, 200,
  260, 391, 463; ix. 172
Lye (Leigh, Mershe), Green, ii. 319,
  389, 391
man., ii. 123
nonconf., ii. 22
pk., ii. 322
pop., ii. 226
prehist. rem., i. 331
priory, ii. 46, **123–4**
rector, *see* Gray, Ric.
timber, ii. 322
trades and ind., ii. 249, 257
Witsand, Hankin de, constable of Pevensey, i. 500
Wittering (unspecified), i. 506 *n*; ii. 3;
  iv. 218 *n*
Wittering, East, ii. 43, 408; iv. 198, 201,
  215–17
 adv., iv. 203, 217
 boundary, iv. 198–9, 202
 Bracklesham, *q.v.*
 ch., ii. 339, 349–50, 367–8; iv. *216*,
  216–17
 coins, i. 326, 329
 dom. archit., iv. 215
 fossils, i. 27
 Hundredsteddle Farm, iv. 198–9, 202
 man., iv. 202, 215–16, 219
 pop., ii. 221
 rectory, ii. 37
 Somerley, iv. 198
  man., iv. 216
  prebend, iv. 216–17
 Thorney, East, iv. 208, 215
  man., iv. 216
  prebend, iv. 208, 215–17; prebendary, *see* Garland, Hen. de
Wittering, West, ii. 43, 291 *n*; iii. 90,
  154 *n*; iv. 198, **217–21**
 adv., iv. 221
 battery, ii. 152
 birds, i. 291
 boundary, iv. 198–9, 202
 Cakeham (Cackham), iii. 52, 98, 102
  chap., ii. 379, 386
  coins, i. 331
  Green, iv. 218
  man., iv. 216, 218–19; ho., iv. 134,
   217–18
  pk., iv. 217
  tower, ii. 163, 334*, 386
 char., iv. 221
 ch., iv. 147, 218–21, *219*
  accessories, ii. 352, 355, 359–61,
   379
  archit., ii. 329, 334–5, 337, 340,
   344, 349–50, 371–3
 coins, i. 326, 331
 dom. archit., iv. 218
 earthworks, i. 478
 fossils, i. 15, 28
 geology, i. 14, 21–2
 guild, iv. 221
 Horemouth, *see* Chich.: harbour
 inc., iv. 218
 lands in, ii. 408, 437
 man., iv. 202, 218–19
 mill, iv. 218
 pop., ii. 221
 port, iii. 90, 96, 100–2
 prebend (Wightring), ii. 48, 404–6;
  iv. 205, 219, 221; prebendary, *see*
  Seffrid the treasurer
 prehist. rem., i. 331
 signal station, ii. 163
 tithes, iv. 221
 warren, iv. 217
Wittersham (Kent), ii. 411
Wittman, Wm., and his w. Eliz., iii. 161
Wivelridge, *see* Peasmarsh
Wivelsfield, i. 55; ii. 44; vii. 92, **119–24**,
  148, 179
 adv., vii. 123–4
 birds, i. 284
 char., vii. 124
 ch., ii. 34, 36, 68; vii. *121, 122*, 122–3
  accessories, ii. 250, 351–2, 355, 378

Wivelsfield
ch. (*cont.*):
architt., ii. 340, 344, 349–51, 365, 372, 378
dom. archit., ii. 389; vii. 119–20, *120, 121*
earthworks, i. 478
Green, vii. 94, 119–20
man., ii. 187; vii. 120–2
pop., ii. 225
rly., ii. 225 *n*
Suss. County Lunatic Asylum, ii. 225 *n*
tanning, ii. 260
Wlenchemere priory, *see* Shulbred
Wlencing (Wulfencing), i. 334, 481; ii. 291; iii. 82
Wlfhun, *see* Wulfhun
Wlfwin (fl. 1147), vii. 256 *n*
Wode, *see* Wood
Wodehorne, *see* Woodhorne
Wodehuse, *see* Woodhouse
Wodering, *see* Pagham: Wythering
Wodewey, Jn., ii. 412
Wodhull, Jn. de, ix. 92
Wody (Wodye):
Jn. (fl. 1491), and his w. Agnes, vii. 100
Jn. (fl. 1510), and his w. Anne, vii. 100
Woflet, *see* Wayflete
Woking (Surr.):
hund., iv. 73, 91 *n*
man., vii. 217
Wokingdon, fam., arms, ix. 209
Wokingham (Berks.), ii. 250; iv. 46
Woknolle:
Geof., ix. 198
Joan, m. Wm. Lunsford, ix. 198
Joan, w. of Wal., ix. 198
Reynold de, ix. 198
Wal. de, ix. 198
Wolbeding, *see* Woolbeding
Wolbedinge:
Alan de, iv. 85
Alice, w. of Ralph de, iv. 85
Bonenee de, m. Wm. de Beaumes, iv. 85
Cecily, w. of Rog. de, iv. 85
Jn. de, iv. 85
Ralph de (d. by 1192), iv. 85
Ralph de (d. 1265), iv. 85
Rog. de, iv. 85
Wolbergh:
Anne de, vii. 196
Jn. de, vii. 196
Thos. de (? two of this name), vii. 196
Wm. de, vii. 196
Wolf, *see* Woolfe
Wolfardesbridge, *see* Woolbeding: Woolmer Bridge
Wolfe, *see* Woolfe
Wolseley:
Frances Garnet, Vctss. Wolseley, vii. 265
Garnet, iii. 62
Wolsey, Thos., cardinal, ii. 16–17, 69, 80, 88, 144, 402; iv. 80, 130; ix. 139, 214
Wolstonbury, *see* Pyecombe
Wolverhampton (Staffs.), ii. 12, 416
Wolversbridge, *see* Woolbeding: Woolmer Bridge
Wolverton, Ld., *see* Glyn
Wolwardebrugge, *see* Woolbeding: Woolmer Bridge
Wolwin (? Wulwin), vii. 279
Wonham, Dan., iv. 226
Wood (Wode):
Charlotte, m. Wm. Davidson, vii. 189
Edw., vii. 69
Geo., canon of Chich., iii. 115
Jas. (d. 1759), vii. 180, 188 *n*
Jas. (d. 1806), vii. 180, 189
Jas. (d. 1831), vii. 189
Jas. (d. 1897), vii. 189
Jas. Russell, ii. 434
Joan atte, vii. 230

Jn. (fl. 1473), ix. 263
Jn. (fl. 1479), ii. 94
Jn. (d. 1485), iv. 51
Jn. (fl. 1631), vii. 69
Jn. (fl. 1697), ii. 249; ix. 23
Jn. (d. 1791), vii. 180
Jn. (d. 1818), vii. 180
Jn. (fl. 1831), vii. 189
Lawson, ix. 172
Marg., m. Thos. Drewell, iv. 51
Martha, *see* Stapley
Mary, m. Jn. Cripps, vii. 100
Nic., ii. 412
Peter atte, and his w. Lawrentia, vii. 230
Sir Rob. (fl. *c.* 1600), iv. 223
Rob. (fl. 1766), ix. 202
Thos. a, vii. 143
(or Din), Thos., vii. 247
and see Awood; Bosco; Woods
wood allowance, ii. 294, 302, 304, 313–16, 318, 322–4
wood (wood-mote, wood playt) courts, *see* courts
Woodard, Nat., curate of New Shoreham, ii. 431–3
Woodard schools, ii. 431–4; vii. 127
Woodbridge, A.E., ii. 453
Woodcock:
Edw., vii. 207
Hen., vii. 158
Ursula, m. Pury Cust, vii. 207
Woodcote, *see* Westhampnett
Woodgate, *see* Aldingbourne
Woodhorne (Wodehorne):
Alan of, iv. 162
his s., *see* Ralph
Peter de, iv. 167
Woodhorne, *see* Oving
Woodhouse (Wodehuse):
Sim. atte, iv. 136 *n*
Wm., ix. 70
Woodingdean, *see* Ovingdean
Woodland, Jn., and his w. Agnes, vii. 96
Woodman:
Edw., ii. 247
Ric., ii. 22, 247; ix. 206
Mr., vii. 267
Woodmancote, ii. 43–4
adv., ii. 92
ch., ii. 250, 337
man., vii. 147
pop., ii. 219
rector, *see* Shore, Phil.
Woodman's Green, *see* Linch
Woodmansterne (Surr.), ix. 257
Woodruffe (Woodrooffe):
Isaac, vii. 238
Mary Ann, *see* Woods
Woods:
Caroline, w. of Edm., iii. 144
Charlotte, iii. 144
Edm. (fl. after *c.* 1700), iv. 169
Edm. (fl. 1805), iv. 188–9
Edm. (d. 1833), iii. 144
Emma, iii. 144
Frances, iii. 144
Geo. Hen., rector of Singleton, iv. 120
Hen. Geo. (? two of this name), ii. 432; iv. 170
Herb., vii. 121
J.W., iv. 107
Jn., iv. 99
Kath., iv. 170
Kath., w. of Edm., iii. 144
Martha, iv. 124
Mary, iv. 99
Mary Ann, m. —— Woodruffe, iii. 144
Ric., ii. 100
S.M.J., ii. 475
W. Layland, iv. 107
fam., iv. 107, 169
and see Awood; Bosco; Wood
Woodside, *see* Hailsham
Woodstock (Oxon.), ii. 53

Woodville:
Eliz., *see* Elizabeth
Sir Ric., ix. 69
Woodward:
Hannah, *see* Smith
Jn., vii. 113
Mat., iv. 123
Thos., canon of Chich., iii. 147
W.A., vii. 113
Wm., ix. 89
fam., vii. 113
Woodyer:
Jn., vii. 121
Thos., iv. 230; vii. 121
his w., iv. 230
wool production, ii. 176, 188, 274, 281–5
and see textile inds.: wool
wool, tax on, i. 505
wool trade, iii. 91, 97, 101–2; vii. 32
Woolavington, Ld., *see* Buchanan
Woolavington (East Lavington), i. 493; ii. 43; iv. 28, 40, 58, 62, 65
adv., iv. 60
botany, i. 67
earthworks, i. 480
foxhunting, ii. 442
man., iv. 58–60, 65, 95, 185
nonconf., ii. 41
pk., ii. 296–7, 305
pop., ii. 218
rector, *see* Manning, Hen.
Woolavington Common, iv. 54
Woolbeding (Wolbeding), ii. 43; iv. 7, 40, 65, **84–7**
adv., iv. 87
bridge, ii. 394; iv. 85
ch., iv. 84–7, *84, 86*
accessories, ii. 351, 353, 355, 364
architt., ii. 348–9, 364, 379
dom. archit., ii. 392; iv. 84–5
fortifications, i. 492
insects, i. 120, 213, 216–17
man., ii. 174; iv. 36, 66, 85–7, 158
mill, iv. 85
pop., ii. 221
Radford, iv. 84
rector, *see* Otway, Humph.
Woolbeding Ho., iv. 50, 84–5, *84*
Woolmer Bridge (Wolfardesbridge, Wolversbridge, Wolwardebrugge), ii. 174; iv. 85
Woolfe (Wolf, Wolfe):
Nic., i. 519; ii. 29
Nic. (? another), iii. 81
Wm., i. 513–14
——, i. 514
Woolger (Wulgar), Thos., mayor of Chich., iii. 92
Wooll, Jn., ii. 428
Woolley, Fred., ii. 415
Woolley (Hunts.), iv. 111 *n*
Woolven, Mary, *see* Hammond
Woolwich (London, formerly Kent), ii. 242, 249
Woolynchmere priory, *see* Shulbred
Wooton, *see* Wootton
Wootton, Geo., ii. 470–1
Wootton (in E. Chiltington), *see* Chiltington, East
Wootton (Wooton) (? in Folkington), ii. 86
Yeldelond, ii. 86
Worcester, earl of, *see* Tiptoft
Worcester, ix. 104 *n*
battle, i. 527–8; iv. 115
bp., i. 496
Worcestershire, ii. 263; *and see* Evesham; Kempsey; Worcester
Worde, Wynkyn de, ii. 405
Worge, Geo., ii. 238
Workman, Hen., and his w. Alice, vii. 229
works, villeins', ii. 232; vii. 55, 58, 74, 95, 157, 183, 203, 213, 225, 265–6, 269–70
Worldham:
Isabel, w. of Peter de, iv. 91–2
Peter de, iv. 91–2

Wormedale, Jn. de, abbot of Roberts-
 bridge, ii. 73
Wormegay, Alice de, m. Rainald de
 Warenne, vii. 110
Worrell (Worrall):
 Ric., ii. 165
 Wm., ix. 248
Worsley:
 Sir Ric., iv. 189
 Sir Rob., and his w. Frances, iv. 189
 fam., iv. 189
Worth:
 Jn. de, prior of Michelham, ii. 79
 Peter de, vii. 235
Worth, i. 536; ii. 43–4, 206; vii. 125,
 192–200
 adv., vii. 199–200
 Burleigh Arches, ii. 3, 117; vii. 92,
  125, 196–7
 char., vii. 200
 Chase, ii. 311
 ch., vii. 197–9, *197, 198, 199*
  accessories, ii. 352–3, 355–6, 359,
   379
  archit., ii. 312, 340, 342, 348–9,
   351, 362, *363*, 364, 377
  Copthorne, ii. 44, 312–13, 480; vii.
   192
  ch., vii. 199
  horn, ii. 201, 313
 Crabbet pk., ii. 310–11, 313
 Crawley Down, ii. 44; vii. 192, 199–
  200
 dom. archit., vii. 192–4
 earthworks, i. 478
 forest, i. 50, 68, 110, 166, 513; ii. 189,
  233, 245–6, 293, 297, 299, 310–
  13; vii. 2–3, 133–4, 192
  bounds, ii. 310
  High Beeches warren, i. 55; ii. 313
  Old House warren, ii. 313
 Huntsland, ii. 313
 inc., ii. 313; vii. 196
 insects, i. 212
 man., ii. 311–12; vii. 2–3, 53 *n*, 54,
  96, 134, 194–7; ix. 278
 Paddockhurst, ii. 462
 pk., ii. 312–13, 463; vii. 196
 poor relief, vii. 200
 pop., ii. 224
 rly., ii. 224 *n*; vii. 192
 rectors, *see* Bethune, Geo.; Liddell,
  Chas.
 Strudgate:
  forest, vii. 195
  man., vii. 196
 Three Bridges, i. 110, 166, 174, 212–
  14, 216–20, 223–5, 301; vii. 192,
  200
 Tilgate:
  botany, i. 60–1
  forest, ii. 312
  fossils, i. 37
  insects, i. 120–1, 132, 143–4, 146,
   148–57, 162, 172, 174, 176–7,
   180–1, 184–6, 218–21, 229, 231–3
  man., ii. 313
 Tinsley Green, vii. 192
 trades and ind., ii. 237, 241 *n*, 247,
  249, 257
 Turner's Hill, i. 55; ii. 463; iii. 43; vii.
  192, 199–200
 Warren furnace, ii. 249
 Worth Lodge, ii. 313
 and see Half Smock
Worth (Kent), iii. 52
Wörth (Germany), vii. 197
Worthing, i. 254, 276; ii. 43
 birds, i. 276, 279–81, 283, 286, 292,
  297
 botany, i. 66, 68
 coins, i. 331
 crustaceans, i. 250, 253, 262–3
 fossils, i. 22, 30
 geology, i. 13, 20, 45
 insects, i. 115–16, 124, 126, 128–9,
  131–5, 137–8, 142, 144–5, 151,
  160, 163, 165, 167, 168 *n*, 172–5,

 177–82, 184–210, 215, 217–18,
  224, 227–32
 mammals, i. 304
 militia, i. 534
 museum, iii. 15–17, 49, 52–4, 60,
  67–8
 navigation lights, ii. 163
 prehist. rem., i. 320, 331
 rly., iii. 68
 resort, ii. 204
 Rom. rem., iii. 3–4, 47, *50*, 68
 sch., ii. 397
 shipping, ii. 155
 signal station, ii. 163
 spiders, i. 239, 241–3
 sport, ii. 448, 453, 460, 478, 481
 trades and ind., ii. 235, 254, 269–70
Worthyall, Jn., warden of St. Mary's
 hosp., Chich., ii. 102
Worting:
 Isabel, *see* St. John
 Sir Thos., iv. 143 *n*
Wotton:
 Honor, m. Wm. Burrell, ix. 228
 Jn. (fl. 1614), iv. 223
 Jn. (fl. *c.* 1700), ix. 228
Wotton (Surr.):
 ch., ii. 328 *n*
 hund., iv. 91
Wotton under Edge (Glos.), ii. 402
wreck, right of, i. 504; ii. 146; iv. 200,
 206; vii. 2, 233–4, 254, 284; ix. 37,
 49, 84, 118, 175
wrecking, ii. 132, 136, 146, 148, 158–9
Wrefordi, iv. 30 *n*
Wren, Sir Chris., ii. 391–2; iii. 74, 76,
 112
Wrenn, H.F., ix. 250
wrestling, *see* sport
Wretham (Suff.), vii. 4, 99 *n*
Wright, Jn., warden of St. Mary's hosp.,
 Chich., ii. 102
Wriothesley (Wriothesly):
 Hen., earl of Southampton, ii. 28; iv.
  78
 Mary Anne, m. —— Ferrers, iv. 102
 Thos., Ld. Wriothesley, earl of
  Southampton, ii. 54; iv. 102
Wrotham, Eustace de, ii. 87
Wrotham (Kent), ii. 252; iv. 185
Wrothe, Rob., master of hosp. of Holy
 Cross, Winchelsea, iii. 107
Wulfencing, *see* Wlencing
Wulfhere, king of Mercia, i. 333*, 482;
 ii. 1
Wulfhun (Wlfhun), bp. of Selsey, iv.
 110
Wulfnoth, father of Earl Godwin, i. 484;
 iv. 91
Wulfred, abp. of Cant., i. 349
Wulfric, moneyer, iii. 83
Wulfric (fl. 960), ii. 3, 292; iv. 83; vii.
 206
Wulfwin, *see* Wulwine
Wulgar, *see* Woolger
Wulwin (fl. 1196), vii. 256 *n*
Wulwine (Wulfwin) (fl. 1163), vii. 33
Wulwyn (fl. before 1005), ix. 49
Wul-, Wulf-, *and see* Ul-; Wol-
Wunstan, moneyer, iii. 83
Wyatt (Wiatt):
 Jas., iii. 78; iv. 121, 142; ix. 131
 Jn. (fl. 1535), iv. 170
 Jn. (fl. 1561), and his w., ii. 197
 O.N., iii. 89 *n*
 Ric., ii. 165
 Thos., vii. 57
Wyavill, *see* Wyville
Wybarne:
 Benj., ix. 196, 254
 Edw. (d. *c.* 1624), ix. 196*, 254
 Edw. (fl. 1632), ix. 254
 Jn. (fl. before 1469), ix. 254
 Jn. (d. 1490), ix. 254, 256
 Jn. (d. 1591), ix. 196, 254
 Jn. (d. by 1612), ix. 254
 Jn. (fl. 1682), ix. 254
 Thos., ix. 196

 Wm., ix. 196, 254
 ——, ix. 254
Wybbyshay, Steph., vii. 117
Wych (Wich):
 Nic. de, dean of South Malling coll.,
  ii. 118
 St. Ric. de, chancellor of Cant., bp. of
  Chich., i. 505 *n*; ii. 8, 10–11, 47,
  49, 87, 93–6, 108, 111, 347; iii.
  85–6, 109–10, 121, 125 *n*, 132,
  133 *n*, 134, 144 *n*, 165; iv. 152,
  217, 233; vii. 15, 40, 69, 163; ix.
  94, 118
 arms, iii. *110*
 and see Chich.: cath.: shrine
Wych Cross, *see* Maresfield
Wychard:
 Phil., iv. 157
 Sybil, *see* Hunston
Wyck, *see* Wyke
Wyckham, *see* Steyning: Wickham
Wycliffe (Wickliffe, Wiclif):
 Jas., ii. 422–3*
 Jn., ii. 14
Wydere, Jn., vii. 36
Wye (Kent), ii. 52, 54; ix. 150
Wyflise, Ric. de, rector of Slindon, ii.
 186
Wyghtring (Wyghtryng), *see* Withringes
Wyhus (unidentified), ii. 89, 230
Wyk, la (unidentified), vii. 2
Wyke (Wyck):
 Hen. a (fl. after 1508), ix. 197
 Hen. (fl. 1539, ? another), ix. 214, 220
 Jn. (d. by 1269), iv. 42 *n*
 Jn. a (fl. 1508), ix. 197
 Randell de, ii. 105
 Rog. de, iv. 171
 and see Wykes
Wyke, *see* Rumboldswyke
Wyke, cross of (? in Beckley), ix. 144*
Wyke, la, wood, ii. 302
Wykeford, *see* Wykford
Wykeham (Wickham, Wikham):
 Jn., ii. 141, 234
 Wm. of, bp. of Winchester, ii. 111,
  421; iii. 111, 116, 122, 124, 159;
  ix. 228
 arms, iii. 111, 122, 159
Wykemer, Adam de, dean of South
 Malling coll., ii. 119
Wykes:
 Christiane de, ? m. —— de Mere-
  worth, iv. 171
 Godeheude, iv. 171
 (or Warham), Hubert de, *see* Warham
 Joan, *see* Martin
 Jn. de, iv. 171
 Ladereyna de, *see* Baseville
 Nichole, w. of Rog. de, iv. 171
 Rob., dean of South Malling coll., ii.
  119
 Rog. de, iv. 171
 (or Mereworth), Wal. de, *see* Mere-
  worth
 Wal. de, iv. 171
 fam., iv. 171
 and see Wyke
Wykford (Wykeford):
 Jn. de, iv. 42
 Marg. de, *see* Baseville
 Nic., iv. 76
Wykley (Wakle), Nic., ii. 404
Wylcombe (Wilcombe):
 Alice, vii. 100
 Jn., vii. 100
 Nic., i. 510; vii. 100
 Peter, vii. 100
 Rob., and his w. Alice, vii. 100
 Thos., vii. 67
Wylde, *see* Wild
Wylehale (Willehale):
 Jas. de, iv. 231
 Nic. de, iv. 231
 Rob. de (fl. 1248), iv. 231
 Rob. de (fl. 1296), iv. 231
 Wal. de, iv. 231
 Wm. de, iv. 231

Wylesham, *see* Wilsham
Wylet, *see* Veulettes
Wylford, *see* Wilford
Wylman, Jn., and his w. Joan, iv. 231
Wymbissh, *see* Wimbis
Wymburn, Gilb. de, prior of Sele, ii. 61–2
Wyming, *see* Gymming
Wympler, Rob. le, ii. 256
Wyn (Win):
  Jn., M.P. for Chich., iii. 98
  Jn. (jr.), M.P. and mayor of Chich., iii. 91, 98
  Ric., prior of Chich. Dominican friary, ii. 94
Wynch, Hen., ix. 192
Wynchelse, *see* Winchelsea
Wyndam, *see* Wyndham
Wyndesor, *see* Windsor
Wyndham (Wyndam):
  Chas., earl of Egremont, iv. 62; vii. 71
  Chas. Hen., Ld. Leconfield, ii. 444; iv. 36, 62, 64 *n*, 65, 175
  Frances, m. Nat. Palmer, iv. 150
  Geo., Ld. Leconfield, i. 535; ii. 444–6, 448; iv. 7, 56; vii. 208
  Geo. Hugh, iv. 24
  Geo. O'Brien, earl of Egremont, ii. 207, 238, 444, 455–8, 461; iii. 24; iv. 24, 36, 64, 76, 175; vii. 208
  Hen., ii. 445
  Hen., Ld. Leconfield, i. 306–7; ii. 444–5, 448; iv. 9; vii. 208
  Percy, iii. 100
  Sir Percy Chas. Hugh, iv. 24
  Sir Wm. (fl. before 1682), iv. 150
  Sir Wm. (fl. 1710), ii. 444
  arms, vii. *208*
Wyndham Hive, Chas., iv. 24
Wyndham (Windeham, Windham) and Ewhurst hund., i. 538; ii. 220; vii. 1, 3 *n*, 125, 189 *n*
Wyndsor, *see* Windsor
Wynendaal (Belgium), battle, iv. 121
Wyngremouth, Giles de, dean of South Malling coll., ii. 119
Wynter, *see* Winter
Wyntereshull, Wm. de, iv. 129
Wyon, E.A., ix. 85
Wyot, ii. 296, 307
Wyreham, Wm., iv. 160
Wysdon, *see* Wisden
Wysebech, Thos., ii. 123
Wyseman, *see* Wiseman
Wysham:
  Jn. de, and his w. Hawise, vii. 142
  Sir Wm., vii. 142
Wystringes (Wystryng), *see* Withringes
Wytham:
  Amy de, *see* St. George
  Jn. de, iv. 105
Wythard, Jn., ii. 185
Wythering, *see* Pagham
Wythering Haven, *see* Pagham: harbour
Wythines, Jn., dean of Battle, ix. 111
Wythyham, *see* Withyham
Wytthauwere, Jn. le, ii. 259
Wyville (Weyvile, Weyvyle, Wyavill, Wyvell, Wyvile, Wyvill):
  Agatha, *see* Radmylde
  Joan, w. of Thos. de, iv. 241, 243–4
  Jn. de (fl. 1261), iv. 123
  Jn. (fl. 1376), ix. 240
  Marg., prioress of Easebourne, ii. 85
  Marmaduke, vii. 41 *n*
  Peter, *see* Quivil
  Ric. de (fl. 1230), vii. 242

  Ric. de (fl. 1242, ? another), vii. 242
  Ric. (d. 1415), ix. 241
  Ric. (d. 1417), vii. 70–1, 73 *n*, 229, 232, 242
  Thos. de, ix. 240, 243

Y.M.C.A., iii. 167
Yalding (Yalden, Yaldwyn):
  Jas. Hen., iv. 72 *n*
  Marg., m. Geo. Coquerell, iv. 62
  Wm., iv. 81
  Mr., iv. 72
  fam., iv. 72 *n*
  and see Yelding
Yalding (Kent), iv. 149
Yaldwyn, *see* Yalding
Yapton (Abberton), ii. 42–3, 81, 205
  adv., ii. 108, 119
  Bilsham, ii. 338, 376
  ch.:
    accessories, ii. 351, 353, 355, 358, 360, 362, 365
    archit., ii. 335, 340, 342–3, *343*, *345*, 346, 348–50, 365, *366*, 368, 370–2, 374
  dom. archit., ii. 382, 392
  insects, i. 220
  man., ii. 109, 119; iv. 65
  pop., ii. 217
  textile ind., ii. 257
  tithes, ii. 263
  Wildbridge, iv. 112
  workho., ii. 210
Yarmouth, Sybil of, ii. 104
Yarmouth, Great (Norf.), ii. 107, 262
  fair, ix. 37, 55
  fishery, ii. 126–7, 156 *n*, 160, 265–8; ix. 34, 37, 70
  relations with Cinque Ports, ii. 132–7; ix. 9, 37–8
Yarranton, And., vii. 63
Yarrell, Wm., i. 275–7
Yarum, Thos., iv. 153 *n*
Yates, Thos., ii. 421
Yeldelond, *see* Wootton (? in Folkington)
Yelding:
  Jn. (fl. 1444), ix. 241
  Jn. (fl. 1564), ix. 241, 244
  Marg., w. of Jn., ix. 241
  Wm., ix. 241
  fam., ix. 241
  and see Yalding
Yenser, Jn., and his w. Julia, iv. 231
Yeo, R., ii. 447
Yeoman, Steph., iv. 102
Yevegod, Jn., ix. 278
Ylgate, Thos., vii. 263
Yngolf, Sim., vii. 189 *n*
Yngworth, Ric., bp. of Dover, iii. 86 *n*
Yong (Yonge), *see* Young
Yoo, Jn., and his w. Marg., vii. 106
York:
  Rob., abbot of Durford, ii. 91
  Wm., and his w. Phoebe, ix. 215
  and see Yorke
York:
  dchss. of, *see* Holland, Joan; Mowbray, Anne; Nevill, Cecily
  dukes of, *see* James II; Richard
York, i. 349, 485; ii. 72, 398–9, 402, 404
  abps., *see* Bayeux; Frewen, Accepted; Kemp, Jn.; Wilfrid
Yorke, Phil., earl of Hardwicke, vii. 248
Yorkshire, i. 168 *n*, 291, 318; ii. 65, 86, 128, 256, 469–70, 473; iii. 85; iv. 56, 157

  East Riding, *see* Beverley; Holderness; Hull
  North Riding, *see* Arden; Boroughbridge; Egglestone; Scarborough; Sedbergh; Stamford Bridge; Whitby
  West Riding, *see* Dewsbury; Doncaster; Halifax; Harthill; Hipperholme; Roche; Sheffield; Towton; Wakefield
Young (Yong, Yonge):
  A.E., ii. 473
  Alice, m. Thos. Bonham, iv. 56
  Anne, m. —— Tilley, iii. 162
  Ant., iv. 56
  C.H., ii. 472 *n*
  Chas., iii. 162
  Francis, bailiff of Rye, ix. 50
  Hen., ix. 192
  Hugh, ii. 99
  J.V., ii. 476
  Jn., bp. of Gallipoli, dean of Chich., prior of Shulbred, warden of New College, Oxford, ii. 51, 82; iv. 105
  Jn., bailiff of Lewes, vii. 20, 24 *n*
  Jn. (fl. 1580), iii. 80
  Capt. Jn. (fl. 1588), iii. 102
  Juliana, prioress of Rusper, ii. 63–4
  Nic., vii. 17
  Ric., mayor of Chich., iii. 162
  Ric., iv. 78
  Thos., iii. 116 *n*
  W.A., ii. 472 *n*
  Wm. (fl. 1541), iv. 56
  Wm. (fl. 1779), ii. 166
  Maj., i. 526
  Mr., ii. 410
Younger, Sir Rob., Ld. Blanesburgh, ix. 74
Younsmere (Iwonesmere, Youngsmere) hund., i. 537; ii. 225; vii. 1, 3 *n*, 81, **221–2**
Ypres, Jn. de, ix. 40, 41 *n*
Ypres Tower, *see* Rye: defences
Yugoslavia, *see* Istria; Siscia

Zeeland (Zealand, Netherlands), ii. 141–2
Zetland, earl of, *see* Dundas
Zierikzee (Netherlands), iii. 102
Zoetman (Zoctmann), Cornelius, ii. 261; ix. 162
Zoological Society, i. 283, 301
zoology, *see* marine zoology
Zouche (Zouch):
  Alan la (fl. 1303), iv. 112, 158, 159 *n*
  Alan la (d. 1346), iv. 66, 112, 158, 171
  Alice la, *see* Thony
  Chas., and his w. Dorothy, vii. 54, 58
  Francis, vii. 54, 58
  Sir Hugh la, iv. 112, 158, 171
  Joan, w. of Sir Hugh la, m. 2 Sir Jn. Pelham, i. 512; iv. 158, 171; ix. 3, 79, 125
  Maud la, m. Rob. de Holland, iv. 159 *n*
  Rog. la, iv. 66, 158
  Wm. la, iv. 171
  fam., iv. 65, 73, 158
Zouche:
  Lady, *see* Arundel, Eliz. de
  Ld., *see* Bishop, Sir Cecil; Curzon, Rob.
Zurich (Switzerland), ii. 424

CORRIGENDA TO
VOLUMES I—IV, VII, AND IX

Vol. I, page xv, line 27, *for* CLAUD *read* CLAUDE
    "   "   11, line 21, *for* Kingstone *read* Kingston near Lewes
    "   "   27, last line, *for* Selsea *read* Selsey
    "   "   31, line 9, *for* Scellescomb *read* Saddlescombe
    "   "   36, line 20, *for* Hawkbourne *read* Hawksbourne
    "   "   53, line 9 from end, *for* Colegate *read* Colgate
    "   "   56, line 19 from end, *for* Berwick, Alfriston and Climping, *read* Berwick and Alfriston,
    "   "   59, line 24, *for* Hanmer *read* Stanmer
    "   "   60*b*, line 18, for *Sedlescomb* read *Sedlescombe*
    "   "   68*b*, line 9 from end, for *Colegate* read *Colgate*
    "   "   109*a*, line 29, *for* Dunston *read* Duncton
    "   "   111, line 9 from end, *for* Selsea *read* Selsey
    "   "   113, line 24, *for* Aldwich *read* Aldwick
    "   "   114, line 24, *for* Welberton *read* Walberton
    "   "   118, line 2, *for* Binstead *read* Binsted
    "   "   125*a*, line 3, *for* Beaufort *read* Beauport
    "   "   129*b*, line 2, for *Seddlescombe* read *Sedlescombe*
    "   "   134*a*, line 20, for *Peasemarsh* read *Peasmarsh*
    "   "   143*b*, line 3 from end, for *Glynd* read *Glynde*
    "   "   162*a*, line 37, for *Peasemarsh* read *Peasmarsh*
    "   "   165, note 2, *for* Bevingdean *read* Bevendean
    "   "   172*a*, line 14 from end, for *Bevingdean* read *Bevendean*
    "   "   222*b*, line 20 from end, for *Chauctonbury* read *Chanctonbury*
    "   "   276*a*, line 6, *for* Stanmore *read* Stanmer
    "   "   284*a*, line 22 from end, *for* Shillingbee *read* Shillinglee
    "   "   284*b*, line 14, *for* Oafham *read* Offham
    "   "   287*a*, line 2 from end, *for* Eskden *read* East Dean
    "   "   295*a*, line 28, *for* Weighton *read* Heighton
    "   "   302*a*, line 6 from end, *for* Pettering *read* Peppering
    "   "   322, line 12, *for* Streatham *read* Stretham
    "   "   323, note 2, *for* Hinover *read* Hindover
    "   "   326, line 5, *for* Attrebates *read* Atrebates
    "   "   328, *delete lines 16–17*
    "   "   328, *after line 21 insert* ARLINGTON. – Neolithic scraper of horseshoe form found in a barrow at Windover Hill [Evans, *Stone Imp.* 308].
    "   "   333, line 16, *for* Wulthere *read* Wulfhere
    "   "   335, line 3, *for* Hydney *read* Hydneye
    "   "   370, line 19, *for* Washington *read* Westmeston
    "   "   467, line 3, *delete* , also known as MOUNT HARRY,
    "   "   467, line 4, *for* Clapham *read* Angmering
    "   "   467, caption of upper fig., *delete* , OR MOUNT HARRY
    "   "   489, line 5 from end, *for* Tunbridge *read* Tonbridge
    "   "   553*b*, *s.v.* Washington *delete* 370,
    "   "   553*b*, *s.v.* Westmeston *after* 368, *insert* 370,

Vol. II, page 1, line 16, *for* bishop of Northumbria *read* archbishop of York
    "   "   12, lines 16–17, *for* later rectors . . . in 1337.[97] *read* a later rector was Jocelin, cardinal bishop of Albano.[96]
    "   "   12, *notes 96 and 97 to be amalgamated as note 96*
    "   "   14, line 17, *for* abbots of Battle and *read* abbot of Battle, prior of
    "   "   15, line 22, *for* 1432 *read* 1431
    "   "   16, line 2, *for* Bridham *read* Birdham
    "   "   16, line 15 from end, *for* the Italian Bernardi *read* Lambert Barnard
    "   "   43, *s.v.* Deanery of Dallington, 1906 *after* Ewhurst, *add* Hooe,
    "   "   43, *s.v.* Deanery of Hastings, 1906 *for* Hove *read* Hooe
    "   "   51*a*, line 16 from end, *for* Thomas Lambrook *read* Lambrook Thomas
    "   "   52*b*, line 18 from end, *for* monastery *read* manor and church
    "   "   61*b*, line 1, *for* John *read* William
    "   "   63*a*, Ramstede nunnery, line 9, *for* 1202 *read* 1204
    "   "   68*a*, line 7, *for* Jerusalem, Sicily *read* Jerusalem and Sicily
    "   "   68*b*, line 29, *for* Ardruin *read* Androin
    "   "   89*b*, line 32, *for* Sonworth *read* Sunworth
    "   "   108*b*, lines 6–5 from end, *for* Sevenhampton *read* Seavington
    "   "   131, note 2, *for* Wittering *read* Wythering in Pagham,
    "   "   138, line 13 from end, *for* Wittering *read* Wythering
    "   "   138, note 11, *for* Anesford *read* Avisford
    "   "   151, line 15 from end, *for* 10 *read* 100
    "   "   152, line 9, *for* Everingham *read* Erringham
    "   "   203, line 7 from end, *for* Awister *read* Awsiter
    "   "   209, note 321, *for* Suffolk *read* Sussex
    "   "   235*b*, line 24, *for* Clarke *read* Clark
    "   "   241*b*, lines 4–5, *for* West Rother Canal *read* Rother Navigation
    "   "   241*b*, line 5, *for* Arun and Wey *read* Wey and Arun
    "   "   243, note 31, *add at end* The missing half of the letter has since been discovered in Sloane MS. 4059, fols. 17–18.
    "   "   250*a*, line 17, *for* Eastbourne *read* Easebourne
    "   "   250*a*, line 7 from end, *for* 1615 *read* 1613
    "   "   250*a*, line 6 from end, *before* Beeding *insert* Upper
    "   "   250*b*, line 17, *for* 1628 *read* 1624
    "   "   253*b*, line 21 from end, *for* two *read* ten

Vol. II, page 265*b*, line 32, *delete* or trawlers
"   "   267*a*, line 31, *for* thirty *read* fifteen
"   "   267*a*, line 32, *before* of *insert* all *and delete* fifteen,
"   "   267*a*, line 33, *for* above 20 tons *read* 20 tons or above
"   "   291, note 9, *for* Keymer *read* Keynor
"   "   297, line 3, *for* Thomas *read* Christopher
"   "   303, line 26, *for* Normansland *read* Nomansland
"   "   303, line 27, *for* Merdon *read* Marden
"   "   324, line 2 from end, *for* William, count *read* Alice, countess
"   "   324, last line, *for* his *read* her
"   "   324, last line, *for* 1248 *read* 1249
"   "   325, line 16 from end, *for* son *read* successor
"   "   330, line 14, *for* King John *read* Henry II
"   "   330, line 19, *for* Robert *read* Alured
"   "   331, line 27, *for* Sedlescombe *read* Saddlescombe
"   "   331, line 18 from end, *for* Hospitallers *read* Templars
"   "   334, line 26, *for* East *read* West
"   "   338, line 24, *for* Pagham *read* North Mundham
"   "   353, line 16 from end, *for* Newark *read* Newick
"   "   354, line 12, *for* the Bernardis *read* Lambert Barnard
"   "   356, line 13 from end, *for* Horsham *read* Hastings
"   "   361, line 18 from end, *for* Lord Hoo, 1453 *read* Sir Thomas Hoo, d. 1486
"   "   361, line 7 from end, *for* Shelley *read* Shirley
"   "   371, line 30 from end, *for* North *read* South
"   "   378*a*, line 5 from end, *for* Lord Hoo (*c.* 1403) *read* Sir Thomas Hoo (d. 1486)
"   "   382, line 17 from end, *for* South *read* North
"   "   387, line 26 from end, *for* Racton House, Lordington *read* Lordington House, Racton
"   "   389, line 28, *for* Groomhall *read* Broomhall
"   "   392, line 4 from end, *for* one of the Bernardis *read* Lambert Barnard
"   "   392, line 2 from end, *for* Theodore Bernardi *read* Lambert Barnard
"   "   404, line 1, *for* P *read* T
"   "   409, line 24, *for* vicar *read* incumbent *and after* Peter's *insert* , North Street,
"   "   420, line 30, *for* Edward *read* Edmund
"   "   420, lines 37 and 45, *for* Sicklecroft *read* Sicklemore
"   "   420, line 51, *for* 1675 *read* 1677 *and for* Hulton *read* Hutton
"   "   420, line 2 from end, *for* Worthing *read* Wartling
"   "   420, line 2 from end, *for* became vicar *read* became rector
"   "   422, line 19 from end, *for* Haynes *read* Bayne
"   "   422, line 15 from end, *for* by the person who supplied it *read* for Lewknor
"   "   422, last line, *delete* famous *and for* John *read* James
"   "   423, line 7, *for* Robert Atkins *read* Francis Osgood
"   "   423, line 25, *for* Atkins *read* Osgood
"   "   423, line 26, *for* 1786 *read* 1773
"   "   423, lines 20 and 17 from end, *for* Price *read* Pirie
"   "   428, line 9 from end, *delete* son of
"   "   434, Ardingly, line 3 from end, *for* G.T. *read* F.K.
"   "   441*a*, line 16, *for* Dainley *read* Downley
"   "   441*a*, line 20, *for* 1525 *read* 1524
"   "   441*b*, line 14 from end, *for* Seven *read* Levin
"   "   452*b*, last line, *for* Barham *read* Barnham
"   "   466*a*, line 6, *for* Guildford *read* Wey and Arun
"   "   466*a*, line 8, *for* Wye *read* Wey

Vol. III, page 4, line 17, *for* Redford *read* Redfold
"   "   9, lines 14 and 23, *for* Antonine's *read* Antonine
"   "   30, line 33, *for* West Hythe *read* Lympne
"   "   64, line 3, *for* Redford *read* Redfold
"   "   77*a*, line 6 from end, *for* Walter *read* William

Vol. IV, page ix, line 4 from end, *for* Merston *read* Chithurst
"   "   6*b*, last line, *for* 1546 *read* 1543
"   "   16, note 50, *for* cxic *read* lxix
"   "   17*b*, line 14 from end, *for* Edmund Ford *read* Edmund. Edmund Ford
"   "   20*b*, line 12 from end, *for* Femer *read* Fenner
"   "   30, note 5, *for* exchanged *read* by way of exchange granted
"   "   51*a*, line 40, *for* 1056 *read* 1086
"   "   56*b*, line 4, *for* 1549 *read* 1547
"   "   61*b*, lines 4 and 9, *for* Moselingthorpe *read* Buslingthorpe
"   "   61, note 24, *for* 326 *read* 690
"   "   77*b*, line 7, *for* 1460 *read* 1468
"   "   77*b*, line 14, *for* As early as 1384 dower was *read* Before 1381 dower had been
"   "   79*a*, line 32, *for* Crullfield *read* Cryfield
"   "   85, note 27, *for* 530 *read* 1530
"   "   91*b*, Compton, line 16, *for* Michael *read* Luke
"   "   93*b*, line 15, *for* Mountagu *read* Montagu
"   "   95*a*, lines 18–17 from end, *for* 1607 *read* 1606 (*twice*)
"   "   97*b*, line 27, *for* 1636 *read* 1635
"   "   97*b*, line 33, *delete* is said to have
"   "   97*b*, line 34, *after* May *insert* , who changed his name to Knight in accordance with her will
"   "   97*b*, line 34, *for* 1738 *read* 1745 *and after* back *insert* from him
"   "   97, note 11, *for* 163. *read* 164; *Table of Private Acts, 1727–1812.*
"   "   98*b*, line 8, *for* 1550 *read* 1549
"   "   105*a*, line 18, *for* de *read* le
"   "   112*a*, line 34, *for* 1386 *read* 1586
"   "   122*a*, line 20, *for* 1307 *read* 1306
"   "   122, note 16, *for* x *read* ix
"   "   129*b*, line 6 from end, *for* Elizabeth *read* the heir Elizabeth Knight
"   "   134*b*, line 11, *for* Lindsey *read* Lidsey

INDEX TO VOLUMES I–IV, VII, AND IX

Vol. IV, page 142*b*, line 16, *for* c. 1720 *read* in 1697
" " 142, note 7, *add at end* Goodwood Estate Archives.
" " 145*a*, line 5, *for* first husband *read* son
" " 153*a*, line 17, *for* 448 *read* 1147
" " 153*b*, line 12, *for* 2nd *read* 5th
" plate facing page 157, *for* MERSTON *read* CHITHURST
" page 157*b*, line 29, *for* 1628 *read* 1626
" " 159*a*, line 29, *for* Glew *read* Glen
" " 162*b*, last line, *for* to *read* of
" " 167, note 19, *for* iv, 144 *read* ii, 92
" " 168*a*, line 6, *for* Joan his wife *read* Isabel his wife
" " 171*a*, last line, *for* Abbey *read* priory
" " 184*a*, line 25, *for* William *read* John
" " 184*a*, line 16 from end, *delete* (afterwards Vice-Admiral Sir)
" " 184*a*, line 15 from end, *after* Berkeley *insert* (later 1st Lord Fitzhardinge)

Vol. IV, page 184*a*, line 15 from end, *for* cousin *read* son
" " 184*a*, lines 15–14 from end, *delete* , Lord Fitzhardinge,
" " 184*a*, line 13 from end, *for* v.c. *read* V.C.
" " 184*b*, line 2, *for* Pagham *read* North Mundham
" " 184, note 54, *add at end* G.E.C., *Complete Peerage* (2nd edn.), v. 411–12.
" " 184, note 55, *add at end* G.E.C., op. cit. v. 655.
" " 192*b*, line 7 from end, *after* daughter *insert* Alice
" " 202*a*, line 6, *for* Duke *read* ealdorman
" " 202*b*, line 4 from end, *for* 1422 *read* 1421
" " 220, note 33, *for* 1545 *read* 1546

Vol. VII, page 3*b*, line 8, *for* John, Duke *read* Henry, earl
" " 4*b*, line 8, *for* seconds on *read* second son
" " 19*a*, line 27, *for* Charlotte *read* Caroline
" " 29*a*, line 2 from end, *for* E. Wynne Baxter *read* Wynne E. Baxter
" " 37*a*, line 11, *for* 1612 *read* 1616
" " 37*a*, line 7 from end, *for* 1638 *read* 1635
" " 37*b*, line 13, *for* ARNACORITA *read* ANNACORITA
" " 37*b*, line 14, *for* in Lombardic characters except in *read* partly in Lombardic and partly in Roman characters;
" " 37*b*, line 16, *delete* , which
" " 37, note 29, *delete* ; but see Comber, op. cit. 254.
" " 54*b*, line 18, *for* son *read* grandson
" " 64*a*, line 11 from end, *for* 4th *read* 3rd
" " 64*a*, line 7 from end, *for* 5th *read* 4th
" " 64*a*, line 2 from end, *for* 3rd *read* 2nd
" " 71*a*, line 14, *for* 5th *read* 6th
" " 71*a*, lines 30 and 36, *for* 5th *read* 4th
" " 81*b*, line 9 from end, *for* grandson *read* son
" " 85*a*, line 12, *for* 1634 *read* 1631
" " 85*a*, line 14, *for* 3 *read* 30
" " 101*a*, line 41, *after* Wyndham *add* (or William)
" " 109*a*, line 13, *for* 1843 *read* 1854
" " 109*a*, line 13, *delete* a
" " 109*a*, lines 15–16, *for* Bishop.⁴ ... Oxford, *read* Bishop of Oxford,⁴
" " 109*a*, line 17, *for* , and *read* ;
" " 109, *add at start of note* 4 *Burke's Peerage* (1931 edn.), 559–60;
" " 141*b*, line 11 from end, *for* 1415 *read* 1440
" " 156*a*, line 20, *for* 1415 *read* 1439
" " 156*b*, line 10, *for* Marton *read* Morton
" " 190*a*, line 3, *for* Margaret *read* Margery
" " 196*b*, line 32, *delete* Earl
" " 216*b*, last line, *for* Joan *read* Elizabeth
" " 223, note 8, *for* xlxiv *read* clxiv
" " 224*a*, line 17, *for* 1806 *read* 1086
" " 226*b*, line 2, *delete* Earl
" " 229*a*, line 10, *for* Geruard *read* Garuerd
" " 239*a*, line 9, *delete* Earl
" " 244*b*, Brighton, line 8, *for* 1730 *read* 1720
" " 244*b*, Brighton, line 13, *for* vicar *read* rector
" " 245*a*, line 26, *after* houses *add* taxed
" " 245*a*, line 19 from end, *for* 1748 *read* 1749
" " 245*a*, line 14 from end, *for* 1722 *read* 1723
" " 245*a*, line 11 from end, *for* 1757 *read* 1758
" " 245*a*, 4 from end, *for* toW est *read* to West *and for* 1738 *read* 1773
" " 245*b*, lines 5–6, *for* published in 1773 *read* drawn in 1761
" " 245, note 17, *for* 5684, fol. 47. *read* 5683, fol. 59 (65).
" " 246*a*, line 9, *for* in 1730 *read* c. 1720
" " 246*a*, line 25 from end, *for* 1748 *read* 1749
" " 246, note 37, *for* Grose, op. cit. iii. *read* Add. MS. 5683, fol. 59
" " 246, note 50, *after* Ibid. *insert* 1656–7, p. 352;
" " 247*b*, line 10 from end, *for* 1737 *read* 1736
" " 248*a*, line 30, *for* Old Shoreham Road *read* road to New Shoreham
" " 248*b*, lines 2–3, *for* 635 new houses were built *read* the number of houses increased by 635
" " 248*b*, line 14, *for* Wickels *read* Wichelo
" " 252*b*, line 16, *for* £25 8*s*. *read* 25*s*. 8*d*.
" " 253*a*, line 37, *delete* west
" " 253*a*, lines 38–40, *delete* In 1665 ... the cliff.⁶⁶
" " 253*a*, line 41, *for* 1734 *read* 1774
" " 253*b*, line 4 from end, *for* 5th *read* 4th
" " 253, note 65, *for* 528 *read* 530
" " 253, *delete* note. 66
" " 253, note 67, *add at end* 529–31.

Vol. VII, page 255*a*, line 1, *for* 1683 *read* 1483
        "   "   257*b*, lines 24–5, *after* taken *insert* in February 1443 *and delete* in February 1442
        "   "   258*a*, lines 9–10, *for* married . . . husband *read* wife of Sir Henry Knyvett (her second husband) and later of John Vaughan.[45] She and Vaughan
        "   "   258*b*, lines 36–8, *for* Mary's moiety ... Attree, [82] who *read* both moieties to William Attree,[81] one in 1806.[82] He
        "   "   262*a*, line 26, *for* WINIFRED *read* WILFRID
        "   "   262*b*, line 37, *for* in 1730 *read c.* 1720
                262*b*, lines 42–3, *for* In 1730 *read* About 1720
        "   "   263*b*, line 16 from end, *for* Wilfred *read* Wilfrid
        "   "   271, note 64, lines 4–5, *for* Ernley in Manwode *read* Earnley in Manhood hund.
        "   "   274, lines 9 and 12, *for* farm *read* fine

Vol. IX, page 3*b*, line 12 from end, *for* third *read* second
        "   "   9*b*, line 22, *for* Ralph *read* Ranulph
        "   "   37*b*, line 24, *for* Anglesea *read* Anglesey
        "   "   56*b*, lines 38–40, *for* His daughter ... John's *read* John Fynes in 1585 quitclaimed the manor to his mother Agnes's second husband John Threele and her sister Joan's husband Thomas Culpeper. Thomas and Joan released their rights to Threele in 1598.[26] Threele's
        "   "   82*b*, line 14, *delete* (q.v.)
        "   "   *82b, line 14, for* 1554 *read* 1556
        "   "   86*a*, last line, *for* rector *read* vicar
        "   "   87*b*, line 4 from end, *for* 1422 *read* 1430
        "   "   106*a*, line 3 from end, *for* survived him for one year *read* died in 1717
        "   "   111, note 4, *for* 560, *read* 569
        "   "   111, note 6, *for first sentence read* Pursuant to Order in Council of 1845 the special privileges ceased to exist in 1846.
        "   "   126*b*, line 23, *for* Mabeuse *read* Mabuse
        "   "   144*a*, last line, *for* Wyte *read* Wyke
        "   "   153*a*, line 32, *for* in 1443 *read* (by 1443)
        "   "   193, line 8, *for* 'Achingeworde'.[3] *read* 'Achingeworde'[3] [evidently Etchingwood in Buxted].
        "   "   195*b*, line 10 from end, *for* 'Bellingham' *read* 'Belingham'
        "   "   196*a*, line 7, *for* Earls *read* Dukes *and for* earl *read* duke
        "   "   196*b*, line 8 from end, *for* brother *read* nephew
        "   "   196*b*, line 8 from end, *for* 1625 *read* 1624
        "   "   196, note 40, *for* v, 407. *read* ccccvii, 103.
        "   "   197*a*, line 8, *for* Earls *read* Dukes
        "   "   202*a*, line 34, *for* about 1379 *read* in 1377
        "   "   206*b*, line 20 from end, *for* who *read* whose son Edward
        "   "   212*a*, line 34, *before* 1294 *insert* 1293 or
        "   "   213*a*, line 21, *for* 1379 *read* 1381
        "   "   214*a*, line 12, *for* in 1615 *read* before 1616
        "   "   214*a*, line 30, *for* Christchurch *read* Christ Church
        "   "   221*b*, line 2, *for* James *read* John
        "   "   227*a*, line 15 from end, *for* 1765 *read* 1755
        "   "   229*a*, line 3, *for* John *read* James
        "   "   229*a*, line 4, *for* 1586 *read* 1506
        "   "   229*a*, line 20, *delete* William's elder son
        "   "   229*a*, line 21, *after* 1293 *insert* or 1294
        "   "   230*b*, lines 26–7, *for* in 1614 *read* before 1616
        "   "   241*b*, line 9, *after* latter *insert* or another John Bolney
        "   "   242*b*, line 10 from end, *for* Fuller *read* Palmer
        "   "   248*a*, line 18, *for* who *read* whose half brother Sir Thomas Hoo
        "   "   248*a*, line 19, *for* Elizabeth, *read* his youngest daughter Elizabeth.
        "   "   248*a*, *delete line 20*
        "   "   248*a*, line 25, *for* 1542 *read* 1534
        "   "   262, note 3, *for a.* 1190) *read* (*c.* 1090)
        "   "   263*a*, line 8 from end, *for* brother *read* uncle
        "   "   266*b*, last line, *for* Oswald *read* Osward